For
Brune
XMAS 2006

Jon

EX LIBRIS

THE
Unquiet
Grave

THE Unquiet Grave

The FBI
and the Struggle for the
Soul of Indian Country

STEVE HENDRICKS

THUNDER'S MOUTH PRESS
NEW YORK

THE UNQUIET GRAVE:
The FBI and the Struggle for the Soul of Indian Country

Published by
Thunder's Mouth Press
An imprint of Avalon Publishing Group, Inc.
245 West 17th Street, 11th floor
New York, NY 10011

AVALON
publishing group incorporated

Library of Congress Cataloging-in-Publication Data is available.

ISBN-10: 1-56025-735-0
ISBN-13: 978-1-56025-735-6

9 8 7 6 5 4 3 2 1

Book design by Maria E. Torres

Printed in the United States of America
Distributed by Publishers Group West

I wrote this book for the Lakota nation,
who deserve better than my nation has given them.

Contents

The utmost good faith shall always be observed towards the Indians; their land and property shall never be taken from them without their consent; and in their property, rights and liberty, they shall never be invaded or disturbed, unless in just and lawful wars authorized by Congress . . .

Northwest Ordinance of 1789

A NOTE TO THE READER

To keep this book to a readable length, I have condemned a mass of detail to the endnotes. Readers interested in my choices about what to put in the endnotes and what to put in the book proper, as well as choices about diction and style, may want to read the introduction to the endnotes and the About the Book section before starting on the main text. Most readers will miss little by going straight to chapter one.

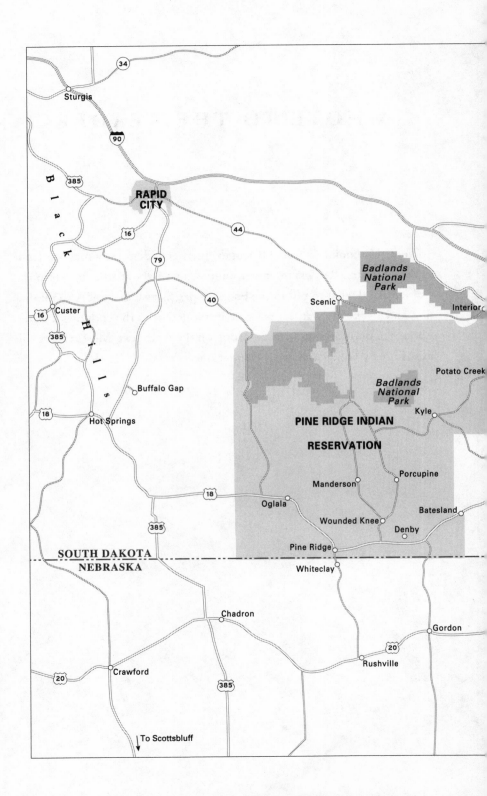

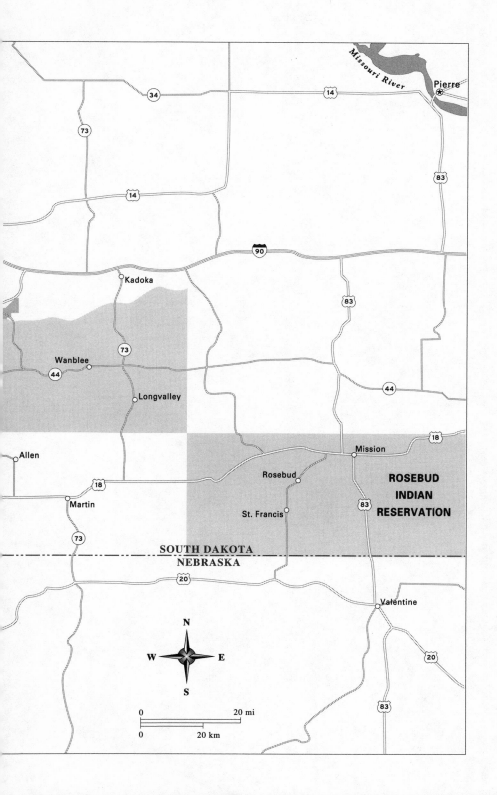

THEN

CHAPTER 1

AS THE FBI told the story, it happened like this.

On February 24, at a quarter to three in the afternoon, a rancher on that part of the South Dakota steppe that crumbles into the Badlands was looking for a place to run a fence line when he turned a bend in a gully and found, curled on its left side, clothed in a maroon jacket and blue jeans, and looking for all the world like someone sleeping in perfect peace, a corpse. Its place of rest was the bottom of an embankment twenty feet high and not fifty steps from Highway 73 but hidden from the road by the embankment. The nearest settlement lay ten miles to the southwest, at a smattering of chipboard federal houses called Wanblee; a few miles to the north, the Pine Ridge Indian Reservation, on which the corpse rested, petered out into one of continental America's emptier expanses. The body lay, if not in the precise middle of nowhere, hard on the edge of it.

Roger Amiotte did not approach the body. He returned to his truck, drove the mile back to his house, and called the Bureau of Indian Affairs police in Kyle, the next outpost past Wanblee. The police had an officer at his place in twenty minutes. The officer was followed by deputy sheriffs from Kadoka, the county seat, then by two BIA investigators and a special agent of the Federal Bureau of Investigation from the town of Pine Ridge, the reservation capital ninety miles off. A search of the scene showed no sign of crime: no violence to the body, no bullet casings or gunpowder, no scuff marks in the scrub, nothing so much as a footprint. A few tufts of dark hair clung to the face of the blond embankment, suggesting the unfortunate had fallen over it.

"When they were hauling the body off," Amiotte would later say, "one of the cops said—I thought it was pretty tactless—he said, 'Well, I guess there must not have been a rape involved, her pants are still on.' *Her* pants. That was my first clue she was a woman. I didn't get too close, and you couldn't tell one way or the other from a distance." She had no identification on her.

As the sun fell, Jane Doe was loaded into an ambulance and driven to the Indian Health Service hospital in Pine Ridge, where next afternoon an autopsy was performed. The pathologist judged her an Indian of twenty to twenty-five years, five feet two inches, 110 pounds, and light complexion, though dehydration and exposure had darkened her. She had borne a child or children and had surrendered a gallbladder to a surgeon and, nearer to death, had had sexual intercourse of a voluntary nature. She had died, the pathologist eventually said—the precise moment of his saying so is a matter of some importance and uncertainty—of frostbite and had lain in the elements for seven to ten days. Her decay was so severe that her fingerprints could not be taken at the hospital, so the FBI asked that her hands be chopped off and forwarded to its laboratory in Washington. The doctor amputated them, and they were sent east. While the lab worked, the authorities on Pine Ridge tried to identify the woman, but none of their leads proved fruitful. Her decomposition worsening, she was moved to a mortuary, but the body proved too far gone to preserve. On March 2, 1976, a week after her discovery, Jane Doe was given a Catholic service and a pauper's burial in an unmarked grave by order of the BIA police.

The next afternoon, the FBI Identification Division in Washington called the FBI field office in Rapid City, which oversaw operations on Pine Ridge. It was Ash Wednesday, the day on which believers since the Middle Ages have darkened their foreheads in reminder of the approach of Judgment Day. Washington told Rapid City that the lab had lifted prints from the woman's severed hands and the Identification Division had matched them to Anna Mae Aquash, a federal fugitive and luminary in the American Indian Movement. It took two days to find her family in the

Canadian Maritimes—Aquash was a Mi'kmaq tribeswoman, a Nova Scotian by birth—at which point the press was also notified.

That was the FBI's story.

Neither the family of Anna Mae Aquash nor her colleagues in AIM believed she had died of exposure. The Aquash they knew was too smart to have taken an underdressed stroll in the prairie winter, and even if she had she was too strong a backpacker and too shrewd an improviser to have succumbed to the cold. And she never—*never*—traveled alone on Pine Ridge, which was then in a state of anarchy just shy of civil war. Her friends and family thought it as likely she had died of exposure—alone, on Pine Ridge—as of a paper cut. They wanted her body unearthed and a second autopsy performed.

The government beat them to it. On March 9, six days after Aquash was identified, the FBI asked for and a federal judge ordered a post-post-mortem. Two days later a backhoe was sent to Holy Rosary Cemetery, outside the town of Pine Ridge, and the grave dug up. Candy Hamilton, a friend of Aquash's, stood vigil.

"After I got there," Hamilton said years later, "Dave Price and Bill Wood and Gary Adams showed up. They were about the worst of the FBI agents on the reservation, though they did sort of keep their distance from me that morning. I had always sworn no matter what they did, they were never gonna see me cry, but I'd already gotten started before they got there. I heard one of them say, 'Well, she's *crying.*' It wasn't a sympathetic tone. They were making jokes and laughing and all that over there."

Special Agent Wood eventually introduced himself to Hamilton.

She said she knew who he was.

He asked if she had information about how Aquash had died.

She told him to go to hell.

In half an hour, the pine vault holding Aquash was lifted from the ground, loaded onto a flatbed truck, and driven to the hospital. There waited Dr. Garry Peterson, deputy medical examiner for greater Minneapolis. Peterson had been hastily retained by the Wounded Knee Legal

Defense/Offense Committee, AIM's legal arm. When the FBI had announced it would hire a pathologist to re-autopsy Aquash, WKLDOC (pronounced "Wickle-dock") had asked that Dr. Peterson be allowed to observe. The government's men had replied that they wanted to get started immediately but, out of kindness, would wait a day for the family's observer. But that morning at the hospital, the FBI agents told Dr. Peterson their doctor was not coming. They did not say why. They said only that if a second necropsy were to be had, Peterson would have to do it. Peterson had brought none of his tools, and the hospital was ill-equipped. (The original autopsy on Aquash, like all Pine Ridge autopsies, was the work of a pathologist who came from off the reservation, kit in tow.) Peterson asked the staff to gather what equipment they could and sent Special Agent Price to Sioux Nation, the general store in Pine Ridge, to fetch a butcher knife. A clutch of Aquash's friends, women chiefly, marked time outside the autopsy room.

"I thought, 'Oh shoot, these agents are having it much too easy today because we're all so upset,' " Candy Hamilton recalled.

"So I started quarreling with Wood. I said, 'Her family's coming and we want her jewelry and personal items to give to them.'

"He said, 'Well, that's all evidence now, you can't have any of that.'

"I said, 'That's not evidence—you couldn't even identify her by 'em. We want it.'

"He just sneered and walked out."

Hamilton is a squat woman with a voice metered in the Cumberlands and a chin that comes at you like a shovel. She was one of many white do-gooders who came to Pine Ridge in the 1970s for the cause of Indian rights and one of the few who stayed after the moment expired. She divided her time between freelance reporting and volunteering for WKLDOC.

"Well, Wood came back in and was way across the room from me, and he said, 'Candy, you want something of Annie Mae's? Here'—and he threw a box across the room at me—'take her hands.' I caught it, and all the women turned and looked and said, 'What's that?' And I said, 'He says it's her *hands*.' You could hear them rattling in there. Everybody was horrified. They hadn't started the autopsy yet, so I went in the room where Peterson was. They still had her all covered up. I told him, 'It's really important for her to have all her body together. Could you put these in with her or put them back on her or something?' And he did, he sewed them back on at the end of the autopsy."

When Dr. Peterson's tools were at last assembled, he unsealed the pine vault and with the help of Agents Wood and Adams removed the cloth-covered coffin inside. The coffin was opened and the body, wrapped in plastic and cloth, was extracted and unwrapped. It was coated in a disinfectant of such pungency that Agent Adams had to excuse himself and revisit his breakfast.

No sooner had Peterson brushed the disinfectant from Aquash than he noticed a lump in her left temple, just above the eye. It looked and felt like a bullet. He suspended his examination while a radiologist took the body for X rays, which confirmed that the lump was a metal object the size and shape of a slug. The body was returned to Peterson, and in seconds he found a hole at the base of the skull. It was surrounded by a circle of dried blood and gunpowder two inches in diameter.

"You could not believe it," he would later say. "I mean, the hole was so plain in the back of her neck. And in the front you could *feel* the lump. You could see the bullet from across the street."

Even before he opened her skull, Dr. Peterson concluded that Anna Mae Aquash had died of a different kind of exposure—as it turned out, exposure to a .32-caliber, copper-jacketed bullet.

It fell to Norman Zigrossi to explain how the government had missed a bullet in the head of a corpse and failed to recognize in her a fugitive whom federal officers had not only arrested more than once but were also searching for at the time her body was found. Zigrossi was the assistant special agent in charge of the FBI's Rapid City resident agency, which meant he ran the office. A sad-eyed man of languid posture but fleet speech, he would soon become infamous in Indian Country for saying of its occupants, "They're a conquered nation, and when you're conquered, the people you're conquered by dictate your future." He called his agents, not inaccurately, "a colonial police force."

Zigrossi saw no mischief in the first autopsy. He said a small-caliber head wound could cause almost no bleeding and could be nearly undetectable once a body had begun to decompose. In proof thereof, he said that no one—none of the paramedics or nurses or doctors or lawmen—who had seen the body had detected the least sign of injury. As for the FBI's not recognizing Aquash, no agents had been at the autopsy, and the lone agent who saw Aquash at Amiotte's ranch did not identify her for the good reason that he had never seen a picture of her. The newspapers of western Dakota, in the manner of the provincial press everywhere, printed Zigrossi's claims without corroboration and returned to alfalfa futures and car-dealership openings.

A few less tractable observers, all from beyond Dakota, nosed further. Freelancer Kevin McKiernan, whose reporting on Pine Ridge remains a gift to history, found a nurse by the name of Inez Hodges who had been on duty the night Aquash was brought to the hospital. Hodges had seen the Jane Doe in the morgue and had instantly noticed an odd and obvious mark on the woman's eye socket: the lodged bullet, although she did not diagnose it as such. She also saw a swath of blood on the white plastic sheet beneath the woman's head. Its plain source was a raised crater at the base of the skull. Hodges showed her findings to a co-worker, whose name the FBI knows but to this day will not release. (To do so, says the FBI, would violate the witness's privacy.)

Kevin McKiernan also found Dr. Stephen Shanker, who had pronounced Aquash dead on arrival. Shanker was just out of medical school, and his experience in matters postmortem was elementary. Nonetheless, in the first moments of his exam, he noticed that the hair on the back of Aquash's head was matted with dried blood. He put his hand there and got a palmful of blood, apparently freshly thawed. A moment's probing brought him to the bullet hole. His analysis was unequivocal—"she hadn't died of natural causes; it looked like a police matter"—and he assumed the autopsy the next day would analyze the wound more extensively. Both Shanker and Hodges said they were stunned by the exposure ruling and that after the bullet was finally found they expected authorities to interview them about what they had seen. The authorities did not—at least not until a public outcry was raised months later.

McKiernan and other reporters also spoke with Dr. W. O. Brown, the resident pathologist at West Nebraska General Hospital in Scottsbluff and the contract coroner for the Bureau of Indian Affairs. Two or three dozen times a year, Dr. Brown flew his private plane to Pine Ridge to look over a corpse (or, more nearly, to overlook one). Of his work on Aquash, he was unrepentant. "A little bullet isn't hard to overlook," he said. "It certainly isn't the first time a bullet was overlooked." And, "Why all the interest in this case? It seems awfully routine, you know. So they found an Indian body—so a body was found." And, "I suppose the Indians will never let that woman die. AIM's trying to stir up all the trouble they can. It's a matter of record that Indians use every little incident that they can to create a situation over. They distort facts and use it to their advantage to further their cause. But I've tried to remain neutral. I don't think I'm prejudiced."

The day after Dr. Peterson found the bullet, Dr. Brown was sure of this much: he had missed it only because the hospital's X-ray machine had been broken. But he soon reversed course: the machine had been in fine fettle and he had merely chosen not to use it because X-rays were "too time-consuming," "too awkward," and "at times unsuccessful." And anyway, since "it's fairly common for Indians like these to die of an overdose," why bother X-raying them? (His tests showed that Aquash's blood was free of drugs or alcohol.) When other excuses failed him, he said he had cut short his exam because the body was "stinky" and "decomposed"—conditions one might have thought were as routine in his work as soot in a chimneysweep's.

But from his verdict he did not swerve. It was the frost that had taken Anna Mae Aquash, not the bullet. The bullet, he said, may have pierced the brain casing, but not the brain proper. *If* it had entered the casing, it *might* have started a chain of events that incapacitated Aquash and left her at the mercy of the cold, but the shot did not kill her. A lesser faith might have been shaken by having missed, progressively, the stained sheet beneath Aquash's head, her gunpowdered and bloodied hair, the hole through several layers of bone, the bloodied masses of soft tissue (including the brain, through which the bullet had in fact passed and which Brown had removed and examined before dumping it in Aquash's chest with other dissected organs), and finally the bullet itself. But Brown's faith was hardened by a steady diet of errata. Among other "errors" in the autopsy, he claimed to have dissected and measured Aquash's stomach, one of her kidneys, and her adrenal glands, but Dr. Peterson found all of these organs attached, unopened, and with metrics quite different from Brown's. And although Dr. Brown reported that Aquash had not been raped and had been dead no more than ten days, Peterson concluded that rape could not be ruled out and Aquash could have been killed weeks, even months, before she was found. Whether these other errors argued that Brown had missed the bullet purposely or incompetently was anyone's guess.

The FBI was in a better position to guess than most. Although Norm Zigrossi said none of his men had been at the autopsy, a nurse who helped with the autopsy told reporters that she had given Aquash's amputated hands to Agent David Price. A BIA investigator at the autopsy, Nathan Merrick, said he "thought" two FBI agents had been there, one of whom was Price. Dr. Brown said on one occasion that a couple of agents "may" have been at the autopsy and on another that agents had wandered in and out of the procedure. The doctor finally settled on the position that no agents had been there at any time. It is this position that the FBI has taken before Congress and other inquirers ever since.

It is not true. FBI reports released under the Freedom of Information Act would eventually prove that four agents—Price, Wood, Donald Dealing, and John Munis—were in the autopsy room, some just before and some just after the procedure. Price even photographed Aquash's face. Zigrossi had either lied or been lied to about his agents' presence.

"In the 1980s we had the pleasure of deposing David Price," Ken Tilsen, the senior-most lawyer of WKLDOC, would later say. "Price, to my mind, must be the most evil living agent in an organization that trained thousands of agents in the practice of evil. When we asked him whether he was at the autopsy, his answer was, 'I wasn't there.'

" 'Okay, then, why did the doctor's assistant say she gave you the hands?'

" 'Well, I was outside the room.'

" 'I see. Was there a window in the door?'

" 'Yeah.'

" 'Did you look through the window?'

" 'I may have.'

" 'But you weren't at the autopsy?'

" 'Oh, no. No, no, noooo.' "

Asked what he remembered in 2003, Norman Zigrossi said, "I know all about the first autopsy. I'll never forget it. Now, I can tell you which of our agents were there, and that was Price and Woods"—he meant Wood.

Was he saying that Price and Wood were in the room while Brown was working on Aquash?

"That's correct."

Zigrossi was unaware he was making a confession. He seemed merely to have forgotten his original story and was now saying what he remembered, which unfortunately for his credibility was the truth.

As at the autopsy, so at the crime scene. Zigrossi said only one FBI agent (eventually named as Donald Dealing) had gone to Roger Amiotte's ranch, but witnesses counted four agents. Amiotte remembered Price and Wood by name. A BIA officer also remembered Price—yet the officer's boss, BIA police chief Ken Sayers, tried to claim the officer was not there. Sayers said only three BIA policemen went to the scene, but witnesses counted as many as six, including Sayers, who in turn denied he had been at Amiotte's.

"When we asked Price whether he was at the crime scene," WKLDOC's Ken Tilsen said, "his first thing was, 'I wasn't assigned to her.'

" 'Okay. Were you there?'

" 'I wasn't working that day.'

" 'That wasn't the question. Were you there?'

" 'I don't remember.' "

Months after the body was found and after much harrying by Kevin McKiernan, Zigrossi said that while only Agent Dealing had gone to Amiotte's ranch on assignment, others might have gone "out of curiosity." To go to Amiotte's "out of curiosity" meant making a three-hour round-trip from either the town of Pine Ridge or Rapid City, where agents were stationed. Because the FBI had jurisdiction over reservation deaths only if they were criminal in nature and because even then the "colonial police force" tended not to be interested in Indian corpses, reporters thought it odd for even one agent, let alone four, to go to Amiotte's. In later years Zigrossi dismissed such talk as nonsense. He said that after two of his men were killed on the reservation in a shootout the year before, he dispatched agents to every unattended death to see if there might be a tie between the new corpse and the agents' killers. This was news to reporters.

Whoever and however many the agents at the scene were, what they saw was another story the FBI could not keep straight. The night the body was found, agents in Rapid City cabled Washington that there was "no indication of fowl [sic] play." But the same cable assigned the case the title "Possible Manslaughter." There was no explanation how manslaughter had been suspected in the absence of evidence of foul play. The FBI would later say its agents were just suspicious about a dead body turning up in the middle of nowhere. But if this innocent explanation were true, agents should have re-titled the case after Dr. Brown's autopsy concluded that the woman had died innocently. But the "Possible Manslaughter" title continued to appear on documents from Rapid City even after Brown's autopsy and, still more incredibly, after Aquash's burial. The FBI would offer an explanation for this oddity too: its agents did not know about Brown's exposure finding until eight days later. That is, the four agents who went to the autopsy were so uninterested in its outcome that neither then nor over the next week did they bother to ask what Jane Doe had died of. Only after the FBI learned that the dead and buried woman was Aquash did they ask what Dr. Brown had found. (They asked by way of a chat on March 4 between Agent Wood and Dr. Brown.) Agent Wood swore to all of this before the judge who ordered Aquash exhumed.

The only hitch in these claims is that an FBI cable released under the Freedom of Information Act says otherwise: the FBI knew of Brown's exposure finding at some unidentified point before Wood's chat with Brown on March 4. No doubt (although the cable does not say as much) the FBI knew of the exposure finding the day Brown made it. Whenever, precisely, the FBI knew, the cable is at odds with Wood's sworn testimony and points to a cover-up. Wood may also have been attempting a cover-up when he swore in court that Brown told him in their chat that during his autopsy he had seen "an obvious injury . . . a small contusion on the head." Brown, of course, said exactly the opposite in his autopsy report and on every other occasion that he was asked about the autopsy. It is impossible to sort out all the lies here, but probably Wood or Brown—knowing that when Aquash was exhumed and re-autopsied, the bullet would be found—decided it would look better if the authorities had seen a bump and missed a bullet than if they had missed everything, and thus concocted the "obvious injury."

The Dakota press did not notice the many contradictions. The same newspapers that on February 25 had quoted FBI agents saying there was no hint of foul play, on March 4 quoted Wood saying there had been a big hint of foul play. When, only a few weeks later, the FBI reversed course again—dropping Wood's claim of the obvious injury and resurrecting the original claim of no hint of violence (which has remained the official line ever since)—the press, not having spotted the first change in course, did not spot the reversion.

The agents who sent Aquash's hands to Washington were working in a long tradition. In four of the New World's five centuries, frontier capitals had paid bounties for Native body parts in proof that their owners had been exterminated. As a grisly byproduct, scalps and hands, ears and genitals became trophies in the saloons and on the saddle horns of the Americas. Even in 1976, when Aquash was dismembered, the museums of civilized North America displayed the skeletons and mummified heads of tribal elders—grandparents and great-grandparents of those still living. The FBI agents who had Aquash's hands severed could not have known they were carrying on a tradition that would make a martyr of Aquash, that songs would be sung about her and ceremonies held in her honor and newborns named for her decades after their deed. Agents did, however, know to be bashful about their handiwork. Early press releases said Aquash's "fingerprints" had been sent to Washington but neglected to say her fingers had gone with them. When the particulars were outed, the FBI described amputation as a standard practice for identification in many jurisdictions, but it could point to no such jurisdiction in North America. Over the years, the FBI refused to say whether its agents had considered other, less gruesome, means of identification. It said only that "it was impossible to obtain fingerprints" on Pine Ridge.

The claim did not sit right with Garry Peterson. "All fingers," he wrote in his autopsy report, "show distinct fingerprint ridges although the finger pads appear somewhat wrinkled." Dr. Peterson said afterward that anyone trained in taking prints—that is, any FBI agent or BIA officer—should have been able to print the fingers. Had better results been wanted, the agents could have asked Dr. Brown to inject fluid beneath the dehydrated fingertips. If all else had failed, Brown could have severed only the fingertips (as the FBI lab eventually did), putting each tip in the corresponding finger of a latex glove and sending those to Washington. There was no justification for taking the entire hands.

A naïf might read into the FBI's claim that "it was impossible to obtain fingerprints" a suggestion that someone had tried. This was not so. The lawmen who had gone to Dr. Brown's autopsy eventually said they were too afraid of destroying even a single print to gently daub a pinky with ink and press it to paper. Far safer, they thought, to have the hands sawn off, immersed in a formaldehyde-filled jar, and mailed to Washington. That the lab could make casts of the prints even after two thousand miles of jostling against glass and that Dr. Peterson found the fingers still printable after their return to Pine Ridge suggested something about their original state.

"One question," Ken Tilsen later said, "that the FBI could never answer about cutting off her hands was, why not wait?" Tilsen in latter years was a man of bare pate and bad angina but still, as he had been in the 1970s, an adherent of the querulous detail, which he piled one atop the next with compounding weight. He carried himself accordingly, chest forward, like a stevedore or beauty queen, but the aggressive effect was tempered by a wrinkled, deliberate voice conveying lawyerly gravitas. "Even if the FBI thought they had to cut off her hands, basic decency requires that you wait more than a day to see if other people might recognize her, particularly since Pine Ridge was and is a small place where everybody knows everybody. They didn't even pause before taking that drastic step. When I asked experts about the motivation for this, what they told me was that the primary result of removing her hands and sending them to the lab—rather than taking the fingerprints at the hospital—was to increase the length of time it took to identify her. [Indeed, once during Aquash's life the FBI had identified her in twenty-four hours from prints lifted off her in the field.]

"Now, why would they want to delay the identification? I have always suspected it was because the FBI was afraid of what they would find if they dug into this case. They knew this was Anna Mae Aquash, and they were afraid that some of their people—not necessarily FBI agents, I have never believed even David Price was capable of pulling the trigger, but their allies, their friends—were involved, and they didn't want to find out. They wanted the trail to go cold. Any of the agents who saw Anna Mae should have been able to identify her. They had her photograph and they had a description of her. She was a fugitive—and not just any fugitive. They believed she had information about the killing of the two FBI agents on

Pine Ridge in 1975, to the investigation of which the FBI had devoted every imaginable resource, and they believed she had been traveling with some of the alleged killers. Moreover, before she disappeared, she was scheduled to appear in court. But the day before her trial, she jumps bond and walks out of the same hotel where the FBI was staying. David Price was, I think, staying in that very hotel. She literally walked out from under their noses. After that, they *had* to be hunting all over for her. A few months later, a woman shows up dead on the same reservation where Anna Mae lived. The body is in the middle of nowhere. It is inconceivable that this woman just wandered off on a drunk and died of exposure, miles from the nearest bar or for that matter any human habitation. The agents look her over. She's an Indian of attractive build. She's about the right age, about the right height, right weight. She's wearing the very distinctive jewelry she always wore. Only a few of the FBI's important fugitives are women, fewer still are Indian women, and fewer still are Indian women from Pine Ridge. Yet the FBI wants us to believe that not one of those agents at the scene or the hospital thinks, 'Hmmm, I wonder if this is our fugitive?' For any of these agents, that is virtually impossible to believe. For David Price it is absolutely impossible."

It was "absolutely impossible" because Price knew Aquash. Less than a year before she turned up dead, he had questioned her about a murder. Several months after that, he had arrested her in a raid, by some accounts recognizing her on sight. He had almost certainly lied about being at Amiotte's, and he had lied about or obscured his proximity to the first autopsy, at which he had photographed her face. At the time he took those pictures, he had been in possession of pictures of the living Aquash. And although he would later swear he was not looking for her, internal FBI documents would eventually prove that just days before her body was found, he was helping to coordinate the hunt for her. And then there is the story that Aquash told her peers, which was that in the last months of her life Agent Price had given Aquash a choice: cooperate with the FBI, or he would see her dead before the year was out.

She had told him to go fuck himself. (Price has consistently and vehemently denied the story.)

* * *

To believe the FBI's claim that its agents did not recognize Aquash was to believe its claim that she was thoroughly decayed. That she was decayed was not in question. How badly decayed was.

"Her face was pure black with exposure and dehydration," David Price once said, "and she had no eyes! *You* try to identify a girl you've only seen twice in your life and [identified] the second time only because she identified herself!" The FBI's press officers have said the same thing through the decades, if with less spirit. Price's claim is supported by a BIA policeman who knew Aquash slightly and said he did not recognize her when he saw her in the morgue.

But other witnesses have said differently. Dr. Peterson, while cautioning that it is harder to identify a rotted corpse than most people think, said Aquash's condition "wasn't bad, even after burial and exhumation." The workers at the hospital who saw Aquash before the first autopsy were more adamant: Jane Doe could have been identified by anyone who knew her. Journalist Kevin McKiernan said that pictures from the second autopsy "showed facial features that appeared identifiable" but also that someone who did not know Aquash well might have needed leading—say, with lineup photos—to identify her. Ken Tilsen said no one who knew Aquash failed to recognize her from the second-autopsy pictures. And Candy Hamilton said Aquash was "totally recognizable" in the pictures.

The FBI could make the question moot by releasing its photos from the two autopsies. It will not. To do so, say Aquash's dismemberers, would violate norms of decency. The FBI does, however, say that its agents showed the pictures to people on the reservation and that this is proof that agents were trying to identify Jane Doe. But the FBI will not say to whom it showed the pictures, and the only person known to have seen them is one Myrtle Poor Bear. In Poor Bear's story, Agents Price and Wood showed her the pictures as a threat. They said Aquash had been blackened by fire, not frostbite, and that if Poor Bear did not agree to lie under oath that she had seen AIM's Leonard Peltier kill the two FBI agents in 1975, Poor Bear would end up like Aquash. Poor Bear perjured herself. Price and Wood said Poor Bear's claim of having been threatened was a lie. The irony of their saying so about a witness who said they made her commit perjury was apparently lost on them. Whatever the truth of Poor Bear's story, the FBI has never explained why its agents were showing pictures of someone whose face was rotten beyond recognizing. If Aquash was, as the FBI claimed, beyond identifying, what good did it do to show the pictures? Surely the mere fact of showing them (if true) proves she was at least potentially identifiable.

"The other thing they say about their great efforts to identify her," Candy Hamilton said, "is they put out a flyer about this unidentified woman. But no one ever saw it. After we found out it was Annie Mae, I dug around on the bulletin board at Sioux Nation and finally found one sign buried under a whole bunch of other stuff. That's the only one I ever saw or heard of. It had the wrong age, wrong size—five-six or something. And she was teeny. I mean, I'm five-four, and I felt like I towered over her."

The flyer does not survive, but the BIA memo on which it was based does. It says Dr. Brown measured the body at five feet two inches and 110 pounds. How Aquash grew to five feet six or so in the flyer is a mystery. (When Brown released his autopsy report two weeks later, Aquash mutated again: five feet four and 105.) Hamilton said the flyer mentioned none of Aquash's identifying traits—her gallbladder scar, her partial dental plate, her childbearing, her jewelry—though all were noted in Brown's autopsy. The jewelry, her friends have said, would have given her away in an instant. Three decades later Roger Amiotte still remembered her "big butterfly bracelet with great big wings of silver and a body of turquoise—stuck out about yay, wider than my wrist. It was unique." The FBI thought the bracelet unusual enough to show a local jeweler (who knew neither its owner nor its maker), but the agents did not show it to the public.

After several days in the hospital morgue, Aquash's corpse was sent to a mortuary just over the state line in Nebraska. But the mortuary, according to BIA police chief Sayers, "told us they couldn't keep it in the state it was," so Sayers ordered the body buried. Yet mortician Tom Chamberlain told another story: the body, he agreed, was beyond embalming, but it was not bad off, certainly not beyond keeping. He had coated it with disinfectant and put it in his unheated garage, where he was certain it could have stayed a week or more in the cold weather—only, Sayers had called him a day or so after the body's arrival and insisted it be buried. Chamberlain said he had asked just how Sayers intended to do that when the corpse had not been identified and had neither a death certificate nor a burial permit attached to it. Sayers did not have an immediate answer.

"Darnedest thing I ever saw," Chamberlain said. "Been doing this for over fifty years and haven't run into a case like this yet."

A friend of Aquash's who had other funereal business visited Chamberlain's at this time and overheard Chamberlain on the phone saying he wouldn't bury an unidentified body without approval from the state licensing office. The friend, Gladys Bissonette, offered to look at the Jane Doe, but Chamberlain told her he had been ordered to let only "authorized" people see the body. Another friend of Aquash's, Lou Beane, said she visited Chamberlain's and heard him say he had a corpse out back with a bullet in its head. The undertaker denied Bissonette's claims; he was not asked about Beane's before his own undertaking.

In the end, Chief Sayers prevailed on a priest at Holy Rosary Mission to bury the woman. No burial certificate ever surfaced, and neither church nor funeral parlor kept their usual records for processing a body. The priest at Holy Rosary later explained that he had buried the woman without the required paperwork because last rites were a sacrament he had to give all comers.

Toward the burial the FBI took an attitude similar to its attitude toward the first autopsy: it knew nothing of the BIA's work. Only after the deed was done, Agent Wood swore in court, did the FBI learn Aquash had been buried. But again there is evidence to the contrary. Inmates from the Pine Ridge jail who buried Aquash on March 2 also exhumed her on March 11. They said the same men in suits attended both affairs. Candy Hamilton said the only suits at the March 11 exhumation were on FBI agents. Ergo the FBI seems to have attended the March 2 burial. Then, too, a report from Agent Wood said that on March 2, BIA officer Merrick told him the body "was being buried at Holy Rosary Cemetery on March 2, 1976." "Was being buried," meaning *at that moment being buried* or *soon to be buried*, was rather different from what Wood told the court: Aquash "had been buried" by the time he learned about it.

Say you have a body that has not been identified. Say you think it is deteriorating and needs to be buried. Say you have chopped off its hands and sent them to a lab, and the lab has succeeded in lifting prints and is trying to match the prints to those in its files, and it has told you this. Say also that a match can typically be made or ruled out in a fairly short time—hours if the prints are unusual in their characteristics, a few days if they are common. Say a need arises to bury the body, and you happen to call the lab on the day of the burial. Would you not, before you put the body in the ground, ask the lab how much longer it needed to make an identification?

Not if you were Agent Wood. Although he spoke with the lab on March 2, he was, according to repeated statements from the FBI, as surprised as anyone to learn on March 3 that the just-buried woman had been identified a day too late. But once more his claim is not borne out by FBI documents. The key manuscript is Aquash's FBI Identification Record, a form on which FBI headquarters in Washington records a person's vital statistics and run-ins with the law. Aquash's death was logged on her identification record as "received" on March 2, the day she was buried. Headquarters could not have marked her death as received into her record unless it knew her identity. Which is to say the FBI apparently identified Aquash either on or before the day its agents buried her—not the next day, as publicly claimed. The FBI could clarify precisely when Aquash was identified by releasing notes from its lab and fingerprint units, but the FBI refuses to do so. The FBI has released just one other paper on Aquash from its identification division, and it was doctored before it was made public. The paper *is* a short memo saying simply that the lab had identified Aquash. What is doctored is the date, which in the released version reads "March 10, 1976." The "10" has been sandwiched into a space that originally held only one digit, which digit was apparently whited-out and replaced with the "10." Perhaps the doctoring was harmless. Or perhaps the original digit was a damning 1 or 2, indicating the FBI knew who Aquash was before her burial on March 2.

Against all of these hints of a cover-up, the FBI has long defended itself by noting that it was Agent Wood who secured the court order to have Aquash exhumed. According to the FBI, "immediately" on learning Aquash was Jane Doe, Wood went to work on the exhumation papers. Had he wanted Aquash to stay buried, the FBI has said, he would have done nothing of the kind. But neither the FBI nor the office of the U.S. attorney, which drafted the exhumation request, has produced any evidence that they started working on the request until March 8, five days after Aquash was identified. March 8 happened to be the day a lawyer from WKLDOC went to the FBI's Rapid City office and demanded a copy of Dr. Brown's autopsy report. The lawyer, Bruce Ellison, said WKLDOC did not believe Aquash had died of exposure and strongly insinuated the Bureau was hiding something. Agent Tom Greene, who spoke with Ellison, could have deflected the charge by saying the FBI was at that moment working to exhume Aquash. He did not. It is possible, then, that the FBI moved to exhume Aquash only after it became clear that WKLDOC would do so. Regardless, the FBI was in no hurry to dig up a body that it had called "terribly decomposed" and that, day by day, was decomposing further, to the harm of whatever story it had to tell. Of course, anyone who knew there was a bullet in its skull need not have hurried.

The first time a director of the FBI spoke publicly about the Aquash case was in May 1976, three months after the body had been found. Till then, Clarence Kelley's FBI had ducked questions by saying that because the case was open, the Bureau couldn't discuss it without compromising the investigation. It was a dubious argument. The questions being put to the FBI— who was at the crime scene? was Aquash identifiable? when was she identified?—would have compromised only its agents. Kelley agreed to speak only after the *Washington Star* and *Minneapolis Tribune* ran page-one exposés about the case, which in turn prompted Attorney General Edward Levi, Kelley's superior, to promise an investigation by the Justice Department. Kelley ordered his own investigation first. The objectivity of the probe may be measured by the fact that Agent Wood was one of the investigating agents. Together, the FBI's investigation and the press reports told Kelley that witnesses had seen four FBI agents at the crime scene, that hospital staff had seen the bullet wound, and that mortician Tom Chamberlain had said Aquash did not need to be buried immediately. But when Kelley spoke to the public, he said that only one agent had been at the scene, that no one there or at the hospital had seen any sign of violence, and that Chamberlain had declared the body needed to be buried. Kelley also knew the entrance wound had been obvious, but he implied it was not by calling it "small." He knew the lodged bullet had been visible to the naked eye, but he implied the opposite by saying it had settled "behind" Aquash's eye socket. He knew Dr. Peterson had diagnosed the bullet wound in a few seconds, but he implied the opposite by saying Peterson made his diagnosis only after X rays were taken. The FBI has reiterated Kelley's falsehoods, with only the smallest of changes, ever since. In recent years, it has even said that Dr. Brown made his exposure finding after only a "cursory" look at the body, not a full autopsy.

Attorney General Levi assigned the Justice Department's General Crimes Division to look into the FBI. The relationship between the lawyers of General Crimes and the agents of the FBI was that of coaches to their star players. What General Crimes investigated and what it concluded, Levi never said. The investigation simply disappeared. Reporters with sources inside the Justice Department said the investigation was never completed; apparently Levi accepted Kelley's internal inquiry in its place. When the U.S. Commission on Civil Rights asked about the General Crimes investigation, the Justice Department ignored the query, although it was required by law to answer. When USCCR persisted, Assistant

Attorney General Richard Thornburgh (later attorney general under Reagan and the elder Bush) finally replied, "You may be assured that our review of this matter was thorough. However, in my opinion it would be inappropriate to forward to your office investigative reports on matters that are currently under investigation." From time to time over the years, members of Congress were asked by their constituents about FBI wrong-doing in the case, and the legislators in turn asked the FBI for explanations. The standard reply from the FBI read, "We believe the allegations . . . lack the specificity necessary for an investigation. Accordingly, no action on our part is warranted."

The man whose autopsy was at the center of the scandal, Dr. Brown, was never investigated—unless a lone phone call from Norman Zigrossi counted as an investigation. Of the phone call, Zigrossi later recalled, "I said to him, 'Did you realize that we had to do another autopsy and they found a bullet in her head?'

" 'Oh well,' he said, 'you can't get 'em all.'

"I said, 'You realize what that does to me?'

"He said, 'I'm sorry. I'm human, okay?'

"I said, 'Okay, you may have to testify to that someday.'

"He said, 'That's fine, I'll testify.'

"What could I do? I can't chew out an old man who tells me he did the best he could. And I believe that's exactly what happened. I have no reason to believe anything different."

The FBI was not known for such solicitude with, say, members of the American Indian Movement who offered thin alibis.

Five years after Aquash's death, at a congressional hearing to reauthorize the FBI, a committeeman asked the FBI whether, given the suspicion that continued to surround the case, the FBI would ever investigate Dr. Brown's role. (The doctor himself had since died.) The FBI functionary at the microphone said the Bureau saw no point in doing so: "I don't think anything could come of it." The committee accepted the answer and moved on. But Indian Country has never moved on.

CHAPTER 2

THE PINE RIDGE Indian Reservation, bereft of the faintest commercial pulse, has always lived on transfusions from beyond. In the early 1970s, the transfusors—the business class of border towns like Gordon and Rushville, Nebraska, and Hot Springs, Kadoka, and Interior, South Dakota—tended to speak of the aid they gave the Lakotas in terms usually reserved for the aid Florence Nightingale gave the wounded of Crimea. They seldom mentioned that the aid was most generous in their bars, somewhat less in their shops, and least of all in their banks, where it was most needed. The Indians who peopled Pine Ridge, the Oglala band of the Lakota* nation, were less rosy about the relationship. They had endless stories of being cheated in their transactions, of being presumed thieves and drunkards until proven otherwise, and of being humiliated and harassed by border-town police. Reporters from outside the region tended to compare the western reaches of Nebraska and South Dakota to Mississippi of a decade earlier, and Mississippi usually got the better of the comparison.

Against this background the events of February 12, 1972, were unexceptional. What was exceptional was the response. On that Friday a quartet of men from the border town of Gordon passed the afternoon in the honored Western pastime of coyote-hunting, then repaired to town to drink.

---

* Outsiders have long known the Lakotas as the *Sioux*, a corruption of the word their enemies the Ojibwas used for them: *Nadouessioux*, meaning "adders." *Lakota*, meaning "friends," is what the Lakotas call themselves. For obvious reasons, it is the preferred term.

At about ten o'clock that night, their talk turned to "busting an Indian," another Western pastime they had enjoyed before. They drove Main Street until they found a prospect. One of the group (by now a quintet—they had picked up a girlfriend) got out and shoved the Indian around, but the Indian only walked away. A few blocks later, they made a more determined assault—whether on the same Indian or a different one is not clear. The victim in any case was Raymond Yellow Thunder, an Oglala ranch hand of middle age, a kindly but not particularly prosperous soul who had gone to Gordon to drink off a midwinter workweek. The four men stepped from the car and took turns beating him, for how hard or how long again is not clear. Then they stripped him from the belt down, stuffed him into the trunk of the car, and drove around town for a couple of hours. At midnight they stopped at the Legion Hall, where a dance was being held, hauled Yellow Thunder from the trunk, and shoved him through a side door of the hall half-naked and slightly bloody. They slammed the door behind him. A story would later spread that Yellow Thunder was forced to dance before the legionnaires, but this was not, it seems, true. The legionnaires later convincingly said that several people rushed to Yellow Thunder's aid, one man tugging Yellow Thunder's shirt down over his loins while others asked if he needed help. Yellow Thunder said he had had enough help from the whites of Gordon, thanks, and went out into the winter night. Gordon's gentry would later point to the help they offered Yellow Thunder as proof of the town's humanity. But if anyone at the Legion Hall saw a need to call the police after the bruised, bloody, pantless, and bootless Indian walked out into the frozen night, it is not recorded.

Yellow Thunder had not been freed long before his attackers came across him again. They shoved him back in the trunk of their car—whether beating him further is not known—drove him around some more, and finally let him go at a Laundromat. They were good enough to throw his clothes out with him before driving home. En route they boasted of their sport at an all-night truck stop. Meanwhile Yellow Thunder shuffled to the city jail, where Deputy Sheriff John Paul, as befit his apostolic name, took in the wanderer. Deputy Paul had done so before, opening a cell on occasion when Yellow Thunder needed to sleep off a wet night. Paul later said that by the time Yellow Thunder arrived, he had heard about the incident at the Legion Hall. Yellow Thunder told Paul he was the victim. Paul said he noticed no injuries to Yellow Thunder beyond a scratch on the cheek and some bruises on his head. He did not call a doctor. He did not take a statement about the beating and kidnapping. He did not ask his colleagues on patrol to find the assailants. Yellow Thunder went to sleep. At seven in the morning, he awoke and left Paul's care. By now he was staggering, but still the deputy did not call a doctor. Later that day an acquaintance of Yellow Thunder's named George Ghost Dog saw him in the cab of a pickup truck in a used-car lot. Deputy Paul's claim of mild injuries notwithstanding, Ghost Dog said Yellow Thunder had a fat lip and a bloodied face. He asked Yellow Thunder if he was all right. Yes, Yellow Thunder said, he would make it.

He did not. A week later he was found, still in the cab, stiffly frozen. An autopsy was ordered, and western Nebraska's ubiquitous pathologist, W. O. Brown, was called. Dr. Brown determined that exposure to the cold had been a factor in Yellow Thunder's death, but, unlike in Aquash's case four years later, Brown did not claim that exposure was the chief cause of death. Yellow Thunder died, he said, from a massive subdural hematoma—a hemorrhaged pond of blood—that covered the entire right side of his brain. The hemorrhage was caused by a blow to the forehead by "some instrument." Brown also recorded several bruises and lacerations on Yellow Thunder's head, on his right side, and on his right leg. The wound where Yellow Thunder had been struck on the forehead was visible, but the pond of blood beneath the skin was not. Suspicion was cast on Brown's autopsy when Yellow Thunder's family asked to see the body and was denied until a mortician had touched it up. Rumors spread that the authorities had something to hide, that Yellow Thunder had been tortured or burned with cigarettes or mutilated, even castrated.

There was also controversy about what the authorities did after the autopsy. The county attorney said he pressed charges against the assailants—brothers Melvin and Leslie Hare and their friends Bernard Ludder, Robert Bayliss, and Jeanette Thompson—almost immediately, a mere two days after the body was found. But Yellow Thunder's family, who lived on Pine Ridge, said the attorney dragged his prosecutorial feet and at first pressed no charges. The family begged the government of the Oglala Sioux Tribe to intervene, but the tribe did little. The charges, however they arose, were not to Indians' liking: false imprisonment and manslaughter in the second degree. Nor was the bail: $6,250 a head. Indians said, rightly, that had Yellow Thunder been white and his attackers red, a murder charge would have been brought, the bail would have been beyond paying, and County Attorney Mike Smith would not have been calling the killing a "cruel practical joke" and the killers "pranksters."

The American Indian Movement was holding a conference at the other end of Nebraska, in Omaha, when Yellow Thunder's body was found. AIM was then in its toddlerhood, having been founded in Minnesota's Twin Cities in 1968, a late start by the standards of twentieth-century rights movements. Indians took longer than blacks and other minorities to mobilize in part because they were more thoroughly oppressed and in part because their population was tiny and diffuse. Scattered thinly across the West and all but vanished in most of the East, Indians totaled less than 1 percent of the American population and by any measure were the poorest, most diseased, and worst educated race in America. Indians did, however, come together forcefully at last, notably in 1969, when an indigenous armada sailed to Alcatraz Island in San Francisco Bay and seized the abandoned prison there. Citing laws that required surplus federal land to be given to Indians, the occupiers demanded the island be reborn as an Indian educational center. Alcatraz, they wrote, was ideal for Indian use, "as determined by the white man's own standards" because:

It is isolated from modern facilities, and without adequate means of transportation.

It has no fresh running water.

It has inadequate sanitation facilities.

There are no oil or mineral rights.

There is no industry and so unemployment is very great.

There are no health care facilities.

The soil is rocky and nonproductive, and the land does not support game.

There are no educational facilities.

The population has always exceeded the land base.

The population has always been held as prisoners and kept dependent on others.

The occupiers did not get their center. They did, however, hold the rock for eighteen months and draw attention to the sorry state of Indian Country. The activism proved contagious. Impudent tribes in Washington state called more loudly for their treaty-guaranteed share of salmon runs, Indians in Milwaukee seized an abandoned Coast Guard station on Lake Michigan and demanded its repatriation, the Six Nations (the Iroquois) of New York threatened to shut down highways that crossed their reservations if parts of their broken treaties were not restored, and on and on it went in small but ever more numerous pockets of America.

AIM was but one of the agitators, but it soon gained preeminence. It got its start policing the Minneapolis police, especially in the bars that catered to the Midwestern Indians who gravitated to the Twin Cities. These were low-end taverns prone to brawls, and when the brawls broke out, the police tended to arrest every Native in sight, guilt or innocence be damned. Often the Indians were beaten ruthlessly. AIM took to the bars with foot patrols that were equipped with police scanners, walkie-talkies, and cameras. When a fight started, AIM often arrived before the cops. They told Indians who were being arrested of their rights, and they photographed the police at work. They were thanked with blackjacks to the head, arrests, and indictments for "interfering" with the law. The AIMers persisted. They held public hearings about the abuse. They published their photographs. The press, particularly in Minneapolis, responded favorably. (The press of St. Paul was more McCarthyite; it tinted all agitators Red, the more so if they were red.) In a remarkably short time, the police beatings and indiscriminate arrests came to a stop, and AIM was lionized. Chapters of the group sprouted around the country wherever three Indians could find the cash for a case of Schlitz and a target for their frustration. Detractors called the chapters red pimples on the white skin of America just waiting to burst. To AIMers this was high praise. AIM's work expanded into quieter services, like finding decent housing and jobs for urban Indians, who had long had neither, and founding "survival schools" for Indian children who had left or been rejected by white schools. But AIM garnered most of its following and nearly all of its headlines from its rowdier deeds. When AIM co-founder Clyde Bellecourt bellowed in his speeches, "We're the landlords of this country, the rent is due, and we're here to collect!"—only a cigar-store Indian could resist smiling.

After Raymond Yellow Thunder was killed, his relatives asked AIM to come to Gordon from its conference in Omaha. Over three days, 1,400 Indians from fourscore tribes descended noisily on the town. Gordon's census doubled. The protesters were led by Dennis Banks and Russell Means, whose charisma was such that they were often taken for AIM's only leaders, which they were not. They were, however, incomparable.

Banks was the senior of the two. Deeply handsome, he had a sandstone face scored by crevasses that ran from jaw to nostril and an escarpment of brow that overhung darkly ruminative eyes. His hair ran to his scapulae. He was the more circumspect of the pair, more guarded in his speech, but not incapable of turning an incendiary phrase when he chose. "For every rifle on the street pointed at an Indian," he said before one confrontation with police, "I'm going to have ten rifles aimed at a white man."

Banks shared a common history with many Indians of his generation and of several previous generations. Born in either 1932 or 1937 (the usual sources for such data, including Banks, are unreliable) on the Leech Lake

Reservation of Minnesota's Ojibwa people, he was taken from his family at the age of five by the federal government and forced into the first of a long series of boarding schools. The schools were run by the Bureau of Indian Affairs on the infamous dictum of "killing the Indian to save the man." On admittance, students had their long, ceremonial hair shorn and traditional clothes burned. Their religions and languages were banned. Rooms were Spartan, board was scarce, regulations were Catholic, and the pedagogy was military. All too often the children were beaten or sexually assaulted by their warders or older students. To thrive required the talents customary to all internment camps: lying, thieving, bullying, toadying. To emerge merely deracinated after a dozen years of this was a victory; the more usual fate was to emerge criminal as well. Banks fit the second bill. After a tour with the air force, he served two tours with the Minnesota State Penitentiary, first for burglary, then for parole violation. During his second stint, he met several other thoughtful Indians who talked about the reasons so many of their people had landed in jail and on skid row. Some of these men, including Banks, would found AIM after their release. The group was begotten, in the phrase favored by Indians, in the iron house.

Russell Means had been relieved of his culture more subtly, although also by federal policy. He was born on Pine Ridge in 1939 but was reared in California, thanks to a BIA program that moved Indians from reservations to cities. The benevolent idea behind the program was that since efforts to bring jobs to Indians had consistently failed, Indians would be brought to jobs. But the program also had a sinister motive, which was to get Indians off land that whites wanted. For centuries America had pushed Indians onto unwanted lands, only later to decide those lands were desirable for one thing or another: uranium or coal, gas or timber, rangeland or farmland. So the BIA paid Indians' bus fare to cities—sometimes on threat of cutting off food and housing on the reservation—set them up in dismal apartments, and entrusted them to the free market. Badly schooled by the BIA and under-skilled from years of joblessness, most of the émigrés couldn't find work or couldn't keep it when they did. The great majority traded poverty among family, friends, and culture for poverty in a foreign land. Most eventually returned to the reservation, worse off now since their land had been bought or leased by whites.

The Means family was in the small minority that did okay. Although entirely estranged from their culture, the Meanses found a toe hold in the American middle class, a humble prosperity. Russell grew tall and erect of gait with a wide, agreeable forehead, a mouth nearly as broad, and a hair-line that was in retreat in front and that was defined in back by long, twin plaits. As a teenager he was an occasional delinquent. As an adult he worked variously as an accountant, a dance instructor, and, in 1970, a part-time director of a small Indian center in Cleveland. After the rise of AIM, he traded the quieter activism of Ohio for the ferment of the Plains, where his skill at giving a good quote made him popular with both Indians and the reporters who covered them. "You have made red niggers of my people!" he would shout. Or, "For America to live, Europe must die!" What passed for calm commentary from Means was, "If the federal government once again turns a deaf ear and closes its eyes to the Indians, their Indian Wars will start all over again. There will be death. I don't consider that a threat. That's reality." Neither Means nor Banks held title to a small ego.

In Gordon, Banks and Means convened a people's grand jury to hear grievances. Foremost of these were alleged rapes of Indian girls by white policemen and alleged swindlings by white storekeepers. AIM threatened to boycott the town, and the Oglala Sioux Tribe, till then not prone to activism, announced that it would drain its accounts from Gordon's banks. The accounts probably totaled no more than $1 million, but even modest sums meant a lot in a town of Gordon's size. City officials met with Banks, Means, and other AIMers and soon agreed to concessions: the city would create a human rights board to hear complaints, and a policeman accused of rape and other barbarisms was suspended. AIM would later say that it had won the indictments, or more severe indictments, of Yellow Thunder's killers. These claims were untrue. AIM did, however, secure a second autopsy of Yellow Thunder (the post-postmortem was a minor staple of

Indian Country), which confirmed the findings of the first autopsy. By then, however, the rumors of torture, cigarette burns, and castration had grown wings, and the second autopsy did little to clip them. Indians had simply been lied to too often to trust so-called facts. Today the rumors are still spoken of as the truth throughout much of the Plains.

During the protests in Gordon, AIM asked federal prosecutors to bolster the tepid state indictments with federal civil rights charges, as was sometimes done in the South when local officials treated lynchers lightly. But the Department of Justice demurred, and three months after AIM left Gordon, Yellow Thunder's killers were tried in state court. Charges against the lone female defendant, Jeanette Thompson, had by then been dropped, and another defendant, Bernard Ludder, had pleaded to kidnapping (for which he was fined $250) and turned on his friends. Melvin and Leslie Hare and Robert Bayliss were convicted and given sentences of two, six, and four years respectively. They served an unknown fraction of the sentences.

In hindsight, AIM's critics would say the group didn't win much that was tangible or enduring in Gordon. The human rights board, for example, proved to be mostly ineffective, and the sentences were mere slaps. But the group's less tangible victories should not be underrated. AIM had taken a yearning for dignity that so many Indians had long felt but had never been able to distill, and distilled it—potently. What AIM would do with its success was another matter.

The Indians who seized the Bureau of Indian Affairs in Washington, D.C., eight months after the Yellow Thunder protests did not start with that intention. They had intended to channel the roiling tributaries of Indian activism into a single stream, which they called the Trail of Broken Treaties. The Trail consisted of Indians from every part of America who packed themselves into ailing autos and descended in caravans toward Washington. It was a long journey, the westernmost caravans starting weeks before the rendezvous in Washington on November 1, 1972. Most of the caravanners stopped en route at AIM headquarters in Minneapolis–

St. Paul, where their leaders drafted a twenty-point platform that they called, with commendable directness, the Twenty Points. The Points called on the United States to restore its several hundred broken treaties with Indian nations. At the time the treaties were signed, the government guaranteed them for all time—"as long as the rivers shall run and the grass shall grow" in the most common phrase—but Congress annulled most of the provisions a few years after signing them, and the Supreme Court approved the annulments. (The idiom *Indian giving*, for a gift quickly taken back, was born in this era; *white giving* would have been more apt.) The treaties with the Lakota nations were exemplars of the pattern. In 1868 America guaranteed the Lakotas sovereign title to half of western South Dakota and a large share of four other states, thenceforth and for all time to be known as the Great Sioux Reserve. Six years later, Lieutenant Colonel George Armstrong Custer was ordered into the Lakotas' sacred Black Hills, in breach of treaty, and found gold. Envoys from Washington hastened west, first to barter for and then, that failing, to demand the Lakotas give up their land. The Lakotas were not in the best shape to refuse: the great bison herds, source of their food and shelter, had been famously slaughtered, and the rations guaranteed by treaty in return for the land already ceded were always short. But although a few Lakotas wanted to sell to the *wasicu*, the white man (literally *one who steals the fat*), the mass of Lakotas followed Little Big Man, who said, "I will kill the first chief who speaks for selling the Black Hills."

Many in the government thought this a good offer—extermination had always been the cleanest route to Native title—but after debate the nation opted for other means. It loosed miners on the Hills and dispatched cavalry to corral "hostile" Indians who were living, as permitted by treaty, nomadically rather than at the government's underfed and diseased reservation encampments. Custer's unprovoked and suicidal attack on the Lakota, Cheyenne, and Arapaho nations at the Greasy Grass (Little Bighorn to the white man) was the climax of the campaign. The anticlimax was America's revenge. So ruthless was the reprisal that the Indian holdouts withered in months. But even after the last Lakotas were confined to the agency camps with all their agonies, the government could not convince three-fourths of the adult men, as required by treaty, to surrender the Black Hills. So Congress severed their rations and threatened to take not just the Hills but most of the Lakotas' remaining land as well. Children died. Liquor and bribes were plied. Even so, nine in ten men refused to sign. Congress declared one in ten enough and voted theft into law in 1877. In subsequent years more of the same would carve the Great Sioux Reservation into ever smaller plots. Pine Ridge was the biggest of these; other reservations were winnowed to the size of modestly prosperous ranches.

The Lakotas were not long in suing for their land. The most important suit was brought in the early 1900s and dragged on for the better part of the century. Finally, in 1975, a federal appeals court proclaimed the obvious: "A more ripe and rank case of dishonorable dealing will never, in all probability, be found in our history." But although the Supreme Court did not disagree, neither did it return an acre. In 1980, the high court ordered the Lakotas to settle all their land claims, for the Black Hills and elsewhere, for $106 million. The hills alone had yielded $4 billion in minerals and timber and billions untold in tourism and real estate. The Indians refused to receive the settlement. "A used car for every Lakota," they scoffed, and the math bore them out. Today the money sits in escrow, steadily approaching $1 billion, but the poorest of America's poor want nothing of it.

Other land thefts had more modern origins. During World War II, for example, the Oglalas lost 525 square miles of Pine Ridge to the Department of War for a bombing range. The inhabitants of the range were given ten days' notice to gather what they could and get off. For their land and improvements—fences, barns, houses, and so on—they were paid dimes on the dollar (white appraisers took a dim view of Indian property) and for their moving costs they were paid even less. What land the government did not buy outright at these prices it leased at three pennies an acre. The residents were told they could return after the war, but the air force kept the land until 1968, at which time Congress gave it not to the Oglalas but to the National Park Service for inclusion in Badlands National Monument, under whose stewardship the tract's rich uranium deposits were not protected from mining.

There were still more artful dodges for acquiring Indian land. In the eyes of the law, Indians, even in the 1970s, were children—legally wards of the state. This condition, which continues today, was a holdover from the nineteenth century, when most Indians were unschooled in the language, commerce, and laws of America and the government sought both to protect Indians from rapacious whites and to keep Indians in submission. (Much of American's Indian policy can be read as a convenient marriage of benign and malign motives.) In consequence of their legal status, Indians could own land on reservations after a fashion, but they were never permitted to own it outright. Instead, their lands were held in trust by the Department of the Interior, parent of the BIA, which was supposed to manage the property for Indians' benefit. Lacking clear title, Indians could not use their land as collateral for loans. Lacking loans (and jobs), Indians had no capital to buy the tools, supplies, and animals to work their land for profit. Their only recourse was to lease the land, sell it to non-Indians, or leave it be. Land-hungry whites—farmers, ranchers, timber harvesters, miners—were only too happy to rent or buy, and the BIA was only too happy to broker the deals, sweetening them with below-market appraisals. On Pine Ridge in the early 1970s, the BIA leased land for an average of $1 an acre per year and sold it for an average of $40 an acre. Millions of acres slipped through Indian hands in this way. Indians who held on to their land tended to be mixed-bloods, descendants of Indians who had married whites and so had better access to capital. For the most part, mixed-bloods also held the few jobs on the reservations, ran the tribal governments, and retained little of their language, religion, and culture.

Corruption in matters related to land flourished. On Pine Ridge a BIA realty officer named Tom Conroy, a mixed-blood Oglala, used his post to buy so many tracts that he became the third-largest landowner on the reservation. When the General Accounting Office, Congress's investigative arm, examined Conroy's books in 1973, it found that the BIA had known as early as 1952 that Conroy was buying land without using sealed bids, but the BIA had done nothing. When the BIA determined in 1964 that Conroy had underpaid on his parcels by $25,939—something like $170,000 in today's money, a regal sum on Pine Ridge—it did not ask him to pay the difference because, the BIA reasoned, the BIA itself was selling Oglala land at fire sale prices. A few Oglalas kicked up a fuss about the BIA's decision, and the matter was brought to a deputy solicitor of the Interior Department. The solicitor saw nothing amiss and retroactively ratified Conroy's purchases. The GAO's exposure of this history in 1973 led to no publicity and no change in Conroy's finances. Conroy was but an extreme example of a rot that, under the BIA, infected all of America's roughly three hundred Indian reservations.

For the surrender of their rich lands in the nineteenth and earlier centuries, the small nations of Indian America had been promised schools, houses, medicine, and food in perpetuity, a deal that struck Americans of the time, correctly, as a bargain for the millions of square miles on which America would grow and prosper. But subsequent generations of Americans parted with their coin grudgingly, and by the time of the Trail of Broken Treaties in 1972, as AIM pamphleteered, "Indian male life expectancy is 44.5 years. For every white child that is born and lives, one Indian child will die. Suicide is 15 times the national average. Malnutrition on reservations is common. Unemployment is 90 percent. School dropout rate is 75 percent. The average annual Indian family income is $1,000 (on some reservations it is $500). Ninety-five percent of housing is substandard." A couple of these statistics, notably the child death rate, were exaggerated, but most were grimly accurate.

A people who were poor, angry, badly schooled, and politically exiled did not often stage the sort of political events that moved the American people to act on their behalf. The 1963 March on Washington is remembered precisely because it was an exception to the rule. The Indians who planned the Trail of Broken Treaties were truer to type and blundered badly by staging their arrival in Washington a few days before the Nixon-McGovern election. They expected their influence would be greatest on the eve of the election, but in fact the nation's reporters and politicians were strewn about the country on campaigns, and the Trailers only guaranteed themselves obscurity.

Typically, when Indian delegations came to Washington, the BIA extended them small courtesies, like helping find lodging and schedule meetings. But three weeks before the Trailers arrived, an assistant secretary of the Interior named Harrison Loesch forbade the BIA from helping them. The insult was compounded just before their arrival when the National Park Service denied the Trailers a permit to hold religious services at the Iwo Jima Memorial in Arlington National Cemetery. One of the flag bearers depicted in the iconic memorial was a Pima Indian named Ira Hayes. Hayes had come home from his flag-raising in the Pacific a hero, but after the commendations were bestowed and the tickertape swept away, he returned to his reservation to find bigotry and poverty unchanged. He took to the bottle and on a drunken night passed out in a waterlogged ditch and drowned. Many of the Trailers were veterans just back from Vietnam. Others had served in the Korean War and World War II. All felt the affront from the Park Service deeply.

The mood worsened when the first of the Trailers arrived in Washington on November 1 and found they were to lodge in the cold basement of a ghetto church occupied by rats. The Trail's inexperienced advance team was partly to blame for the poor lodging, but so too the order by Harrison Loesch denying the Trailers help. After a miserable night, Trailers by the hundred decamped from the church to the BIA headquarters in Foggy Bottom and squatted there on the understandable theory that the building belonged to them. Loesch, his hand forced, promised to help them find better billets and in the meantime let them stay in the building's auditorium. Indians continued to arrive from around the country, and by day's end, with the crowd in the BIA's auditorium numbering a thousand, Loesch arranged for them to move temporarily to a roomier hall in the nearby Department of Labor. But the Trail's leaders sensed that they had the BIA in a bind and agreed to go only if Loesch set up a meeting for them with the White House, which till then had snubbed the Trail. In a few hours, a meeting was arranged.

Dennis Banks was announcing this détente at a press conference in the BIA auditorium when a riot broke out at the building's entrance. The government would later say the Indians started the riot, which is how the story played in the news media, but the claim was not true. Earlier in the day the Department of the Interior had asked the D.C. police to clear the building at five o'clock. When the détente was reached, nobody thought to tell the police that the eviction was off. A few minutes after five, the police charged—a rare instance, wags later said, of work done at the BIA after hours—and the Indians fought back. The would-be evictors were evicted in a few minutes. Several combatants on both sides were bloodied. The Trailers, unjustly attacked and afraid of a second charge, heaped office furniture in front of every exit and fashioned weapons from broken-off table legs and envelope openers, which they brandished on the front steps of the BIA headquarters. Photos of the scene were headed for the front pages of the morning papers.

The White House dispatched an aide, Bradley Patterson, to negotiate with the Trailers, and a new deal was struck: the Indians would spend the night where they were and next morning would move to the Labor auditorium, where food and cots would await them. From there, the rank and file would be sent to better lodging while Banks, Means, and other leaders discussed the Twenty Points with the White House. The next morning, Friday November 3, the Trailers filed out of the BIA building, but as the last of them were about to leave, the first returned and said the door at Labor had been locked. The Indians feared a setup—maybe the Labor auditorium was a decoy just to get them out of the BIA. They quickly reoccupied their bastion and strung a banner across the front that read NATIVE AMERICAN EMBASSY. They were there to stay. It would turn out that there had been no setup, only incompetence. "Perhaps only the BIA could have managed successive failures of this magnitude," historians Paul Smith and Robert Warrior wrote. "The locked door was the result of a decision by a minor functionary who believed that only after everyone had left the BIA building could anyone enter the Labor Department."

More negotiations followed, but they were sterile. The Indians recognized the value of a hostage, even if it was one of Washington's uglier edifices, and they declared themselves fine in the BIA building. All they wanted now were serious negotiations on the Twenty Points. The White House dispatched Leonard Garment, senior counsel to and confidante of Nixon, and Roger Morton, secretary of the interior, whom the Indians called "Secretary of His Limousine." Garment and Morton said the administration was not inclined to renegotiate treaties under threat, and the talks that followed soaked up the pre-election weekend. On Monday, election eve, the White House won a court order for the forceful eviction of the Indians at six that evening. Phone lines to the building were cut, and the White House gave an ultimatum. Many of the diplomats of the Native American Embassy sang death songs, painted their faces, made Molotov cocktails, and perched typewriters on upper-story windowsills to use like boiling oil on the parapets of a castle. Only eighteen months earlier, the Ohio National Guard had shot dead four antiwar protesters; reporters inside the BIA building did not find the Indians' fears hyperbolic. Other Trailers, their patience worn from days of small slights and decades of large ones, snapped on learning of the ultimatum. They ripped files from cabinets and art from walls, they overturned desks and bookcases and refrigerators and anything else that could be overturned, and they spray-painted graffiti throughout the hallways. In minutes, the interior of Interior's building was wrecked, its records in hopeless disarray. When the vandalism was reported in the press a few days later, the Trailers lost much of their reservoir of public goodwill.

It was something of an anticlimax when the promised attack did not come. President Nixon, not caring for an election-eve massacre, ordered his aides to find out just how little mollifying the Indians would require to leave town. The answer, as it happened, was not much. The occupiers were wearing down under the fear of attack and the uncomfortable, unhygienic quarters. The Trailers told Nixon's aides that if the White House promised to make a formal reply to the Twenty Points and paid for the Trailers' trip home, they would go. Nixon's aides agreed and handed over $66,500 in small bills. Historians Smith and Warrior synopsized, not inaccurately, "It was the most important act of Indian resistance since the defeat of Custer at Little Big Horn, yet after all the vows of victory or death, everyone agreed to leave in exchange for gas money home." With the Indians out of the Native American Embassy, the reelected Nixonians gave the Twenty Points due consideration, duly declared them fanciful, and assumed that would be the end of that. They would not be so lucky.

The Trail had a postlude, an augury of things to come. Before vacating the BIA, the Natives had backed a U-Haul to the building's loading dock and packed it with ten tons of documents. Dennis Banks later said his people first made photocopies of the documents, but "in the end we ran out of copy paper and took the originals." It was a claim worthy of an ambassador under Nixon, himself a great handler of documents. The stolen papers showed how the BIA was bamboozling Indians of their land and of royalties from land leases. Copies of the damning papers were given to reporters, few of whom cared. One who did was Jack Anderson, author of the muck-raking and widely syndicated Washington Merry-Go-Round column. Anderson turned the documents into scathing articles that ran in scores of papers. The government responded to the revelations by investigating Anderson's main source.

The source was Hank Adams, an Assiniboine Sioux from Montana who lived among the fishing tribes of Washington state. Adams was a lay lawyer who, with a small group of other leaders, ultimately secured the fishing rights that Washington's tribes had been promised by treaty but were long denied. For his pains, he had been shot in the gut by anti-Indian vigilantes in 1970, and neither the state nor the federal government had ever shown much interest in finding his would-be assassins. Adams was not an AIMer. The group was too raucous for his tastes. But he recognized AIM's power and supported its leaders where he could. It was he who conceived of and wrote the Twenty Points, and after the Trail reached Washington he served as a mediator between Trailers and the White House. After the occupation, Adams set himself to retrieving the stolen BIA documents, which had been dispersed in odd lots to dozens of reservations across the country. He had alerted the government to his work, and the FBI thanked him by arresting him as he was readying a load of documents for return to the BIA. The FBI's mistake was arresting Les Whitten too. Whitten was Jack Anderson's co-writer. At the time of the sting, Whitten and Adams were meeting to discuss some of the more incriminating documents.

The sting turned out to be the work of John Arellano, a Mexican-American undercover agent who had infiltrated the Trail for the D.C. police in the guise of a Pueblo Indian. At the time he was assigned, the Trailers had committed no crimes nor shown intent to do so with the exception of some en route shoplifting—not excusable but also not the sort of vice to which undercover cops were normally detailed. At some point during the Trail, the FBI federalized Arellano's spying and put him on its own payroll. Photos from the occupation show Arellano on the BIA barricades, shaking an amputated table leg at his fellow cops. He later testified in court that an assistant attorney general, Henry Peterson, gave him authority to wiretap the Trailers. If so, it was a major breach of law: only a judge could authorize a wiretap, and no judge had done so. (Arellano said he never set up the tap.) After the Trailers left town, Arellano stayed in Washington and ran errands for the handful of Indian leaders who remained. In January 1974, Hank Adams asked Arellano to take several boxes of recovered papers to the BIA. When Arellano failed to show, reporter Whitten offered his car. Whitten and Adams were arrested in Adams's driveway. Only after Jack Anderson raised hell about the arrests in fifty states were the charges against Adams and Whitten dropped. Later that year, on Columbus Day, an anniversary Indians have long associated with infiltration of their ranks, the D.C. police gave Arellano a medal for his outstanding covert work.

Jack Anderson's columns aside, the post-Trail press about the protesters was almost wholly condemnatory, the ravaged BIA building serving as proof of their depravity. The media's censure allowed federal and state governments to deal with activist Indians mostly as they pleased. Dissidents on many reservations reported that jobs, housing, and other necessities controlled by the BIA were withdrawn from them and given to more quiescent Indians. More potent warnings were also issued. By one report, the National Guard of Washington state practiced mock invasions of Indian reservations in which actual Indians were designated by name to be killed—and the tribes of Washington were among the most civil of American activists (too civil, by the lights of some of their Indian peers). Most Indians returning from the Trail were not headed to the comparative enlightenment of Puget Sound. Most were headed to the Plains.

AIM directed as many Trailers as it could to Scottsbluff, Nebraska, where they were paired with Mexican fieldworkers for protests against the deep racism in city and county governments. (Dr. W. O. Brown, perhaps not incidentally, made his home in Scottsbluff.) There were Gordon-style mass marches and citizens' grand juries that led to a lawsuit that in turn led to a court order that enjoined local governments from violating minority rights. It was one of the more sweeping civil rights orders ever issued beyond the South, but national reporters largely ignored it. Reporters did not, however, ignore a melee that broke out between AIM and police in which Russell Means was arrested. AIM was again sullied by violence and again reminded that nothing won the media's attention like a good fight. According to the local police, after Means was arrested he somehow smuggled a gun into his jail cell. Means, however, said he had been searched upon his arrest, searched again at his booking, and searched yet again when put into his cell, after which he went to sleep. He was later awakened by officers who were standing outside his cell, pointing shotguns at him, and daring him to pick up a gun on the floor of the cell. He declined. Means had a well-earned reputation for playing loose with facts; if he claimed mountains, molehills could not be ruled out. But in this case the official account—that a prisoner who should have been searched at least on his arrest and again at the jailhouse had smuggled a revolver inside, only to leave it in plain view on the floor—was the more incredible tale.

Means's story matched those of other agitators in Indian Country. One such story was told by Richard Erdoes, an artist and photographer who came to South Dakota about the time of Means's jailing to sketch Lakota medicine men for *Time* and *Life*.

"I vass horrivied to learn zerr verr Nazis here in America," Erdoes said decades later in the rich accent of his native Vienna (which, for readability, is reproduced only in this first sentence). "I was in Berlin, you see, when the Nazis came to power. My friends and I printed anti-Nazi leaflets and glued them to the walls of houses at night, and eventually my best friend was hanged. His family had to pay for the hanging. It was not free. Another friend of mine was taken to Buchenwald concentration camp and died there. By sheer dumb luck, I was able to escape to Austria. When Austria was seized by the Nazis I escaped to Paris, and when Paris was seized by the Nazis I escaped to Dieppe, and when Dieppe was seized by the Nazis I escaped to England, and eventually I came to New York. Years later, I came to Rosebud Reservation to sketch old Henry Crow Dog and John Fire Lame Deer, and I found the Nazis here. What happened was that one day I was driving around to draw some landscapes, when very suddenly two pickup trucks appeared behind me with guns in the racks and cowboy types at the wheels and ran me off the road. My camper ended up lying on its side in a ditch. I climbed vertically out the door, walked two miles back to Crow Dog's, and said, 'Somebody tried to kill me.'

"There was much merriment and laughter, and they said, 'No, if they wanted to kill you, you would be dead. They just wanted to give you a taste.'

"I said, 'A taste of what? I am just here to sketch.'

"They said, 'Well, your van has a New York license plate.'

" 'What does that mean?' "

The Crow Dogs explained that a white rancher named Baxter Berry, son of a former governor, had lately killed an unarmed Indian. Erdoes's New

York license plates and his affiliation with *Time* and *Life* had led locals to believe he was investigating the case.

"I had not come to cover the Baxter Berry case," he said, "but now I was mad, so I decided I would cover the case. The man Baxter Berry had killed was Norman Little Brave, a Pentecostal preacher known as a sober man and a hard worker. I went to the courthouse and asked why Baxter Berry had killed him. I was told Little Brave had threatened him. I asked what Little Brave had threatened Baxter Berry with, what weapon, and I was told with nothing, just words. I asked why Baxter Berry had to shoot him if he was unarmed, and I was told, 'You know how those Indians are.' There was no investigation. Baxter Berry did not even show up at his own trial. He was acquitted of course. Justifiable self-defense.

"I called in the story to New York, and the next morning, two state troopers woke me up at my hotel and put cuffs on me. I said, 'What have I done?' They said, 'You have stolen a mirror.' They dragged me to my car. Sure enough there was a huge mirror in the car. I did not put it there. I said, 'I work for *Time* and *Life*. They have a very good legal department. I am not a poor Indian with whom you can do as you please.'

"One of the men, he shook his fist in my face. He said very grandly, 'I cancel my subscription to *Life*.'

"I laughed of course, and he pulled a gun on me. The other guy held him back. He said, 'You better disappear from here. We do not like your kind.'

"I said, 'What kind might this be?'

"He said, 'We don't want any of you Fucking. Jewish. Faggot. Commie. Bastards. From New York.' "

"I said, 'You have it all wrong. I am only the smallest bit Jewish, and I am heterosexual. I do not associate with Communists, and I was conceived by my father and mother, who were married. And as you can tell from my accent I am not from New York. The only thing you got right was 'fucking,' but I have a nicer word for it. I call it 'making love.'

"He was not made happy by this. He said, 'You will be out of here by tomorrow.'

"I said, 'I will not. I will stay here until I get my work done and I will do as I please. If you don't like it, go to hell.'

"I went back to Crow Dog and Lame Deer and said, 'It's outrageous how you are treated here. Anything I can do, put me to use."

When Leonard Crow Dog, Henry's son, was later charged with crimes arising from his activism, Erdoes coordinated his defense team. Eventually Erdoes co-wrote the autobiographies of the Crow Dog family and of Dennis Banks.

In later years, revisionists would say that red people never had it as bad on the High Plains as black people had it in the South. To the extent that the revision stuck, it was largely because the sins of the Plains did not receive the national scrutiny of those of the South. Today nearly every schoolchild can tell you something of the black civil rights movement; maybe one in a thousand can speak of the red. That a vicious, officially sanctioned anti-Indianism survived in America well into the 1970s is a fact lost to history.

Eight months before the Trail of Broken Treaties, the Oglala Sioux Tribe inaugurated a new president, and he, Dick Wilson, was not partial to AIM. "Nothing but a bunch of sponges," he said of the group. "Here in Pine Ridge they bum off my poor people—poor Indians living on welfare. They're social misfits. Their lawlessness, their tactics of violence give the rest of us a bad name." After the Trail, when AIMers started showing up around Pine Ridge, President Wilson warned, "If they want a showdown, the Oglala Sioux are ready for it. They used one of our dead people to capitalize on"—he meant Raymond Yellow Thunder. "Let them try some live ones now. We mean it." He said if Russell Means was fool enough to set foot on his native reservation, he himself would cut off Means's braids, stuff him in a dress, and dump him at the reservation border. Reporters could not get enough of the president.

"The long-awaited Dick Wilson enters, a brick of a man with a stomach that matches his ego," one dispatch read. "He slams the screen door and straddles a kitchen chair with the cockiness expected from an ex-plumber who now makes $13,500 a year on a reservation where the average annual income is $1,800."

"His tradition," reporter Kevin McKiernan remembered, "was that of the South Boston strongman of the 1930s. And he had a fetching oafness, like one of the Three Stooges with a double-barreled shotgun. AIM couldn't have asked for a better foil."

The president dressed the part. He favored dark glasses and a habiliment of High Plains haute: two parts polyester, one part snakeskin. His hair was martially buzzed, his head was of medicine ball proportions, and the blood vessels of his cheeks suggested he was not afraid of a good tipple. His body was less brick than well-filled bag. It was hard to look at the man without thinking of sausage.

Wilson was accused of malfeasance even before taking the oath of office. During his campaign, he was said to have taken $10,000 from one or two white businessmen in return for, according to one story, promising his patrons what amounted to a bootleg franchise on the dry reservation or, according to another story, a sweetheart construction deal. On election day Wilson allegedly imported unregistered voters and paid for votes with hooch and greenbacks. Once in office, he was accused of buying tribal land worth $80,000 for a mere $20,000 and of stealing and selling a tribal truck. (The truck, in any event, disappeared during his reign and could not be accounted for.) Wilson also engineered a 50 percent raise to the $9,000 presidential salary, then, it seems, helped himself to another $5,000 yearly under the table. He tried to commandeer the tribe's housing funds for a private slush, and when the tribal housing board refused to go along, he created a parallel board, ignored the original board, and did as he pleased. He was a great believer in nepotism. He fired the director of the tribe's Head Start preschool program and replaced her with his wife, he gave a fat consulting fee to his brother for little or no work, and he named his son the director of a jobs program. Although the tribal constitution required him to keep a budget, he refused to do so, with the result that in 1974, two years into his tenure, an accounting firm said the tribe's books were in such chaos that there was no telling whether or how much Wilson was skimming.

The Bureau of Indians Affairs, in its capacity of guardian over its Indian wards, had to approve virtually every act of the tribe—financial or otherwise —and could have vetoed nearly any measure that it thought would hurt the tribe. The BIA hardly ever saw anything amiss with Wilson. In one egregious example, the tribal secretary told the BIA that Wilson had forged his (the secretary's) name on checks totaling $69,000. The BIA replied that the secretary's signature may well have been forged but it was not the BIA's job to do anything about it. The BIA's job, the secretary was lectured, was merely to verify that the paperwork had been filled out. Since the paperwork had a signature purporting to be the secretary's, who was the BIA to decide whether it was really his?

Wilson's corruption was not only or even mainly financial. It was political, and it was for the anti-AIM bent of the corruption that the BIA supported him. For example, the constitution and bylaws of the Oglala Sioux Tribe required the president to call the tribal council into session four times a year. Wilson called the council into its first session on time, in July 1972, but he quickly adjourned it and thereafter illegally ran most of the tribe's affairs through a small executive committee under his control. One of the executive committee's more notorious acts was to outlaw the assembly of three or more people with the means to riot. So broadly worded was the statute that "means to riot" included vocal chords. Any threesome on a street corner—for that matter, any threesome in a living room—who were out of favor with Wilson were subject to arrest. The BIA area office approved the statute and wrote Wilson, "The Tribe is to be complimented for their efforts in developing this ordinance and their attempt to improve the criminal justice services on the Pine Ridge Reservation."

In November 1972, as the Trail of Broken Treaties came to an end, Wilson ordered all tribal employees to Billy Mills Hall, the hangar-like civic center in the town of Pine Ridge. (Olympic gold medalist Billy Mills was an Oglala.) Since the tribe was the largest employer on the destitute reservation, it was a large gathering. Wilson announced that the Trailers were bound for Pine Ridge, that they meant to hold a victory dance at Billy Mills, but that the dance was a Trojan horse, that AIM's true end was the sacking of the tribal and BIA headquarters. The crowd was appropriately riled, and the tribal council, which Wilson called briefly into session, passed an ordinance banning AIM from the hall. If Wilson's critics were right, ordinance 72-55 was supposed to do no more. But when 72-55 appeared in the statute book, it empowered Wilson to throw anyone who supported AIM off the reservation or out of a tribal job. "Wilson had the people of Pine Ridge so paranoid," said Dave Long, the vice president of the tribe and one of the few dissidents on the council, "that when a few AIM members were seen in Rushville, over the Nebraska line, the tribal buildings in Pine Ridge were evacuated."

AIM came to the reservation nonetheless, and Wilson made good on his new powers. No sooner did Russell Means set foot on the reservation than he was jailed and chaperoned to the reservation line. (While in jail, a turnkey who knew Means let him out of his cell to play checkers. Wilson got wind of his liberty, came to the jail, and shouted Means back to his cell, where he taunted him.) Dennis Banks was also arrested, while officiating at a wedding, jailed, and escorted to the frontier. So too AIMers who had lived their entire lives on Pine Ridge. One was Vice President Long, whom Wilson stripped of his post without pay or due process, even though by law Long was removable only by impeachment. Means and Long filed a complaint with the prosecutors of the U.S. attorney's office in Rapid City, noting that Wilson's despotisms were expressly forbidden by the Indian Civil Rights Act of 1968. They asked that Wilson be charged with violating their civil rights. The prosecutors said they would give the matter consideration, which was all they gave it. If the prosecutors were disinclined to let so trivial a thing as an act of Congress stand in the way of Wilson's harassment of AIM, perhaps it because the Justice Department, of which the U.S. Attorney's Office was a subsidiary, had just asked the FBI, in the aftermath of the Trail of Broken Treaties, to step up its monitoring and infiltration of AIM.

Of his many innovations, Wilson's finest was his goon squad—pedagogues he dispersed around Pine Ridge to educate his opponents. The lessons they offered were corporeal, and it did not take many lessons before the reservation was quite literally beaten into submission. The goons received their name from their enemies, but they took to the epithet proudly. *Goon*, they said, stood for Guardian of the Oglala Nation. After the Trail of Broken Treaties, Wilson asked to put the goons on the federal payroll, and Stan Lyman, the BIA superintendent on Pine Ridge, thought the idea capital. So too Lyman's boss, BIA area director Wyman Babby. In November or thereabouts, $60,000 was forwarded to Wilson. By some reports the money came from the Office of Employment Opportunity, the same federal jobs program from which the White House had taken $66,500 to send the Trailers home from Washington. If so, the symmetry of welcoming AIM back to the Plains via the same bankroll that sent them from Washington must have pleased Wilson. The federalized goons were to be deputized by the BIA police, but the scheme ran afoul of Richard Colhoff, the BIA's chief of police on Pine Ridge. Colhoff said the goons were a public nuisance. In fact, they were the source of most of the trouble on the reservation, and even had they been upstanding citizens, Colhoff said that deputizing a group of untrained men for riot control was madness. He did not further endear himself to his superiors by adding that he would treat AIMers with neither more nor less severity than anyone else in his jurisdiction. Colhoff was no saint. His officers had been accused of driving arrestees into the darkened prairie and beating them. But he had a measure of decency that Superintendent Lyman and President Wilson could not abide. They howled to Director Babby, who found Colhoff an assignment on another reservation. Two-thirds of the tribal council petitioned Babby to keep Colhoff on Pine Ridge, but Babby ignored them. With Colhoff gone, Wilson ordered every able-bodied man employed by the tribe to Billy Mills Hall for riot training. Some came willingly, others out of fear of losing their jobs. There were brief tutorials in judo and the use of nightsticks, followed by the distribution of paychecks. More tutorials and paychecks followed.

Long accustomed to abuse and fearful of the goons, the Oglalas of Pine

Ridge were slow to chafe. But by the end of 1972, six of the reservation's eight district councils, which functioned as neighborhood councils do in a large city, called on Wilson and Lyman to resign. Come January 1973, when Wilson again refused to call the tribal council into session, several councilmen circulated a petition for his impeachment. Petitions to impeach were as common on Pine Ridge as pawn tickets. Of the six presidents before Wilson, six had faced them. In ordinary times, nobody beyond the reservation would have noticed another such petition, but these were not ordinary times.

In the small hours of a Sunday morning at the end of January 1973, a Lakota named Wesley Bad Heart Bull was knifed to death in the Black Hills village of Buffalo Gap. A white man named Darld Schmitz admitted to the killing and was charged with second-degree manslaughter before being released on $5,000 bond. Here, to AIM, was the case of Raymond Yellow Thunder all over again. The truth was more rumpled.

On the night of his death, Bad Heart Bull had gone to Bill's Bar with friends, who were admitted entry while he was turned away. The barkeep knew something of Bad Heart Bull's nineteen arrests for assault, drunkenness, and disturbing the peace. At the time, although the barman didn't know it, Bad Heart Bull was being sought for rupturing a rival's nose, cheekbone, and windpipe over a bottle of wine. While his friends drank inside Bill's, Bad Heart Bull stood in the gravel street—Buffalo Gap was one of those crossroad hamlets without a foot of asphalt to its name—and may or may not have rattled a foot-long length of logging chain at passersby. At 2:00 a.m. Bill's closed and a white patron, Jim Geary by birth, Mad Dog by nickname, came out and challenged Bad Heart Bull to a fight. Mad Dog had told friends earlier in the evening that he was "gonna get me an Indian," but his bark proved worse than his bite: one blow from Bad Heart Bull's chain left him cold on the gravel. By some accounts Bad Heart Bull continued to beat Mad Dog even as he lay prone. By others Bad Heart Bull did nothing of the kind. In any case, soon after Mad Dog fell, several shots rang out. Apparently they came from some distance away and had nothing to do with the quarrel outside Bill's. In the story told by Bad Heart Bull's friends, as Bad Heart Bull turned to see where the shots came from, Darld Schmitz, till then a spectator, stuck a knife in his chest.

Schmitz was known as a barroom tough himself. That night he was celebrating the birth of his third child by taking his mistress and friends out on the town as his postpartum wife lay in the hospital. In the story told by Schmitz's camp, his mistress, a distant cousin of Bad Heart Bull, thought she could stop Bad Heart Bull from savaging the unconscious Mad Dog. But as she tried to grab her cousin, he threatened her, and Schmitz sallied to her rescue. Bad Heart Bull supposedly swung his chain at Schmitz, who ducked and thrust a small pocketknife into Bad Heart Bull's chest before fleeing into the night. Schmitz's camp did not mention the distracting gunshots.

On being stabbed, Bad Heart Bull fell but was soon back on his feet and may or may not have continued whipping Mad Dog until he weakened and was overpowered. After he finally collapsed, friends loaded the fallen men into separate cars and rushed them toward the hospital in Hot Springs, fifteen miles southwest, but Bad Heart Bull's car was of Indian vintage, it sprung an oil leak, and the engine burned up and ground to a halt. Mad Dog's handlers stopped and loaded the unconscious Bad Heart Bull next to his victim, but by the time they arrived at the hospital, Bad Heart Bull was dead. Schmitz's cut had nicked his aorta, just enough for it to bleed out. (The beaten Mad Dog lay a month in the hospital before recuperating enough to return home.) Later that morning Schmitz was arrested in the nearby town of Custer. He still had the knife, which he gave to the police, and he admitted having stabbed Bad Heart Bull but said he had done so with cause. He was charged with manslaughter and released almost immediately on light bond.

As the prosecutor of Raymond Yellow Thunder's killers had done the year before, the prosecutor for Custer County, Hobart Gates, looked favorably on the claims coming from the camp of the white defendant and skeptically on those from the camp of the Indian victim. Prosecutor Gates defended his manslaughter charge by saying that in such tawdry circumstances, no jury would convict a man of murder. He meant no jury of twelve white people (nearly all of South Dakota's juries at the time were white as rock salt) would convict a white man of murdering an Indian in such circumstances. AIM replied that had the killer been Indian, the charge would have been murder. And indeed, two years later, when a lesser leader of AIM named Dick Marshall killed a man in similar circumstances— shooting him without premeditation in a Black Hills barroom scuffle—he was charged not only with murder but with murder in the first degree. (Myrtle Poor Bear, who perjured herself after the FBI threatened her with photos of the dead Aquash, was also prevailed on by the FBI to perjure herself to convict Dick Marshall.)

Dennis Banks and Russell Means rallied AIMers to the town of Custer, which billed itself "The Town with the Gunsmoke Flavor," for a confrontation with Hobart Gates. They spoke of the rendezvous in the same words Crazy Horse had used before his rendezvous with the town's namesake: "Today is a good day to die." On February 6, 1973, a hundred or so AIMers—well shy of the thousand AIM had predicted—were met by police in riot gear. The police allowed only a few of them into the public building for the meeting with Gates. Banks, Means, and a couple of others went inside and harangued Gates. Meanwhile, hard words passed between AIMers and lawmen on the courthouse steps, and the verbal soon became physical. First shoves, then punches were offered. Probably AIM started it, either when a protester charged police from the outside or when one of the AIMers inside struck a policeman in the foyer. (By another, unlikely account, the fight began when an officer shoved Sarah Bad Heart Bull, mother of the slain Wesley, down the courthouse steps. That she was shoved is indisputable; whether she was shoved as prelude to riot or, more likely, after it started is less clear.) Once fists were thrown, it took no time for brawl to become riot. The police were generous with clubs and teargas, and more than one Indian was knocked unconscious, but the Indians wrestled away several police batons, and at least one policeman was knocked unconscious too. Dozens on both sides were bloodied. Several of the Indians seized a nearby gas station, made firebombs, and tried in vain to burn the stone courthouse. They had more success with the wooden Chamber of Commerce building, which burned to the ground. The Chamber's immolation featured prominently in wire-service reports, most of which implied the building was a substantial edifice. In fact, it was slightly grander in size than a Pine Ridge two-seater. A much more substantial arson was the torching of two police cruisers. The riot stretched across the afternoon, now surging, now relenting, now surging again. The sheriff deputized white citizens and called for reinforcements from officers of the state Fish and Game Department. Not until early evening was the rebellion fully quelled, by which time about two dozen Indians had been arrested, including Banks and Means. Banks had jumped out a courthouse window and commandeered a gas truck—for the purpose, he later said, of moving it away from the arsonists. Authorities suggested the opposite motive. Means was arrested in the foyer of the building, where he had traded fists with officers inside.

In the week after the riot the Black Hills fairly crawled with National Guardsmen and state troopers. Indians were stopped, searched, and arrested for the crime of driving with red skin. Gun shops saw a run on their wares by the white citizenry. A few days after the riot, an Indian and an Anglo got into a barroom scrap in Rapid City, the metropole of western Dakota, and the Indian was arrested. Even in the calmest of times, Rapid City could not be accused of enlightened race relations. Indians called it Rapist City or Racist City. Many years later, the man who became Rapid's chief of police would say of the 1970s, "It was a different era. When I first became a policeman here, if you found a drunk Indian downtown, you'd put him in a garbage can. And when he got out, he was sober enough to leave, and that's just the way things were." AIM asked the city fathers to shut the bars until tempers cooled. The fathers declined. The next night, enraged Indians went from bar to bar smashing mirrors and windows, ripping out barstools and tables, and brawling with white barmen and patrons. The next day, the city closed the bars. It was against this backdrop that the impeachment trial of Dick Wilson was to proceed in two weeks.

* * *

Wilson answered the call for his impeachment in the traditional manner of those who found themselves encircled by hostile redskins: he called the cavalry. The U.S. Marshals Service, perhaps the least understood of federal law enforcers (its mandate was shipping federal prisoners and guarding federal buildings), sent its Special Operations Group to Wilson's rescue. SOG, in the words of its director, was a domestic "strike force" that had been created in response to protests in the 1960s that targeted federal buildings and land. In training and tactics, SOG was so like the Green Berets that its creators were accused of having formed the group to skirt the congressional ban on using the armed forces domestically. (The military could be used at home only on explicit presidential or congressional order; SOG could be used merely on the attorney general's say-so.) The sixty-five marshals of SOG who came to Pine Ridge in mid-February 1973 were dressed loudly in jumpsuits of sky blue and were not shy about displaying their rifles and side arms. They built sandbag bulwarks atop the BIA building and trained machine guns on the street below. Wry Oglalas called their makeshift citadel Fort Wilson. Eventually the SOG force on Pine Ridge grew to 110 men, which was the entire national complement.

The BIA police also heeded Wilson's call, adding forty officers from other reservations to the dozen normally on duty in Pine Ridge. The FBI and the U.S. attorney's office for South Dakota, neither of which had previously taken an interest in crime on Pine Ridge, also established offices in Fort Wilson. The FBI agent in charge of the entire Minnesota-Dakota region and the U.S. attorney both took up residence. Stan Lyman, the BIA superintendent, wrote in his diary, "There was an elaborate radio and communication post set up, with all kinds of radios and telephones and control panels. One big officer was sitting there, typing out everything that happened and phoning it in, every hour on the hour, to the director of marshals in Washington, D.C. Everybody had a gas mask. If grenades were to be used, they would be fired from shotguns; the shotguns and grenades were all laid out, ready to fire. Should gas be used, a big fan was set up in front of the window to blow it away from the building. The window had already been taken out to form a lookout post." So many lawmen were wedged into the BIA building that the BIA had to shut down almost all of its normal administrative operations on Pine Ridge.

All of this, it is important to remember, was in response to an entirely lawful move by the tribal council to impeach its president. AIM may have rioted at Custer, but the group had neither publicly threatened nor privately plotted against Wilson, and the impeachment in any case was being pushed not by AIM but by residents of Pine Ridge, where the only high crimes and misdemeanors that were known to have been committed had been committed by the man the United States was circling its wagons around. Had Nixon garrisoned Washington thus before his impeachment, or had any state governor done so, the nation would have been in a froth. But America did not blink at the equivalent taking place on Indian reservations, perhaps because beyond South Dakota the media gave it almost no coverage.

Wilson's trial by the tribal council began on February 22, 1973. By law, he was supposed to give his accusers sufficient time to gather witnesses and evidence. He did not. He was also supposed to recuse himself during the trial, in this case yielding the gavel to Dave Long, his enemy in the vice presidency. He did not. The BIA could have forced him to do so, but it did not. Wilson called his trial to order and proceeded to screen *Anarchy— USA*, a film by the John Birch Society that linked the civil rights movement to godless Communism and godless Communism to revolution in Algeria and elsewhere. Wilson hardly needed to add that such would be the fate of Pine Ridge if he were removed from office and replaced with a president soft on AIM. When the film concluded, Wilson adjourned for the day. Next day, he called supporters to enumerate his virtues and refused to recognize his critics. At times, he stood behind allied council members and whispered instructions in their ears. The dissidents on the council—by some stories a trio, by others a sextet—walked out. The remaining councilors gave Wilson a vote of confidence and adjourned. That night Wilson and his family, claiming threats against their lives, stayed holed up in Fort

Wilson. The next morning, BIA police escorted the family off the reservation while Wilson remained in his fastness.

Wilson's enemies retreated to the small community of Calico, a few miles northwest of Pine Ridge, where they had been holding mass meetings for weeks. The Oglala Sioux Civil Rights Organization, as the assemblage called itself, now asked the marshals of Fort Wilson for protection from Wilson's goons, but the marshals declined. So OSCRO invited AIM to stand guard and help strategize. For five nights after the failed impeachment, tiny Calico Hall filled with Oglalas by the hundreds. Late arrivals stood several deep on the frozen ground outside. Again and again the congregants reviewed their predicament: Wilson, through brutality, graft, and patronage, had a lock on the tribal council, and the BIA had thrown the dead bolt against administrative appeal. (The BIA's Stan Lyman would soon declare, "Whether the tribal president is corrupt or not is rather beside the issue. This is a matter of revolution!") The U.S. attorney had refused to prosecute Wilson for the boldest of crimes, and civil suits faced the tallest of odds, for reasons that will soon become clear. The dissidents could try to vote Wilson out, but the next tribal elections were a year off, and Wilson, who had bought the last election and had strengthened his hold since, looked a good bet to steal the next one too. The options— lawful options—did not look good.

On the night of February 27, 1973, the leaders of the Calico meetings recessed for a caucus with a few of Pine Ridge's most respected elders. They asked the elders' advice.

"Go to Wounded Knee," the elders said. "Make your stand there."

They did.

CHAPTER 3

IN 1890, AFTER the last of the nomadic Indians had been confined to reservations, there arose among the Paiutes of Nevada a new religion. Its prophet, Wovoka, said God knew His red children were suffering and He was prepared to return them to Eden. All He required was that they live peacefully, work hard, and perform a dance, the ghost dance, which God had taught Wovoka. The Indian Bureau, predecessor of the BIA, permitted the faith to spread—peaceful living and hard work were precisely what were wanted of the Indian. But as the religion crept eastward, it mutated. The ghost dance soon promised not merely an earthly Eden for Indians but also the annihilation of whites. In its turn to militancy, the religion acquired an amulet: the ghost dance shirt, which, when worn by a person of faith, was said to make him impervious to gunfire. By the end of 1890, believers in Dakota were ghost-dancing incessantly. The Indian Bureau sought to quash the dancing, but the Indians had been made bold by their bulletproof shirts and ignored the orders to cease from reservation superintendents. The superintendents were a shabby lot, their positions doled out by a system of spoils rather than merit. On Pine Ridge the Oglalas called the superintendent Young Man Afraid of Indians. Addled by the dancers' chants, Young Man Afraid wrote the army, "Indians are dancing in the snow and are wild and crazy . . . *We need protection and we need it now.*"

General Nelson Miles, commander of the Division of the Missouri, took a Baptist view of the dancing and sent companies to seize the dancers' headmen. Sitting Bull, elder of the Hunkpapa band of Lakota, was captured—first, on

Standing Rock Reservation in what is now northern South Dakota. As he was being led away, gunfire of uncertain provenance broke out and he was shot dead along with thirteen others. His end recalled that of Crazy Horse, who had been murdered in 1877 after surrendering to the army. The martyrdom of Sitting Bull did not ease tensions on the once Great Sioux Reserve, but within a few weeks General Miles had bloodlessly rounded up all the ghost-dancing bands save one, led by a chief named Big Foot, whose group had been swollen with the survivors of Sitting Bull's dancers. In late December the Seventh Cavalry intercepted Big Foot in the Badlands. The Seventh was the same that Custer had gotten annihilated on the Little Big Horn, and the reconstituted body was of a vengeful disposition. The cavalrymen marched the few hundred Lakotas to Wounded Knee Creek where the next day, December 29, 1890, Colonel James Forsyth had them encircled. Forsyth mounted Hotchkiss machine guns on the surrounding hilltops and demanded the Indians' weapons. The tense surrender of guns was barely underway when a shot was fired. Neither the shooter nor his motive will ever be known, but his shot was followed by a bloodletting the likes of which the Plains had never seen. Probably in the ensuing panic the Lakotas tried to mount a defense, but it would not have amounted to much. Their aged guns were trifles compared with the soldiers', and their ranks were short on warriors and long on unarmed women, children, and elders. The cavaliers loosed their Hotchkisses on the Indians nonetheless. Abdomens and skulls were exploded like so many watermelons. The bullets severed limbs like leaves from trees. Great pools of blood seeped over the snow as men and women, infants and the infirm fell in heaps. What the big guns missed, scores of carbines picked off. Long after the Indians stopped firing, the soldiers continued. Fleeing children were pursued for miles through frozen creekbeds before being shot in the back. The ghost-dance shirts had offered a thin defense against Manifest Destiny.

The army said the mass grave it dug the next day held 146 Lakotas, of whom 44 were women and 18 children. One of the murdered was Big Foot. The army reported another 51 Indians wounded, 7 of whom eventually died. The Lakotas said their dead numbered more like 350. On the cavalry's side, the army claimed 25 killed and 39 wounded. Most (perhaps all) were killed by their comrades' crossfire. The army said then—and says now—that what happened at Wounded Knee was a pitched battle among equals, and it awarded twenty Congressional Medals of Honor to the Seventh for bravery at the "Battle of Wounded Knee." The names of Colonel Forsyth and General Miles were bestowed on two Montana county seats known to posterity as tolerable places to piss on the road to Billings. Lakotas have tried several times to have the medals stripped from the cavalrymen but have always failed. In 1975, Senator James Abourezk of South Dakota proposed that the government compensate the heirs of the massacre's victims with a niggardly $3,000 apiece—a total burden on the Treasury of about $600,000. The army fought the bill, and Congress sided with the army. The press gave the matter the smallest blip of attention, and the nation left the Indians to their open wound.

Eight decades after the massacre, the village of Wounded Knee on the Pine Ridge Reservation was known mainly by its trading post. The post was a descendent of one of the many franchises the Indian Bureau had granted white businessmen to keep Indians in food (usually rotten), clothing (usually thin), and hardware (usually frail). General William Tecumseh Sherman had observed in the nineteenth century, "A reservation is a parcel of land inhabited by Indians and surrounded by thieves," but the trading post franchises brought the thieves onto the reservations. The Wounded Knee Trading Post was a superior specimen. Its owners, the Gildersleeve and Czywczynski families, had strewn billboards for seventy-five miles that announced, SEE THE WOUNDED KNEE MASSACRE SITE, VISIT THE MASS GRAVE. POSTCARDS, CURIOS, DON'T MISS IT! The postcards showed slaughtered Indians, including Chief Big Foot, frozen in the 1890 snow. The traders enlivened their commerce with beadwork, quilts, and other curios bought low from Oglalas and sold high. A Catholic priest once watched Mrs. Czywczynski barter a beader to a stingy $3.50 for an exquisite work, then turn around and sell it for $12.00.

The traders doubled as creditors, lending their Indian patrons $10 at humble interest of $2.25 a week. As village postmasters, they also offered a rudimentary auto-payment—opening the mail of customers who had run tabs, cashing their checks without asking, paying their bills at the post, and calling other shopkeepers across the reservation to see if debts were owed them too. There had been calls to boycott the post, but none had worked. The post was the only store for a dozen miles, and the many car-less Oglalas of Wounded Knee had no choice but to buy groceries and other wares at its inflated prices. Years later Clive Gildersleeve was called to testify about his business practices, and he invoked his Fifth Amendment right not to incriminate himself ninety-nine times.

On the night of February 27, 1973, the critics of Dick Wilson at Calico Hall piled into fifty-odd cars and drove south to the town of Pine Ridge. The marshals and policemen at Fort Wilson braced for an attack, but they were assaulted only with horns and middle fingers. The caravan continued east through town on U.S. Highway 18, then turned north toward Wounded Knee on the reservation road known as the Big Foot Trail. The leaders of the caravan had told their three hundred followers that they were merely going to Porcupine, north of Wounded Knee, in order to use a large meeting hall there. The secrecy about their true destination was meant to foil spies—presciently, as it turned out. When the lead cars stopped at Wounded Knee and the followers were told they were going to occupy the village, few complained.

Greater Wounded Knee consisted of a downtown and a residential neighborhood separated from one another by an open half-mile and an immense economic gulf. Downtown, known as "white Wounded Knee," held three churches, the trading post, a museum attached to the post, and the homes of the handful of whites who ran commercial and ecclesiastical Wounded Knee. Most of the structures had running water and reliable heat, which could not be said of Indian Wounded Knee. One of the churches, Sacred Heart, sat at the head of the mass grave of the victims of the 1890 massacre. The unsubtle intrusion of the conqueror's religion on the sacred ground of the conquered was a great affront to many Indians. Both church and grave sat atop a modest rise that, after the caravanners turned the church into a dining hall, came to be known as Fry Bread Hill.

On arriving in downtown Wounded Knee, some protesters went first to the mass grave, where they prayed and begged their ancestors' guidance in what they were about to do. Others, more secular, set about pillaging the trading post and museum. Russell Means recalled later that among the museum's displays was a nineteenth-century ledger of cattle receipts on Pine Ridge: "The cavalry captain in charge had made up names for the Indians who received that beef—'Shits In His Food,' 'She Comes Nine Times,' 'Fucks His Daughter,' and 'Maggot Dick,' to recall a few. When I first had seen that vile book in 1967, I got so mad I had to leave. When we took over in 1973, we burned it." Means did not see a "Never Again" value in such artifacts.

White Wounded Knee was a gerontocracy. Of the eleven residents at home that night, seven were sixty-eight or older. They were rousted from their beds, told that Wounded Knee was being reclaimed, and ushered into a single house where they were put under guard, partly for their protection but mainly as hostages. For the most part, they were politely handled, but Father Paul Manhart, vicar of Sacred Heart, had his hands tied behind his back for a time, as though his captors feared he would bless them.

In Wounded Knee the usurpers had chosen a difficult spot to defend. The village sat exposed at the bottom of a broad valley broken by a few dry washes, a few small hills, and a very few stands of trees. Attackers could sit on the valley rim and fire at most everything below. The occupiers blocked the roads coming into town, parked their cars facing away from downtown, and shone their headlights in the direction of the attack that was sure to come. Then they sent a list of demands toward Pine Ridge. The listbearer got a mile before he ran into a roadblock already set up by the FBI.

Since the Trail of Broken Treaties, the FBI had cultivated moles inside both AIM and the Oglala Sioux Civil Rights Organization, and the moles had kept the Bureau informed of the activists' movements—sometimes quite skillfully, sometimes not. In an instance of the latter, a pair of under-cover agents infiltrated AIM meetings in Rapid City the week before activists seized Wounded Knee. But after only three days, the moles came under suspicion and had to be removed. In a more successful example, on the day Wounded Knee was taken, the FBI monitored Russell Means as he drove from Rushville, Nebraska, to Pine Ridge. The identities and methods of his watchers remain unknown, but Means was on the reservation all of three minutes before two of Wilson's goons, Poker Joe Merrival and Glen Three Stars, tried to thrash him. Means got away, but a friend, Gary Thomas, the federal legal aid lawyer on Pine Ridge, was not so lucky and was beaten. Afterward Thomas lodged a complaint with the BIA police and FBI and produced two witnesses, but the authorities ignored him. That evening, two hours before the congregants at Calico Hall left for Wounded Knee, moles tipped Fort Wilson to their departure. The moles had, however, been fooled by the feint to Porcupine and told their handlers that AIM and OSCRO were headed there.

Joseph Trimbach, the FBI agent in charge of the three-state region, was on the FBI roadblock when the occupiers' demands were brought out. Originally the demands were three: that the U.S. government unbreak America's 371 broken treaties with Indian nations, that it root out the rot in the BIA, and that it investigate the tribal governments of every Lakota reservation. Later, the demands were augmented: Dick Wilson, Stan Lyman, and Wyman Babby were to be fired; the beatings of Wilson's goon squad were to be probed; and the White House was to meet with the occupiers. Trimbach passed the demands upward, asked Washington for help, and loaded for bear. Come the morning, he was in command of 250 FBI agents, U.S. marshals, and BIA officers, a dozen armored personnel carriers mounted with machine gun turrets, tens of thousands of rounds of ammunition, and even a Phantom jet. His manpower would soon double. Dick Wilson, not wanting to be outdone, outfitted his goons with clubs, football helmets, and those most potent of reservation killers—six packs. Against this array the 300 occupiers of Wounded Knee had maybe

100 men of combat age and an arsenal of deer rifles. Ammunition was scant.

The first night of the occupation, nothing more than scattered shots were exchanged. The second brought little more. But the tranquility was not to last.

The rebels took advantage of the initial calm to fashion a city-state. They empowered a junta and made it modestly accountable to a daily meeting of the populace. Former paratroopers built bunkers, carpenters made a dormitory of the trading post, a house was converted to a field hospital, and church basements became kitchens. The SEE MASS GRAVE sign was pulled down. In its place arose a mock graffito offering $50 for one of Russell Means's braids, $100 for the pair, and $1,000 with his head attached. Another draftsman offered two pouches of Bull Durham for Dick Wilson, pickled.

The romance of liberating the storied hamlet had the desired effect on the world beyond. Reporters and camera crews flocked to Pine Ridge. By the reckoning of historians Paul Smith and Robert Warrior, the occupation received more media attention in its first week than all the Indian activism of the previous decade combined. "The American Indian commands respect for his rights only so long as he inspires terror for his rifle," General George Crook, the old Indian hunter, had said. Marrying the terror of the rifle to the sanctity of Wounded Knee was a quintessentially AIM improvement. It was no small testament to AIM's savvy that opinion polls showed that a majority of Americans supported their seizure of an American town by force of arms.

Not all the press, however, was favorable. The hostage-taking sat particularly poorly with reporters, and at AIM's request, Senator Abourezk flew out immediately to negotiate the captives' release. He was joined by his senior South Dakota colleague, George McGovern, fresh from his defeat in the fall presidential race against Nixon. McGovern had a reputation as an unabashed liberal, but Indians of the Plains did not know him as such. "It is ridiculous to talk about [honoring] treaties abrogated by an act of

Congress over a hundred years ago," McGovern once said of Indian grievances. "If you start with the wrongs that go back a hundred years or more,
every government that exists on the face of the earth probably would have
to fall." Of Wounded Knee's new masters he opined, "They're rip-off artists
exploiting the Indian problem for their own selfish needs."

"We asked to see Senator Abourezk," Russell Means replied. "We did
not ask to see Senator McGovern. Senator McGovern typifies three individuals of the last century: General Crook, General Sheridan, and General
Custer." But Means let McGovern into Wounded Knee anyway, and once
inside, the senator learned the prisoners were no more. They had been set
free, but they had refused to leave.

"The fact is," octogenarian Wilbur Reigert told reporters, "we as a group
of hostages decided to stay to save AIM and our own property. Had we
not, those troops would have come down here and killed all of these
people. The real hostages are the AIM people."

McGovern was positively downcast—defeated once more.

Thereafter, the government faced a quandary. It could seize the village,
but only at cost of filling a lot of coffins. Or it could pursue negotiations,
but at the cost of giving the Indians several more days, possibly weeks, to
put their grievances before reporters, who were inclined to skepticism
about the government's claim that AIM was a menace to the nation. After
much internal debate, the White House chose to negotiate rather than
attack. That did not mean the government intended to tolerate a critical
press. The Justice Department cabled its enforcers on Pine Ridge, "Do not
let newspaper personnel in the Wounded Knee area. . . . No TV coverage
of the Wounded Knee area, authority Attorney General." When reporters
complained that the government was trying to muzzle them, the Justice
Department said it was just looking out for the reporters' safety. The
reporters said they could look out for themselves fine. But Justice was not
moved until national TV networks called the government's attention to the
First Amendment. Even then, Justice relented only slightly, allowing reporters
no closer to Wounded Knee than the government roadblocks.

Crafty reporters found their way inside the village anyway, usually slipping through the government perimeter with the AIM pack trains that resupplied the village nightly. Once inside Wounded Knee, the journalists found the facts different from those on offer from the government. The Justice Department, for example, had tried to justify the heavy weaponry on its side by saying the rebels had an M-60 machine gun. But reporters inside Wounded Knee found there were no M-60s and in fact most of the Indian rifles were three shots from falling apart. Another time, an armored personnel carrier tried to flush Indians from a bunker, and the Indians returned fire. Back in Pine Ridge, a government spokesman said the Indians had fired first and that the APC had been nowhere near the bunker. When a reporter said that was untrue, the spokesman said the reporter didn't know what he was talking about. The reporter said he had the whole thing on video.

"Don't you think that destroys your credibility," the reporter said, "telling us [the APCs were] 'two to three miles away,' when we have documentation—on film—that those APCs came to within at least five hundred yards of the bunkers?"

The spokesman sputtered.

After several such embarrassments, the government relented and let journalists into Wounded Knee for visits of a few hours, but reporters who parked their cars at the FBI's roadblock and walked into the village often returned to slashed tires and smashed windshields. Invariably the agents on the roadblock had seen nothing. Only after the vandalism was mentioned in *Newsweek* did it stop. The harassment was worse for reporters who were considered "alternative," "underground," or "leftist"—that is, reporters without the protection of a large corporate parent. Many were arrested by the FBI, BIA, and Marshals Service, charged with a manufactured crime like interfering with an officer, and escorted to the reservation line. One reporter arrested by the FBI protested that she had done nothing wrong and said the agents would have to drag her to jail kicking and screaming. The agents gave her a choice: come with them peacefully, or go with Dick

Wilson's pals in the BIA police. The agents counseled against the latter course, as they could not guarantee her safety with the police. She went with the FBI. Another arrested reporter invoked the protections of the Constitution and was told, "There are no constitutional rights on the reservation"— in practice, an impeccable legal opinion. Still another journalist, an artist named Paul Collins, received more vigorous guidance.

Many years later Collins said, "I published a story in *Ebony*, which got read by a lot of people, and I became a threat to Dick Wilson. So I get picked up and taken in, and Dick says to his goons, 'Why don't you take Paul out for a ride and let's see if we can't get an understanding?'

"I said to him, 'We can get an understanding right here. You don't have to take me anywhere.'

"He said, 'No, we want him to see some of our beautiful South Dakota sights.'

"I said, 'In the dead of night?'

"So they took me in their car, Wilson's goons did, and dropped me in Nebraska. It was just over this hill. They drive off back up the hill, and then I hear this binnnnng, binnnnng. I realized they were shooting at me—actually shooting at me. So I dove in a hole. I wasn't there too long when I heard this whuuump, whuuump, whuuump. It was the rotors of a helicopter. A searchlight came on, and I didn't know what to expect next. But then this voice comes over a loudspeaker.

" 'Is there a Paul Collins down there?'

"I stood up and said, 'You bet I'm here.'

"The helicopter was sent out by a friend of mine, Guy Vander Jagt, who was a congressman and had been watching out for me."

Not everyone on Pine Ridge had congressmen watching out for them.

What started as a cold war at Wounded Knee soon turned hot. A head that popped above a bunker, a patrol that ventured too near an enemy position, simple ennui—all were occasion for gunfire. Usually the shots were few. Always they threatened to become larger firefights, free-for-alls involving hundreds of combatants in dozens of bunkers on both sides. Vietnam veterans in each camp said that several of the firefights on Pine Ridge were worse than anything they had endured in Indochina. The government, better supplied with ammunition, got off more and heavier rounds—an estimated 500,000 by the end of the siege, 7,000 a day. (Senator McGovern praised the lawmen for their "incredible restraint.") The rebels, starved for ammunition, chose their shots more carefully and passed much of the occupation lying on floors thinking sympathetically of the Vietcong.

A week and a half into the occupation, the government declared a ceasefire and lifted its roadblocks on the theory that the Indians were tired, terrified, hungry, and cold and would leave if given the chance. But during the truce, immigrants to Wounded Knee outnumbered emigrants from, and the government had to restore the roadblocks and cancel the ceasefire.

"I'm sure as hell planning on changing their lifestyle," declared Wayne Colburn, the director of the U.S. Marshals Service, who had been on the siege lines since the second day. "If this means starving, if it means being cold, not reading the evening papers, not being able to watch television, not making telephone calls, not being able to get soap to wash their clothes with, that's what's going to be done"—and he cut off the electricity, water, and phone service into Wounded Knee.

"Nobody had the heart to tell Colburn," an AIM wit wrote, "that doing without food and electricity, that being hungry and cold is not a novel experience for Indians."

The rebels marked the end of the ceasefire by declaring their independence: henceforth Wounded Knee would be the Independent Oglala Nation. Passports were issued to the citizenry, and ION's diplomatic corps radioed the federal forces, "Lay down your weapons, and you will be treated in accordance with the Geneva Convention." Russell Means told reporters with his usual meekness, "Any spies who violate our borders will be subject to international law and will face a firing squad." Some days later the cattle of white ranchers found their way onto the barbecue pits of the new nation, and the U.S. Attorney charged ION's governors with cattle rustling. Dennis Banks protested. These were no mere cows. They were illegal aliens. They had strayed across the international frontier without documentation and had naturally come under suspicion of being FBI infiltrators. How was ION to tell whether they were really cows other than by skinning them?

The theatrics—the mix of grandiosity, mirth, and bellicosity—lured new citizens, Indian and non, from every corner of the country. The newcomers, those who made it through the government lines anyway, brought badly needed supplies, and their heroic inbound hikes boosted the morale of residents. Once inside, the new citizens were introduced to the sweat lodge, the pipe, the red road, and other foundations of Native religions. For many Indians, it was their first exposure to their traditional culture. One of the occupiers later said, "We had guys coming in there alcoholic, and days after getting there they were straight. This will be hard to believe, but they never had withdrawal symptoms—no DTs, nothing. That was the power of the cause we were working for, the heritage we were reclaiming. We were reclaiming it for all Indians, for the generations that had it stolen from them."

It would be hard to overstate the pride that Natives throughout America took in the takeover of Wounded Knee. For more than a century, throughout much of Indian Country, the very word *Indian* had been synonymous with and appended to *dirty* or *drunk* or *stupid*. Wounded Knee did not change this state of affairs, but it did change Indians' acceptance of it—and did so very nearly overnight. The day was coming when whites, whatever they thought, could not speak of Indians in such terms. Wounded Knee marked the overthrow not just of a forgotten hamlet but of the established order. Indian Country, its enduring poverty and despair notwithstanding, would never be the same again.

Whenever the names of ION's citizens could be learned, the U.S. attorney put them before a grand jury and shook out indictments like salt at a pretzel stand. It was to counter these charges that the Wounded Knee Legal Defense/Offense Committee was formed. WKLDOC was an all-volunteer corps of lawyers, investigators, and press hands who were shunted to South Dakota by the National Lawyers Guild and other liberal groups. Most WKLDOCkers stayed a few days or weeks—whatever vacation they could afford—but a small nucleus stayed years. They ate by the sufferance of food stamps and the economy of hot dogs and slept four or fourteen or forty to a room that was generally two months' shy of condemnation. Nearly all, in Dick Wilson's phrase, were "white hippies." Wilson knew that without WKLDOC's legal and investigative help, AIM would be doomed in the long run, and he tried to throw the hippies off the reservation. He was overruled by a federal judge who did not care for WKLDOC himself but who was bound by Supreme Court precedent to let the legal team represent its clients on Pine Ridge. The most Wilson could do was deport the judge's process-server and the white clergymen who had come to mediate the siege. "Dope pushers," Wilson said of the latter. "Or if they're not pushing it, they're sure as hell using it." Of the chief mediator, he added, "The Reverend John Adams is the most arrogant son of a bitch I ever met." ("I am an *ordained* son of a bitch," the Reverend Adams amended before departing.)

The WKLDOCkers knew that when their clients eventually appeared in court they could hardly claim they had committed no crimes. WKLDOC would have to prove that the seizure of Wounded Knee was justified, and to do that, it would have to show that armed rebellion was the only recourse left an aching, oppressed people. To do *that*, WKLDOC had to compile testimony about the crimes of Wilson and his goons, which, although common knowledge on the reservation, had never been documented. So WKLDOCkers drove the byways of Pine Ridge and interviewed witnesses and swore out affidavits. The tales they gathered, while not probative, were persuasive in their weight.

In one, Corraine Brave said that she and her sister-in-law were hitchhiking home when they were picked up by goons Glen Three Stars and Charlie Richards, who drove them to Denby Dam. "At the spillway," Brave attested, "they threatened to throw us into the water and told us that if I didn't admit having been in Wounded Knee they would shoot me. At this time the men were pointing a gun at my chest and the gun was cocked. When Charlie finally realized that we were telling the truth, he said that he was sorry but that he was just doing his job and we were then taken to Pine Ridge."

In another story, Edward Cooper and a friend told of being arrested by BIA policemen as they tried to sneak into Wounded Knee. They were taken to the jail and told to put their hands on the wall and spread their legs. A previously broken pelvis kept Cooper from spreading to the officers' satisfaction, and one of the policemen kicked his leg out. Cooper spun around in agony. "But I remembered I was on a peaceful mission," he recalled, "so I dropped my hands. At that point, the jailer started punching me in the upper chest and face. I didn't try to defend myself, only dropped down and doubled over. An assistant to the jailer whipped out his black-jack and hit me from behind at the base of my skull, then from above on the crown of my head, then on my eye from underneath. 'Fuck with us, we'll fuck with you,' he was saying. And, 'These guys with long hair, they think they can run the world.' Two other jailers came to the aid of the two already on me. The four of them beat me to the ground, punching me and kicking me."

Gary Thomas, the legal aid lawyer beaten by Wilson's goons, reported that not long after his beating, Wilson told him to get off the reservation or his goons would kill him. Thomas did as bade. For years the government left his post unfilled—which in practice meant that the poor of Pine Ridge, which was to say most of Pine Ridge, went lawyerless.

Hobart Keith, a tribal councilman and Wilson critic, also told of having been beaten by a goon. The goon was Glen Three Stars, the same who had beaten Gary Thomas and threatened Corraine Brave. Keith had reliable witnesses, but tribal prosecutors refused to indict. Keith said he would go to federal court, and his case was so strong, it seemed that even the federal prosecutors might have to act. To head them off, tribal prosecutors belatedly charged Three Stars with assault. He was brought to the courtroom of

Judge Dorothy Richards, a Wilson appointee who in her last job, as clerk of court, had been accused of embezzling court fees. After Wilson elevated Richards to the bench, she allegedly had fees and fines paid directly to her, notwithstanding a ban on the handling of cash by judges. She was also alleged to have falsified the arrest records of defendants in order to bring harsher sentences on them and to have taken the furniture and appliances from a home for troubled youth and had them installed in her own house. When Three Stars appeared before her, she convicted him without ado and sentenced him to ten minutes in jail and a nickel in fine. Jeopardy was thus attached to his offense, and Keith could not pursue it in federal court. BIA superintendent Stan Lyman wrote approvingly in his diary, "The judge said she had just made the punishment fit the crime."

Other critics of Wilson told of being denied trials by jury on the excuse that funds to pay jurors had suddenly dried up. Others said that when juries were empanelled, they were handpicked by Wilson's executive committee. Others reported that judges simply refused to call their courts to order to hear complaints. Still others were turned away well before reaching a courtroom, by tribal prosecutors whose offices just happened to close whenever complainants appeared, or by policemen who just happened to run out of complaint forms. WKLDOC piled up these stories like tailings from a grim mine, and they would later prove useful in the trials of AIMers charged with seizing Wounded Knee. But by the time the stories were compiled, Wounded Knee was weeks old, and by then the mainstream press had tired of Pine Ridge and could not be bothered to sift through them. Most of the grievances were so much dust in the wind.

When the Independent Oglala Nation demanded Wilson's ouster, federal officials said that if the Oglalas wanted rid of him, they could vote him out. ION took the government at its word, and it proposed to scrap both the president and the constitution for which he stood. The tribe's constitution, like the constitutions of most Indian nations, was written by the U.S. government and forced on the tribe in the 1930s. In many respects it was an enlightened instrument, for example by giving the tribal council the right to run many of the tribe's day-to-day affairs. But in its utter disregard for traditional Oglala government—a matrix of clans, societies, and chiefs dating back centuries—and in its awarding of near-total veto power to the BIA, the constitution was mostly one more mallet for bludgeoning the culture out of the Oglalas. The document did, however, have a mechanism for its own dissolution: one-third of eligible voters had to call for a constitutional referendum, whereupon the question of dissolving the charter would be put to a vote.

Activists of the Oglala Sioux Civil Rights Organization who had remained outside Wounded Knee collected the necessary signatures and sent them to the BIA, which had to call the referendum. The BIA, with its usual haste in urgent matters, let a month pass before replying and then said it would not call an election because OSCRO did not have enough signatures. OSCRO said the BIA must be mistaken. In 1969, the last year for which voter rolls were available, 3,104 Oglalas had been registered. Since one-third of 3,104 was 1,035, and since OSCRO had 1,460 signatures, the BIA had to call an election. The BIA answered that it was true that in 1969 there had been 3,104 eligible voters. But, said the BIA, by 1973 the number of eligible voters had swollen to 9,518. Thus OSCRO would need one-third of 9,518, or 3,172 signatures, which was 1,700 more than it had gathered. OSCRO asked how in the hell the number of eligible voters had tripled in four years. The BIA replied that after OSCRO had sent in its petition to dissolve the government, the BIA had redefined the term "eligible voter," hence the tripling. OSCRO demanded to know how the BIA could change the definition when the tribe's constitution and bylaws were quite clear about who was an eligible voter, to wit: enrolled members of the Oglala Sioux Tribe who were twenty-one years or older, who lived on the reservation, and who had registered to vote. The BIA answered that the tribe's constitution and bylaws were irrelevant. It was using a definition in federal regulations—regulations the BIA had written—which said that eighteen-year-olds (not twenty-one-year-olds), nonresident

Oglalas (not just those on Pine Ridge), and the unregistered (not just those who had registered) were all eligible to vote. OSCRO rejoined, correctly, that the BIA's regulations could not supersede the tribal constitution. But the group added that even if the regulations did trump, they did not say that off-reservation and unregistered Oglalas could vote; the BIA had pulled these conditions out of thin air. Cornered, the BIA admitted "ambiguity" about these conditions, but surely, the BIA explained, on so grand an issue as a con-stitutional referendum, the regulations had *meant* to allow off-reservation and unregistered "voters" to vote. This exchange between OSCRO and the BIA stretched over several months, long after the guns were laid down at Wounded Knee, and at this last rejoinder from the BIA, OSCRO gave up.

"It looks to me," Senator Jim Abourezk observed, "like the BIA is making the voter-eligibility figures higher and lower when it wants. In this case, the BIA is a law unto itself." He was right. Even he had no more power to move the BIA than did OSCRO.

As the occupation of Wounded Knee entered its second month, Wilson or one of his goons—the author is not clear—posted a notice urging Oglalas to "march into Wounded Knee and Kill Tokas [non-Oglala Indians], wasicus [whites], hasapas [blacks] and spiolas [Mexicans]. They want to be martyrs? We will make it another Little Big Horn!! and any one of their beatnik friends can be a stand-in for Yellow Hair." The flyer evinced some confusion about which side of history Wilson and his goons were on: they were more in the tradition of the Indians who found it profitable to scout for Custer than of the Indians who killed him. But historical confusion notwithstanding, the next day Wilson and fifty mixed-bloods answered the call—sort of. Instead of invading Wounded Knee and killing the occu-pants, they set up a roadblock on the Big Foot Trail between Wounded Knee and Pine Ridge, a few hundred yards in front of the FBI roadblock. To reach the FBI barricade and Wounded Knee beyond, travelers first had to pass through the goons, who stuck their guns in the faces of all comers as the FBI watched. When WKLDOC's lawyers arrived to visit their clients, the goons refused to let them pass. The lawyers sent a message to the FBI agents up the road, reminding them of the court order permitting them to see their clients. The agents in turn caucused with President Wilson. Would he consider lifting his illegal roadblock, at least for a few days?

Wilson said he would not.

Would he consider letting through a team of mediators consisting of Senator Abourezk, a minister, and a WKLDOC lawyer?

He would not.

The agents offered WKLDOC their regrets. What could they do?

The WKLDOCkers suggested that on occasion the FBI had been known to arrest lawbreakers, but their suggestion went unheeded. WKLDOC went back to court. Judge Andrew Bogue, one of two federal judges in South Dakota and the judge of first resort for cases in the western half of the state, said he saw no reason why the goons should have to remove their illegal road-block. In fact, as far as he was concerned, they could continue to stop travelers so long as the government did not abet their lawbreaking. Unfortunately, Supreme Court precedent left him no choice but to order the goons to let the lawyers through. The goons grudgingly let them pass.

The BIA's idea of complying with Bogue's order not to support the goons was to send cases of C-rations, two-way radios, and Port-A-Potties to the roadblock. The FBI complied by giving the goons boxes of shotgun shells and rifle cartridges. Eventually the government parked an APC with the goons. The goons showed their gratitude by continuing to level their rifles at all travelers, federal and WKLDOC alike.

Things continued thus for a couple of weeks, until one day the goons turned away mediators from the Justice Department on grounds that they were overly sympathetic to AIM. Wayne Colburn, the director of the Marshals Service, had by then grown tired of having shotguns pointed at him whenever he approached the roadblock. When he heard of the mediators being turned away, he grabbed two of his marshals, put the rest on alert, and sped to the roadblock to set the goons straight. FBI agents up the road had heard over the radio that Colburn was coming and tipped the goons, who had rifles at hand and spines erect when the marshals stepped out of their van. Hoping not to inflame the Wilsonites any more than necessary, the marshalls left their guns in the van—a decision they soon regretted. Colburn gave the goons a choice: let the mediators through, or join him on a ride to jail. The goons said they intended to do neither and gripped their rifles more determinedly. The discussion did not improve from there.

"If there is going to be bloodshed," one of the goons eventually said, "let it start here."

Colburn later said he believed at this point that he and his men might well be murdered. That outcome was averted when one of the marshals sidled back to the van on pretense of using the radio, grabbed a gun instead, and spun on the advancing goons. Colburn told them to get their asses up against the van. Several tense moments passed before they complied.

As they did, an FBI agent appeared and told Colburn that there was really no need to arrest such good friends as these.

"If you're not going to help," Colburn answered, "you might as well get back up against that van yourself."

The agent said he was under no obligation to follow the orders of a U.S. marshal.

"Your ideas on jurisdiction," Colburn said, "mean about as much to me as piss falling from the sky." He told the agent to clear the hell out of the way, and the agent did.

Colburn put eleven goons in cuffs and carted them to Pine Ridge, where Dick Wilson watched them processed and forwarded to Rapid City in a cool fury. Eight of the goons were eventually arraigned in federal court. In a press conference after the arraignment, their leader, John Hussman, professed bafflement about why they were arrested. He said the goons had been deputized by Dick Wilson and had had the help of the BIA. "And since we set up the roadblock, four Federal Bureau of Investigation agents had been working with us in twelve-hour shifts."

That night other goons reestablished the roadblock. Before Colburn could dismantle it again, FBI agents prevailed on the goons to temporarily disband it. They promised that higher-ups in Washington were at that moment working on a deal to let the roadblock stand, if only the goons wouldn't stir things up in the meantime. But by next morning the deal had not come off, and Wilson and a hundred angry goons set up the roadblock once more. While they were doing so, a furious teleconference was concluding between Colburn in Pine Ridge and L. Patrick Gray, the FBI's acting director, in Washington. The arbiter of the discussion was a senior official at the Justice Department, perhaps Attorney General Richard Kleindienst himself. Colburn demanded the roadblock come down; Gray demanded it be kept in place but brought under FBI control. The arbiter sided with Gray.

That afternoon Colburn had to drive through the roadblock again. With him were the top negotiators on Pine Ridge from the Justice and Interior departments, Richard Hellstern and Kent Frizzell. As they approached the roadblock, a teenager with a rifle ordered Frizzell, who was driving, to roll down his window. Frizzell told the kid if he wanted the window rolled down he could do it his goddamned self. The kid leveled his weapon at Frizzell's head, cocked it, and ordered him out. As Frizzell started to comply, Colburn jumped out of the car and put the barrel of his automatic rifle within smelling distance of the kid's nose.

"Pull that trigger," he said, "and you're a dead man."

An FBI agent stepped between them and suggested the boy might lower his gun.

"I'll lower mine when he lowers his," the boy said. He was shaking but firm.

Tender negotiation ensued, and Colburn lowered his gun, followed by the kid.

At a press briefing the next day, the government's Richard Hellstern said the event he had witnessed was nothing worthy of bold type: "Words were exchanged and weapons raised, but fortunately cooler heads prevailed."

Dick Wilson, however, held up a finger and thumb with a quarter inch of air between them. "We came *this* far from shooting Frizzell and Colburn," he said and broke into an enormous grin.

Hellstern was asked what charges would be brought against the teenager. He said none. In fact the government had just decided to train the goons and put them on the federal payroll.

A few days later the teenager's rifle was discovered to have a hair trigger. The discovery was made when the gun blew a hole in a car radiator after a slight jostle. The kid's trembling could have cost Frizzell half his skull.

The first two or three hundred thousand bullets fired at Wounded Knee came to rest in dirt, wood, and body parts that, mercifully, were not vital. Then in late March, U.S. Marshal Lloyd Grimm took a bullet to the spine and became a paraplegic. A few weeks later AIMer Frank Clearwater, who had just hiked into Wounded Knee and was sleeping off the trek, was shot through the skull by a bullet that pierced the thin wall of the house in which he lay. He never woke. At April's end another AIMer, Buddy Lamont, was flushed from his bunker during a firefight and shot through the heart. He died in an instant.

Death took the snap out of the occupiers. ION's leaders, who till then had done as much to prolong the siege as they had to end it, began to sue more determinedly for peace. In early May an accord was reached: the Justice Department, which had lately begun to investigate civil rights abuses on Pine Ridge, would see the investigation to its conclusion; Wilson's tribal accounts would be audited; and the White House would send a delegation to Pine Ridge to talk about broken treaties. In return, the citizens of ION would surrender their guns and submit to arrest. The stand-down took place on May 8, seventy-one days after Wounded Knee was seized. Most of ION's citizenry snuck out of the village before the surrender. Before leaving, they dug a hole beside the mass grave of Big Foot's people and there laid Buddy Lamont. (Frank Clearwater was buried elsewhere.) The headstone they erected read, "Two thousand came to Wounded Knee in 1973. One stayed."

It should have said "Two." For Lamont had company in subterranean Wounded Knee, another new arrival. Thirty years would have to pass before his companion in death would become known.

CHAPTER 4

THE HOUSE OF Paul Thunder Horse sat down a country lane just off Highway 27, a few minutes' drive from Wounded Knee. On the midnight in question, Thunder Horse and friends were driving home from a social outing, spread over two cars, and had just turned down the lane when sparks flared in the dirt before them. The report of gunfire was close behind. To those in the cars, it sounded as if guns of at least two calibers were being fired at them. Dallas Little Bear, driving the first car, told the children in the backseat to stop screaming and get down.

"But I'm hit, Daddy!" his daughter cried. "Daddy, they got me."

Little Bear stopped the car, ran around to the passenger side, and asked for Mary Ann to be handed out to him. Even in the dark, he could tell the wound was bad—blood was flowing freely from one of her eyes. The bullets did not let up, so he passed his daughter back into the car, hurried back to the wheel, and made a dash for the highway (the car behind him having already done so). Shots followed them down the lane. It was a long twenty minutes to the hospital in Pine Ridge, but Mary Ann Little Bear survived. Her eye, however, did not. She was nine years old.

The police were called. Well after daylight, a complement of BIA officers and FBI agents arrived at Paul Thunder Horse's house. At least half a dozen adults had witnessed the shooting, either from one of the cars or from the nearby houses, but the lawmen spoke to only a few of them, and to those only briefly. They took no official statements nor even, so far as the interviewees could see, notes. Nor did they photograph the bullet holes in the cars or the houses, nor collect the lodged bullets.

The witnesses were unanimous about where the shots had come from: the property of the Francis Randalls, 250 yards up the way. The Randalls were goons; the Little Bears and Thunder Horses were AIM sympathizers. The lawmen made a brief visit to the Randall house and may have confiscated a couple of pistols, but these would not have been the crime weapons since bullets from pistols would not have carried 250 yards. No arrests were made.

Later that day, Dallas and Roselyn Little Bear went to the police station in Pine Ridge to swear out a complaint. In Roselyn's account, they appeared before a white man, whom they assumed was a BIA police officer or an FBI agent. "He showed me two plastic bags full of shells that he said had been picked up at Randall's place," she said at the time. "He told us that he didn't want to arrest anyone because he didn't have enough evidence. We asked him if we could sign a complaint against John Hussman, Woody Richards, and Francis Randall." Richards and Hussman were sons-in-law of the Randalls; their cars had been parked in front of the Randall house at the time of the shooting. "He told us we couldn't."

The night Mary Ann Little Bear was shot was not the first time guns had been fired from the Randall place. Six or seven weeks earlier, according to witnesses, someone at the Randalls' had shot up the Thunder Horse house. John Hussman's truck had been parked in front of the Randall house on that occasion too. The law had been called, BIA officers and FBI agents had come, brief questions had been asked of witnesses, and a few pictures had been taken of the bullet holes in the house. But if Hussman or the Randalls were ever questioned, no one saw it. Certainly they were never arrested. The fact of this earlier shooting did not make the police more inclined to arrest the alleged shooters of Mary Ann Little Bear. Instead, the BIA police announced to the press that Mary Ann Little Bear had been maimed in an "exchange of gunfire," the implication being that both sides were to blame. There was no evidence then—or now—that the victims "exchanged" a single shot, or even had a gun with which to do so.

The Independent Oglala Nation had fallen three months before Mary Ann Little Bear was shot, but AIMers still lived in every community on the reservation and WKLDOC had set up shop in nearby Rapid City. When the BIA and FBI refused to arrest the shooters, AIM sent armed men to guard the Thunder Horse house and WKLDOC sent a team of investigators. The government that barely stirred itself on behalf of Mary Ann Little Bear now mustered fourteen BIA police, FBI agents, and U.S. marshals to threaten the AIMers with arrest. Perhaps because of the AIMers' arms, or perhaps because of the presence of white WKLDOCkers, no arrests were made. After the law departed, WKLDOC's investigators examined Dallas Little Bear's car. They found that the bullet that struck Mary Ann had passed through the driver's door and through the front seat before ricocheting off the passenger-side door and finding her eye. It was the indirect path that had kept the bullet from penetrating her brain. A second bullet had pierced the driver's side door, had somehow missed all seven riders, and had lodged in one of the seats, where a WKLDOC investigator dug it out. The FBI agents who had looked at the car that morning had been in such a hurry that they missed the second bullet completely.

The WKLDOCkers took statements from sixteen adults and teenagers who had been in the cars and nearby houses. Most were AIM partisans. But at least one householder who was not partial to AIM verified the AIMers' claims: the shots had come from the Randall place, and the victims had fired none in return. The only witness who differed was the wife of Woody Richards, one of the alleged shooters. She told the WKL-DOCkers that Woody had been in the Randall house on the night of the attack (as had she) but that he hadn't done any shooting. In fact, by her reckoning, most of the shots had come *from* the Thunder Horse house *toward* the Randall place. Ms. Richards's testimony would not have fared well in most courtrooms.

The WKLDOCkers collected other evidence that had been overlooked or ignored by the government's investigators, including more shells from the Randall property. When they tried to photograph the shells *in situ*, Woody Richards greeted them with a rifle and said, "Snap one picture, and I'll shoot you dead." The investigators settled for filching a few of the shells.

When their work was done, they offered to give the FBI, BIA, and U.S. attorney's office the witness statements they had collected as well as the shells from the Randalls' land and the bullet from the Little Bears' car. The government declined them all. WKLDOC took the story to reporters, but with Wounded Knee already in the distant past the national press showed little interest in Pine Ridge. Certainly reporters would not return for so small an event as the maiming of a child. Newspapers in West River, as South Dakota west of the Missouri was known, found a few inches for the shooting but none for the government's refusal to investigate or prosecute.

The shooting of Mary Ann Little Bear fell into a class of crimes that the accord that ended Wounded Knee was supposed to address—namely, human rights abuses condoned or ignored by the local law. The Civil Rights Division of the Justice Department had started its inquiry into such abuses before Wounded Knee fell and in a few weeks fielded fifty-five complaints. The Civil Rights Division sent the FBI to investigate. A short time later the young lawyer overseeing Civil Rights' work, Dennis Ickes, reported his findings to the leaders of ION. Ickes (pronounced ICK-ees) said that in eleven of the fifty-five cases, when FBI agents went to the victims' houses and asked about the complaints, the victims said no such crime had occurred. "I don't know whether those people are afraid to tell us the truth, or whether in fact nothing happened," Ickes allowed, but there was nothing to be done in such cases. In each of the other forty-four cases, Ickes eventually determined that based on the FBI's investigation, there was "no prosecutive merit" in the complaint—nothing that would convince a grand jury to indict or a petit jury to convict. In other words, the aggrieved of Pine Ridge were suffering mass hallucination. There was no brutality in Wilson's dominion.

ION's leaders replied that sending FBI agents to investigate crimes the FBI had ignored in the first place might not be the best way to get the truth from terrified victims. They asked Ickes whether the Civil Rights Division had ever investigated its investigators—ever, say, prosecuted an FBI agent or a U.S. marshal. Ickes had to admit that no, that had never happened in the history of the Civil Rights Division. The FBI's representative at Wounded Knee took offense at the question, with its suggestion that his men might be biased against AIMers. "We will go anywhere, at any time, under any circumstances to receive a legitimate complaint," he said. *Legitimate* was the rub. If the death threat against Gary Thomas—a white lawyer with two witnesses—was not legitimate, if the attempted beating of the eminent Russell Means and the certain beating of Councilman Hobart Gates were not legitimate, how could a complaint from an Indian who lived in a tarpaper shack stand a chance?

Any doubts on this question were put to rest by the shooting of Mary Ann Little Bear. Even Oglalas who had long ago accepted being trod upon were sickened that the Justice Department would abandon an innocent child rather than confront Wilson's goons. A very few people may still have clung to the hope that the government might yet be shocked, or forced, to revoke the carte blanche it had given Wilson. But these hopes were dashed after Pedro Bissonette was killed.

On Pine Ridge, men who disagreed with Dick Wilson tended to do so quietly, his goons being a convincing deterrent to clamor. It was therefore mostly women who picketed the tribal buildings and filed complaints and prodded their fellow Oglalas to plot at Calico Hall. Whether women were less harassed by the goons or simply less cowed was an open question, even among themselves. But whatever the case, the women who led the struggle against Wilson were not comfortable doing so absent their men. Politics among the Oglalas had long been a male domain, at least on the surface, and feminism had pierced the domain only so far by the 1970s. The women who nourished the rebellion thought, probably rightly, that men would not join the struggle if only women led. At one of the meetings before Wounded Knee was seized,

Ellen Moves Camp, one of the fiery female leaders, demanded of the crowd at Calico Hall, "Where are all our men?!"

One hollered back, "I'm right here!" This was Pedro Aloysius Bissonette, and it was not an empty boast.

Bissonette, who pronounced his name PEE-dro BISS-uh-net, was a co-founder of the Oglala Sioux Civil Rights Organization and a frequent, voluble, and seemingly fearless detractor of Wilson. When Wounded Knee was seized, he was the only resident of Pine Ridge to join the rebels' ruling junta. On the night of October 17, 1973, five months after Wounded Knee fell, he was driving toward the town of Pine Ridge from the east when a pair of BIA policemen who had a warrant for his arrest saw his car and followed him. Bissonette turned off the highway, drove forty or fifty feet down a dirt road, and stopped. The officers pulled behind him and ordered him to step out of his car with his hands up. He did not. The order was given again, and then again. He finally emerged, but his hands were not up. Officer Joe Clifford had stepped out of the police car on the driver's side, and Officer Evans Rencountre had stepped out on the passenger's side, each with a gun. They approached Bissonette on opposite sides of his car.

"You afraid?" Bissonette said, noting their weapons. The officers would later say that he seemed drunk. "You going to shoot me?"

The officers told him to step away from his car, but instead he leaned into the front seat, grabbed a rifle, and, ignoring Clifford, strode around the front of the car to where Rencountre stood. As Bissonette raised his rifle, Rencountre pointed his shotgun at him and pulled the trigger—but the gun jammed. Rencountre beat a retreat down a roadside ditch back toward the police car, and Bissonette followed, his rifle still aimed at him. On the roadbed above, Clifford took aim at Bissonette and fired, but his gun failed as well. He tried again—still no luck. Later he would discover the gun had not been loaded. He retrieved a shotgun—probably from the police car, though possibly he had it at his side—and tried once more. The third time was the proverbial charm. The blast ripped open Bissonette's chest and spun him around. He murmured something as he fell—the officers could not hear what it was—and by the time they came to his side, his breathing and pulse were already weak. They called an ambulance, which, as the hospital was only a few miles to the west, arrived quickly. Neither on the way to the emergency room nor on arrival could Bissonette be resuscitated. He was declared dead at 10:10 p.m., twenty minutes after the officers had pulled behind him. That anyway, in time, was the story the Bureau of Indian Affairs told.

Mark Lane, Esq., believed hardly a word of it. Lane was inflexible, hyperbolic, and bullying, detested even by many of his WKLDOC colleagues. He was also everlastingly curious, dogged in pursuit of facts, and brilliant in the cultivation of witnesses. He had quite literally written the book on conspiracy—*Rush to Judgment*, a denunciation of the official inquiry into President Kennedy's assassination—and he needed little convincing that there was more to Bissonette's killing than the self-defense that the police were claiming. To Lane's mind, Bissonette was the most important witness in the upcoming trials of the occupiers of Wounded Knee. Bissonette was knowledgeable enough to catalog the many sins of Dick Wilson and personable enough to do it in a way that even a white jury might find moving. It was exceedingly convenient for the government to have Bissonette out of the way. A few hours before he was shot, Bissonette had called Lane. He said he was coming to Rapid City to turn himself in for the outstanding warrant, which stemmed from a string of lesser charges. He said he wanted to put those charges behind him so he could focus on helping his people. The next thing Lane heard, Bissonette was dead.

Lane grabbed two of his aides and drove immediately from the WKLDOC office in Rapid City to the hospital morgue in Pine Ridge. They found Bissonette on a gurney, drained of color, with seven small holes describing a compact circle on the right side of his breast. Among and near the holes were several bruises, most the size of dimes but one the size of a silver dollar. On Bissonette's right hand were two small entry wounds and a grisly exit wound. Lane took photographs, then left to examine the crime scene and secure permission from Bissonette's mother to have the body released to WKLDOC for autopsy.

As Lane went about his work, Len Cavise, a young WKLDOCker in Rapid City, called U.S. Attorney William Clayton. Cavise said WKLDOC wanted its own autopsy on Bissonette and asked that the government not perform one in the meantime. Clayton agreed. But a few hours later, shortly before 5:00 a.m., a nurse at the hospital called WKLDOC to say Bissonette's body was gone. Lane rushed back to the morgue and, sure enough, Bissonette was not there. He demanded to see the form that authorized the removal of the body. It was produced, but the blanks for who had taken Bissonette, when he had been taken, and where he had been taken were empty. The hospital staff purported to know nothing. So too, at first, the Pine Ridge police. But eventually WKLDOC discovered that Bissonette's body had been flown to Scottsbluff, under the care of Dr. W. O. Brown.

Len Cavise in Rapid City called U.S. Attorney Clayton back and asked what in God's name was the body doing in Scottsbluff.

Clayton said he had no idea. Everything was being done on the orders of the BIA police.

What of Clayton's promise, Cavise demanded, that there would be no government autopsy?

Clayton said he had promised no such thing.

Cavise said Clayton most certainly had.

"If you're going to say I told you that," Clayton said, "then I'm not going to talk to you." He hung up.

Cavise tracked Fred Nichol, the chief federal judge for South Dakota, to a Pierre motel, roused him from bed, and asked for an injunction against the government's autopsy. Nichol said he would look into it and get back to Cavise within the hour. Next Cavise called the police chief on Pine Ridge, Del Eastman, who admitted at last that he had sent the body to Scottsbluff. But he had done so, he said, "under direct orders from Bill Clayton" (a claim Clayton denied). Cavise hung up and called Dr. Brown's office in Scottsbluff and asked if Brown was performing an autopsy despite the wish of Bissonette's mother that WKLDOC oversee the autopsy. An aide to Brown refused to answer, but Cavise persisted and was finally told yes, an autopsy was being performed but there was nothing to be done about it since the job was almost done. (This was later proven untrue: the autopsy had not yet begun.)

Judge Nichol called Cavise back. He too had been told the autopsy was nearly done but said it hardly mattered: he would not enjoin a pathologist whom the government said was competent unless he suspected the government of trying to hide something. As yet, he had no reason to think so. A few days later U.S. Attorney Clayton asked Judge Nichol to authorize the autopsy retroactively. Clayton claimed that the government had received permission for the autopsy from Theresa Perkins, sometimes called Theresa Bissonette, who had once been either Bissonette's girlfriend or his common-law wife (depending on one's definition). But the couple had been long estranged when Bissonette was shot, and the permission she had granted, if any, was of doubtful legality. Moreover, Perkins was the sister of the man who killed Bissonette, BIA officer Joe Clifford. She had a rather plangent motive for a postmortem friendly to the government. Judge Nichol, who probably knew none of this, granted Clayton's request for the retroactive authorization.

Throughout the night of Bissonette's killing, Mark Lane spoke several times with Police Chief Eastman. According to Lane, at first "Eastman insisted only one bullet had struck Pedro in the chest. He was doing that because he did not know that we had already seen the body and, in fact, that I had photographed the body. I told him, 'Well, you're a liar. He was hit in the chest by seven penetrating missiles.'

"He said, 'How do you know?'

"I said, 'Because I have seen the body.'

"He paused and said, 'Well, you might be mistaken.'

"I said, 'Sure, I might be mistaken. And the other five witnesses in the room might also be mistaken.' There was a pause, and I said, 'How did all that happen with one bullet?'

"He said, 'Well, it was a shotgun.'

"That's when they changed the story, when they knew that we had seen the body."

A newsman apparently verified that Eastman originally said Bissonette was killed by a single shot from a pistol.

There were other problems in Eastman's story. He apparently said at first that the gun Bissonette had pointed at Officer Rencountre was a shotgun. Later he seems to have said that it was a high-powered rifle of a type common to the BIA stockpile—that is, a gun that could easily have been planted. (The gun was finally described as a Winchester A303, a .30-06 rifle.) Lane doubted Bissonette had a gun at all: he had never known Bissonette to carry one; nor, he said, did anyone he asked. Eastman also told Lane that Bissonette had been killed beside his car, but when Lane visited the scene, he found a pool of blood forty-five feet from where the police said Bissonette had fallen. Either Bissonette had been killed at the site of the bloodstain, or he had been moved there after being killed—neither of which possibilities fit the police story. Lane also doubted Eastman's claim that Bissonette was shot a little before ten o'clock. Lane turned up two Pine Ridge residents, Verlean Ice and Goldie Little Crow, who said that just after nine o'clock, forty-five minutes before the supposed time of the shooting, they drove by Bissonette's car, which was parked on the roadside surrounded by five police cars with red lights flashing and officers milling about and taking measurements. Another Pine Ridge couple, John and Cordila Attack Him, told Lane that they had turned on their police scanner at around nine o'clock and heard the police say someone had been shot. There were no other shootings on Pine Ridge the night Bissonette was killed.

On the morning after the killing, Mark Lane held a press conference. He told reporters that at 9:00 p.m. the night before, Bissonette had been taken from his car to a roadside ditch where he was beaten and tear-gassed. Lane said the large bruise on Bissonette's chest was made by a teargas canister, the smaller bruises on his chest were caused by fists, and there were other markings on Bissonette's body that seemed to be gas burns. After this torture, a small-caliber pistol was put to Bissonette's chest and the trigger was pulled seven times. He was left to bleed for nearly an hour and was dead or all but by the time the ambulance was called.

In Indian Country today, among those who remember Pedro Bissonette, it is Lane's version of the killing that prevails, as unshakably as the BIA's version prevails among the government. Neither is right.

Pounding hell out of white guys was such fun that Pedro Bissonette grew up to become an amateur boxer, and a good one. He was short but solid, confidently handsome, quick to grin, irrepressible of spirit. At the age of sixteen a rodeo horse fell on him and broke his back, but he refused to lie in bed two months to recuperate. He suffered compressed vertebrae as a result but for the rest of his life never complained of the pain. As an adult, after his own boxing days were over, he tutored teens in sparring, as much to teach dignity as sport, and he dreamed of founding a training camp with money that never came to hand. He was fluent in both Lakota and English, and he used these skills to help less Anglicized elders navigate the BIA's bureaucracy, for example by wrestling loose disability checks that were stuck in red tape and deciphering lease agreements written in incomprehensible legalese. For such work he was beloved by elders. When the anti-Wilsonites wanted to convince the traditional (and traditionally apolitical) Oglala chiefs to support their drive to impeach Wilson, it was Bissonette who talked the chiefs into it. By the time he joined the junta that ruled Wounded Knee, Dick Wilson was calling him Pine Ridge's biggest traitor, the Oglala who let AIM onto the reservation. His followers, as more than one WKLDOCker would later say, "looked up to him like a god."

Bissonette was also a hothead. His closest friend, Poker Joe Merrival, would later recall that their friendship began when Bissonette stepped from a car, got into Poker's face, and said, "I hear you're the toughest guy around. You want to fight?"

Poker did not want to fight. "I got a better idea," he said. "Why don't we beat up on some white guys?"

So together they patronized the border-town bars where ranch hands abused Indians, and in the course of brawling with cowboys, became the best of friends. As it happened, Merrival was one of Wilson's most trusted goons. He was one of the pair who tried to jump Russell Means a few hours before Wounded Knee was taken, and he had also been appointed by Wilson to shadow AIM at public protests and report on their doings. It was Bissonette's unique talent, alone among leaders of OSCRO and AIM, to somehow maintain friendships on both sides of the AIM-goon divide.

Another of his talents was finding trouble. It was not unusual for an angry young man in Indian Country to compile the kind of record of criminal indictments that Bissonette did before Wounded Knee. But after Wounded Knee, the indictments assumed unusual importance. The greatest of the charges was assault on a federal officer; its origins were tangled. Some months before the assault, Theresa Perkins put a bullet into Bissonette's breast, narrowly missing his heart. Perkins was apparently angry over his attentions to other women. Bissonette recovered, refused to press charges, and tried to reconcile with her. But the reconciliation went poorly. In his version of events, when it seemed she was reaching for a gun to shoot him again, he backhanded her and broke her jaw. She was not as shy as he about pressing charges, and he was swiftly indicted. When Bissonette learned of the charge, he went to the police station with Poker Joe and, it seems, tried to threaten officers into withdrawing the complaint. When that failed, Poker knocked one of the officers flat. On their way out the door, a welfare worker who had denied benefits to one of Bissonette's relatives had the bad luck to cross their path. Bissonette knocked the welfare worker to the ground, and he may have threatened the man with worse. Arrest warrants were issued for both Bissonette and Poker.

The next night BIA police stopped the pair as they were driving into Pine Ridge and said they would have to come downtown. Bissonette and Poker said there were some white guys they needed to "take care of" first and asked if they could turn themselves in tomorrow. When the officers said they would have to come along, Bissonette accused them of being Uncle Tomahawks—toadies for whites. The conversation deteriorated from there, and Bissonette supposedly said, "You're going to have to kill me to take me in." He went to the trunk of the car, opened it, and said, "You want a shootout? You ready to die?"

"Don't do that, Pete," Poker said and slammed the trunk shut. The trunk was later discovered to have a homemade club in it, though what it held at the time of the confrontation is unknown.

The police led Poker away, but before they could grab Bissonette, he jumped into the car, gunned it down the road, and came back toward them. Most of them scattered as he passed by, but one was pinned against a car and clipped by Bissonette. The officer landed on his back with cracked vertebrae. In the chaos Poker Joe bolted into a darkened field and the police unloaded their guns after him but did not hit him. Bissonette was charged with assaulting a federal officer, Poker with flight. The next day Bissonette surrendered at the police station. He made bond quickly, but again he fought with Theresa Perkins, again was arrested, and again was released. All the while he was leading the resistance to Dick Wilson. His police record was not a problem for his followers. Any Indian who had not been hauled into court had an uncle or a cousin or two or three who had.

Then came Wounded Knee. Suddenly Bissonette was hosting press conferences before reporters from around the globe, testifying to the evils of Dick Wilson and the BIA and America's ongoing colonization of Indians. The FBI asked its spies in Wounded Knee to gather information on him, and Justice Department officials wrote memos about the danger he posed. Eventually the U.S. attorney's office won eleven indictments against him for alleged crimes at Wounded Knee with sentences totaling nearly a century. Bissonette went into hiding after Wounded Knee, but he was quickly betrayed by a mole and arrested. Where the other leaders made bail easily enough, Bissonette's many prior arrests and his impending trial for running over the BIA officer gave the government grounds for setting his bond unattainably high. He sat in jail.

WKLDOC had a policy of defending clients only on their Wounded Knee charges and leaving them to their own devices on other charges. So

Bissonette was appointed a lawyer by the court, one Robert Warder. According to Bissonette, Warder disregarded his ideas about how to prepare his defense and told him he was not only guilty but possibly crazy. Warder said Bissonette needed a psychiatric evaluation, but Bissonette refused to be evaluated. Warder then announced that he had brokered a fine deal: Bissonette would plead guilty to assaulting the policeman and be given probation on that count, and his many other charges—the alleged assaults on Theresa Perkins as well as the eleven charges for riot, kidnapping, and conspiracy at Wounded Knee—would be dropped entirely. In return, he would testify against Banks, Means, and the other leaders of Wounded Knee. In the meantime the government would house him at a military base, like a Mafia wise guy turned state's evidence. Starting immediately, he was to see no one save Warder and his jailers. Warder said he had already cleared the deal with both the prosecutor and his good friend Judge Andrew Bogue, and he reminded Bissonette that if he did not take the deal, he was looking at ninety years in a box. Bissonette told friends that Warder pressed him so zealously that he felt brainwashed. He asked Judge Bogue for a new lawyer, but Bogue said Bissonette could have Warder or no one. Bogue was apparently not concerned that Warder was also representing other Wounded Knee defendants—the very people Warder was advising Bissonette to turn against.

Bissonette rejected Warder's offer. "I will stand with my brothers and sisters," he wrote. "I will live for them and if it is necessary to stop the terrible things that happen to Indians on the Pine Ridge Reservation I am ready to die for them." Die he would, but the terrible things would continue for some time.

While all of this was unfolding, Bissonette received an unexpected jailhouse visit from two FBI agents who said they wanted to know about civil rights abuses on Pine Ridge, a topic dear to Bissonette. He agreed to talk to them. But the questions they asked had nothing to do with rights violations. They wanted to know only about the shooting of a U.S. marshal at Wounded Knee. Bissonette said he could not answer without his lawyer—a WKLDOC lawyer since the questions were about Wounded Knee—and said he would talk with them only about civil rights complaints, as agreed. The agents persisted for half an hour, and more than once Bissonette nearly came to blows with them. When they finally left, Bissonette called WKLDOC, and a WKLDOCker called the senior FBI agent in Rapid City and asked just what the Bureau was doing illegally questioning one of WKLDOC's clients without his lawyer.

The agent answered that the FBI was just investigating civil rights complaints. Wasn't that what WKLDOC wanted?

Meanwhile WKLDOC lawyers who tried to visit Bissonette in jail were evicted on Judge Bogue's orders. All of which led WKLDOC to conclude that where Wounded Knee defendants were concerned, there was no such thing as a charge that was unrelated to Wounded Knee. WKLDOC hurriedly found two lawyers to represent Bissonette on his assault charge and asked for a brief continuance to build his defense since his trial was only a few days off. But Judge Bogue would not grant the continuance, nor would he allow WKLDOC to represent Bissonette (no matter that Warder, having expected Bissonette to take his deal, was apparently also ill-prepared for trial).

When Bogue gaveled Bissonette's trial into session, Bissonette turned his back to Warder at the defense table and remained in that posture for the rest of the trial. When a WKLDOC lawyer asked if she could advise Bissonette from within the bar, Bogue said no, but when she asked that his refusal be entered into the record, he relented. In the meantime WKLDOC appealed Bogue's refusal to let the group represent Bissonette. A panel of the Eighth U.S. Circuit Court of Appeals granted an immediate oral argument—a sign that it took the matter seriously—and although it denied the appeal, it did so only because the appeal would be mooted if Bissonette were acquitted at trial. The panel made clear that if Bissonette were convicted, he could revive the appeal. It was a hint to Bogue that he would likely be reversed. Bogue took the hint. Just before Bissonette's case went to the jury, he dismissed all charges, notwithstanding that the defendant was guilty as Cain. It would not be the last time the government had to set an AIM wrongdoer free because its own wrongdoings were of greater consequence.

On a late September day in 1973, four months after his trial, Bissonette allegedly fired a shot over the heads of goons in Whiteclay, Nebraska, a village just south of Pine Ridge consisting of little more than bars for liquoring the residents of the dry reservation. Those who claimed to have witnessed the shot were not known for their integrity—goon Charles Winters, for example, would later have a hand in a particularly senseless murder—but their stories mostly agreed. The sheriff of Sheridan County was not known for involving himself in the bloodless quarrels of the Indians who enriched Whiteclay's taverners, but he issued a warrant for Bissonette's arrest. Given the witnesses and the sheriff, most WKL-DOCkers saw the warrant as a ploy to harass Bissonette. In Mark Lane's view, it was a license to kill him.

After the warrant was issued, Bissonette fled Pine Ridge and worked for a short time as a welder on the Northern Cheyenne Reservation of eastern Montana. But the police discovered his whereabouts when he made a phone call to Dennis Banks, whose line was tapped, and a friendly tribal judge tipped Bissonette that the police were coming for him. He fled again, this time for Colorado. But as he drove south from Montana, he decided he didn't want to live on the lam, and so, on the night of October 16, he drove back to Pine Ridge. The next morning, his last, he went to Poker Joe's place and talked about how to rid the reservation of Wilson. Poker had started to sour on his boss, and the pair resolved that they would stand for office in the upcoming elections. (After Bissonette was killed, Poker filed for president but was eclipsed by a contest between Wilson and Russell Means.) Bissonette told Poker he was going to turn himself in that evening but in Rapid City since "the cops on Pine Ridge jack around too much."

Later that day Bissonette had a run-in with police, a prelude to his fatal encounter that night. Three decades later the FBI still refuses to release key documents about the encounter or the names of the witnesses to it, so much remains unknown. What is known is that at half past three in the afternoon, Bissonette picked up a hitchhiker near the town of Pine Ridge and drove her to a homestead north of town. Shortly before they entered the homestead, Bissonette noticed that a BIA police car was following him. He turned into the long driveway of the homestead, and the police car followed a respectful distance behind. He stopped the car at the house, told his hitchhiker to take cover, and stepped out with a rifle. The two BIA officers inside the police car later said that Bissonette pointed his rifle at them, but as there were children and other innocents outside the house, they decided to U-turn and wait for Bissonette back at the highway. When they did so, Bissonette fired a shot at them, which encouraged them in their retreat. A few minutes later Bissonette came racing by them onto the highway and, after passing a bus and a car that the police could not pass, got away. The BIA in Pine Ridge dispatched every available officer on a manhunt that covered a large swath of the reservation. Houses that Bissonette was known to frequent were searched, patrols cruised the highway looking for his car, and a couple of FBI agents who were in Pine Ridge immediately joined the hunt as well. When darkness fell, the hunt was suspended, but officers were told to remain on the lookout for Bissonette, who was to be considered armed and dangerous. By one account, the officers were instructed to shoot to kill. The entire episode, if true, made the fatal shooting that night much more understandable.

But while most of the story as the BIA told it was true, the crucial point—that Bissonette had fired on police—was almost certainly not. The hitchhiker, for one, told the FBI later that although Bissonette did step out of the car at the homestead with a rifle, he neither pointed it at the police nor fired it. The radio log of the BIA police supports the hitcher's account: it shows that the policemen who were supposedly fired on never radioed the shooting to the dispatcher—despite being in constant contact with the dispatcher and despite having several idle minutes at the highwayside to call in the shot. This would have been a rather large error for one officer to make. For two officers, it was nearly unthinkable.

After Bissonette eluded the police, he visited friends on the eastern end of the reservation (the police were searching the western end) and from one of their houses called WKLDOC. WKLDOC aide Sand Brim remembered, "Mark [Lane] got on the phone and said, 'Get off the reservation right now! Get out!' There was some talk about taking back roads. But Pedro wanted to go by a relative's house, then to his mom's—she lived near Pine Ridge. Mark was really urging him not to do it. 'Do not do it! Do not! Come out!' The next phone call we got, they had killed him."

After Bissonette was shot, AIM called on supporters around the country to come to Pine Ridge for his wake and funeral. With his usual restraint, Dick Wilson declared, "The Oglala Sioux have organized and are prepared for the AIM invasion. This announcement is intended to warn these invaders that their invasion will be met with resistance by the Oglala Sioux. Enter at your own risk." He sent his goons to the hilltops around the home of Bissonette's mother, where the wake of several days was being held. "If you have to shoot them," goon leader Duane Brewer was heard telling his men, "shoot them all, women and children too."

The BIA police stopped mourners as they came and went from the wake, searching their cars and persons without warrants. Several were arrested for drunkenness despite having drunk nothing. Bissonette's cousin Floyd Running Hand was one of the arrestees. When he demanded to make a phone call, his jailers choked him until he blacked out. He awoke in the hospital, where doctors were told he had tried to hang himself. He was told if he wanted to leave the hospital alive, he would agree. He did. Another arrestee, John Iverson, was hauled before Judge Dorothy Richards, to whom he complained that he had asked for a breathalyzer test to prove his sobriety only to be refused by the police. Judge Richards laughed. Pine Ridge didn't have breathalyzer equipment, she said, then she nicked him $20 and gave him fifteen minutes to get off the reservation.

AIMers came to the funeral nonetheless—from New Mexico and Minnesota and Washington and California—and took up armed positions at the Bissonette place opposite the goons. Between the weaponry, the harassment from the Wilsonites, and the certainty among AIMers that Bissonette had been assassinated, a single eager finger or careless word could have touched off a bloody battle. It was thus to considerable alarm when shortly before dawn one morning, Dick Wilson's car came swerving into the wake. AIM's sentries proved cool of head and stopped the car without incident. At the wheel they found a drunken teenager who said Wilson had paid him and given him the car to drive into the compound. AIM presumed, reasonably, that Wilson had been trying to provoke a firefight with the kid as sacrifice. WKLDOC filed a complaint with the BIA police accusing Wilson of trying to incite violence and corrupting a minor, but when reporters asked the police if they were going to arrest Wilson, they said they hadn't received WKLDOC's complaint. Later they said they had received it but that they could do nothing about it because it had been improperly filed. (This was apparently untrue.)

The FBI had jurisdiction over crimes of violence on the reservation, but it also took no interest in the complaint. Perhaps the FBI was too busy investigating the mourners—a job it had begun several days earlier by slipping spies inside the mourning caravans. The resulting espionage, both en route and at the wake, appears to have been nearly round-the-clock, but if the FBI found so much as a misdemeanor committed by the mourners, it has never said so. To this day the FBI censors almost every word of its several-hundred-page dossier on the espionage. The censors reject the notion that they are still withholding the documents because the documents would show the FBI was spying illegally on peaceful mourners. The FBI says it is only trying to keep secret the identity of informers who might still be alive; it is just an unfortunate side effect that releasing even a few words about the informers' work could blow their cover. The FBI hastens to add that if anyone can prove that any of the informers are dead, the Bureau would gladly release their reports. The difficulty of proving people dead without knowing their names does not concern the FBI.

* * *

The inquiry into who killed Pedro Bissonette was entrusted to Dennis Ickes, the same young lawyer from the Justice Department who had investigated abuses on Pine Ridge (and who had determined, in effect, that the Oglalas were hallucinating en masse). A few days into the Bissonette inquiry, Mark Lane said of Ickes's work, "He has evidently found it sufficient to speak only to FBI agents and the BIA police. When told of statements that WKLDOC investigators had received, he did not express any interest in getting the information from witnesses. He stated only that if everything we said was true, he would be 'very depressed.' " Decades later Ickes confirmed that he spoke only to government sources, but he said there was nothing wrong with that. It was the policy of the Civil Rights Division, he explained, to leave the gumshoeing to the FBI, which, after all, had agents who were trained in on-the-ground investigation. He was a mere lawyer, not a detective, and if the FBI did not speak to the witnesses who said Bissonette had been killed earlier in the evening, who was he to second-guess them? Ickes seemed not to recognize that the FBI and the police force that the FBI was investigating had been allies and that the man who had been killed had been an enemy of both.

Even so, the FBI's limited investigation turned up information that disturbed Ickes in 1973. For example, Dr. Brown found in his autopsy that the blast that killed Bissonette (Brown said it came from a shotgun) penetrated his chest on a horizontal trajectory—that is, on a course parallel to the ground. But officers Clifford and Rencountre had said that when Clifford shot Bissonette, Clifford was standing on the road and Bissonette was in a ditch—meaning the shot should have entered Bissonette's chest at a downward angle. Dr. Brown also found that the shot pierced Bissonette more or less perpendicular to his chest—that is, on a straight line from his front to his back. But in the police story, Bissonette was standing almost in profile to Clifford—meaning the shot should have entered his body at a sharply right-to-left angle. Dr. Brown's findings, of course, are automatically suspect, but in this case a second autopsy commissioned by Mark Lane confirmed most of Brown's conclusions. Ickes was also concerned by some discrepancies (it is not precisely clear which discrepancies) between how Clifford and Rencountre said Bissonette was holding his gun and what the ballistics suggested. And while Clifford and Rencountre said they had requested backup, Ickes noted that the police radio log showed no such request. Whether or not they had called for backup, Ickes could not understand why they had tried by themselves to arrest a man who was supposedly armed and dangerous and who was making no move to escape instead of waiting for reinforcements.

This was not to say Ickes agreed with Lane that the police had beaten, gassed, and shot an unarmed Bissonette seven times—nor should he have. The second autopsy confirmed that Bissonette had been killed by a single shotgun blast and probably had not been beaten beforehand. The small bruises on Bissonette's chest that Lane had attributed to a beating had, in fact, been made by lesser pellets from the fatal shot. The silver-dollar-sized bruise on Bissonette's chest turned out to have been made not by a teargas canister but by the shell that held the pellet wad. Ickes also believed Bissonette had a gun, but he seemed to doubt that Bissonette had been pointing it at one of the officers. Certainly if Bissonette had wanted to shoot, he had plenty of time to do so with the officers' misfires. That he did not shoot, even after they tried to shoot him, seemed to indicate a strong restraint on his part.

Ickes summarized his findings for his superiors and recommended that a grand jury investigate the shooting—a much weaker course than asking that the grand jury indict Officer Clifford. If the grand jury found wrongdoing, and if the Civil Rights Division agreed, and if the U.S. attorney for South Dakota agreed as well, then, Ickes counseled, Clifford should be indicted. It was a lot of ifs. Ickes further recommended that an indictment for murder or manslaughter would be inappropriate and, should the grand jury want to indict, Clifford should be charged with violating Bissonette's civil rights. The punishment for violating someone's civil rights was more symbolic than substantial.

Ickes seems to have been concerned that the Justice Department would reject even this tepid course, for he felt compelled to explain that the government had lost all credibility as a law enforcer on Pine Ridge and that the Justice Department needed at least to *appear* to be doing something on the case. Coming from the man whose job it had been to ensure the government's credibility on Pine Ridge, this was quite an admission. An even more important admission was Ickes's explanation for how the government's credibility had evaporated. He wrote,

> Since January, 1973, we have investigated approximately 25 complaints of police misconduct, of which approximately 13 revealed that incidents had occurred. This Office submitted one prosecutive summary to the Front Office recommending prosecution of ▬▬,* a BIA officer; but the request was denied. No other requests concerning the 13 have been submitted, inasmuch as the injuries to victims were minor, or in that evidence of specific intent on the part of police officers was not strong.

In other words, the Justice Department had decided that at least half of the complaints about police brutality on Pine Ridge were true, but only one prosecution had been contemplated and that one had been quashed by Washington. For the next three decades, the federal government claimed just the opposite: it knew of no police misconduct on Pine Ridge; certainly no allegations of misconduct had ever been substantiated. Ickes's memo makes plain, even if he was right that the beatings were minor (and there are hints in his memo that suggest a "minor" injury meant any short of coma), that the Justice Department saw nothing wrong with a steady current of lesser brutality.

Ickes's supervisors approved his mild recommendation for an investigative

---

* Blackened blocks represent passages censored by the government. Short blocks (like this: ▬▬) usually indicate only one or two censored words. Long blocks (like this: ▬▬▬▬▬) indicate censorship of many words.

grand jury, and for two days in December 1973, the jury heard testimony. Who testified and what was said are not known. (The federal government keeps grand jury records sealed, no matter how many decades have passed or how strong a smell of mischief surrounds the proceedings.) What is known is that when Mark Lane appeared before the jurors at the end of the second day, he learned that the U.S. attorney had not called, and had no plans to call, people he considered key witnesses. He accused the prosecutors of a whitewash, and he told the jurors the facts as he saw them and the names of people they should call. If Lane can be believed, one juror told him, "It's good that we finally heard from the other side."

Lane's account was probably right, for the jury convened again to hear more testimony two months later. One of those who testified was a Catholic priest from Pine Ridge by the name of Charles. Father Charles said he had recently been menaced by three drunken BIA policemen who mistook him for an AIMer. One of the policemen was Joe Clifford, who was forced to resign over the incident. That was as much punishment as Clifford ever endured from the government. The grand jury, whatever it found, did not indict him, and WKLDOC never heard another word from authorities about the killing.

At the end of 2003, I went to the law enforcement building of the Oglala Sioux Tribe and found Joe Clifford, who was working for his old employer once more, albeit now as a janitor. A stocky man of late middle age, he was on break, leaning against a door and staring out its narrow window. I introduced myself and asked about the shooting of Pedro Bissonette. He said, politely enough, that he did not want to talk. I told him that the evidence I had seen did not cast him in the most favorable light and maybe he would like to tell his side of the story. He said some things were better left unsaid.

"Let it rest," he said. "Just let it rest."

Not long after, I visited the home of Evans Rencountre, just outside Pine Ridge. Everyone I had spoken to called Evans "Binky," which seemed altogether too playful in the context of my visit. On the evening of my visit, a party was in progress. A reveler at the door told me it was Evans's birthday and invited me in amid glares.

A somewhat leaner version of Joe Clifford strode up to me and said, "So you want to know what happened." It was a challenge, not a question, and a fair bit of liquor was behind it. The speaker, Rencountre, seemed almost to be weighing whether to continue with words or with fists. Eventually he settled on interrogating me about my background so that, as he said, he could come fuck up me and my family if I fucked up him or his. When he was satisfied with my answers, he said, in the choppy voice of a police report, "I was a trainee cop. Young guy. I got to work at thirteen-thirty that day. My wife took me. I didn't even make it to the office—got to the corner, had a code red. Officer's down, officer had been shot. So I jumped out. All I had was my thirty-eight, a shotgun. I heard it was two officers were shot at earlier. We cruised that night looking for what the memo said was one fugitive. Then we were told to look for Pedro Bissonette in a dark car. So we stopped every dark car we could find. We found him at the turnoff to Johnson Holy Rock's. There was a light post on the right. Nothing on the left. No cars coming. All we did is, we stopped the car, asked him to step out. He stepped out with his rifle and pointed it at me. And he said—all Pedro said to Joe and I was, 'I'm an Indian' and 'Let me go.' That was it. And he cocks his rifle and came at me. My shotgun was fucked up. It jammed, so I backed off and dropped it. The only thing that saved me was Joe. Joe's was loaded, and he hit the safety and saved my life." He did not mention any misfires of Clifford's gun. For a long while after he had stopped speaking, he gave me a look that I could not decipher.

"Scratch all that," he finally said. "You want to know the truth?"

I said I did.

"That's part of it right there," his son Frank said. Frank was a young, muscled man with a head shaven close as a kiwi and a background in prison for homicide. He urged his dad to tell the truth.

I asked the elder Rencountre what the truth was.

"Nobody ever came to question me," he said. "The FBI, gun enforcement agents, nobody. What we did was right. We did everything by the book. Didn't try to lie. Pedro was my cousin"—which came as a surprise to me. "I see him every day. *Every* day. Don't you ever get that close to someone and watch them die. It hurts. Nobody cares how I feel. The only one who cares is my son."

He asked Frank to get up and get me something that turned out be a polished piece of wood with a picture of an Indian pasted on it—art.

"Here," he said, "this is yours. No one ever leaves this house without getting something." He set it on the table and asked me to take it when I left, but later, after Frank and I had gone out for a case of beer and come back, the gift was gone.

From time to time throughout the evening, Evans returned to his story, but he rarely added details of any importance.

"Just tell him, Pop," Frank would interject every ten or fifteen minutes. "You told him part of it, Pop. Tell him the rest."

Once, after a reflective pause, Evans said slowly, "Pedro—Pedro was the best thing that ever happened to Pine Ridge. Because he brought us all together." In tone and diction, this was almost exactly what Bissonette's many admirers in AIM had said. But whatever Evans Rencountre thought the whole truth about the killing of his cousin was, he never told me.

Not long before this book went to press, the FBI gave me part of the file on its investigation into Bissonette's death. The statements of Clifford and Rencountre (who, despite Rencountre's memory, apparently did speak to the FBI) were so thoroughly censored that it was impossible to tell exactly what they had said about the shooting. But another FBI document, which seems to have been written early in the investigation, summarized their claims by saying, "BISSONETTE fired at them when they attempted to apprehend him." If true, this was news. All the public accounts said that Bissonette had only pointed his gun at Rencountre, not that he had fired a shot (which he clearly had not). Another FBI document said that while

Bissonette's body was at Dr. Brown's clinic in Scottsbluff, the FBI tested his hands "in [an] effort to prove he had been firing a weapon prior to his having been shot." An effort to *prove* he had been firing, rather than to *find out whether* he had been firing did not suggest impartiality on the FBI's part. After the test came back negative, the claim that Bissonette had fired on the police disappeared (it seems) from the FBI documents. All of which makes it appear that Clifford and Rencountre—or someone—may have first tried to justify the shooting by saying Bissonette shot at the officers, then, that story being unsupportable, settled for Bissonette's merely having charged them with a loaded gun.

The FBI will reveal no more about its investigation. Its lawyers say that most of its file is lost but that even were it not, the FBI would not release much of it. The FBI is worried about violating Clifford's and Rencountre's right to privacy. Under the circumstances, it is not hard to understand why throughout Indian Country people still believe the BIA assassinated a leader of the Indian rights movement and the FBI covered it up.

CHAPTER 5

ANNA MAE PICTOU was born in 1945 into the same mortifying poverty known to aborigines the world over. Her particular instance was the small Mi'kmaq Reserve of Nova Scotia in the Canadian Maritimes. At a young age, she, her two sisters, and a brother were abandoned by parents suffering from too much drink, too little money, and too few chances to change either circumstance. The children grew up in the shuttled homes and bad schools customary in such situations, and the first opportunity Pictou had to leave home, she took. For decades Mi'kmaqs had migrated across the Gulf of Maine to pick berries and potatoes in New England and returned home at harvest's end. Pictou joined the harvest at seventeen, but rather than go back to Canada at the end of the season, she went to Boston with another Mi'kmaq teen, Jake Maloney, with whom she had fallen in love. They settled into a cramped flat, found work in the factories of sub-urban Boston, and began to accumulate the trappings of the American good life. Photos of the period show Pictou with her hair piled into an unbecoming but trendy beehive. In her later years, she would roll her eyes at the mention of her "apple" period—apples being red of skin but white at the core—but trying on the values and styles of white America before deciding they did not fit was a phase nearly every Indian activist of her generation passed through.

She and Maloney married too young, had two daughters too young, and quickly found themselves fighting about the usual antagonisms—bills, housework, love and the lack of it. Often as not, the fights were lubricated by alcohol, which did not help their union. Nor did a dalliance that Maloney had, nor that his paramour was a student at the karate studio he had founded with the family savings. The marriage finally collapsed in 1969. Pictou, mother of two, was twenty-four.

Divorce suited her. She began to shed the more unnatural of her Anglo imitations, and she found a purpose in the betterment of her people. In 1970 she helped found the Boston Indian Council, which tried to put Natives into decent jobs, houses, and schools. Eventually she quit her job in a sewing factory to teach Indian children about their history and culture at an experimental school. At the time it was just shy of heretical to suggest that there was more to Indian history than scalping whites and getting shot by the cavalry. Pictou adored the work. But a few months after she started, the school ran out of money and closed, and she went to work at a day care for minority children. On the side, she earned a high school equivalency degree and took courses at Wheelock College. She won a scholarship to Brandeis University, which, had she accepted, would have put her in the tiny cadre of Indians attending the four-year colleges in North America. She turned the scholarship down, apparently because she was loathe to give up her volunteer work with the Indian Council. She soon founded a job-placement program at the council and funneled many Indians, eventually including herself, into a General Motors assembly line in Framingham. The union wage was a godsend to a people who were used to making minimum wage, if that.

The American Indian Movement came into Pictou's life on Thanksgiving 1970. The descendants of the Plymouth Pilgrims who took part in the first Thanksgiving had long commemorated the holiday with celebrations that made no mention of the holocaust—military and biological—that befell the Indian participants of the first feast. In 1970 AIM declared Thanksgiving a Day of Mourning and held its own commemoration at Plymouth. Pictou went. It was a gay time. The AIMers poured blood-red paint over the rock to symbolize the fate of their ancestors and commandeered a replica of the *Mayflower* from bewildered tourists. Pictou returned to

Boston enthusiastic about AIM. Two years later, when the group announced the Trail of Broken Treaties, she took leave of her assembly line to go to Washington and ended up barricaded inside the BIA building, one of the thousand or so in AIM's supporting cast. With her on the trip was an Ojibwa artist named Nogeeshik Aquash, with whom she had fallen in love. They doted on one another, but their love was as volatile as hers with Maloney and as prone to bitter fights and jealousies. The mortar that held it together was a shared passion for Indian rights and for preserving what remained of Indian cultures. They returned from the Trail determined to do more for their people but uncertain of precisely what.

The answer came when Wounded Knee was seized in February 1973. Pictou took another leave from the assembly line, put her daughters in the care of her family, and traveled with Nogeeshik to AIM headquarters in St. Paul, where they presented themselves for duty. Their bona fides were checked and deemed sufficient, and Bill Means, brother of Russell, drove them to Crow Dog's Paradise on South Dakota's Rosebud Reservation. The Paradise was a wooded ravine where medicine men Henry and Leonard Crow Dog, father and son, made their home. (Henry was one of the sages whom Richard Erdoes, the journalist for *Time* and *Life*, had come to sketch when he was accosted by cowboys and cops.) The Crow Dogs were so steeped in the old ways that Henry had forbidden Leonard from attending white schools and instead raised him in accordance with centuries of traditional teaching. Henry spoke no English, and Leonard spoke it only haltingly. Both Crow Dogs were immensely important to AIM because they reconnected AIM's many deracinated activists with their stolen spiritual past. Much of the religious reawakening that occurred at Wounded Knee could be attributed to Leonard Crow Dog, who was inside the village for much of the occupation. The Crow Dogs were also important to AIM for draping a mantle of holiness on the group's militant shoulders and for letting AIM use the Paradise—an hour's drive from Wounded Knee but beyond Dick Wilson's jurisdiction—as its staging ground for the pack trains that kept the besieged village in food, armament, and recruits.

Anna Mae and Nogeeshik rested briefly at the Paradise then were driven to a drop-off point on Pine Ridge laden with gear. Under cover of night, they and others were guided through gulleys and over ridges to Wounded Knee. Michael Denny, a Potawatomi who packed in with Pictou and Aquash, remembered of her, "She was carrying a pack filled with medical supplies. When we got close to Wounded Knee, we had to hit the ground several times and get back up and run for cover from U.S. government gunfire. Anna Mae had to do this too, and it amazed me that she had the physical strength with the heavy backpack—and she was small—to do this, and I realized she had strength in her heart too."

They arrived in the village shortly before dawn. Like all initiates, they were brought before the leaders of the Independent Oglala Nation, partly in welcome, partly for another vetting. Dennis Banks asked Aquash and Pictou what they wanted to do, and they said they wanted to be assigned to a bunker. When Banks suggested Pictou might prefer the kitchen, she replied that she would not mind doing her share of cooking and cleaning but she had not come to Wounded Knee to get stuck behind pots and pans. They were given weapons and sent to a bunker.

"Most of the people at Wounded Knee were kids, people in their late teens or early twenties," said Kevin McKiernan, who was the only reporter to stay inside Wounded Knee throughout the siege and who shared the floor of a trailer with Anna Mae and Nogeeshik for a month. "Anna Mae stood out in part because she was older"—twenty-eight—"and had more of the self-confidence that comes with age. She was also a seeker and a learner, and she was more urbane than most of the people there. She would study people, quietly. She wasn't loud. She was not overly deferential to Nogeeshik, but she was traditional in the sense that if one of them would talk first, it would be him. If she was serious, she also had a funny bone. She teased me for 'the sins of the white man.' I liked her enormously, and people seemed to like both of them."

One of McKiernan's photographs from Wounded Knee shows Pictou digging a bunker with a seven iron. She is bent over, glancing back over her shoulder at him with a look that acknowledges both the hopelessness of chipping through the frozen soil and the certainty that since the bunker has already been hacked four feet deep, it can, bit by bit, be made deeper. Another photograph caught Pictou in the middle of a large and winsome laugh as Nogeeshik hopped in front of her on a pogo stick.

But not everyone at Wounded Knee liked Pictou. Her friend Mary Moore (later Mary Crow Dog, wife of Leonard) wrote that Pictou fought with a group of women called the Pie Patrol (about whose anatomical name Moore professed chaste confusion: "there were no pies and they did not do much patrolling as far as I could see"). Moore wrote of the patrol, "They were loud-mouth city women, very media conscious, hugging the limelight. They were bossy, too, trying to order us around [and] getting all the credit and glory while we did the shit work, scrubbing dishes or making sleeping bags out of old jackets. Annie Mae gave these women a piece of her mind and I took her side." Moore was too hard on the Pie Patrol. Many of the patrollers, like Madonna Gilbert, cousin to Russell Means, and Lorelei DeCora Means, wife of Russell's brother Ted, did great amounts of work in the shadow of their more famous male relatives. But Moore was right that the patrollers did not like Pictou. Probably they resented that she was less retiring in front of the men, that she was toting a weapon and "manning" a bunker, and so on. Whatever the origin of the animosity, it would follow Pictou to her final hours.

In early April, a few weeks after Anna Mae and Nogeeshik arrived at Wounded Knee, Mary Moore delivered herself of a son, whom she named Pedro for her friend Pedro Bissonette. Pictou was one of the midwives. The next day, Anna Mae and Nogeeshik were wed before the citizens of the Independent Oglala Nation. McKiernan's photographs show them by turns cheerful and solemn, alternately caught in the sanctity and the joy of the moment. The bride's gown was a field coat over blue jeans. Her dark hair was styled, as usual, in a curtain to her scapulae, and her large eyes were at once captivated and captivating. The groom, who was given to dandified dress even in normal times, wore a hat for the occasion that was straight off a musketeer. Above his rakish goatee he sported a grin of triumphal proportions. The birth of Pedro Moore and the nuptials of the Aquashes were taken for good omens, for declarations of faith in the young nation, and AIM widely publicized them as such. The disintegration of the Aquash marriage, not a year later, would receive less promotion.

The Aquashes honeymooned inside ION for two weeks. On April 25, a few days after Frank Clearwater was killed and a few days before Buddy Lamont would be, they walked out of the new nation and into the welcoming embrace of the BIA police. The police took them to the town of Kyle, north of Wounded Knee, where they were charged with breaking Dick Wilson's law that banned three or more people from gathering in one place. The next morning "Annie Mae Aguash" and her husband were interviewed briefly—whether by the FBI or BIA is unclear—and released. Her interview lasted sixteen minutes, an indication of how unimportant she was to authorities. This would soon change.

The Aquashes returned to Boston determined to set up a school for Indian children along the lines of the school that Anna Mae had taught at a few years before, but the idea never came together. In early 1974 they left Boston for good and divided their time between Ottawa, where they staged a show of Indian art and fashion, and St. Paul, where Dennis Banks and Russell Means were being tried for crimes at Wounded Knee. Eventually the Aquashes settled full-time in St. Paul. Indians by the score were doing likewise to support Banks and Means for the length of their eight-month trial. But the courtroom was so small that many could not get in, so Anna Mae put the idle feminine fingers to work (the masculine being unsuited by temperament) sewing ribbon shirts. These were shirts of ordinary manufacture onto which brightly colored ribbons were stitched. Their origins lay in the drab castoffs that missionaries had given Indians for the last two or three centuries and that Indians in turn enlivened with buttons, military braids, medals, and any other scrap of color that could sustain a suture. Anna Mae's idea was to sell the shirts for the benefit of the Banks-Means defense fund, but the shirts turned out to be so popular that nearly all of the seamstresses gave them away to their admiring menfolk for nothing.

Aquash found other outlets for her energy at the overlapping AIM and WKLDOC offices, doing everything from clerical work to writing press releases to planning fundraisers. She also tutored students at the Red Schoolhouse, AIM's school for Indian children who had either dropped out or been kicked out of public school. She was especially keen on teaching students how to use libraries to research their heritage. She hoped, if ever resources came her way, to research and write a history of North American Indians from the Indians' perspective—one of many ideas that expired with her on the Badlands floor.

Her marriage fared poorly in St. Paul. Both Aquashes were drinkers (though presently Anna Mae would wean herself), and when they drank, they fought. Nogeeshik sometimes beat her, although not with impunity. She had learned karate from Jake Maloney and apparently could land enough punches to disable the slender Nogeeshik. She was prone to depression and may have considered suicide during this period, particularly when drunk. In one unsubtle cry for help, she covered her arms in ketchup—ersatz slashed wrists. The marriage to Nogeeshik ended like the one to Maloney: he took up with another woman, and Anna Mae bade him goodbye. She was said to have punctuated her farewell by aerating his car with a shotgun, but Nogeeshik later said the story was not true. After their separation, Anna Mae reverted to the name Pictou, or tried to, but the surname she had taken at the iconic wedding at Wounded Knee would not be discarded so easily. To the small public who followed Indian affairs she remained Anna Mae Aquash, and would continue so even in death.

Into this emotional void stepped Dennis Banks. Banks was a known appreciator of the feminine form, his taste famously catholic. He advertised his appetite by wearing a beret embroidered with a Playboy bunny, and his caresses were so widespread that it was said he might single-handedly cure the underpopulation of Indian America. When he published his autobiography in 2004, at an age when many men are content to see their line increase by means of grandchildren and great-grandchildren, he was still adding to his immediate brood, which might explain why he miscounted them. In 1974 Banks was married to a much younger Lakota woman, Kamook Nichols, a friend of Aquash. But friendship did not stop Aquash from falling in love with Banks, and they began an affair that summer. A few weeks into their liaison, Banks flew to Ontario to mediate a standoff between Indians and police at Anicinabe Park, and Aquash crossed four hundred miles by thumb and foot to be with him. She had to creep the last few miles through a police-pocked forest and swim across a frigid bay. Her devotion was total. But if Banks ever showed her more loyalty than a bull shows one of his heifers, it is nowhere recorded. Today he acknowledges having had nothing more than a friendship with her.

After their rendezvous in Ontario, Aquash continued east to Nova Scotia to see her daughters and, on arriving, was enraged to learn that Jake Maloney had taken custody of them without telling her. There was no denying, however, that she had been an absentee mother for more than a year. If she wanted to regain custody, she would have to settle into a paying job and keep a stable household, which in practice meant giving up her activism. She agonized about what to do, but in the end she chose her cause over her family and prayed that someday her girls would grow to understand.

She returned to St. Paul for a few illicit weeks with Banks, but he soon sent her to Los Angeles, where to gossips she became "Dennis's West Coast woman." Her brief was to revitalize AIM's California office, a potentially lucrative satellite since many of Hollywood's stars sympathized with the Indian cause from the bottom of their capacious pockets. Aquash came to Los Angeles a new woman: Joanna Jason. She meant the alias to fool the FBI, which she assumed, correctly, had penetrated AIM with informers and would be watching her, but the ruse did not work. Her liaison with Banks, her rise to AIM's leadership, and her mandate to raise funds from the rich had attracted the FBI's attention. Before coming to Los Angeles, her FBI dossier was a few unenlightening pages. After Los Angeles, her file swelled to the size of a small book.

Nearly all of the informers' reports on her and her colleagues in California depict a group struggling just to stay afloat. In December, for example, months after Aquash had arrived in Los Angeles, moles said that she was still trying to raise the small sum to rent an office. When she finally managed to do so and opened shop on Venice's Avenue 23, she and her staff were so short of cash that all of them slept there, zoning to the contrary notwithstanding. For weeks, the chapter's grandest fundraising event was a garage sale. Later, when actor Marlon Brando donated a parcel of land, it proved so undesirable the AIMers doubted they could sell it for profit.

"Our biggest problem," a spy quoted Aquash, "is that we don't have the funding to call halfway across the country to find out who is representing who in the Wounded Knee trials. There's no money to pay for long-distance calls. The phone bill last month was one hundred and ninety-two dollars. The salary I make feeds us. We're waiting for somebody to call us about the government's presentation in the trial at Lincoln because we can't afford to call them. If we have any money, we'll be able to put out a newsletter. But we have postage costs, printing costs, money for mats, and so on."

The group's hand-to-mouth existence did not stop the FBI from seeing in Aquash a threat to the republic. FBI agents prevailed on state officials to search driver's license registries, welfare rolls, and other state databases for information on her. Given that she was under suspicion of no criminal activity, the search was probably illegal. It was certainly fruitless. Meanwhile the FBI's informers inside Los Angeles AIM reported on her most pedantic activities. When she handed out leaflets at an art exhibit, it was duly noted. When she recruited a volunteer to lick envelopes, it was duly noted. When she wrote a press release in support of Wounded Knee defendants, it as duly noted. The petty espionage was supplemented with petty theft. Utility bills, message slips, and other missives meant for Aquash all found their way into her FBI file. Their contents—"Joanna, ███████ will call tomorrow and feed tape of Lincoln to us"; "Joanna, ███████ called regarding printed checks"—did not exactly reveal crimes against the state.

By law the FBI was entitled to spy on people to solve past or ongoing crimes or to prevent imminent ones. But none of the snooping on Aquash in California in 1974 turned up evidence of criminal activity. Decades later, when the FBI was asked by what rationale it had spied on Aquash during this time, agents said Los Angeles AIM was a fair target because national AIM had broken a multitude of laws in its seizure of Wounded Knee the year before. It was a rationale that, if consistently applied, should have set the FBI to infiltrating Republican precinct committees in Boise and Louisville in the years after Watergate.

CHAPTER 6

THE GOVERNMENT OF the Oglala Sioux Tribe was volatile by design, if not precisely by intention. The tribal constitution required that presidential elections be held every two years, which meant new presidents were barely settled into office when voters were allowed to throw them out— and usually did. At the time Dick Wilson took the presidency in 1972, decades had passed since a president had succeeded himself. Wilson's solution to this problem was a formula known to strongmen the world over: hire those you can, terrorize those you can't. As the election of 1974 drew near, Wilson could state his importance to his tribespeople succinctly: "When I took office, there was two hundred and fourteen tribal employees. Today there are seven hundred and fifty-two." The growth had been made possible by a once-stingy federal government that gave the tribe $24 million a year during Wilson's reign—whether specifically to keep him in power or by happy coincidence is unclear.

At the end of 1973, Russell Means declared he would stand for president in the primary election of January 1974. Other contenders declared too, but the only fight worth talking about was between Wilson and Means. Wilson told his people that electing Means was as good as giving their reservation to the Communists, the clergy, and the white hippie lawyers of WKLDOC. But in the primary Means drew 150 more votes than Wilson and the field narrowed to the two of them for a February runoff. Two weeks before the runoff, Wilson named Glen Three Stars chief election judge. Three Stars was the goon who had been sentenced to ten minutes in jail and a nickel in fine for manhandling Councilman Hobart Keith. He was the same who had attacked Means at the Sioux Nation grocery, the same who had threatened Corraine Brave's life at Denby Dam. He also had convictions for forgery and grand larceny. The least that could be said of such a résumé was that Judge Three Stars would know fraud and intimidation when he saw them. One of the other two members appointed by Wilson to the three-man election board was also a former felon. Means asked the Justice Department and Senator Jim Abourezk to send teams to monitor the election, but both declined to do so, although apparently the Justice Department had a couple of staff in Pine Ridge on election day.

No sooner had balloting begun on February 7 than disturbing reports began trickling into AIM. Foes of Wilson said they tried to vote but were turned away from polling stations. Poll-watchers were barred too, first at the precinct polls, later at the building in Pine Ridge where the election board counted the ballots. Non-Indians were said to have voted, and drunks flourished crisp bills in bars—payment, they said, for casting pro-Wilson ballots. In one district an election judge let a Wilson man take a stack of ballots from a polling station and return them marked; the Wilson man said he had taken them to elderly "shut-ins." In another district, Potato Creek, forty people were registered to vote but eighty-three ballots were cast. The Justice Department's staff in Pine Ridge saw nothing. When the election board tallied the votes, Wilson was declared to have beaten Means by a count of 1,709 to 1,530.

A reporter asked Wilson if he would be conciliatory to his defeated rival.

"No," the president said, "I'd still like to challenge him to a fistfight." He gave AIM ten days to get off the reservation "or else."

"I accept the challenge 'or else,' " Means answered.

WKLDOC contested the results by filing a challenge, as required by law, with Three Stars's election board. The board recommended the tribal council dismiss the complaint, and the council, which by law had five days to act on the recommendation, did nothing. As the days turned to weeks and Wilson's April inauguration looked to become a *fait accompli*, WKLDOC filed suit in federal court. *Russell Means et al. v. Richard Wilson et al.* was placed on the docket of Judge Andrew Bogue, the same who had tried Pedro Bissonette. Judge Bogue had earlier made clear his views on AIM by calling the occupiers of Wounded Knee "hotheads," "hoodlums," and "criminals and fugitives from justice." He said he knew for a fact (at a time when no facts had come before him) that the rebels had initiated every exchange of gunfire and so were to blame for all of the shooting at Wounded Knee. He suggested that the lawyers who defended the occupiers should be indicted alongside them. All of these observations Judge Bogue made knowing that when the occupiers were brought to court, he would be charged with giving them a fair hearing.

On receiving *Means v. Wilson*, Bogue declared himself offended by the sloth of WKLDOC on so time-sensitive an issue as the seating of a tribal president. He was not impressed that WKLDOC had filed its complaint with the election board immediately, that it had given the tribal council extra but not unreasonable time to act, or that WKLDOC had alerted him that it would appeal to him should the council do nothing. The judge said the tardy filing was inexcusable for a group like WKLDOC, which had sixty to eighty attorneys at its disposal. (In fact, WKLDOC never had more than a handful of lawyers in South Dakota at any one time, and nearly all of them worked pro bono and were eternally behind as they tried to manage the defense of 275 people charged with crimes at Wounded Knee.) WKLDOC asked Bogue to enjoin Wilson from being re-seated while Bogue weighed the larger question of whether Wilson stole the election. Bogue denied the request. His deep concern about timeliness notwithstanding, he then took six months—a quarter of Wilson's term—to issue a decision on the election.

During those six months, WKLDOC documented each of its election-day charges, and the U.S. Commission on Civil Rights found enough evidence of fraud to launch a major investigation. Even U.S. Attorney General William Saxbe, not known as a friend of AIM, declared that voting laws on Pine Ridge had been so wantonly violated that a new election should be held. Saxbe could have brought criminal charges against Wilson for stealing the election, or he could have used his clout to force a new election. He did neither. Instead, his department submitted an amicus brief in *Means v. Wilson* detailing the fraud. Bogue threw the brief out. He said it proved that the Justice Department was biased in favor of AIM—a charge never before or since leveled by a person of sound mind. In the end, Bogue ruled that the election would stand. He did not claim the vote had been free and fair. Indeed, he acknowledged the possibility of fraud. But he said the law did not require a fraud-free election, so Wilson's theft could stand. The sliver of truth in Bogue's opinion was that other courts had held that when thousands of votes are cast, every last ballot need not be free of fraud. Bogue conveniently ignored that those courts had also held that the fraud should not be so great as to swing an election or undermine faith in the democratic process.

Shortly after Bogue ruled, the U.S. Commission on Civil Rights concluded its investigation and reported that there had been "massive irregularities" during the election, that nearly all of WKLDOC's charges could be confirmed, and that in no way could the election be considered valid. USCCR heaped blame on the Bureau of Indian Affairs, which by law was required to supervise the elections but which steadfastly refused to do so. Officials at the BIA, as if to underscore USCCR's point that their agency was corrupt, said they had read USCCR's report but declined to make a single counterargument and declared the election would stand.

WKLDOC appealed Bogue's decision first to an unsympathetic panel of the Eighth Circuit and then to the U.S. Supreme Court, which in 1976 declined to hear the case. By then, Wilson's second term had expired and a new election had been held. The Supreme Court was probably of the view that the new election made Means's appeal moot. That the Oglala people might deserve a judicial accounting for the stolen election, or that those who stole it and those who let it be stolen should be held answerable for their deeds did not, apparently, impress the justices of America's highest court.

* * *

After Wounded Knee, WKLDOC prepared the defense of its clients from an office improvised out of the spare rooms of a fraternity house of the National College of Business in Rapid City. The mingling of leftist J.D.s and future CEOs amounted to something of a cultural exchange. Late in the summer of 1973, the WKLDOCkers noticed that their comings and goings at the frat house were being scrutinized by clean-cut men, sometimes on foot, sometimes in late-model unmarked cars. WKLDOC started patrolling the neighborhood in hope of learning the voyeurs' identities. A night or two after the foot patrols began, two young WKLDOCkers, Jeanne Davies and Fritz Feiten, spotted one of the unmarked cars. It was empty of occupants but had a two-way, police-style radio inside, so Feiten wrote down the car's license plate number. As he did so, two men stepped out of a car across the street and walked up to him and Davies. They flashed FBI badges. "H-u-g-h-e-s," Davies copied into a notebook and started to write his badge number, but Agent Hughes retracted the badge, snatched Davies's paper, and ordered them to put their hands on the car. The WKLDOCkers asked if they were under arrest.

"No," said one agent.

"We'll see," said the other.

More agents arrived, and a battery of questions was put to Davies and Feiten about what they were doing. When the WKLDOCkers refused to give any information beyond their names, the questions turned to taunts, then to arrests. They were walked to the county jail a few blocks away and booked for creating a public nuisance. WKLDOC had them bailed out soon enough, but on their way out the door the FBI added a federal charge—interfering with witnesses to a judicial proceeding—and the pair were re-arrested. No federal witnesses had been involved in the incident on the street, save the FBI agents themselves, and they were not the sort of witnesses the law contemplated. But because it was Saturday night and a federal magistrate was unavailable to review the complaint, Davies and Feiten were kept locked up over the weekend, which was the real motive behind the complaint. Come Monday, the magistrate immediately dismissed the federal charge, and the city attorney did the same with the municipal public-nuisance charge. The FBI never received a reprimand for what was clearly harassment of legal workers.

Feiten and Davies were out of jail all of a few hours when lawmen and lawyers collided again, this time at a motel across from the frat house. Of Rapid City's many hostelries, the FBI happened to have billeted its out-of-town agents in a motel within eye- and earshot of WKLDOC's office—a pure coincidence, the FBI later said. Lawyers Mark Lane and Lake Headley made a tour of the premises and saw two of their law enforcement shadows in the lobby, so Lane took photos of the lobby that happened, by pure coincidence, to capture the agents on film. One of them rose and demanded the lawyers leave. Headley said the man needed to identify himself and the authority on which he was giving the order. The man replied by grabbing Headley's arm and ushering him toward the street. As Lane later attested, "After they had both tried to force Mr. Headley out of the door, Mr. Headley informed the first FBI agent that he was under citizen's arrest for assault and battery. Mr. Headley then asked a woman employee at the motor inn to please notify the police." When the second agent became unruly, Headley put him under arrest too. "Following the South Dakota Citizen's Arrest statute," Lane wrote, "Mr. Headley did not touch either of the men or put them into physical custody." When the police came, Headley passed his prisoners to the officers, who declined to take them captive. One of Headley's prisoners was Agent David Price, soon to make Anna Mae Aquash's acquaintance.

While this was happening inside the motel, WKLDOCkers on patrol outside saw two more agents sitting in a car and snapped their pictures. The agent in the driver's seat, later identified as Maurice Pearson, climbed out and demanded that the photographer, lawyer Anthony Muller, desist. When Muller asked why, Pearson, addressing Muller by the honorifics "pukeface," "motherfucker," and "long-haired asshole," said if ever he found Muller alone, he would "beat the shit out of" him. Pearson climbed back into his car, and Muller took another photo. Out popped Pearson again, this time joined by a second agent who came from down the street. The new agent added a few honorifics of his own to Pearson's, tried to jerk Muller's camera from around his neck, and, failing, tried to remove the lens to expose the film. When Muller informed the agent that he was committing an assault, the agent smashed the camera in Muller's face. One of the agents, in WKLDOC's account, "stated that he would get two witnesses of his own to fabricate an event and have Mr. Muller arrested for assault on a federal officer." Roger Finzel, another WKLDOC lawyer who was present, made a citizen's arrest of the threat-maker, whereupon Agent Pearson told Finzel that if he didn't get the hell out of there, he would be "beaten all over the street."

The police arrived, heard out both sides, and then, in an act without precedent in West River Dakota, arrested one of the agents (it is not clear which) and took him to the police station. The WKLDOCkers followed. As they topped the front steps, Agent Pearson emerged from the building and shoved one of the legal workers, Carolyn Mugar, back down them, and Mugar made the now customary citizen's arrest. She also demanded that police take Pearson into custody, and they did. Both agents were soon released, but three days later the city attorney charged Pearson with assault and issued a warrant for his re-arrest. Pearson left town the same day.

Joseph Trimbach, the FBI agent in charge of the Dakotas and Minnesota, said Pearson's departure from Rapid City was just a coincidence; he was not fleeing an arrest warrant, only being rotated back to his home office in California. When reporters asked if the FBI would return Pearson to Rapid City to face the charge, Trimbach scoffed at the idea. "This is a trumped-up charge," he said. "There is no basis for it. . . . It is absurd on its face that FBI agents would harass the militant Indians or their representatives." He denied that his men had been put under citizen's arrest, although they most certainly had, and he added that the arrests of Davies and Feiten had been "valid arrests," although they most certainly had not.

On the night the Rapid City attorney issued the warrant for Pearson, an anonymous caller phoned the WKLDOC office and said, "If you don't get that girl out of town, we're going to kill her." WKLDOC assumed "that girl" was Mugar and the caller was an FBI agent. By way of reply, AIM issued a wanted poster for Agent Pearson along with an all-points bulletin that read,

> Those who harbor this fugitive from justice should be informed that all appropriate legal action will be taken against them. This applies to the director of the F.B.I., Nixon and others who are in a position of authority. Fugitive Pierson [sic] is armed and must be considered fairly dangerous (after his assault on an unsuspecting woman who was holding a camera in her hand at the time.) AIM offers a reward of one case of beer for actions leading to the arrest of this fugitive.

The anonymous call was not the only mystery WKLDOC credited to the government. The committee's mail routinely arrived three to six days later than was typical for Rapid City, or it never came at all. The phone lines in the fraternity sometimes gave off a loud whine like a vacuum cleaner and at other times gave off an echo-like feedback, like that produced by a microphone. One time a legal worker picked up a phone to make a call and heard not a dial tone but faint conversations, among which she caught the phrase "Bob Warder—that's your job." Warder was Pedro Bissonette's court-appointed lawyer; this was around the time of Bissonette's trial. On another night WKLDOCkers noticed a small red dot, like the endpoint of a very fine light, playing against their windowsill. Its origins were never determined, but much later the WKLDOCkers learned of lasers that could reproduce conversations from the vibrations that voices made against windows. Whether these and other mysteries were evidence of FBI surveillance or of WKLDOC paranoia will never be known. What is known is that the FBI's overt spying made WKLDOC and AIM extremely sensitive to and—eventually and ineluctably—paranoid about the FBI's covert spying. Which was, as we shall see, the point.

WKLDOC filed suit against the FBI for creating a climate that scared its clients from meeting with their lawyers: the FBI had cast a pall over the constitutional right to a fair defense. The case went to Judge Bogue, who said the plaintiffs' claims of having been illegally spied on, both on the street and over the phone, were entirely speculative but that even if they were true, the spying was so trifling that it did not require judicial remedy. "It might be noted," Bogue opined, "that many of the acts complained of by the Plaintiffs seem to have been occasioned by the activities of the Plaintiffs themselves. The incidents, occurring while investigating F.B.I. automobiles, photographing agents, and investigating the Defendants' housing, seem to have occurred when the Wounded Knee Legal Defense/Offense Committee was taking the action to the Defendants. It appears that many of these incidents may have been avoidable by Plaintiffs." It was the same logic that held a woman need not fear being beaten by her husband if she did not raise her voice. Bogue dismissed the case.

Dennis Banks and Russell Means were the first of the Wounded Knee defendants to be tried for the takeover. They asked Bogue to recuse himself for blatant bias, and much to their surprise he did. (He probably assumed an appellate court would remove him if he did not remove himself.) The case fell to Fred Nichol, a prairie moderate, former prosecutor, and chief federal judge for South Dakota. Nichol intended to try the case in the state until WKLDOC commissioned a survey of bias among South Dakotans. To the question "What should be done about Indian militants, American Indian Movement members, and other Indians who demonstrate claiming they haven't been given equal rights?" the most common answers were "Jail 'em" and "Shoot 'em." Judge Nichol moved the trial to St. Paul. It started in January 1974.

Banks and Means served as their own co-counsel, backed by some of the country's most accomplished trial lawyers. These including the gifted embellisher Mark Lane, the meticulous Ken Tilsen, and the wild-haired, brass-tongued Bill Kunstler, whose clientele included Martin Luther King

Jr., Black Panther Stokely Carmichael, the Chicago Seven from the 1968 Democratic Convention, and the antiwar Berrigan brothers. On the other side were arrayed the resources of the nation, but the nation, as embodied by assistant U.S. attorneys R. D. Hurd and David Gienapp—whose vitae consisted of embezzlement prosecutions and the like—seemed less than invincible.

Hurd and Gienapp argued a straightforward criminal case: Banks and Means had conspired to riot, seize, and hold Wounded Knee and then had done so, along the way destroying property, taking hostages, and firing on officers of the law. The defendants denied everything, but this was just a pro forma defense. Their real argument was that even if the jury found they had acted entirely as accused, their acts were justified by the horror that was Pine Ridge—indeed, the horror that was Indian America. Every time the Oglalas and their allies in AIM tried to right the reservation's many wrongs, federal and tribal governments blocked them with duplicity, persecution, and terror. The Indians had been left no choice but to break the law.

The key to this defense lay in destroying the government's credibility, and Banks and Means caught a break early when the prosecution called a witness to disparage a petition signed by 70 percent of the permanent residents of Wounded Knee. The petition had called on the government to abandon the siege—at least, the original petition had done so. The copy the government produced at trial was doctored to seem weaker. On cross-examination, the defense proved that the FBI had had custody of the petition at the time it was doctored. An FBI agent was called to the stand to explain how the document had been altered. The agent was at a loss. He said the FBI had a lot of files on Wounded Knee and it was hard to keep them all straight. Perhaps there had been a clerical error. Judge Nichol declared himself "greatly disturbed" by this answer. "I used to think the FBI was one of the greatest bureaus that ever came down the pike. I think it's deteriorated, and I don't care how many FBI agents are here in court listening to me."

The discussion about files led Judge Nichol to ask exactly how many the FBI had on Wounded Knee. He was astounded to learn 315,000. WKLDOC was astounded too. The government was bound by law to give the defense nearly all of its files that might help exonerate the defendants, but Banks and Means had not received anything approaching 315,000. They asked Judge Nichol to find out whether all appropriate files had been handed over, and Nichol forced the prosecution to give the defense 200 of the unseen files as a test. Half of the 200 files turned out to be relevant to the defense and should have been handed over months earlier. Prosecutor Hurd excused the lapse by saying the papers were unimportant, but the law did not make an exception for "unimportance." Hurd pledged to be more fastidious in reviewing the government's paperwork.

Not long later the prosecution called Special Agent in Charge Joseph Trimbach to the stand, and WKLDOC took the opportunity to ask him whether the FBI had wiretapped the sole phone line that had been left running into Wounded Knee. The line was used only for negotiations between the besiegers and the besieged and for privileged conversations between the besieged and their attorneys. A tap on the phone would have been illegal without a court order, which the FBI did not have. Trimbach testified there had been no tap.

But he was followed to the stand by Joe Pourier, a lineman for Bison State, the phone company that served Pine Ridge. "He was a goon," WKLDOC's Sand Brim remembered of Pourier. "But he had been a child-hood friend of Pedro Bissonette, and when Pedro was killed, Joe Pourier, like Poker Joe Merrival, flipped. Mark Lane patiently and painstakingly cultivated his friendship, and Pourier would come sit on our porch and drink schnapps with us. After he testified, he was threatened with death—Poker Joe was shot at too—and we had to get him off the reservation."

Pourier testified that he had set up a phone at one of the government roadblocks and tied it into the phone line that came out of Wounded Knee so that the occupiers and the government could speak directly. That much was perfectly legal. But Pourier had also rigged the government's phone to work as a party line, a line the government could pick up and, anytime the occupiers were talking to their attorneys, eavesdrop on the conversation. It was a low-tech wiretap, but it was a wiretap all the same—and, without a court order, illegal.

When the defendants asked the government to produce the records for Pourier's work, the government said the records had been destroyed. When the defendants pressed for other papers related to the tap, the government surrendered a Justice Department memo requesting the tap and FBI reports summarizing five tapped conversations. One of the FBI reports acknowledged that the FBI did not have a court order for the tap but said it hoped to get one soon. It never did. When Banks and Means asked why they had not been given the documents to begin with, the prosecutors said they had meant no harm; it was just that they had so many papers, they didn't know these particular ones existed.

"You see, that's the disturbing thing," Judge Nichol said. "We're always finding out that the head of the bureau or the guy at the top never seems to know anything."

"Well, that's true, Your Honor," prosecutor Gienapp agreed.

Joseph Trimbach was called back to the stand and asked why he had said the FBI had not wiretapped the defendants when it most assuredly had. Did he know about the tap at the time, or were his subordinates running amok?

Trimbach said he must have known at the time, only to have forgotten about it later. There was a lot to remember, he said.

The defense replied that even if it were true that he had forgotten during his earlier appearance on the stand, that did not explain why he had refused to hand over the papers about the tap during pretrial discovery. Wasn't it he, the defense said, who ultimately determined which of the FBI's documents were released?

Trimbach replied that while he may have technically authorized the withholding of the papers, he hadn't really made the decision. His aides, see, were forever sticking papers under his nose, and he didn't always read them before signing them.

At this, Judge Nichol noted that a senior official of the FBI had just sent him a birthday greeting and he was "crushed to find out that [the well-wisher] may not have written the letter after all."

Before dismissing Trimbach, the defense asked whether he was aware that it was illegal to run a wiretap without a court order.

Of course, Trimbach said. But he had never thought of the party line as a wiretap. Had he known it was considered a tap, why naturally he would have gotten a court order before letting it be installed.

But hardly had Trimbach stepped off the stand than WKLDOC pried another paper loose from the FBI, this one an affidavit in which the affiant, whose name had been doctored out, formally requested that a judge legalize the wiretap. That is, the FBI's affiant acknowledged that it needed a judge's approval to listen in on the party line. Nichol forced the government to release an undoctored copy of the affidavit, and the affiant turned out to be none other than Joseph Trimbach. Once more Trimbach was called back to the stand.

Had he known about his own affidavit, the defense asked, or had that just been stuck under his nose too?

Trimbach answered that he must have read it—only he couldn't recall having done so. In fact, he couldn't recall a single thing about the affidavit.

The defense asked why the affadavit that Trimbach originally released to Banks and Means was missing the part of the page that bore his name and signature.

Trimbach said he had no idea.

Prosecutor R. D. Hurd was also quizzed by judge and defendants about what and when he had known of the wiretap papers. Hurd admitted that he had first seen Trimbach's affidavit months before but had not given it to the defense as required by law. He also admitted that he hadn't bothered to correct Trimbach when Trimbach testified under oath that he knew nothing about the wiretap. Like Trimbach, Hurd claimed there was no malice in his actions. He had simply forgotten all about the wiretap papers, which, it seemed, carried an amnesial contagion. It was almost anticlimactic when a

Justice Department memo was released saying that the FBI knew the tap was illegal but had decided to keep it in place anyway.

The newly found memo did, however, give the defense a chance to summon to the stand the number-two man at the FBI, Mark Felt. Decades later Felt would be revealed—and lionized—as Deep Throat, the shadowy source who helped Bob Woodward and Carl Bernstein expose Watergate. But Felt was no angel. He was a consummate counterintelligence man with a long list of covert crimes to his credit. When the defense asked Felt if the Justice Department memo was accurate, he freely admitted it was and said he saw nothing wrong with the unauthorized wiretap, which perhaps explained why his men in the field saw nothing wrong with it either.

Toward the end of the testimony about the wiretap, Banks and Means demanded that U.S. Attorney William Clayton charge Trimbach, several other FBI agents, and Clayton's own assistant U.S. attorneys, Hurd and Gienapp, with crimes ranging from perjury to illegal wiretapping. But Clayton (the same who had spirited away Pedro Bissonette's body in the middle of the night) declined to indict his colleagues. So Banks and Means asked Judge Nichol to dismiss the case on grounds of malicious prosecution. Nichol, however, said that while the episode troubled him greatly, it was not grounds for dismissal.

The defendants took matters into their own hands. When one of the last of the wiretappers left the stand, Banks rose and said, "We are placing this man under citizen's arrest." Nichol told Banks that witnesses could not be arrested inside the courthouse, to which Banks replied that they would arrest him outside. As marshals hustled the witness, FBI agent Gerald Bertinot, from the courtroom, Banks, Means, and a claque of supporters pursued him out the door, through the courthouse, across a skyway, through another building, and onto the street before he finally escaped into a waiting car and was whisked away.

Far more grave than wiretapping was the defendants' charge that the government secretly—and illegally—used the U.S. Army and Air Force at

Wounded Knee. The Posse Comitatus Act of 1878 forbade the president from sending federal troops against citizens unless he or Congress explicitly and publicly ordered the forces sent. (*Posse comitatus* is Latin for "force of the county" but connotes something closer to "lynch mob.") During Wounded Knee neither the president nor Congress had ordered the armed forces deployed, yet, if AIM was right, they had come to Wounded Knee all the same. The proof, AIM said, was in the armored personnel carriers and other heavy weaponry used by the feds. The government brushed off the charge by saying the equipment belonged to the South Dakota National Guard. State national guards, although funded mainly with federal dollars, were units of individual states and could be dispatched by governors without violating the Posse Comitatus Act. It was the National Guard of Ohio that had been used to lethal effect against demonstrators at Kent State in 1970. Because AIM could prove no differently, the charge lay dormant until mid-trial, when a reporter called WKLDOC's Ken Tilsen to ask if he had seen a certain Senate report about Wounded Knee. Tilsen said he knew of the report—the prosecution had given him a copy—but he had seen nothing in it of interest. The reporter was surprised: what about the section discussing the Pentagon's involvement at Wounded Knee? Tilsen said his copy of the report said nothing of the kind. The reporter sent Tilsen his copy, whereupon Tilsen learned that the copy the prosecution had given him had been doctored: the section discussing the Pentagon's role at Wounded Knee—a role that had been quietly approved by the White House—had been excised. The reporter had chanced across an uncensored copy when a secretary in the prosecutors' office sent it to him by mistake.

Judge Nichol, so apprised, asked what the prosecution had to say for itself. R. D. Hurd said he had no idea how Tilsen could have been given a doctored version because his office had only one version—the true and correct one. But when the same question was put to one of Hurd's assistants, the assistant said there were two versions in the office: one with and one without the section on the Pentagon. Asked why only the shorter version was given to Tilsen, the assistant speculated that there had been a copying error.

"This is about the most bizarre explanation I've heard," Judge Nichol said, noting that only "the grossest kind of a fluke" had brought the document to light.

"Aren't you getting kind of tired," he asked Hurd, "of explaining your own negligence in some of these matters?"

"No, Judge," Hurd said. "I'm getting used to it, as a matter of fact." This was a progression. Earlier Hurd had said, "I don't enjoy trying a case where I have egg on my face every day."

The testimony about the Senate report led to the release of more documents. The documents and related examinations on the stand showed that Army Vice Chief of Staff (later White House Chief of Staff) Alexander Haig had ordered two colonels to Wounded Knee to oversee the siege and to do so in civilian garb—the latter an order they had never been given in their long military careers. Both colonels admitted in court that army trucks loaded with matériel were driven to points near, but not too near, Wounded Knee and that the matériel was transferred to civilian trucks that were driven to Wounded Knee by soldiers in civilian clothes. The matériel included 16 armored personnel carriers, 400,000 rounds of ammunition, 120 sniper rifles, and 20 grenade launchers. The U.S. Air Force contributed a Phantom jet and three helicopters. The army also sent a chemical warfare team to teach the marshals and FBI agents how to use the grenade launchers, and it put 200 Airborne troops in Colorado on twenty-four-hour alert for an assault on Wounded Knee. Colonel Volney Warner, one of the pair sent by Haig, coordinated and oversaw the government's strategy at the siege and drew up the rules of engagement. (The Pentagon eventually claimed that Warner had a restraining influence on the marshals and agents. When he first arrived at Wounded Knee, he asked if the civilian officers were shooting to kill. "Rifles," he was supposedly told, "are for that purpose." He changed the protocol to shoot to wound.) All of this activity by the armed forces had been approved secretly, in varying degrees of specificity, by Haig, Pentagon counsel (later counsel to President Nixon on Watergate) Fred Buzhardt, Attorney General Richard Kleindienst, and Nixon himself.

Confronted with this evidence, the prosecution shifted its argument: "The Pentagon had no role at Wounded Knee" became "The Pentagon had no *real* role at Wounded Knee." But even as prosecutors were saying so, the Defense Department released a report that expanded on the army's restraining influence during the siege. It turned out that the FBI's Joseph Trimbach had lobbied the army to invade the village with 2,000 GIs. He was apparently undeterred by the certain knowledge that scores—maybe hundreds—of combatants would die. His scheme was vetoed by Colonel Warner. While this news reflected well on the Pentagon in one respect, it was hard for the government to say the Pentagon was not involved at Wounded Knee in any "real" way when one of its colonels was calling the shots. So the government shifted its argument again: the Pentagon *was* really involved, but it was only by an oversight that neither the president nor Congress had publicly authorized the Pentagon's involvement. And since it was plain that the president wanted the military there, it hardly mattered that he had not issued a public order.

This was a bold argument, but neither Nichol nor judges in other Wounded Knee trials accepted it. One of the other judges, Warren Urbom, on the federal bench of Nebraska, rebutted, "Congress could have passed and may yet pass legislation to permit the use of the Army or Air Force without presidential order. But it has not done so. The people could have amended or could yet amend the Constitution to permit use of the military services under whatever circumstances they declare. But they have not done so. I am bound to follow the law as it is, not as it will or could become."

Judge Nichol was of the same mind. He concluded that the armed forces had been used illegally at Wounded Knee, but he also concluded that the case of *U.S. v. Banks and Means* afforded no remedy against the government for this crime—save for dismissing the charges against Banks and Means, which he still was not prepared to do. If AIM wanted to hold the Pentagon accountable, Nichol said, it would have to file a separate suit.

WKLDOC did, naming as defendants General Haig, Attorney General

Kleindienst, Colonel Warner, and other men of war. (Nixon, having been pardoned by Ford, could not be sued.) Hoping to avoid Judge Bogue's courtroom, WKLDOC filed its claim in Washington, D.C., but a federal judge there ruled that the case should have been filed in South Dakota and dismissed it. WKLDOC appealed and two years later won a reversal. After more maneuvering, the case was transferred to Dakota anyway, where it landed in front of Judge Donald Porter, newly appointed to the federal bench but no kindlier to AIM than Bogue. By the time Judge Porter heard arguments and ruled, it was 1982, seven years after the suit was first filed.

Porter held that even if government officials had violated the Posse Comitatus Act at Wounded Knee, they could not be sued because the act did not specifically authorize suits in cases where the law was broken. In effect, Porter declared the venerable act a dead letter, all but unenforceable. WKLDOC appealed, and after four more years of briefs and arguments, an appellate court reversed Porter. The court said that the Constitution's protections against search and seizure gave citizens an implicit right to sue government officials who turned the armed forces against them. The government appealed, and two more years passed before the U.S. Supreme Court declined to hear the government's case, at which point the suit finally returned to Porter.

The government now made a new argument: the men of war were immune from suit because they were public officials performing official deeds. The slight truth in this argument was that officials who broke the law while performing official acts could indeed be immune from suit *if* they did not know or could not have been expected to know that they were breaking the law. Judge Porter ruled that although the defendants had dressed their military men in civilian clothes, cloaked their shipments of military arms in civilian trucks, held all meetings between military and civilian officials in secrecy, and denied any military involvement until it was inescapably proven, the defendants had no idea that what they were doing was illegal. Case dismissed. The plaintiffs could have appealed, but it was now 1989, fourteen years after the suit had first been brought.

WKLDOC had long since disbanded, one of the original Oglala plaintiffs had died of old age, and the case had staggered along by the sufferance of a few pro bono lawyers. The remaining plaintiffs withdrew their claim. Neither the government nor the men who ran it were ever held to account for turning the armed forces of the nation against its people. Today hardly anyone recalls that so historic a breach even occurred.

The government's case in *U.S. v. Banks and Means* filled weeks, then months, then the better part of a year. In all that time, the prosecutors failed to tie the defendants to most of the charges against them and discredited themselves in the process. Hurd and Gienapp hoped to rectify their problems with a final witness. Ordinarily, they were required to name their witnesses in advance, but they received permission from Judge Nichol to make their last call a surprise. He turned out to be Louis Moves Camp, son of Ellen Moves Camp, one of the peppery Oglala women behind the takeover of Wounded Knee. When her son walked into the courtroom in St. Paul, she jumped to her feet and screamed, "Louie! What are you doing?" Judge Nichol had to order her dragged from the court, whereupon she fainted.

Order restored, the prosecutors asked Louie Moves Camp a series of questions designed to pin Banks and Means to the many charges against them. Over two days, he testified that the preparations to seize Wounded Knee were not spontaneous but a long-planned conspiracy led by Banks and Means, that both defendants had stolen $1,000 from the trading post, and that they had ordered hostages taken, bunkers built, Molotov cocktails made, and federal troops fired upon. By the end of Moves Camp's direct examination, he had tied Banks and Means to virtually every count against them.

On cross-examination the defense asked Moves Camp why witnesses said he was in California for most of the 71-day occupation while Moves Camp claimed he was in Wounded Knee for nearly all of the siege.

Moves Camp said the witnesses must be lying.

The defense produced a newspaper article and a photograph that showed Moves Camp lecturing about Wounded Knee, during the time in question, at a Bay Area university. Counsel asked again: was Moves Camp sure he was in Wounded Knee when he claimed?

Moves Camp sputtered, then admitted he had been in Wounded Knee only briefly, after which he went to California.

The defense demanded to know how the government, which had had Moves Camp in its custody the last several months, had failed to learn he was a liar when the defense had uncovered his California travels even before he was off the stand. Judge Nichol was eager to hear the answer too, but Prosecutor Hurd said he could not really explain it. Moves Camp had just seemed like a reliable guy, so everyone had taken him at his word. Hurd's claim was undermined, however, when he admitted that he had asked the FBI to give Moves Camp a lie detector test and Joseph Trimbach had refused.

"Since when," Judge Nichol asked, "does the head of the [regional] FBI start telling the prosecution that they can't have a lie detector test if they want to?"

Moves Camp's wife was called to the stand, and she testified that Louie had told her that in return for testifying he would be given lots of money and a new house, and his many criminal charges—which allegedly included armed robbery, assault with a deadly weapon, and assault causing bodily harm—would be dismissed.

There was still more to the story. After Moves Camp first took the stand, Rachel Tilsen, wife of Ken, received a call from a woman who lived in Wisconsin, just across the state line from St. Paul. The woman said Moves Camp had been in Wisconsin a few days earlier and while there had been accused of rape. The charges had been hushed up by the FBI. Rachel Tilsen asked the woman how she knew this, and the woman said she was the wife of the county attorney. Her husband was furious because the FBI had spirited Moves Camp to Minnesota to protect him from indictment. Her husband was keeping mum about the incident, but she was not. She said she felt for the girl who had been raped and thought the whole thing an outrage.

The next day defense attorney Mark Lane asked R. D. Hurd at a bench conference whether Moves Camp "was jailed for a serious charge, which may be rape."

"I can answer you there," Hurd said. "He has not been arrested on anything more than public intoxication."

Lane said he wanted the details.

"I don't think any of that is relevant and material," Hurd said. "You can't impeach a witness as showing that he was arrested for public intoxication."

Judge Nichol said Lane could question Moves Camp about the matter if he wanted, and Lane did.

"Were you arrested in Wisconsin this past month?" he asked the witness.

"No," Moves Camp said.

"Do you know a girl named Brenda?"

"No."

"Do you know the sheriff of River Falls, Wisconsin?"

"No."

"These people mean nothing to you?"

"No."

Lane then entered into the record a sheriff's report of a rape allegation made by a young woman named Brenda against a man named Louie Moves Camp.

Judge Nichol said Hurd had better have a good explanation.

He did not.

The story that came out was that the FBI had installed Moves Camp at a Wisconsin dude ranch—partly to prepare him for his testimony in St. Paul and partly to protect him from ill-wishers in AIM. His chaperones were the ubiquitous Agent David Price and a Price protégé, Agent Ronald Williams. (Williams would later be killed in the 1975 shootout with AIMers in the Pine Ridge community of Oglala.) One evening not long before Moves Camp was to testify, Price, Williams, and Moves Camp went bar hopping—Price downed five scotch-and-waters, Williams managed nine, and Moves Camp outdid them both with a tally not recorded. (Judge Nichol complimented the agents on keeping pace with their witness.) At the last bar, Moves Camp told Price and Williams that he wanted to take a teenager named Brenda back to his room. The agents said they couldn't sanction such an arrangement, but instead of taking Moves Camp home, they left him in the bar with Brenda. The next morning Moves Camp called Price from a café and said Brenda had gone to the police and accused him of rape. Price told Moves Camp not to worry about it, he would talk to the police, then Price went back to sleep. ("If you've eaten with Louie, you'd understand that," Price explained. "He usually eats two breakfasts.") Later that day Price met with County Attorney Robert Lindsay and subsequently no charges were brought against Moves Camp.

Lindsay was called to the stand and asked about his chat with Price. He acknowledged that Price had told him Moves Camp was an important witness. But he said this information had not influenced his decision about pressing charges. He was influenced instead by witnesses who had watched Moves Camp and Brenda having sex and who said the act was consensual. (Brenda vehemently denied the claim.)

The defense asked why, if Lindsay was not pressured to drop the case, his wife had told Rachel Tilsen a totally different story.

Lindsay said he didn't know.

Asked what exactly he had told his wife, he declined to say; the conversation was protected by spousal immunity.

Judge Nichol called Agent Price into his chambers. The transcript of their discussion is sealed, but according to Ken Tilsen, who was there, "Nichol found the behavior of the FBI agents—taking a witness on a drinking spree—incredible. It was also incredible that they could not recall who did what when, or how they happened to leave River Falls without Louie Moves Camp that night. Were they too drunk? Was he too drunk? You could not tell from the record because there was no written report on any of this. I believed the lack of a record was a deliberate effort to prevent the discovery of the facts—it meant we could not confront Price with any contemporaneous writing. Judge Nichol also seemed to doubt Price's claim that when he told Louie Moves Camp on the morning after the alleged rape that he would he would 'take care of it,' he only meant he would *ask* about the charges, not try to influence them."

Back in court, Agent Williams was called to the stand, with Price scheduled to follow. Neither man said much that was revelatory, but as defense attorney Bill Kunstler was questioning Williams, he noticed that a side door to the courtroom—the door through which witnesses entered—had opened a crack. Kunstler motioned wordlessly to Judge Nichol for silence, then crept over to the door and jerked it open. Two FBI agents who had been leaning on the door, obviously eavesdropping on Williams's testimony, tumbled into the well of the court. Kunstler accused them, no doubt correctly, of intending to illegally pass the contents of Agent Williams's examination to Agent Price, who was secluded in a witness room. But after questioning the eavesdroppers, Judge Nichol let them go with only a stern warning.

The Louie Moves Camp affair concluded with prosecutor Hurd being called to the stand, where he was asked how it was possible that he had not known Moves Camp had been arrested for rape.

Sheepishly, Hurd admitted he had known all along.

Hadn't Hurd, the defense asked, said to Judge Nichol only days ago that Louie Moves Camp had been accused of nothing more than drunkenness?

Yes, Hurd said, he had said that.

Nichol simmered. The prosecution rested.

Banks and Means thought the government's case so weak that they called only a few witnesses in their defense before resting. Judge Nichol gave the case to the jury and dismissed the alternates, but hours later one of the twelve remaining jurors became violently ill and had to be hospitalized. Her dismissal from the jury entitled either side to ask for a retrial, but with eight months of litigation behind them, Nichol urged both camps to let the eleven survivors come to a verdict. The defense readily agreed; the prosecution did not. The alternate jurors who had been dismissed had derided the government's case to the press and acquittal was in the air. Hurd told reporters he thought the jury could not be trusted, that it seemed likely they would reach the "wrong" verdict, and he demanded a mistrial. Nichol, his patience sorely tried by the government's many sins, snapped. In an hour-long courtroom harangue, he said Hurd had slandered the American system of justice when he spoke of jurors reaching a wrong verdict, and he upbraided both the prosecution and the FBI for "seeking convictions at the expense of justice."

"The waters of justice have been polluted," Nichol concluded, "and dismissal, I believe, is the appropriate cure for the pollution in this case." He threw out all the remaining charges against Banks and Means.

It was an enormously important decision, or should have been. But as the trial's foremost historian, John Sayer, wrote, "To a public saturated with misconduct at the highest levels of government, the escapades of the FBI at a trial somewhere in the Midwest could not have mattered much. It all might have made for great television if watching Watergate had not become a full-time job by the spring of 1974."

Days after Nichol dismissed the case, the Justice Department named R. D. Hurd and David Gienapp two of the nation's outstanding assistant U.S. attorneys. Banks likened the commendations to the Congressional Medals of Honor given the Seventh Cavalry after the massacre at Wounded Knee.

In the following months, both the FBI and the U.S. attorney's office undertook postmortems to determine what had gone wrong at the trial. Much of the FBI's analysis focused on Joseph Trimbach, but in the end the Bureau concluded that neither he nor his agents had done anything—not a thing—wrong. The postmortem from the U.S. attorney's office, which also examined other political trials in which the government had fared poorly, reached a similar conclusion: the prosecutors were blameless. The guilty parties, it turned out, were the radical lawyers who convinced naïve jurors that the government was evil, the limp judges who did not reign in the lawyers, and the soft reporters who gave sympathetic coverage to the whole spectacle. The Justice Department recommended the White House solve the problem by appointing judges who were more willing to clamp down on "extremists."

Of the 562 arrests and 185 federal indictments stemming from Wounded Knee, the government won just 15 convictions—11 for felonies, 4 for misdemeanors. The conviction rate of 7.7 percent was one-tenth the average for criminal trials in the federal courts of the Eighth Circuit. The government, simply put, could not convince Americans that the Indians had done wrong to turn to violence.

But losing the trials did not mean losing the fight against AIM—quite the contrary. As prosecutor David Gienapp said years later, "To some extent, the prosecutions accomplished as much by getting dismissed or an acquittal as they would have had there been a conviction, because Russell Means and Dennis Banks realized even if you get off, sitting nine months in a courtroom isn't what they want to do." Gienapp was speaking not merely with the advantage of hindsight; the strategy was one the government consciously pursued at the time. At the end of the siege, for example, Colonel Volney Warner urged the Justice Department to throw the proverbial book at AIM. "AIM's most militant leaders and followers, over three hundred," he wrote, "are under indictment, in jail, or warrants are out for their arrest. The government can win even if no one goes to prison." It was not a new strategy. FBI Director J. Edgar Hoover had used the same plan in the late 1960s to kneecap the Black Panthers.

By the end of the Banks-Means trial, the strategy was beginning to have the desired effect. AIM was spending something like three of its every four hours and dollars just to keep its members out of jail, which did not leave much time or money for the betterment of its people or the recruitment of new followers or calm thought about its future or past. It was the sort of strain that could lead a group to do desperate things.

CHAPTER 7

UNTIL HIS APPOINTMENT as special prosecutor of AIM, the Sicangu Lakotas of the Rosebud Reservation, just east of Pine Ridge, held Bill Janklow in high esteem. The young legal-aid lawyer had seen to the acquittal of dozens of Indians on the worst of charges—murder, rape, assault, and the like—at a time when Indians rarely beat shoplifting raps. He had also successfully sued the nearby town of Winner and the state of South Dakota, the former for discriminating against Indians in city services, the latter in the selection of juries. He had a reputation for passion on behalf of his clients. Once, when a judge was making ceaseless rulings against a client, Janklow rose and demanded, "What time does this railroad station close?" The judge was not amused by the reference to railroading and threatened Janklow with contempt. Another judge fined Janklow $10 for backtalking, made it $20 when he did not let up, and raised it to $30 before Janklow pulled out his checkbook, slapped a $100 writ on the table, and said, "There! I've got seven more coming." For clients arrested after hours, Janklow left a coffee can stuffed with bail money on his porch. Years later Russell Means, who lived on Rosebud in the late 1960s, still fondly recalled the Christmas that he and a Santa-costumed Janklow drove the reservation giving gifts to families so poor that the walls of their shacks were made of cardboard.

It was thus something of a surprise when the state attorney general appointed Janklow to prosecute the AIMers who had rioted at the Custer Courthouse three weeks before Wounded Knee was seized. The Custer prosecutions were to South Dakota what the Wounded Knee prosecutions were to the U.S. government: an enormously important chance to cut off AIM at the knees. At first, Janklow was level of head and calm of speech. But the former civil rights lawyer was not oblivious to his state's ire toward AIM, and he soon warmed to the moment. His initial promises merely to seek justice soon became declarations that he would "put American Indian Movement leaders in jail, if not under it."

He was as good as his word. While AIM outmaneuvered federal prosecutors on the Wounded Knee charges, Janklow scored conviction after conviction for the Custer riot. Among the more famous was his conviction of Sarah Bad Heart Bull, mother of Wesley, whose slaying had led to the confrontation at Custer. Wesley's killer, Darld Schmitz, had faced just ten years for manslaughter (and was eventually acquitted), but for brawling over the light charge against Schmitz, Janklow prosecuted Sarah Bad Heart Bull for crimes whose penalties totaled up to forty years. After she was convicted, most observers predicted a sentence of probation, but Janklow sought and won a jail term of one to three years. When reporters from out of state suggested that racism might explain the difference in the justice given Darld Schmitz and the justice given Sarah Bad Heart Bull, Janklow declared that not only had the trial been free of racial animus but so too was the entire system of justice in South Dakota.

This was quite a claim not only because of his own prior lawsuits against the state but because of a mid-trial assault on Bad Heart Bull's supporters that he and Judge Joseph Bottum had jointly overseen. The assault had a prelude. A few days earlier, Judge Bottum held Bad Heart Bull's WKLDOC attorneys in contempt—a holding neither unusual nor necessarily inappropriate. But while Bottum only scolded the white lawyers on the defense team, he had the lone Indian lawyer, Ramon Roubideaux, jailed overnight. The next day, the Indians in the courtroom refused to stand for Bottum, who retaliated by limiting their number to twenty and having them (but not other spectators) filed through metal detectors and frisked. When the Indians still refused to stand for the judge, he ordered the court cleared, but they refused to leave. Three clergymen who were there told writer Peter Matthiessen what happened next: "a jump-suited tactical squad, twenty-four strong, backed up by an equal number of ordinary police out in the corridor, burst into the courtroom like an SS troop. Everyone in the place jumped up in alarm. These robot figures—clad in helmets with face shields, steel-toed combat boots, and metal-knuckled gloves, and armed with forty-inch clubs with steel-ball ends, as well as revolvers, Mace, handcuffs, and even gas masks—attacked the unarmed and outnumbered Indians without bothering to order them out of the room. The first man they reached was knocked unconscious, and, trying to defend themselves, the desperate Indians fought back as best they could; a wild melee took place before the twenty were subdued. The injured included Custer defendant Dave Hill, who suffered permanent impairment of his vision in one eye, poked by a nightstick.

" 'They were asking for it,' Judge Bottum told the horrified bishops, 'so I let 'em have it.' "

"Janklow was standing outside the doors of the courtroom," Karen Northcott, one of WKLDOC's most devoted workers, later said, "and he was the one who ordered the riot squad through the doors. I still remember him looking through the courtroom window, and his expression as the troopers rushed in was like someone rubbing his hands with glee, with a child's delight."

Janklow would later admit that he had informers among the Indian protesters who had alerted him to their civil disobedience. The victims, Russell Means among them, were charged with riot. Of the many felony indictments Means earned from his activism in the 1970s, this was the only one for which he was ever convicted.

For such deeds Janklow became a hero to white South Dakotans. In mid-1974 he parlayed his renown into a run for the office of his boss, Attorney General Kermit Sande, a Democrat. Janklow, a Republican, reminded voters that he was the only prosecutor ever to have "convicted AIM," and he promised that if elected, he would take leave of his duties in the capital to personally prosecute Dennis Banks, whose trial for riot at Custer was on hold while his Wounded Knee trial dragged on. Janklow predicted he would send Banks to prison for so long that AIM would have folded up shop before he got out. Banks bore the brunt of Janklow's attacks because Janklow could not stir himself to the same vitriol against his old friend Means. Banks, as it were, got Means's share.

Banks was not one to take a punch without returning it, and he entertained several ideas for undermining Janklow's campaign. None seemed right until Bill Means, brother of Russell, received a call from a friend named John Arcoren. Arcoren, known to all as Johnny Cake, said that when Janklow lived on Rosebud in the 1960s, he had raped Johnny Cake's adopted daughter. Means took the story to a young Oglala lawyer named Mario Gonzalez who served part-time as chief judge of the Rosebud Tribal Court. A few months earlier, Judge Gonzalez had endeared himself to AIM when BIA policemen tried to arrest Russell Means for fighting with police on Rosebud. The case had come to Gonzalez, who had ruled that the federal officers had no authority to arrest Means. He reasoned that the Fort Laramie Treaty of 1868, the same that had promised the Black Hills to the Lakotas for all time, had given the Lakotas exclusive jurisdiction over crimes committed by Indians on Lakota lands. Since the U.S. government had broken the treaty illegally, the treaty was still valid; hence, Judge Gonzalez held, the agents could not arrest Means. In the American West this was heresy on a grand scale, something akin to ruling slavery unconstitutional in the antebellum South. To say the treaty was still valid was to say the Lakotas owned title to most of the Dakotas and a nice portion of Montana, Wyoming, and Nebraska. It was a paper rebellion. The government appealed Gonzalez's decision to Judge Bogue, who vacated it immediately. AIMers loved Gonzalez all the same for thumbing his nose at the feds. When Bill Means brought Johnny Cake's story to Gonzalez, the judge thought the matter should be looked into, and, more than a trifle injudiciously, he passed what he knew to Dennis Banks. Banks heard Gonzalez out, then told confidantes that if there was anything to the rape claim, he was going to have Janklow's ass.

* * *

On a Saturday night in January 1967, Jancita Eagle Deer was checked out of her dormitory at the Rosebud Boarding School in Mission, South Dakota, by Bill Janklow. Eagle Deer was a full-blooded Lakota with bobbed hair of pitch, eyelashes of a length other girls would sell fingers for, a full-cheeked smile, and a frame of pleasing proportions. She was fifteen. Her parents had been unable to care for her, owing to the same alcoholism and despair that had cleaved Anna Mae Aquash from her parents, and she had been placed with foster parents, John and Yvonne Arcoren. With the help of attorney Janklow, the Arcorens were in the process of adopting Eagle Deer. Janklow had also helped Eagle Deer gain admittance to the BIA boarding school in Mission, where he lived, and since the Arcorens lived twenty miles away in St. Francis, Janklow assumed an avuncular posture toward the girl. On that Saturday night, he brought her home for dinner with his family, after which she was to go to a dance. At five minutes before eight—the time would assume some importance—Janklow drove her the half-mile downtown, but the dance hall was unlit: they were too early.

"We might as well drive around until the dance starts," Janklow said.

"Can I go to a movie?" Eagle Deer said.

He replied, in her version of the story, "Wouldn't you rather drink with me?"

"I'd rather go to the dance."

They may have briefly driven around the town, a sprinkling of bruised buildings and rutted streets that would not have sustained much driving, but soon they headed west into the countryside on U.S. Highway 18. A few miles from town, he turned the car north on a dirt section-line track and, in the story Eagle Deer told—all of what follows is Eagle Deer's story, all of which Janklow has repeatedly and vehemently denied—drove until he reached a small rise where a gate blocked their progress. They were in the middle of rangeland, the nearest home a half-mile off and invisible in the night. He leaned across her seat, pushed a lever, and as the seat fell back pushed her back with it. She tried to get up, but he held her down.

"The first time I saw you in my office, I was crazy about you," he said. "And I have been ever since." He asked her to come away with him.

She said he had a wife and children.

"To hell with them. I'll get a divorce."

Not knowing what else to say, she said his wife was nice and he shouldn't divorce her, but he was unbuttoning her blouse and seemed not to hear. She hit him and said she wanted to go back to town, but he kept unbuttoning, so she kept hitting.

"Goddamn, what are you so frightened about?" he said. "I won't hurt you."

He got her blouse unbuttoned, unbuckled his belt, and unzipped his pants. He raised her skirt and tried to pull down her underwear. She was flailing, and it took some doing to get the underwear off, but at last he mounted her. The rape, according to Jancita Eagle Deer of the eighth grade, lasted about ten minutes. What she felt or thought, whether she continued to struggle or went limp, what precisely her assailant was alleged to have done—the sounds and smells and touch of her particular hell—is nowhere recorded.

When Janklow was sated, he got off her and told her to put her underwear on. She did and pulled her skirt back down and buttoned her blouse. He reassembled himself, put the car in gear, and started back to town. The dashboard clock read 8:50.

They were silent until Janklow took three dollar bills from his wallet and gave them to her. She wouldn't tell anyone, would she?

She took the money without comment.

He said he was going to Denver on Wednesday and asked if she would come along.

"If I could take one of my girlfriends," she said.

"Forget it."

They drove on in silence.

"What if I wanted to check you out of the dorm? What would you do?"

"I don't know."

When they arrived downtown, he let her out at the dance hall and told her to come back home after the dance. She did not. Next morning, he saw her on the street with friends, ordered her into his car, and drove her home. He sent his wife to the store and yelled at Eagle Deer for staying out all night. She asked him to take her back to school. At one o'clock on Sunday afternoon he did, and she went directly to a dormitory matron, Catherine Bordeaux, who could see she had been crying. Eagle Deer said she had been raped and told the foregoing story.

"Are you sure what you're saying is true?" Bordeaux said when Eagle Deer had finished. "A false statement could get you in a lot of trouble."

"He took advantage of me," Eagle Deer said. "And I have proof."

She unbuttoned her shirt, revealing what Bordeaux described as a nickel-sized "discoloration of the skin" on her upper left breast. Another hickey was visible on the right side of her neck. Eagle Deer credited both to Janklow.

While they were talking, the phone rang. It was Janklow, and he asked to talk to Eagle Deer, but Bordeaux said the girl was distraught and didn't want to speak with him. She hung up and went to tell her supervisor, Kaye Lord, about Eagle Deer's claim. While Lord and Bordeaux were talking, an aide rushed up to them and said that Janklow had stormed into the office where Eagle Deer was waiting and that it sounded "like big trouble in there"—the girl crying, the man hollering. Lord went to the office and sent Eagle Deer out. When the tearful girl emerged, she told Bordeaux in the hallway, "Mr. Janklow told me not to get him into trouble. He said he would buy me everything I wanted."

Inside the office, Kaye Lord found Janklow pacing. She said, "I think you had better tell me your side of the story."

He agreed. He said the night before, Eagle Deer had had supper with his family, after which she had asked to have a couple of drinks. He had said no. A little before eight, she asked if she could go to the dance, and a few minutes later he drove her downtown. Because the dance hall was darkened, he wouldn't let her out of the car. She asked if he would buy her peppermint schnapps, and he said, "Of course not." They drove around for maybe thirty-five minutes. At about ten minutes to nine, he let her off at the dance hall and told her to come home by a quarter of two. She didn't, and he picked her up in Mission the next morning. In the afternoon he dropped her at her dormitory. That was it. He asked to see Eagle Deer.

Lord said it would be too upsetting and suggested he leave. After he did, she called Eagle Deer back into the office and asked to hear her side. Eagle Deer told the same story she had told Bordeaux and showed Lord the hickey on her breast. Lord called Eagle Deer's stepparents and the school's principal, but not for several hours did she call the BIA police, and not until Monday morning, thirty-six hours after the alleged rape, did a doctor at the Rosebud Hospital examine Eagle Deer.

On that Monday an investigator of the BIA, Peter Pitchlynn, began an inquiry, and on Wednesday he made a report to the FBI. The FBI made its own investigation and made report to the U.S. attorney. A month later, an assistant U.S. attorney wrote the FBI that "there is insufficient evidence to support the allegations of the victim, and said allegations are unfounded." Janklow was not prosecuted.

In 1974 AIM reconstructed much of the story with the help of BIA investigator Pitchlynn, since retired and living in Tulsa, Kaye Lord, also no longer with the BIA and living in western South Dakota, and Jancita Eagle Deer herself, then living in Des Moines, Iowa. Their recollections were compelling and left Banks and his associates with no doubt that Janklow had raped Eagle Deer. But there was no proof, no investigative reports from Pitchlynn or the FBI, no medical exam, no physical evidence. The case was a classic he-said/she-said. Most of Banks's advisers thought that to attack Janklow with the evidence then available, in the midst of his campaign for attorney general, would smack of a smear, and a cheap one at that. The consensus was to let the charge lie.

Banks agreed more evidence was needed, but he refused to let the charge lie. He asked his staff to dig deeper. Eventually, through means that still are not clear, some documents were harvested from the government. By one unlikely account, Banks was given a copy of the FBI's report on the alleged rape. Much more probably, Banks was shown Peter Pitchlynn's BIA report by officials of the Rosebud tribal government who were friendly to AIM. Whatever the origin and nature of the new discoveries, they convinced Banks to file a claim against Janklow. He did so, in Rosebud Tribal Court, in October 1974, three weeks before election day. Because tribal courts do not have jurisdiction over major crimes on reservations (federal courts do), AIM accused Janklow not of rape *per se* but of conduct unbecoming a member of the tribal bar. (Janklow had been a member of the bar since his legal aid days on Rosebud.) In addition to the rape claim, Banks accused Janklow of drunken driving, disobeying police officers, perjury, and malpractice. Judge Gonzalez received the complaint, ordered a hearing to determine whether the would-be attorney general should be disbarred, and appointed Banks special prosecutor—a rare turnabout of an Indian prosecuting his white prosecutor. The hearing was set for Halloween, five days before voters were to cast their ballots.

Even before the rape charge was raised, it had been a rough campaign. A few weeks earlier, Janklow had refined his "in jail, if not under it" position on AIM to the latter: "The only way to deal with these kinds of people is to put a bullet in their heads. Put a bullet in a guy's head, and he won't bother you anymore." When reporters asked if he really meant it, he said, "If it helps people understand my position, let 'em repeat it."

A short while later, Attorney General Kermit Sande held a press conference on the evils of Janklow when the subject strode in and, to the delight of reporters, swapped insults with his rival. Janklow accused Sande of incompetence and mismanagement. Sande accused Janklow of having been a juvenile delinquent, and he said that after Janklow had filed for office, his criminal record had mysteriously gone missing from his hometown courthouse. Reporters asked Janklow if it was true that he had a criminal past.

"I do not now have and never in my life have I had a criminal record." But he added, "Nineteen years ago, in Moody County, a petition of delinquency was filed against me. It was dismissed. I never appeared in court."

Reporters asked about the nature of the delinquency petition, and Janklow said it had been an "assault" involving several juveniles. The victim had been a seventeen-year-old girl.

Did "assault" mean "rape"?

"It didn't go that far," Janklow said. "It was preliminary to that type of thing, but there was no actual rape involved."

After being accused of the assault, Janklow had been given a choice of entering jail or entering the Marines Corps. He enlisted the next day.

Eight days before the election, a small weekly newspaper of discreetly leftist views called a press conference in Sioux Falls. The featured speakers were Jancita Eagle Deer and Peter Pitchlynn. Eagle Deer, looking exhausted and frail, was given the microphone first. She said, in a voice almost too faint to be heard, that seven years ago she had been raped by Bill Janklow. Reporters asked her to speak up. She did for a few moments, but her voice dribbled back down again. The reporters asked again, she tried again, failed again. After a few minutes, the host, publisher Richard Barnes, suggested that Eagle Deer take some time to collect herself and gave the podium to Peter Pitchlynn.

Pitchlynn said that when he investigated the case in 1967 he believed Eagle Deer's claim that Janklow had raped her, and he still believed her today. He had recommended Janklow be prosecuted. He assumed the FBI agent who had investigated the case after him, and whose investigation trumped his, had disagreed, but he didn't know. The agent and the assistant U.S. attorney who declined to prosecute were both white; Pitchlynn was Indian.

When the microphone was returned to Eagle Deer, a man named Jeremiah Murphy took over the questioning. Murphy was not a reporter but a lawyer, Bill Janklow's lawyer to be precise.

"Wasn't Bill Janklow your guardian?" he asked Eagle Deer.

"No, sir," she said. "It was my foster parents, Mr. and Mrs. Johnny Arcoren."

"But didn't Bill get you into this girl's dorm, and didn't he sign as your guardian?"

"No, he didn't get me—"

"Why do the records show that?"

Eagle Deer said she had no idea.

"Another question. To constitute a rape there must be penetration. According to the prosecutor's office on the Rosebud Reservation and the doctor's reports at the Rosebud Hospital, there was no penetration. How could it be rape?"

"There was," she protested.

"The doctor's report shows there was no penetration, nothing happened, no physical abuse to you, no marks on your body whatsoever."

"That's not true."

"It's right there in black and white, on the reservation, in the hospital."

"I guess Bill Janklow bought the doctor out—and the tribal chairman—" stammered Eagle Deer, clearly grasping at reeds.

"The records are still there," Murphy said. "I looked at them last week." He changed direction. "Isn't it also true that you showed up on Bill Janklow's doorstep since he's been in Pierre? You've been to his house, you've called him on the telephone?"

"Yes, I called him once about two years ago."

"And you've been at his house in Pierre."

"No, I've never been to his house."

"Now, there's hotel records that show that you were in Pierre."

"Yes, I was in Pierre."

"And you were at his house, and Bill Janklow paid for the room so that you'd stay away from his house."

"I've never been at his house. He told me he would help me if ever I needed help. And so I called him. I was going through a divorce and, uh—"

"Well, if this man raped you, why in the hell would you call him for help? You said he's threatened your life, you said he's raped you. And then you call this man and say, 'Would you help me get a divorce?'"

Murphy did not subscribe to the theory that victims could become psychologically attached to their victimizers.

"I didn't ask him to help me get a divorce," Eagle Deer said. "I figured he would probably do me some good if he would just help me."

Murphy turned to the investigator. "Mr. Pitchlynn, you stated that you hadn't been in contact with anybody in regard to this matter"—actually, Pitchlynn had told reporters the opposite: "interested parties" had called him recently. "Did you receive a phone call from Bill Janklow Friday night at eight o'clock?"

"Somewhere around that time, yes."

"Isn't it true, Mr. Pitchlynn, that you said that the American Indian Movement had contacted you?"

"Well, I didn't know they were American Indian Movement at that time. Some party, I think his name was Durham, Doug Durham, contacted me."

"Did the man named Durham identify himself as being associated with any movement? I mean, didn't you ask him who he was, or what he represented?"

"No. He said he was working on this case in connection with the Rosebud Sioux Tribe," which was true enough since Rosebud tribal president Bob Burnette was helping Durham.

The conference continued in this vein for several minutes. With each question, Murphy became angrier and angier. Finally he ejaculated, "Somebody's after Bill Janklow's ass! . . . I've never been upset in my life, but there's a man out there with a family, with some kids that he's got to explain to in the morning things that were put on the television about him."

Publisher Richard Barnes interjected, "Well, what about Jancita when she was a kid?"

"Jancita, when she was a kid, was represented by the man who's now Attorney General Kermit Sande's campaign chairman—Harold Doyle, the United States district attorney at the time. She was represented by good people. There was no case. It was a put-up job. You've been calling all over the state. Why didn't you call and check the records on the reservation? You'll find out that you need the U.S. attorney before you look at the damn things."

With that, Murphy shoved papers at Eagle Deer, Pitchlynn, and Barnes—summonses for a defamation lawsuit Janklow intended to file against them—and the conference came to a close. Years later Janklow said that a reporter leaving the conference was heard to mutter, "The only thing that got raped in this was the press."

Pitchlynn said after the conference, "It looked like a trap to me."

Minus the reporter's word "only," both were right.

To the Dakota press, a match between an articulate white man and a fumbling Indian woman was no match at all, and articles that ran over the following days said or implied that Janklow had been smeared. The reporters never asked how Jeremiah Murphy had seen the papers he said he had seen, papers like Eagle Deer's school and medical records. These were personal documents, protected by law from prying eyes like Murphy's, as any lawyer would have known. Nor did the press ask Murphy or the U.S. attorney by what rationale the latter had let the former see these papers. Nor did reporters ask the candidate for attorney general why his lawyer was subverting privacy law. Nor, above all, did reporters investigate the truth or falsity of the competing stories told by Murphy and Eagle Deer. They simply decreed Eagle Deer wrong.

A few days later, the Court of the Rosebud Sioux Tribe, Judge Mario Gonzalez presiding, convened to hear evidence *In re Disbarment of William Janklow*. The only reporter in attendance was Minnesota freelancer Kevin McKiernan. Janklow did not attend either, though Gonzalez had ordered him to appear and show cause why he should not be disbarred. Gonzalez had also ordered a BIA police officer to bring the BIA's file on the alleged rape, but the officer's superiors ordered him not to give Gonzalez the "confidential" file. This was a large insult. Virtually every court in the nation was entitled to review police records when relevant to a case at hand. For the BIA to say that Judge Gonzalez could not see the records was tantamount to saying that his court was no court. There was irony in this turn of events because tribal courts had been created a century before by the Indian Bureau to strip traditional chiefs of power and give it to Indian judges who could be kept servile. The creator considered its creation legitimate only so long as it remained docile. Gonzalez answered the BIA's insult by jailing the officer who refused to hand over the file and promising the same for his superiors if they set foot on the reservation. Judge Bogue immediately reversed Gonzalez and, more insult to injury, misspelled his name.

Dennis Banks proceeded with his case, calling twenty witnesses against Janklow. One swore that Janklow had shot dogs from a motorcycle while riding through Rosebud's housing projects. Another said Janklow had prosecuted a tribal official while employed by the tribe, which, if true, was a major conflict of interest. Still another said that police on Crow Creek Reservation had stopped Janklow for driving "all over the road," whereupon he had staggered out of his car half-dressed, his genitals one with the South Dakota winter, and announced, "No sonofabitch Indian can arrest me." In that episode, Janklow was supposedly taken to a drunk tank, jailed overnight, and released the next morning in borrowed pants. Gonzalez had asked for the BIA's records on that matter as well, but they too had been withheld from him. The charge was later proven partly correct and partly incorrect: Janklow was arrested for wild driving and sassing an officer, but he was neither drunk nor nude nor jailed overnight—all of which would have been made plain had the BIA given Gonzalez the requested file.

There was also the matter of rape. Eagle Deer testified, in Gonzalez's words, "in obvious discomfort at reliving old horrors." He found her testimony entirely credible. Kaye Lord and others recounted the rape as Eagle Deer had told them, and Eagle Deer's medical records, unlike her police file, were produced by the hospital. Contrary to the press-conference claim of Jeremiah Murphy, the records contained evidence of some kind, not made explicit by Judge Gonzalez, that was consistent with a claim of sexual assault.

"Furthermore," Gonzalez wrote, "the evidence indicates that an obstruction of justice followed the rape. When a complaint was being made to the Bureau of Indian Affairs Special Officer, Janklow was there. No relief or representation was possible through the Legal Services Program since Mr. Janklow ran it. . . . [T]estimony indicates that as recently as two months ago, Mr. Janklow offered Miss Eagledeer's grandfather money after inquiring about her. The depth of the suffering which Miss Eagledeer conveyed in her testimony cannot be reproduced through words on paper. Feeling shame, she left the Rosebud Reservation and returned only once until today. Her foster parents testifyed [sic] that her grades and interest in school fell after she was raped. She still feels frightened and inhibited by the beastly act committed against her by Mr. Janklow. It can only be hoped that she will come to realize that she should hold her head up proud for she has no guilt. She is a victim."

Gonzalez disbarred Janklow from tribal court, then went one better and issued a warrant for his arrest. The warrant was a dead letter, certain to be overturned in federal court were it ever served on him. Still, it was not every day that a court of law ordered the arrest of the odds-on favorite for attorney general—a court of law, it needs saying, that was neither more nor less biased than the typical South Dakota court. The newspapers of the state might have been expected to give at least a few paragraphs to the warrant, to the disbarment, or to the finding that Janklow had raped Eagle Deer. They did not. Janklow's prosecution of AIM might be news, but AIM's prosecution of Janklow was flimflam.

Five days after his disbarment, two of three voters in South Dakota cast ballots for Janklow, and he became the state's foremost enforcer of the law.

CHAPTER 8

ON A RESERVATION of dirt streets, no scheduled air service, and none foreseeable, a council of the Oglala Sioux Tribe ordered a field leveled, a band of tarmac long enough to land jetliners laid, and, in lieu of a control tower to guide the air traffic, a windsock installed. The council gave its creation the feverish name Pine Ridge Airport. Its asphalt could have filled every pothole on the reservation.

To this port on the afternoon of February 26, 1975, a team from WKLDOC flew. They had come from Iowa, where several Wounded Knee trials were being held, to research a case. Their vessel was a rented single-prop. On landing, they were met by local WKLDOCkers who drove them to Wounded Knee, where they went about their work without event. They were then driven back to their plane, but it was not as they had left it. It was bleeding air. Rounds of what appeared to be number-four shot had ventilated the fuselage, cabin, engine compartment, and wings, making it unfit to fly. The group's chauffer, lawyer Roger Finzel (one of those who had been threatened by the FBI on the streets of Rapid City in 1973), suggested they get back in his car and leave immediately. While one of the team snapped hurried photographs of the damage, the others moved legal files from the plane to the car. As they did so, they noticed cars whipping in and out of the parking lot of the nearby tribal planning building, a goon redoubt. The cars seemed to be taking women and children away.

The six WKLDOCkers squeezed back into Finzel's convertible and made for the exit, but before they could reach it they were cut off by a dozen cars that raced off the nearby highway and into the airport parking lot. Dick Wilson's car was in the lead. He stuck an arm out the window and pointed to the convertible, and the following cars encircled it and came to a halt. Out stepped twenty-five or thirty goons. One sat on a pickup fender with a pump-action shotgun leveled at the convertible's windshield. The WKLDOCkers rolled up windows and punched door locks, as the goons tried the handles without luck. Because it was winter, the roof of the convertible was on. A tall, muscled specimen walked up to the driver's side of the car and yelled at the WKLDOCkers to get out. Finzel knew him as Duane Brewer, an ex-policeman and Vietnam veteran who ran the tribe's highway safety program. If WKLDOC could be believed, the only safety the highwaymen guaranteed was that of their own paychecks; the program was little more than a shell for putting goons on the federal payroll. Finzel answered Brewer that the WKLDOCkers were just fine where they were.

"I can't hear you through the window!" Brewer shouted.

"I can hear you fine!" Finzel shouted back.

This opinion wrought bedlam. Brewer kicked at the window, and the rest of the goons, as if on cue, swarmed over the hood and trunk and stomped on the windshield and rear glass. One of them stuck a knife in the convertible's roof and ripped a hole above Finzel's head. Hands rushed through, one tugging Finzel's hair, another punching his face. A second gash was made over the backseat, and Bernard Escamilla, the Wounded Knee defendant whose case the WKLDOCkers had come to investigate, was pounded with fists and boots. The car was rocked wildly, glass began to shatter. Brewer yelled something about Finzel having been involved in an incident at the tribal courthouse.

"There must be a mistake!" Finzel screamed. "Get Dick Wilson! He knows I wasn't there."

"You want Wilson?" Brewer said.

Everything stopped.

"Here he is."

Wilson emerged from behind his men like Moses parting the Red Sea. "What do you want us to do with them, Dick?" Brewer said.

Wilson surveyed his quarry for a long moment. Then he grinned. "Stomp 'em," he said. "I want you to stomp 'em."

The chaos resumed as if it had never stopped. The windshield was pulverized, the rest of the roof was ripped off, the rear window was kicked in. Fists, knives, and boots surged into the car.

Eda Gordon, an investigator who lived with Finzel on the reservation, yelled to her colleagues that they were sitting ducks and should get out of the car. William Rossmoore, the lawyer who had piloted the plane, heeded Gordon's advice, springing out of the shotgun seat and running for his life. He made it twenty or thirty yards before being beaten into the ice and muck of a nearby ditch. Each time he rose, a boot crashed into his ribs or calves and down he went again. Eventually he stopped trying to get up, but the boots kept coming all the same.

Finzel emerged from the driver's seat to savage blows on the head, jaw, and nose. A punch to the stomach sent him crumpled to the ground, where kick upon kick upon kick ensued. He lost consciousness, regained it briefly, passed out again. Eda Gordon followed Finzel out of the car and wrapped her tiny frame around him in meager defense. She would later guess ten men had ganged him. At one point a teenager with a hunting knife jerked Finzel's head back by his ponytail—Gordon assumed to slit his throat—and she pulled his head back down and covered his neck with her arms. The teenager settled for cutting Finzel's hair, a short-haired Indian scalping a long-haired white man.

Bernard Escamilla, who had been well-battered even before leaving the car, was thrashed to the asphalt on emerging and kicked mercilessly in the gut. He rolled over to protect himself but succeeded only in transferring the kicks to his back. He managed to stagger up once, but a fist smashed his skull and he wilted.

Throughout, investigator Kathi James and lawyer Martha Copleman were trapped in the backseat by a knife-wielding goon, who demanded to know what was in the boxes on their laps. "None of your business," Copleman dared, and the goon slashed up the files, hinting the two women might be next.

The madness stopped without explanation as instantaneously as it had started.

An older man with a bloated face brought Escamilla to his feet and wrapped a tender arm around him, as though the best of friends. "You Chicanos have got no business on the Pine Ridge Reservation or with AIM," he said, and he ordered Escamilla to the driver's seat. Escamilla limpingly obeyed. Finzel, having regained consciousness, was ordered to his feet too, but he could get to the car only with the help of Gordon and James. Rossmoore hobbled back covered in muck and bruises.

"Don't come back," one of the goons, probably Brewer, told the victims. "If you do, we'll kill you. And if you tell anyone what happened here, we'll kill you."

While the blocking cars were being cleared, Escamilla was given a couple more bashes to the face. He nudged the car forward, and Brewer shouted, "Come back here so I can hit you a couple more times." But the last goon car had moved aside and Escamilla stomped on the gas. In his rush out of the parking lot and onto the highway, he nearly crashed head-first into an oncoming bus.

At the reservation village of Oglala, a haven of AIM supporters, the WKL-DOCkers stopped and begged a ride to Rapid City. They did not dare go to the hospital in Pine Ridge, and the convertible—glassless, roofless, light-less, and radioless (the radio had been ripped out during the assault)—was in no shape for a February drive. While they waited for another car, Gordon called the U.S. Marshals Service in Rapid City and, without much hope, asked for help. Marshal Bruce Jacobs said the situation Gordon described didn't sound like a job for his men. It sounded like a police matter. Gordon asked if this was the same Marshals Service that two years earlier had swathed Wilson in sandbags and machine guns before there had even been a hint of violence—the same Marshals Service that for ten weeks at Wounded Knee had blockaded, fired on, and otherwise policed the occupiers. When Jacobs referred her again to the BIA police, Gordon said there was no prayer the BIA's pot would interfere with Wilson's kettle. Jacobs said he found that very hard to believe.

Gordon hung up, called the police anyway, and got no answer. Impossible, she thought. The BIA had dispatchers in Pine Ridge round the clock. Next she dialed the FBI in Rapid City and asked for their help. Agent Jack McCarty invited her to come to the office in Rapid and make a complaint —tomorrow. As Gordon told the story (McCarty could not be found for comment, and the FBI would not help locate him), McCarty was awfully sorry, but it was getting to be closing time, and by the time the WKL-DOCkers made the hour-long drive to town, there wouldn't be anyone around to hear a grievance. Gordon suggested that McCarty send agents to Pine Ridge immediately, but McCarty said only that the FBI might send someone, after a complaint had been filed. It would depend on the contents of the complaint. During the negotiations that ended Wounded Knee, the FBI had said, "We will go anywhere, at any time, under any circumstances to receive a legitimate complaint." Apparently having one's plane shot up and car destroyed and body beaten senseless did not count as legitimate.

Gordon hung up and called friends in Pine Ridge, who told her the town was in anarchy. Goons had set up roadblocks on the main thoroughfares, and a goon mob had attacked two of Wilson's critics outside the tribal buildings. The critics, Councilmen Severt Young Bear and Marvin Ghost Bear, had fled to the police station, but as they ran inside, all the officers ran out. Only a single jailer remained, which explained why no one had answered Gordon's call. The mob told the councilmen that if they tried to leave, they would be killed. Young Bear, not coincidentally, was Gordon and Finzel's landlord. He and Ghost Bear were the chairman and secretary of the tribal law and order committee—satire knew no limits on Wilson's Pine Ridge.

Gordon rang Agent McCarty again and told him about the roadblocks, the barricaded councilmen, the abdication by the police. People could be killed, she said. She begged him to send agents to the reservation immediately. McCarty heard her out, said he could promise nothing, and hung up. To this day, no documents have emerged to show that the FBI made so much as a phone call to the reservation on that chaotic day, let alone dispatched agents to investigate. A couple of weeks later, the regional FBI office held a press conference to say that agitators on Pine Ridge were confused about the FBI's role. "We *investigate* violations of the federal law over which we have jurisdiction," said Agent Phil Enlow, chief deputy to Joseph Trimbach. "We are not a law *enforcement* agency, nor are we in charge of maintaining order in a community." Those who had seen the FBI enforcing the law and maintaining order minutes after Wounded Knee was taken, or who had seen the FBI jumping into the manhunt for Pedro Bissonette minutes after it started could be excused their confusion.

Councilmen Young Bear and Ghost Bear stayed holed up in the police building for nearly four hours. When none of the Pine Ridge police could be persuaded to return and extract them, a patrol from beyond the town was begged to come (by whom is not clear) and did. On being liberated, Ghost Bear fled to Rapid City and settled there, but the goons so harassed him even in Rapid that for several months afterward he had to change his address regularly. Young Bear stayed on the reservation in his native Porcupine, where anti-Wilson sentiment was strong, but he could leave home only furtively, and AIM stationed armed guards at his house. Even these did not deter goons from cruising back and forth in front of his property and shouting death threats for the rest of Wilson's reign.

The WKLDOCkers were finally lent a car and arrived at St. John's Hospital in Rapid City late on the night of the attack. Rossmoore, Gordon, Finzel, and Escamilla were treated for multiple contusions. Three doctors and two dozen X rays were required to rule out broken bones in Finzel's head, neck, chest, back, and legs, all of which were badly contused. Several of his muscles had been ripped from his bones, and cartilage in his ribcage had been ruptured. Escamilla had a broken arm, and his viscera were bruised and possibly bleeding. He was kept in the hospital for two days to make sure none of his organs gave out. Rossmoore had sprains that took months to heal. Gordon suffered from knifed hands. For months the victims dreamed of fists, boots, and knives. The women dreamed of rape. They were always certain they would be killed, and they woke up screaming.

After twenty-four hours, the police maxim holds, most leads go cold, most evidence is tainted. Forty-eight hours after the beating, the FBI got around to talking with Duane Brewer. He was indignant about being questioned, and he accused the FBI and its parent, the Justice Department, of coziness with AIM. Why were they always investigating the good people of Pine Ridge and letting the Communists and terrorists off the hook? His homily was interrupted by his wife, who pronounced supper ready, at which point the agents said they didn't want to keep Brewer from his meal, and they left. Years later Brewer would say he was so well acquainted with several agents that they often supplied him and his goons with ammunition.

Agents also made a tardy visit to Dick Wilson, who was of Brewer's mind.

"You don't swarm down here when there's an attack on me or my people," the president said. "People that are for law and order have no civil rights anymore."

The agents told Wilson his men were not cooperating with their investigation. Would he ask them to talk?

He said he would not, and the agents departed.

The FBI's leisurely investigation nonetheless turned up one fact on which the goons and AIM agreed: there had been a prologue to whatever had happened at the airport. Earlier that afternoon Dick Marshall, an Oglala and low-level AIM leader, had an appearance in tribal court on a charge of disorderly conduct. (Marshall said he had only been resisting a goon attack, for which he was charged with a trumped-up crime.) Marshall came to court with a vanful of friends, including Russell Means, and demanded a trial by jury rather than by one of Wilson's judges. In the story AIM told, Chief Judge Theodore "Red" Tibbetts, a Wilson man, was so flummoxed by the demand and by the show of support for Marshall that he closed the court. A small crowd of police and goons had gathered in the parking lot outside the court building, having been tipped by an informer to the incursion of "an AIM caravan" on Pine Ridge. The informer had swollen the van by a couple of syllables. Probably he or she had done so because the second anniversary of the takeover of Wounded Knee was the next day and authorities on Pine Ridge were expecting an invasion. In any case, the words *AIM caravan* kicked up emotion like dust on a dirt road. As the AIMers left court, Duane Brewer made a line across the parking lot for Russell Means.

"You had your fun at Wounded Knee while the rest of the people on the reservation suffered," Brewer said. "You want to bump heads?"

Means said he did not want to bump heads, and he climbed into the van.

A BIA police captain, Joseph "Skee" Jacobs, told Brewer to calm down, but Brewer ignored him, turned to Marshall, and asked if he wanted to bump heads. Marshall demurred too and got in the van. Brewer settled for smashing Means in the face through an open window. Means was ready to bump heads now, but his cohorts, fearing a setup, held him in his seat and the van sped off.

Captain Jacobs and several of his officers had ringside seats to the assault, but they merely held Brewer until the van left, then let him go and watched as he hopped in his car and sped off after the AIMers. Apparently Brewer radioed ahead for other goons to stop the van because when the AIMers neared the airport, a few miles to the east, a car emerged from the parking lot of the tribal planning building and blocked the highway.

"Let's ram that sucker!" Means said, and the driver of the van, Tom Poor Bear, jammed the accelerator. The goons in the car reversed their makeshift roadblock off the highway in a hurry, and as the van passed, the AIMers threw open the sliding door and emptied their shotguns at the car. Other cars pulled out of the planning center to give chase, but the AIM crew stopped and fired on them too and the goons backed off. The AIMers drove on to Wounded Knee without being further molested. Within the hour, the planeload of WKLDOCkers landed at Pine Ridge Airport, completely ignorant of these events.

In the meantime, Brewer returned to tribal headquarters and blackened the eyes of a court officer who had held him back when he was attacking the AIMers. "I don't want a police report about this," Brewer told the officer. "If there is one, I'll kill you."

The next day, Wilson and fifteen or twenty carloads of goons marked the anniversary of Wounded Knee by driving to Fry Bread Hill and, from a perch beside the grave of the victims of the 1890 massacre, firing pot-shots at passersby. When they grew bored, they drove to the anti-Wilson community of Porcupine, set up roadblocks, and barked threats at the townspeople, who cowered in their basements.

After the FBI's first interview with Brewer, agents visited him twice more. His denial fell away by pieces. First he acknowledged assaulting Means and chasing the van. Then he said he had threatened Councilmen Young Bear and Ghost Bear but that he knew nothing about an incident at the airport. Later he allowed that he had heard something about the air-port affair but wasn't sure what exactly had happened. Still later he said he had been present at the beating.

"I saw some of it," he said. "The women covered the men, but we didn't touch the women. We are not women beaters." More than that he would not say.

Dick Wilson was revisited by the FBI too, but he stuck to his story: he had not been present for any part of the beating and knew nothing about it. He did allow, however, that when he heard Means, Marshall, and their vanmates had shot up the airport, he drove out to investigate and saw a lot of people standing around, maybe a hundred. "If they come back," he quoted himself, "stomp their ass." Later in the day he found a mob outside the police station and was told that Councilmen Young Bear and Ghost Bear were trapped inside. "They ought to have the hell stomped out of 'em," Wilson quoted himself again.

The FBI agents said Wilson's words *stomp 'em* echoed what he had allegedly said during the airport assault. Did he know anything about this?

Hell of a coincidence, Wilson said.

In the course of its investigation, the FBI administered exactly two lie-detector tests. The subjects were Roger Finzel and Eda Gordon. Both passed.

While the FBI investigated, WKLDOC asked the BIA what it was going to do about the disintegration of its police force on February 26. The BIA said there was nothing to be done: accounts of the day's events were so conflicted, it was too hard to tell what had happened. "Since we have no data," Wayne Adkinson, the BIA's new superintendent on Pine Ridge, said, "we can't assign the blame to anyone."

The WKLDOCkers asked Judge Bogue to jail Wilson for violating the order, still in effect, that Bogue had issued during Wounded Knee that enjoined Wilson from interfering with legal workers. Bogue declined. Instead he offered to have U.S. marshals escort the legal workers as they went about their work on Pine Ridge. Since these were the same marshals who had rebuffed Gordon when she had begged for help and who, in addition, had been accused of pro-Wilson mischief before, during, and after Wounded Knee, WKLDOC forsook Bogue's generosity: it was hard to imagine convincing terrified witnesses to come forward with what they knew while their terrorizers looked on.

When the FBI finished its investigation, it forwarded the results to U.S. Attorney Bill Clayton, who reviewed the findings. Clayton had six articulate victims, half of them lawyers, five of them (not irrelevantly in South Dakota at the time) white, and all willing to testify. Two bystanders had also promised to come forward. Medical records attested to severe injuries, and a car and plane had been demonstrably demolished. The beater-in-chief, Duane Brewer, had lied about, then admitted taking part in the attack and had also admitted assaulting a court officer on the same afternoon. The beating's overseer, Dick Wilson, had lied about not being at the airport and had confessed ordering his goons to stomp his enemies. The crimes had escalated until a police station was deserted and elected officials were held hostage. Clayton called a grand jury into session, presented facts, produced witnesses. In a few days he had his men: Russell Means, Dick

Marshall, and Tom Poor Bear were indicted for firing on the goons from their van. Wilson and his goons walked.

That, as they say, might have been that, had not syndicated columnist Jack Anderson picked up a phone and called Dakota. In the three years since the Trail of Broken Treaties, when Anderson published columns about the rot in the BIA, he had kept abreast of events in Indian Country. Now he asked Clayton's office why the grand jury had not believed the WKLDOCkers' claims about the beating and what, if anything, Clayton had done to convince jurors otherwise. Anderson made clear his belief, common among reporters, that a prosecutor with a lobotomy and a lisp could get a grand jury to indict a ham sandwich for jaywalking. Five days after Anderson started raising questions—two months after the beating—U.S. Attorney General Edward Levi announced that Dick Wilson and six of his goons (including Brewer and Dick Wilson Jr.) would be indicted.

The Plains did not exactly shudder with the weight of the indictments: misdemeanor assault and misdemeanor conspiracy, both of which carried maximum penalties of six months in jail and $500 in fines. No charges were brought for the storming of the police station, the holding of hostages, or the destruction of the car and plane, and the defendants would remain free without bond until trial. Pedro Bissonette, for alleged crimes at Wounded Knee, none of which had caused bodily harm, had faced nearly a century in jail, and his bond had been $150,000. The charges were what they were because America was largely unaware of the beating at the airport (Anderson's columns did not stir other reporters to write about it), and Attorney General Levi felt none of the pressure to bring major indictments against Wilson that, say, Attorney General Robert Kennedy had felt a decade before to bring against Ku Klux Klansmen who had brutalized civil rights workers in the South.

Nobody in AIM doubted that even such attention as the beating was getting was the result of the victims' white skin and polished voices. In the year before the beating, twenty-six people had been murdered in South Dakota, twenty-three of them had been on Pine Ridge, and nearly all of the victims had been Indians. The murder rate on the reservation was eight times that of Detroit, then America's most homicidal city. Yet the national press almost entirely ignored the story. WKLDOC tried to interest reporters in the more sensational murders, like the case of the Eagle Hawk family, whose car was rammed by goons, killing the mother, her four-month-old daughter, and three-year-old nephew. Goons threatened the survivors in the hospital, and the authorities declared the murder a routine auto accident. But reporters didn't bite. A few dead Indians in an out-of-the-way corner of an out-of-the-way state didn't count for much individually, and collectively they were not seen as the alarming result of systemic racism. The reporters and editors who hastened Jim Crow to his grave would not do the same for bigotry against Indians.

After Attorney General Levi announced the misdemeanor indictments, Wilson and his men had themselves charged in tribal court, à la Glen Three Stars, for the same misdemeanors. They pleaded no contest, were fined $10 a head (sentences having stiffened since Three Stars's nickel fine), and went to a federal magistrate with the argument that to be tried in federal court for the same crimes would constitute double jeopardy. For good measure, they noted that the federal charges against them were so light, the U.S. government had no authority to prosecute them in the first place. They were probably right: under federal law only the most serious crimes committed on reservations could be prosecuted in federal court; lesser crimes, like the ones the feds had accused them of, were the jurisdiction of tribal court. The magistrate, with apparently wobbly logic (his opinion does not survive), denied the defendants' motion to dismiss the case and ordered trial to proceed under Judge Bogue. The Wilsonites said they would appeal after trial, and there was good reason to believe they would prevail.

As trial approached, the defendants' lawyers moved to suppress the statements that Wilson and Brewer had given the FBI because, they argued, the agents had not read them their rights. Dennis Ickes of the Justice Department's Civil Rights Division, who was prosecuting the case with a pair of U.S. attorney Clayton's assistants, could have argued that the motion was nonsense: the FBI did not have to read a person his rights until he was taken into custody, and neither Wilson nor Brewer had been in custody when questioned. But Ickes said, incredibly, that since the statements "contained nothing incriminating," it was fine by him if they were suppressed. He also dismissed a dozen or so witnesses, some of whom apparently would have testified that the goons had boasted about the beating. Ickes may have thought he didn't need the witnesses because two of the defendants, Fred and Everett Brewer (cousins of Duane), turned state's evidence. If so, it was an amateur discard. Hours before the Brewers were to testify, they reneged on their plea agreements. Judge Bogue could have jailed them for contempt until they testified, but instead he approved their reneging. Ickes had to go to trial with few or no witnesses to corroborate the beating, aside from the victims—long-haired out-of-state rabble-rousers who were unlikely candidates for the sympathy of a West River jury.

Dick Wilson was tried first, separately from his men, with the counsel of John Fitzgerald, a onetime lawyer for the Boston Mafia who had moved west in 1973 after starting his car one morning and setting off a massive bomb. One leg lighter but miraculously alive, Fitzgerald had offered his services to WKLDOC, most of whose members blanched at the offer. But the iconoclastic Mark Lane brought him into the fold, and Fitzgerald was soon sitting in on strategy sessions for the Custer trials. A few weeks later, special prosecutor Bill Janklow announced that he was hiring a new assistant to help with the Custer cases—one John Fitzgerald. WKLDOC made a noisy protest, and even some anti-AIMers in South Dakota thought Janklow's move in poor taste. Janklow was forced into a rare volte-face and the offer to Fitzgerald was withdrawn. But WKLDOC could not convince either Judge Joseph Bottum on the state bench (he of the riot in the courtroom at Sioux Falls) or Judge Bogue on the federal bench that Janklow, as WLKDOC alleged, had illegally invaded the defense camp.

At the trial of Dick Wilson, Fitzgerald told the jury with straight face that Wilson was not at the airport on February 26 but that even if the jury decided he had been and that he had ordered the car stopped, Wilson would have been well within tribal law to do so. The law in question was one Wilson had passed permitting the president to stop and search cars if he feared AIM was taking over the reservation. It seems (transcripts do not survive) that Fitzgerald did not bother to prove AIM *was* taking over the reservation. Instead he focused on the fact that there were a pistol and rifle in the trunk of Finzel's convertible, and he repeatedly reminded jurors that the so-called victims were arrivistes whose only purpose in South Dakota was to give succor to AIM. In the same way that AIM had turned *U.S. v. Banks and Means* into a trial of the government, Fitzgerald turned *U.S. v. Wilson* into a trial of AIM. Ickes and his fellow prosecutors seem to have countered Fitzgerald incompetently, indifferently, or not at all.

Judge Bogue's rulings did not help. At one point he ejected students from an AIM survival school who had come to watch the trial on the pretense that they were whispering too loudly. In truth, he was furious that they had held protest signs outside the courthouse—"the most outrageous thing that I have seen for a long time," an obvious bid to influence the jury. He called on the students' teacher to explain herself, and she, Madonna Gilbert, referred him to the First Amendment. "That's the most ridiculous, most asinine thing I ever heard of," said Bogue, who proceeded to question each juror about whether the signs of children had influenced them to convict the defendant. The jurors said that they hadn't even noticed the signs.

The trial lasted four days, and the jury deliberated four hours before acquitting Wilson of all counts. Of the twelve jurors, twelve were white.

"It was a justifiable stomping," Wilson explained to reporters.

Ickes asked the WKLDOCkers if they wanted the remaining goons taken to trial, and the WKLDOCkers said they had had their fill of the Justice Department's justice and had better things to spend their time on. The goons were bargained to simple assault and given a year's probation (two years for Brewer, with his extra assault on the court officer). But five weeks after the last plea was made, all of the goons were discharged from probation on account of their not having beaten anyone unconscious in the interim. On Pine Ridge, the prevailing opinion was that if white lawyers fared this badly when they took Dick Wilson to trial, mere Indians didn't have a prayer.

CHAPTER 9

FIVE MONTHS AFTER Bill Janklow was elected attorney general of South Dakota, President Ford nominated him to the board of directors of his old employer, the Legal Services Corporation. Although the post was of minor consequence, it required confirmation by the Senate, and a hearing on Janklow's qualifications was scheduled. On the day of the hearing, Janklow took a seat in the room of the Senate Labor Committee while other business was conducted, but when the chairman asked him to approach, he was nowhere to be seen. Committee staff searched the Capitol for hours without finding him. It was not until that night that reporters located him, back home in Pierre. He told them he had left the hearing room when a network television crew arrived because he did not did care for his past to be debated before the entire nation.

By "his past," he meant the rape charge. Six days before the hearing, the Senate committee had been presented with a bill of particulars against Janklow. The presenter was Jimmie Durham, who ran a group called the International Indian Treaty Council (an offshoot of AIM that worked for indigenous rights worldwide). Durham told the Senate that Janklow had raped Eagle Deer and had committed other crimes as enumerated in Judge Gonzalez's Rosebud courtroom. Durham also said that since becoming attorney general, Janklow had sent eighty state troopers to assault a pork plant that was seized by Indians on the Yankton Reservation. The assault was illegal because only the federal and tribal governments had jurisdiction over reservation crimes; Janklow's troopers had no more authority to quell a disturbance on Yankton than in Omaha. About his taking the law into his own hands, Janklow was brazen. "Once it becomes clear that the federal government isn't going to do its job," he told Dakota's admiring press, "we'll take action." Jimmie Durham asked whether the U.S. Senate wanted to confirm a self-described vigilante to oversee a federal legal program.

After Janklow fled Capitol Hill, some of his allies suggested that his flight looked a bit like admitting guilt. They said if he wanted a political future, he needed to put the rape charge to rest once and for all. Janklow, as it happened, was not friendless in the Senate. South Dakota's Jim Abourezk was an old law school classmate. One summer during school, Abourezk had leased a Black Hills restaurant and hired Janklow to work the bar while Russ Means and Madonna Gilbert danced in Indian regalia for tourists. Democrat Abourezk and Republican Janklow had stayed close since then, notwithstanding opposing views on AIM and other matters. After Janklow skipped his confirmation hearing, they talked. What was said is not clear, but around this time Abourezk told his colleague Alan Cranston, the California Democrat who chaired the Senate Labor Committee, that he knew Janklow and he did not believe Janklow had raped Jancita Eagle Deer. Previously Cranston's committee said it would not call Janklow back for another hearing—his nomination had appeared to be dead—but around the time of Abourezk's chat with Cranston, the committee set a date for a re-hearing and asked the White House to look into the alleged rape. The White House turned to the FBI.

The FBI had already examined Janklow's background before his first hearing, as was customary with nominees for Senate confirmation, and had, presumably, deemed the rape charge as baseless then as it must have in 1967. Now the FBI examined the rape claim again and rushed its findings to the White House. On June 11, three weeks after his retreat, Janklow returned to Capitol Hill and appeared before the committee. Chairman Cranston said that the White House had sent him a letter about the FBI's inquiry. The letter read, "This investigation included 45 substantive interviews in several different states, comprising some 375 FBI agent hours. The results of this investigation and two previous investigations which have been communicated to the committee indicate that these allegations"—meaning the rape charge and all the rest raised by Durham—"are simply unfounded."

Said Cranston, "This committee has discussed these results at length with both the White House and the Federal Bureau of Investigation and concurs fully in Mr. Buchen's conclusion"—Philip Buchen was the White House counsel who wrote the letter—"that the allegations against you are totally unfounded." Cranston hoped the latest investigation would silence the spurious charges for good.

Senator Jacob Javits of New York, one of the last of a liberal Republican breed, concurred and declared the exoneration of Republican Janklow by a Democrat-controlled Senate "a vindication of our system. . . . We all can be very proud that this was the result, and you should take satisfaction from it rather than laboring under any feeling that you have been harassed. You have really proved something very, very useful and important to our country."

The committee recommended approval, and the full Senate confirmed Janklow unanimously. But what proof led the Senate, FBI, and White House to pronounce Janklow clean—what, exactly, the FBI turned up in its 45 interviews and 375 agent hours—reporters never asked. Men of both parties (and men they all were) had decreed Janklow innocent, and that was enough for the press.

Nor did reporters ask whether it was just a coincidence (as Janklow claimed) or something darker (as AIM claimed) that two months before Janklow's confirmation his chief accuser was struck and killed by a car. Jancita Eagle Deer died hundreds of miles from home, on a remote highway, on foot, and no one could explain how she had arrived there or where she was going. Her death, said the Nebraska State Patrol, was an accident.

In March 1975, a month before Jancita Eagle Deer was killed, Dennis Banks and fellow AIMer Vernon Bellecourt drove from St. Paul to Des

Moines to talk with their colleague Doug Durham (no relation to Jimmie Durham, who was soon to testify about Janklow before the Senate committee). Finding Durham at home, Banks and Bellecourt took him to a motel where the Rev. John Adams of the National Council of Churches was staying. Adams was the minister Dick Wilson had called an arrogant son of a bitch.

"We showed Doug a 302 FBI document without revealing the signature," Banks later remembered. (A 302 was an agent's report.) "He said, 'What have I been telling you? There's a pig who has infiltrated our organization.' He pretended to be very angry. Then Vernon uncovered Doug's signature at the bottom. Vern said, 'Okay, Doug, read this one then.'

"Doug said, 'But I looked at it already.'

"Vern said, 'Look at the bottom.'

"Doug stared for a moment at his own signature, turning white as a sheet as the blood drained from his face. He stammered, 'Well, what do you want to know? Do you want me to admit that I work for the FBI? *Yes, I do*. I work for them, and I have done so for a long time.' "

Doug Durham was AIM's national director of security. His job was to sniff out FBI infiltrators in AIM.

AIM had discovered Durham's treachery only by chance. Two years earlier, during the siege of Wounded Knee, a man named Lon Smith offered to buy guns in Phoenix and give them to AIMers for use at the siege. AIM agreed, and an AIM foursome went to Arizona to pick up the guns. But as soon as the guns were handed over, the AIMers were arrested for plotting to break federal anti-riot laws. In pretrial hearings, Lon Smith emerged as the government's star witness; the government, it seemed, had set the AIMers up. Reporter Ron Ridenhour, who helped break the story of the My Lai massacre, took an interest in Smith and discovered that he was also behind a scheme in which families of soldiers missing in Vietnam paid $10,000 to have their loved ones found. Smith claimed he could find them because he had served seven years in the Central Intelligence Agency and had innumerable contacts in Southeast Asia. (The CIA will neither confirm nor deny Smith's résumé.) When Smith failed to deliver, the families complained to authorities, and Smith became the subject of a fraud investigation, which, when Ridenhour reported as much, rather dampened Smith's credibility in the AIM gun-running case, which in turn was dismissed. Sometime before the dismissal, however, Doug Durham testified in a proceeding for the case. The details about Durham's testimony—what he said, whether he spoke incognito or openly, whether his testimony was merely submitted in writing or delivered in person—are sketchy. In any event, WKLDOCkers did not learn of Durham's testimony until much later, when, in preparation for one of the Wounded Knee trials, they requested papers on the gun-running affair from the government. The prosecutors of that case, as required by law, handed over either Durham's testimony or some of his informer's reports or both. The confrontation in Des Moines with Banks and Bellecourt followed.

At the confrontation, the two AIMers told Durham they wanted him to confess his sins to their lawyers in Chicago. Perhaps because he was afraid to do otherwise or perhaps because he was eager to loose a long-tied tongue, Durham went to Chicago that weekend and talked to WKLDOC's Ken Tilsen and Len Cavise. The story of the FBI's most devastating infiltrator inside AIM took nine hours to tell.

Douglass Frank Durham joined the Marine Corps in 1956, fresh from Des Moines's Roosevelt High School. In later life Durham would say he passed his three-year tour of duty quietly as a cook, a military policeman, or both, after which he returned to Des Moines to drive a dairy route. But as a younger man he told another tale: he had served in a joint CIA-Marine unit and on his discharge from the Corps in 1959 continued in the CIA's employ. The Agency trained him in the arts of the clandestine trade— demolition, safecracking, lock-picking, scuba-diving, aviation, forgery, disguise, and more. In time he was "sheepdipped"—that is, all his links to the U.S. government were hidden—and stationed in Retalhuleu, Guatemala, whence he flew missions of an unclear nature, perhaps running guns, perhaps committing sabotage. By one account, Durham claimed to have worked with the CIA's secret army of *gusanos*, literally "worms," the Cuban exiles who invaded the Bay of Pigs in 1961. He left the CIA that year. All of this may have been fantasy, or it may not have. The CIA will say nothing of Durham's claims and is shielded by law from having to. What is certain is that in 1962 Durham joined the Des Moines Police Department, where he became known for what were delicately called "unorthodox" tactics. More than one supervisor took to telling him, "Des Moines isn't Cuba, Doug."

Len Cavise, one of the WKLDOC lawyers who interviewed Durham in Chicago, later said of Durham's believability, "He had a desperate need to feel important. He always wanted to impress people. Three or four times that weekend he got the biggest charge out of very, very quickly listing all the ingredients on a Big Mac—must have been twenty-five things—down to the sesame seeds. But even though I knew he was pathological in some way, I bought a very high percentage of what he said. Maybe that's a function of who I was then, or maybe he only lied about things I couldn't check. But where I could cross-check him, he checked out." Durham did not claim a past in the CIA to Cavise.

At the Des Moines Police Department, Durham's first undercover job was buying liquor sold illegally on the street in paper cups. He was soon promoted from street patrol to vice squad, but not long later his wife died and he abruptly resigned.

"There was no evidence of foul play," Durham later said of her death, "although there was lots of talk by some people around the police station. It was the loss of my wife, taking care of my son, and trying to work different shifts that led me to quit—although I was advised later when getting into undercover work that I should tell everyone I got caught working with burglary gangs and stuff like that and that I got booted off the force."

In fact, there *was* evidence of foul play and Durham *was* booted off the force. Donna Exline Durham and her husband had quarreled and he had beaten her, apparently severely, although the beating was not immediately fatal. A day or two later, she stopped by her in-laws' house, said she wasn't feeling well, and went home to rest. She died a few hours later, eight months pregnant with their second child, who died too. Durham said the cause of death was swelling of the brain, but one member of his family later claimed to have seen two different death certificates, one citing pneumonia and one claiming the cause was unknown—as if, perhaps, the authorities couldn't get the alibi right. The Exline family threatened a lawsuit, and the police department quietly reviewed the matter and had Durham examined by a psychiatrist. The psychiatrist concluded that his patient had a "paranoid schizoid personality," was prone to "uncontrollable outbursts of violence," was "unable to tell right from wrong," and was "unfit for employment involving public trust." He recommended Durham be committed to a mental institution. According to Paula Giese, an AIM investigator who researched Durham's career after AIM exposed him, "Durham was allowed to make a deal—he was not prosecuted or committed, but he was supposed to commit himself for treatment. He was fired, with this understanding, in October of 1964."

Durham did not commit himself. Instead he became a restaurateur. Giese's research convinced her that Durham's three restaurants were Mafia fronts where heroin deals were brokered, gangland hijackings were plotted, and $30,000 might change hands in an hour's gambling. Giese was a gifted investigator but credulous in matters Durham. She believed, for instance, that Durham had finagled planes from the Iowa Air National Guard for drug runs to Mexico and Canada, which was almost certainly untrue. Probably she also overstated Durham's ties to the Mob. That said, at least one of Durham's restaurants did become a hangout for a rough crowd, and the police department recruited their erstwhile employee to eavesdrop on his patrons and wire the tables in the restaurant to record conversations.

His relationship with the cops thus rekindled, Durham was given other covert work. Not all of it was glamorous. On one job he was sent to photograph a gathering of "subversives" who turned out to be housewives protesting the closure of a city park. He photographed them anyway. Soon he was freelancing for police departments in other Midwestern cities, but he again had trouble staying on the right side of the law. In 1969 he was charged with receiving stolen airplane parts. He cried setup.

"I got a pretty good attorney," he said in 1975, "Larry Scalise, a nice Italian fellow who had been attorney general for Iowa and was defending quite a few criminals at the time. This case got as far as the preliminary hearing, and the witness against me, a guy named Barry Douglass, never showed up—disappeared, nobody's ever heard from him since. He was scared to death I was going to have him hit, and I was accused quietly of having eliminated this guy. Which, no, I didn't." Absent the witness, the case melted.

A year later Durham was indicted again, this time for extorting money from a man whom he had threatened with Mob violence. He was convicted at trial, but the Iowa Supreme Court threw out his conviction on grounds of improper venue: Durham had committed the extortion in Des Moines but had been charged and tried in another jurisdiction, apparently because state prosecutors were afraid of his ties to the police and prosecutors of Des Moines.

None of which deterred the Des Moines police from continuing to work with Durham, as citizens learned in the spring of 1972, when a grand jury publicly chastised ten police officers for fencing tens of thousands of dollars of purloined sportswear. It was Durham who had stolen the sportswear, from a factory where he was working undercover to catch—of all the ironies—a sportswear thief. In the course of its investigation, the grand jury found all manner of rot among police and prosecutors, and said the fact that police had any dealings with Durham was grounds for presuming the entire department corrupt. But the corruption was so thorough, the jury was stymied in its collection of evidence and Durham could not be indicted.

Unlike the jurors, the FBI saw no reason to avoid so crooked a character as Durham. He started working for the Bureau in 1971, apparently infiltrating cigarette-smuggling and gambling rings in Nebraska. Other jobs may have followed in the course of the next year or two. In the middle of March 1973, a few weeks after AIM took Wounded Knee, a leftist weekly in Des Moines named *Pax Today* asked Durham to take photographs inside the occupied village. Durham, who had a small photography business, said yes and then called the FBI. He offered to share his photos if agents would arrange for him and two *Pax* editors to get through the roadblocks. The arrangements were made, the *Pax* team went to Wounded Knee for an afternoon, and on their return the FBI paid Durham $150 for his wares. AIM later suspected that *Pax*, with its tiny circulation and obscure origins, was an FBI or CIA front—one of the several false news services that the spymasters did indeed create to spread "disinformation" among the Left. But *Pax* was nothing of the kind. A few years earlier, its young publisher, Chris Eckhardt, had been a plaintiff in a Supreme Court case, *Tinker v. Des Moines Independent Community School District*, that became a landmark in students' rights of free speech. It was a testament to the suspicions that arose in AIM after Durham was exposed that even highly credentialed leftists like Eckhardt were suspected of betrayal.

After Wounded Knee, the FBI encouraged Durham to burrow into AIM, and Durham got in touch with the director of the Iowa chapter, Harvey Major. He told Major that although he was only a quarter Chippewa (a plausible lie, given his dark hair, broad cheekbones, and olive skin), after going to Wounded Knee he was a hundred percent AIM. Major invited him to join the chapter. At the time, Iowa AIM was occupying the lawn of the First Church of the Open Bible, a well-propertied sect that had its headquarters in Des Moines. The AIMers were demanding $50,000 from the church for past sins against Indians. Durham put the group's demands in writing, soon became the chief negotiator, and eventually won a few concessions. After this success, Durham was made the chapter's publicity officer, then its second-in-command, from which post he made demands on other churches. According to one minister, Durham's "strong moral argument, complete with scriptural quotations" was the deciding factor in a vote by Iowa's United Methodists to give AIM $100,000: $85,000 for Dennis Banks's bond on Wounded Knee charges and $15,000 for a proposed Indian center.

Doubts about Durham's intentions arose early. The Rev. John Adams later wrote, "One minister suggested to me that Doug Durham was working for the FBI and recommended that I check it out with the Bureau. I didn't, for by this time, Doug was a leader and questions were constantly being raised about most of the leaders of AIM. As a matter of fact, at Wounded Knee I once had been interrogated for more than an hour because circumstances led some Indians to conclude that I was an FBI agent. Moreover, the FBI would not have acknowledged that Doug was their operative—or they might have said he was, even if he was not, simply to discredit him as an AIM representative."

In August 1973, four months after joining Iowa AIM, Durham led a platoon of ten armed AIMers in seizing a floor of the state education building in Des Moines. Their hodgepodge of demands—money for an Indian center, better treatment of imprisoned Indians—was only lightly tied to the building they had seized and made the takeover seem gratuitous. The AIMers reinforced this impression by quickly capitulating to police (whom Durham had tipped before the takeover) without winning a single concession. The pointless violence lost Iowa AIM much of its support. Durham would later claim that his raid was meant to help the chapter. "We had one violence-prone man," he explained, "who wanted to seize the statehouse at gunpoint and kidnap the governor. I helped neutralize that threat by suggesting the alternate plan to Banks and Means of taking over the office building for three hours." But while it was true that Iowa AIM, like the rest of AIM, had violence-prone members, it was also true that Durham was among their number. He had urged or would soon urge the kidnapping of governors, the bombing of statehouses, and the commission of crimes of similar grandeur. In all probability, the raid on the education building was Durham's brainchild and for that reason was an important marker in his career inside AIM—the moment he crossed the line that separated mere informers from agents provocateur. The latter was one of the clandestine arts in which the FBI had long experience.

* * *

When Congress created a Bureau of Investigation within the Department of Justice in 1908, its members were so worried about siring a secret police that they forbade agents from carrying weapons, making arrests, or investigating any but a narrow set of special crimes (which is why the FBI's agents are officially titled "special agents"). The restraint did not endure. Soon agents were permitted to carry weapons and make arrests for a broad range of crimes. During the First World War, as fears grew that Bolsheviks and Kaiser sympathizers were secreted throughout the land, Attorney General A. Mitchell Palmer created a Radical Division inside the Bureau, the frank charge of which was to spy on the nation. The division's mandate was not far from that of the secret police Congress had once feared, but now Congress raised hardly a protest. The main targets of the Radical Division were Communists, but anyone whose views were out of favor with the Bureau or the White House it served was a candidate for espionage. In one latterly notorious example, Senators Burton Wheeler and Thomas Walsh, who made a withering critique of the oil leases that President Warren Harding gave friends at Teapot Dome, Wyoming, had their phones tapped and homes burgled by agents looking for compromising information on them. (The spies came up dry.) The division also specialized in compiling lists of "extremists," and in 1919 and 1920, Attorney General Palmer used the lists to arrest leftists by the thousands. These were the infamous Palmer Raids, and at first they were devastating to the Left. But the Left fought back in the press, and Palmer's namesake raids eventually became bywords for tyranny. The Radical Division was abolished a few years later. It would not stay dead long.

In 1924, a young lawyer named John Edgar Hoover was appointed director of the Bureau, and among his first acts was to ask that the Radical Division, renamed the General Intelligence Division, be restored. "Terror by index cards," one congressman called it, but Hoover got his division. He set his agents to compiling detention lists of the very sort used in the Palmer Raids. Heads of labor unions, eminent reporters, even members of

Congress were slated for arrest in the event of national crisis. By the 1930s so many thousands of names were on the detention lists, they made those of the Palmer Raids look like back-of-envelope scribbles. The lists proved disturbing to Francis Biddle, Franklin Roosevelt's attorney general, and he ordered Hoover to discard them. Hoover complied by changing the name of the "detention lists" to "security index" and reporting back to Biddle that the lists were no more. It was a model of evasion Hoover would resort to again and again in his long career.

The "subversives" on Hoover's index were not merely tabbed for future arrest. Their phones were tapped, their mail was opened, their movements were watched, and their ranks were perforated by informers who, if they could not be cultivated from within, were inserted from without. The intelligence the FBI gathered in this manner almost never uncovered crimes, so at first glance the exercise would seem to have benefited Hoover little. But Hoover quickly hit on the idea of giving his political patrons dossiers on their opponents' foibles—financial troubles, say, or sexual "aberrations," or associations with supposed subversives. The Roosevelt White House, apparently the first recipient of Hoover's illegal files, thanked him for his diligence, and Hoover gave similar files to every president through Nixon. None saw fit to refuse them. The complicity of the Oval Office was important since it gave Hoover the immunity to do largely as he pleased with the security index and much else. He soon compiled dossiers on every rising politician, every second-tier labor organizer, every junior reporter of questionable politics, and then, as needed, used the findings bluntly. A senator who suggested the FBI's budget should be trimmed might receive a visit from agents who, just as a courtesy, wanted to let the senator know that a prostitute had mentioned his taste for spankings. A single visit of this kind was usually enough to achieve the desired change in the senator's pronouncements. But sometimes further persuasion was required. In 1970, for example, Congressman William Anderson, a Tennessean of war-hero pedigree, denounced Hoover for tyranny. Soon newspapers in his district were reporting that Representative Anderson might have engaged prostitutes, and he lost the next election. Years later, FBI files revealed that Hoover's agents had shown Anderson's picture to whorehouse madams and asked whether he was a frequenter of their establishments. A lone madam said the congressman or someone like him "might" have been a guest, which "news" Hoover spilled to reporters in Tennessee. There is no mystery why J. Edgar Hoover was widely reckoned the most untouchable man in Washington until his death in 1972.

As Hoover's power grew, his spying on the country assumed stupendous proportions. The Communist Party USA, which never had more than 80,000 members and which by the 1950s had atrophied to maybe 5,000, was nonetheless infiltrated by 1,500 FBI operatives in that decade. (Hoover once bemoaned that the FBI, through the dues of its infiltrators, was the largest single financial supporter of the party.) By the end of the 1950s the FBI had amassed 432,000 files on civil libertarians, labor unionists, peaceniks, and other "subversives" and had placed 5,000 informants among them. The numbers trebled over the next decade. Yet only 2 percent of the FBI's "domestic security" investigations led to prosecutions (let alone convictions), which is to say that 98 percent of those spied on seem to have done nothing wrong. Critics called the FBI's intelligence-gathering stupidly scattershot and cripplingly inefficient. The criticisms, while true in part, overlooked the value of paranoia. The prospect of a fed under every bed made activists second-guess every new ally and wonder with every conversation whether unfriendly ears might hear it. Many groups became paralyzed by fear, suspicion, and bitter recriminations about informers in their midst.

"If you have good intelligence," an FBI spy chief candidly told Congress in the 1970s, "you can seed distrust, sow misinformation. The same technique is used in the foreign field."

Hoover's obsession with radicals reached its apotheosis with the black civil rights movement, which rose to prominence in the 1950s. Hoover sent scores, perhaps hundreds, of informers into groups led by Martin Luther King Jr. and his allies. A few informers also infiltrated the Ku Klux Klan, but when the FBI was tipped to imminent attacks on civil rights workers, more than once Hoover looked the other way and let protestors be bludgeoned by Klansmen nearly to death. In 1963, after King gave his "I Have a Dream" speech, which to rational minds was the century's nonpareil among demands for dignity, one of Hoover's top aides wrote, "We must mark him now, if we have not done so before, as the most dangerous Negro of the future in this nation from the standpoint of Communism, the Negro, and national security." Hoover agreed. He had King's motel rooms bugged to capture his extramarital affairs, and then shared the tapes with presidents, congressmen, and King's wife. When King was named the winner of the Nobel Peace Prize in 1964, FBI agents sent him an unsigned letter with the adultery tapes enclosed and suggested he kill himself before the award ceremony:

> King, look into your heart. You know you are a complete fraud and a great liability to all of us Negroes . . . King, there is only one thing left for you to do. You know what it is. You have just thirty-four days in which to do this . . . You better take it before your filthy, abnormal fraudulent self is bared to the nation.

As King's power diminished in the late 1960s (and was extinguished with his assassination in 1968) and the power of black nationalists like the Black Panther Party grew, Hoover re-directed his agents to the latter. His counterintelligence chief ordered agents to do whatever was needed to "prevent the rise of a messiah who could unify and electrify the militant black nationalist movement." Agents provocateur were sent among the Panthers, often posing as disgruntled ex-cops who had seen the light, just as Durham would later do with AIM. Sometimes the ex-cop had stolen police files before he crossed over, in which case the files invariably "revealed" that certain Panthers were police informers. Schisms, exiles, and gunfights followed. In 1969, after two Panthers in San Diego were killed by former allies and a general bloodletting broke out, the FBI field office wrote Hoover, "Shootings, beatings and a high degree of unrest continues to prevail in the ghetto area of San Diego. Although no specific counter-intelligence action can be credited with contributing to this over-all situation, it is felt that a substantial amount of unrest is directly attributable to this program."

Two victims of Hoover's machinations who might stand for the faceless many were Jean Seberg and Geronimo Pratt. Seberg was a white actress who infuriated Hoover by giving money to the Black Panthers. He ordered that she "should be neutralized" with a counterintelligence program, or COINTELPRO in FBI idiom. His agents planted a lie with gossip columnists that Seberg, who was pregnant, had been made so not by her white husband but by a Black Panther lover. The gossips put the tale in print, and the traumatized Seberg went into labor prematurely. Her baby died two days after being born. Seberg held an open-casket funeral to show the gossips the child was white, then she tried to kill herself. She failed, but she made seven more attempts, usually on the anniversary of her daughter's birth. In 1979 she finally succeeded. "The COINTELPRO attack on her," wrote Richard Gid Powers, one of Hoover's foremost biographers, "was no different from hundreds of other documented attacks on obscure radicals and their friends, stories that were never told because the victims were not glamorous, nor famous, and, in many of the worst cases, not white." One of the unfamous and unwhite was Geronimo Pratt. A mid-level leader of the Black Panthers in California, Pratt was framed by the FBI for a 1968 murder the Bureau knew he didn't commit and sent to prison for what was supposed to be the rest of his life. For twenty-seven years, while Pratt enjoyed penitentiary beatings and sadistically long stretches in solitary confinement, the FBI suppressed the evidence of his innocence. He was fully exonerated only in 1997 after a series of desperate lawsuits, and he became one of the very rare victims of COINTELPRO to win a cash settlement from the FBI.

COINTELPRO was kept hidden from the public until a March night in 1971, when a posse that called itself the Citizens' Commission to Investigate the FBI burgled an FBI office in Media, Pennsylvania, and took reports that described dozens of COINTELPRO actions. The burglars sent copies of the reports to Senator George McGovern because of his reputation as a courageous liberal. But McGovern had his eye on the presidency and apparently feared being tainted by the burgled goods or, perhaps, by whatever Hoover might manufacture about him. The senator returned the papers to the FBI. Reporters, fortunately, were more interested in the mail from the Citizens' Commission, and exposés followed. Within days, Hoover declared an immediate end to COINTELPRO, but his critics were not convinced. They assumed Hoover would continue his dark arts under another name, and in fact it was later revealed that in his memo "ending" COINTELPRO, he told agents that if they continued to find a need for counterintelligence, they should submit requests to headquarters for case-by-case approval. Congress would later find that COINTELPRO had died more in name than deed. Well into the 1980s the FBI was found to have burgled offices of leftist groups, like the Committee in Support of the People of El Salvador (CISPES), which had done nothing more illegal than oppose Latin American death squads that were backed by the Reagan Administration. Exactly how long COINTELPRO lived on remains unclear.

Dennis Banks saw in the provocations of Doug Durham neither indiscretions nor incitements but a warrior's zeal. Banks met Durham in Iowa early in the summer of 1973, just after Wounded Knee, and they got to know one another better later that summer at the annual sun dance at Crow Dog's Paradise. Durham offered AIM his skills as a pilot, ex-cop, and photographer. "Once a pig, always a pig," Vernon Bellecourt warned, but there was no other objection, so Durham's offer was accepted. A few weeks later Banks was indicted for his part in the riot at the Custer Courthouse, and he fled to a hidden cabin in the Canadian sub-Arctic. When he gave no sign of returning to Rapid City for an October court appearance—which, if missed, would have resulted in the forfeit of his $105,000 bond, $85,000 of which came from Methodist collection plates—the Rev. John Adams tried to find him to convince him to return. After a few phone calls, Adams was given a number in Edmonton that, when he dialed it, was answered by Durham. Durham told Adams that Banks had put him in Edmonton as an intermediary. Adams explained his problem, and Durham professed concern. But he said, "Every message I try to get through to Dennis is getting garbled by the next intermediary. I need to fly directly to him, but I'd have to rent a float plane to do it."

Adams forwarded him cash, and Durham flew to Banks's northern hideout. Once there, Durham convinced Banks that forfeiting the Methodists' money would be foolish, and he flew Banks back to the States, dipping low across the U.S.-Canadian border to avoid radar. Banks made his court appearance without incident.

"This whole sequence adds to the puzzle," Adams later wrote. "Durham, by bringing back Dennis Banks, helped him avoid arrest as a fugitive, enabled Banks to effect his own decision to return to the U.S., gave assistance to the Movement by returning its national executive director, saved the $85,000 which the Iowa annual conference would have lost if Banks had forfeited his bond—and undoubtedly gained information which he, as a paid operative, reported to the FBI."

Durham gained more than information. Until the Canadian flights, AIM's trust in him was only tentative, and the FBI, despite having worked with him before, treated him as a freelancer. After the trip, Banks made him his bodyguard, pilot, and confidante, and the FBI hired him full-time. Over the next year Durham was rarely far from Banks. When the Banks-Means trial began in early 1974, Banks made Durham chief of security for the defense team. Later he made him chief of security for all of AIM. From these posts, the agent provocateur gave interviews to reporters and advice to AIM chapters, scrutinized the bona fides of new recruits and current members, and had access to AIM's mail, financial accounts, and nearly all of its other records. AIM would later say Durham stole $100,000 from WKLDOC and AIM, an estimate that can be neither proved nor disproved because the records have been destroyed and because, even if they hadn't been, one or more genuine AIMers were dipping into the coffers as well.

As Durham grew closer to Banks, several people in Banks's inner circle—including his brother Mark, his lover Anna Mae Aquash, and a few of his senior staff—told him the suspiciously skilled and "un-Indian" Durham was either a spy or a deceiver in other ways. But for more than a year Banks would not hear them. Then late in 1974, while Banks was visiting actor and supporter Marlon Brando in Hollywood, Vernon Bellecourt called and said, "I have some very, very important news, but I cannot give it to you over the phone. I am here with Clyde, and we need to talk with you immediately." Banks flew to Minneapolis. The news was the FBI report signed by Durham.

According to Banks, "Vernon called a meeting. There were seven or eight of us present—Russ and his brothers Ted and Bill, Clyde and Vernon Bellecourt, Herb Powless, and Annie Mae. We talked about what to do, trying to estimate the damage Durham had done to AIM. And I must speak the truth in saying that some of those present suggested that we kill him. One of our group, expressing his rage, said, 'We ought to just take him out and shoot him, and go bury him someplace.' " If Banks can be believed—and for reasons that will become clear, he almost certainly cannot—"Annie Mae said, 'I was the first to suspect Doug. It's up to me to take care of this. I'll take him out if you want me to.' And she absolutely meant it." In Banks's story, he and Vernon Bellecourt turned Aquash and the others from assassination. Instead, Durham would be watched in the hope that he would lead AIM to more spies. He did not.

A few weeks later, in January 1975, Menominee Indians in northeastern Wisconsin seized an abandoned novitiate on what was once tribal land and demanded that the monastic order that owned the novitiate give it to the tribe. AIMers set up quarters nearby, and Durham and Aquash handled press operations from a shared motel room.

"One of the proofs that Durham was a provocateur, not just an informer," reporter Kevin McKiernan said years later, "was that during the Menominee takeover he pissed off the anti-Indian vigilantes up there, almost to the point of violence. The vigilantes called themselves WHAM, the White America Movement, and they were patrolling the woods looking for an excuse to get into a gunfight. Before coming to the takeover, Durham had stolen an airplane in Milwaukee, and he had run up a huge bill in one of the little towns around there that he wouldn't pay. All of this was leaked to the WHAM guys by the cops or the FBI, and so was Durham's criminal record—real or false I don't know. When I would interview the WHAM guys, they would talk about how awful Durham was and that since his record showed ties to the Mob, he was proof AIM was run by the Mob. WHAM devised a plan the gist of which was that if any of their guys was taken out, they would take out some AIM guys. So Durham's work came damn close to getting some people assassinated. Ironically, Durham was one of the people on WHAM's hit list."

Before the occupation ended, Durham packed up and left quietly. Perhaps the FBI evacuated him to protect him from WHAM. Or perhaps he sensed the game was up after AIM shut him out of sensitive deliberations, in which case he may have feared violence from the Indians. His disappearance led to the confrontation by Banks and Bellecourt several weeks later in Des Moines.

On March 13, 1975, AIM held a press conference in Chicago's federal building with Doug Durham as the headliner. He told reporters that for two years he had infiltrated AIM, during which time the FBI had paid him $1,000 to $1,100 a month ($3,500 to $4,000 in today's money). He said he was ashamed of having thoroughly subverted so virtuous a group as AIM.

"I exercised so much control," he said, "that you couldn't see Dennis or Russell without going through me, you couldn't contact any other chapter without going through me, and if you wanted money, you had to see me."

Reporters asked whether he had informed for the FBI when he worked for the defense team during the Banks-Means trial.

He said he had.

They asked whether he had given the government information that was material to the defense.

He said, "I gave—on some occasions I gave information that was material to the defense. I was asked not to involve myself in the defense proceedings; however, by the nature of the position I had attained in AIM, it was impossible to avoid access or privy to this information. I was one of the only non-defendants allowed into the exclusive defense committee chambers with conversations between attorneys and clients."

During the trial, Judge Nichol had ordered the FBI to review a list of WKLDOCkers and to say whether any informers were among them. Prosecutor R. D. Hurd and FBI regional director Joseph Trimbach both swore there were none—but Durham's name had been on the list. After Durham was exposed, WKLDOC went back to Judge Nichol and told him he had been lied to. Nichol called on Hurd to explain, and Hurd admitted that he had known that an FBI informer was "very close to one of the defendants." But, said Hurd, the FBI had told him that the informer had been instructed to inform only about violence, not about defense strategy, so Hurd had not considered him to have penetrated the defense. Hurd's excuse was irrelevant. Nichol had ordered the government to admit to every informer who had even "arguably" had any "contact with" the defense camp—not just to informers who were illegally spying on defense strategy.

Trimbach, for his part, said he had had no idea Durham was an informer. Yet no sooner did he say so than one of his subordinates, Agent Ray Williams, said that he (Williams) had had dozens of contacts with Durham during the trial and that Trimbach knew about them from the start. Trimbach also said that after Durham was exposed, he looked into the matter and found that Durham had revealed nothing about the Banks-Means defense. AIM, he said, could trust him on that score.

WKLDOC asked Nichol to punish several FBI agents and prosecutors, including Trimbach and Hurd, for perjury and for violating the defendants' right to a fair trial. After much consideration, Nichol wrote, "I recognize that a court may, in the exercise of its discretion, institute contempt proceedings to vindicate and reinforce the integrity and power of the court.

[But] I conclude that it would be unwise for the court to pursue this matter. If we were in the midst of trial, with Means' and Banks' right to a fair trial in potential jeopardy, my conclusion would possibly differ. On the contrary, the Means' and Banks' indictments have been dismissed, which, in a sense, is the ultimate remedial relief."

Nichol either did not understand or did not care that Durham was one of many, that there was a broader corruption inside the government, and that while dismissing the case against Banks and Means was good for them, it did little to deter the FBI from doing the same to other defendants. The very week that Nichol declined to punish the government, a witness took the stand in another political trial, one arising from the riot at New York's Attica Prison in 1971. The witness said that for a year and a half she had reported to the FBI, illegally, on the trial strategy of the defendants. Similar revelations preceded and followed Nichol's decision, including the revelation that WKLDOC had been penetrated in 1973 by a husband and wife team, Harry (Gi) and Jill Schafer. The Schafers had come to WKLDOC's Rapid City office during Wounded Knee and immediately started badgering its staff to import guns. They also spread rumors that worsened already deep rifts inside Wounded Knee between local Oglalas on one side and AIMers from beyond Pine Ridge on the other. When WKLDOC grew suspicious and banned the couple from its office, Gi threatened WKLDOC's Ken Tilsen with death. *The New York Times* exposed the Schafers in the spring of 1975, within days of Durham's exposure, and reported that the Schafers had set up a fundraising front that diverted money meant for WKLDOC. Jill said they had the FBI's permission for the diversion. Their names, like Durham's, had been on the list of WKLDOCkers that the FBI certified was free of informers. But Judge Nichol found no more cause to punish the government for lying about the Schafers than he had for Durham.

WKLDOC appealed Nichol's inaction to the Eighth Circuit, and a three-judge panel agreed that the prosecutors of *U.S. v. Banks and Means* had either lied to Nichol or had themselves been lied to by the FBI. But the panel sided with Nichol in his decision that no one in the government need be punished. Justice, the panel held, had been served via dismissal of the defendants' case. If anyone in any branch of the Justice Department was sanctioned for invading the defense teams of the 1970s, the event was never publicized.

A point overlooked by nearly all of the reporters at the Chicago press conference and by most commentators thereafter was that in eighteen months at the top of AIM, with nearly unlimited access to its files and its leaders, Durham either never found evidence of an important crime, or he did but the government did not pursue prosecution. The latter possiblity is just short of unimaginable. In other words, if there was a legal basis for Durham's protracted, pervasive espionage, it has never been made public.

On the night of Friday, April 4, 1975, two weeks after Durham was unmasked, two teenagers in a Pontiac GTO were careering across the southern Nebraska plain when they collided with a woman on foot. A suitcase she was carrying was impaled on the bumper of their car, the rest of her belongings were scattered across 70 feet, and her body was thrown 150 feet from the point of impact. When deputy sheriffs arrived, they found Jancita Eagle Deer lying partly across the road, perpendicular to traffic, and had badly mangled—dead beyond question. The boys who hit her said she had been standing in the middle of their driving lane and appeared to be weaving and disheveled. They hit her, they said, at fifty or fifty-five miles per hour and did not stop to see whether she was alive or dead, or even to move her out of traffic. Instead they continued to a nearby farmhouse and called the police. The deputies believed the boys' general story but did not find the details convincing. Their survey of the accident scene suggested that Eagle Deer had been standing not in the middle of the lane but much closer to the shoulder and that the boys had been driving much faster than fifty-five. They had hit her because they were driving recklessly. The officers, however, did not issue so much as a written warning to the driver. Coincidentally or not, the driver belonged to one of the more prosperous families of the nearby town of Aurora and, unlike his victim, was white.

AIM could not believe that there was no connection between Eagle Deer's death and her recently resurrected rape charge against Janklow, and it sent a pair of investigators to Aurora. They found on the roadside one of Eagle Deer's shoes and several items from her purse, which did not impress them with the diligence of the sheriff's office. The AIMers also noted that there were no skid marks on the road, which suggested that the boys had neither swerved nor braked before the crash. But they could prove no more and went home. A few months later AIM's Paula Giese made a more thorough investigation. She apparently spoke with the boys, who said that Eagle Deer had been "trying to flag them down. They assumed she had been pushed from a car by 'some guy she wouldn't put out for' and had a few laughs about this. As they sped toward her, they expected her to jump out of the way, but they struck her." Giese concluded that the boys had been criminally reckless but did not kill Eagle Deer intentionally.

She wondered, however, about Doug Durham. During her investigation, Giese learned that on Eagle Deer's final afternoon, she had left South Dakota's Rosebud Reservation for Des Moines with a dark-haired man in a late-sixties blue Chevrolet. The two of them were last seen in Valentine, Nebraska, just south of Rosebud. The logical route from Valentine to Des Moines passed a hundred miles north of where Eagle Deer was killed. No one could explain her presence outside Aurora. Giese suspected that the dark-haired man was Durham and that if Eagle Deer had indeed been unsteady and disheveled just before her death, it was because Durham had beaten her and kicked her out of his car, perhaps while it was moving— though why he had done so in south-central Nebraska, Giese was not certain. Giese had reason for her suspicions: eight months before her end, Durham had taken Eagle Deer for a lover and had quickly become her batterer.

The two had met in the summer of 1974. When Johnny Cake came to AIM that July with his story about the rape of Eagle Deer, it was Durham whom Dennis Banks sent to investigate the claim. By coincidence, Durham and Eagle Deer both lived in Des Moines at the time. They had even crossed paths fifteen months earlier, when Durham saw Eagle Deer and her daughter on a sidewalk and asked to take their picture because, he said, they made such a pretty pair. Eagle Deer consented, Durham took the photo, and she forgot all about it until he showed up at her house in 1974 to investigate the rape. After Durham was exposed, AIMers suspected that he had been "casing" Eagle Deer as part of a long-range plot to get her to accuse Janklow of the rape. Durham had surmised, so the thinking went, that the accusation would backfire and help elect Janklow. The suspicion, still current in parts of Indian Country, was entirely fanciful. At the time Durham photographed Eagle Deer, he knew nothing of the rape claim, and Janklow was an obscure lawyer with no known political aspirations. In all likelihood Durham took Eagle Deer's picture in an effort to build files on Iowa's small Indian population. If the method was literally scattershot, it was no more so than the rest of the FBI's intelligence-gathering.

After they re-met, Durham brought Eagle Deer to the AIM office in St. Paul, seducing her en route.

"About fifteen seconds after I first laid eyes on her," Paula Giese wrote, "Jancita blurted out to me the story of the rape, the fact, as she saw it, that she was going to marry Durham, a few facts about his twenty-thousand-dollar a year salary in AIM, which caused my jaw to drop even further, and some facts about the near-fatal illness for which she was going to help him get cured. I felt it was hopeless to enlighten her, although in seven months of working 'under' Durham at the AIM house, I already knew he was a rotten character so far as women are concerned and I also knew he didn't have leukemia, although he had for a while conned me into excusing a lot on grounds that he'd soon be dead."

Eagle Deer told AIM the story of the rape, and AIM declined at first to press it. When Eagle Deer dropped out of sight, Giese assumed Durham had taken her back to Des Moines. In fact, he had set her up in a Twin

Cities apartment. "She was kept drunk," Giese later claimed, "and a few Indian women became aware that Durham was, in effect, pimping for her." He was also beating her. Once, when she threatened to leave him, he said if she did so, AIM would take her daughter and raise her "as an Indian" on a reservation. Eagle Deer stayed put.

Meanwhile Durham revived her rape claim against Janklow. It was he who set up the press conference in Sioux Falls that featured Eagle Deer and Peter Pitchlynn just before Janklow's election. And it was probably he (or maybe one of his FBI handlers) who tipped Janklow's camp to the press conference, thereby enabling Janklow's lawyer Jeremiah Murphy to come armed with enough research to discredit Eagle Deer. (Janklow's election campaign was not the first in which the FBI had meddled. In 1948, J. Edgar Hoover gave Thomas Dewey intelligence on his rivals for the Republican presidential nomination. In return, President Dewey was supposed to elevate Hoover first to attorney general, then to the Supreme Court. Truman's upset threw sand in those gears.) Janklow would have won his race for attorney general even without the sympathy he gained from the discredited attack that Durham probably engineered. But that fact is irrelevant to the integrity of the electoral process, which suffers any time it is manipulated by those in power, and it will never be known how much Janklow's mandate to fight AIM was increased by the FBI's mischief.

Three months after Eagle Deer was killed, Paula Giese received a call at the AIM office from a man who would not give his name but whose stiff manner and diction made her think he was a lawman.

"I understand you are interested in Doug Durham and are investigating the death of a young Indian girl, Jancita Eagle Deer," the man said. "You might like to know that the license of the car that picked her up on the afternoon of April 4"—the day of her death—"was checked. The car belongs to Durham's father."

The man did not explain how a license plate number had been found for the car, nor did he say anything else before hanging up. Giese did some digging and found that, sure enough, Durham's father owned a 1967 blue Chevrolet—a match, perhaps, for the blue Chevy of late '60s vintage that had been driven by Eagle Deer's dark-haired companion. Giese also learned that Durham often drove his father's car when he thought his own was too conspicuous, but her investigation stalled there.

Several weeks later, in December 1975, Giese drove to Des Moines to meet relatives of Eagle Deer with whom she had been living when she was killed. As Giese approached their house in the country, she was stopped by two police cars, both of which had three or four officers inside—not a typical rural patrol. They detained her for an hour on pretense of a broken turn signal and threatened her with jail. While she waited for them to decide her fate, she heard a police dispatcher say something about the FBI. She had set up the appointment with Eagle Deer's family only that morning—in fact, she had never spoken with them before—and neither she nor they had told anyone about the meeting. Giese concluded, no doubt rightly, that the FBI had sent the police to intercept her after learning about the meeting via a tap on either her phone or the phone of Eagle Deer's relatives. In the end the police allowed her to proceed to the relatives' house, shaken but without a detour to jail.

The relatives, the Sheldahls, told Giese that when the Nebraska police gave them Eagle Deer's personal effects, her address book was missing. Eagle Deer had always kept the book with her and, according to one witness, had it when she left Rosebud on the day of her death. The Sheldahls said the FBI had questioned them more than once about the address book's whereabouts. They also said that not long after Eagle Deer's death, their house was broken into. Nothing of value was taken, but Eagle Deer's papers had been gone through and some may have been removed. The Sheldahls were certain that Durham or his colleagues were responsible for the break-in. "But what can we do?" one of the Sheldahls said. "Those people have so much power."

Giese never learned anything more about Durham's involvement in Eagle Deer's last hours. Not long later she descended into fits of paranoia.

During one fit, she threw herself out a second-story window because, she said, "they" were coming to get her. When she died in 1997, she was half crazy and wholly alone, one more forgotten casualty of the FBI's counter-intelligence programs. It was weeks before her body was found, and she had begun to decay into the floorboards.

Durham's entanglement with Eagle Deer, the occurrence of her death so soon after she had resurrected the rape charge, and the many small mysteries that followed her demise—why did a presumptive lawman call Giese in secret with information about Durham? why was the Sheldahls' house broken into?—prompted many rational people to believe the most irrational of theories. To this day in Indian Country, people will tell you that Durham ran over Eagle Deer and left her on the highway to be run over again. Or that he shoved her from his car into the path of the one that struck her. Or that he threw her from an airplane onto the highway, where she was run over. The FBI could have snuffed much of this paranoia with a public inquiry into what, exactly, its provocateur had done inside AIM and to what extent he had abused—physically and psychologically—one of his targets. But paranoia in Indian Country was not something the FBI cared to snuff.

CHAPTER 10

IN THE SUMMER of 1975, members of the American Indian Movement from across the country gathered in Farmington, New Mexico, for their annual convention. It was a fractious time. Doug Durham and Gi and Jill Schafer had been exposed only weeks before, and AIMers presumed not only that more agents were among them but that since Durham had wormed his way to the right hand of Banks, the infiltrators could be anywhere. Suspicion stole into every mind. For many it was a short leap to the paranoia that COINTELPRO was meant to induce.

In Farmington the suspicions settled on Anna Mae Aquash. She had worked in many of the same places as Durham—he had, for example, followed her to the West Coast office (from which she expelled him for disruptive behavior)—and a theory then current in AIM held that FBI operatives worked in pairs, *viz.* the Schafers. That Aquash had often denounced Durham as an informer only proved the FBI's cunning. Durham himself had exposed an informer or two in his time—bit players whom the FBI, it was now clear, had been willing to give up to secure his cover. Aquash was also close to Banks, as Durham had been. Banks had ended their affair for reasons not entirely clear earlier that year, but they were still close, and the thought of what confidences might have passed in bed or would continue to pass out of bed gnawed at several AIMers. Foremost of the suspicious was Vernon Bellecourt, who, after Durham was outed, took the job of AIM's security chief. During the convention in Farmington, Bellecourt ordered Bob Robideau, Dino Butler, and Leonard

Peltier—whose names would soon become famous in Indian Country for other reasons—to interrogate Aquash. (According to Robideau, Banks was also "a party to" the order.) They drove her to a deserted mesa and parked. While Robideau and Butler stayed with the car, Peltier walked Aquash over a rise and accused her of being an agent. She said that was bullshit. In the story Aquash later told several friends, Peltier then put a gun to her head and told her to confess. In some versions of the story, he stuck the barrel in her mouth.

"If you believe all that stuff about me," Aquash told him, "I give you permission to pull the trigger."

He did not.

Peltier (pronounced pell-TEER) has always denied Aquash's account of what happened on the mesa. He has said he vetted her mildly, was convinced of her good faith, and came away her friend. There was never a possibility of murdering her. But others have said that Bellecourt had ordered Peltier, Robideau, and Butler to kill Aquash where she stood if they decided she was an informer. Some AIMers also recalled a heated exchange in Farmington between Bellecourt and Banks, the latter apparently furious over the technique of the former. But the veracity of such accounts is hard to judge.

It is certain, however, that Aquash was neither the first nor the last to endure such an interrogation. At the Menominee takeover of the novitiate in Wisconsin four months earlier, the takeover from which Durham made his abrupt exit, several AIMers were accused of espionage. A young reporter named Paul DeMain recalled much later, "I was at this big party outside the occupation, and all of a sudden I notice everyone's cleared out but this one individual who went into the kitchen and came out with an AR-15 pointed at me. He says, 'Who are you? We know you've been taking notes and making records.' I did some fast talking. I had been staying with a local leader who was very respected, and I stuck his name into the discussion several times. I have always thought that if it hadn't been for my association with that leader, I might have ended up buried in the woods back outside that cabin." Decades after that encounter, DeMain would become the reporter most responsible—and in method and tone most controversial (he would, for example, make the ludicrous charge that AIM ran a "COINTELPRO program . . . as sophisticated as the one run by the FBI")—for solving the murder of Aquash. Among the reporters who would help him solve Aquash's murder was Minnie Two Shoes, an AIMer who was also interrogated at the Menominee takeover. The answers Two Shoes gave her interrogator were apparently less convincing than DeMain's, and she was exiled.

After the interrogation in Farmington, Aquash was terrified, disconsolate, and quietly a-rage. She thought of returning to Canada, where there was no shortage of work to be done on behalf of Indians and where she would be able to see her daughters more often. But she wanted to clear her name, and her fidelity to AIM was absolute. She stayed until death took her.

The FBI had not lost interest in Aquash since its invasive chronicling of her activities in Los Angeles in the fall of 1974. Throughout the first half of 1975, informers recorded her movements as she traveled around the country, albeit in less detail than had been done in Los Angeles, where the FBI's network of moles was clearly more extensive. The reports continued to show an AIM more expiring than expanding. For example, after Aquash traveled from Los Angeles to Wisconsin for the novitiate takeover, she was tracked to AIM headquarters in St. Paul, where informers said she and her staff spent weeks just raising gas money to get back to California. Shortly after she returned to Los Angeles, she left for Shiprock, New Mexico, where Diné (Navajo) activists had seized an electronics factory whose owners were accused of mistreating workers. The FBI monitored Aquash on her way to Shiprock but lost track of her once she slipped into the factory. She was among a small team who sifted through the company's records and turned up documents that proved many of the workers' claims. (Not that the proof did them much good. The owners simply packed up the equipment and moved the factory to the Third World, where labor was cheaper and more quiescent.) Aquash did not return to Los Angeles after Shiprock; instead she went to the Pine Ridge village of Oglala and settled there with other migratory AIMers.

Around the time she arrived in Oglala, the Canadian government began spying on her family in Nova Scotia. The extent of Canada's espionage is not clear. But after Aquash was murdered, her brother-in-law, who was a constable, was told by a colleague that the Royal Canadian Mounted Police had had him (the brother-in-law) and his wife (Aquash's sister) under surveillance throughout the spring of 1975. Another friend of the family reported that Mounties had interviewed her that spring about Aquash. Decades later, documents released from the FBI would show that the Bureau had asked the Mounties for the spying.

The FBI's request of Canada coincided with dire, if vague, reports about what Aquash and the other newly arrived AIMers were doing in Oglala. By the account of one informer, "AQUASH had brought in funds and possibly foreign representatives" for an enterprise that other informers called a "special AIM project" or a "secret AIM project." The FBI read into the project its worst nightmare, which was that AIM was planning a popular revolt even bigger than Wounded Knee or, failing that, scattered terrorist attacks. The rumors coming out of Oglala—rumors of a secret project bankrolled from overseas and based just a few ridges west of Wounded Knee—led the Bureau to mass agents on Pine Ridge. The agents' charge was to learn what AIM was doing and defuse it if they could or, if they could not, to be on hand when the chaos erupted. To all appearances, the tone inside the FBI was alarmist verging on paranoid. It was no small irony of COINTELPRO that it inspired hysteria in the targeters as well as the targeted.

The FBI learned nothing about the secret project, and with reason: there was nothing to learn. The only "foreign representative" Aquash had brought to Oglala was herself, the extent of her funds was cigarette money, and the secret work was not secret—it was overt social service. The two or three dozen AIMers who settled in Oglala had been invited there by elders seeking help, on behalf of the desperately poor community, with the rudiments of life. The AIMers planted gardens, brought meals to the homebound, fixed broken-down cars, and started sewing circles. Along the way they educated people about treaty rights and other matters political. Aquash was one of the most fervent of the workers, but her only sedition was plotting to replace the over-larded, over-starched, over-processed surplus foods that the government gave Indians with fresher, healthier nourishment. She was beloved for her efforts.

"Anna Mae left her home and her two kids and her good job for us," Roselyn Jumping Bull said shortly after Aquash was murdered. "She told me, 'After I realized how you people live, I didn't want none of the things I had before. I left everything because I wanted to show you I love you people and want to help you.' That's why I liked her. None of the other girls ever talk like that."

"She was a quiet person when she lived among us in Oglala," Ellen Moves Camp remembered, "always beading and sewing and doing things. She was always in the middle of things, but she wasn't mouthy about what she did."

Aquash adopted Oglala as home and said that when she died she wanted to be buried there and lie among her friends for all time.

The proximity of a mass of FBI agents to a mass of AIMers added to the unease of Pine Ridge, which was uneasy enough under the despotism of Dick Wilson. AIMers and agents were forever brushing against one another in the reservation's few small towns and on its narrow byways, and every chance encounter added to the tension. In AIM after the exposure of Durham, the certain result was more paranoia. It did not help that the FBI, till then blasé about crime on Pine Ridge, suddenly took an interest in the subject, particularly in the case of crimes that might implicate AIM or be used to pressure a suspect to become an informer inside AIM.

One crime in which the FBI took an intense interest was the murder of Jeanette Bissonette, a cousin of Pedro. On March 26, 1975, Bissonette was driving home from the wake of a friend (also murdered) when she stopped on a dirt lane and was shot by a sniper. Because she was shot near the homestead of Dick Wilson's brother, and because her car was similar to Wilson's, the FBI speculated that in the dark AIM had killed her by mistake. (This was, unlike many of the FBI's accusations against AIM, at least plausible.) Agent David Price took the case and came to Oglala to ask Aquash, among others, what she knew about the shooting. To this day the FBI will not disclose whether Aquash told Price anything beyond her name or, if she did, what either she or Price said. But it is certain that Price's visit did not help Aquash with the nascent rumors that she was an informer. It was not that anyone thought that if she were an informer, she would speak with her FBI handler by the light of day. But anyone visited by the FBI could be pressured to inform. Word that the FBI had paid her a visit traveled fast, and the interrogation in Farmington followed a few weeks later.

Even after Farmington, Aquash might have lived a comparatively quiet life on Pine Ridge, doing her social work and putting the suspicions about her to rest and deciding where next to turn her energy. But that possibility evaporated after a small piece of hell was loosed on Oglala that summer.

At a quarter to noon on June 26, 1975, two FBI agents in separate cars were driving on Highway 18 near Oglala when they came upon a red truck that they suspected of harboring one Jimmy Eagle. A few days earlier Eagle had allegedly beaten a drinking buddy and made off with his cowboy boots. It was the sort of crime the FBI would not have paid much mind before the "secret AIM project." On June 25, the day before the agents spotted the truck, they tried to serve a warrant for Eagle's arrest at the Jumping Bull ranch, where he was believed to live. Coincidentally or not, the ranch was also home to most of the Indians involved in the "secret AIM project," including Dennis Banks. (Aquash, though, lived in a trailer a few miles up the road, perhaps because she was out of favor.) When Agents Ron Williams and Jack Coler saw the red truck on June 26, they radioed the FBI dispatcher in Rapid City that they were going to pursue it. They did so at a good clip—the Indians in the truck were clearly aware the unmarked cars were tailing them—and when the truck pulled off the highway into the Jumping Bull ranch, the agents followed. The truck continued down a dirt road, over a low ridge, and into a small valley, where it stopped next to a smattering of outbuildings. At about that moment, or perhaps a little before, Agent Williams radioed to base, "It looks like these guys are going to shoot at us."

He did not say what made it look that way. Possibly someone in the moving truck stuck a gun out a window. Possibly after the truck stopped, its occupants took up defensive positions, guns in hand. Certainly on Wilson's Pine Ridge most AIMers carried weapons, and most of them, on being chased by two unmarked cars, would probably have brandished their arms. Whatever the case, the agents stopped their cars on a treeless expanse of bottomland, a respectful distance from the Indians, and a shot was fired. Countless analyses would follow, but the author of the shot, whether agent or Indian, was never discovered. Williams and Coler stepped out of their cars, naked but for the cover the cars afforded, and the Indians from the truck scurried behind buildings and trees. They were quickly reinforced by AIMers whose camp lay just over the next ridge and whose peace had been disturbed by the gunfire. The firefight began in earnest.

"We got a problem here," Williams radioed to Rapid City. "We are in a little valley in Oglala, South Dakota, pinned down in a crossfire between two houses." He asked for backup and was told it was already en route in the form of agents only a few miles away.

The radio was silent for a minute, then Williams came back on the air, his plea more urgent: "Get to the high ground and give us some covering fire!"

There was more silence, then, "Hurry up and get here, or we are going to be dead men!"

At about this time, a BIA police officer and an FBI agent arrived at the ranch from separate directions on Highway 18. But as they approached the top of the first ridge, they came under a hail of fire, and each car had a tire shot out. They were forced to make a zigzagging retreat in reverse to the highway. The FBI agent, Gary Adams, radioed

Williams that he hadn't been able to top the rise and so couldn't see him in the valley below.

"Keep coming!" Williams begged. "I'm down here!"

Several more minutes passed before Williams came back to his handset and panted faintly, "I'm hit."

They were his last recorded words.

Peter Matthiessen later made an exhaustive investigation of what happened during the shootout, which formed the heart of his 1983 book *In the Spirit of Crazy Horse.* Matthiessen concluded (as did the FBI) that after Coler and Williams stopped their cars on the valley floor, Coler went to his trunk, got out a rifle, and crouched behind the trunk to trade fire with the AIMers. Almost immediately an incoming bullet passed through the trunk lid, splayed like shrapnel, and nearly tore off his right arm. He may have tried to get a tourniquet on the shredded bicep, or shock may have overcome him almost instantly. In either case, the artery bled clean and he passed out. Williams meanwhile was returning fire from behind his door with a handgun, an ineffective weapon across the hundred-yard gap between him and his adversaries. Over the next several minutes, he sustained several wounds, none of which was fatal. At some point he recognized the futility of his situation, cast his gun aside, and took off his shirt to stanch the bleeding from Coler's arm. Probably by the time he did so, Coler was dead or near enough to it that his efforts were moot. The AIMers approached. Who and how many they were are still unknown, but among them were Leonard Peltier, Dino Butler, and Bob Robideau— the same trio who had interrogated Aquash in New Mexico a few weeks before. The FBI later said that as the AIMers drew near, Williams begged for his and Coler's lives and, that failing, begged on behalf of their families. It was an unprovable but not unreasonable guess. One of the AIMers put a high-powered rifle to Williams's forehead, pulled the trigger, and scattered his brain about the valley floor. When the FBI later recovered his body, the fingers of his right hand were found to be nearly severed, suggesting he had raised them before his face in a final, futile gesture of self-defense. A similar coup de grâce, probably superfluous, was fired into the head of the prone Coler.

The AIMers searched the agents, took their guns, and moved one of their cars into the woods to listen on the police radio to the urgent talk about the response being assembled against them. It was massive. A BIA SWAT team was on maneuvers near Oglala that day, and its members were quickly directed to the Jumping Bull ranch. Other BIA officers and FBI agents descended from the nearby town of Pine Ridge. Goons arrived. Roadblocks were set up. A spotter plane was sent aloft. The AIMers—maybe fifteen or twenty in number (Dennis Banks, incidentally, was elsewhere that afternoon)—decided to make a break through a wooded creekbed with two of their number left behind to cover them. One of the rearguard, Joe Killsright Stuntz, took a federal bullet between the eyes and fell lifeless, but not before buying his friends' escape: the police had yet to cinch their cordon around the ranch, and as they exchanged shots with Stuntz and the other AIMer, the rest of the AIMers slipped through a gap and into the surrounding hills, where they were covered by the falling night. From there they made their way to friends' houses.

Within hours of the first shots, the FBI's Joseph Trimbach was back on Pine Ridge, this time with a sniper team from Minneapolis. A forty-man SWAT team was also flying in from Washington, agents and arms were coming from Denver and Chicago, and a chemical-warfare team was being assembled. By the next day, Trimbach had a force of two hundred agents, dressed in camouflage, armed to the marrow, with armored personnel carriers at their backs and planes and helicopters overhead. This was the same FBI that only a few months before, when the WKL-DOCkers had been beaten at the airport and the police had abandoned their station to the goon mob, claimed to be a mere investigative agency, not a law enforcer of the policing and arrest-making variety. Trimbach's FBI militia was supplemented by imported BIA police, U.S. marshals, and state troopers, the last flown from Pierre under the personal command of Attorney General Bill Janklow, who, as at Yankton, had no authority for an incursion on an Indian reservation but was making good on his promise that the law was irrelevant.

Trimbach, Janklow, and other authorities justified their overwhelming response by telling reporters, who uncritically told the public, that the agents had been led into a "cold-blooded ambush" that had been mounted by AIM "guerrillas" from "sophisticated bunkers" and "fortifications." After wounding the agents, the guerrillas had "taken them from their cars" and "stripped them to their waists." As Williams pleaded on behalf of Coler's young wife and child, the killers "shot [them] repeatedly in their heads" and "riddled" their bodies "with machine-gun bullets." Nearly all of the details were bunkum. In truth, the AIMers were as unprepared for the "ambush" as the agents, the "bunkers" were root cellars, the "fortifications" were rickety outbuildings, and the AIMers had no machine guns.

"It is patently clear," the U.S. Commission on Civil Rights concluded, "that many of the statements [from officials] that have been released regarding the incident are either false, unsubstantiated, or directly misleading." USCCR fingered the FBI and Janklow for most of the manipulation. ("Sobsisters," Janklow said of his critics. "They excuse these crimes as some type of social disorder. They're soft on the Indians just because they're a minority group.") The *Columbia Journalism Review*, dean of media watchers, agreed with USCCR's assessment but also piled scorn on the reporters who parroted the official propaganda without verification.

But such re-evaluations came later, and from out of state. At the time in lower Dakota the outrage against AIM over the killings was undiluted, which left the federal government and Dick Wilson free to do as they wished.

Said Wilson, "The Oglalas don't like what happened. And if the FBI don't get 'em, the Oglalas will."

"What do you mean?" a reporter asked.

"Just what I said. We have our own way of punishing people that way."

"Shooting on the reservation?"

"You said it. We'll take care of 'em."

The manhunt for the agents' killers spread across Pine Ridge house by house. Its methods were not subtle. At the home of Wallace Little, age seventy-five, twelve vans unloaded a posse of fifty agents and police officers in battle dress. Little asked to see a search warrant, which they could not produce, so he ordered them off his property. The posse told him to get the hell out of the way and ransacked his house. They found nothing.

James Brings Yellow of Oglala, who had been in ill health, was likewise trespassed upon. The stress of the incursion sent him to the hospital, where he died a few days later.

USCCR condemned the "full-scale military-type invasion," which would have been obscene in any circumstances but which was all the worse given the FBI's years of apathy toward murdered Indians. USCCR said the trampling on civil liberties "would not be tolerated in any non-Indian community in the United States," which was mostly right: New Rochelle and New Canaan would not have tolerated it; New Haven and Newark were another story. Kevin McKiernan later discovered that from 1973 to 1976 the FBI sent 2,600 personnel (agents and support staff) through its Rapid City office, which had a normal complement of fewer than a dozen agents. Pine Ridge, with a population of not quite 15,000, had been turned into an FBI proving ground—a boot camp, in the words of a senior agent in Rapid City—in a way that no other community in the country had endured before or has since.

Congress saw no evil. A few years earlier, the Senate had created a committee to investigate the many abuses by the FBI and CIA that were coming to light in the press. The Church Committee, so named for its chairman Frank Church, turned its attention to the FBI's penetration of AIM after Doug Durham was outed in the spring of 1975. Hearings were scheduled for that summer. But after the killings at Oglala in June, the committee postponed the hearings. The senators explained that they did not want to interfere with the FBI's investigation on Pine Ridge. No doubt they also feared looking as if they were coddling the agents' killers. That the FBI might have contributed to the agents' deaths—by its support for Wilson, its riddling of

AIM with operatives, and its recent escalations on Pine Ridge—either did not occur to the Church Committee or, perhaps, seemed too nuanced an argument to reduce to a sound bite. Whatever the committee's motive, by the time the FBI caught the killers of Agents Williams and Coler, Congress's interest in intelligence abuses had waned, and the hearings on how the FBI had undermined AIM were never held.

Anna Mae Aquash was not in Oglala on the day of the shootout. She had left the day before, June 25, for Cedar Rapids, Iowa, where Leonard Crow Dog and two other leaders of Wounded Knee, Carter Camp and Stan Holder, had been convicted in one of the government's rare trial victories over the occupiers. Aquash had planned to speak at a rally for the three AIMers, but when she heard about the shootout she immediately returned to Pine Ridge. It took her no time to find her fugitive friends in hiding on the reservation.

"I'm never gonna leave you guys again," she told them, and she was true to her word.

The FBI quickly compiled a list of the AIMers who frequented the Jumping Bull ranch where the shootout occurred. From that list, the FBI distilled a second roll of people who were probably present on the day of the shootout. Aquash was not on the second list, but she was on the first and so was among those whom the FBI badly wanted to find. Candy Hamilton, the friend of Aquash who would stand watch at her autopsy, later said, "One day in July of '75, Annie Mae and I were here in Oglala at the house where the defense committee's office was. The FBI pulled up— they weren't hard to spot in their fancy cars and camouflage—and Annie Mae took one look at them and went right up into the little crawl space in the attic. I told somebody, 'Go get a car and get Annie Mae.' I forget who it was drove up for her. But when they did, some guys distracted the FBIs, yelling and hollering. We used to yell at them, they'd yell back—it was like a ritual. While they were being distracted, Annie Mae walked out of the house, got in the car, and they drove off. We didn't know at the time that it was Annie Mae they were looking for. But we found out later that at the same time a bunch of agents were over in the housing going door to door asking for Annie Mae.

"The episode was important because even though she avoided them, it made her look bad, which served the FBI well. All the people who had been at the shootout couldn't testify about it. They would have been indicted for murder just for looking out a window during the shooting. So they're all in hiding, and the FBI is going around saying these people at Jumping Bull's were getting ready to unleash Armageddon. Annie Mae was the most articulate person who was in that group who was not at the shootout. At trial she could have said that what the people at Jumping Bull's were really doing was standing up for treaty rights and planting gardens. She could also talk about all the harassment from the FBI. So here would be this tiny, beautiful woman who's so clear and smart, laying this all out for a jury. You don't think that didn't keep the FBI awake some nights? Clearly they never thought they were going to lose one of those trials from the shootout, but still they didn't need any super-good witnesses. If suspicions were raised about Annie Mae and somebody got her out of the way, so much the better."

Aquash kept a low profile through July. In early August she went to Crow Dog's Paradise on the Rosebud Reservation for the annual sun dance, the weeklong rite of regeneration through sacrifice that in Indian Country was akin to Easter in purpose and Christmas in importance. At gatherings of AIMers, even spiritual ones, the group's leaders tended to go through Pabst and pot like old Cadillacs through oil. Aquash was an exception, having given up alcohol the year before on the belief that leadership in AIM demanded rectitude. Usually she kept her disapproval of her colleagues' carousing to herself. But after the shootout at Oglala, when every law enforcer in West River was looking for a reason to raid an AIM camp, and when one drunk driver or one drug tip could give them all the excuse they needed, Aquash told a besotted Russell Means that his carrying on was practically suicidal. She told a wobbly Leonard Crow Dog that he had

all the dignity of a pickled pope. Neither man took the criticism construc-
tively. Crow Dog called her an informer and ordered her off his land. The
epithet *informer* had become common in AIM, often said in heat but
seldom literally meant, a bit like *motherfucker* or *cocksucker*. But Aquash's
recent interrogation by Peltier gave Crow Dog's insult unusual gravity, and
the whispers about her grew louder. She left Crow Dog's for a camp just
down the road, on the property of Diane and Al Running, Crow Dog's
sister and brother-in-law. For the next several weeks she seems to have
alternated between the Runnings' place and her trailer in Oglala.

"She was scared of everybody," her friend Geraldine Janis later said of
this period. "She never did tell me why. All she said was, 'I don't trust
nobody.' She lived all alone out there [in Oglala]. I'd bring her to my house
so she could take a shower, or I'd drive her to town for food and cigarettes.
She was too scared to go alone."

She was camped at the Runnings' in the early morning of September 5,
1975, when she was awakened by a shout of "FBI! Come out of the tent!"
When she unzipped the flap and crawled out, Agent David Price was
standing over her.

A series of confrontations had preceded Price's arrival at Aquash's campsite.
A week earlier, Frank Running, the teenage son of Al and Diane Running
and nephew of Crow Dog, was allegedly beaten by two men, Robert Beck
and William McCloskey. If WKLDOC was right, Beck and McCloskey
were seen fraternizing with FBI agents shortly thereafter. A few nights later
the two men and their wives descended boisterously on Crow Dog's place
and demanded that young Frank be handed over. Instead, the intruders
were taken prisoner by Crow Dog and the Runnings. If the government is
right, Crow Dog and Al and Frank Running beat Beck and McCloskey
severely and made them sign statements confessing various crimes. After
being let go, one of the victims had to be "hospitalized with broken back,
jaw, and severe facial injuries."

AIMers found the government's claims preposterous. Crow Dog, they said, was a medicine man, a pacifist who never carried a gun and would never have let such an event take place in his presence. But while Crow Dog was indeed religious and gunless, he was no pacifist. He had once been convicted of menacing a suspected informer with a chainsaw, and he regularly and fiercely beat his wife Mary. The claims of Beck and McCloskey may or may not have been true, but they were at least plausible. It was also plausible, as AIM speculated, that the FBI had sent Beck and McCloskey to Crow Dog's to provoke an assault. Certainly once the assault was committed, the FBI used it as a pretense to mount a raid far out of proportion to the alleged crime. Not forty-eight hours after Beck and McCloskey limped into the hospital, a hundred FBI agents on foot, in helicopters, and in inflatable rafts swept down on the riparian homesteads of Crow Dog and the Runnings.

David Price was one of the raiders. He later reported that after he entered the Running property, he came upon a good-sized tent and shouted for its occupants to come out. There was a fair amount of rustling before a lone woman emerged. She made no immediate impression on him. He asked her to identify herself, and she said she was Anna Mae Pictou, at which point he remembered that he had interviewed her five months earlier about Jeanette Bissonette's murder. He asked her more questions about the murder, but she said she knew nothing and refused to talk.

AIM's version of their meeting, which seems to have come mainly from Aquash (though perhaps there were other witnesses too), was rather different: Price recognized her instantly, shouting, "You! I've been looking everywhere for you!" As it happened, Price *was* looking for her. At least, FBI documents later showed that he had a photograph of her, and since Aquash was among those the FBI most wanted to find, and since Price was the only agent who had ever met her, and since he was deeply, emotionally involved in the murder investigation of his slain friends, it would have been odd if he had *not* been assigned to search for Aquash. Minimally he would have refreshed his memory about her. Probably he later claimed not to have recognized her because he didn't want people to think he had also recognized her when she turned up dead at Roger Amiotte's ranch several months later.

Price directed Aquash to stand in a row of other AIMers while the FBI searched the camp. In a statement recorded by Candy Hamilton a week later, Aquash said of the agents, "They were all over the place, dumping things and just tearing things apart. I could hear things crashing inside the house, falling off, breaking or smashing. I could hear comments coming from them from inside: 'Oh, look at *this*.' They would laugh at something. They seemed to be having an awful lot of fun. They emptied medicine bags and threw about medicine pipes and confiscated eagle feathers and varieties of beadwork and those objects that are used in sacred ceremonies. . . .

"I have seen that there is something that is disturbing the agents very much. There is something wrong somewheres. It is not only the raid that they seemed to be interested in. There were a lot of other things about Indian people in general that they are very, very concerned with. I think they most definitely want to destroy the Indian nation if it will not be subdued to the living condition of a so-called reservation. They definitely are out to destroy our concept of freedom."

Other AIMers told similar stories. One said he was interrogated with an M-16 held to his head. Dino Butler, a prime suspect in the killings at Oglala, said the agent who arrested him didn't know who he was until one of his comrades said, "Hey, you know who you got there? That's fucking Dino Butler. Why did you take him alive?"

"Did he have a gun on him?" another agent asked.

"A forty-five, loaded," the arresting agent said.

"You should have shot the son of a bitch right there."

Butler said that on the hour-long drive to the FBI office in Pierre he was repeatedly threatened with death. He arrived sound of body but not necessarily of mind.

In his search of Aquah's tent, Price found a sawed-off M-1 carbine, loaded and with the serial number obliterated; three hand grenades filled with shrapnel; and a "brown 'government type' briefcase" containing five bundles of dynamite, thirty sticks per bundle, each neatly tied with red yarn. The FBI lab later analyzed the briefcase and concluded that "a human hair found therein appears to have identical characteristics of one located on the hairbrush used by deceased S[pecial] A[gent] JACK R. COLER." Price told Aquash she was under arrest for possession of illegal weapons and asked if she was a Canadian citizen. She replied that she was a Native American. He retorted that she'd be back in Canada before the day was out. He tried several times to get her to talk about AIM and the shootout at Oglala, but she said nothing.

When he left her to rejoin the search, Aquash said to a friend standing with her, "You know what that guy said to me? He said that it was AIM leadership that killed Buddy and Frank at Wounded Knee. The man's crazy! He's just trying to start trouble."

Price, no doubt, was trying to start trouble. But although he was wrong that AIM had killed Buddy Lamont and Frank Clearwater at Wounded Knee (both were shot by government men), he may have known something about a similar event at Wounded Knee that AIM would just as soon have kept buried.

After being driven to Pierre, Aquash was interviewed by two FBI agents, Fred Coward and Jeanette Morgan, the latter one of the FBI's tiny female minority. (J. Edgar Hoover had fired the few female agents when he took over the Bureau in the 1920s and thereafter barred women from contaminating his agent rolls—his secretarial rolls were another matter. Only on his death in 1972 were women again permitted to become agents.) Agents Coward and Morgan later reported that they asked Aquash what she knew about the killings at Oglala and that she said she had nothing to say—she had been in Cedar Rapids that day. They suggested, although they knew otherwise, that she had been in Oglala. She said she had not. They asked again what she knew of the shootings, and again she said she knew nothing. They moved on to harmless topics like her background, then circled back to Oglala. Again she pled ignorance. The interview continued in this vein for half an hour until, after yet another question about the shootings,

> PICTOU put her head down on the desk to which she was sitting at and did not reply to the question. PICTOU advised at this point that "you can either shoot me or throw me in jail as those are the two choices that I am taking." PICTOU was asked specifically what she meant by this to which she replied "that's what your [sic] going to do with me anyway." PICTOU was advised by the interviewing Agents that they had been very cooperative, polite, and had responded to her personal requests for cigarettes, coffee, and the use of the bathroom and this was certainly not a display or attitude to which she indicated that the Agents would do.

The agents wrote that Aquash then requested an attorney, and they immediately ended the interview, as law required, and had her booked into the county jail, whereupon she was allowed her statutory phone call.

But Aquash told Candy Hamilton quite a different story. She said she had demanded to see a lawyer even before the interview began—which would have been more in keeping with her shrewdness—but "the agent told me that I could not make my call unless I talked to him first. I told him they can't do that.

"He said, 'You know, you're not going to get a call through unless you talk to us first.' He said, 'I want to talk to you about an incident that happened in Oglala on June 26 where two men were killed.'

"I told him, 'Three.'

"He said, 'Okay, three,' but he was a bit unnerved by my referring to the fact that there were three rather than two."

Aquash said she continued to ask for a lawyer but was refused until she put her head down on the table and told the agents to kill her or jail her. She also told Hamilton and other friends that in addition to the interview with Agents Coward and Morgan, she had another with David Price. Price's interview occurred much more informally; apparently he spoke to her while she was awaiting questioning by Coward and Morgan. (There appears to be no record in Aquash's FBI file of an interview by Price in Pierre.)

"Price tried to get her to roll over," said John Trudell, Aquash's friend who served for several years as AIM's chairman and chief spokesman. "What she told me was that he knew she had been having custody problems with her kids, and he didn't have anything else on her. So he tried to get her to become an informer by telling her that he could help her get her kids and give her a new identity and money and that kind of crap if she would cooperate. She told him to go fuck himself, which was when he said he would see her dead within a year." (Price, again, has denied these claims.)

The bail for Aquash and several of her colleagues, including Butler, Crow Dog, and Al Running, was set at $5,000 apiece—not an extravagant sum, but far more than any of them had. AIM and WKLDOC were by this time starved of cash, and it appeared that all of them would sit in jail for quite a while.

"But I went before the magistrate," Aquash told Hamilton, "and he made a statement that I had been indicted, and my lawyer said, 'No, she has *not* been indicted.' The magistrate was really surprised. He looked at the—the prosecutor, I think you call him; I know he's not on my side—and asked him, 'She hasn't been indicted?' And he said, 'Oh, no.' Evidently that made a totally different circumstance because he [the magistrate] said, 'Well, we can release her on ten percent of her bond.' "

It still took four days for her friends to raise the $500 to free her. But her release was swift compared to that of her jailmates, who had all been indicted before the raid on other charges (mostly related to the Beck-McCloskey beating) and were not eligible for bond reduction. They sat in jail for weeks. Aquash's quick emancipation drew suspicion to her again. Had the FBI wanted to keep her in jail, her doubters said, it could have made sure she was promptly indicted. Perhaps agents hoped she would lead them—wittingly or not—to one of the suspects still at large for the killings at Oglala. In later years AIM would be ridiculed for suspecting someone as devoted as Aquash of cracking in Pierre. Critics said AIM should have considered that Aquash's indictment was tardy simply because she was less important than the likes of Dino Butler or because the FBI and U.S. attorney's office were incompetent. Either supposition might have been true. But so too were AIM's concerns that a loyalist had cracked—although as it happened, Aquash was not the one. Al Running, threatened with a long sentence for beating Beck and McCloskey, turned informer either while jailed in Pierre or immediately after. Like Aquash, he was released before his cellmates on light bond, but with less justification than she since he had already been indicted. If his release did not attract the suspicion that Aquash's did, it was probably because he was an in-law of Crow Dog and so theoretically beyond reproach.

On her release from jail, Aquash called her sisters in Canada and, speaking in Mi'kmaq to foil wiretappers, said, "These men that are in the woods all over this place want to kill me, if the FBI don't get me first." She did not explain who "these men" were. Her sisters urged her to come home, but she said she couldn't desert the Oglalas, whom she had come to love. "If you could see the people, the way they're treated here, you'd understand."

A few days later, Aquash drove from Rapid City to Denver and from there flew with Nilak Butler, Dino's wife, to Los Angeles. They were arrested as they stepped off the plane. FBI documents would later show that the FBI had been tipped to their arrival by the man who chauffeured them to Denver, John Stewart, alias Darryl Blue Lake. (Not long later, Stewart allegedly drained the checking account of a WKLDOC affiliate in Oglala and disappeared.) In Los Angeles the FBI was less interested in Aquash than in Butler, who had been at the Jumping Bulls' during the firefight and was still a fugitive. She was interrogated and jailed for two weeks before making bail, while Aquash was questioned only briefly at the airport and released. (Aquash apparently refused to tell the FBI anything, but again the FBI declines to make the record of her interview public.) There was a legal rationale for Aquash's speedy release: she had not violated the terms of her bond, either by traveling to California or by being in the company of a fugitive whom she was not trying to hide, and no new charges had been levied against her. But once again she had been cut loose while others sat in jail, and clearly someone in AIM had tipped the FBI to her and Butler's arrival. Suspicion fell on Aquash once more.

The suspicion was all the greater because Dennis Banks and Leonard Peltier were in Los Angeles at that moment. By then both men were fugitives hotly sought by the FBI: Peltier for killing the agents at Oglala, Banks for skipping a sentencing hearing a few weeks earlier, after Bill Janklow convicted him of rioting at Custer. It did not help Aquash that the reason Banks and Peltier were in Los Angeles was to raise money for arms to strike back at the government. AIMers wondered if Aquash was supposed to lead the FBI to the two leaders while they performed this delicate errand. Decades later, documents released by the FBI would show that agents did indeed know Banks and Peltier were in California and hoped for Aquash's (unwitting) help in finding them: "SA CORDOVA will attempt to surveil or otherwise monitor AQUASH's whereabouts to determine if she has knowledge regarding the whereabouts of BANKS or PELTIER."

Aquash stayed in Los Angeles for a month under the watchful eyes of informers. Her sole purpose, the informers noted, was to raise bail money and publicity for her colleagues imprisoned in Pierre—above all, for her accuser Leonard Crow Dog and her one-time assistant interrogator Dino Butler. The work was wearying, often demeaning, and nearly always unsuccessful, which did not deter the moles from spying on her minutely. In one instance Aquash organized a protest that drew only a dozen protesters, but a spy noted solemnly, "It has been determined that ███ allegedly made up all the posters used at the demonstration: 'How much more blood must flow? As long as the grass shall grow,' 'President Ford, isn't it time you met your landlord?' "

Banks and Peltier found more success in California. They visited actor Marlon Brando, who gave them a motor home and $10,000, and they immediately invested part of the windfall in ten rifles. As the FBI had hoped, Aquash did rendezvous with them, but apparently she wasn't tailed. At least, the FBI has released no record to that effect. In early October, Banks, Peltier, and Aquash returned to Pine Ridge, by some accounts traveling together for part of the trip, by other accounts traveling separately the entire time.

On arriving in South Dakota, Aquash was given a letter from the court-appointed lawyer who was defending her on her weapons charges, Robert Riter. She hated the man. "She doesn't trust him," an informer told the FBI, "because he tried to get her to plead guilty on one point and then he would get her off on another." Riter's letter memorialized the plea bargain: Aquash would testify against Dino and Nilak Butler for killing the agents, the government would drop the more severe of her two weapons charges, and she would plead guilty to the lesser one. She scoffed and gave the letter to a friend, Dorothy Brings Him Back, who was, incidentally, the estranged wife of informer John Stewart.

"If you think it's important," Aquash told her, "keep it."

Brings Him Back apparently did, to Aquash's regret.

Early on the morning of Columbus Day 1975, Pine Ridge awoke to the blasts of bombs. The BIA office building, the tribal law enforcement building, and the local power plant were all damaged. As bombings go, the damage was mild: cubby-sized holes were blown in the walls of the buildings, windows were shattered, parts of town briefly lost power. The bombs had been set to explode at a time when no one was present, so no one was injured. AIM fingered Dick Wilson. Wilson fingered AIM.

"If any more AIM members, or any others, come onto this reservation bearing arms," he said, "they will be taking their lives into their own hands. I grew up on law and order, and I am a law-abiding citizen; however, I have given up on the so-called law and order we have had and am taking the law into my own hands."

That day or soon after, Marlon Brando's motor home headed northwest from Pine Ridge in a caravan with a couple of cars. Aboard were Aquash, Peltier, Dennis Banks, his wife Kamook Banks, their young child, Kamook's sister Bernie Nichols, and a few others. A week and a half later they stopped on the far side of Puget Sound on the Port Madison Reservation, where AIMers John and Nancy Chiquiti took them in.

Years later Bob Robideau said of this period, "We decided that the time had come for armed resistance against the oppression on Pine Ridge, and this time it wasn't going to be no Wounded Knee. We planned to take over the whole reservation, put in the traditional Oglala leaders, and those leaders agreed. A small group could handle it if it was done right, and we had accumulated about thirty people, which was enough to take out the police station, the courthouse, all the seats of authority; after that, we would set up roadblocks. That was going to happen as soon as we had sufficient armament and equipment. But we had an untrained and undisciplined group, with too many leaders, and things started to break down. One group split away in Colorado; then some of our Chicano volunteers got killed in a big fight down there among themselves. By the time we headed north from Colorado, we were back down to our original group and Dennis." (Robideau was not with the group that went to Puget Sound—he had gone on an errand in a different direction and was arrested when his ammunition-laden car exploded in Kansas.)

Once the AIMers reached the Chiquitis' place in Washington, they put out a call for explosives and weapons. By and by, friends came to Port Madison with two hundred sticks of dynamite and ten assault rifles. The AIMers judged this armory, together with the rifles they had bought in Los Angeles, sufficient to seize a reservation the size of Connecticut and hold it, come what may, against the United States of America. They needed only to re-form their army to carry out the plan. All things considered, the insurrectionists were fortunate that insurrection in their own ranks spared them this suicide.

While they were in the Northwest, Aquash missed a pretrial hearing on her weapons charges. She had called WKLDOC beforehand to ask about court appearances in Pierre and was told either that she had no hearing or that she had one but did not need to attend—wrong in either case. When she failed to show, a judge issued a bench warrant for her arrest and she became, for the first time in her life, a federal fugitive. Four days later, on November 14, the AIMers left the Chiquitis for their Pine Ridge reckoning. They were influenced in their departure by the appearance of a small airplane that passed over the Chiquiti compound two days in a row. The AIMers took the plane, correctly, for FBI reconnaissance. It was later revealed that the FBI had also sent agents sneaking through the woods around the compound to record the license plates of the motor home and the other cars. It remains a mystery why the FBI did not arrest the lot of them then and there. The Bureau knew Banks and Peltier were in the group, and their status as wanted fugitives had only increased since their trip to Los Angeles. Banks later claimed that the FBI let them go because it wanted to ambush them either while they were en route to or after they had arrived on Pine Ridge. His theory is plausible, but there is little evidence to support it.

The AIMers drove south to Portland, then east across northern Oregon. At ten o'clock that night, as they approached the Idaho line, a police car pulled behind the motor home and signaled for it to stop. Earlier that day the FBI had issued an all-points bulletin describing the caravan, noting that its occupants were armed and dangerous, and directing any officer who saw the AIMers not to stop them but to alert the FBI to their whereabouts. Oregon State Patrolman Ken Griffiths had only skimmed the bulletin and missed the crucial word *not*. As the motor home pulled to the side of the road, Griffiths pulled behind it, and a station wagon in the caravan that Griffiths had not noticed till then stopped about a hundred yards behind him. A third car in the caravan drove on. Griffiths stepped out of his car, shotgun in hand, and walked to the right rear bumper of the motor home. He hollered for the occupants to come out. Leonard Peltier was the first to emerge, followed by Aquash, Kamook Banks, and the Bankses' eighteen-month-old daughter. "There was quite a bit of milling about of these subjects," Griffiths later wrote, "with the male yelling, 'Watch the women and children.' " He asked if anyone was still inside but received no answer. Griffiths asked again, still with no answer.

"Answer me, goddamnit! Anyone else still in there?"

"No," Peltier finally said.

But hardly was the syllable spoken than, as Griffith recalled, "The backup lights of the motor home came on, the vehicle backed up a very short distance, and at the very same time the motor home sped off and the male suspect [Peltier] jumped over the right-of-way fence, while using the women and children as a shield. As the male was in the act of clearing the fence, writer observed a flash coming from him, then heard the report of a small calibre firearm. The women and child scurried north from this location toward the parked station wagon. As the male subject had cleared the fence and was fleeing into the darkness, writer fired two rounds toward the suspect with the shotgun, evidently causing no problem to the suspect, as he fled the area, not to be seen again."

AIMers later derided Griffiths's account, which required first that Peltier had fired on a patrolman he knew to be armed, second that he had done so while scaling a fence, third that he had used women and a child—*AIM* women and child—as cover, and fourth that Dennis Banks, at the wheel of the motor home, had abandoned his eight months' pregnant wife, his child, and his ex-lover to this melee. But in fact over the years the AIMers themselves, including Banks, would say that Griffiths had the story just about right. The only unresolved point was whether it was Peltier or Banks who had fired the shot. Banks said he had, but he was probably only trying to deflect blame from Peltier.

Banks abandoned the motor home a few miles down the road and fled on foot. The police who arrived minutes later found a small armory inside: seven fifty-pound cases of DuPont seventy-percent dynamite; dozens of blasting caps; yards of leg wire and detonation cord; guns in every cabinet and cranny, all with obliterated serial numbers; and six pocket watches with screws drilled into their faces so that their moving minute-hands, when they came into contact with the screws, could trigger bombs. None of this arsenal was registered, and one of the guns, the FBI lab later reported, "was examined and found to contain the [partial] serial number 622056 in two locations, which is the digit portion of the serial number of the .357 magnum Smith & Wesson, Model 19, revolver issued to SA JACK R. COLER."

As the manhunt for Banks and Peltier spread across five states and two Canadian provinces, Aquash, Nichols, and two AIMers who had been in the station wagon, Russ Redner and Kenny Loud Hawk, were jailed and assigned an unattainable bond of $100,000 apiece. The papers that federal prosecutors filed to indict them included an intriguing claim. The FBI, the papers said, had been tipped to the presence of the AIM caravan at the Chiquitis' by two informers, identified only as "Informant A and Informant B." (Hoover had insisted that his agents call informers *informants* because he thought it made them sound more like professionals and less like snitches.) According to the papers, Informer A had logged more than a hundred reports with the FBI. Informer B had logged twenty. Both were said to be reliable. The quantity of A and B's reports implied that they were long-time informers. Many senior AIMers presumed that one or both had been—*must* have been—inside the caravan. The presumption, while predictable amid the COINTELPRO-inspired paranoia, was foolish because the caravanners had been quite bold in their movements: they had held a celebratory clambake on their arrival at the Chiquitis', well-wishers had come and gone throughout their stay, Peltier, who used to live in Seattle, had gone out on the town with old friends, and Banks had even given a speech at a fundraising party. Any of a hundred people could have been A or B. But senior AIMers assumed A or B must have been close to the leaders, and their suspicions narrowed to Aquash. Her track had collided with the arrest of her colleagues too many times.

A reporter who interviewed her in jail later said, "Anna Mae only had one thing to tell me. She said, 'If they take me back to South Dakota, I'll be murdered.' " She did not say who her murderers would be.

She was less grim in a jailhouse letter to her sisters: "I'm sure that as soon as I return to South Dakota I will be harassed. I am sure I will be sent up. My efforts to raise the consciousness of whites who are so against Indians here in the states was bound to be stopped by the FBI sooner or later. But, no sweat, I'm Indian all the way and always will be. I'm not going to stop fighting until I die and I hope I am a good example of a human being and my tribe. I have the support of the American Indian Movement behind me and I have no worries. I feel great."

On November 22, 1975, Aquash was flown back to Pierre to be tried on her weapons charges. On November 24, the day before her trial, she appeared in front of Judge Robert Mehrige, a moderate from Virginia who had been imported to South Dakota to help with the backlog of AIM cases. Judge Mehrige asked Aquash why she had missed her earlier court date, and she told him about the wrong information WKLDOC had given her. Since coming to South Dakota, Mehrige had come to believe that the government was overzealous in its prosecution of Indians and alarmist about the threat they posed. He took Aquash at her word. And since neither she nor her colleagues had been indicted for the Oregon arrest (that would come a few days later), he set her free on her own recognizance. Even her lawyer was surprised by the judge's lenience.

That night, Aquash checked into the St. Charles Hotel with other AIMers, but at daybreak she was gone. When she did not appear at trial, a furious Mehrige issued a warrant for her arrest, and she became a fugitive for a second and final time. Her co-defendants, Nilak and Dino Butler, were tried on weapons charges without her and acquitted. (The government could not prove that the weapons attributed to the Butlers were theirs.) Had Aquash stayed, she probably would have been acquitted too. Why she left is not known. One of her sisters, Rebecca Julian, said that before Aquash was transferred from Oregon to Pierre, she had said "she would not run because whatever they blamed her for, she didn't do it, and running would only make her look guilty."

To AIMers, Aquash's latest deliverance was again inexplicable.

WKLDOC's Bruce Ellison, counsel for Dino and Nilak Butler, expressed the common fear in his diary: "We were all staying in the same adjoining rooms. We all knew that we were under extremely heavy surveillance everywhere we went. Well, somehow she made it out. Hopefully, she disappeared without being tailed."

But had she? And if so, how? And why had she been set free on her own recognizance in the first place? The woman kept slipping from the law in the unlikeliest of circumstances.

CHAPTER 11

IN 1976, THE bicentennial year of the American republic, Dick Wilson stood for reelection to an unprecedented third term as president of the Oglala Sioux Tribe. Russell Means, his rival from 1974, was preoccupied with various trials, so Wilson was opposed instead by a moderate named Al Trimble. Trimble had been the BIA superintendent on Pine Ridge when Wilson was first elected in 1972, but the two men had quickly run afoul of one another and the BIA had transferred Trimble to Albuquerque. He remained in exile for a time, but as the tribal election of 1976 drew near, he quit the BIA, announced he would challenge Wilson, and returned to Pine Ridge, an Oglala de Gaulle. After the scandalous 1974 election, the balloting in 1976 took place under the scrutiny of a large team of neutral observers. The vote, in consequence, was mostly free and fair, and Wilson, unaided by fraud, was outpolled.

The Wilsonites, however, did not depart quietly. Before Trimble was inaugurated, one of Wilson's lieutenants let it be known that the town of Wanblee, where the vote had run three to one in favor of Trimble, "needed straightening out." A more emphatic warning was given a few days later to an AIMer from Wanblee named Richard Lee Lamont.

"Richard Lee was in Pine Ridge," Charlie Abourezk, son of Senator Jim, said many years later, "and some of Wilson's goon squad accosted him—hit him in the back of the head, knocked him on the floor, and told him something to the effect of, 'You tell those AIM fuckers in Wanblee that we're coming out to get 'em.' Richard Lee came back to Wanblee and told us about it. This was two weeks before the incident with Byron."

The incident with Byron took place on January 31, 1976, a Saturday. It was the custom of goons from Pine Ridge to drive to Wanblee on weekends and socialize with like-minded relatives there. Irrigated with bootlegged beer, the gatherings usually lasted through the day and well into the night. On January 31, the party was held across the street from the house of Guy and Pearl Dull Knife, who were AIMers. Shortly before noon the Dull Knifes and their friend Byron DeSersa came home from their own beer run, and as they stepped out of the car, the goons shouted obscenities at them.

"In those days," Guy Dull Knife said much later, "people would shoot at each other for no reason, no reason at all. So we got out our guns—Byron had a twenty-two, and I had my sawed-off M-1—and went outside. When we did, the goons fired up in the air. We did too, then we ran in the house. That's when they opened up. The whole house got sprayed. Bullets and Sheetrock were flying everywhere. It was a wonder my dad wasn't killed. He was upstairs, but some guys rushed him down to the basement where the walls were cement. We were pinned down, couldn't go anywhere because so many rounds were coming at us. By the end of it, there were three hundred bullet holes in my house. You could see outside through the holes. Soon enough, the cops came charging into the house and arrested me."

The number of holes in Dull Knife's account might have enjoyed some inflation over the years, but most of the rest happened as he said. A possible exception is the matter of who fired first. The goons, for all their dubious reliability, later told the FBI with convincing consistency that Dull Knife had fired the first shot. The FBI, which was likewise untrustworthy on the day's events for reasons that will become clear, quoted one of Dull Knife's friends and Dull Knife's father—each plausibly—saying that Dull Knife had shot first. Yet even many of the goons conceded that Dull Knife had shot not at them but only up in the air, for which offense they had filled his house with lead. By all accounts, Byron DeSersa had fired no shots at all.

The police who arrested Guy and Pearl Dull Knife did so not because they concluded Guy had started the gunfight but because after arriving at the scene, they asked headquarters to check the Dull Knifes' police records and headquarters radioed back that both Dull Knifes had warrants outstanding for their arrest. The warrants had been issued for a charge no longer known and were of so pressing a nature that they had lain unserved for nearly a year and the Dull Knifes had never been told of them. But the police now found it expedient to serve them, and for good measure they seized Guy's gun and DeSersa's too, although the latter seems to have been both lawfully registered and unloaded.

"I came by during all this," Charlie Abourezk said, "and while I was talking with the police about what was going on, I noticed some activity kind of kitty-corner from Guy and Pearl's house. I think it was the home of Lonnie Bettelyoun and his sister, Shirley. They were Wilson supporters. The people were out in front of the house, fingering us and being pretty menacing. One guy had a rifle with a scope on it, and he was waving it at us right in front of the BIA police. They didn't even seem to care. So I said, 'You gonna do anything about those guys?' And one of the BIA cops said, 'Don't worry about it.' They were just arresting Guy and Pearl on those old warrants and taking them to Pine Ridge, and you could *see* the bullet holes in the front of their house."

The FBI later reported that the BIA officers did not even walk across the street to speak to the goons, let alone confiscate their guns. One officer explained his indifference by saying he could see only one gun among the people across the street.

After the police left, an AIMer named Webster Poor Bear ventured over to the goon house. "If you guys want to have a gunfight," the goons later quoted him, "we're next door with seventeen rifles." Chuck Richards accepted the challenge on behalf of the goons. Richards was the head of a clan so brutal, they were known as the Manson Family and he as Charlie

Manson. He suggested a change of location for the duel, and Poor Bear agreed to Interior Junction, a crossroads several miles west of town. That afternoon at the appointed time, a half dozen carloads of goons drove west to the junction (some AIMers probably drove there too, although this is less certain), but when they arrived they found two police cars parked there. Probably the police had been tipped to the shootout. The foiled goons drove back toward Wanblee but stopped short of town to see if any AIMers would pass by on their way back from the aborted shootout.

While this was going on, Byron DeSersa loaded four friends into his car and, in the story the friends later told, drove west from Wanblee to find another friend in the small community of Potato Creek. The site of the would-be shootout was on their route, and possibly DeSersa and friends were really headed there, but the evidence for this speculation is thin and the FBI did not believe it. Not finding their friend in Potato Creek, they turned around and drove back toward Wanblee and passed the goons loitering on the roadside just after sunset.

The goons gave chase. When DeSersa noticed them in his rearview mirror, he flattened the accelerator of his Grand Prix until he was driving eighty-five or ninety miles an hour, but his lead nonetheless melted steadily. At an S-curve a mile out of Wanblee, his transmission jammed in fourth gear, and by the time he got it unstalled, the first goon car, a large black sedan, had pulled alongside him.

"Get down!" someone in DeSersa's car shouted.

An instant later a gun roared from the black sedan. Three or four more shots followed in quick succession, and glass and metal exploded throughout the cabin of the Grand Prix. A cloud of smoke and debris swirled around everything.

"Oh Christ, man, I'm hit!" DeSersa screamed. "I'm hit bad!"

George Bettelyoun, sitting behind DeSersa, told him to stop the car. (Bettelyoun was of the same extended family as the goon Bettelyouns who lived across the street from the Dull Knifes; the Bettelyoun family, like many on Pine Ridge, was divided between AIM and goon.)

"I can't," DeSersa said. He was in tears. "I'm hit bad."

Lester Jack, sitting in the front passenger seat, urged DeSersa not to lose control, and this much DeSersa was able to do for his passengers. He kept the Grand Prix in its lane until it slowed of its own accord and coasted into the roadside ditch.

George Bettelyoun later said, "The black car that shot us up went past us and stopped. I was thinking they were going to come back and start shooting again. The other guys in our car, they got out and started running up the bank on the side of the road. I tried to get Byron out, but he said, 'I can't move. My leg—.' So I looked over the seat, and his leg was almost blew off. There was a hole in there right through the center. So I said, 'Get out. They're gonna kill you.' I knew they weren't shooting to play around after I seen that hole in his leg. So he crawled across the seat and got out the door, and I tried to help him up that bank. But he couldn't make it. He said, 'Go on.' So I just took off. It was all open country there. There's no cover whatsoever, just a fence line that the weeds are piled up on."

Bettelyoun, Jack, and a third passenger took refuge up the hill at the fence. The fourth passenger, a teenager, forsook the thin cover, sprinted over the long hill, and did not stop until he reached Wanblee. Meanwhile the rest of the goon caravan drove past DeSersa's ditched car, then one of their number U-turned and came back. As the car passed, a woman shouted at the prone AIMers, "That should teach you, you dirty fucking Indians!"—a not atypical insult in that era for an Indian with a lot of white blood to hurl at one with less. The goon car U-turned once more, passed the AIMers a final time, and drove on to Wanblee. In the coming months there would be disagreement about whether those in DeSersa's car were armed and, if so, whether they fired on the passing goons from the fence line. The goons said yes on both counts, DeSersa's passengers no. The FBI never found evidence of firing by the AIMers, and it seems unlikely that, had the AIMers been armed or firing, the goons would have made a second pass just to taunt them.

By the time the goons had driven away and the AIMers emerged from hiding, DeSersa was unconscious. Webster Poor Bear happened onto the scene, probably returning from the aborted shootout, and tied a tourniquet on the man who had taken the bullet meant for him. Then he sped into Wanblee to find a doctor, the lone clinic being closed on Saturday evenings. The rest of the group loaded DeSersa into his Grand Prix but discovered that one of the goons' rounds had hit the fuse panel and disabled the headlights. Night had fallen on the unlit road, and DeSersa's friends were forced to drive at a crawl, doors ajar, watching for the highway lines by the dim cabin light. It was the longest mile of their lives. More bottomless minutes awaited them at the clinic before Poor Bear arrived with the doctor.

Bruce Pegram, MD, thought his patient was dead—he had no pulse in his carotid artery and no blood pressure—but he had him wheeled into the clinic anyway and on closer inspection noticed a faint heartbeat and rare, very shallow breaths. He bore down on the honeycombed flesh where DeSersa's right thigh had been, but the pressure proved unnecessary: DeSersa had no blood left to bleed. Another doctor arrived and together they tried to insert an intravenous line into DeSersa's arm, but his collapsed blood vessels made the job impossible. As they slashed open the arm in a desperate attempt to get a needle in, DeSersa went into cardiopulmonary arrest. In one of those ironies that would seem contrived were fact fiction, a BIA policeman who had arrived performed mouth-to-mouth resuscitation. The police force that would not protect him in life would try to revive him in death. The resuscitation failed, and DeSersa was pronounced dead at 6:10 p.m.

Mostly dead, that is. AIMers had assembled in the clinic's waiting room and were in a dark mood. They had beer on their breath, and at least one had a shotgun in hand. Dr. Pegram did not care to be around when they learned their friend was dead, so he packed the body into an ambulance and said that DeSersa needed attention only the hospital in Pine Ridge could offer. This, strictly speaking, was true: the hospital had the reservation's only morgue. While the ambulance was en route, a medic radioed the dispatcher that DeSersa's condition had worsened and he had died. The transmission was heard over the many police scanners on the reservation, and to this day, most of DeSersa's friends think he died in the ambulance.

At the morgue in Pine Ridge the body was kept under guard until midnight, when it was transferred for autopsy to the pathological firm of Brown and Armstrong in Scottsbluff. This was three weeks before W. O. Brown conducted his peculiar postmortem of Anna Mae Aquash. There is no sign that the police secured approval for the autopsy from DeSersa's wife. Dr. Alvin Armstrong concluded that DeSersa had been drinking but not drunk. His body, save for the wounds he had received that night, was normal and healthy. Armstrong described the incidental wounds as a half-inch-wide gash on the left forearm caused by a grazing bullet and two other superficial gashes across the top of both thighs caused by either a bullet or a metal fragment. The mortal injuries were to the right thigh, the worst being "a gaping, perforating wound that measured up to 25 mm [an inch] in diameter. Surrounding this were innumerable smaller irregularly sized and irregularly spaced penetrating wounds." Two missiles had passed through the leg entirely. Other fragments had lodged in the flesh. But although the damage was savage, months later Dr. Pegram of the Wanblee clinic would testify that DeSersa need not have died had pressure been applied to his leg in time. The extra minutes of drive-by menace from the goons were all that were required to bleed him to death.

Byron DeSersa was the great-grandson of medicine man Nicholas Black Elk, author of the book of wisdom *Black Elk Speaks*, and the son of Aaron DeSersa, publisher of *Crazy Horse News*. The latter was an anti-Wilson journal of irregular frequency, inventive grammar, and strong opinion on and off the editorial page. During Wounded Knee, Aaron DeSersa had been one of AIM's spokesmen outside the occupied village, and for his extravagant pronouncements, not always supported by fact, reporters had christened him Chief Sitting Bullshit. Many AIMers saw in Byron's murder an assassination—payback for his father's muckraking. But there was no truth to the theory. He was just the unfortunate who had stopped the bullet.

Like Anna Mae Aquash, Byron DeSersa was one of the few Indians of his generation to attend college and one of the many among those few who did not finish. Instead he matriculated in a study-abroad program in Vietnam, courtesy of the U.S. Army. He survived and returned to find work as an investigator in the legal aid office of the Rosebud Reservation. His boss was Bill Janklow. Several years after DeSersa's murder, Janklow claimed him for one of his informers inside AIM. But there has never been a jot of proof for the claim. Indeed, the evidence in DeSersa's FBI file contradicts Janklow at every turn. During the occupation of Wounded Knee, for example, DeSersa was a frequent *subject* of informers' reports. One mole whom DeSersa mistook for a friend snuck out of Wounded Knee with him, watched as he bought a rifle and bullets to take back inside, then wrote up the incident for the FBI. Another informer "described DECIRSA [sic] as the one who earlier during the siege of Wounded Knee had taken shots at the airplanes during flyovers."

After the armistice at Wounded Knee, DeSersa traveled to Seattle, where he soon wound up in a hospital bed with a hole in his head. The story he mumbled to the local police through a wired jaw was that he was visiting friends in West Seattle when a gun was tossed to him. It went off as he reached for it, the bullet passing through his cheek and exiting behind his right ear. The people who brought him to the hospital vouched for his story, and the police accepted it, but neither gun nor bullet was ever produced.

The FBI was not convinced. Informers, one of whom was almost certainly Gi or Jill Schafer, reported that DeSersa had gone to Washington to foment another Wounded Knee. The target, the informers said, was Frank's Landing, a village on the Nisqually Reservation where Indians were protesting violations of their fishing rights with growing success. One informer told the FBI that DeSersa was shot when a fight erupted over his mission. (The informer named the shooter, but the FBI to this day will not divulge the name.) FBI agents visited the bedridden DeSersa and suggested he was trying to beget another Wounded Knee. He mumbled that there would be more Wounded Knees but he was not trying to start one in Washington. He said little more, the agents left, and nothing came of the episode. Some months later, federal prosecutors dismissed charges that had been pending against him for alleged crimes at Wounded Knee, and the FBI and its informers lost interest in him. They did not pay DeSersa much heed again until he lay cold on a Pine Ridge gurney.

After firing the fatal shots, DeSersa's murderers drove back to their party in Wanblee and spilled out of the house into the yard and street. Richard Lee Lamont, the man waylaid by goons in Pine Ridge weeks before, lived down the block. He and a friend had the misfortune to step out of the house just then and drive away, and as they did, the goons fired on them with what Lamont guessed was twenty rounds. Two of the rounds struck the car, but Lamont and his friend escaped otherwise unscathed. It was not the first assault on the Lamonts that day. That afternoon, after the Dull Knifes' place was shot up, Chuck Richards had put a gun to the throat of Lamont's wife Amelia and said if he couldn't kill her husband, he would kill her. Friends had dragged Richards away. Amelia Lamont did not think reporting the incident to police would do any good and so did not. Richard Lee did not think reporting the latest shooting would do any good either, so he and his friend continued to the high school gym in Wanblee to watch a basketball tournament where, for a few hours anyway, they might forget the madness around them. They were not there long when a neighbor arrived and said the police had come to the Lamonts' house and wanted to talk to Richard Lee. He drove home, but no sooner did he step from his car than he was fired on by the goons. He fled to a cluster of four police cars.

"They were still shooting," Lamont later told Kevin McKiernan, "and the policeman just told me to get the hell out of there 'cuz they were shooting at me."

Why, McKiernan asked, would a policeman say such a thing?

"He was scared," Lamont said. "He didn't want to get out and do anything about it. So I ran right behind the cop car and hid because they were still shooting. And then he told me to get out of his way too. He probably would have ran over me if I didn't."

All four of the police cars sped off and left Lamont to find his own cover. The FBI would eventually decide that Lamont was telling the truth about the episode. But the FBI noted that Lamont had been unable to identify the shooter or to prove with certainty that he was the intended victim of the shots. To the discerning minds of the FBI, these facts negated the responsibility of the police to act, or even to stick around.

About this time, Charlie Abourezk returned to Wanblee from Pine Ridge, where he had bailed out Guy and Pearl Dull Knife. He found the village in anarchy. "These guys who killed Byron knew the BIA cops weren't doing anything to approach them, so they were fearless. A lot more BIA were called in. I don't remember how many units, but more than we'd ever seen before." One observer counted eighteen police cars. "They were at the entrances to the housing and all over, but they weren't going to the house where these guys were. The guys had moved their vehicles covered-wagon style around the front of the house, and they were just randomly shooting at houses of people they thought were AIM supporters. Later that night the FBI comes down, but they only sent two agents. They set up over at the clinic, but they weren't going around anywhere. They were just interviewing people we brought to them. So I made some pretty strong statements. I said, 'You guys get over there. If you're too scared to go in, at least go over there and identify who's in the house so you can follow it up later.' The FBI agent told me—he says, 'We're not a police department, we're an investigative unit,' and they refused to go."

Two years later the director of the FBI, William Webster, wrote just the opposite to a critic: ". . . it is clear that Federal officers, including Special Agents of the FBI, are lawfully empowered to enter upon and perform investigative and *law enforcement* functions on the Pine Ridge and Rosebud Indian Reservations" (emphasis added).

"After the FBI got done questioning everybody," George Bettelyoun told Kevin McKiernan, "they said, 'You boys watch yourselves,' and they left. And then they didn't come back till Monday morning."

McKiernan asked if he had heard Bettelyoun right: "They told you, an eyewitness to the murder, just to watch yourself over the weekend?"

"Yeah," Bettelyoun said. "Right there, see, the FBI, they say they're an investigative watchyoucallit and they only handle so many major crimes. Well, there's a major crime committed, a murder, and they just walked away from it. That was where you feel helpless, you know."

Bettelyoun had drawn the agents' attention to the black sedan driven by the goons who shot DeSersa. It was easily identified by two four-foot aerials on its trunk, and it sat in plain view, beside the cars of the other goon revelers, all night.

"After the FBI left," Abourezk said, "I went back to my house with some friends. It was kitty-corner from the house where the guys who killed Byron were, a quarter-block away at most. As we were walking up the steps, we could hear 'em yelling at us, saying stuff. I said, 'Aw, ignore 'em. Let's just go in.' Just as I was walking in the door and the screen door was closing—WHAP! Round hits right above my head. Later on, the FBI dug it out. It was a forty-four, and that's what had gone through Byron's door too. As soon as that hit, I yelled, 'Hit the deck,' and everybody dropped to the floor. It sounded like hail. You could just hear all those bullets hitting the house. We crawled down to the basement and broke a window in the back. My friends boosted me up, and I crawled out to go get help. There was a streetlight in the back, and when I hit that light, those guys must have saw me between the houses because there was more gunfire. I ran across that clearing and flagged down Chuck Twiss, who was a tribal police officer—dead now. He drove me around and pulled into my driveway, and all those guys who shot at me went back inside. The police came inside and were looking at the bullet holes in my house, but they didn't do anything more than that. At one point, we were standing in front of a window, and one of the officers said, 'Get away from that window. Those guys shooting from that house are crazy—and they're still shooting!' They fired at houses most of the night. Next door to me, Minnie High Horse was in her bed and a round went right through the windowsill next to where she was laying. Just missed her."

Later that night a firebomb was thrown through a window of the Dull Knifes' house. The Dull Knifes had been too wary to return home, but a friend was sleeping in their basement when the upstairs bedroom exploded in flames. A BIA officer, in a burst of initiative that must have been at odds with the training manual on Pine Ridge, drove to the house and helped the friend extinguish the fire before it spread. A second firebomb was reserved for the Lamont family.

"We were standing outside talking to policemen," Richard Lee Lamont said, "and two goons came from next door, number two-twelve, and one of them threw a firebomb at my house. It dropped to the ground and burned outside. Then these people who had just firebombed my house ran back to their house. I said to the policemen, 'Oh, if you can't arrest them, I'm going to go over there and do something about it 'cuz that's my family.' I said, 'My little girls could have got burnt up, 'cuz that was their bedroom that it hit.'

"And they said, 'Are you threatening us? We'll take you to jail.'

"I said, 'No, I'm not threatening nobody. I'm just asking you guys to do something about it.'

"And they said, 'Well, we'll see.'

"They never did go to that house. All they did was took three pictures. Instead of taking a statement from me, they took a statement from a person that wasn't even involved around there, didn't even see it."

The FBI would later lie to reporters that no one had been home in either firebombing and that both bombings were "probably unrelated" to DeSersa's murder. The FBI did not mention that one of the targets had been a children's bedroom or that policemen had witnessed one of the attacks. The local press did not question the FBI's claims.

At three in the morning, nine hours after DeSersa was murdered, the BIA assembled a SWAT team and sent it with a search warrant to the house where the goons were celebrating. But an hour before the team arrived, the goons were tipped—either by a friendly lawman or by a transmission they had overheard on a police scanner—and moved their murderers' ball down the block. Their cars were visible from where the SWAT team stood, but the team did not so much as walk down the street and knock on the door to question the killers. The people of Wanblee could bear no more. A caucus of the citizenry sent word to the goons that if they were not out of town in twenty-four hours, they would be evicted by force of arms.

On Sunday morning, just before noon, the goons took their leave. "But before they left," Abourezk said, "we saw them loading weapons that looked like AR-15s or M-16s into a vehicle, and two of these guys had on bulletproof vests that looked like government-issue, which was real curious. When they finally left, they turned on their lights and honked their horns, kind of did a little victory lap around the housing." BIA police and deputy sheriffs escorted them out of town. "Instead of going the short way back to Pine Ridge, they drove out around through Longvalley and Martin, down to Highway 18. What we found out later when we saw discovery for the trials was that they got stopped by some tribal cops near Martin, I think. This was in the radio logs. The cops who stopped them radioed into Pine Ridge, and the log showed that the person who called back—you could tell from the code number—was the captain, Skee Jacobs. Well, two of his kids were with this group. The officers who stopped them said, 'Should we hold 'em?' And Jacobs said, 'No, let 'em go. They're okay, they're local people.'

"Later I married Byron's wife. Her brother, Ted Big Crow, was a BIA police officer then, and he told me that he stopped these guys on their way back to Pine Ridge"—this was a separate stop, apparently, from the one near Martin. "He was mad. These guys had just killed his brother-in-law, you know. So as they were coming home, he drove outside of Pine Ridge and called for backup. He put his car across the road sideways, turned the red lights on, got his shotgun out, laid it on the hood. He pulled his other weapon, and he waited for them. None of the other cops came to back him up except for his cousin, Pat Mills. When they all pulled up and Ted stopped them, he made 'em spread-eagle on the ground and went and searched the car and couldn't find any weapons. But one of the girls was really shaking and scared, so he pulled her aside and says, 'What's going on?' She says, 'These guys are really bad, and they've got their weapons hidden under the back seat.' And so he went and lifted the back seat and found all these guns, which he took. But he didn't arrest anybody. He just identified who was there—I think that helped with the investigation some-what—and then let them go. They all drove into Dick Wilson's house and partied up over there."

While the killers partied up, the people of Wanblee demanded an accounting from the BIA and FBI.

"I'll be the first to admit," said Norman Zigrossi, the FBI agent in charge of western South Dakota, "there were some mistakes made by law enforcement. Anybody with any common sense can see that."

The mistakes, however, were the BIA's. Zigrossi reminded reporters that it was the BIA that was responsible for on-the-ground policing, whereas, as one of his men explained, the FBI was "an investigative agency and is not empowered to furnish protection." The distinction was again lost on Oglalas, who had been invaded only a few months earlier by an army of FBI agents hunting for their comrades' killers. Also, even if the FBI was only "an investigative agency," why did its agents refuse even to investigate the crime while the criminals were conveniently parked at a single address, their guns still smelling of smoke? None of these consider-ations concerned Zigrossi, who soon retracted even his criticism of the BIA and declared every one of the complaints against the government "nonspecific and unfounded."

The BIA was not so churlish as to disagree. "The officers who responded handled the investigation to the best of their ability to prevent further vio-lence," BIA police chief Ken Sayers said. "There is nothing at the present time to confirm that there was actual shooting at anybody during the night—only sporadic gunfire by unidentified people who seemed to be shooting in the air to distract the officers' attention and not specifically at any certain thing." In the BIA, episodic gunfire to confuse the police was nothing to get exercised about.

The local press gave brief and gentle scrutiny to the abdication of the BIA and FBI, and only one reporter from beyond the state, Kevin McKiernan, gave the matter serious consideration. In consequence, hardly anyone knew that the U.S. government had abandoned an Indian town—again—to murderous thugs with whom it was allied. Once more the silence of the news media guaranteed that neither the lawmen directly involved in the events nor their superiors were ever held responsible.

On the Sunday night after the goons left Wanblee, Charles Winters, known to friends as Elmer, short for Elmer Fudd, told his uncle, BIA police captain Skee Jacobs, that he had been in the car that had chased Byron DeSersa and that it was he who had fired the fatal shot. Winters said he was too tired to make a full confession just then, but if Uncle Skee would let him sleep, he would tell everything in the morning. Uncle Skee was solicitous of the confessed murderer and left him in peace. The next morning, Jacobs picked up Winters and drove him to the police station, where Winters told a clutch of BIA and FBI men that he did not, in fact, kill Byron DeSersa.

His listeners said they were confused. Had he not told his uncle the opposite just last night?

Winters quivered, but his tongue held tight. Questions were pressed upon him, and his quivering turned to quaking. Eventually he asked for a trash can and vomited into it. Exhausted, he finally admitted he was the killer.

The FBI hurried out a press release that announced, a trifle grandiosely, that the killer had been "apprehended through the investigative efforts of the Bureau of Indian Affairs and the FBI." The release was meant to ward off the increasingly warm questions that Senator Abourezk and others had been asking about Wanblee. The release had one other flaw: Elmer Fudd did not kill Byron DeSersa, and the FBI already suspected as much.

Even with its anemic investigation, the FBI had already developed a prime suspect by Sunday morning. Agents knew (because AIMers told them on Saturday) that the murder vehicle was a black 1970 Oldsmobile owned by Lonnie Bettelyoun, a goon who was the younger brother of Chuck "Manson" Richards (and a cousin of AIMer George Bettelyoun). Agents also knew or strongly suspected that one of the guns that was used on DeSersa was a large pistol of a kind owned by Lonnie Bettelyoun. They had pegged Bettelyoun as the most likely killer; a close second and third were two of his three passengers, Dale Janis and Billy Dean Wilson, the last a son of President Dick. Elmer Fudd was the third passenger in the car and as such could have shot DeSersa, but he was believed to be a follower rather than a leader and was not a principle suspect. Nonetheless, his confession followed by recantation followed by confession did not stir official suspicion, nor did it prompt vigorous additional investigation. In fact, although none of the people in Bettelyoun's car had gone into hiding after the murder, the FBI was in no hurry to interview them. Two or three days later, a pair of FBI agents happened upon Lonnie Bettelyoun in his car, and their questions of him were almost precious:

Had he or his car been involved in DeSersa's murder?

Bettelyoun said no.

Was he sure?

Yep, he was sure.

The agents took a few pictures of the car and let him be. There is no sign that the FBI then—or ever—asked to inspect the car or sought a warrant to do so, even though one of the agents noted that the right rear passenger door had "what appears to be an indentation as a result of a rifle being fired *from* the vehicle" (emphasis added).

DeSersa's Grand Prix was not so neglected. It was dusted and combed from bumper to bumper, its smallest contents tabbed, bagged, and sent to the FBI lab. Eight months after the crime, agents in the field were still asking the lab to test such trifles from the car as paper cups and scrap paper. The agents making the requests said they wanted to know if such objects yielded the killers' fingerprints—a prospect they must have known to be fanciful since the killers had never been inside DeSersa's car. In all probability they were really hoping to learn that someone in DeSersa's car had fired a gun; the FBI had ordered DeSersa's hands tested for just that purpose. The tests of both hands and car came back negative.

DeSersa was barely cold before the goons who had been in the cars behind Lonnie Bettelyoun's black Oldsmobile started spilling their stories to friends. The FBI belatedly took their statements. Almost to a person, the witnesses said that as the black car pulled alongside DeSersa's car, Bettelyoun drew his .44-Magnum pistol, and Elmer Winters, weaponless in the front passenger seat, slumped down so Bettelyoun could shoot across him. Billy Wilson, in the seat behind Winters, stuck what was believed to be a .22-caliber rifle out the window and squeezed the trigger. Dale Janis, in the seat behind Bettelyoun, pointed a .243 lever-action rifle across Wilson and fired. (One of Janis's shots probably fell short, causing the interior dent in Bettelyoun's rear passenger door.) At the party afterward, Bettelyoun showed off a snub-nosed revolver and said, "This is the gun I used on DeSersa." Other goons quoted Bettelyoun's riders saying that Bettelyoun had ordered them to fire. The ballistics evidence eventually confirmed the general story (and showed that Bettelyoun's shot had either missed DeSersa or only grazed him; it was a round from Janis or Wilson that had chewed through DeSersa's thigh). In brief, Elmer Winters had almost certainly been coerced into taking the fall.

The FBI knew this much within a week or two of the murder, but it sat on the evidence for nearly a month before telling the U.S. attorney's office. The prosecutors in turn let five months pass before seeking indictments for Bettelyoun, Wilson, and Janis, and they brought those only after Winters recanted his confession for a second and final time. AIMers took the reluctant indictments as proof that the feds were in league with the goons, that the government, too, wanted Winters to take the fall. It was not an implausible theory. But equally possible was that the prosecutors, like prosecutors everywhere, simply did not relish reopening a case that had already been "solved." The prosecutors' file on the case might shed light on the question, but the file, the U.S. attorney's office asks the public to understand, has been lost.

Decades later, under pressure from a Freedom of Information Act lawsuit, the FBI released its file on DeSersa's murder. Although heavily censored, the file shows that a lawman—never before mentioned in the few public discussions of the case—arrived at the goons' party just as Bettelyoun, Wilson, Janis, and Winters returned from the shooting of DeSersa. The lawman was either the sheriff or a deputy sheriff of Jackson County, which overlapped the northeastern corner of Pine Ridge. (His name and rank have been censored by the FBI.) By the lawman's telling, as soon as he arrived at the goons' house, it came under withering gunfire for several minutes, which he experienced but did not see because he was hunkered behind a refrigerator for the duration. Of several party-goers interviewed by the FBI, the lawman was the only one to recall such an attack. After the supposed assault died down, he neglected to take statements from witnesses, collect evidence, or radio news of the attack to his comrades in the BIA or his own sheriff's office, as might have been expected of an officer who had just endured a fusillade in his own jurisdiction. The man merely stayed at the party for the next several hours and commiserated with the goons about their lot while drinking what he described as endless cups of coffee. Goons said Elmer Winters passed out from drinking so much coffee.

"At no time while he was at Wanblee," the FBI summarized, "did he hear any mention of BYRON DE SERSA nor did he see or receive any information regarding firebombs or any other shooting other than" the attack on the goons' house. The lawman did not hear Lonnie Bettelyoun say, as goons in the house heard, "We just warmed up a car." He did not hear Dale Janis say, as others heard, "I think I hit the driver." He did not hear Billy Wilson say, as others did, that the people who stayed in the house had missed all the fun on the highway. Of seven party-goers interviewed by the FBI, five said the place was abuzz with the shooting of

DeSersa. Of the two who said otherwise, one lied out of fear for his life; the other, it seems, out of fear for his badge.

The FBI agents on the case must have known the lawman was lying since they juxtaposed his incredible story with the more credible claims from other party-goers and since they returned to interview him a second time. (He told the same story.) But after the second interview, the lawman was never again disturbed about the DeSersa case, and his presence at the festivities was never mentioned in FBI documents thereafter.

After his final recantation, Elmer Winters struck a deal. He would testify against the shooters and plead to accessory after the fact, a crime that carried a maximum sentence of ten years, and the government would drop the murder charge against him. Judge Bogue approved the deal and gave Winters five years.

Dale Janis, who was only sixteen, was tried separately from Bettelyoun and Wilson, who were adults. R. D. Hurd was among his prosecutors. Little is known about the trial since neither a transcript nor talkative witnesses survive, but apparently Janis admitted firing his gun in the general direction of DeSersa's car but said he hadn't meant to hurt anyone. He had fired, he claimed, only because a gun barrel had poked out of DeSersa's car and he wanted to scare the guy with the gun into putting it away. The jury deliberated a few hours before convicting him of murder in the second degree. In the four months between conviction and sentencing, Judge Bogue permitted the murderer to remain at large on light bond. When Janis was finally incarcerated, he served until his eighteenth birthday, a term of not two years.

After Janis's conviction, the prosecutors expected Bettelyoun and Wilson to take a plea bargain. They did not. Their defense was captained by John Fitzgerald, the car-bombed ex–Mob lawyer who had seen to Dick Wilson's acquittal for the beating of the WKLDOCkers at the airport. Bettelyoun and Wilson repeated Janis's lie that a gun had poked out DeSersa's car, but they did not repeat his claim to have fired only in warning. They said they had shot to kill and would do so again if they had to—they were not ashamed of having defended their lives. Their argument should have been easily disgraced since all but one of the goons in the trailing cars and everyone in DeSersa's car claimed that no gun had been pointed at the goons. (The lone witness who said otherwise also claimed that DeSersa had sideswiped Bettelyoun's car—a claim the FBI had debunked through analysis of the paint on DeSersa's Grand Prix and nearly a dozen witness statements.) But on March 2, 1977, Wilson and Bettelyoun were found not guilty. The errors of the prosecution, the calculations of the defense, the impressions of the jury are nowhere recorded.

The order of acquittal was hardly stamped when Elmer Winters petitioned Judge Bogue to reduce his five-year sentence because, he said, he had been true to his word and testified against his erstwhile friends. One might have thought Winters rewarded enough by his plea bargain, but the U.S. attorney supported his cry for mercy, and Bogue lopped two years off his term. Like Janis, Winters spent fewer than two years behind bars.

Over the decades, AIMers have often pointed to the case of Byron DeSersa as an exemplar of the goons having gotten away with murder. If the truth was not quite that, it was close enough to moot the difference.

CHAPTER 12

LATE ON OCTOBER 10, 1974, a few weeks after the end of the Banks-Means trial and a few months before Doug Durham was exposed, the sheriff's office of Ventura County, California, received a distress call from a man who had just come from a place called AIM Camp 13 and who said he had seen a body on the ground that was bloody and looking bad. Camp 13 lay in Box Canyon, a badland coulee whose arid terrain was favored by Hollywood's makers of spaghetti Westerns. Only a few years earlier Box Canyon had achieved notoriety as the home of Spahn Ranch, whence the Manson "family" had carried out the Tate-LaBianca murders. Sheriff's deputies responded quickly to the call on the night of October 10, arriving at the camp around midnight. At the entrance they found a taxi of the Red-and-White Company with blood on the seats, and in a nearby drainpipe was the body of a man soon identified as the cabdriver. George Aird was dead of seventeen stab wounds. He was twenty-six-years old.

The deputies searched the camp's buildings and in one found a young woman in a shower washing blood from her hair and from under her fingernails. The clothes she had just taken off were also bloodstained. Her name was Marcie Eaglestaff. Hours later, deputies found two more blood-soaked people crouching behind a building. Marvin Redshirt, a twenty-six-year-old Oglala from Pine Ridge, said he and his girlfriend had been asleep in the hills above the camp when they heard a commotion and came down to see what it was. They were bloody because they had skinned some animals earlier in the evening. But his girlfriend, Holly

Broussard, a nineteen-year-old native of Long Beach, said that she and Redshirt had been not in the hills but hiding in the camp. In her pocket, deputies found the keys to George Aird's cab and a pocketknife coated in blood. Eaglestaff, Redshirt, and Broussard were taken to jail and booked for crimes ranging from robbery to murder. It seemed, as the crime writers say, an open-and-shut case.

It was not. Within weeks all three were granted immunity in return for testifying that two mid-tier AIM leaders had committed the murder. (Eaglestaff, Redshirt, and Broussard were not AIMers themselves, although they had lived at AIM Camp 13.) One of the mid-tier leaders was Paul Durant, an Ojibwa who had run an Indian center in Brooklyn and co-founded AIM's Chicago chapter. Durant was lank of build and aquiline of nose, with melancholy eyes set deep in a drawn face. He went by the name Skyhorse. The other leader was Richard Billings, a Tuscarora-Mohawk known to friends, sensibly enough, as Mohawk. He too had co-founded Chicago AIM and had once helped seize an abandoned naval base on Lake Michigan that became Chicago's Indian Village. At twenty-six, Mohawk was Skyhorse's junior by three years, but wide eyes, smooth cheeks, and a puckish grin made him seem younger by a decade. On the night of the murder, Skyhorse and Mohawk had been at or near Camp 13, but they had fled the scene because, they later explained, if they had stayed at the camp they would at best have been manhandled by police and at worse have been charged with a crime they did not commit. They were arrested in Phoenix in late October and returned to jail in Ventura County, where they were charged with murder.

The National Lawyers Guild and the California Civil Liberties Union believed Skyhorse and Mohawk were being framed, and they created a defense committee to represent the pair. But AIM made an investigation of its own and concluded that Skyhorse and Mohawk were indeed guilty. The murder had already dampened Hollywood's charity toward AIM (it occurred early in Anna Mae Aquash's first foray to Los Angeles, and many of her fundraising travails could be blamed on the crime), and AIM did not want to make matters worse by giving succor to the killers. AIM urged the lawyers to disband their defense committee, and the lawyers did. Only in 1976, after Skyhorse and Mohawk had sat in jail for a year and a half, did anyone think it important that AIM's investigation had been conducted by Douglass Durham.

After the fall of Wounded Knee in 1973, many veterans of the takeover found themselves in California, and that autumn AIM's Los Angeles chapter leased the camp in Box Canyon as a retreat for the weary occupiers. By early 1974, most of the AIMers left for the Banks-Means trial in St. Paul, and the Los Angeles chapter apparently stopped paying the lease. But a few persistent campers cobbled together the rent and stayed. Their informal leader was a man who had been kicked out of the WKLDOC office in Rapid City because, as AIM's Paula Giese wrote, "he had beaten an elderly Indian woman severely, raped a 15-year-old Indian girl, burned some file material from the legal office, and been stopped from burning the building." AIM warned its California members that the man was probably a police agent, but those who stayed at the camp either did not know or did not care. They were less activists than addicts, living for the eighty-proof and angel dust for which the camp, under the disreputable leader, became known.

In February or March of 1974, Doug Durham told people in St. Paul that "a man"—perhaps meaning the leader—"has given us some land in the California hills for a training camp, if you know what I mean." Durham told AIM's staff that they would teach guerrilla strategy and tactics at the camp, which struck them as bizarre since virtually none of them knew anything and didn't want to know anything about fighting a guerrilla war. Durham named the place AIM Camp 13, probably for the implication that AIM had a dozen other such camps and for the Ian Fleming-esque sound. Some months later Durham abandoned his guerrilla-training intentions for want of support and, no doubt, because other provocations were more ripe.

The bacchanals at Camp 13 continued throughout 1974 to the embarrassment of AIMers in Los Angeles, who begged St. Paul to find a way to close the camp. AIM's headquarters unwisely dispatched Skyhorse and Mohawk. Both men were prone to drink and quickly became more problem than solution. In early October, Banks and Durham made a fundraising trip to California and took an afternoon to inspect the camp. Banks later claimed disgust at what he saw, but he either could not or would not close the place. A few days after his visit, two of the campers robbed a neighbor in Box Canyon, striking him several times and menacing him with a four-foot fishing gaff—a crime the press inflated, apparently with encouragement from the sheriff's office, to a "torture-robbery." When George Aird was murdered two days later, reporters were primed to believe the sheriff's description of a grisly ritual killing in which the victim was scalped to the beat of war drums and the singing of the AIM anthem. Pictures of the abandoned cab parked in front of a sign reading AIM CAMP 13 were headed for page one.

Reporters called St. Paul for AIM's reaction to the murder, and Paula Giese said that AIM condemned it but knew no more details than the press did, save that Redshirt, Broussard, and Eaglestaff did not appear to be AIM members. When Durham heard her, he dressed her down almost violently for so limp a response and forbade her to speak to reporters. Thereafter he took all calls on the matter and said that since whites had once scalped Indians, it was about time Indians returned the favor. He pledged AIM's total support for the three arrestees, who, he said, were AIMers "all the way," and he added that if the sheriff did not free them immediately, AIM would send an army to bust them from jail. Durham then moved the press operation to his apartment, to which he flew a young woman from Louisiana named Veronica "Raven Hawk" Keene. Keene claimed Choctaw blood, but her complexion was pale, her eyes blue, and her hair and eyelashes appeared to have been dyed black: light brown showed at the roots. Durham had brought her to St. Paul once before, in February 1974, to work as a secretary in the AIM office, mostly on the Banks-Means trial. She had left after only a month. Some AIMers recalled that she was evicted after being caught taking security files from the office. Others said she left when Judge Nichol ordered the government to identify infiltrators in the defense camp. After Aird's killing, she and Durham encouraged the claims of scalping and ritual murder—which was how the story played in several news outlets across the country.

The deal that Marvin Redshirt struck for immunity required him to take a lie detector test to verify that he had not stabbed George Aird. If he passed, he would be allowed to plead guilty to a charge of aiding and abetting and be given a sentence of probation. If he failed, he would have to plead to assault with a deadly weapon and be sentenced to six months in jail. He failed. Asked to explain his failure, he finally admitted having stabbed Aird, but he said Skyhorse and Mohawk had forced him to do it after Aird was already dead in order to implicate him. Redshirt served some portion of his six months, after which, according to Giese, prosecutors helped him win a college scholarship, which was neither the usual fate of a convicted felon nor the usual role of prosecutors. Redshirt flunked out of the academy, but this failure was smoothed over by Louis Broussard—real estate investor, retired naval commander, and father of Redshirt's girlfriend Holly—who installed him in an apartment rent-free and found him a job on a naval base.

Meanwhile Skyhorse and Mohawk were left to public defenders, one of whom had represented Redshirt in his deal with the government—that is, in his deal to testify against Skyhorse and Mohawk. The defender apparently saw no conflict of interest therein. Over the objection of his client, Skyhorse's lawyer arranged a pretrial hearing to examine his sanity. One of the expert witnesses at the hearing was Doug Durham. Durham claimed a PhD in psychology and apparently said he was a practicing psychologist or a professor of psychology, and he esteemed himself expert in "the Indian mind." No transcript of his testimony survives, so the full extent of his perjury is not known. A couple of years later, after he was exposed for an infiltrator and his deception at Skyhorse's hearing was deduced,

AIMers tried to have him charged with perjury. But Ventura's prosecutors refused to indict. A real psychologist who examined Skyhorse concluded he was sane but added, "Paul believes the CIA or feds are trying to implant a device in his head. That the authorities are trying to get him to turn against his people. That his mail, phone conversations, etc., are monitored. Paul is paranoid."

"Perhaps," a reporter later wrote, "Paul Durant was in far greater touch with the realities in his life than anyone gave him credit for."

Skyhorse and Mohawk searched for other lawyers among the nation's legal defense groups without luck. The Southern Poverty Law Center, which defended only death-penalty cases, wrote in reply to Skyhorse, "We have spoken with Richard Erwin of the Public Defender's office. Erwin assures us that you do not face the death penalty and will at most be convicted of second-degree murder." In fact, the gas chamber was still a possibility in the event that Skyhorse and Mohawk were convicted. Stymied, the defendants took to protesting their lawyers' deeds at pretrial hearings. But the several judges who sat on the case variously ignored them or, in one instance, had them dragged from court—"insane troublemakers," that judge called them. Eventually the lawyers simply waived their clients' pretrial appearances. Justice would proceed without the accused.

Throughout this time, Skyhorse and Mohawk were housed in a windowless "minimax security unit" in the gut of the decrepit Ventura County Jail. They were usually confined solitarily, separate even from each other, and were rarely permitted to leave their cages or to have visitors. Perhaps Durham's threats to bust AIMers out of jail had had effect. Skyhorse took to the weekly chapel service not for salvation but for the window through which the sun shone and the sound of another human voice. Both prisoners claimed they were regularly beaten and chained to bars for hours at a stretch. Skyhorse said he was once shackled naked for days on the floor of a cell in an inch of standing water, and Mohawk claimed to have been thrashed so badly he could no longer straighten his left arm. They were also drugged—Skyhorse with the sedatives Thorazine, Stelazine, and Mellaril,

Mohawk with drugs he did not know—and felt eternally sluggish and unable to concentrate. Much later, when they were permitted to become advisory counsel in their case, they found it nearly impossible in their mental and physical state to prepare a defense.

Late 1974 passed in this way to early 1976, when Skyhorse received an issue of *Akwesasne Notes*, the chronicle of the Indian rights movement. Till then, his jailers had denied him the newspaper. The issue he received had an article about Doug Durham's work for the FBI. In their isolation, Skyhorse and Mohawk had not heard about Durham's exposure a year before. The news came as a bolt of understanding, and Skyhorse hurried off a letter to *Akwesasne Notes* that read in part,

> My acquaintances have questioned my position as being paranoid, hateful, and just who do I think I am that the state would go to all the trouble [to frame me]. I hope I am not being egotistical, but I believe I am a victim of this plot.
>
> I met with Doug Durham at least three times just prior to my arrest. He even came out to the encampment where all the events that surround my imprisonment occurred. I invited him there seeking his help. At the time of our meetings, I remember I felt he was interrogating me. At the time, I felt he was just being weird.
>
> When the decision to repudiate us from AIM was made, Durham was the responsible source. When one of the co-defendants (at that time, 1974) was able to make $100,000 bond (her father is a retired Navy commander and a millionaire), Durham met with her.

At nearly the same time that Skyhorse learned of Durham, he received a letter from his prosecutor that said he was required by law to tell the defendants that another paid informer of the FBI had penetrated their ranks. The informer was Virginia DeLuce, treasurer and co-founder of AIM's Los Angeles chapter and known in the movement as Blue Dove. DeLuce had been a B-movie star and pinup girl of the World War II era with credits including *Jitterbug* with Laurel and Hardy, *Cover Girl* with Rita Hayworth and Gene Kelly, and many forgettable episodes of *Sergeant Bilko*. Later, youth fading, she settled in Arizona, where she may have written a book about the Diné (if so, it had a minimal distribution) and where she became friendly with Arizona's foremost reactionary, Barry Goldwater. When Indians seized Alcatraz in 1969, she took part and was given the name Blue Dove by Tuscarora medicine man Wallace "Mad Bear" Anderson. From then on, she was a regular in AIM. She was also active in Chicano rights groups, prisoner-support groups, and the American Friends Service Committee, the political arm of the Quakers. Whether she at first believed in the goals of these organizations and later became disillusioned is unknown, but she claimed she did not start spying for the FBI until 1971, a couple of years into her affiliation with most of the groups. She ratted on them all.

As treasurer of AIM's Los Angeles chapter, it was DeLuce who first paid the rent on Camp 13 in the fall of 1973. AIMers suspected her in hindsight of continuing to pay the rent after AIM disavowed the camp, the idea being to embarrass AIM with the orgy-like atmosphere and hurt AIM's fundraising. AIMers also suspected, not unreasonably, that either the FBI gave her the money for the ongoing rent or she siphoned it from AIM's treasury. On the day George Aird was murdered, DeLuce drove Skyhorse and Mohawk from Camp 13 to a rally in Los Angeles that was very thinly attended—one of those thankless protests that Aquash helped organize—where they were apparently photographed by an undercover agent who was perhaps DeLuce. (After the murder, the photos were used to identify and arrest them in Phoenix.) When the rally was done, DeLuce drove them back to the camp, dropping them off a few hours before Aird was killed. All of which, when discovered, led AIMers to wonder whether the FBI had planned the murder so as to destroy Skyhorse, Mohawk, and the Los Angeles chapter. The FBI did not, in fact, have such foresight, but as in other cases, once the murder occurred, the government wasted no time using it to achieve foul ends.

The government disclosed DeLuce to Skyhorse and Mohawk only after a mighty internal struggle. The district attorney for Ventura County, John Dobroth, told the FBI that he needed to call DeLuce as a witness at trial: she was the only person of upstanding character who could put Skyhorse and Mohawk at Camp 13 shortly before the murder. Agents in the FBI's Los Angeles office told Dobroth that DeLuce was one of their best informers—almost certainly, she was one of the spies who had made detailed reports on Aquash—and they did not want her burned. Dobroth said he had no choice and would call her. In the story AIM later uncovered, the FBI appealed for help to the U.S. attorney for California. The U.S. attorney had no direct authority over Dobroth, who worked for the state, but the attorney's influence in legal circles was great. Someone in the U.S. attorney's office apparently spoke to Dobroth, but Dobroth continued to hold steady. So the FBI called the Justice Department in Washington, and Justice applied pressure as well. At this, Dobroth supposedly declared, "Unless someone with the power to fire me orders me not to call her, I'm going to use her." Dobroth was not fired, but he did receive an unexpected promotion, and the case fell to his assistant, Michael Bradbury. Bradbury, however, persisted in demanding DeLuce as a witness, and he sent Skyhorse the letter exposing her. Soon after, Bradbury either removed himself or was removed from the case.

The court had allotted Skyhorse and Mohawk a meager $500 to hire private investigators, and the defendants decided to use the sum to find DeLuce, who had disappeared after her exposure. But the investigators were themselves investigated—tailed, they said, by sheriff's deputies, FBI agents, or both.

"Before this," one of the investigators said, "I didn't believe the federal government had any involvement in this case. Now I have no doubt of it."

When Paula Giese saw Skyhorse's letter to *Akwesasne Notes* in the spring of 1976, she had no trouble believing that the government had framed the pair. She wrote them, but her letters came back from the jail stamped "Not Here." She tracked down their lawyers and offered her considerable help.

Andrew Marsh, Mohawk's lawyer, did not return her calls. Fred Kosmo, Skyhorse's lawyer, said the case was "open and shut"; Skyhorse, he said, was guilty as Nixon.

In the summer of 1976 the entertainment at the annual gala of the Ventura County Bar Association was a skit called *People v. Tonto*. The scene: a courtroom. The year: 1985. The setup: a case that had dragged on for a decade. The curtain lifted, and Tonto rose from the defense table to make, in *vox primitive*, motion 2,001 for mistrial. He said the gavel used by the judge had been made by a company that had polluted Lake Erie and thereby destroyed the livelihood of Indians. Ergo, the judge was a racist.

"Motion denied!" bellowed the judge to applause from the audience. The judge then called the Lone Ranger to the stand and heaved a considerable sigh of relief. The skit proceeded in this fashion through the grand finale, in which Tonto and the rest of the company sang, "Oompahpah! Oompahpah! Tonto don't want the trial to end 'cuz we're having so much fun. Oompahpah!" There was much laughter and applause, including from Judge Marvin Lewis, before whom Skyhorse and Mohawk were to be tried.

After the applause drained away, a Cherokee teacher named Sharon Sperling stood and softly said, "I have two brothers up in Ventura County Jail who are fighting for their lives, and you are making fun of it. They are not laughing. You should be ashamed of yourselves." She left in tears. The skit's author was the lawyer who had negotiated Holly Broussard's immunity deal.

When Skyhorse and Mohawk learned of the skit, they demanded Judge Lewis recuse himself. The judge offered a brief courtroom apology but said recusal was hardly called for. The defendants appealed, and an appalled California Supreme Court disqualified not just Lewis but the entire bench of Ventura County. Venue for the trial was changed to Los Angeles. The defendents had no way of knowing they had exchanged Ventura's fire for Los Angeles's frying pan.

The trial was finally scheduled to begin in early 1977, two and a half years after Skyhorse and Mohawk's arrest. By then, thanks mostly to Paula Giese, a defense committee of slender funds but impressive pro bono lawyers had been reestablished, and the defendants had won a few small legal rights, like the right to interview witnesses. That right proved a mixed blessing. The interviews had to take place in a glass chamber of the jail known as the aquarium, where a wall with a tightly grilled speaking hole separated the defendants from the interviewees while a guard watched and listened from a few feet away. At the end of one interview, guards searched Mohawk and found—or "found"—a packet of heroin on him. Since he had been searched before entering the aquarium, the witness with whom he was meeting was implicated in having slipped him the drugs—a virtually impossible feat—and was thus discredited for trial purposes. Perhaps not incidentally, the witness was important. She had shared a cell with Holly Broussard and Marcie Eaglestaff after they were first arrested and had overheard Eaglestaff say of Skyhorse and Mohawk, "I could cut them loose if I wanted to. But I'm going to say they did it like the prosecutors want so I can get out. Then I'm going to disappear and not testify against them."

Another jailhouse visitor on whom suspicion was cast was Sharon Sperling, the Cherokee who spoke tearfully at the Ventura Bar dinner. After one of her visits, guards "found" two marijuana joints in Skyhorse's pocket, and Sperling had to fear for her public school job. Still another visitor, legal worker Julie Evening Lily, was investigated and found to have an expired license plate. This discovery prompted a computer search that turned up an erroneous warrant for her arrest. She was jailed three days before the matter was sorted out. Other visitors, mostly women, said that police questioned them for hours before allowing them to see Skyhorse and Mohawk and that after their visits they received obscene phone calls and death threats.

In February 1977, a few weeks before trial was to start, Skyhorse and Mohawk were admitted to a hospital emergency room badly roughed up. They told their defense team that half a dozen guards had taken turns on them. Doctors found both men suffering from blurred vision, headaches, fatigue, and inability to concentrate. Mohawk's sight and thought were so compromised that beating-induced brain damage could not be ruled out. They were also addicted to painkillers given to them after previous beatings, and they were so malnourished that it was hard to say which of their disorders had been caused by the beatings and which by lack of nutrients. The doctors declared the defendants medically unfit to stand trial, and the court was forced to hospitalize them until their condition improved. Not until May 1977 did the trial finally begin, by which time Skyhorse and Mohawk had been behind bars longer than any pretrial defendants in the history of California.

At trial the facts on which both the prosecution and the defense agreed were these: Marvin Redshirt, Holly Broussard, and Marcie Eaglestaff wiled away the afternoon of October 10, 1974, on whiskey, wine, and cigarettes that Broussard had shoplifted that morning. In the evening the threesome decided to move their party from Camp 13 to the house of David Carradine, star of TV's *Kung Fu*. Carradine had a vigorous social relationship with Indians. A few weeks earlier he had flown to St. Paul and provided "refreshments," not entirely legal, for Doug Durham's birthday party. Redshirt, Broussard, and Eaglestaff drove to Carradine's house with two friends, Roland Knox and Le War Lance. (The latter would become the subject of Ian Frazier's book *On the Rez*.) Carradine was not home, but War Lance, who had a key, decided to stay. Knox left in the car for parts unknown, the original trio called a cab for the long ride back to Camp 13, and George Aird arrived for the last fare of his life. At that point, accounts differed.

The prosecution pinned its case on the testimony of Marvin Redshirt and put him on the stand first. He said the cab ride was uneventful but that when they arrived at the camp, Skyhorse and Mohawk walked up to Aird and insulted him without provocation, which inspired him, Redshirt, to punch the cabbie. Soon others were assaulting him too. The details from there are murky—no trial transcript survives—but eventually Aird was lying on the ground and Holly Broussard was kicking him and Skyhorse and Mohawk were stabbing him. Skyhorse and Mohawk finally killed him, then gave the knife to Redshirt and made him stick it in the corpse once. He did.

On cross-examination, the defense reminded Redshirt that he told investigators he was drunk when he had stabbed Aird. Just now he said he was not drunk. Which was it?

He was not drunk, he said.

Had he lied?

Yes, Redshirt said, he had.

Why?

To protect himself.

The defense then walked Redshirt through a series of other lies he had made: that he had no previous arrests for drunk and disorderly conduct, that he had never stabbed or kicked Aird, that Skyhorse and Mohawk had been along for the cab ride, that he knew nothing about a cabdriver or a murder.

Redshirt admitted lying about them all, and more.

"How many times have you lied?" defense attorney Skipp Glenn asked.

"Approximately a thousand times," the prosecution's star witness said. "One lie leads to the next one to cover it up."

The defense then produced a tape recording on which Redshirt said that he always took care of "number one." Was making a deal with prosecutors to beat a murder rap taking care of number one?

Yes, he said, it was.

Had he bought his freedom by offering to testify against Skyhorse and Mohawk?

Yes, he said, he had.

The defense excused him.

Within the hour, the prosecutors capitulated. They offered to dismiss the murder charges if Skyhorse and Mohawk would plead no contest to a few lesser counts. With the gas chamber looming, the defendants readily agreed, and papers were submitted to the court for approval that was practically pro forma. To everyone's dismay, Judge Floyd Dodson scuttled the deal and ordered the trial to continue.

Judge Dodson, it happened, was sitting on the case by special appointment, having lost re-election in Santa Barbara County the previous fall. (Critics had accused him of intemperance on the bench and financial conflicts of interest; he had lost in a landslide.) Under California law, judges who left office due to electoral defeat could not be appointed to temporary sittings, but judges who left office due to retirement could. To preserve the possibility of a temporary appointment, Dodson "retired" from his Santa Barbara judgeship the day before he was to be turned out of his chambers. Almost immediately, the chief justice of the California Supreme Court named him visiting judge for the Skyhorse-Mohawk trial in Los Angeles. Had Dodson agreed to end the trial, his $50,000 salary (about $150,000 today) would have come to an abrupt end.

Defense lawyers suggested that the judge's income might be impairing his judgment and asked him to disqualify himself. He refused. On appeal, the state supreme court, which by then had a new chief justice, concluded that Dodson had gamed the system and that in the future all judges defeated at the polls, including "self-retirees" à la Dodson, would be barred from temporary postings. But the court also said that since the trial of Skyhorse and Mohawk was already underway, it would not be proper to remove Dodson, and the decision to accept or reject the plea bargain would remain his. The bid to kill two men continued, no matter that even its prosecutors thought it unwarranted.

Perhaps to save face, the prosecution called month after month of witnesses, but these did not reflect well on the government. The immunized Holly Broussard admitted to joining in the murder as a kind of sport—"he was being brutally beaten, and I wanted to be a part of it"—and said that she, Redshirt, and Eaglestaff had tormented Aird partly because they didn't have the cab fare, partly because they had discovered that Aird's wife was black (he was white, and the murderers did not approve of this form of interracial union), and partly because they were fascinated with the occult and were curious about what it would be like to torture someone. Broussard also said that the district attorney had asked her to buy a pocketknife like the one the police had taken from her on the night of the murder. When the defense asked why the D.A. had made that surprising request, Broussard said the D.A. told her the original knife had been lost. Several police officers were then called to the stand and asked if the murder weapon, coated in blood and perhaps fingerprints, had indeed been lost. They said it had: it had been put on the hood of a patrol car at the crime scene, never to be seen again. But a lone officer followed his colleagues to the stand and said otherwise. He was at the stationhouse on the night of the murder and saw the knife, which had been brought in by officers in the field. He had even talked with his supervisor about having seen it. But the supervisor was called to the stand and said his subordinate didn't know what he was talking about.

Holly Broussard's was not the only dagger that went missing. Two months after the murder, a caretaker at the camp found a twelve-inch blade in an outdoor oven and gave it to the sheriff's office. The blade, which had no handle, was coated in rust-colored stains that may have been blood. Sheriff's deputies testified that they had meant to send the blade to the lab for testing but by mistake it had been sent to the property room, where by another mistake it was destroyed. Either the police of Ventura County were breathtakingly incompetent, or they had an aversion to preserving murder weapons.

Another witness who took the stand, Carmella Fish, said prosecutors badgered her for months to perjure herself. They wanted her to testify that she had seen Skyhorse and Mohawk at the crime scene, but she repeatedly told them she had seen nothing of the sort. She said she had driven into the camp, had seen Redshirt and Eaglestaff standing over Aird's bloodied body with a rope around his neck, and had left immediately to call the police. The prosecutors' harassment of her peaked in 1976, when the case was first set for trial. Fish was living in Albuquerque, so the prosecutors said they would wire her money to fly back to Los Angeles. When she arrived at the Western Union office, she was handcuffed and then, she said—incredibly yet credibly—flown to Wisconsin, where she was jailed and questioned by an investigator from the Ventura County prosecutor's office (who was apparently in Wisconsin on other business). In this compelling setting, the investigator "mentally forced" her to say she had seen Skyhorse and Mohawk standing over Aird's body. She recanted her statement after leaving police custody.

While such matters were filling months of trial, a brawl broke out between guards and inmates in the Los Angeles County Jail, and Skyhorse and Mohawk were badly beaten. Six guards were called to the stand to say Skyhorse and Mohawk had started the fight, which, prosecutors argued, proved they were unfit to serve as co-counsel. The prosecution asked Judge Dodson to revoke their rights of self-representation. The defense answered with thirteen inmates, all of whom said the guards had started the fight and some of whom said Skyhorse and Mohawk had tried to break it up. One inmate also said that on another occasion a guard told him, "If you kill Skyhorse and Mohawk, you can get anything you want." The guard allegedly gave the inmate a shank to do the job and heroin in down payment. The prosecution rebutted with an inmate of its own who said Skyhorse had forced him to perform fellatio on Mohawk while he, Skyhorse, watched. "Do it," Skyhorse supposedly said, "or I'll butcher you like I did the cabdriver." Two other inmates had seen it all. But the defense rebutted by showing that the prosecution's inmate had made a career out of supplying incriminating information that met police needs and that he had, to boot, recently been declared criminally insane. The defense also obtained affidavits from him and his two supposed witnesses saying they were promised lighter sentences for lying about the forced fellatio. Judge Dodson weighed the evidence and said it permitted only one conclusion: Skyhorse and Mohawk were unfit to serve as counsel; he revoked their rights to do so.

The prosecution's last attempt to tie Skyhorse and Mohawk to the murder was through a witness named Frank Sexton, who testified that he had seen Skyhorse and Mohawk on the night of the crime and that Skyhorse's pants had been covered with blood. But on cross-examination, Sexton said that at the time he saw the blood, he had been in the middle of a two-week bender on PCP, LSD, peyote, marijuana, Benzedrine, methamphetamines, heroin, and mescaline. Also, he couldn't recall being "straight" for any two consecutive days in the last five years, he said his memory was "all fucked up," and he agreed that the "blood" on Skyhorse may well have been mud. By the time the prosecution rested, a year had passed since Judge Dodson denied the deal to end the case.

The defense had only one important matter to explore: why did the FBI, which had no jurisdiction in a state murder case, become so involved in this one? Why, for example, were FBI agents among the early responders to the crime scene? The defense put the question to a police sergeant who arrived at the camp in the hours after the murder, but the sergeant said no FBI agents had been at the scene. The defense prodded, apparently producing evidence to the contrary, and the sergeant allowed that maybe an agent had come—although, if so, the sergeant didn't know the man. The defense prodded further, and finally the sergeant admitted that multiple agents had been at the scene and he had known them well enough to introduce to other cops.

The defense subpoenaed Doug Durham and ten other FBI employees, but the FBI refused to honor the subpoenas, and the prosecution asked Dodson to quash them. He did. He also quashed every other attempt by the defense to establish the obvious—that Skyhorse and Mohawk had been framed. The question of whether the FBI had tried to send two innocent men to the gas chamber was, Dodson ruled, irrelevant and inadmissible. It was not the FBI that was on trial, he lectured. It was Skyhorse and Mohawk. The frustrated defense rested.

On May 24, 1978, the jury acquitted the Indians of all charges. It was Skyhorse's thirty-third birthday. He had entered jail at twenty-nine.

* * *

The acquittal of Skyhorse and Mohawk was a dénouement for AIM. Two and half years earlier, Leonard Peltier had been arrested in Canada, where he had fled after the bust of Marlon Brando's motor home, and was charged with the murder of the FBI agents at Oglala. Bob Robideau and Dino Butler were already in custody in the United States for the same crime. While Peltier fought extradition, they were tried before Judge Edward McManus, a moderate from Iowa. Like Judge Nichol in St. Paul and unlike Judge Dodson in Los Angeles, Judge McManus allowed the defendants to offer a political defense, which was that the government, through the provocations of COINTELPRO and the buildup in response to the "secret AIM project" and the blind support for Dick Wilson, had made Pine Ridge toxic—and ultimately lethal—with paranoia. Agents Coler and Williams, charging into the AIM camp, were doomed as much by the FBI's own devilry as by AIM's bullets. The jury agreed, and Robideau and Butler were acquitted.

Canada extradited Peltier largely on the testimony of Myrtle Poor Bear. Poor Bear was the woman who eventually alleged that Agents David Price and Bill Wood showed her pictures of the blackened Aquash and threatened her with a similar fate if she did not implicate Peltier. Under the agents' tutelage, Poor Bear signed three affidavits. In the first, she said she was Peltier's girlfriend (which was untrue), she was familiar with the AIM camp at the Jumping Bull ranch (also untrue), and she was not present when the agents were killed (true). The second affidavit was a mostly verbatim copy of the first, except now Poor Bear claimed she *had* been present during the shootout and had seen Peltier kill the agents. The third affidavit restated the second. The FBI gave the Canadian government and Peltier's lawyers only the last two incriminating affidavits. The exculpatory first was withheld—a grossly illegal omission. Many months after Peltier was extradited, his prosecutor admitted that anyone who spent a few minutes with Poor Bear should have known she was "incompetent in the utter, utter, utter, ultimate sense of incompetency." Price and Wood had spent entire days with Poor Bear. They had kept her secluded, effectively under house arrest (some would argue kidnapped), in a Black Hills motel. They knew she was utterly, utterly, utterly incompetent, which was why they had used her.

Peltier's trial was assigned to Judge Paul Benson, a North Dakotan whose views on AIM were similar to Judge Bogue's and who ruled Poor Bear's perjurious affidavits immaterial. The defense was forbidden even to mention them. So too evidence that the FBI had coerced other witnesses, fabricated statements, and doctored ballistics—all of which the FBI had undeniably done. When defense lawyers tried to show that the government was responsible for the anarchy on Pine Ridge and, in turn, that whoever shot the agents had done so in justifiable self-defense, Benson ruled the lawyers out of order. The government, he admonished (prefiguring Judge Dodson in Los Angeles), was not the party on trial. Peltier was. He was convicted in 1977 and sentenced to two life terms, which he is serving still.

From the seizure of Wounded Knee in 1973 to the acquittal of Skyhorse and Mohawk in 1978, the American Indian Movement was unvaryingly under indictment, in jail, on trial, or on the lam. AIM achieved much nonetheless. It was largely AIM that made Indians proud again to be Indians, and it was that reborn dignity that quickened the pace at which tribes demanded amends from America—demanded, say, that reservation lands be returned to tribal control or that Indian children be given decent schools or that the federal government stop trampling on tribal sovereignty. Roger Finzel, the WKLDOCker beaten unconscious at the Pine Ridge airport, later said he knew AIM had "won" when he went to Dick Wilson's trial for the beating and saw goons in the courthouse reading the old treaties and speaking of their abrogation with the same learned outrage as AIMers.

The government's persecution of AIM stopped its achievements cold. It was a swift, not a gradual, end. Within a year of Wounded Knee's surrender, AIM abandoned most of its work securing Indian rights in favor or merely trying to survive the government's attack. Within another year, the embittered group turned from militance-with-occasional-violence to violence-with-occasional-militance. The violence—both by and to AIM—drove away activists, turned press and public opinion against AIM and convinced donors to cinch their purses. By the time Peltier was convicted in 1977, AIM was fast disintegrating. By the time Skyhorse and Mohawk were acquitted a year later, there was hardly enough left of AIM to throw a victory party.

NOW

CHAPTER 13

THE CADILLAC THAT killed Randy Scott was headed south on Moody County 13. Scott, on a motorcycle, was westbound on County 14, which crossed 13 in the level farm country of southeastern South Dakota. Just before the intersection, Scott's friend Terry Johnson, also on a motorcycle, glanced in his rearview mirror and saw Scott looking fine. After the intersection, Johnson glanced again, but Scott was not there. An enormous cloud of dust was.

A family in a motor home a few hundred yards behind Scott had a clear view of his last moments. They said that as soon as Johnson's motorcycle passed through the crossroads, a big white car raced into the intersection from the north, and Scott's motorcycle ran smack into the side of it. Then everything went smoky with dust and debris. The motorcycles, the family said, were doing sixty miles an hour or so; the Cadillac was doing at least that. Scott could not have seen the car until the last instant because a tall cornfield at the corner of the crossroads completely obscured the view to the north.

Another family was approaching the junction from the south and had a head-on look at the Cadillac as it drove toward them. They said the Cadillac didn't appear to slow down in the least before running the stop sign on its side of the intersection. When the motorcycle hit the car, it was, they said, as if an auto parts store exploded—gears and springs, rubber and spokes, washers and chrome flying everywhere.

Investigators later determined that Randy Scott's 700-pound Harley-Davidson hit the rear, driver-side door of the 3,900-pound Cadillac

DeVille and bowed the car's frame inward two feet. This in turn caused the roof to cave in, the trunk to buckle, and the windshield to shatter into a thousand-odd pieces. The Harley fared worse. Its headlight, front tire, and gauges exploded on impact, and its frame compressed front to back. Forks, pedals, and handlebars twisted like pipe cleaners, the engine casing popped open, and the gas tanks imploded. In the half second in which these events occurred, motorcycle and car were locked in a skid of maybe thirty feet. Then the Cadillac spun free and through a highway sign—nearly hitting the northbound family—before coming to a stop in a ditch 300 feet beyond. When the Harley was released from the Cadillac, it took the outer panel of the driver-side door with it and soared through the air before crashing and coming to a halt 150 feet from the point of impact. Randy Scott did not go with his bike. He was thrown free of it but not, unfortunately, of the car. His chest and abdomen caught the popped-open lid of the trunk and tore it from its hinges, all but disemboweling him, yet still he flew over and beyond the crossroads before landing in a tumbling, corkscrewing skid that ended 100 feet from the spot of the collision. The witnesses found him a minute or two later, lying face up with grisly lacerations and no pulse. In life Scott was a farmer of soybeans. Death had come for him in a soybean field.

Patty Jenkins, of the northbound family, stepped out of her car and jogged over to the Cadillac, where a passenger was helping a bejowled man of prosperous girth slide across the driver's seat and out the passenger-side door. She asked if they were okay, and the passenger said they were. The driver, she saw on closer inspection, was Bill Janklow.

Ten minutes later the first deputy sheriff arrived. He and two more officers who came later questioned Janklow about the crash, and Janklow told them the same story: "I was going south, going to Brandon, and I was coming down the road, and as I came up to this place, there was a car on the left-hand side of the road that came right across towards me. I was slowing up for that stop sign and I just raced around it. I gunned around him. When I tried to—when I tried to miss them, I gunned it."

Janklow, in other words, had had to race through the stop sign to avoid an oncoming car. Of the six witnesses to the wreck, excluding Janklow and his passenger, not a one had seen a car swerving head-on for Janklow. The date was August 16, 2003, seven months into Janklow's first term in Congress.

Attorney General Janklow became Governor Janklow in 1979. He did so on the back of the American Indian Movement. If there were other factors in his ascension, as of course there were, none was more important than having AIM for a foil. In 1976, one year into Janklow's term as attorney general, Dennis Banks was captured outside San Francisco. Banks had lived on the run since his encounter with the Oregon State Patrol in Marlon Brando's motor home the previous November, and he had been wanted before that for fleeing his conviction, at the hands of Janklow, for the Custer riot. On his arrest, Banks told California's governor, Jerry Brown, that he feared for his life in a penitentiary run by Janklow, and he drew Brown's attention to Janklow's *mot* that the only way to deal with AIMers was to put bullets in their brains. When Janklow demanded Banks be returned to South Dakota, Brown rebuffed him. Banks enjoyed asylum in California as long as Brown remained governor.

By way of reply, Janklow announced, "We feel there is a beacon in California saying, 'Give us your felons, your pickpockets, your crooked masses yearning to be free.' So we are going to send to California every crook in the state. Anyone with a felony conviction who has not hurt anybody will be invited to go to Sacramento, and as long as they stay in California we won't do anything. We believe in equal treatment."

He was nearly as good as his word. For seven years he gave accused (not convicted) nonviolent felons a choice between a one-way ticket to the Golden State and prosecution. No one turned down the ticket. It was just one example of Janklow's lavish exploitation of AIM to his advantage.

South Dakotans made Janklow governor two and a half years later. By then, AIM was all but expired (the group would continue to exist—it still does today—but more in name than fact), and Janklow transformed his anti-AIMism into a more ecumenical law-and-orderism punctuated by the same bravado he had used against AIM—as, for example, when he declared that anyone found with dynamite would be detonated with it, or when he tried to take a side arm into the U.S. Supreme Court, where he was arguing a case. He held the governor's mansion for two four-year terms before being forced into early retirement by term limits. But he returned in 1995 for two more terms, upon the expiration of which he was sent to Congress. He won most of his races by enormous margins.

In Janklow's repeated and decisive victories Indians tended to see what blacks saw in Strom Thurmond's: the inconsequence of their past. It was not that the latter-day Janklow, any more than the latter-day Thurmond, continued to express the barbarisms on which he had risen to power. But his continued presence in power said that to a great many people the malignant history of South Dakota, under whose legacy Indians still suffered daily, was so much water under the bridge, nothing to get worked up about. Janklow confused matters, as did Thurmond, by making the occasional generous gesture to old enemies. For example, after Dennis Banks tired of exile and finally entered a South Dakota prison in 1985, Janklow gave him a furlough to attend his grandfather's funeral. Meanwhile the governer continued his assaults on Indian interests at a lower pitch: pursuing court cases that chipped away at tribal sovereignty, backing commercial ventures next to sacred Lakota sites, elevating the perjurious R. D. Hurd and the ex–Mob lawyer John Fitzgerald to the South Dakota bench, and so on.

And although not precisely by intention, Janklow did more than any other individual to keep the government's subversion of AIM from becoming widely known. It had been Janklow's habit, from the start of his political career, to retaliate against critics by any means necessary. Reporters who wrote unfavorable stories found themselves blacklisted at state agencies, unable to interview officials they needed for their articles. Other reporters were fired or "reassigned" after Janklow threatened their weak-kneed publishers. Such tactics sufficed to make most reporters self-censoring in their coverage of the governor, but where more persuasion was needed, Janklow did not hesitate to sue. His libel suits were legion. Time and again, they were judged unfounded at best and frivolous at worst, as when he sought $6 million from WKLDOC for saying in court (where such statements are protected) that he had been seen drunk in a bar. It mattered not a whit that his claims were almost always quickly dismissed. It still cost his critics to defend against them. And there was always the chance that even a frivolous claim might not be thrown out quickly.

Such was the case with his suit against *Newsweek*, which in 1983 ran a story that said, accurately enough, that Janklow had been disbarred from tribal court for raping Jancita Eagle Deer. Through ceaseless motions and appeals, Janklow kept the empty claim in court for years before it was finally thrown out. Viking Press and Peter Matthiessen endured worse after they published *In the Spirit of Crazy Horse* in 1983. Matthiessen's epic of how the government framed Leonard Peltier mentioned Eagle Deer's rape allegation and other stains on Janklow's name almost in passing, for which trespasses Janklow demanded millions. No doubt encouraged by Janklow's suit, Agent David Price brought a similar claim. Viking mounted a vigorous defense, but on advice of counsel the publishing house stifled the promotion of *Crazy Horse* and didn't release a paperback edition until the suits were dismissed—eight years later. A book that might have become a bestseller instead reached a more modest audience. Viking later estimated its defense costs at nearly $1 million, and writers and publishers took heed. From 1983 until the publication of *The Unquiet Grave* in 2006, no major publishing house produced a book that broached Janklow's pursuit of AIM or his alleged rape of Eagle Deer—or, more importantly, the government's broader struggle against AIM.

Janklow made a more intentional assault on AIM's carcass in 2000, when, during the last days of the Clinton presidency, activists sought a pardon for Leonard Peltier, then marking his twenty-fifth year in prison. Among those calling for Peltier's freedom were Nobel Peace Prize winners

Bishop Desmond Tutu and Rigoberta Menchú, activists Coretta Scott King, Sister Helen Prejean, and Gloria Steinem, writers Kurt Vonnegut and William Styron, and entertainers Robert Redford and Barbra Streisand. When rumors surfaced that Clinton was inclined to pardon Peltier, Janklow hurried to the White House where, according to both Janklow and White House sources, he made the decisive argument against clemency. Clinton pardoned the likes of fugitive campaign donor Marc Rich instead, and Peltier stayed in Leavenworth.

"Had we known that pardons were for sale," an aging Vernon Bellecourt said, "we would have contacted millions of friends to send one dollar apiece to a pardons pool."

When Janklow was elected to Congress in 2002, Hank Adams, the Assiniboine who had negotiated the end of the Trail of Broken Treaties, asked the House of Representatives to investigate him. Adams drew Congress's attention to Janklow's illegal incursions on the Yankton and Pine Ridge reservations and to Judge Gonzalez's finding that he had raped Jancita Eagle Deer. Adams suggested that if the House agreed that Janklow had committed such crimes, it should refuse to seat him. Congress ignored Adams entirely.

The Native press, however, gave Adams a trace of ink, and the story came to my attention in this way. I was curious about why an Indian leader who commanded the respect of nearly all who knew him was, after so many years, still pursuing Janklow, whom I had never heard of and whose crimes, real or alleged, were older than I. After speaking with Adams, I asked the FBI and BIA to produce their reports on Eagle Deer's rape claim. Both bureaus acknowledged that they should have the reports, but both said they couldn't find them. I called Janklow's congressional office and told his press secretary that I presumed Janklow had the reports and that I also presumed he would share them since he had (as I had learned) often said that the FBI's investigation in 1975 had cleared him beyond doubt. The press secretary said Janklow would gladly share them and promised to send them next day, but a week passed with no reports. I called the secretary back to inquire of their whereabouts and was told that Janklow had decided I didn't need the reports after all. He added, "Bill said to tell you that he does not want you to have a reckless disregard for the truth"—*reckless disregard for the truth* being the judicial standard for libel.

The reports, as it turned out, had already entered the public domain by another route. When Janklow sued Matthiessen, Viking Press, and *Newsweek* in 1983, he opened himself to the possibility that the defendants would ask for his FBI and BIA files. They did just that, and the documents were entered into the court record, where I found them decades later in the archives of several states. The most important records were archived in South Dakota, but the local press had either never looked at them or, if they had, had never printed what they saw.

Even in their heavily censored state, the reports made plain why Janklow did not want people to see them. To begin with, his alibi for the rape was deeply flawed. He had first told his alibi to Kaye Lord, the boarding school supervisor, on the afternoon after the alleged rape, his story being that he and Eagle Deer had left his house for the dance hall at 8:00 p.m., that they found the dance hall dark and went for a drive to kill time, and that they returned to the dance hall at about 8:45 p.m. The starting time of 8:00 and the ending time of 8:45 roughly matched what Eagle Deer told Lord. But the next day Janklow changed his alibi. He now told BIA investigator Peter Pitchlynn that the drive had started at 8:00 but had lasted only until 8:15—just long enough to get to the darkened field several miles from town and come directly back, but nowhere near long enough for a rape.

This was not the only improvement Janklow's alibi enjoyed in the following days. When Janklow spoke with Kaye Lord, he didn't mention anyone who could verify his story. But days later he led the FBI to three witnesses, all of whom said Janklow had returned to the dance hall in town no later than 8:20. The most formidable of the witnesses was the town's police chief, Jim Deuchar, a friend of Janklow. Deuchar told the FBI that Janklow came to the police station, just to chat, at 8:20. He remembered the time precisely because he was making an entry in the police log when

Janklow walked in. (There is no sign the log was ever produced.) Deuchar also told the FBI that a few minutes after Janklow arrived, Eagle Deer wandered over from the dance hall, where Janklow had dropped her off, and tried to get Janklow to buy her peppermint schnapps. Janklow said no and she left.

Janklow's other witnesses were a pair of sisters named Amy and Patty Wright, aged fifteen and thirteen. The Wrights said, essentially, that they met Eagle Deer in Mission at 8:20 as she was getting out of Janklow's car and stayed with her for the next several hours.

The trouble with Janklow's new witnesses was that their stories could not simultaneously be true. If the Wright girls were with Eagle Deer from the moment she stepped out of Janklow's car, then they had to have been with her at the police station. But Police Chief Deuchar did not say that the Wrights had come with Eagle Deer to the station, nor did the girls say they had done so. Someone was, or all of them were, lying. Coincidentally or not, after Janklow rose to power, the mother of the Wright girls became known as one of Janklow's most favored supporters on the Rosebud Reservation. Coincidentally or not, as an adult, one of the Wright girls was given to boasting that she could get Governor Janklow on the phone in under five minutes any time of day, any day of the week.

The investigative reports show that the FBI agent on the case, John Penrod, neither noticed the contradictions in the alibi nor asked Janklow or his witnesses about them. Nor did Penrod collect physical evidence, like the clothes worn by Eagle Deer and Janklow. Nor did he search Janklow's car. Nor did he look for tire tracks at the scene of the alleged rape, which would have been important because Janklow said he had pulled into the little-traveled field only to U-turn, while Eagle Deer said he had driven a half-mile into it and parked. Asked decades later why he had forgone this legwork, Penrod explained that on the Indian reservations of West River Dakota, the U.S. attorney discouraged such exertions.

"You'd wait to see if he wanted to prosecute," Penrod said. "Then, if he did, you'd gather that kind of evidence."

But a decision to prosecute could be weeks in coming—in Eagle Deer's case, it was over a month—by which point most of the evidence would have disappeared or been contaminated. Ronald Clabaugh, the assistant U.S. attorney who reviewed the case in 1967, said Penrod's memory was wrong; his office never frowned on the collection of evidence. But Penrod worked the reservations for nine years and was firm in his recollection.

The documents from the court archives also shed light on Eagle Deer's rape exam. The doctor who performed it was fresh out of medical school and had to find a book on how to do the exam. Even then, he didn't know that the lapse of thirty-six hours between the alleged rape and his exam would sharply cut the odds of finding semen. The doctor also didn't know that he needed to swab for semen outside Eagle Deer's vagina and comb her groin for foreign pubic hairs. When she complained of a tender thigh, he didn't see in her complaint a possible symptom of sexual assault. (A doctor who testified before Judge Gonzalez seven years later did.) And because he didn't examine Eagle Deer beyond her pubis, he completely missed the nickel-sized hickey on her breast, visible in an investigative photo. The most the doctor could have reasonably concluded from the exam was that Eagle Deer had exhibited symptoms consistent with rape but that rape could be neither proven nor disproven. The doctor, however, said no semen meant no rape, and Agent Penrod and Assistant U.S. Attorney Clabaugh agreed.

Nothing in Penrod's report suggests that Janklow benefited from favorable treatment *per se*. He seems to have benefited "merely" from, on the one hand, the deference accorded a white male lawyer whose accuser was an Indian girl and, on the other, an institutional reluctance by the federal prosecutor to pursue a "trivial" charge like rape. (The reluctance continues today. Andrea Smith, a professor of Native American Studies at the University of Michigan, has found evidence of gross, ongoing under-prosecution of reservation rapes, but she has been unable to pinpoint the extent of the under-prosecution because no U.S. attorney will tell her how many rape complaints are received or prosecuted on reservations.) But if Janklow's exoneration in 1967 was generic, his exoneration in 1975, when the rape claim was re-investigated for his Senate confirmation, seems to have resulted from a more intentional cover-up. The Ford White House touted the re-investigation's "45 substantive interviews in several different states, comprising some 375 FBI agent hours." But Janklow's FBI file and other court papers show that 28 of the 45 interviews did not even discuss the subject of rape. They were, it seems, interviews of the "Is the nominee a Communist?" type—common to background checks of the time but irrelevant to real investigation. Of the remaining 17 interviews, the FBI's censorship is too severe to say whether any touched on the rape, but it is clear that nearly all of the 45 interviews were brief and not "substantive." It also appears that in 1975 the FBI did not re-interview any of the original finders of fact: not Agent Penrod (who was still in the FBI's employ), not BIA officer Pitchlynn, not prosecutor Clabaugh, not the doctor, and not school administrator Lord. Nor is there any sign from 1975 that the FBI examined Janklow's changed alibi, the conflicting alibis of his witnesses, the shoddiness of the rape exam, or Penrod's failure to collect physical evidence. There seems, in short, to have been absolutely nothing to support the White House's claim of an extensive inquiry. The senators who cleared Janklow were snowed.

The motive for the deception, and its place of origin, can only be guessed. Maybe the FBI deceived the White House, or maybe they were in cahoots. Maybe the cover-up was bureaucratic rather than political in intent: the FBI simply didn't want to admit having botched the 1967 investigation. Maybe the re-investigators were as incompetent or indifferent as the original investigators and never noticed that Janklow had been given a pass eight years before. Or maybe more sinister forces were at work. The re-investigation took place at the same moment that the FBI was in a near frenzy over the "secret AIM project," and Attorney General Janklow was the FBI's most potent ally in the state where both the project and the heart of the FBI's covert fight against AIM were located. Unquestionably, the FBI would not have wanted Janklow disabled. Whether this predilection led the FBI to lie to the White House and the Senate about its "re-investigation," only the FBI can say. It will not, of course. After I found the censored investigative reports, I gave their case numbers to the FBI and asked it to search for them again and, if found, to release uncensored copies. The FBI at last found the reports but refused to release any part of them, even those parts already in the public domain. I sued, and the Bureau released some of the already public parts. As this book went to press, my lawsuit to win the release of the remainder was entering its fourth year.

The rules that govern the bar of the U.S. Supreme Court say that when a member is disbarred from another court, he or she is, *ipso facto*, disbarred from the Supreme Court. After Janklow was elected to Congress in 2002, a law student named David Harris who had spent part of his childhood on the Rosebud Reservation sent the Supreme Court a copy of Judge Gonzalez's order disbarring Janklow from tribal court. Harris told the justices that, given the rules of their bar, they had to disbar the congressman. The court ignored him.

I called the court to ask why. A spokeswoman told me that for a member of the Supreme Court bar to be expelled, the lower court making the initial disbarment had to request the Supreme Court to do the same. In this case, the tribal court had not done so, so the Supreme Court would not disbar Janklow. The spokeswoman also said that the lower court had to be the highest court in its jurisdiction, which a tribal court was not. I confessed my puzzlement. I had a copy of the rules of the Supreme Court bar open before me, and nowhere could I find the requirements she was citing. There followed much ummming and ahhhing from her end of the line, until finally she said that the requirements were not actually *written* in the rules; they were just *sort of implied*. To my layman's ear, it sounded a tad arbitrary for the highest court in the land to ignore its written rules and make up new ones as it went along. The practice was, however, consistent with Indian jurisprudence, whose guiding precedent was that binding treaties that no longer served America's acquisitive purposes could be broken at whim. As the spokeswoman did not seem the type who would profit from a discussion of these points, I said only that even if she were right about what the rules were, she had erred on at least one part of their application, namely that the Rosebud Tribal Court was not the highest in its jurisdiction. That court, I said, was and is the rough equivalent of a state supreme court, the venue of last resort for non-federal issues on the sovereign reservation. The spokeswoman rejoined, with admirable finality, that tribal courts did not "count," that only a federal court or state supreme court did. It sounded to me like another made-up rule.

The spokeswoman didn't know it, but she was granting Janklow a reprieve he had been granted before. In 1974, Judge Gonzalez alerted the federal and state bars of South Dakota that he had dismissed Janklow from the tribal bar and asked them to do likewise. As with the U.S. Supreme Court, the federal bar of South Dakota was required to disbar any member disbarred elsewhere. But Judge Fred Nichol, who oversaw the bar, let Janklow's membership stand, probably because he was loathe to insult a sitting attorney general. The state bar association was required to investigate the merits of Gonzalez's disbarment and decide whether to do the same. The bar's investigation consisted of a phone call to Harold Doyle, who had been the U.S. attorney in 1967. Doyle was asked if he had made a mistake by not prosecuting Janklow for rape. He said no, and that was that.

It seemed to me newsworthy that the Supreme Court had broken its rules for a sitting congressman who a lower court decided had raped an Indian child, that the FBI or White House or both had deceived the Senate about the alleged rape, that before that the FBI and U.S. attorney had given the congressman a pass on the rape charge (and that reservation rapes were still badly under-prosecuted today), and that by virtue of the government's compassion, the alleged rapist had risen to become the George Wallace of Indian Country. I suggested as much to editors at dozens of newspapers and magazines, but they all declined even the briefest of articles. The more candid editors said that since their readers knew nothing about modern Indian history, it would require too many column inches to educate them enough to care. The most candid said that Bill Janklow might be the George Wallace of Indian Country, but to the rest of America he was a two-bit congressman from a one-bit state. In these explanations lay a neat summary of why Indian Country has been neglected so thoroughly since the end of the Indian wars.

A lone exception to the media blackout was a columnist for the *Washington Post* named Richard Leiby. Leiby had become interested in the story after talking to law student David Harris, and in the course of his research he received a bootleg audiotape of the testimony Jancita Eagle Deer gave before Judge Gonzalez in 1974. Gonzalez, now retired, has the master tape, but his fear of Janklow is such that he will not distribute copies. He is wont to offer reporters to listen to it in person, only to rescind the offer, presumably in fright, after they have traveled considerable distance to do so. Leiby was deeply moved by Eagle Deer's testimony.

"It was devastating," he said, "utterly convincing. You cannot listen to her without getting chills and feeling she is telling the absolute truth."

He wrote a column to this effect, supported by evidence from my investigation, and gave it to his editors, who spiked it. As it happened, what Post Company owned *Newsweek*, and Janklow's suit against the magazine two decades earlier had not faded from corporate memory. The conglomerate did not care to court another lawsuit over so "minor" an event by so "minor" a politician.

After Randy Scott was killed, the South Dakota press made a belated investigation into Janklow's driving record—belated because Janklow had long been notorious for recklessness on the road. The press found that nine months earlier, on the very spot where he killed Scott, Janklow had roared past a stop sign into the intersection at maybe ninety miles per hour and missed smashing into a family in a minivan by inches. Jennifer Walters, riding in the van, called 911 on her cell phone and reported the feral Cadillac. An hour later the Moody County dispatcher called her back and said a deputy sheriff had found the car—it was driving ninety-two—but had let the driver go without ticketing him. Did Ms. Walters still care to file a complaint?

Walters asked why the deputy had let the driver go.

The dispatcher chuckled. "It was Governor Janklow."

"I was just a little concerned," Walters told reporters after Scott was killed, "about who he was and who I am and carrying things any farther. I also believed nothing would ever be done, so I just let it drop and thank my stars that I'm alive."

Her assessment that nothing would be done was validated by other reportorial discoveries, including that since 1994, police had caught Janklow speeding more than twenty times—driving eighty-four in a construction zone signed for forty, passing cars with reckless swerves into oncoming traffic, racing down the highway with flashing police lights that Janklow had installed and illegally used on his private cars—and let him off every time. During this period Janklow caused at least seven wrecks but never had his license suspended. In three of the wrecks, he claimed, as he would on the day he killed Randy Scott, that a car or animal entered his lane and forced him to swerve. Witnesses never saw the other cars or animals, one of which the police derided as a "phantom vehicle." Had reporters read the court papers from his libel suits fifteen years before, they would also have found a deposition in which Janklow was asked, "How many times have you been stopped for speeding?"

"Lots," he answered.

"What is lots? Thirty times?"

"For speeding? Yes. Oh, gosh yes."

"Closer to one hundred times?"

"I think it would probably be more than fifty. I never kept track, but it is a lot."

"Do you know that you were stopped over three hundred times for speeding in the last fifteen years?"

"No."

"Would you deny over two hundred times in the last twenty years?"

"Yes. Probably."

The revelations prompted the state's Republican governor, Mike Rounds, to declare that the state patrol was doing a fine job and he wasn't planning on changing much of anything. An outcry forced him to make a desultory investigation, but he withheld the findings from the press until forced to release them. When finally made public, they showed that state troopers had showered Janklow with even more favorable treatment than the press had discovered, which prompted the imperturbable Rounds to say that none of the troopers or their superiors would be fired or even demoted or reprimanded. He declared the matter closed, and the state press corps did not push him further.

A few weeks after Randy Scott was killed, the state's attorney for Moody County, a former Republican only recently converted to Democracy, charged Janklow with three misdemeanors and manslaughter in the second degree. The latter was a felony punishable by ten years in prison and $10,000 in fines. (Janklow's people had lobbied for a single reckless-driving charge, a misdemeanor with a maximum of one year in jail and $1,000 in fines.) The congressman was tried in December 2003 in Flandreau, seat of Moody County, which by chance was his boyhood home. During his four gubernatorial terms, Janklow had blessed Flandreau's 2,376 residents with an egg-production co-op, a community center, a swimming pool, and an airport—Janklow International, wits called the last. In return, citizens had given him their votes in diluvial quantity. Observers wondered how impartial a local jury would be.

Come the trial, Janklow mounted a defense unique in the annals of American law: innocence by reason of hypoglycemia—by reason, that is, of low blood sugar. His lawyer explained that on the morning of the accident, the diabetic Janklow had given himself his usual insulin shot but then had neglected to eat during the rest of the day. This in turn caused a serious imbalance in his blood sugar. Normally Janklow would have noticed that he was becoming weak and that his mind was becoming less clear, but he had recently been prescribed a new medicine, a beta-blocker, which masked the signs of his weakness. By the time he drove through the cross-roads of routes 13 and 14, he was, quite unintentionally, in a very dangerous state, his mind too badly fogged to comprehend the stop sign or to assess his own condition. The defense found a doctor to testify for the less outlandish parts of the theory, but more credible doctors, speaking for the prosecution, said that while beta-blockers could stop a person from shaking or sweating, they would in no way keep him from noticing that his body had gone weak or his mind cloudy.

Janklow's counsel could not find an expert to explain other holes in the hypoglycemic argument, for example how, if Janklow was foggy of mind just before the crash, he was entirely clearheaded just after it; or why the medics who came immediately to the scene saw no signs of hypoglycemia in Janklow, even though they knew he was diabetic and specifically looked for such signs. Janklow's lawyer *did* explain why just after the crash Janklow offered an entirely different defense for running the stop sign—in the form of the car coming at him—from the blood-sugar defense on offer in court: the oncoming car had been a hallucination, and the hallucination further proved Janklow's dire hypoglycemia. The only trouble with this tidy claim was that Janklow's passenger, his congressional chief of staff Chris Braendlin, also said just after the crash that he had seen the oncoming car. Perhaps hypoglycemic hallucinations were contagious. Janklow's lawyer did not say.

On the last day of the weeklong trial, Janklow took the stand, and the prosecution, unable to ask him about the crash (he said a bang on the head during the wreck eventually erased his memory of it), queried him about his prior driving record. Was it generally his practice, the prosecution asked, to stop at stop signs?

"Always," Janklow said. But he added, "Unless I have a reason not to. There are times I've been going on emergency stuff, on important stuff."

"Have you run stop signs late at night when you are by yourself?"

"I probably have."

"Or if you're just running late?"

"I probably have."

"Do you go through them at a high rate of speed?"

"I probably have."

The jury deliberated five hours before convicting him of all counts.

South Dakotans hailed the verdict as proof that no man in their state was above the law, but the remarks from the jurors afterward made the principle seem less certain. To a person, the jurors thought Janklow was telling the truth as best he could recall it, and they all believed either that the masked-hypoglycemia defense was an accurate description of what had happened or that it was quite plausible.

"I felt he was honest," said the jury foreman, a forty-four-year-old dispatcher of trucks and seller of insurance. "I believe the man has a lot of character."

In the early deliberations, six of twelve jurors had wanted to acquit on all counts. They eventually voted to convict only because they thought a diabetic should have known not to skip meals before driving. They reached their verdict, they said, with the greatest of reluctance.

Indians tended to find in the jurors' remarks not a redemption of justice in Dakota but the reverse. That the jurors had refused to see Janklow for what he was and that they had convicted him of killing a *white* man only with difficulty went a long way to explaining why he never had been and never would be held to account for wronging Indians.

Janklow's sentencing hearing followed his conviction by a month. Among those who testified to the strength of his character was Larry Wright, brother of alibi witnesses Amy and Patty. "Contrary to belief," Wright said, "he's not a racist. Look at me. My skin is brown." Loyal at the beginning, the family remained so to the end.

At the close of the hearing, Judge Rodney Steele opined that Janklow had been a distinguished public servant and that because his conviction had forced him to resign from Congress, he had already endured a "special" humiliation, hence was not in need of harsh sentencing. He jailed

Janklow for 100 of a possible 3,650 days. For killing nobody, Sarah Bad Heart Bull, Dennis Banks, and Russell Means had been sentenced by South Dakota judges to multiples of Janklow's sentence. Judge Steele further decreed that if Janklow stayed aright of the law for three years, his conviction would be sealed—in effect erased from his record, as if Randy Scott had never been killed. Later that day, the Scott family filed a civil suit against Janklow for wrongful death. Their lawyer said they would seek millions.

CHAPTER 14

"**LADIES AND GENTLEMEN**, on a December morning in 1975 a little red Ford Pinto wagon pulled up to the edge of a road about three miles north of the junction of Highway 73 and 44. The driver of that little red car was Theda Clarke. There were three passengers in the car: the defendant, Arlo Looking Cloud; fellow by the name of John Graham; and Anna Mae Aquash. After Anna Mae was taken out of the car, she was walked by the defendant and by Mr. Graham from the edge of the road out to the edge of that cliff." The prosecutor pointed to an aerial photograph on the courtroom video screen. "All the way out there she was begging them not to kill her. When they got to the edge of the cliff and she realized that her pleas were to no avail, she asked to have time to pray. While she was praying, she was shot in the back of her head. Her body was either thrown or fell over the cliff, came to rest right there where that white mark is. Stayed there for about two and a half months until a rancher riding fence found it. After Anna Mae was killed, the defendant and Mr. Graham walked back to the car and three people drove back to Denver."

U.S. Attorney James McMahon was all line and angle, a Grant Wood portrait come to life. His gestures were as spare as his frame, his tone without affect, his suit a shade of businessman's overcast. He appeared in every respect a man on guard against the moment of passion that might cost him any of twelve votes. He told the jury that Anna Mae Aquash had been arrested in Oregon in the fall of 1975 and brought to Pierre for trial, but she had jumped bond—had called a friend in Rapid City, who had come to Pierre and given her a ride to Denver. There Aquash was received by a member of the American Indian Movement named Theda Clarke, who in turn delivered her to the apartment of Troy Lynn Yellow Wood, also of AIM.

"She was not initially being held against her will," McMahon said of Aquash. "She spent Thanksgiving there. She spent into December there. But she was very scared while she was there. The first part of December, a call came from South Dakota down to Denver, by Angie Janis. Said that Anna Mae was an informant, she was wanted back in South Dakota. A meeting was convened at the home of Troy Lynn Yellow Wood. Theda Clarke was there, and of course Troy Lynn Yellow Wood was there. Angie Janis was there. There were some members of the Crusade for Justice there, which was a Chicano organization out of Denver that had close ties with the AIM people. And there were other people there who have not yet been identified. The defendant Arlo Looking Cloud was there, and John Graham was there, and their job during this meeting was, they kept Anna Mae Aquash in a separate room under guard.

"When the meeting ended, Theda Clarke came to the room and said, 'Let's go.' They got Anna Mae up and they tied her wrists together. Anna Mae was crying. She said, 'I don't want to go. If I go back to South Dakota, you will never see me alive again.' Troy Lynn Yellow Wood had a conversation with Theda Clarke, said she didn't understand why they were taking her. Theda Clarke said, 'She is going one way or the other.' The defendant, Mr. Looking Cloud, and John Graham marched her out of the apartment, put her in the hatch end of that little red Pinto car that was owned by Theda Clarke, tied up. Then the two of them got in the car along with Theda Clarke. They drove all night to Rapid City. Early in the morning they went to an empty apartment that was owned by Thelma Rios, another AIM member in Rapid. The defendant, Mr. Looking Cloud, and John Graham kept Anna Mae Aquash under guard all day.

"Some point late in the afternoon Anna Mae was taken to a house that had been set up for what was called the Wounded Knee Legal Defense/Offense Committee. There was another meeting at that time involving Anna Mae. When they left that house, the defendant, Mr. Graham, and Theda Clarke again took Anna Mae. They put her back in the little red Pinto, again bound up, tied up. The defendant was now driving, and they headed south toward the Pine Ridge Indian Reservation. They first went to a small town, Allen, South Dakota, on the Pine Ridge Reservation, then went to Rosebud. They stop at a house in Rosebud in the wee hours of the morning. Theda Clarke and John Graham go in the house, and the defendant stays in the car and guards Anna Mae. While they are in that car, she begs him to let her go. She tells him she knows she is going to be killed, and she begs to be set free. The defendant refuses. Theda Clarke and John Graham come out of the house, they get into the car, and they start driving north toward Wanblee. Approximately three miles north of the intersection of Highway 73 and Highway 44 is where they pulled over and walked her out to the cliff.

"From the time in Denver, when Anna Mae Aquash was taken, bound, and put into that little red Pinto, when she was hauled bound and tied up to Rapid City, when she was hauled bound and tied up down to the Pine Ridge Reservation, to the Rosebud Reservation, and out to that cliff on the south edge of the Badlands where she was killed, Mr. Looking Cloud was there every step of the way. And when we are done with the evidence, ladies and gentlemen, we are going to ask you to find him guilty."

Defense attorney Tim Rensch was James McMahon's inverse. His sideburns were carved to rakish points, his goatee was nearly as acute, and his belly and ease were those of a barman. In a coat of sportscaster beige, slacks of tightly checkered green, and a tie of arresting yellow, he presented *Esquire*'s idea of an esquire.

"Arlo Looking Cloud didn't kill anybody," Rensch told the jury. "Arlo Looking Cloud, the evidence in this case will show, didn't *help* kill Mrs. Pictou-Aquash. What Arlo Looking Cloud became embroiled in was simply being in the wrong place at the wrong time. You see, in December of 1975, Arlo lived in a place near the projects down in Denver. He had a job selling art, making paintings, things of that nature. He had a little boy.

Up to that point in his life, he had had some problems with alcohol and with drugs, but he was doing well. And this weekend in early December of 1975 his path would change. The woman who lived with him, Charlotte Zephier, was going on a trip that weekend. And what does Arlo do, the twenty-two-year-old young man that he is? He goes out on the town and drinks all night. He sleeps all day, and he wakes up in the afternoon with a splitting headache, and he decides to go downtown again and try to find his friend Joe Morgan, and that's what changed his fate. His intent was not to kill somebody or help premeditate the end of a human being. His intent was to go drinking because he had a hangover. He appears on the steps of Troy Lynn Yellow Wood's and knocks on the door to see if his friend Joe Morgan is there, and Troy Lynn doesn't answer. Theda Clarke is there.

"Theda Clarke is a fifty-ish Indian woman who owns a bar in Colorado. Arlo had known her from before. She would give him some drinks, let him drink in her bar, things of this nature. Theda, on this night, says to young Arlo, 'Hey, we want you to drive up to Rapid City for us.' Arlo doesn't really want to drive up to Rapid City for her. You will find evidence in this case that Theda Clarke, well, she was older, she was pushy, and when she asked Arlo to drive to Rapid City, Arlo said, 'Okay, I will do it.' As he steps into the house of Yellow Wood's, they shoo him right down to the basement, and as he comes down the steps, he sees an individual he had never met before by the name of John Graham. There was also a young woman laying on the couch under a blanket, but they don't introduce her to Arlo. Arlo meets John Graham, also known as John Boy. They converse, don't talk really about much, and suddenly this John Graham is talking about a rope, and Theda is talking about a rope, and John Graham takes this young woman off of the couch, has her get up, and ties her hands behind her back. Arlo Looking Cloud doesn't know what their relationship is, doesn't really know what is going on. But he knows enough not to ask questions.

"Well, John Boy leads this young woman, who turns out to be Anna Mae Pictou-Aquash, up these steps on this night in December of 1975. Arlo through the years has made statements about this. And you will find in this case that for thirty years, approximately, Arlo has been, well, not a productive member of society. He's lived on the streets. He has been drunk. He has used drugs. He has abused his body. He has done many things that affect his memory and his ability to communicate about events." Here Rensch extended a gentle hand in the direction of his client, who in press photographs had appeared a coal-eyed incendiary with cheeks roughened from hard living and a mustache of a vaguely sinister Manchurian cut. But in the drab modern courtroom in Rapid City's drab federal courthouse in February 2004, the defendant turned out to be a wisp of a man, nearly pigmy in height and unsteady of carriage and gaze—more mystified than Manchurian. The Arlo Looking Cloud of fifty might, with a great strain to mind and body, have been able to snuff a grasshopper. More than once during the trial of his life, he would fall asleep at the defense table.

"But that night," Rensch continued, "this twenty-two-year-old boy who was there walked up those stairs, and, yes, he thought something was amiss and he didn't do anything to stop it. And as they go out into the car, this poor lady is put into the back and Arlo drives. He doesn't make any excuses about driving, but he thought they were just going to Rapid City. Theda mentioned something about this girl talking too much. Nothing about, 'We are going to take her to Rapid and she is going to be interrogated.' Nothing about, 'Please help us kill this woman in furtherance of the movement.' So they drove all night to Rapid City. Arlo drives some of the time, he sleeps some of the time. There isn't much conversation in this car. Arlo knows something isn't fitting right here, but he is not asking questions, and Theda and John Boy act as though they know what is going on—act as though they heard something about what might happen—but they don't talk to Arlo about it.

"They get to Rapid City in the early morning hours, and they drive to an apartment that is up by the mall out by the highway, Knollwood Heights. There is no furniture in the apartment. John Graham sleeps in a room with Ms. Pictou-Aquash, Arlo sleeps on the floor. Arlo wakes up at some point in the day and he takes the car down to put gas in it. He runs into a friend, and they spend a period of time together. Then Arlo goes back to the Knollwood Heights apartment, and Theda and John Boy are mad at him because he has gone with the car. They say, 'We have to go to the reservation,' and everybody gets in the car. They drive down to the reservation. Arlo drives for a period of time, remembers stopping, remembers sleeping, remembers switching drivers. Ultimately they end up out in front of a house in Rosebud near the hospital.

"At this time, he is with Anna Mae, with Ms. Pictou-Aquash, and John Boy Patton Graham and Theda Clarke go into this house. They don't tell Arlo what they are going in for. Arlo doesn't know what they are going in for. He doesn't remember Ms. Pictou-Aquash begging to be let go at that point. I guess the evidence will have to bear itself out on that. But nonetheless there's never been any discussion about anybody killing anybody up to that point in time. John Boy and Theda come out of this house, and Arlo is thinking, 'Well, maybe I can finally get back to Denver.' They come out, they get into this Pinto, they drive toward Kadoka. Arlo doesn't know what they are driving toward Kadoka for. Theda is driving. John Boy is there. And they act as though they know what is going to happen, but nobody talks about it. On that lonely highway going straight up on the map to Kadoka, Theda Clarke pulls a U-turn and goes back and forth several times and stops on the side of the road. John Boy Patton gets out of that car— John Boy Patton who is bigger than Arlo—and John Boy Patton tells Ms. Pictou-Aquash to get out of the car and begins leading her off into the ditch. Either John Boy or Theda say to Arlo, 'Come on, get out here.' Arlo gets out of that car, he starts to walk up there. He doesn't march her up to the side of the cliff. He doesn't grab her arm. He is following along, not knowing what is going to happen, and he is thinking they are going to let her go way out here. Then he hears her start to pray, and in his mind he starts to think, 'We are going to pray.'

"BAM! At that point John Boy Patton pulls out a gun and shoots this woman in the back of the head. Arlo reels from it. Arlo did not know that was going to happen. She falls over this cliff, the white shale cliff of the

Badlands, and John Boy Patton turns around, and he looks at him, and he has a gun. And what does this young twenty-two-year-old man do? He says to Graham, 'Give me the gun.' Graham reaches out, hands him the gun. And Arlo fires the gun over the ravine until the gun is empty, and he did it because he was afraid this man who just put a bullet in this woman's head would do the same to him. And he hands the gun back, relieved that the gun is empty. They walk back to the vehicle. They get in. They start going back to Denver. They stop at a bridge, and John Boy Patton—John Graham—wants to bury the pistol. Arlo wants to help bury the pistol, then no one else will get shot. They go down below the bridge, and Arlo helps dig that hole, and they bury the pistol, and they drive to Denver.

"When they get to Denver, Arlo Looking Cloud falls off the face of the earth as it relates to the American Indian Movement. While he lived close to Troy Lynn, and he will see her, and while he may see Theda from time to time because they live in the same town, he stays away from the American Indian Movement. You will hear evidence in this case that on the other hand Mr. Graham—John Boy Patton—had a meteoric rise in the American Indian Movement. At the close of this case I will be asking you to decide whether or not the government can prove beyond a reasonable doubt that Arlo Looking Cloud aided and abetted a murder and had the *intent* for somebody to die. I will ask you to look at his words and understand that a young man who was merely present at something so horrible as a murder is not responsible in the way the shooter is."

The opening arguments in *U.S. v. Fritz Arlo Looking Cloud* were remarkable, if for anything, for the breadth of their agreement: AIMers had held Aquash in Denver and taken her by force first to Rapid City and then to Pine Ridge and Rosebud, where, late in the night, a person or persons unseen decided she would die. The question for the jurors was a narrow one: what did Arlo Looking Cloud know, and when did he know it? But for the spectators who filled the gallery—onetime FBI hands like Joseph Trimbach, who interrupted a Floridian retirement to attend; paunchy AIMers like Russell Means and Vernon Bellecourt, who had long ago fallen out and now tried not to meet eyes; and a mass of reporters not seen in such density at an Indian trial since *U.S. v. Banks and Means*—the question they hoped, or feared, to have answered was who *else* knew what, and when?

The prosecution called for Nathan Merrick, and a broad-faced man attired in the canvas formality of a rancher at church came to the stand. Merrick had been a criminal investigator for the BIA in February 1976 and was among those who went to Roger Amiotte's ranch the day Aquash's body was found. He testified uneventfully about a routine crime-scene investigation until the prosecution asked, "Mr. Merrick, did you have any idea what the cause of death was at that time?"

"At that time," Merrick said, "looking at the body and the way the condition was, general consensus was that she probably was murdered or killed by someone. There was blood underneath of her head, the hair coming from the side of the ravine. And I just felt that somebody threw her down in the ditch, down into the ravine."

This was an astonishment, or should have been. For twenty-eight years, the government had said that until the second autopsy none of its lawmen had seen any sign that Aquash had died violently—no hint at all of trauma to the body, save the decay of exposure. Yet now Merrick was saying not only had he seen blood but the *consensus* of the many BIA officers, FBI agents, and deputy sheriffs on the scene was that the victim had been murdered.

Defense lawyer Rensch, whose client had an interest in proving the government untrustworthy, might have been expected to draw the jury's attention to Merrick's revelation. He did not. He might also, since the jurors had been told nothing of the controversies surrounding Aquash's corpse, have been expected to use Merrick's revelation to explore those controversies. He did not do that either. Not then, nor for the rest of the trial, would jurors hear a word about the great many lies the government had told about its handling of Aquash's body.

Nor did reporters bring Merrick's revelation to light, probably because they didn't know what they were hearing. Few of them were learned in Indian affairs, and anyway most of their employers had charged them with covering only what was said in court. Their stenography yielded a crop of articles declaring "AIM on trial," which was both true and untrue. The FBI, for any who listened closely, was on trial too.

Some months after he testified, Nate Merrick said he couldn't recall who else at the crime scene had been party to the consensus of murder. Asked whether, given the consensus, he had not thought it odd when Dr. Brown ruled the Jane Doe dead of exposure, he said he had not. He had just assumed that he and his fellow officers misdiagnosed the blood on Aquash's head: what they thought was the work of a murderer must have been caused by Aquash's stumbling over the ledge. But even if Merrick was telling the truth, his story didn't explain why the government denied that its men saw blood or suspected foul play when they saw and suspected just that.

Not long later, the FBI released documents that said Aquash's clothes had blood on them. How much blood—whether microscopic or visible to the naked eye—is not clear. The FBI has laboratory notes that probably say, but it refuses to release them.

Donald Dealing, retired from twenty-six years in the FBI but still possessed of the trim anonymity that the Bureau favored in its agents, was called to the stand to discuss what he had seen at the crime scene. He too contradicted a claim cherished by the FBI. The Bureau had long held that he was the only agent who went to the crime scene on the afternoon the body was found. But he said there had been other agents. He did not say who and how many, and Tim Rensch did not ask, but after the trial other FBI officials also referred to "agents" at the scene (also without saying who or how many). Dealing's contradiction slipped by reporters as cleanly as Merrick's did.

On cross-examination, Rensch asked, "Have you ever heard of COINTELPRO?"

There was a long pause. "Yes," Dealing finally said.

Did the FBI, Rensch said, cultivate informers in AIM under COIN-TELPRO?

"I frankly don't—" Dealing started, then began again, "I have heard about COINTELPRO through media and that sort of a thing, but I frankly have never been involved in whatever that was. So I don't know what that is, I am sorry."

That he knew nothing about a program that had nearly consumed the FBI during his tenure reflected poorly either on his powers of observation or on his veracity. But Tim Rensch did not prod him further.

Dealing was followed to the stand by another FBI retiree, Bill Wood, who was an affable-looking grandfather of small ears, close-set eyes, and thin nose. Ten years and twenty pounds ago, he might have passed for George W. Bush. He told the court that he had overseen the Aquash case in the first years after the murder but had not been able to solve it. Rensch seemed skeptical.

"Now, in December of 1975," he asked, "there were informants within the American Indian Movement, were there not, sir?"

"I don't personally know that, no," Wood said.

This was another remarkable claim. December 1975 was only a few months after Agents Williams and Coler were killed at Oglala. The FBI, which riddled AIM with informers even in calm times, penetrated the group all the more thoroughly after the killings. For years Wood's beat had been the American Indian Movement. Yet he had heard nothing about informers in the group? It was hard to swallow.

"Did you personally handle any informants in December of 1975?" Rensch asked.

"Yes, sir, I think I probably had some informants at that time."

"In December of 1975 were you personally in contact with or receiving information from any known operative of the FBI within the American Indian Movement?"

"No, sir."

"You didn't receive any information in December of 1975 from any informant of the FBI about the circumstances surrounding Ms. Aquash's death, did you?"

"No, sir, I did not."

This answer had the advantage of agreeing with what the FBI had said for a quarter century: the murder had been unsolvable for so long because no one would talk to the FBI. But the claim was untrue. After the trial, some of the papers from Wood's file on the case were released under pressure of a Freedom of Information Act lawsuit. One of the heavily censored papers read,

> On December 19, 1975 [which was to say, one week after Aquash was murdered] ████████ advised that an unidentified Indian female was ██ ████████ Colorado. The three Indian members of AIM (all of Denver, Colorado) identified as ████████ (phonetic), ████████ and ████████ allegedly ██ ██ ████████. . . . Source claims the rumors are that ████████ who stays at the ████████, Colorado and ████████ Colorado, committed the actual murder. Others who may have knowledge of the murder are ████████ Colorado and ████████, South Dakota.

The report also said the victim "was supposed to have been from Canada," "was suspected of being an FBI informant," and had been arrested over the summer at the raid on the Crow Dog and Running properties. The only AIMer who could have met the description, as the FBI knew, was Aquash. In short, the FBI knew at least the outlines of Aquash's kidnapping and killing, and probably knew the names of her killers, within *days* of the murder.

The FBI may also have known something of Aquash's fate even before she was murdered. A hint of such (and at this point it is no more than a hint) is raised by an FBI report of December 8, 1975, two or three days before the supposed date of the murder. The only part of the report the FBI will release reads,

█████ source advised Anna Mae Aquash, Indian female ████████
██
██
██
██

Perhaps this scrap has nothing to do with Aquash's kidnapping. But if so, why, after thirty years, does the FBI refuse to release even the slightest indication of what its source advised? Certainly the only *legal* justification for the censorship is that the information bears on the ongoing murder case.

Regardless of what the FBI knew before the murder, after agents were tipped to it that December, they apparently did not try to find or learn anything about Looking Cloud, Graham, and Clarke (or whatever threesome from Denver the tipster had mentioned). At least, the FBI has released no papers to that effect. This, to repeat, was at a time when AIMers everywhere were being spied on, arrested, interrogated, and indicted on any pretense that arose. Yet here the FBI learned that AIMers committed a murder, and it did nothing to look into it. This is, to put it mildly, suspicious. Odder still, after Aquash's body was found, Agent Wood told the U.S. attorney in report after report that the FBI had turned up nothing on the case: only "negative results concerning any positive information regarding AQUASH's death," in Woods' tangled words. He supported his claim by giving the prosecutor sheaves of false leads and dead ends and mentioning only briefly the tip from Denver. He seems to have portrayed the tip as just another red herring, even though he soon knew, as other documents in his file show, that it was accurate.

Skeptics have long believed that the FBI knew who killed Aquash but refused to "solve" the case for fear of where it would lead—maybe to an FBI operative directly involved in the murder or maybe to the less direct but equally unsavory tactics of COINTELPRO, which nudged AIM in a murderous direction. "For years the identity of Anna Mae's killers was an open secret," said Paul DeMain, editor of the small biweekly *News from Indian Country*. "Hundreds, literally hundreds of people knew who killed her and how." In the late 1990s, DeMain and other amateurs solved the case. Then he published the killers' names, thereby depriving the government of its claim that the case could not be cracked. Even so, four more years passed before prosecutors indicted Looking Cloud and Graham. (Theda Clarke has escaped indictment on the grounds of having Alzheimer's, although when I visited her she was entirely lucid. Graham, a Canadian, is fighting extradition from Vancouver.) Wood's papers from Aquash's file are the final proof that the FBI's skeptics were right.

But again Tim Rensch alerted the jury to none of this mischief. Instead, he said to Wood, "Do you know what COINTELPRO is, sir?"

"I have heard the term," Wood replied.

"Did you ever take active efforts to snitch-jacket a person?"

Wood cocked his head and squinted, the personification of confusion. "To do what?"

"Snitch-jacket a person."

"I don't know how you are using that term, sir."

"Did you ever take active efforts to start rumors that people who were not informants *were* informants?"

"Absolutely not. *No.*"

"Were you ever trained in any way to have informants or operatives say that people who weren't really informants *were* informants to create dissension within the American Indian Movement?"

"As far as I know, that wasn't a technique that was used."

"Did you ever do that?"

"No, sir."

"Now, you knew that Ms. Aquash was approached by the FBI and they wanted her to be an informant, did you not know that, sir?"

"No, sir, I did not." (His file said the opposite.)

"Did you ever take part in steps to damage the reputation of people who refused to become informants?"

"No, *sir*. I mean, that wasn't a part of what we *did*."

"So back in 1975, as far as you know, there was no effort by the Federal Bureau of Investigation to plant rumors and create dissension within the American Indian Movement. Is that your testimony?"

"I never did that, and I don't know of anyone else that was doing that."

Rensch dismissed the witness without apprising the jury of the mass of evidence to the contrary. Rensch did not even tell the jury what COINTELPRO was.

Kamook Nichols was a casting director with a star's anatomy. She strode to the stand in a plum pantsuit that flowed fluently over her contours. Her skin was lithe, her deportment erect, her hair cropped but thick. "Dennis Banks's trophy wife," her detractors had said years ago, but she had since parted ways with Banks, and she mounted the stand now, molars clenched and lips drawn to a scowl, the star witness against the movement her husband had built. It was not the sort of act one normally associated with trophy wives. As she settled into her chair, a pew of FBI agents and U.S. marshals in the gallery leaned forward and in unison gripped the back of the bench in front of them. Their knuckles turned white, but they did not notice.

U.S. Attorney McMahon directed Nichols to the AIM convention in Farmington, New Mexico, in June 1975 and asked if she had heard that Leonard Peltier had confronted Aquash there. Rensch objected. Nichols hadn't been present at the so-called confrontation, so whatever she had to say would be hearsay. Also, the confrontation had nothing to do with Looking Cloud's guilt or innocence, so it was irrelevant. Rensch accused McMahon of trying to turn the jury against AIM and, by association, Looking Cloud.

Judge Laurence Piersol, a man of Einsteinian hair and mumbled ruminations, had in his lawyer days defended reporters sued by Bill Janklow for libel. He agreed with Rensch that Nichols's observations would be hearsay but not that they would be irrelevant. They might speak to whether Aquash knew she would be killed and so might reveal her state of mind before her death, which in turn might reveal whether Looking Cloud knew or should have known of her doom. Piersol ruled that Nichols could answer. For this and similar rulings, AIMers accused Piersol of being the prosecution's patsy, but his rulings were grounded in precedent and there was no sign at trial that he was biased against AIM.

Permitted to speak, Nichols said of Peltier, "I heard that he had taken her away from the camp in a car and had put a gun to her head, and that he wanted to know if she was an informant."

"Did you hear what her response was?"

"She told him that if he believed that, he should go ahead and shoot her."

McMahon asked if there were other times that AIMers accused Aquash, and Nichols told of an event some weeks later. She and her husband Dennis were in a motel in Custer when "Leonard Crow Dog came in, and he was very angry. He was yelling, and he told Dennis that he had kicked Anna Mae off of his property. She was a fed. He didn't want her on his property."

McMahon asked if there were other times.

Nichols recalled an episode some weeks later, in October 1975, at the home of AIMer David Hill in Oglala. "We got to Dave's house," she said, "and Dave and Leonard [Peltier] took Anna Mae into the adjoining room, and they were making her make bombs."

"Why were they doing that?"

"For the sake of the fingerprints being on the bomb."

"Were you there when they placed the bombs?"

"Yes."

"Who placed the bombs?"

"Dave Hill and Leonard got out of the car and told Anna Mae to get out with them, and they laid the bombs by the two power plants in Pine Ridge." These were the bombs that exploded on Columbus Day 1975.

McMahon asked Nichols about the drive to Washington state, after the bombings, in Marlon Brando's motor home. He wanted to know why Aquash was along.

"I think Anna Mae was there," Nichols said, "because Dennis and Leonard were watching her."

"While you were camping in Washington state, was Anna Mae allowed to leave by herself?"

"No."

"Was she being watched?"

"Somebody always went around with her."

"Were there allegations or accusations made toward her while you were camping in Washington state?"

"Yes."

"Who made those?"

"Leonard."

"Did you hear him?"

"Yes."

"What did he say?"

"He said that he believed she was a fed and that he was going to get some truth serum and give it to her so that she would tell the truth."

"While you were in Washington, were there any discussions in which sensitive material that you wouldn't have wanted in the hands of law enforcement was discussed?"

"Yes," she said. She started to cry. "We were sitting at the table in this motor home. Anna Mae was sitting by me, and my sister was on the other side, and Dennis was standing in the aisle. Leonard alternated between sitting and standing, and he started talking about June 26, and he put his hand like this"—she pointed her index finger and thumb, gunlike—"and started talking about the two FBI agents."

"Tell the court as best you remember exactly what he said."

"Exactly what he said?"

"Exactly what he said."

"He said, 'The motherfucker was begging for his life, but I shot him anyway.' "

At this, the agents and marshals gripping the bench back let go as one, slumped in their pew, and traded knowing smiles: Peltier may have been railroaded, but it was for a crime he had committed. (After the trial, Nichols's sister, Bernie Lafferty, said she too had heard Peltier talk about killing the agents and giving Aquash truth serum.)

McMahon asked Nichols what day she learned of Aquash's death, and Nichols said February 24, 1976—the day Aquash had been found, a week before she was publicly identified.

"How do you remember it was February 24th?" McMahon said.

"Because Dennis called me."

"Dennis Banks?"

"Yes."

"How did you relate that call to the date of February 24th?"

"When he called, I was sitting at the desk in our office, and I looked at the calendar and it was my nephew's birthday. And I was remembering it was my nephew's birthday and I needed to call him, and Dennis told me they had found Anna Mae."

Banks was in California at the time. He had no legitimate way of knowing that the Jane Doe was Aquash, which was to say, if Nichols was right, Banks was either involved in the AIM discussions preceding Aquash's death or had been told about her death (directly or indirectly) by someone who was.

Nichols said that a few months later she went to Pine Ridge and learned the story of how Aquash had been killed, but she did not go to the FBI with what she knew until the late 1990s. The FBI eventually wired her for sound and sent her to visit her old AIM colleagues in hope of learning something about the murder, or so Nichols said. AIMers suspected the FBI was looking for other dirt as well, probably about Peltier. In the year before the Looking Cloud trial, the government paid Nichols $49,000, partly for travel but mostly to move her to secret locations. The first move was merely precautionary, but the second, she testified, was essential because Banks had learned her new address. Forty-odd thousand dollars was so lavish a sum for two moves that doubters speculated the feds were padding her expense account in lieu of putting her on the payroll.

On cross-examination, Rensch asked Nichols about the trip west in Brando's motor home.

"It is your position before this jury," he said, "that Ms. Pictou-Aquash wanted to get away and no one would let her go, is that right?"

"She told my sister she asked to go home, and they told her she couldn't."

"Were you there when she said that?"

"No."

"Your sister was one of the people who was watching her, wasn't she?"

"My sister was traveling with her. They never directly said to my sister, 'We are going to go to the store, and you keep an eye on her.'"

"No one ever directly said to you that someone was to keep an eye on Ms. Pictou-Aquash, isn't that true?"

"No, it was never said to me."

"Did you at any point out there on the West Coast hear anybody say that they should keep an eye on Ms. Pictou-Aquash?"

"No. They just did. She was never alone."

"Did you believe that she was being held prisoner, or her freedom of movement was being restricted during that time?"

"I think if she wanted to leave, there would have been an incident."

Arlo Looking Cloud, Rensch implied, had found himself in an equally ambiguous situation, aware that Aquash was not free to leave but unaware that anything fatal awaited her.

Nichols left the stand. Seven months later, she married one of the government's lead investigators in the Aquash case, BIA policeman Bob Ecoffey, a onetime goon.

Mathalene White Bear of El Monte, California, was a lean woman of not quite fifty years, long dark hair just starting to grizzle, and a sad countenance.

She took the stand and said that her friend Anna Mae Aquash had stayed with her on her last trip to Los Angeles, in September 1975. It was the trip in which Aquash met Banks and Peltier after Marlon Brando gave them his motor home. Aquash was seeking refuge.

"What was she seeking refuge from?" McMahon said.

"She didn't get too specific, but she was afraid of threats that had been made on her life." (After the trial, White Bear was more forthcoming. Aquash, she said, was afraid of David Price's alleged threat, made only a week or two earlier, to see her dead before the year was out.)

"Did the two of you make any type of arrangements whereby she could signal you if she was in danger?"

"Yes, we did. Before she left, she gave me some messages for her daughters, then she showed me a ring. It was a very unusual ring—silver and a sort of S-filigree shape. She also gave me a phone number. She told me that hopefully the next time I seen that ring it would be on her finger. But if it were to come to me another way, then I was to call that phone number."

"Do you know whose phone number it was?"

"At the time I wasn't really sure."

"Did you find out?"

"Yeah. John Trudell," AIM's chairman.

McMahon walked her through the next few weeks, and White Bear, weeping softly, said that in November Aquash called and identified herself by a code name. She said she was staying with a couple (later discovered to be Theda Clarke and her husband, who lived outside Denver) and was all right and was waiting to be told where to go. She called again a week or two later from Troy Lynn Yellow Wood's.

"She was a little more upset," White Bear remembered, "a little more distraught. She said she felt like she was being caged in. The people she was with had her afraid to go outside. She was being watched, and for her own safety they kept her indoors."

A third and final call came a few days later, in early December: "She was scared. She was being trapped and she knew something was going wrong.

I offered to go get her, or do something, and she said, 'We will see about that.' She told me, 'Have you heard from anyone?' and I told her no. And she says, 'Tell my—' 'Tell my' something, and then the phone went dead." White Bear broke into sobs.

McMahon waited for her to stop crying with all the emotion of concrete drying. Finally he said, "Did you ever receive anything from her in the mail?"

"Yes. Within three, four days, something like that, I got a little box in the mail. There was no return address on it, and when I opened it up, all that was in there was the silver ring."

She called John Trudell, as Aquash had instructed, and the next day he arrived at White Bear's house and picked up the ring.

"Then what did you do?"

"Then," White Bear said, "I spent twenty-eight years of *hell* waiting to find out what happened."

After the trial, White Bear said that she once asked Trudell what he had done upon receiving the ring, which she took for a distress signal. In her recollection, Trudell said he made inquiries about Aquash but by that time she was already "untraceable."

Trudell's memory differed. He said (correctly, on this point) that Aquash had sent the ring not from Yellow Wood's apartment in Denver but from jail in Oregon, where a WKLDOC lawyer had smuggled it out. The arrival of the ring just after Aquash was kidnapped from Yellow Wood's was something of a coincidence. Trudell also said (again correctly) that the ring came with a letter and the purpose of the ring was to prove that Aquash had written it. In Trudell's memory, the letter said that when FBI agents interrogated Aquash in Portland, they accidentally let her see papers mentioning Informers A and B, the betrayers of the AIM caravan. Aquash asked Trudell to spread the word about the informers. Trudell's memory on this last point is perhaps suspect because by the time Aquash wrote the letter, the government had already publicly disclosed A and B—they were not a secret she needed to alert friends to.

But as Trudell remembered, "It smelled like a setup. I thought the papers had been intentionally left for her to see, in order to create more paranoia and shit. I didn't do much with the information because I wasn't going to go waving a flag about infiltrators inside our community like the FBI wanted." Trudell did not say so, but surely he wondered, if only for a moment, whether Aquash was knowingly trying to "create more paranoia and shit."

The ring was not a distress signal from Denver, but a phone call to Trudell from Troy Lynn Yellow Wood was. She called to say that Aquash had been kidnapped from her apartment. Trudell was then under indictment on a firearms charge, and by the terms of his bond he was not supposed to travel beyond Nevada and southern California.

"So I called Dennis Banks," he said, "and told him I was concerned. I called *him* because he was in a position to do something about it. I wasn't. The people who took Annie Mae were not going to listen to me. They were all loyal to him, and I had no pull with them. Russell [Means], Clyde [Bellecourt], Vernon [Bellecourt]—they all could have swayed those people, depending on what they knew and when they knew it. I don't remember exactly what I said to Banks, but I expressed my concern. He said he would look into it."

Whether Banks did or not, Trudell's call did not have the desired effect, and he apparently did no more to help the woman he called his friend.

Twenty-nine years before Angie Janis appeared in court, she was Angie Begay, resident of Denver, late of Pine Ridge, lover of John Graham. On the stand in 2004 she cast her eyes toward her knees and seemed to shrink with each answer. After a few minutes, she looked in danger of disappearing entirely, an occurrence that would have suited her fine. McMahon's assistant Robert Mandel asked her about a day in December 1975 when Janis (pronounced juh-NEECE) received a phone call from Thelma Rios in Rapid City. Rios owned the empty apartment in Rapid to which Clarke, Graham, and Looking Cloud drove Aquash.

"What did Thelma Rios say to you at that time?" Mandel said.

"I can't remember the exact words," Janis answered in a near-whisper, "but something to do with Anna Mae was an informant and needs to come back to Rapid, something like that."

"What were you supposed to do?"

"Just tell someone in Denver. Theda or John Boy, Theda Clarke or John Boy, I don't remember who exactly I told."

Janis went to Yellow Wood's and delivered the message, and a meeting of low-level AIMers and two or three members of the Crusade for Justice was hastily convened.

"Do you remember what was being discussed at that meeting?" Mandel said.

"That she was an informant, and—I don't know. Someone mentioned what they do—the Crusade mentioned what they do to informants."

"What did they say they did with informants?"

"He made some kind of motion. They go like this to them, he said." She drew a finger across her throat.

"They kill them?"

"Yes."

"Cut their throats?"

"Yeah."

"What was Anna Mae's condition when she was taken from the basement?"

"She was tied up. I think her wrists were tied, and they had her on, like, a board or something—her hands were tied to the board. They carried her out."

"What did you think was happening to her at that time?"

"I don't know. I just thought they were taking her back to Rapid to question her, that nothing bad would happen to her. I didn't think anything bad was going to happen."

"In spite of the fact that she was carried out of there tied up?"

"Yes. Because there were other informants before her and nothing ever happened to them—John Durham." She meant Doug.

"Did you at some point find out that Anna Mae Aquash had been murdered?"

"Yes."

"Well, did you think her death was connected to when she was taken away from the house there in Denver?"

"Yes."

"Did you ever discuss that with anyone?"

"No."

"Did you ever think of going to law enforcement about it?"

"Yes, I did."

"Did you do so?"

"No."

"Why not?"

"Scared."

"Are you scared as you sit here today talking about it?"

"Yeah."

She was delivered to Rensch.

"Did you consider her a friend?" the defense attorney said.

"I did."

"You liked her, and you didn't think anything bad was going to happen to her other than just some questioning, did you?"

"No, I didn't."

So too, Rensch implied, Arlo Looking Cloud.

The prosecution called Candy Hamilton. In her southern drawl, Hamilton explained that in December 1975 she had been subpoenaed to testify at a trial in Sioux Falls, which lay at the other end of the state from Oglala, where she was living. She didn't have a car, so she found a ride to Rapid City, spent the night, and next day got a ride to Sioux Falls. It was the night in Rapid that interested prosecutor Mandel. Hamilton had spent it with Thelma Rios, who, unbeknown to Hamilton, had called Angie Janis in Colorado earlier that day to demand Aquash be brought to Rapid. While Hamilton slept in Rios's home, Aquash was installed, under guard, in Rios's apartment. Next morning, Hamilton awoke to the voices of Rios and WKLDOC lawyer

Bruce Ellison. She said they sounded "jumpy" and "urgent," and they left in a hurry for the WKLDOC office. Later Hamilton went to the office too. It was in a converted house, and Hamilton worked most of the day in an upstairs room. She came downstairs once, to the kitchen in the back of the house, and there saw her friend Aquash, who had been crying.

"We exchanged greetings," Hamilton said, "and then I said to her that people in Oglala really missed her, and that I did, and that strange as it might seem, that Oglala could be a really safe place for her to stay."

What, Mandel said, was Aquash's reply?

"She said, 'Well, I don't think I will get to' or 'I don't think I will'—something to that effect. We talked maybe another—less than a minute probably, and she said, 'Well, I have to go back in there now,' and went back to that front room."

Hamilton never saw Aquash again.

In the front room, for the better part of the day, was where AIM accused and interrogated Aquash about being an informer. Hamilton didn't see the people in the room, but she heard their voices and identified them as Ellison, Rios, Ted Means, his wife Lorelei DeCora Means, Clyde Bellecourt, Madonna Gilbert, and a man Hamilton knew only as Red. Most of them were leaders of AIM; Clyde Bellecourt was a co-founder. Exactly what happened in the room was not brought out at trial, but editor Paul DeMain and AIMer Bob Robideau have said the "evidence" against Aquash included the letter from her attorney promising a light charge in her weapons case if she turned on her comrades. This was the letter Aquash had off-handedly given her friend Dorothy Brings Him Back two months earlier. According to Bob Robideau, Bruce Ellison told him that he, Ellison, brought the letter to the interrogation. Ellison has denied it, has further denied any part in the interrogation, and has refused to answer questions about it before a grand jury. He has even claimed, fancifully, that there was no interrogation at all. The others allegedly in the front room that day have either made similar denials or have refused to talk.

That evening, Hamilton rode to Sioux Falls with Clyde Bellecourt, Ted

Means, Webster Poor Bear, and a man she did not know. They stopped en route at the house of Bill Means, on the Rosebud Reservation, near Rosebud Hospital.

"Bill Means," Mandel said, "also known by the nickname *Kills?*"

"Yes," Hamilton said. She said the men went into the house wordlessly, without inviting her to join them. She assumed at the time that they were going to smoke a joint and knew she didn't partake. After what seemed a long time, Ted Means and Clyde Bellecourt came back out and, with Hamilton, drove to Sioux Falls in silence.

"That's a long drive not to say anything on," Mandel observed.

"Yes."

"After you found out about the death of Anna Mae Pictou-Aquash, did you ever have any discussions with anybody about it?"

"Well," Hamilton said, "with a great many people. I asked Madonna what became of Anna Mae after they talked to her, and she said, 'Oh, we just told her to get out of there.' "

"Madonna Gilbert?"

"Yes."

Hamilton was passed to Rensch, who led her back to her talk with Aquash in the kitchen of the WKLDOC house. How far was it, he wanted to know, from where they had been standing to the back door? "Are we talking ten feet?"

"Oh, no, probably like three or four steps."

"The back door was visible from the kitchen?"

"Yes."

"Who else was in the kitchen at the time?"

"Just the two of us."

Aquash could have walked right out?

She could have.

"She didn't ask you to help her in any way, did she?"

"No."

Hours before her doom, Aquash must not have known she would be killed. Probably, Rensch implied, her interrogators were not certain either, or else why would they have given her so easy a chance to escape? Rensch's point, although he did not say as much, was that if neither Aquash nor her interrogators knew she would be killed, Arlo Looking Cloud, a mere foot soldier who wasn't even at the interrogation, could hardly have known.

Rensch asked if Hamilton had once heard an AIMer named John Stewart call Aquash an informer.

Hamilton said she had.

"Who was John Stewart?"

"He was a man who lived in Oglala. He was from Rosebud originally, but he was living in Oglala and he turned out to be an FBI informer." Stewart was the mole who had tipped the FBI to the arrival of Aquash and Nilak Butler at Los Angeles International Airport.

"Where were you when you heard this FBI informant say that Ms. Pictou-Aquash was an informant?"

"Probably at a meeting in somebody's house in Oglala. It wasn't just a personal conversation."

"When would that have been?"

"Probably around October, November. October probably of '75."

But Rensch did not explain to the jury why it was important that an FBI operative had abetted the lie that would lead to Aquash's murder.

Hair pulled to a tight bun, glasses tipped slightly toward the end of her nose, Cleo Gates looked more like the accountant she had become than the protester she had been in the 1970s. She was asked to recall a night in December 1975 when she and her husband Dick Marshall received unexpected guests at their home in Allen, on the Pine Ridge Reservation. She said the four visitors came not long before midnight. They were Theda Clarke, Arlo Looking Cloud, John Graham, and Anna Mae Aquash. She did not know it, but they had come from the interrogation in Rapid City. Clarke asked to speak to Marshall privately, and she, Graham, and Looking Cloud went into a bedroom with him. Gates was left alone with Aquash in the living room for several minutes.

"She was real quiet," Gates remembered. "I asked her if she wanted coffee because there was food, and I thought maybe she might be hungry. She had a cup of coffee, I think, and she might have ate a doughnut, and that was it. She didn't offer any conversation. Actually I didn't know her, so I wasn't really sure what to say to her myself." Eventually the others came out of the bedroom. "Dick said, 'They want us to keep her here.' I said, 'What for?' 'I don't know, just keep her here.' And I said no."

"Why did you say no?" prosecutor Mandel asked.

"Because this was Anna Mae, and people were saying she was an informer. I never knew her myself, so I didn't—wasn't sure. So I just told Dick no. I said, 'I don't think we should.' Dick went back and told them and they left. They weren't there very long."

In the minutes that Cleo Gates was alone with her guest, Aquash's hands were not tied. The front door was steps away, unlocked, unguarded. Other houses were just steps beyond. A phone was in the room, Gates's car was outside, but Aquash did not ask for help or seek it herself. Gates said she had sensed no danger either.

"I didn't think anything of it until they found her," Gates said on another occasion. "Then I thought, 'Oh, my God,' and I shut my mouth. You couldn't trust the cops, you couldn't trust your friends, you couldn't trust anybody. Who was I going to tell?"

Troy Lynn Yellow Wood took the stand in a bustle of energy ill-confined by the witness chair or her fifty-some years. U.S. Attorney McMahon asked her to recall a conversation that she had had with Looking Cloud and John Trudell in 1988. She did so reluctantly—Looking Cloud, she said, was like a brother to her—but eventually she admitted that Looking Cloud had spoken of Aquash's kidnapping and murder.

McMahon asked what Looking Cloud said about the stop at the house near the Rosebud hospital, the stop at which Graham and Clarke had gone inside and Looking Cloud and Aquash had stayed in the car.

Yellow Wood answered, "He said that she told him they were deciding her fate in there and he should just let her go."

"Didn't she beg him to let her go?"

"I think she asked him, you know, very sincerely."

McMahon gave her a dubious look.

"I guess you could say begging," Yellow Wood allowed.

"And he wouldn't let her go?"

"He said that he couldn't do that. She told him that they were going to be—whatever they decided in there, he was probably going to have to carry it through. He told her that wasn't going to happen. He didn't believe that."

"He wouldn't let her go, would he?"

"No," she said, then added quietly, "he said he couldn't do that."

McMahon asked what happened after Graham and Clarke returned to the car.

"He said they drove into the Badlands. He said that they got out of the car and that Theda stayed in the car and that he and John Boy walked up a hill."

"What was Anna Mae saying as they walked up that hill?"

"That she asked them to let her go, that they didn't have to do that to her."

"Was she crying?"

"She was crying, I think."

"And she was telling them that she had two young daughters?"

"I don't know that."

"Did she tell them she hadn't done anything wrong to anybody?"

"Yes."

On cross-examination, Rensch said, "When you listened to Arlo, it was your impression that when she was shot, it was a total surprise to him."

"Yes."

"When you listened to what Arlo described to John Trudell, it was your impression that he didn't want her to die, isn't that true?"

"I don't believe he ever thought it would happen."

"Well, was it your impression in listening to his words that he wanted her to die?"

"No."

"Did you ever hear him say that he was in any way in control of the situation?"

"He was never in control."

John Trudell had chaired AIM from 1973 to 1979, after which he became a musician and poet. He took the stand in black shoes, black pants, black belt, black shirt, black leather jacket, black hair, black goatee. It was hard to believe a man so small could be covered in so much black. McMahon asked how he learned that Aquash had been killed.

"It was in a conversation I had with Dennis Banks in Berkeley sometime in '76," Trudell said. "February, March, sometime in '76. At this time I didn't know there had been a body found, and Dennis mentioned to me, he said, 'Well, that body they found in Pine Ridge'—or 'Wanblee,' he said—'I think it is Anna Mae.' "

Trudell had told the same story decades before—but with two important differences. In the earlier version, Trudell had not credited Banks with the exculpatory words *I think*. Banks had had no doubt about the body's identity, saying flatly, "That is Annie Mae." The second difference was that in Trudell's earlier version, he had been more certain of the date on which Banks made his statement—and the date made that statement more incriminating. "Dennis told me," Trudell had said, "she had been shot in the back of the head. He told me this in February, about the 25th or 26th of February." On February 25 or 26, the fact of a bullet in the back of Aquash's head had not been made public. Nor had her identity. So far as anyone publicly knew, the body was that of a Jane Doe who had died of frostbite.

Defense attorney Rensch directed Trudell to the talk he and Troy Lynn Yellow Wood had with Looking Cloud in 1988.

"When you were speaking to him," Rensch said, "was it clear to you that the fact that she was killed was a surprise to him?"

"See, after they left that house," Trudell said, meaning Bill Means's house on Rosebud, "I don't know about surprises anymore, all right, because somebody said to do this. But up until the time they went to that house, I don't think he expected that she would be killed."

"You just said, *At that house somebody said to do this.*"

"Yes."

"What are you referring to?"

"Well, John Boy and Arlo and Theda, they weren't decision-makers. I mean, they couldn't give this kind of order. They did what they were told."

"Do you recall Arlo saying that anybody at that house said anything about Ms. Pictou-Aquash being killed?"

"That was the impression of what I got out of what he told me."

"I want to know if you heard from Arlo's mouth something about him knowing that she was going to be killed."

"When they left that house, they knew."

"Did Arlo *tell* you that he knew, or are you making an assumption?"

"I am very careful about making an assumption on this. It's just that— when John Boy and Theda came out of that house, Theda took some of Anna Mae's jewelry."

The prosecution's final witness was, in a sense, Arlo Looking Cloud. Rensch would not let his feeble client take the stand, but Looking Cloud had given a videotaped statement to the Denver police on his arrest in 2003, and the tape was now played on the courtroom screen. On it, a nearly inert Looking Cloud stared blankly at an interrogation-room table opposite his inquisitor, Bob Ecoffey, a mellow-voiced bear of a man who directed the BIA police nationwide and was soon to become the bridegroom of Kamook Nichols. Ecoffey asked Looking Cloud if he had drunk alcohol that day.

"A little," Looking Cloud told the tabletop.

Ecoffey did not ask how "little." Instead he asked what happened to Aquash in December 1975.

Looking Cloud spoke in a halting voice just above a murmur. He said Aquash had been bound at the wrists in Denver and driven through the night to Rapid City. He didn't know about an interrogation in Rapid, wasn't part of it anyway, and at no point knew the bigger plan: "They didn't tell me nothing." They left Rapid less than twenty-four hours after getting there and took Aquash to Pine Ridge. He skipped the stop at Bill Means's house on Rosebud, said they eventually drove toward Kadoka. As the sky turned blue with dawn, Theda stopped the car. John Boy got out and untied Anna Mae, and Looking Cloud got out too. He saw the pistol, but he thought they would just scare her with it. They walked her to the edge of the cliff, and John Boy fired the shot. The drive back was quiet.

"If anything happens," Theda said, "I did it."

From the time they left Denver to the time of the murder, Aquash never said a word to Looking Cloud, or so he claimed. The prosecution rested its case.

Tim Rensch opened Looking Cloud's defense by summoning David Price to the stand. "The most hated FBI agent in America," WKLDOC had called a younger Price, but the older model displayed none of the restless arrogance credited to the youth. He mounted the dais almost gingerly. His gray suit held more color than his cheeks. He was just a few months away from a mandatory retirement that it did not appear he would enjoy.

"Did you personally take part in cultivating informants or contacts within the American Indian Movement in 1975?" Rensch asked.

"Yes, sir," Price said (with more honesty than his supposedly informerless partner Bill Wood).

"Did you know an informant named John Stewart?"

"I don't know that John Stewart was an informant."

"Did you know a John Stewart?"

"I had contact with a John Stewart."

But Rensch did not ask what kind of contact, nor did he ask anything else about Stewart. He simply dropped the provocative matter of the operative who had helped snitch-jacket Aquash and moved on.

"At any of the points that you spoke with Ms. Pictou-Aquash, did you attempt to cultivate her as an informant?"

"No, sir."

"At any of those points did you ask her if she would provide information relative to the activities of the American Indian Movement?"

"I asked her on April 10, 1975, about the murder of Jeanette Bissonette."

Price did not mention his effort to pry information from her during the raid on Al Running's or his alleged threat to see her dead if she did not inform for him. Rensch did not ask about those matters either.

"In 1975," Rensch said, "how many informants did you regularly deal with that were involved in the American Indian Movement?"

"Very few," Price said.

And with that, Rensch dismissed his witness. The jurors did not hear that Price had almost certainly lied about being at the crime scene, that he had lied about or obscured his proximity to the first autopsy, that he had probably lied about being able to identify Aquash. Nor did jurors hear anything further about the FBI's sabotage of AIM, because when Price left the stand, Rensch rested his case. It had lasted five minutes. Evidently he was so certain of having discredited the prosecution on his cross-examinations that he felt no need to mount an affirmative defense.

Closing arguments were made and the jurors sent away to deliberate. Four hours later they convicted Arlo Looking Cloud of murder in the first degree.

CHAPTER 15

IN 1988 A Montana ranch foreman named Barry Clausen, who, as he tells the story, was working with the law to catch traffickers in illegal weapons until he himself was unjustly indicted for trafficking, told a sheriff that one of the buyers of the illegal arms was a dilettante rancher named John Durham. John had a brother named Doug. Clausen had known both men for several years.

"You know Doug Durham?" the sheriff said. "What do you know about the ballistic reports—you know, the killing of the FBI agents on Pine Ridge?"

Clausen said he knew nothing about the reports; he barely even knew about the killings.

"The ballistic reports," the sheriff said, "show it was Durham's gun that killed the agents. Durham did it."

Clausen asked where the sheriff had gotten his information, and after some coyness the sheriff named an FBI agent in Butte. The agent would not talk to Clausen, but Clausen determined that after he cleared up the unfortunate business with the gunrunning, he would investigate Durham. His investigation, such as it was, remains the only firsthand account of what became of the man for whose sins, as AIMers like to say, Anna Mae Aquash died.

Clausen first met the Durhams in 1984, four years before his talk with the Montana sheriff. John Durham had a ranch in Montana but lived mainly in Texas, and he asked Clausen to ship some horses from the

Rockies south. Clausen took the job and, with his wife Lindy, drove the horses to a ranch outside Dallas owned by John's brother Doug. With its long, curved driveway ending at a manor house, its kidney-shaped pool, and its graceful stables in the bucolic background, the spread could have passed for a set from the city's eponymous TV show. The Clausens found Doug and his wife Jan welcoming, if slightly eccentric. The focal point of their living room was an enormous organ built to Doug's specifications, and there were enough guns about the place to outfit a platoon. When Doug showed the Clausens to bed for the night, he advised, "Don't leave the room until I let you know the night security system is deactivated. You'd probably set off more alarms than a fire."

The Clausens and the Durhams became fast friends. While Lindy and Jan spent days shopping in town, Doug showed Barry his computers, which were surplus from NASA—"the best and largest computer system money could buy," Clausen judged. A few years earlier Durham had taught himself several computer languages and started a data-management company. His clients included the Dallas County Sheriff's Office, for which he designed an arrest-tracking system. So well did Durham and the sheriff get on that the latter put a police car, radio, and expense account at the disposal of the former. Durham may also have installed data systems for the FBI, as he claimed to Clausen. Certainly he was a close friend of the agent in charge of the FBI's Dallas office, Dave Gillis. It was Gillis who convinced Durham to buy the hobby ranch in Texas after his exposure by AIM, and Gillis's ranch was but a mile from Durham's as the mockingbird flies. The two men were frequent visitors at each other's homes. All of which is to say that none of Durham's many crimes—his perjury in the Skyhorse-Mohawk trial, his effort to lure AIM into training guerrillas, his seizure of the state office building in Iowa, his wholesale abuse of Jancita Eagle Deer—stopped the FBI or the local law from staying snug with him. To catch crooks, the Bureau often said, you had to work with a few. But the Bureau always portrayed its relationships with criminals as expedients, born of realpolitik and lasting only as long as needed. In truth, some lawmen just liked crooks—*their* crooks anyway. Crooked AIMers would have enjoyed a different reception from the nation's sheriffs and FBI agents.

A few days into the Clausens' visit, Durham offered Barry a job with a starting annual salary of $100,000.

"Lindy gasped," Clausen remembered, "and I asked, 'Doing what?'

" 'For $100,000 a year, does it matter?'

"Doug looked at Lindy and said, 'Barry's job would mean a lot of traveling and he's going to need a secretary. The position is yours at $30,000, if you're interested.'

"She said, 'If he's making $100,000 a year, why in the world would I want to work?' "

While Clausen weighed the offer over the next few days, Durham tutored him in his computer system. Clausen is coquettish about what he saw on the computers. He says only that many of the files were government-related and that "I have always wondered if someone such as myself was authorized to read them." In the end, he declined Durham's offer, though not out of suspicion over a $100,000 job with no description. It was simply, he said, that the ranching life in Montana was so good, and he and Lindy didn't want to leave it.

But the money ate at him. Two years later Doug's brother John made the same overture—"no suit, no tie, but the same amount of money"—and Clausen jumped. A job description was finally tendered: Clausen was to sell software and hardware for Digital Pro Corporation, which John Durham owned and which catered to the data-management needs of oil companies. Clausen did not think $100,000 overly generous for a computer novice to peddle computers. He drove to Dallas and reported to work at the Durham family's commercial empire, which was composed of subsidiaries that rose and fell with the frequency of storefront churches. One company was little more than a room of cubicles from which phone salesmen tried to con investors into backing oil exploration.

"It was a glorified pyramid scheme," Doug's son Dennis Durham later said of that company. "You'd get a hundred investors, each putting up $10,000. It only cost $40,000 to drill a well, so you'd drill it, it'd come up dry, and you'd say, 'Sorry, investors,' and pocket a lot of cash. Every once in a while Doug would hit oil, which would help him get more investors. He got lucky enough times that he began to think of himself as an oilman, and that was the downfall of the business. He went overboard on the exploration."

While Clausen was getting settled in Dallas, he stayed at Doug's ranch in a large touring bus that Doug had ordered to spec at a cost of $225,000 (about $500,000 today) and that was equipped with video cameras and other surveillance tools. Much later, Clausen learned from a source whom he will not name but who was probably the FBI's Dave Gillis that the FBI used the bus as a command post during "certain events in Dallas." (Gillis did not respond to requests for an interview.) Eventually, Clausen moved out of the bus and into a more spacious guest suite owned by Digital Pro. Some weeks later he decided to visit Galveston for a weekend. A Digital Pro vice president asked if the company could put up some out-of-town guests in the suite while he was gone. Clausen said fine and went to Galveston, but it rained all weekend and he returned early to Dallas. When he walked into the suite, he found two men huddled over a pile of goods spread atop a coffee table.

"It didn't take a genius to figure out what the stacks of money and bags of white powder meant," Clausen recalled. "My hands rose up between my eyes and those sitting near the tables, and I said, 'I just live here, I didn't see a thing.' "

He went to his room "in shock." Half an hour later, one of the men opened the door and said by way of introduction, "I could have killed you, you know." The man said his name was Kelly and he had talked to the vice president at Digital Pro, who in turn had said Clausen was "all right," so Kelly let Clausen live. Kelly bade him good night and suggested he not leave the suite. Next morning at breakfast, Clausen's new friends talked "about killing people as other people talk about killing flies." When

Clausen looked concerned, Kelly said, "Hey, don't worry. We've got Gillis and Durham covering for our ass." It was Kelly who enlightened Clausen to the reason for his liberal salary: on his traveling sales calls, the demonstration computers he carried would be stuffed full of cocaine.

Clausen remained with Digital Pro just long enough, he has claimed, to investigate the company's criminal activity. Once he gathered what intelligence he could, he called the Texas State Police, which stung the coke ring. Jim Menece, Digital Pro's aptly titled vice president, was arrested with twenty-five pounds of cocaine worth perhaps $1 million and was sentenced to eight years in prison. (There is no evidence that John Durham was involved in his vice president's extracurricular activities.) Clausen returned to Montana, and there ended, for the moment, his association with the Durhams. If Clausen's account is shamelessly self-serving, several of its details—his cooperation with police, the sting, Menece's conviction—were nonetheless verifiably true.

A few years later, when the Montana sheriff told Clausen that Doug Durham killed the agents at Oglala, Clausen tried to call his old friend but couldn't find him. Another scandal had befallen Durham, and he had since lowered his profile. The scandal began when which his oil business failed and his creditors tried to foreclose on the computers he had put up as collateral. Durham told the creditors that he had installed those computers at the Dallas County Jail and if they wanted them back, they could foreclose on the sheriff. This situation—along with revelations about the car and other perks the sheriff had given Durham—made headlines in Dallas, and for a time a gaggle of reporters camped outside the Durham ranch in hope of peppering him with questions. Durham feared AIM and other old acquaintances would learn his whereabouts, and he changed his address.

Clausen called Dave Gillis to ask for Durham's new address and took the opportunity to ask about Gillis's supposed involvement (per the boast of Kelly) in the drug operation at Digital Pro. Gillis said there was nothing to it. The drug ring had only used his and Durham's names to make people think, quite slanderously, that they had the protection of a senior FBI agent and a rich businessman. Gillis had known nothing of the drug trafficking, nor had Doug. Clausen believed him—justifiably or not, it is impossible to say—but he still thought Durham had murdered the agents at Oglala.

In the latter part of 2003, I became acquainted with Dennis Durham, second of Doug's three sons. He was a good-looking man with brown, swept-back hair, his father's wide cheekbones and knowing eyes, a pocked face, broken nose, and missing bicuspid. We met initially by letter because Dennis was in his third year of a twenty-seven-year stretch with the Iowa Department of Corrections. The same institution, as it happened, housed the son of Jancita Eagle Deer, whom his father had ruined—the falling tide had stranded all boats. (David Foell, Eagle Deer's son, was serving life without parole for a murder-for-hire.) Dennis's crime was habitual burglary, one of his father's trades, and I asked if Doug had trained him.

"No," he wrote back. "My dad taught me many things, but to break the law was not one. Bend it, maybe. Ha ha." He explained that his parents had divorced and that he had grown up partly at his father's ranch in Texas, where he developed a cocaine addiction, again unrelated to the family's extralegal enterprises. He left Dallas to escape the abundant coke there and returned to his native Des Moines. He did well for a time, but in Iowa the drug of plenty was methamphetamine. "So I unwittingly exchanged a coke habit for a meth habit. Hence the crime, to pay for the habit."

Dennis's knowledge of his father's undercover work was modest. He had been a child for most of Doug's covert career, and later in life the once self-aggrandizing Doug was no longer talkative about his past. (No one else in Durham's family wanted to talk about it either.) But Dennis was certain that his father had been trained at the FBI proving ground in Quantico, Virginia, and he was also certain that Doug had said he was trained by the CIA—although what, if anything, he did for the CIA, Dennis did not know. According to Dennis, throughout his father's many scandals in Des Moines and in Dallas, he was never out of favor with the police or FBI, whose officers and agents were always stopping by for coffee or borrowing the houseboat for a vacation. But the scandals in Dallas eventually reached such a pitch that "one day he got in that customized forty-two-foot Blue-bird of his, with its floor safe, alarm system, video surveillance, and the whole nine yards, and took off. When he first ordered that thing from the factory in Georgia, I thought to myself that this would be his getaway vehicle if danger came. And that's exactly what it was when Doug fled Texas for Florida."

Doug settled for a time in the Bradenton-Sarasota area, where he man-aged an RV park. Sometime later he left there in a hurry too, for reasons unknown. He was rumored over the next few years (almost certainly wrongly) to have been making the rounds of the Eastern powwow circuit, or to have advised New York in its gambling struggles against the Mohawks, or to have moved into a cultish communal home in Dallas. Dennis, who was mostly estranged from his father, knew only that Doug lived in Canada during this period. Perhaps the elder Durham feared pros-ecution in the U.S. Later, however, he returned to the States and settled in a trailer park near Quartzsite, Arizona. I had traced him to the region about the time I met Dennis but had been unable to find a specific address. After getting to know Dennis, I asked if he could help.

"Doug's dead," his next letter began abruptly. He had died a few weeks earlier, about the time I had mailed Dennis my last letter. He explained that his father had been receiving chemotherapy for a lymphoma in his neck when his heart all but gave out under the strain. There were AIMers, I thought on reading this, who would appreciate that a failure of heart brought Durham to death's door. The heart trouble was followed by a stroke that left him brain dead.

"The doctors had a hard time finding a family member to unplug him," Dennis wrote. "John David, Dwight, and Carol (his brothers and sister) wanted nothing to do with him. Ditto for his children. But his son Daniel finally agreed to fly out and gave authorization to turn off life support. I must say I'm neither sad or happy. It's hard to get emotional about someone who had as few emotions themself—not that I'm hollow, in fact

I'm quite sensitive. I guess he died inside all of us over time, and we dealt with that already in our own way."

I would not get my interview with Doug. On the other hand, death theoretically threw open his FBI files to the public. I wrote the Bureau a letter of condolence noting the details of the hospital where their man had expired and the mortuary that had handled the body and asked to see his files. The FBI replied with regrets that the files could not be released without a death certificate, which Nevada law barred me from obtaining, or an obituary, which no newspaper had run because none of Durham's kin had commissioned one. I was stymied. My pleasure, a few days later, on realizing *I* could commission Durham's obituary was somewhat unbecoming in a reporter. I gave the particulars to the Las Vegas *Review Journal*, which asked whether I wanted to suggest a charity to which donations could be made in the deceased's memory. I resisted the urge to name the American Indian Movement. The file-processors at the FBI had given signs of being a humorless lot, and as I already had a lawsuit pending against them, I didn't want to push my luck. It is one of my life's lasting regrets. The obituary ran, I sent it to the FBI, and the FBI said it would get back to me in a few years. I sued again. My lawyer argued to a federal magistrate that the Freedom of Information Act gave the FBI twenty days to give me the files. The magistrate agreed, then gave the FBI ten times that. As this book went to press, the FBI was just releasing a portion of the files, a summary of which I will post to my Web site, SteveHendricks.org.

In May 2000 the FBI compiled a report titled "Accounting for Native American Deaths, Pine Ridge Reservation, South Dakota." The report was occasioned by a hearing of the U.S. Commission on Civil Rights held six months earlier in Rapid City, which hearing had itself been occasioned by a recent spate of murders of Indians that had all gone unsolved, unprosecuted, or under-prosecuted. USCCR eventually concluded that the police and prosecutors of South Dakota had at best handled the murders callously and at worst turned a blind eye to them. ("Garbage," Governor Janklow said of USCCR's report, which, he added, he had not read "because I don't read garbage.") But the real news at the USCCR hearing was not testimony about the recent killings. The real news was that Lakota after Lakota testified that the cankers of the present existed only because the past was an open wound. It was this wound, they said, that needed healing above all else. Most of their grievances were rooted in Pine Ridge, whose era of lawlessness under Dick Wilson they called the Reign of Terror. They complained that long after both Wilson and AIM were gone, the FBI still refused to re-examine the many unpunished crimes committed during the Reign of Terror.

USCCR summoned the FBI of Rapid City to reply, and its agents told the commissioners they were shocked—shocked—by the critique. They knew of *no* legitimate case on *any* Indian reservation in South Dakota from *any* era that had not been diligently investigated. In fact, aside from a few "nonspecific rumors," the grievances the Indians were testifying to had never been raised with the FBI.

"I am not overwhelmed," USCCR commissioner Christopher Edley, a Harvard Law School professor, told the agents, "with the sense of you all having depths of self-awareness about [Indians] not trusting the FBI."

Edley might have added that the FBI did not have depths of awareness of—or perhaps respect for—the truth. The truth, as scores of FBI documents show, was that the FBI was told repeatedly about the unpunished crimes, and on several occasions agents themselves wrote about them. When, for example, the FBI turned its back on Byron DeSersa's murder, Senator Jim Abourezk demanded an accounting of the FBI's investigations on Pine Ridge. The FBI compiled a list of murders, assaults, and arsons committed in the previous year, and the list seems to show (the FBI's censorship is extensive) that a large majority of the FBI's investigations did not lead to prosecutions, let alone convictions. The list ran fifteen single-spaced pages. Peter Matthiessen's *In the Spirit of Crazy Horse*, published in 1983 and brought to the FBI's attention that year, can be read as a compendium of unsolved crimes on Pine Ridge. Ward Churchill and Jim

Vander Wall's *Agents of Repression*, published in 1988, included an itemized list of unsolved crimes on and around Pine Ridge, which list was expanded and republished in at least a dozen books, articles, and Web sites, many of which were brought to the FBI's notice.

The FBI's "Accounting for Native American Deaths, Pine Ridge" was an internal reply to the criticisms from the USCCR hearing. For the benefit of headquarters in Washington, the FBI's Minneapolis office examined fifty-seven deaths on Pine Ridge from the Wilson era. (Lesser crimes were not considered; apparently bludgeoning a fellow into a coma or burning a house down did not rate.) Minneapolis concluded that, contrary to the allegations, virtually every case had "been solved either through conviction or finding that the death had not been a murder according to the law." The FBI declared itself not guilty, but it did not make the accounting public.

Only after reporters learned of its existence three years later and demanded copies did the FBI release it. The contents suggest the reason for the secrecy. In, for example, the case of Delphine Crow Dog, sister of Leonard and aunt of Jancita Eagle Deer, the accounting reported that she was found dead in a field in December 1972, that AIM claimed she had been beaten to death by a BIA policeman, that an autopsy found she had died of exposure, and that, because of the autopsy, the FBI made no investigation. What the accounting did not say was that the autopsy was conducted by the firm of Brown and Armstrong, the same that later ruled Aquash dead of exposure. There was no explanation why an autopsy from the discredited firm should now be or then have been deemed credible, no word about whether bruises or broken bones or ruptured organs were considered and ruled out. Nor was there any sign that the FBI had interviewed the people who claimed to know the details of the crime, let alone interviewed the alleged murderer. In short, the FBI of 2000 was as little interested in the possibility of foul play as the FBI of 1972 had been.

The cumulative weight of such "re-evaluations" was obscene. The accounting said that brothers Clarence and Vernal Cross were shot by BIA police officers in June 1973, that Clarence died, that AIM claimed the shootings were unprovoked, and that the U.S. attorney decided AIM's claim was groundless and did not indict the officers. What the accounting did not say (but recently released papers do) is that the Justice Department's Civil Rights Division concluded the BIA police had violated the Crosses' civil rights. The Civil Rights Division wanted to prosecute, but the U.S. attorney refused. Also in June 1973, per the accounting, Philip Black Elk was killed when he tried to light his hot water heater and it exploded. AIM said the heater had been tampered with. The accounting said the FBI never investigated the claim. In September 1973, Jackson Washington Cutt was hatcheted to death in front of a witness, but the accounting said the FBI closed the case when the witness recanted his testimony. In the same month, Melvin Spider, who had earlier been beaten by BIA police, was killed by a blow to the head. "Although a suspect was developed," the accounting said, "there was insufficient evidence to charge that person with the death," and the case was closed. In October 1973, Aloysius Long Soldier was shot in the head. AIM called it a murder, the BIA police called it a suicide, and the FBI accepted the BIA's conclusion. The accounting gave no reason why. In November 1973, Allison Fast Horse was shot in the chest with a .22-caliber bullet. The FBI found no leads; case closed. In December 1974, Robert Reddy was stabbed twice through the heart. Agents identified a suspect and made appointments to polygraph him, but the suspect kept breaking the appointments so the FBI closed the case. In April 1975, Hilda Good Buffalo was found dead in her home. There had been a small fire, and the autopsist ruled her dead of carbon monoxide poisoning, even though, as the accounting noted, she had a stab wound in her neck. The accounting did not explain the wound; case closed. In May 1975, Ben Sitting Up was axed to death by Elmer Red Eyes, but "because of his mental condition and because the case lacked evidence," Red Eyes was not prosecuted. In July 1975, Andrew Stewart, nephew of Leonard Crow Dog, was shot in the head, "probably," according to the autopsy, by his own hand. The Crow Dogs said he was murdered. The FBI did not investigate. In March 1976, Cleveland Reddest was killed in a hit-and-run. The FBI found his killer but decided that Reddest had been lying in the road—there was no explanation how that conclusion was drawn—and ruled the death accidental; case closed.

Of the few cases among the fifty-seven that led to prosecutions, most ended in no or minimal jail time. Dorothy Poor Bear, having stabbed Leon Swift Bird to death, was convicted of manslaughter and given a suspended sentence. Antoine Bluebird killed Kenneth Little with a tire iron, was convicted, and received probation. Le Roy Apple stabbed Howard Blue Bird to death, confessed, pleaded to assault, and was sentenced to one year. Arlene Good Voice intentionally ran over and killed Betty Lou Means, pleaded to assault, and was sentenced to eighteen months' probation. Only five of the fifty-seven deaths led to sentences of any length: three in prison terms of ten years; one in a term of fifteen; and one, a double-murder, in twenty. Although the accounting did not say so, nearly all of the accidental deaths were deemed accidental by Drs. Brown and Armstrong. Doubtless some of those deaths *were* accidental. No doubt as well, many of the murders that AIM claimed were politically motivated were not, and even of those that were, not all were killings of AIMers by goons. (Not that the FBI bore no blame for non-political killings. By giving *carte blanche* to murderers—and to rapists, batterers, and thieves—the FBI permitted crime to flourish on Pine Ridge as nowhere else in the country.) But because of the FBI's deceit, the Oglalas will never know which of the deaths were political and which not and which were accidental and which not. What it must feel like, for some Oglalas, to run into the unpunished killers of their loved ones at the gas stations and ball games and powwows of Pine Ridge for the rest of their lives is beyond my power to express. Small wonder that to this day Oglalas distrust the men and women of the FBI who are charged with protecting them.

One distinction of the FBI's accounting is its rare public mention of Doug Durham. The mention occurs in a brief discussion of the death of Jancita Eagle Deer, who, the accounting notes, was allegedly last "seen in the company of federal agent-provocateur Douglass Durham." The accounting explained that "since her death occurred outside the jurisdiction of the FBI, no investigation was conducted by the FBI"—an entirely mendacious claim. The FBI did and does have jurisdiction to investigate its operatives, whether for beating an object of their surveillance or for tampering with an election or for invading a defense camp or for lying in court. If the FBI does not investigate the abuses of its provocateurs, perhaps it is because doing so would leave it rather short-staffed for other work.

When Barry Clausen called the FBI's Dave Gillis to find Durham in 1992, he asked whether Gillis had heard anything about Durham shooting the agents at Oglala. Gillis said he had not, but he had heard about FBI reports that proved Durham's gun was one of the murder weapons. Clausen said he recorded Gillis's statement, but it is apparently an insult to his integrity to share the tape, so he does not. Gillis will not comment.

Gillis gave Causen Durham's new address, and Clausen drove to Texas to see his old friend. Durham was surprised when he showed up on his doorstep but was eventually welcoming. They talked for two days about Durham's work in AIM, the scandals at Digital Pro, and other entries in Durham's résumé. When the conversation turned to the shootout at Oglala, Durham chose his words with care. He said his gun *could* have been used to kill the agents but that he himself was not at Oglala that day. Clausen didn't believe him on the second point, but Durham was right. After his remorseful press conference in Chicago, Durham retracted his regrets and went on an anti-AIM lecture tour sponsored by the John Birch Society. By one account, he was engaged at a lecturing on the day of the shootout. Even if that were not so, none of the many people at the shootout has ever put Durham at the scene—and most of them had an incentive to do so. Moreover, had Durham walked into an AIM camp that summer, he would have been swiftly ushered out or have met an unkinder fate.

Durham's gun, on the other hand, was another matter. Durham said that near the end of his mission in AIM, Dino Butler asked to borrow his van, and Dennis Banks told Durham to let Butler have it. Durham did as told.

"My weapon was in the van," he said to Clausen. "Dino never returned, and my van was later found somewhere in Nebraska. Everything in the van was gone, including my gun and tape recorder."

Dino Butler ended up at the shootout, although the van did not. It was appropriated from Butler by Russell Means, who later said of Durham, "I told Dennis, 'We think he's a fed. So tell him if he wants his van, he has to come to Pine Ridge to get it.' I think everybody knew what that meant, and I leave it to you to surmise." Subtlety not being Means's forte, he added, "If Durham had been a real threat, he would have disappeared and quietly been buried somewhere. But he wasn't, so we exposed him to the news media. That was more valuable to us than taking care of him internally." It was Durham's van that Means, Dick Marshall, and other AIMers used in their running shootout with the goons the day the WKLDOCkers were beaten at the Pine Ridge airport.

Either Clausen learned nothing more from Durham, or he will say no more. What he did learn—that the gun of an FBI provocateur might have killed two FBI agents—was not entirely damning to the FBI. Even if true, an AIMer had still pulled the trigger. But the prospect was a bit like America's arming of Saddam Hussein before sending troops to Iraq to get shot by American arms: just embarrassing enough that the U.S. government did not care to ruminate on it publicly.

CHAPTER 16

DEATH CLINGS TO Wounded Knee. The siege of 1973 had not even ended before rumors of fresh graves—postscripts to the mass grave of 1890—rose from the valley. The decades have not silenced the rumors, only made them murkier and freer of range. The graves are said to lie, variously, behind the occupiers' lines, behind the federal lines, or in the no-man's land in between. In short, anywhere. If the rumors are given credence, it is probably because there are other, verifiable stories of murder narrowly averted at the siege.

There is, for example, the story of a dispute between on one side Pedro Bissonette and his followers and on the other Dennis Banks, Russell Means, and their followers. Bissonette had argued for a more conciliatory stance in negotiations with the government. Banks and Means wanted the opposite. Words turned sharp, guns were drawn, and several people present thought it would come to bloodshed. It did not, because additional partisans of Banks and Means appeared and forced Bissonette's outnumbered faction to lower their weapons.

A similar story circulated about a fight over what to do with a load of dynamite brought into Wounded Knee. The disputants were Banks and followers in one camp and Northwest leaders Bob Free and Sid Mills and their followers in the other. The respective views of the camps have been lost to time, but guns were again drawn and put away only after several fraught minutes. Afterward, Free was offered gifts to assassinate Banks (he declined), and an ally of Free's, Angel Martinez, had to be talked out of doing the job.

Still another story, spare of detail but often and credibly told, is of a debate among the occupiers about whether to assassinate Vernon Belle-court. His supposed crime was squandering money outside the village that might have been spent on weapons for use inside.

The tales of violence and near-violence did not originate only from AIM's side. As told earlier, goons on a roadblock twice pulled guns on Wayne Colburn of the U.S. Marshals Service. And in another story, a goon foot patrol captured twelve men and eight women bound for Wounded Knee and radioed the goon roadblock for a van to take the "hippies" to jail.

"Cut their goddamn hair for 'em," the roadblock answered. "You hold them sonsabitches and shoot 'em if they try to run. Over."

"They ain't got no fight left in 'em," the patrol answered, perhaps sug-gesting they had been beaten already. "Fuck 'em in the face. You want we should stand by or what?"

A U.S. marshal listening to the conversation radioed his superiors, "It appears they have some people in custody behind the roadblocks. There's a lot of talk about weapons and shooting people and so on."

AIM never found a record of twenty people brought to jail, so a rumor grew that the hippies had been killed and buried. It remains widely told, despite its unlikelihood: twenty missing people would have generated inquiries from family and friends, which in turn would have generated investigations by reporters and WKLDOC, which did not happen.

After the stand-down at Wounded Knee, the government, mindful of the rumors, sent agents and marshals to look for fresh graves in the vil-lage and the no-man's land outside. AIM, meanwhile, sent people into the no-man's land and the hills behind the federal lines. Neither side found a thing.

Ray Robinson regarded himself a freedom fighter. Born in the nation's cap-ital during the Great Depression, he lost his youth to poverty, his father to a poker-game shooting, and his education to Jim Crow. He grew tall, well-formed, dark-skinned, angry. Of the last quality he once wrote,

"Because I could not fight the white man legally and win, I decided to take up boxing where the world could watch and see me beat one with my hands." His and Pedro Bissonette's were the same story at different longitude.

Robinson's skill in the ring was, like Bissonette's, insufficient for a paying career, so he looked for other ways to fight the white man. He found what he was looking for in 1964 when a small group of activists passed through Washington on a long walk from Québec to Guantánamo Bay. The walkers were protesting North American relations with Cuba, which Robinson did not much care about, but they were integrated and bound for Dixie, which was to say for trouble with Jim Crow, which Robinson cared about deeply. To walk, he had to lay down his gloves, literally and metaphorically, which did not come easily for him.

"Now come a new thing to me that's called nonviolence, and I'm trying it," he wrote during the walk. "This thing that's called nonviolence is the biggest challenge I have ever tried as a man."

Trouble came to the protesters in Albany, Georgia, where Police Chief Laurie Pritchett jailed them for parading without a permit. Pritchett was one of the few segregationists ever to have gotten the better of Martin Luther King Jr.; he smothered King's Albany Campaign in 1961 and 1962 with hundreds of arrests that were free of the violence typical of Southern bossmen. The Guantánamo protesters went on a hunger strike in Pritchett's jail, and after a few weeks Robinson went one better by refusing water. When his health failed, Pritchett had him hospitalized and ordered frigid orange juice pumped into his stomach by nasal tube. Robinson later said, without exaggeration, that the agony of the nearly freezing fluid coursing through his sinuses was a torture unlike anything he had ever endured. He recovered, was re-jailed, and resumed his total fast. This time Pritchett threatened him with the state mental hospital—a fate, for a black man in Georgia of 1964, not far above the Siberian gulag for a Soviet dissident. Robinson finally capitulated, but not before losing two teeth to malnutrition.

After the walk, Robinson gave himself entirely to the struggle for civil rights. He married a woman equally committed, Cheryl Buswell, and they started a communal farm in Alabama to grow food for activists. By night the Ku Klux Klan burned crosses in their yard. By day, as the communalists farmed the fields, the Klan threw Molotov cocktails at their farmhouse. On one of the daylight assaults, Robinson saw the Klansmen approaching, grabbed a rifle, and ran in front of their car, gun leveled, with an invitation to climb out. The gunless Klansmen accepted, and he escorted them into the living room of the farmhouse, where he sat them down and made a show of setting the gun aside. Then he talked to them about the people at the farm and their nonviolent purpose, and he asked about the lives and hopes of his guests. The conversation, nerve-wracking at first, went on for hours. At the end of the visit, Ray told the Klansmen they were welcome back anytime, in peace.

"And god*damn* if the next day," Cheryl Buswell-Robinson said years later, "that Klan car didn't come driving back up our road and stop right in front of our house. Out steps one of these guys Ray had talked to the day before, and he stayed there all afternoon talking with Ray, helping him with a truck he was fixing."

Before Ray Robinson went to Wounded Knee in 1973, he was best known to America's leading activists, when known at all, for two incidents at the Poor People's Campaign of 1968. The campaign was a protest of U.S. poverty policy conceived of by Martin Luther King and carried out by others after King's assassination. Hank Adams, the soon-to-be negotiator of the Trail of Broken Treaties, was one of a coalition of organizers who met with Attorney General Ramsey Clark before the campaign.

"While I was speaking to Clark," Adams remembered, "someone in the auditorium's balcony began shouting, 'Pick that turkey clean! We're gonna pick this turkey clean!' That person was Ray Robinson, whom I didn't know, and whose name I learned only after the flag-arrest episode at the Supreme Court. The fact is, Ray's actions were viewed as disruptive."

The flag-arrest episode came a few days after Robinson insulted Clark. The U.S. Supreme Court had just issued a decision in *Puyallup Tribe v.*

Department of Game of Washington that further curtailed Indian treaty rights, and the campaign planners decided to deliver a petition of protest to the justices. When court officers refused to let them into the building, Ray, Cheryl, and others tried to break in through a side window and, failing, settled for lowering Old Glory on the flagpole out front—"stupid, stupid, stupid," Cheryl said decades later. The Robinsons and another protester were arrested, and the arrests landed on the front page of *The New York Times*. Among the campaigners there arose speculation, which Adams first heard from Latino activists, that Robinson might be an agent provocateur.

Ray and Cheryl passed the next five years passed more quietly on the farm. In the spring of 1973, Ray went to New Mexico for a congress of Vietnam Veterans Against the War and heard an appeal for volunteers to resupply the beseiged Wounded Knee. By this time, Robinson was a complete convert to the thing called nonviolence, but he couldn't resist the chance to witness an armed uprising of the oppressed against their oppressors. He drove with friends to Rapid City and from there, it seems, was escorted to Crow Dog's Paradise. In the third week of April, he called Cheryl and said he was hiking into Wounded Knee the next night with an AIM guide and other recruits. She begged him not to go. She said they had crops in need of planting, outbuildings in need of fixing, three children in need raising, and more to do besides. He said he was going in. It was the last time Cheryl spoke to him.

His hike in seems to have gone poorly. By at least two accounts, the deep-voiced Robinson talked too loudly, and his companions became suspicious that he might be *trying* to get his group caught by goon or federal patrols. By one story, his guides left him in the dark to be brought in by another group of hikers. In any case, he seems to have entered Wounded Knee under a cloud, one that may have been all the darker for his reputation from the Poor People's Campaign.

Not long after arriving, he took part in a sweat lodge ceremony, the Plains Indian rite in which steam cleanses body and soul. AIMers commonly believed that evil spirits could not abide the heat of a sweat and that informers in particular would be exposed inside the lodge. Doug Durham, it was later noted, assiduously avoided the sweat lodge. Robinson's was run by Leonard Crow Dog, who was renowned for scalding newcomers. "Sweat 'em, don't cook 'em," his wife often teased him. In the middle of the ceremony, Robinson was overcome and had to crawl out of the low-roofed lodge, gasping for air. When he recovered and asked to be let back in, Crow Dog said he had to return the way he had left—backwards, on hands and knees, a posture meant to humiliate him.

This was all bad enough, but Robinson made matters worse by refusing to bear arms and telling the rebels they ought to have occupied Wounded Knee nonviolently.

"If he's the guy I'm thinking of, and there were very few black guys in Wounded Knee—he may have been the only one at that time—he came off as loud, even obnoxious," reporter Kevin McKiernan said years later. "He was something of a bull in a china shop, and I remember thinking, 'That's trouble,' and stayed away from him."

An Oglala named Richard Two Elk, who says he shared a bunker with Robinson, recalled, "He seemed to have difficulty adjusting to the conditions in Wounded Knee—no food, constantly under fire, the unilateral AIM command. Almost immediately he began wanting to open discussion on strategies in the Knee. We in the bunker were not in charge of anything, so it didn't do us any good to talk about it. He didn't want to accept that. Some thought he might be a little disturbed."

As Two Elk told the story, a few days into Robinson's stay in the village, he got into an angry argument with his bunkermates, who radioed the Wounded Knee command post for help defusing him. The command post sent a security squad.

"There were six or seven people who came as part of the security element," Two Elk later wrote, "and in all there were a dozen or so of us in the room. When security entered the house"—the bunker had been built into the side of a house—"Leonard Crow Dog, the only person without a firearm, grabbed the knocker off of our door; it was a piece of thick wood approximately one foot long. The others followed him in and formed a semicircle facing Mr. Robinson. Leonard told Mr. Robinson that he'd need to come with them, to which Mr. Robinson protested with profanity. He rose from the chair where he was seated and seized a butcher knife lying on the table near him and started moving toward Leonard. By this time, security had formed a full circle around Mr. Robinson. The next thing, I heard a loud BANG and saw Mr. Robinson's lower leg spin from the knee and rotate outward. As he started to fall forward, his eyes rolled up and he went down. When Leonard saw he was shot, he told us to get him into the van for transport to the Wounded Knee hospital. Everyone in the security element left in the van and took him to the hospital. That was the last I saw of Mr. Robinson. It was my understanding that he'd been evacuated with the Community Relations Service"—the mediation wing of the Justice Department—"although I don't know that this actually happened. I didn't see a fatal injury. The wound didn't look bad."

There was much in Two Elk's account that was self-serving, improbable, or both: he did not see who shot Robinson; he did not see a bad wound; he thought Robinson had been passed to the government; aside from Crow Dog, who was innocent, he could not remember any of the witnesses to the shooting, although he had shared a bunker with some of them for months; and he claimed that Robinson, a mostly peaceable man who in his better moments could speak calmly with Klansmen who had firebombed his home, had had a heated fight with his bunkermates and then tried to knife Crow Dog while surrounded by a dozen of Crow Dog's armed followers. But if Two Elk was equivocating about much, he was right about the central fact: an AIMer shot Ray Robinson inside Wounded Knee, and he was never seen again.

I stumbled onto the story of Robinson's shooting in the course of other investigations and at the end of 2003 published an article about it. Not long later, editor Paul DeMain convinced Two Elk to speak publicly about what he knew, which prompted others who knew pieces of the story to talk to reporters too, mostly off the record. One source who spoke on the record was Marlette Thunder Horse. A lifelong resident of Wounded Knee, Thunder Horse had been one of the children in the car with nine-year-old Mary Ann Little Bear when she was shot in the eye.

She said, "My uncle Stanley Hollow Horn—we called him Billy—he used to sit outside and cry before he passed in '98. When he'd get like that, he'd say that Ray Robinson, the colored man, was in the bunker with him, and the colored man didn't like the fact that they were using force. He said it should have been a peaceful demonstration. Billy said it was Carter Camp that took him, and Lester Davis [a pseudonym] and Leonard Crow Dog. Billy heard them say that they'd heard Ray talking on a radio to the feds—which how could he do that? He was always around other people. Then my uncle heard a shot. After that, he never saw him again. He said, 'I know they killed him and buried him.'

"He said the AIM leaders threatened him. They said if he ever talked about Ray Robinson, they would come and get him and all his children. So he said he'd take it to the grave. A lot of people tell me, 'There's a bullet waiting for you if you open your big mouth.' But when I heard this year that Cheryl Robinson was looking for her husband, it made me want to cry. I thought, 'Oh God, he's lying right out here in Wounded Knee.' "

Another version of Ray's last moments has him sitting on the stoop of the house-bunker when Crow Dog arrived and summoned him to appear before Dennis Banks.

"In a minute," Robinson said. "I'm eating my oatmeal. I'll go when I'm finished."

The insolence earned him a bullet to the kneecap.

By all accounts, after Robinson was shot, he was taken to the village's makeshift clinic, a two-room affair run by Madonna Gilbert and Lorelei DeCora, both of whom were later accused of guarding and interrogating Anna Mae Aquash in her last hours. (Whether they were present when Robinson was brought to the clinic is not known.) On a wall the clinicians had spray-painted a slogan: BLEEDING ALWAYS STOPS IF YOU

PRESS HARD ENOUGH. But Robinson's bleeding did not stop. He died in the clinic and was buried by cover of night, perhaps on the banks of Wounded Knee Creek, perhaps beneath one of the bunkers.

Stanley Hollow Horn was not the only person threatened with death if he dared speak of the murder. One of Robinson's friends who drove with him to South Dakota, Janie Waller, hiked into Wounded Knee a day or so after him. On her arrival she asked where he was and for answer was brought before some of the leaders of the Independent Oglala Nation— *which* leaders are not clear—and told that if she knew what was good for her, she would never mention the name Ray Robinson again.

By chance, Robinson had another friend in Wounded Knee. Allen Cooper was a Caucasian so fervent for the cause that AIMers called him Crazy Al and gave him the radio handle Honky Killer; he had come to the village in the occupation's second week. Eight years earlier, Cooper and Robinson had fasted together in Laurie Pritchett's jail, but they hadn't seen each other since, and they were amazed to meet again when Robinson hiked into Wounded Knee. They embraced, talked for a spell, then went back to their duties. It was the last Cooper saw of Robinson.

After Robinson was killed, two men came to Cooper's bunker and told him to come with them. "I'd patrolled with these guys, man," Cooper later said. "I was their friend. When they came for me, they couldn't look me in the eye, just looked at the ground as they spoke. They were ashamed of having to carry out this order they'd been given. They took me to one of the buildings downtown and I was chained to a bed. Leonard Crow Dog was there, and he questioned me while Stan Holder—he was the security chief—and Carter Camp—he was also part of the ruling group—stood behind him. Crow Dog started asking if I was an informer, things like that." Cooper will not discuss Crow Dog's questions more specifically, but almost certainly Crow Dog was trying to learn whether Cooper had been in league with the "informer" Robinson or would talk about Robinson's murder. The questions continued for some time.

"It was serious, man. Very, very heavy. Eventually Crow Dog stopped.

He turned his back to me and looked at Holder and Camp. He didn't say a word, and I couldn't see his face, but he was asking their opinion. I cannot tell you the horror I felt. It was indescribable. It was just—just the most terrifying moment of my life. Holder and Camp didn't move or say a thing either. It was dead silent. They both just very slightly, very slowly shook their heads no, meaning I was not an informer. And I was sent back to the bunker."

Cooper's story is supported by an account from, of all the ironies, a genuine informer. He or she told the FBI at the time that "there is a young white male locked up and being held prisoner in Wounded Knee. ███████ advised that this young man's life has been threatened, and the occupants have discussed executing this individual because they think he is a traitor."

Cheryl Buswell-Robinson learned of her husband's disappearance when Janie Waller returned to Alabama and said Ray had gone missing at Wounded Knee. Waller, who has since died in a car wreck, was too terrified to say more. Cheryl enlisted the help of her friend Barbara Deming, a writer who published occasionally with *The New Yorker* and who had marched and fasted in Georgia with Ray and Crazy Al. Deming made an investigation, the sources of which are now mostly lost (and Deming herself is dead), and turned up the story about Ray's having been shot while eating oatmeal. One of Deming's sources said that a Wounded Knee veteran told him, "Yeah, I knew that Ray Robinson. He was a pig and we took care of him." For some time, that was the extent of what Cheryl could learn.

Months later, probably in the fall of 1973, WKLDOCker Sand Brim called Cheryl. Before joining WKLDOC, Brim had worked for black civil rights under Coretta Scott King. Years later, she recalled that she may have have met Robinson once or twice during shared struggles in the South. She may also have seen him in Rapid City, very briefly, just before he went into Wounded Knee.

"When I heard, and I am emphasizing *heard*, that he was killed," Brim said, "it was like a dark cloud covered everything. People were talking with marbles in their mouths."

The Wounded Knee veterans she asked about Robinson would not admit even having seen this singular man, whose large frame, booming voice, and black skin would have been hard to miss—let alone knowing his fate. After Brim learned what little she could, she called the farm in Alabama, and Cheryl, assuming her own phone was bugged, called Brim back from a neighbor's house.

"I'm sorry to tell you," Brim said, "but your husband is dead."

"How? Where? What?" Cheryl remembered saying.

"It was at Wounded Knee. I can't tell you any more than that. I don't know any more, and I'm not even supposed to tell you this much. But I thought you had a right to know."

For the next year Cheryl hoped for another call from someone who had seen or heard about Ray, but the months passed in silence. In the autumn of 1974, she decided it was time to go to St. Paul and speak directly with AIM.

"I met with Clyde Bellecourt," she said. "We were sitting in this tiny little office, and I told him my husband was in Wounded Knee and hadn't come home.

"Clyde said, 'I don't know anything about it.' He said, 'Nope, don't know nothing, never heard anything.'

"I said, 'Well, is Dennis Banks around? Because my understanding is that Ray was sitting eating oatmeal, and Banks summoned him, and he was shot when he didn't come right away.'

" 'Nope, Dennis isn't here.'

" 'Could you call Dennis and set up an appointment for me?'

" 'I don't know where Dennis is at.'

"He wouldn't budge. So I went and met with Ken Tilsen over at WKLDOC. He said the only black person he knew of at Wounded Knee was Ray's friend Janie Waller. He knew about her because she had been processed out after the stand-down and he'd seen the papers. I said, 'Well, Ray went in a day before her. At least that's what Janie told me.' Tilsen said he didn't know anything. When I tried to talk with him about Sand Brim's call and how I was having trouble finding her, he got madder than a wet hen. 'She doesn't know anything! Leave her alone!' Well, how did he know what she knew or didn't know? So then I went to Rapid City, but it was the same there. It was like trying to go through jello. I posted pictures of Ray in the AIM and WKLDOC offices in both cities, but nothing came of them."

Thirty years later, Clyde Bellecourt could not recall having met with Cheryl, and of Ray he said, "I don't know who you're talking about." But the wire-service reporter to whom he said so thought him uneasy.

A curious letter in the archives of an old AIMer documents a part of AIM's response to Cheryl's visit. The letter, from Dennis Banks to an envoy at the Justice Department, said AIM was trying to help Cheryl locate her husband, who had gone missing at Wounded Knee and whose photo was enclosed. The curiosity is that the Justice Department man never got the letter. The original on AIM letterhead (never signed), the carbon copy, the picture of Ray, and even the addressed envelope were all filed away unsent. Maybe Banks had never meant the letter to be sent. Maybe he had only wanted to appear to be doing something about Robinson's disappearance. Or maybe a well-intentioned AIMer had typed the letter without Banks's knowledge, and Banks, on seeing it, declined to sign. Or maybe Doug Durham had a role in the letter, since it was typed by Veronica "Raven Hawk" Keene, the assistant he imported to "help" with media relations after the murder at AIM Camp 13. If so, Durham probably intended the letter to embarrass AIM, only to have Banks (or someone else) nip that plan in the bud.

Another archived document points more strongly to a cover-up. This is a WKLDOC memo written two months after the fall of Wounded Knee by Jeanne Davies, one of the WKLDOCkers whom the FBI jailed in Rapid City on the false charge of interfering with agents. In her memo, Davies wrote that she investigated the whereabouts of a dozen people rumored to have gone missing at Wounded Knee. In each case, she found either the person himself or proof the person was alive. Ray Robinson was among the people "proven" alive. The proof came in a phone call that Davies—or perhaps another WKLDOCker—made to the Robinsons' farm. Someone at the farm supposedly said that within the last two days friends of Ray at Vietnam Veterans Against the War received two postcards from him. Apparently Davies did not think it odd that a man missing for ten weeks would get in touch not with his wife and children but with friends. (Friends, of course, would have been less likely to spot forged handwriting.) Nor did she think it odd that he would do so via postcard. (A postcard would have been easier to fake than a phone call.) Nor did she think it suspicious that the postcards proving his existence should turn up just days before she investigated him. Ken Tilsen, who received Davies's memo, apparently suspected nothing either. There is no evidence that Davies or Tilsen knew, or did not know, that they were party to a cover-up. (Tilsen says he does not remember the memo, and Davies's whereabouts are unknown.) Quite possibly, Robinson's killers orchestrated the mailing of the postcards, then orchestrated Davies's investigation so as to "clear" AIM of the murder.

Other mysteries about Davies's investigation are less explicable. For one, Cheryl said that neither she nor anyone she knew at the farm received a call from WKLDOC asking whether Ray was alive. Nor did she hear about the posthumous postcards from "Ray" until I brought them to her attention three decades later. Perhaps the call to the farm had been invented. Or perhaps the postcards had. Or perhaps someone at the farm, possibly Ray's friend Janie Waller, had been coerced or bluffed into abetting the fraud. The full story may never be known.

After her futile visit to AIM in 1974, Cheryl was in a quandary about what to do next. To turn to the FBI was to deliver herself to the very people who had sabotaged the freedom struggles that she and Ray had worked for. It would also give the Bureau a mallet to batter AIM with. She was heartsore enough that Ray had been killed; that the nation's foremost movement for Indian rights, however flawed, should be brought down in the bargain was almost more than she could bear. She also wondered whether the FBI, through an operative, had somehow been involved in her husband's murder. It was not a fanciful concern. Just such a thing had happened not far from the Robinsons' farm in 1965, when civil rights worker Viola Liuzzo was murdered by Klansmen, one of whom turned out to be an FBI operative. But after her trip to St. Paul and Rapid City, Cheryl's options were few, and in late 1974, more than a year and a half after Ray's death, she filed a missing-person report at the Selma office of the FBI. She was circumspect with the details since she clung to the slim hope that Ray might have gone into hiding, but she appears to have said enough for the FBI to know Ray had been murdered at Wounded Knee. The agents who took her report did so, she said, with indifference bordering on disdain. Not once in the coming months, indeed not once over the next quarter century, did anyone at the FBI follow up with her. Nor, so far as she could tell, did the FBI speak with people who had seen Ray just before he went into Wounded Knee or who might have seen him inside Wounded Knee. Nor could she detect any other sign that the FBI was investigating his disappearance.

There was an ominous parallel in this to Anna Mae Aquash's case: the FBI, told of a crime both grim enough and solvable enough to undo AIM at a time when AIM's undoing was just what the FBI wanted, apparently did nothing, or close to nothing, with the information. Perhaps it was not coincidental that Robinson, like Aquash, was killed while under suspicion of being an FBI mole or that, as recently discovered papers show, Robinson, like Aquash, had been spied on minutely and without regard for the lawfulness of his actions. One example of the intelligence the FBI collected on Robinson was a copy of an intercepted postcard that Cheryl had sent her mother from Paris in the late 1960s. The card said *in toto* that she and Ray were having a hard time finding a room. Perhaps the FBI feared Ray and Cheryl were communicating in code with "Mom." The CIA also kept an eye on Robinson, probably as part of Operation CHAOS, its illegal program for spying on domestic dissidents. A CIA report from 1965, released for reasons unrelated to Ray, summarized his activism and arrests, noted that the FBI had an "extensive" dossier on him, and characterized him as an extremist threat to the nation.

Robinson, in short, fell into that broad category of activists that COINTELPRO was designed, in the memorable phrase of J. Edgar Hoover, "to neutralize." That is not to say the FBI killed Robinson; certainly the available evidence points in the opposite direction. But perhaps agents were only too pleased to learn of his murder and were loath to investigate it, just as agents in San Diego had been when black nationalists killed each other in the COINTELPRO-inspired bloodletting of 1969. Whatever the FBI's motive, its inaction confirmed Cheryl in her belief that the FBI could not be trusted, and her options narrowed to two: speak to the press about Ray's killing, with all the trauma that implied, or keep quiet. Cheryl's children were in diapers and her farm was failing and her husband wasn't coming back in any case. She kept quiet and the killing slumbered thirty years.

In 2004, I and other reporters asked Dennis Banks if a man he had summoned to his presence at Wounded Knee had been shot and killed, but Banks refused to answer. Stan Holder, the security chief who helped interrogate Crazy Al Cooper and whose security team had probably come for Robinson, also spurned interviews. Leonard Crow Dog did not reply to messages, nor did Lorelei DeCora or Madonna Gilbert (now Madonna Thunder Hawk) from the Wounded Knee clinic. Of the several people allegedly involved in Robinson's last minutes, only Carter Camp was loquacious. Camp had been elected chairman of AIM immediately after Wounded Knee, but within weeks of his ascension, he ended an argument with Clyde Bellecourt by putting a bullet in Bellecourt's stomach and thereafter was *persona non grata* in AIM. Much later he was allowed to return to the fold. Camp first spoke publicly about Robinson in 1999, during a week of meetings and rallies in Washington, D.C., in support of Leonard Peltier's petition for clemency. One of Robinson's daughters, Tamara Kamara, attended the events and at one made a tearful plea for information about her father. When she was done, Camp walked up to her and said, "I broke bread with your father." He confirmed that Robinson had been inside Wounded Knee—a fact most AIMers were still denying—but said he had seen Robinson walk out of the village. If Robinson was dead, he told her, it must have been goons or feds who got him. Tamara called her mother in Detroit and told her about the conversation, and Cheryl took the next plane to Washington. She approached Camp the next day with a photograph of Ray.

"I said, 'Carter, look at this picture and see if you remember my husband.' And I positioned myself so I could see the look on his face when I showed him that eight-by-ten. So I uncovered it, and he looked at it, and he looked at it, and he *looked* at it. I swear to God, it was excruciating how long he looked. I didn't say a word, didn't interrupt—just let him commune. He finally turns to me with a pained look on his face, and he says, 'No, I don't remember him.' And he had *just* told my daughter at this very emotional thing yesterday that he had broke bread with Ray and it was 'a hole in my heart' and all that. Ain't that a kick?"

Four years later, when Robinson's murder broke in the press, Camp returned to his original position: he had met Robinson, but he had watched the man walk out of Wounded Knee with his own eyes. The feds must have got him. I got in touch with Camp and asked which story—his original and latest one, or the one he told Cheryl in between, or another one altogether—was true. He replied, in nearly so many words, that the mere act of asking that question proved me a dupe of the FBI and much worse besides, and he wasn't going to tell what he knew to a dupe. I gave him several chances to deny having had a part in Robinson's death, but he never took me up on the offer.

In 2001, after a silence of twenty-seven years, the FBI returned to Cheryl Buswell-Robinson. The agent who appeared on her doorstep in Detroit said he wanted to talk about Ray, and she agreed to speak. But the questions he asked did not seem calculated to solve the killing.

"He wasn't asking," she said, "about what Ray had been wearing, or who had been with him, or how his body might be identified, or anything like that. I suspect they were really working on Anna Mae's case"—Arlo Looking Cloud was shortly to be indicted—"but of course they're not going to tell me that. Well, I didn't want to be part of whatever witch hunt they were on. That part of the world where Ray was killed has had more than its share of suffering. So I said, 'I'd be happy to talk to you with my lawyer here.' And the guy walked away. Never came back. Is there any reason, *any reason*, that I should think the FBI is more trustworthy on Ray's case than it was on Viola Liuzzo's?"

Cheryl next heard from the FBI three years later, just after the story of Ray's murder broke and just before Looking Cloud went to trial. This time Agents Dan Cooper and Marc Vukelich were on the phone from Rapid City. They said they had an open investigation into Ray's death and a grand jury was going to hear evidence on it in the last week of April—coincidentally, the anniversary of Ray's murder, always an emotional time for Cheryl and her family. Cooper and Vukelich said they wanted to talk to Cheryl face-to-face and, according to her, promised that if they could get a good lead on where Ray was buried, they would excavate his remains. Warily, she flew to Rapid City. She returned in an outrage.

"Those bastards lied to me!" she said. "There was no grand jury. They've done nothing, *NOTH-thing*, on the case that I can see. It was all just a ploy to get me out there, some kind of fishing expedition. They showed me pictures of some buildings that AIM had supposedly trashed at Wounded Knee. Had nothing to do with Ray. All I could tell was they wanted to show me how awful AIM was. Then they brought in this racist-ass assistant U.S. attorney who made some foul remarks about Indians before saying he didn't have any evidence that showed Ray was murdered. At least, Ray wasn't murdered with premeditation, and premeditated murder is the only charge with no statue of limitations. It was an accident—was what he said. I said, 'Well, how do you know it was an accident if you don't even have the body? If you dig it up, and there's a bullet hole in the back of his skull, it was premeditated, right?' They didn't give a goddamn. They wouldn't even commit to a cadaver-sniffing dog."

As this book went to press, Cheryl was arranging permission from the Oglala Sioux Tribe to search the washes of Wounded Knee for her husband. She planned to rent a ground-penetrating radar and hire an expert to interpret its data at a cost of thousands of dollars that she did not have. Her three children, grown and with children of their own, said they just wanted their father home.

CHAPTER 17

THE QUESTION OF who ordered the murder of Anna Mae Aquash haunts the legacy of AIM. It should haunt the FBI as well. The operative word is *should*.

Much remains unknown about how the order was arrived at, but what is known is that in November 1975, after the government announced that Informers A and B had betrayed the caravanners in Marlon Brando's motor home, AIM's leaders became obsessed with finding them. Vernon Bellecourt, AIM's security chief after Doug Durham was exposed, coordinated the hunt. The full extent of the hunt, the methods used, the evidence marshaled, and the roster of people involved are still incomplete. But it is certain that in late November or early December, Bellecourt, having spoken with other AIMers in the Midwest, flew to California and met with Dennis Banks, then in hiding in the Bay Area. Not long later, someone called Thelma Rios in Rapid City and ordered that Aquash be brought to Rapid from Denver, and Rios picked up a phone and called Angie Janis in Colorado, who went to Troy Lynn Yellow Wood's and made it happen.

This much could have occurred relatively benignly. Many of the people involved may have thought, as several have since claimed, that because Doug Durham had been questioned and let go, nothing would happen to Aquash.

"When Madonna [Gilbert] told me," Aquash's friend Candy Hamilton said, "that after they got done questioning Annie Mae in Rapid, they just put the fear of God in her and said they never wanted to see her again, I believed her. The sense I got was that at the end of the interrogation, a lot of them didn't want to kill Annie Mae and probably didn't know she'd be killed. But then one or more of the people kept pushing and saying, 'We can't let her go. We just can't let her get away.' Then somewhere, someone high-enough up made the decision that, okay, they weren't gonna let her go."

Hamilton had her suspicions about who might have led the push to kill Aquash, but she declined to name the person or persons, partly because she believed that he or they were dangerous and partly because if she were wrong, she would be doing exactly what the FBI had wanted all along: cannibalizing other activists on the basis of rumor and innuendo.

At the end of the interrogation in Rapid City, more phone calls were made. Banks and Bellecourt were involved from California (or perhaps Bellecourt had returned to the Twin Cities and took part from there), and so were some of the interrogators in South Dakota. The conversations culminated in a call from Bellecourt to Bill Means's house on Rosebud. Whoever answered the phone handed it to Clyde Bellecourt, who had just come from the interrogation in Rapid City (via the drive that Candy Hamilton described at the Looking Cloud trial, the one in which she stayed in the car while Clyde, Ted Means, Webster Poor Bear, and the man she did not know went inside). Vernon told Clyde that Aquash had to be taken care of, or so three sources have said: Russell Means, who got the story from kidnapper Theda Clarke, a relative and loyalist of his; editor Paul DeMain, who got the story from people he will not name; and Robert Pictou-Branscombe, a distant cousin of Aquash who investigated the case in the 1990s and also got the story from people he will not name. Nobody familiar with AIM believes Vernon Bellecourt had the authority or commanded the respect to give such an order and have it carried out. More likely he was a conduit. For whom is the question. Lacking more evidence, I decline to name the possibilities, but they are well known and few.

When Clyde Bellecourt hung up the phone, he apparently passed the order to others at Bill Means's house and then left for Sioux Falls. According to Paul DeMain, who again will not disclose his sources, those who stayed included Bill Means and David Hill. A few hours later Theda Clarke and John Graham walked into the house while Aquash and Looking Cloud stayed in the red Pinto outside. Clarke and Graham were told to kill Aquash, and did.

The cover-up, however, was imperfect. Two dozen people from California to Colorado to Rapid City to Pine Ridge to Rosebud had been involved in Aquash's demise, and some of them talked. Just weeks after Aquash's body was found, Kevin McKiernan reported with certainty that she had been interrogated by AIMers in Rapid City shortly before her death. A few weeks after McKiernan's report, Aquash's wallet turned up in the hands of WKLDOC's Ken Tilsen. Since the wallet was not on her body when it was found, it seemed likely that the killers had passed it to Tilsen, probably through intermediaries.

In 2003, I interviewed or tried to interview the alleged principals in Aquash's last hours. A spokeswoman for Dennis Banks said he would grant me an audience so long as he maintained "editorial control" over the "content" he "contributed" to my story. I replied that no ethical reporter would agree to that and that Banks could take the interview or not, which prompted an obsequious fluster from the flak. *Such* a misunderstanding we had had, she said. Dennis had *never* meant to imply he wanted to *control* what I wrote. (Silly me to have thought "editorial control" meant precisely that.) He just wanted to make sure he was quoted correctly. I said he could record our interview, and she set a date to meet at his home on the Leech Lake Reservation. I flew to Minnesota, but Banks stood me up. He did not respond to messages thereafter. In the past, Banks has maintained his innocence on all things Aquash, to the point of denying even their affair. He has said he never "really" believed she was an informer and that she was in Brando's motor home on the drive west not because she was being watched but because "we needed someone who was not wanted by the law who could go around openly buying whatever we needed." This was a canard. The caravan had several other members who were not fugitives who could and did buy groceries and guns without raising an eyebrow. But in a less guarded moment during a 1994 protest march, Banks told Paul DeMain, "You know, we believe the FBI set us up, that you'll find someone in the government that worked hand in hand to get us to that point." His belief may well have been true, but it was not a ringing claim to innocence.

Bill Means agreed to meet me in a Minneapolis bar, but he too stood me up. I found him at his house, but he did not want to talk there. We finally had a brief meeting at his office in St. Paul. I asked about the part of the conspiracy that supposedly played out at his house on Rosebud.

"It just didn't happen," he said. "Anna Mae was never in a car outside my house, not that I knew of anyway. If she was and I'd known it, I'd have gone out and got her. She was my friend."

Means is a large man with a swollen face enclosed by two plaited braids and, on the day we met, an air of despair. He had answered these questions too often of late.

"So Theda Clarke and John Graham," I said, "never stopped at your house?"

"There were a lot of people coming through my house. I'm not saying those people weren't there. Arlo, I'm not sure about. John Boy and Theda were involved in the sun dance at Crow Dog's, which was not far from my house. They could have been at my house that summer or fall lots of times. But I don't know about that for sure." (The sun dance took place several months before Aquash was shot.)

"Did AIM kill Anna Mae?"

"Anna Mae is a victim of the war between the FBI and AIM. In war, strange things happen, whether it's My Lai or friendly fire. There are victims of war who are totally innocent, and that's what Anna Mae was."

This statement, like Banks's to DeMain, was probably true, but it also had the echo of a troubled conscience.

Clyde Bellecourt was declining interviews, but his brother Vernon met me at his favorite Minneapolis barbecue joint. In his great raspy voice, Vernon said he had never thought Aquash was an informer, much less investigated her for it. Certainly he never passed along an order from

Dennis Banks or anyone else to have Aquash killed. On the role of Clarke, Graham, and Looking Cloud, he invoked the principle of innocent until proven guilty (this was before Looking Cloud's trial). But even if they were guilty, "The American Indian Movement is no more responsible for the acts of a few of its members than the Shriners or American Legion would be for a few of theirs."

I had heard that Bellecourt had been in touch with the three kidnappers over the years to see if they would maintain their silence, so I asked when he had last spoken to them.

He said he hadn't talked to Looking Cloud in nearly thirty years and had never talked to Graham.

"Never?" I said.

"No," he answered. But he added, "Several months ago, probably a year and a half ago, I got a call from him. So I talked to him on the phone. Just a general discussion. He was concerned why people are accusing him. He said, 'Why is it?' That was all the conversation was."

"So that's the only time you've spoken with him?"

"It seems to me I got maybe two—I'm sure the FBI knows how many calls. I have no doubt my phones are tapped, have been for years." He eased into a discussion of Nixon's campaign against AIM.

I eased back to Graham.

"I seen him once," Bellecourt finally said, "fifteen, twenty years ago. I was at an event in Saskatoon, Saskatchewan, when he was there. But that's about it. I've maybe over twenty-seven years seen him once, maybe had two or three brief telephone contacts. Was that gumbo pretty good?"

"Top notch," I said. "How about Theda Clarke?"

"After she had a stroke—half of her body was paralyzed, you know—I went in to see her, like I'd go see any relative who's sick. I've known her whole family more than thirty years now. I've been in to see her twice. The first time, she didn't even recognize me, it had been so long and I had lost so much weight. When I was talking to her, she was kinda in and out. She couldn't hardly remember anything."

The nursing home where Theda Clarke lives is in Crawford, in westernmost Nebraska. Dropping in on someone in Crawford is slightly more convenient than dropping in on someone in Juneau. Dropping in twice—on someone you have not seen for so long that she does not recognize you—evinced a touching concern from Bellecourt.

Not long after our lunch, the Pictou-Aquash family received an audiotape of Bellecourt, or someone sounding a lot like him, that was apparently made without his knowledge. The Bellecourtian speaker said that he had investigated Aquash because he thought she was an informer, that Clyde Bellecourt had been at Bill Means's house when the decision was made to kill Aquash, and that Graham, Looking Cloud, and Clarke had transported Aquash in captivity before killing her. When a reporter asked Bellecourt about the tape in 2004, he rasped, "I have never stated anything like that. To this day I don't know who shot Anna Mae"—as if the denials of today could trump the audio of yesteryear.

I met Ken Tilsen on his deck overlooking the St. Croix River. The deck had a leftist pedigree: it was here, Tilsen said, that his friend Paul Wellstone decided to make his first run for the U.S. Senate. I reminded Tilsen that he had ended up with Aquash's wallet, which he had forwarded to her family with a note that said, "I . . . enclose Anna Mae's billfold, which came to me through a circuitous route." I asked him about the route.

"You know—boy—I've never seen that letter," Tilsen said. "But I'm told it exists. I looked everywhere to see if I could find anything that refreshed my memory about where I got her wallet. I cannot find anything, nor can I think of how I could have gotten it, unless maybe it came from the police or from Garry Peterson"—WKLDOC's pathologist.

"The wallet wasn't on her body," I said.

"I just don't know then."

This answer disturbed me. The phrase in his letter—"through a circuitous route"—seemed intentionally obscure, and it also struck me as odd that although he had known and liked Aquash, and although she had been murdered after an interrogation by members of his group (as he knew when he received the wallet), he had completely forgotten how the potentially incriminating wallet had come to him. It did not help my estimation of Tilsen that Cheryl Buswell-Robinson said he had helped gum up her search for information about her murdered husband or that Peter Matthiessen told me Tilsen had lied to him brazenly, when he was researching *In the Spirit of Crazy Horse*, about Dick Marshall's innocence in the killing of Martin Montileaux. On the other hand, the estimable Kevin McKiernan and many other people swore by Tilsen's integrity. And it was Tilsen who alerted McKiernan to the Aquash story in the first place, which would have been a risky move for a man with something to hide.

I later shared my concerns about the wallet with Tilsen, and he replied with insults to my intelligence and probity. How, he demanded, could I even *think* the wallet had come to him other than by innocent means? Hadn't I considered, say, that Aquash might have left the wallet in Pierre before skipping her court date and that it was forwarded to him from there? Or that she had lost it years before her murder, and it just happened to turn up after her decease?

I had considered several such possibilities, but they were mostly implausible, and I had turned up no evidence to support them, and Tilsen hadn't either. It was telling, I thought, that the normally rational Tilsen became nearly irrational on being asked a question that he himself would have put to David Price had Price's associates grilled Aquash for betraying them, then Aquash had been murdered, then Price had ended up with her wallet, which he had explained by saying only that it had come to him "through a circuitous route" and that he couldn't remember what the route was. I doubted very much that Tilsen had a thing to do with Aquash's death, but I also doubted he wanted anyone to know the truth about it.

In the fall of 2005, I tried to interview David Price, who, strictly speaking, was not a principal in Aquash's last hours but who was not untainted by them either. From his home in Rochester, Minnesota, he asked about my credentials and, when I related them, said it didn't matter how many universities I had graduated from (only one, alas), I was surely working "for a cause." Unless someone he trusted could vouch for me, he wouldn't talk, and he didn't. Most of his colleagues in the FBI were of the same mind.

Had the FBI not sabotaged the rights movements of the postwar era, had it not sent Doug Durham and Gi and Jill Schafer and John Stewart and Virginia DeLuce and others of their kind into AIM, had it not added the virus of Informers A and B to the paranoia it had already created, had it investigated crimes against AIMers on Pine Ridge, had it stanched the perjury and coercion and framing that its agents practiced as a matter of course, had the Justice Department not gone along with every step of this, had the BIA not let Dick Wilson run his own impeachment trial, steal an election, and jerry-rig voter rolls to save his government, had the courts held the FBI or prosecutors accountable for their sins, or had Congress done so, Anna Mae Aquash would not have been killed. To read the news reports of the last few years is to be told that Aquash was murdered because AIM thought she was an infiltrator. This is only half the truth. Aquash was murdered because the government of the United States waged an officially sanctioned, covert war on the country's foremost movement for Indian rights. It was a quiet war, chiefly psychological, with only the occasional shot fired in anger, but like the Cold War, it was war all the same.

The American Indian Movement must share the blame. AIM's defenders have said, rightly, that a people whose near-ancestors were defeated in wars of conquest, stripped of their culture, and swindled at every chance, a people who a century later were still denied decent schools and homes and were sent to penitentiaries almost as a rite of passage, could hardly have avoided falling victim to COINTELPRO. The stratum of Indian Country from which AIM sprang was too angry, too "ghetto," in the word AIMers often used, to answer the provocations of the FBI by turning the other cheek. But a sociological truth cannot absolve individuals, not automatically anyway. The individual men and women who ran AIM were savvy to a person. Some were brilliant. A few were wise. They knew or should have known that only the FBI could separate the snitches from the snitch-jacketed. They knew or should have known that exactly what the FBI wanted was for activists to gamble on the matter and kill one of their own. That AIM's leaders rolled the dice was criminal not merely in the legal sense but in their betrayal of the thousands of their race who had entrusted their hopes to AIM. When AIM's leaders killed Aquash, they killed their own movement as surely as the FBI did.

There are retirees today on both sides of the AIM-FBI divide who are living out a comfortable seniority but who are as deserving of a cage as Arlo Looking Cloud. The difference that separates them still is that only the AIMers stand a chance of being put in one.

Finally, there is the difficult question of David Hill. A Choctaw from Oklahoma, Hill came to AIM in or around 1971 and by the end of 1972 was on friendly terms with most of the group's leaders. He took part in many of the seminal events in AIM's brief history: the Trail of Broken Treaties, the riot at Custer, the police riot at the Sioux Falls Courthouse, the Columbus Day bombings, the trip in Brando's motor home. But he is best known for dynamiting the visitor center at Mount Rushmore in the early morning of June 27, 1975, several hours after the shootout at Oglala. Ten days later, Hill and a young accomplice, one Tony Ament, were arrested for the bombing. In Hill's possession at the time of his arrest were equipment of the kind used in the bombing and a stolen gun with an obliterated serial number. Informers had told the FBI within hours of the Rushmore explosion that Hill had made the bomb, where he had made it, and who had watched him do it. Hill also made other bombs that night, one of which was intended for a police station but which at the last moment was not planted. In short, David Hill was in a tight spot after his arrest, the sort of spot for which Pedro Bissonette, say, would have been threatened with decades in the clink.

Yet Hill was quickly released from jail, and over time his many charges disappeared one by one. There were plausible grounds for several of the dismissals, just as there was for much of the lenience the government showed Aquash. But the dismissal of the bombing charge was hard to explain: it was not every day that the government overlooked a bombing at a national icon, particularly when the FBI was certain its suspect was the bomber. (Hill's FBI file makes clear the FBI never even considered other suspects, save for Ament, who turned out not to have been with Hill at the time of bombing.) Not surprisingly, suspicion arose within AIM that Hill had cut a deal with the feds. Unwise remarks by Hill abetted the suspicion.

"When Dave was in the lockup," an AIMer who asked not to be identified said, "he told us we better make sure we got him out immediately, or he'd end up talking. He said he just couldn't sit in jail. I thought, 'Well, shit, it's a little late for that.' "

If the FBI can be believed, more than one AIMer thought Hill "knew too much" about the killing of the agents at Oglala, and after his release from jail a plot was soon afoot to murder him before he talked. The plot, if there was one, was not carried out. But agents tried to warn Hill about it, and if they succeeded in doing so (the FBI's papers are ambiguous on the point), they almost certainly suggested they could protect him if he became an informer. The sum of these parts is the COINTELPRO conundrum. Did Hill crack? Did the government set him up to make it seem he had? Or did mere circumstance, coincidence, and appearance conspire against him?

In Aquash's final weeks, her path repeatedly crossed Hill's. According to more than one source, in October 1975 they drove Brando's motor home together for part of the trip from Los Angeles to Pine Ridge. Once back in Pine Ridge, as Kamook Nichols and others have said, Hill and Leonard Peltier forced Aquash to make the Columbus Day bombs (with dynamite Hill provided) and denounced her as a snitch. Weeks later, on the eve of Aquash's interrogation at the WKLDOC house, Hill came from Utah to Rapid City, probably to take part in the deliberations on Aquash's fate. And if Paul DeMain was right, Hill was at Bill Means's house when Vernon Bellecourt phoned the order of execution to his brother Clyde. Consequently, Hill has often been suspected of being the reason the government first refused to solve Aquash's murder and then did so only at the level of the triggermen. He was, so the theory ran, the provocateur who was too close to the conspiracy.

In 2003, I spoke with Hill about the suspicions that had dogged him through the decades. He denied any involvement with the FBI (plausibly enough, I thought), but he lied about several matters large and small, including having any role in Aquash's last days. He even claimed he had met Aquash only once.

"And it was so short," he said, "that I hardly remember anything about it. In fact, I thought she had curly hair until I saw a picture of her after she was dead and it was straight."

But lying about Aquash was hardly a probative: if doing so made one an operative, most of AIM's leaders were on the FBI payroll. Having no more to go on, I did not intend to write about Hill, but then two more pieces of information surfaced. The first originated with David Seals, best known for his novel *The Powwow Highway*. In the 1990s Seals interviewed Hill's ex-wife Thelma Rios, and in 2004, on the occasion of the Looking Cloud trial, he published excerpts in which Rios repeatedly said Hill was an agent provocateur. Rios was not guessing—she was certain.

"I should know," she told Seals. "I was goddamn married to him. He's a cop and always was."

Rios's intimacy with Hill simultaneously gave weight to her charge and raised the possibility that she was merely an embittered lover out for revenge. So a month after the interview was published, I asked her to explain exactly how she had known Hill was "a cop."

"I can't help you there," she said, "because I never said it." She explained in the tone a mother uses for a wayward child that she had no idea how that confounded Seals had so misquoted her, but she was going to wring his neck if ever she got her fingers near enough to it. Her denial convinced me less than her original vociferous claims to the contrary. Her denial, in the same conversation with me, of having played any part in Aquash's final days was equally unconvincing.

A year later I chanced into a lunch date with Norman Zigrossi, the agent who had run the FBI's Rapid City office from the day after the Oglala shootout through and beyond the time of Aquash's murder. In retirement Zigrossi was as languid of eye and fleet of speech as he had been in youth; only his hairline had conceded to the passage of the years. Over chicken soup, I said there was one matter about the trials for the Oglala shootout— a subject I knew was close to his heart—that I had never understood: why had the government not put David Hill on the stand? I explained that Hill had told me he had been an operative for the FBI, that a couple of agents had pretty much confirmed it for me, and that Hill also claimed to have watched the murder of Agents Coler and Williams. It seemed to me that if the government had put Hill on the stand, it could have convicted all three defendants, not just Peltier. In truth, of course, Hill had told me no such thing—not about working for the FBI or about witnessing the shootout— nor had any agents. But I had learned in my research that lying to interview subjects to see what they would say was a standard technique of the FBI, and given the chance to practice on one of the practitioners, I thought I should.

Zigrossi answered, with more warmth than our chat had enjoyed to that point, "I know Dave Hill, and Dave Hill had *nothing* for us. No matter what he offered. He would like to have known more than he did. You go through with him point by point, and you ask him where he was that day and what it was he claims to have seen, and you'll find out he wasn't there. As for all this other stuff Hill was supposed to have given us, it never amounted to anything, nothing that we could use anyway."

Zigrossi paused, I gathered in the realization that he had said more than he meant to, then said, "Now, as long as a person is still living, I'm not going to confirm or deny that that person was an informant. But I can tell you that Dave Hill couldn't help us at all."

If Zigrossi was telling the truth, then Hill, minimally, had *wanted* to be an informer. And if that was true, he almost certainly had been one. At least, it is hard to imagine the FBI, days after the killing of the agents, turning down a would-be mole who was intimate with the suspected killers and most of AIM's leaders. To take Zigrossi at his word is to believe the lay theorists on why the government did not want Aquash's murder solved: the

FBI *did* have someone too close to Aquash's murder—someone, no less, who had called her a snitch and forced her to make bombs.

Then again, maybe Zigrossi only wanted me to think Hill was an informer. I couldn't fathom why he would care to nudge me in that direction, but then much of what the FBI did was not fathomable without knowing the secrets the FBI knew.

Then too, perhaps despite trying to be cautious in my assumptions, I read more into Zigrossi's words than I should have. Certainly Hill's FBI file gives no sign that he was an operative, and there are several claims in it throughout much of Aquash's last months that the FBI's agents couldn't even find Hill. To believe the file is to believe Hill is just one more person unfairly besmirched by COINTELPRO, a victim like Aquash. But of course it is impossible to trust the FBI's files in such matters.

In the end, the triumph of the COINTELPRO is that the whole truth will probably never be known.

On March 11, 1976, the body of Anna Mae Aquash, having endured its second autopsy, was returned to her friends and family, who bore it to the Jumping Bull ranch in Oglala. The men of the community feared being caught mourning an informer, so women hacked the grave from the frozen soil. They were inexperienced, and one of their number had to lie in the hole to measure their work.

"We felt like it was our own funeral anyway," one said. "We thought we might as well get used to it."

During the two days of wake, Russell Means and his family drove by on their way to a basketball game but did not stop. Vernon Bellecourt called from Minneapolis to say he would come to the funeral but did not. Dennis Banks, in California, declared the funeral day a national day of mourning for Indians—but not until several days after the fact. On Sunday, March 14, in a driving snow, Aquash was laid to rest next to her friend Joe Killsright Stuntz, who was shot dead in the Oglala firefight and beside whom, Aquash had said, she wanted to lie when her time came.

She lay twenty years without a proper headstone. In 1996 her friends finally raised the money for one and held a small ceremony to place it. The ceremony was scheduled to accommodate Dennis Banks's itinerary, but neither he nor any of AIM's other leaders attended. Banks later said, a bit defensively, "I've been to Annie Mae's grave sixty, seventy, or eighty times." Vernon Bellecourt was another frequent graveside mourner.

In consequence, on a damp April morning in 2004, in the presence of her sisters and daughters, Aquash was lifted once more from the earth. Her elder daughter, Denise Maloney Pictou, explained, "We don't want Vernon Bellecourt holding another ceremony at her grave."

After the indictments of Arlo Looking Cloud and John Graham in 2003, Maloney Pictou assumed the difficult role of speaking for the family. Her statements tended to effusive praise of the BIA, FBI, and U.S. attorney's office—the only entities, she said, that had had the decency, integrity, and perseverance to bring her mother's killers to justice. She belittled critics of those agencies for their "defeatist and negative attitudes" rooted partly in old fears about governmental mischief that were no longer valid (if ever they had been) and partly in AIM propaganda. The bleeding hearts, she said, had been conned: "We have complete faith that those institutions that are mandated to protect our rights will do just that." And of her mother's end: "Her death was not a consequence of political unrest or warfare."

Both concepts would have been lost on her mother.

Denise's younger sister, Deborah Maloney Pictou, was an officer in the Royal Canadian Mounted Police, the same that had spied on her mother and family, at the FBI's behest, when she was a child.

From the disinterment on Pine Ridge, Aquash's remains were shipped across the continent to Pictou Landing, Nova Scotia, where they were given a generous welcome by the Mi'kmaq people. A quiet graveside ceremony followed, and the remains were lowered into the Pictou ancestral plot. They lie there today, two thousand miles from Aquash's enemies and from the friends she had asked to rest among for all time.

POSTSCRIPT

AT THE TIME this book went to press, John Graham continued to fight extradition from Canada for the murder of Anna Mae Aquash. Prosecutors presumed he would be returned but no time soon. Graham maintained his innocence, but he had changed his story about his part in Aquash's abduction and killing so often and so clumsily that it was hard to believe he was right. His best bet of escaping Arlo Looking Cloud's fate probably lay in testifying against more senior conspirators. Of course, he could do so only if the government had an interest in prosecuting the conspirators, which was not at all certain.

I was recently given a partial transcript of an interview between a reporter and an AIMer who is unnamed but who is believed to be Bernie Lafferty, the sister of Kamook Nichols. In the transcript, the interviewee says she served coffee to several leaders of AIM, whom she names, while they talked about the killing of Ray Robinson. The talk apparently took place in the summer of 1973, a few weeks after the stand-down at Wounded Knee. Since I haven't been able to verify the interviewee's account, I will not name the alleged participants in the cover up, although I will say that most of them have declined the chance to discuss their innocence with me.

An exception was Russell Means, who was not in Wounded Knee when Robinson was killed. After reviewing the transcript, he said he had heard AIM accused of a lot of outrageous things, but the murder of a black man inside Wounded Knee took the cake. For believing in such "wacko" rubbish, he adjudged me a "cockeyed" fool deserving of nothing but pity. I asked Means which of the stories he had heard over the years about the killing of Robinson, and he claimed that our exchange, which took place in 2006, was the first. He really did take me for a cockeyed fool.

Aside from the implausibility that any top-tier AIMer hadn't heard of the homicide, I had drawn Means's attention to it by e-mail three years before. I suspected his memory might be impaired by the money he stood to receive from a film about the siege of Wounded Knee. The film was nearing production, and its script was based on his autobiography. The emergence of a murder by AIMers might require adjustments both to the plotline and to Means's income. Or maybe not. When I wrote the producer, Patrick Markey (of *A River Runs Through It* and *The Horse Whisperer*), to ask if the newly discovered killing would be included in the movie, his associate producer replied that the Robinson incident was one of many interesting incidents from Wounded Knee—as if I had pointed out that Dennis Banks had bedded four women, not three, during the siege. It will be interesting to see whether HBO, the network bankrolling the film, bills it as fact or fiction.

The interview transcript, incidentally, has been given to federal prosecutors, probably by editor Paul DeMain, with whom the interview may have originated. Prosecutors said they still had no plans to indict anyone for killing Ray Robinson.

The claim by Kamook Nichols that Leonard Peltier boasted of killing the agents at Oglala has received wide attention, mostly because Peltier's detractors have said it justifies his conviction and will justify denying him parole when he is next eligible for it in 2008. The argument is spurious. It brushes aside the fact that Peltier was denied the right to a fair trial and so could not argue to a jury, as Dino Butler and Bob Robideau did, that even if they found he had killed the agents, the government was more guilty than he. We abridge the right of anyone to a fair trial at peril to us all, even if we forget this truth during times like our neo-McCarthyite present.

I have never met Leonard Peltier, and I doubt I would much like him if I did. I also believe it is far more probable than not that he finished off the agents while one of them begged for their lives. But the man has been imprisoned thirty years in consequence of being railroaded in the most obscene way, and that is suffering enough, particularly since his railroaders have never been jailed a day. He should be set free.

It is easy to forget in this chronicle of intrigue that the thousands of people who gave themselves to AIM did so for the noble goal of freeing a race from the grotesque miseries afflicting it. Many of those miseries, of course, are with Indians still, almost as if AIM and its allied movements had never been. The miseries are fundamentally economic: the Great Depression of the 1930s has nothing on the Eternal Depression of Indian Country.

There is only one honorable solution to the privation of the Lakotas: to return the land we stole from them—at least, to return what is returnable. I use the word "we" rather than "our ancestors" because if we know of the theft, as we do, yet do not right it, we are as guilty as our forebears. This solution is not impractical. A major portion of the once–Great Sioux Reserve, tens of thousands of square miles, is owned by government agencies like the U.S. Forest Service, the U.S. Bureau of Land Management, and state lands departments, and it can be returned to the Lakotas without taking a single parcel from a private landowner. For the ranchers and loggers and others who now use the government lands, the handover could be done gradually so as not to disrupt existing leases. In the meantime, rents from the leases could be paid to the Lakotas. Senator Bill Bradley introduced a bill to do something along these lines in 1987. Naturally, western senators killed it immediately, and so too its successor. But the bill was an important seed that bears replanting. To see it take root and flower would be the work of a generation, or several. But that is true of all progress that endures.

ACKNOWLEDGMENTS

MY DEBTS IN making this book have no end. A few of the larger ones are below.

The Fund for Investigative Journalism, for reasons I still do not understand but am too selfish to argue with, graced me with a grant that made much of this book possible. Many thanks to the Fund's directors, distinguished reporters all.

The law firm of Meloy Trieweiler of Helena, Montana, has so supported my literary and legal endeavors that I hardly know whether to say thanks or give them a byline. Mike Meloy was particularly kind in lending me his associate, Jennifer Hendricks (whom I know in another context), to sue the government for violating the Freedom of Information Act. This book could not have been written without the documents we won from those lawsuits. Special thanks also to Meloy Trieweiler's Denise Roberts and Lorrie Cole for patience and good cheer with my thousand phone calls and frequent commandeering of their office equipment.

Diana Zimmerman and the rest of the crew at Helena's Lewis and Clark Library saved me thousands of dollars with their diligent, amiable, and illimitable fetching of books, magazines, and newspapers from across the continent. They are public servants in the truest sense and deserve triple their present salary, whatever it is. To the rest of Helena's citizenry I give thanks for twice rejecting my assaults on their town's electoral summits, thereby leaving me no choice but to write the damn book.

CounterPunch, the underfunded, underedited, undercirculated, always interesting, and mostly right newsletter of investigation and opinion ran my stories about Indian Country when no one else would. Co-editors Jeffrey St. Clair and Alexander Cockburn have a standing invitation to the microbrews of Knoxville. Visit them at CounterPunch.org.

Two men who funded my education and rescued me from crushing debt, Hugh Stimson and Doug Hurley, here get belated praise and my unfortunately ritual apology for being wretchedly out of touch. These men are saints plain and simple.

Like every reporter chasing a story, I have had many helpful guides. Most are apparent in the book. I give particular thanks to Hank Adams of Frank's Landing Indian Community, who aided my early education in Indian affairs; to Eva Iyotte and Oleta Woodenknife Mednansky of White River, who graciously hosted me several times in Indian Country and did their best to get me drunk; to Robert Quiver of the Lakota Student Alliance, who helped me track down many elusive people on and around Pine Ridge even though his views and mine diverged on several matters; to Rose Baker, of the Turtle Mountain Reservation, who lent me access to the papers of Paula Giese notwithstanding her suspicion about my request; to Karen Northcott, whose enthusiasm about the Wounded Knee Legal Defense/Offense Committee did not hinder her objectivity and who read and helpfully commented on a ghastly early draft; to Ken Tilsen, who gave me access to the WKLDOC archives, even though I later questioned several of his actions severely; to Kevin McKiernan, who helpfully reviewed a draft and whose peerless reportage and raw video footage (the latter preserved in the Academy Film Archive of Los Angeles) gave this book much of its background and foreground; to Peter Matthiessen, who covered related events extraordinarily well in *In the Spirit of Crazy Horse* and who also offered helpful comments on a draft; to David Harris, who helped resurrect the story of Jancita Eagle Deer and who still owes me $150; to the countless Lakotas on Pine Ridge, Rosebud, and other reservations who let me intrude on them for a few minutes or a few hours; and to the scores of others who granted me interviews.

My first editor at Thunder's Mouth Press, Jofie Ferrari-Adler, never doubted the importance of this book and vigorously championed it to his colleagues at the Avalon Publishing Group. When Jofie left for other pursuits, the book fell to John Oakes, publisher of Thunder's Mouth, in whom I was fortunate to have another believer (and a tolerator of many a missed deadline, the result of which was a much better book). Freelance editor Kathryn Schulz made such vast improvements to the text that I probably owe her my next child. Wendie Carr, publicist extraordinaire, has my ever-lasting devotion for her early enthusiasm and grand plans, many of which I'm sure will bear fruit. Howard Zinn and Jim Hightower were exceedingly kind to promote this book when it was still an embarrassing manuscript in need of massive work, and Studs Terkel and Peter Matthiessen later lent their voices with such effusion that I still blush. My mother should blurb me so.

My son was born about the same time as my proposal for this book and turns four with its publication. For letting me abandon him so often to his mother (even if he rather prefers her), he has my loving gratitude. I hope as he grows he will see that my abandonments are for good cause and never more than temporary. Warm thanks to the kind souls of Chelsea Gilfillan, Chasya Roberts, and the whole team at Pete's Place of Helena, Montana, for giving him peace-of-mind care.

Jennifer Hendricks—professor, in-house counsel, mother, laundress, therapist, typist, proofreader, bedmate, breadwinner—has borne me through my many writerly despondencies and has represented me through years of very tangled, very dull, and very important lawsuits to pry secrets from the government. She has done so at great cost first to her private practice and now to her scholarship. I say a prayer weekly that she won't realize how much better she could do than me.

Authors' acknowledgements nearly always lie by omission—specifically, by acknowledging only those worthy of thanks. But for every two people who do a book like mine a kindness, three throw obstacles in its way. A few of these devils should be given their due.

The Federal Bureau of Investigation, the Bureau of Indian Affairs, and the Executive Office of U.S. Attorneys each employs battalions of people whose job is to stop you and me from knowing what they do. These people are called Freedom of Information officers, proving Orwell right. When a citizen asks to see these agencies' papers—that is, our papers, your and my papers—about, say, the government's illegal spying on Jane Doe, the FOIA officers respond that they cannot hand over the papers because to do so would violate Doe's privacy. Such concern for privacy these spymasters have! The king of censors is the FBI's David Hardy, under whose guidance my most important FOIA requests were stalled for months or years, after which they were often answered in so censored a fashion as to be worthless. Hardy and company did not single me out: they treat every citizen of the republic this way.

Hardy was abetted in his stonewalling by the Justice Department, which, particularly under President Bush, gives ridiculous legal color to the FBI's ridiculous censorship and delay. The lawyer at Justice who defended the FBI on most of my complaints was Jeffrey D. Kahn. Kahn was unflaggingly courteous, most reasonable in small but important diplomatic matters like accommodating scheduling requests, and utterly tireless in explaining why it was unthinkable that the writers of the Freedom of Information Act intended to allow information to slip out of the government. That a law should be interpreted justly rather than to the maximum advantage of one's client is a principle on which I diverge from Kahn, his superiors, and his clients.

The FBI and Justice Department are permitted to mock FOIA by a limp federal judiciary that still believes the myth, brilliantly nurtured by J. Edgar Hoover, that all G-men are squeaky clean. The certain fact that for most of the last century the FBI tried to destroy the Left remains heretical to most judges, who let the FBI decide which of its scandalous files should stay hidden. I acknowledge here the Honorable Don Molloy of the federal bench of Missoula, Montana, for keeping this benighted tradition alive in my ongoing FOIA cases. Perhaps one day, after enough books like this one have been published, Molloy and other jurists will see the error of putting blind trust in the FBI.

Congress, if it wished, could so sharpen the teeth of the Freedom of Information Act that no judge could defang it. But Congress does not wish it. There are secrets that leaders of both parties prefer to keep tucked away. The true victims of Congress's inaction are not the reporters who have to bring costly lawsuits (although we are victim enough) but the many Lakotas and people like them who have neither the money nor the expertise to wage years-long lawsuits and so rarely get the documents about how their people were abused. Is it any wonder, to restate what I have said in the book proper, that so many Indians continue to see their recent past as an open wound, that even today they do not trust the government to investigate or prosecute crimes in Indian Country?

To the dozens of newspaper and magazine editors who turned down my pleas to cover Indian Country in more detail—not much detail, mind you; maybe a fifth of what is given to Gaza—kindly read this book as a request for your reconsideration. The next time you say that crimes against Indians in the 1970s are too remote to cover, ask yourself if you have said the same lately about the thirty-year-old crimes of General Augusto Pinochet of Chile or the fifty-year-old crimes of the Ku Klux Klan of Montgomery.

ABOUT THE BOOK

Word Choices

I USE THE term *American Indian* rather than the alternatives—*Native American, indigene, aborigine,* and so on—because it is the word most Indians of the Plains use to describe themselves, because it is simple, euphonious, and familiar to non-Indians, and because although its origins are disputed (possibly it was a mistaken reference to the people of India, possibly it was a reference to people "of God," or *in dios*), it is in any case not derogative in origin. The National Congress of American Indians, the American Indian College Fund, the American Indian Movement, *Indian Country Today, News from Indian Country,* and many other organizations run by and for Indians see no reason to stop using the word. Nor do I.

The term *Indian Country* has a legal and a general meaning. Legally, it is the land held in trust by the U.S. government for tribes, which mostly means reservation land. More generally, it is the area surrounding and including reservations. Indian Country is, simply, where Indians live. When I use the term in the book, it is almost always in the second, more general sense that I mean it.

The secrecy of both the government and AIM have forced me to use qualifiers like *may, perhaps,* and *possibly* more often than I care to. I regret leaving the reader with so much uncertainty about matters so important. But better to call attention to what is known (for example, the fact that a murder took place) than to say nothing because so much remains unknown (for example, precisely how and why the person was murdered). I hope other reporters can discover what I could not.

I sometimes anthropomorphize groups like the FBI, BIA, and AIM: "the FBI wanted X," "AIM thought Y." I do so only when there is strong evidence that the act or belief is institutional. Anyone who thinks an agency like the FBI is not a living organism with its own personality should have his head examined.

The job of the nonfiction writer is to tease the curious and relevant from the dull and irrelevant while staying faithful to what actually happened. I am not sure I have done my duty wisely. The hardest choices always came when a direct quotation held something profound but was so long-winded or cluttered that the profundity was in danger of getting lost. If I had been writing this book mainly for researchers, I would have chopped up the quotations and used ellipses to show every chop. A convoluted sentence such as: "This thing, you know, happened and, um, let's see, there was that other thing, oh yeah, that, as I meant to say a few minutes ago, did too"— would become this: "This thing . . . happened and . . . that . . . did too." But repeated ellipses disrupt the story, tire the eye, and sometimes make a meaning less clear instead of more. My solution was to leave out ellipses when I cut phrases of little historical value—the above example would become "This thing happened and that did too"—but to say in an endnote that I had condensed the quotation. Where I cut a phrase that seemed to have historical or other value (albeit irrelevant to my immediate ends), I have used the traditional ellipses. I recommend that writers who quote a quotation from this book check the endnotes to see whether the quotation was condensed. If it was, please consult the original source or note the condensation in your own work.

A Call for Whistleblowing and Correction

Hundreds of people know secrets that, if told, could add valuably to our knowledge of the events in and around this book. But whistleblowers are rare in AIM, rarer still in the FBI, and rarest of all among the unaffiliated and often scared observers on the sidelines. The silence of the knowing is the same as that of the oft-quoted German verse:

When they came for the Communists,
I did not speak;
I was not a Communist.

When they came for the trade unionists,
I did not speak;
I was not a trade unionist.

When they came for the Jews,
I did not speak;
I was not a Jew.

When they came for me,
there was no one left to speak.

I encourage people who know of related cover-ups or framings, perjuries or frauds, beatings or murders to tell their stories to reporters or editors they trust. Naturally, I welcome hearing such stories myself. I can be reached at Steve@SteveHendricks.org or at P.O. Box 2148, Knoxville, TN 37901-2148. To verify my mailing address in the future, see my Web site, SteveHendricks.org.

Any writer who tries to extract a great many facts from a great many unwilling people will make mistakes. I have surely made them by the dozen. I encourage knowledgeable readers to let me know of them, ideally with countervailing evidence. I will post the more important corrections to my Web site and will ask my publisher to correct any future editions of the book.

On Profiteering

Many Indians are wary of non-Indian writers who come to Indian Country, do a bit of work, then leave with articles or books while their subjects remain in unspeakable poverty. I rarely set foot on a reservation without being attacked as one more "appropriator" or "cultural imperialist" trying to get rich on the backs of Indians. The concerns are understandable—no region of America is more exploited than Indian Country—but I disagree with the argument, implicit when not explicit, that only Indians should write about Indians. For one thing, if non-Indians ignore Indian Country, our (largely) non-Indian federal government is not going to end its abuse and neglect of Indians anytime soon. For another, a writer, like an Indian, ought to be judged not by the color of his skin but the content of his character and the quality of his work. Whether my work and character are good or bad are open to debate. I leave it to the reader to judge.

Writers could nonetheless ease Indians' concerns with at least a rudimentary accounting of their profits. Here is mine. My advance against royalties and a grant I received to investigate this book were both exceedingly modest—much less, combined, than a single year's poverty-level wage—and all of the money was sunk into the cost of researching this book, as was much of my wife's salary. For the four years I worked on the book, I made no money. If the book sells on par with others in its genre, I will pay off a few but not all of my debts and will make no profit. If it sells very well, I will cover my debts and clear maybe a thousand dollars for each year of work. Only if the book becomes a minor bestseller—a rare thing for a serious topic by a first-time author—will I make a profit that approaches a minimum-wage income. If it becomes a major bestseller and gets optioned by Hollywood, I could make serious money. I could also be appointed director of the FBI.

Small Acts that Might Add Up

Readers who are concerned that Congress has never investigated the FBI, BIA, and U.S. attorney's office for the events described in this book should ask their legislators to do so at long last. Names and e-mail addresses of members of Congress can be found at www.Senate.gov and www.House.gov. Members can also be written the old-fashioned way at Senator X, U.S.

Senate, Washington, D.C. 20510; and Representative Y, U.S. House of Representatives, Washington, D.C. 20515.

Readers with even a little money should, I suggest, share some of it with Indian Country. One or all of the following groups would be a good place to start.

The Native American Rights Fund gives critical legal help to tribes across America, including help suing state and federal governments for some of their many sins. One of NARF's most important suits, *Cobell v. Norton*, has for a decade held the BIA's feet to the fire for losing billions— yes, *billions*—of dollars in royalties that should have been paid to more than 300,000 individual Indians. The suit is ongoing, thanks to the liberality of NARF's donors. You can give to NARF online at www.narf.org, by phone at 303-447-8760, or by post at Native American Rights Fund, Attn: Development Department, 1506 Broadway, Boulder, CO 80302.

Donors might also give to America's thirty-four tribal colleges, which turn out distinguished graduates from the poorest pockets of America with shamefully little funding from federal and state governments. (While you're writing Congress, ask them about that one too.) The American Indian College Fund, an umbrella group for the colleges, gives 6,000 scholarships to Indian students each year. At the time of this writing, AICF spent a healthy 87 cents of every dollar on scholarships and other educational programs. Donate to AICF online at www.collegefund.org, by phone at 800-776-3863, or by post at American Indian College Fund, P.O. Box 172449, Denver, CO 80217-9797. E-mail inquiries can be made to donations@collegefund.org.

Most tribal colleges also accept donations directly. The college on Pine Ridge Reservation is Oglala Lakota College, www.olc.edu, 605-455-6000, P.O. Box 490, Piya Wiconi Road, Kyle. SD 57752. On Rosebud Reservation, the college is Sinte Gleska University, www.sinte.edu, 605-856-8100, 101 Antelope Lake Circle, P.O. Box 105, Mission, SD 57555 (send donations to the attention of Sinte Gleska Foundation).

Lakota political groups come and go like Chinook winds. Poverty ensures their instability. A very small group that is currently extant and that has done good work is Defenders of the Black Hills. Their contact information is www.defendblackhills.org, BHDefenders@aol.com, 605-399-1868, P.O. Box 2003, 919 Main—Room 110, Rapid City, SD 57709.

Part of my royalties from sales of this book will go to the Native American Rights Fund and the American Indian College Fund.

ENDNOTES

THE ENDNOTES AS I first wrote them were as long as the book proper. Because printing them in full would have added several hundred pages and several dollars to the book's price, I have pared them by two-thirds for publication. The full notes are posted on my Web site, SteveHendricks.org. I encourage researchers who want more detail to consult the full notes. Bound copies of the full notes will also be placed in several college libraries and historical-society archives in South Dakota, Nebraska, and Minnesota under the title *The Unquiet Grave: The FBI and the Struggle for the Soul of Indian Country: Expanded Endnotes.*

The notes below are densest where my research raises new facts or tries to sift through competing claims about disputed events.

The notes refer often to the WKLDOC Archives. These are, more properly, the Wounded Knee Legal Defense/Offense Committee Archives of the Minnesota Historical Society, St. Paul, Minnesota.

CHAPTER 1

p. 3   On February 24, at a quarter: Interview of Roger Amiotte by author, near Wanblee, S.D., Aug. 2003. See also FBI FD-302 report, interview of Roger Amiotte by SA Donald A. Dealing, Wanblee, S.D., MP 70-11023, interviewed Feb. 24, 1976, transcribed Mar. 5, 1976.

p. 4   The pathologist judged her an Indian: W. O. Brown, pathologist, autopsy of Anna Mae Aquash, autopsy performed Feb. 25, 1976, report issued Mar. 15, 1976. Brown told the FBI that Aquash had had sex within four or five days of her death. (FBI FD-302 report, interview of W. O. Brown by SA A. Wade Shirley, Scottsbluff, Neb., OM 70-1906,

RC 70-11023, interviewed Oct. 8, 1976, transcribed Oct. 12, 1976.) Brown died in the late 1970s.

p. 4 **The next afternoon, the FBI Identification:** The call is mentioned in an FBI teletype from Rapid City to Washington. Although the teletype is stamped 3:47 p.m., the call may have been made earlier. (FBI teletype from Rapid City (4-38)(70-11023), to Director, FBI, et al., re Anna Mae Aquash, et al.—Fugitive, Mar. 3, 1976, 3:47 p.m. URGENT; FBI FD-36 form, teletype, from Rapid City (4-38) (70-11023), to Director, FBI, re Anna Mae Aquash, et al.—Fugitive, March 3, 1976, 3:47 p.m.) Washington followed the call with a teletype: "Finger impressions obtained from deceased hands submitted with reairtel identified as fingerprints of Annie Mae Aquash, aka—fugitive, FBI nr 275229P1." (FBI teletype from Director, to Minneapolis, Rapid City (70-10239), re "Unsub, unknown victim—deceased, Indian female located at Wanblee, South Dakota, February 24, 1976, CIR—Possible Manslaughter," Mar. 3, 1976, 9:02 p.m. URGENT.)

p. 5 **On March 9, six days after:** FBI teletype from ASAC, Rapid City (70-11023) (P), to Director, FBI (Attn.: External Affairs Div. and General Investigative Div.), re "Unsub; Anna Mae Aquash, aka (Deceased)," May 25, 1976.

p. 5 **"After I got there," Hamilton said:** When Hamilton first learned the Jane Doe was Aquash, she went to the cemetery to look for her grave but could not find it. When she returned for the exhumation, she discovered the grave was unmarked. (Interview of Candy Hamilton by author, Oglala, S.D., Aug. 2003.) Price refused to be interviewed for this book, and I could not locate Wood. The FBI declined to put me in touch with him.

p. 5 **They said only that if a second necropsy:** FBI documents show that the doctor the FBI tried to contract to perform the second autopsy said no. (FBI teletype from Rapid City (70-11023) (P), to Director, FBI, re "Unsub; Anna Mae Aquash (Deceased)—Victim, CIR—Murder," Mar. 11, 1976.)

p. 6 **". . . and he threw a box across the room":** If Hamilton interview, *supra.* Ken Stern, whose book is not flawless, quoted Hamilton earlier saying the hands were tossed to Bruce Ellison. (Kenneth S. Stern, *Loud Hawk: The United States versus the American Indian Movement,* Univ. of Okla., 1994, p. 170.) Peter Matthiessen also wrote that Ellison asked for the hands back, although he does not say to whom they were given. (Peter Matthiessen, *In the Spirit of Crazy Horse,* Viking, 1991, p. 261–2.)

p. 7 **When Dr. Peterson's tools were at last:** For details of Peterson's autopsy, see Garry Peterson, pathologist, autopsy of Anna Mae Aquash, Mar. 11, 1976; and FBI FD-302 report, by SA William B. Wood, SA David F. Price, SA J. Gary Adams, Pine Ridge, S.D., RC 70-11023, events of Mar. 11, 1976, transcribed Mar. 22, 1976.

p. 7 **It was coated in a disinfectant:** Hamilton interview, *supra.*

p. 7 **No sooner had Peterson brushed:** Peterson has said many times that he noticed the bullet instantly. (Kevin McKiernan, "Indian woman's death raises many questions," *Minneapolis Tribune,* May 30, 1976, p. 1B; David Weir and Lowell Bergman, "The Killing of Anna Mae Aquash, *Rolling Stone,* Apr. 7, 1977, p. 51ff.)

p. 7 **It was surrounded by a circle of dried blood:** "On the posterior neck, 4 cm. above the base of the occiput and 5 cm. to the right of the midline is a 4 mm. perforation of the skin with a 2 mm. rim of abrasion surrounded by a 1.5 x 2.2 cm area of blackish discoloration. Surrounding this is an area of reddish discoloration measuring 5 x 5 cm. The area is grossly compatible with a gunshot entrance wound." (Peterson autopsy, *supra.*)

p. 7 **"You could not believe it":** Interview of Ken Tilsen by author, Troy, Wis., Aug. 2003. See also Pat Doyle, "Who Killed Anna Mae Aquash?" *Minneapolis Star Tribune,* Jan. 1, 1995.

p. 8 **"They're a conquered nation":** Zigrossi told me in 2003 that his quotations were part of a larger "philosophical discussion, a protracted historical discussion." (Weir and Bergman, *supra.*)

p. 8 **He said a small-caliber head wound:** Associated Press, "FBI defends timing of exhumation request," *Rapid City Journal,* Mar. 13, 1976, p. 13; Associated Press, "FBI denies coverup in death," *The Sunday Columbian,* Mar. 14, 1976, p. 16. Zigrossi also said the FBI could not be held culpable for the mistakes of Dr. Brown because the BIA, not the FBI, contracted him. But the FBI had accepted Dr. Brown's findings for years.

p. 8 **. . . no agents had been at the autopsy:** "No SAs present during February 25, 1976, autopsy." (FBI teletype from Rapid City to Director, Mar. 11, 1976, *supra.*)

p. 8 **Freelancer Kevin McKiernan . . . found a nurse:** (Interview of Kevin McKiernan by author, Santa Barbara, Cal., July 2003; McKiernan, "Indian woman's death, *supra.*) The FBI later confirmed McKiernan's findings in interviews with both nurse Inez Hodges and Dr. Stephen Shanker. The FBI also found a hospital volunteer from Groton, Connecticut, who had been with Shanker and who seconded Shanker's story. (FBI FD-302 report, interview of ■■■■ [Inez Hodges], Public Health Service Hospital, Pine Ridge, S.D., interviewed on June 8, 1976, by SAs ■■■■ and ■■■■ [one of whom was William B. Wood], transcribed June 11, 1976; FBI FD-302 report, interview of ■■■■ [Dr. Stephen Shanker], by SAs ■■■■ and ■■■■ [one of whom was William B. Wood], Public Health Service Hospital, Pine Ridge, S.D., interviewed on May 28, 1976, transcribed June 10, 1976; FBI FD-36 form, teletype from ASAC, Rapid City (70-11023) (P), to New Haven, re Unsub; Anna Mae Aquash, aka—Victim (Deceased), June 1, 1976; FBI teletype from SAC, New Haven (70-902) (RUC), to ASAC, Rapid City (70-11023), re "Unsub; Anna Mae Aquash, aka—Victim (Deceased)," June 3, 1976, 2:30 p.m.)

p. 9 **"A little bullet isn't hard to overlook":** Dr. Brown's quotations can be found in Jerry Oppenheimer, "FBI Under Fire For Conduct in Indian's Death," *Washington Star,*

May 24, 1976, p. A1; McKiernan, "Indian woman's death," *supra*; Johanna Brand, *The Life and Death of Anna Mae Aquash*, James Lorimer & Company, 1993. Much of Brand's account was based on the reporting of Kevin McKiernan. I have condensed some of Brown's quotations slightly.

p. 9 . . . X-ray machine had been broken: "Ontario gun suspect said S. Dakota victim," *The Oregonian*, Mar. 13, 1976, p. B4. At other times, Brown told reporters the choice not to use the X-ray equipment was a "calculated risk."

p. 9 But from his verdict he did not swerve: Brown's autopsy report read, "SUM-MARY: Death is felt to be due to exposure. It is understood that a subsequent examination revealed a bullet wound of the head, which I inadvertently overlooked. Although there were extensive post mortem changes in the brain, I found nothing in the examination of the brain to indicate involvement of this organ by the bullet tract." (Brown autopsy, *supra*.) Another time Brown said, "The bullet may have initiated, or set in progress, the mechanism of death, the proximate cause of which was frostbite." (McKiernan, "Indian woman's death," *supra*.) The FBI offered varying opinions on what Brown thought of the bullet, first saying he acknowledged that the bullet must have killed Aquash, then saying he was sure that she had died only of exposure. (FBI teletype from Rapid City to Director, Mar. 11, 1976, *supra*; FBI teletype from ASAC Rapid City to Director, May 25, 1976, *supra*.) The FBI did not explain the shift.

p. 10 A lesser faith might have been shaken: Peterson noted the presence of blood in the neck and inside the skull, and he traced the path of the gunshot wound through the brain. (Peterson autopsy, *supra*; Weir and Bergman, *supra*.) On the matter of Brown's care-lessness, Kevin McKiernan told me that a janitor from the hospital on Pine Ridge said that Brown tossed him a ball of thread as he walked out the door at the end of one autopsy and told him to sew up the body.

p. 10 . . . a nurse who helped with the autopsy told: Tilsen interview, *supra*.

p. 10 . . . Nathan Merrick, said he "thought": McKiernan, "Indian woman's death," *supra*.

p. 10 Dr. Brown said on one occasion: In Brown's autopsy report, he listed only BIA officers Merrick, Doug Parisian, and James Stensgar as present, but he said differently at other times. (Matthiessen, *supra*, 1991, p. 260; Brown autopsy, *supra*; Brand, *supra*, p. 24; McKiernan, "Indian woman's death," *supra*; Oppenheimer, *supra*.) Norman Zigrossi said Dr. Brown told him that no agents had been at the autopsy. (FBI teletype from ASAC Rapid City to Director, May 25, 1976, *supra*.) The most likely scenario is that agents wandered in and out of the autopsy.

p. 11 Price even photographed Aquash's face: Letter from William H. Webster, FBI Director, to Arthur S. Flemming, U.S. Commission on Civil Rights Chairman, Aug. 7,

1979, p. 9. David Price has said on several occasions that he was the agent who took the photos of Aquash. The FBI has maintained there was no lie about the presence of the agents: when Zigrossi said "no agents were there" or "no agents were at the autopsy," he meant only that agents were not standing at Brown's side while he was wielding the scalpel.

p. 11 "In the 1980s we had the pleasure": Tilsen interview, *supra*. Price has testified, "I did not attend her first autopsy and stayed out of the room during her second autopsy, since that particular procedure is not one that I enjoy observing." (Second affidavit of David Price, *David Price v. Viking Penguin, Peter Matthiessen, and Bruce Ellison*, U.S. Dist. Ct., 4th Div. Minn., Civ. 4-85-819, May 1987.) Price declined my several offers to interview him for this book.

p. 11 "I know all about the first autopsy": Interview of Norman Zigrossi by author, via phone, July 2003. The FBI has maintained through the years—in communications to Congress, the U.S. Commission on Civil Rights, the government of Canada, and the public—that no agents were at the first autopsy. Two directors of the FBI have said so.

p. 11 Zigrossi said only one FBI agent: The FBI has maintained ever since that only one agent went to crime scene. (FBI press release, "Statement of FBI Director Clarence M. Kelley," May 26, 1976; Webster letter, *supra; FBI Authorization: Hearings Before the Sub-committee on Civil and Constitutional Rights of the House Committee on the Judiciary,* 97th Congress, Mar. 19, 24, 25, Apr. 2, 8, 1981, (testimony of Charles Monroe, Apr. 2); FBI report, Office of the Director, "Inquiry Concerning Indian Matters," Jan. 5, 1982, reprinted in FBI Authorization, *supra*.)

p. 11 Amiotte remembered Price and Wood: Amiotte interview, *supra*.

p. 11 A BIA officer also remembered Price: The officer was Doug Parisian. Parisian also said David Price was at the autopsy. (McKiernan, "Indian woman's death . . . " *supra*. See also Brand, *supra*, p. 23.)

p. 11 . . . but witnesses counted as many: Amiotte said so, as did an FBI field report. (FBI FD-302 report by Dealing, events of Feb. 24, 1976, *supra*.) "Chief Sayers . . . denies that he was present and claims that only officers [Nate] Merrick, [Paul] Herman and [Glen] Little Bird and FBI agent Donald Dealing were present." (Brand, *supra*, p. 23.) Zigrossi's eventual admission that more than one officer was at the scene is also recorded by Brand.

p. 12 In later years Zigrossi dismissed such talk: "At that time, anything that moved, especially if someone got killed, we would visit it because we were there to stay, and we stayed till we solved that murder [of the two agents]. And all of those various incidences helped us." (Zigrossi interview, *supra*.) BIA Chief Ken Sayers told the U.S. Commission on Civil Rights the same thing. (Brand, *supra*, p. 23.) Reporter McKiernan doubted the claim: "It may not be impossible that the FBI jumped down there every time a hitchhiker's body was found, but why didn't we hear about it?" (McKiernan interview, *supra*.)

p. 12   The night the body was found, agents . . . cabled: (FBI teletype from Rapid City (70-NEW), to Director, FBI, re "Unsub; Unknown victim—deceased. I/F approximate age 20 found near Wanblee, South Dakota on February 24, 1976. CIR—Possible Manslaughter," Feb. 24, 1976, 10:00 p.m.) Zigrossi said, "There was absolutely no indication of foul play." (Zigrossi interview, *supra*.)

p. 12   The FBI would later say its agents: This argument seems to have first emerged in 1982: "Because of the substantial distance of the body from the road, the teletype also noted that the death may possibly have been the result of manslaughter." (FBI report, "Inquiry Concerning Indian Matters," *supra*.)

p. 12   . . . its agents did not know about Brown's exposure finding: BIA criminal investigator Nate Merrick also seemed to be trying to hide that he knew of Brown's exposure finding. A report he wrote the day after the autopsy discusses many of Brown's findings but omits the small matter of how the woman died. Merrick did not write that Brown failed to tell him the cause of death. Nor did he write that Brown did not know. He simply wrote nothing—as if it were routine for criminal investigators not to investigate whether the dead had died criminally. (Merrick outline/investigative report, *supra*.)

In an FBI report of the same day, an agent claimed, "Preliminary autopsy failed to determine cause of death . . ." This was untrue in two respects. First, there was nothing "preliminary" about Brown's autopsy. Second, Brown had to have determined the cause of death on the day of the autopsy (if ever) because he never saw the body again, and he never claimed to have arrived at a later revelation. That same week, the FBI called the finding one of "possible exposure," although Brown never allowed that his conclusion was merely "possible." (FBI airtel from SAC Minneapolis (70-NEW) (P), to Director, FBI (Att. Latent Fingerprint Sec.), re "Unsub; Unknown Victim–Deceased Indian Female Located at Wanblee, South Dakota, 2/24/76, CIR—Possible Manslaughter," Feb. 26, 1976; FBI FD-36 form from Rapid City to Omaha, Mar. 1, 1976, *supra*; FBI FD-204 report from William Van Roe, Minneapolis, to USA, Sioux Falls (Attn.: AUSA David R. Gienapp), re "Anna Mae Aquash," field office file 4-38, Mar. 11, 1976.)

The FBI would repeat these lies many times over the years. Perhaps the most stunning example was a letter from the FBI to Senator Tom Daschle in 1998, which read, "Additionally, the local pathologist who initially examined the corpse did not perform a full forensic autopsy and, based on a cursory external examination, concluded the cause of death was due to exposure." (Letter from A. Robert Walsh, acting unit chief, for John E. Collingwood, assistant director, FBI Office of Public and Congressional Affairs, to U.S. Senator Tom Daschle, Jan. 27, 1998.)

p. 13   So swore Agent Wood: Wood testified that he called Dr. Brown on March 4, the day after the FBI learned Jane Doe was Aquash. "Doctor Brown advised your affiant that his autopsy on the aforesaid unidentified Indian female had revealed that this individual had died of exposure." (Wood affidavit, *supra*.) In his March 4 conversation with Dr. Brown, Agent Wood did not ask, or did not record if he did ask, how Dr. Brown knew on March 4 what he did not know on February 25. This seems an improbable oversight on the part of Agent Wood. The FBI refused to put me in touch with Wood, and my efforts to locate him failed.

p. 13 The only hitch in this argument is that an FBI cable: FBI teletype from Rapid City (4-38) (70-11023), to Director, FBI, re "Subject Anna Mae Aquash, et al—fugitive," Mar. 3, 1976. The language of this and other documents implies that the FBI knew about Brown's exposure finding on the day of the autopsy.

p. 13 . . . "an obvious injury . . . a small contusion": The claim of an "obvious injury" contradicted the FBI's many statements, both before and after the autopsy, that there was no sign of foul play at the crime scene, nor of a wound to the body.

p. 13 It is impossible to sort out all the lies: Wood may not have secured Brown's collusion in the contusion, although he could have, since Brown released his autopsy report on March 15, eleven days after his (supposed) talk with Wood about the contusion, six days after Wood told the court about the contusion, and four days after Dr. Peterson found the "contusion."

p. 13 The same newspapers that on February 25: "Dr. W. O. Brown told the FBI on March 4, that the woman had died of exposure according to the results of his autopsy, and said that the only obvious injury on the body was a small contusion on the head." (Paul Riley, "FBI denies AIM implication that Aquash was informant," *Rapid City Journal*, Mar. 11, 1976; see also, "Autopsy shows Aquash died of bullet wound," *Rapid City Journal*, Mar. 13, 1976.)

p. 13 When, only a few weeks later, the FBI reversed course: See, e.g., FBI FD-204 report of Van Roe, *supra*.

p. 14 Even in 1976 . . . the museums of civilized: The University of South Dakota had Indian skeletons on display at least as late as the early 1970s. (Paul Chaat Smith and Robert Allen Warrior, *Like a Hurricane: The Indian Movement from Alcatraz to Wounded Knee*, The New Press, 1996, p. 139.) The ghoulish exhibits prompted Congress to enact the Native Graves Protection and Repatriation Act of 1990.

p. 14 The FBI agents who had Aquash's hands severed: The FBI said its agents ordered the hands severed, but the BIA said the two agencies did so jointly. Dr. Brown sometimes said the BIA and FBI gave the order jointly, but another time he apparently said a court gave the order. (Zigrossi interview, *supra*; FBI FD-36 form from Rapid City to Director, FBI, May 25, 1976, *supra*; FBI FD-302 report by SA John Robert Munis, Pine Ridge, S.D., RC 70-11023, events of Feb. 25, 1976, transcribed Mar. 1, 1976; Oppenheimer, *supra*; Brand, *supra*, p. 25; Webster letter, *supra*.)

p. 14   Early press releases said Aquash's "fingerprints": "Fingerprints delayed identification of body," *Rapid City Journal*, Mar. 9, 1976.

p. 14   The lawmen . . . eventually said they were too afraid: Brand, *supra*, p. 25. A
close reading of FBI documents shows that the FBI never claimed that the government's
men had tried taking prints, only that prints were unobtainable.

p. 15   That the lab could make casts: ". . . the fingers were placed in a material called
Duplicast, which is a material that is similar to epoxy . . ." (*U.S. v. Fritz Arlo Looking Cloud*,
U.S. Dist. Ct., S. Div. S.D., CR 03-50020, Feb. 2004, transcript p. 101ff. (testimony of
Kimberly Edwards, forensic examiner, FBI latent fingerprint unit).)

p. 15   "They didn't even pause before taking": Tilsen's claim was verified by Ken
Sayers, BIA police chief. (McKiernan, "Indian woman's death," *supra*.)

p. 15   And in fact once during Aquash's life: The rapid identification was made after
Aquash was arrested in Oregon on November 14, 1975. (FBI FD-302 report by SA Leo B.
App, Jr., Portland, Ore., PD 89-94, events of Nov. 15, 1975, transcribed Nov. 16, 1975.)
Aquash's National Criminal Information Center fingerprint classification was
20131010071353111006.

p. 16   "She's . . . about the right height, right weight": The document declaring
Aquash a fugitive on November 11, 1975, listed her as 5'2", 105 pounds. (FBI FD-65
form, from SAC, Minneapolis (4-38) (P), to Director, FBI, Attn: Special Investigative Div.,
re "Subject Anna Mae Aquash, aka—Fugitive, NFA," Nov. 11, 1975.) On the day of the
first autopsy, the FBI reported that Jane Doe was 5'2", 110 pounds. (FBI FD-302 report
by Munis, events of Feb. 25, 1976.)

p. 16   . . . he had questioned her about a murder: The FBI will not release Price's
interview with Aquash on April 10, 1975, about the murder of Jeanette Bissonette.

p. 16   . . . he had been in possession of pictures of the living Aquash: The FBI had
photos of Aquash as early as November 1972, apparently taken of her either while she was
living in Boston or during her participation in the Trail of Broken Treaties. The Rapid City
office had these photos and others shortly after Agents Ron Coler and Ray Williams were
killed in Oglala in June 1975. Aquash's photo was also taken on her arrests in September
and November 1975. (U.S. Government Memorandum from SAC, Los Angeles (157-
11137) to SAC, Minneapolis (157-4323)(P), re "CHANGED: ANNA MAE AQUASH,"
Oct. 17, 1975; FBI FD-302 report, interview of ▆▆▆▆ by SA Charles T. Stephenson,
Sharps, S.D., MP 70-10239, interviewed July 12, 1975, transcribed July 12, 1975; FBI FD-
302 report, interview of Nogeeshik Aquash by SA John E. Shimota & SA Robert K. Taubert,
Minneapolis, MP 70-11030, interviewed Mar. 19, 1976, transcribed Mar. 23, 1976.)

p. 16   And although he would later swear he was not: For example, in a lawsuit he
brought against Peter Matthiessen and Viking Press, Price attested, "Defendants' supplemental

reply brief also suggests I was actively looking for Ms. Aquash at the time she was murdered. This is not so. Ms. Aquash was a fugitive, but as I explained in my prior affidavit, there was no particular reason to believe she was on Pine Ridge at the time she was murdered. She was simply one of innumerable fugitives nationwide, and I have no recollection of looking for her any more than I was looking for any other fugitive whom I had no particular reason to believe was in my area." (Second affidavit of David Price, *supra*.)

This is a lie. Aquash's body was found on February 24, 1976. On February 18, 1976, Price wrote a memo about the progress on the search for Anna Mae Pictou Aquash, stating, "On 2/12/76 ▆▆▆ advised PICTOU was in ▆▆▆ S.D. at ▆▆▆ with ▆▆▆. These persons were en route ▆▆▆ S.D. via ▆▆▆. They were driving a blue Mustang with temporary South Dakota plates. They were probably going to stay with ▆▆▆. PICTOU was wearing blue jeans, a red scarf, a long brown coat and moccasins. A fisur of the ▆▆▆ area on 2/12/76 and 2/13/76 met with negative results." A "fisur" is physical surveillance—a stakeout. Because Price wrote the memo, in all probability it was he who conducted the stakeout. No doubt he was assigned to oversee the hunt for Aquash because he knew what she looked like from having interviewed her twice. (FBI Memorandum from SA David F. Price, to SAC Minneapolis (4-38), "Anna Mae Aquash, aka Pictou—Fugitive," Feb. 18, 1976.) While Price searched for her in western South Dakota, other agents searched other parts of the country under the coordination of an agent in Minneapolis. (FBI FD-263 report of William Van Roe, Minneapolis, "Anna Mae Aquash, aka Annie May Aquash et al.—Fugitive," investigative period Nov. 24, 1975–Feb. 3, 1976, report issued Feb. 18, 1976.)

p. 16   And then there is the story that Aquash told: Price has strongly denied he ever threatened Aquash.

p. 17   That she was decayed was not in question: For the various opinions on whether the body was identifiable: "She was basically intact but was going skeletal," Roger Amiotte said. (Amiotte interview, *supra*.) Brown's autopsy report said her tissues were "dessicated [sic], of a dark slate color," and in some places showed early mummification. The optic globes were collapsed. (Brown autopsy, *supra*.) Price was quoted in Matthiessen, *supra*, p. 461. The FBI has always maintained that Anna Mae Aquash was unrecognizable "due to the advanced decomposition of her facial features." (FBI press release, Kelley "Statement," *supra*.) The one FBI agent who the FBI admits was at the death scene, Donald Dealing, was less emphatic: "The body appeared to be partially deteriorated." (FBI FD-302 report by Dealing, events of Feb. 24, 1976, *supra*.) The BIA policeman who claimed Aquash for an acquaintance lived and worked on the Rosebud Reservation. (FBI FD-302 report, interview of ▆▆▆ by SA William R. Schroeder and SA William Van Roe, Rosebud, S.D., RC 70-11023, interviewed Nov. 9, 1976, transcribed Nov. 18, 1976.) Peterson was quoted in

Matthiessen, *supra* p. 261. McKiernan is quoted in McKiernan, "Indian woman's death," *supra*, and in McKiernan interview, *supra*.

p. 17 The FBI could make the question moot: The FBI has told me it has the photographs it made of Aquash at both autopsies. At the time this book went to press, my suit against the FBI to release the photos (and other documents) was in its third year. (*Stephen Hendricks v. U.S. Dept. of Justice, et al.*, U.S. Dist. Ct., Helena Div. Mont., CV-03-061-H-CSO.) The FBI once shared the photos with the U.S. Commission on Civil Rights, but USCCR has since destroyed them in accordance with a standard document-destruction schedule.

p. 18 If Aquash was, as the FBI claimed, beyond identifying: Moreover, the pictures were Polaroid instant-prints, a type of image not known for reproducing fine detail. To be potentially recognizable in an instant-print, a face would have been quite intact.

p. 18 "But no one ever saw it": Norm Zigrossi did not even remember posters "because if posters had been posted, if the right agents would have seen the pictures of Jane Doe, we should have identified her." (Zigrossi interview, *supra*.) This comment raises the question of why, since the "right" agents—i.e., agents who knew her—*did* see Aquash, they did not identify her. David Price said efforts to identify Aquash were more extensive. (Price affidavit, *supra*.) Zigrossi added that "hardly anyone came to the morgue anyway to try to identify her. It's not something people want to look at—someone that decayed." A few people went to the hospital to try to look at the body but were turned away. A very few people were permitted to see it, including the family of Myrtle Poor Bear, who thought Myrtle was missing (she was in fact in FBI custody). (Matthiessen, *supra*, p. 446. See also Brand, *supra*, p. 14.)

p. 18 . . . but the BIA memo on which it was based: This was Merrick's outline/investigative report, *supra*, which read in part, "The BIA Area Office, located in Aberdeen, has been notified [of the Jane Doe]. The Area Officer will send out a Missing Person Flyer to the Indian Reservations in the Aberdeen Area."

p. 18 . . . so Sayers ordered the body buried: FBI teletype from ASAC Rapid City to Director, May 25, 1976, *supra*; FBI teletype from Rapid City to Director, Mar. 11, 1976, *supra*; FBI press inquiry, Portland Ore., first released Mar. 12, 1976, updated Mar. 24, 1976. Sayers was quoted in Oppenheimer, *supra*; Zigrossi agreed. (McKiernan, "Indian woman's death," *supra*.) (This is not to say the FBI was uninvolved in the decision to have Aquash buried.) The claims of Chamberlain and Peterson are also found in McKiernan.

p. 19 The friend, Gladys Bissonette, offered: Brand, *supra*, p. 19.

p. 19 Another friend of Aquash's, Lou Beane: Interview of Charlie Abourezk by author, Rapid City, S.D., Aug. 2003.

p. 19 No burial certificate ever surfaced: Letter from Kenneth E. Tilsen,

WKLDOC, to International Indian Treaty Council, July 6, 1976, in WKLDOC Archives; Brand, *supra*, p. 16. My inquiries to South Dakota Department of Health in 2005 turned up neither a burial nor a death certificate.

p. 19 Only after the deed was done, Agent Wood swore: "On March 2, 1976, I was advised by Nathan Merrick . . . that the remains of the unidentified Indian female had been buried . . ." (Wood affidavit, *supra*.) But Merrick said in 2004, at the trial of Arlo Looking Cloud, that he was not on Pine Ridge when the body was buried, having left for a family emergency in Nebraska. Decades later, speaking with me in 2003, Norm Zigrossi agreed with Wood: "I found out she had been buried as a pauper, okay? And I said, 'Who the hell ordered her to be buried?' The FBI routinely does this, but we pay for the burial. We hadn't this time.' "

p. 19 Inmates from the Pine Ridge jail: Brand, *supra*, p. 16, 19.

p. 20 Then, too, a report from Agent Wood: (FBI FD-302 report, interview of ▆▆▆▆▆ [Nathaniel Merrick] by SA William B. Wood, Rapid City, S.D., RC 70-11023, interviewed Mar. 2, 1976, transcribed Mar. 12, 1976.)

p. 20 The key manuscript is Aquash's FBI Identification Record: FBI identification record, Identification Div., 275 229 P1 (Annie Mae Aquash), Apr. 30, 1976. Her death could not have been logged as received on her form if her identity remained unknown until March 3, as the FBI claimed. There is also circumstantial support for the argument that the FBI knew Aquash's identity before March 3: the FBI's many statements about the handling of Aquash's body do not say the body was *identified* on March 3; they say only that Washington *called* Rapid City on March 3 to say the body had been identified. The reader is left to assume the identification was made on March 3, but that is never stated explicitly. (See, e.g., FBI press release, Kelley "Statement," *supra*; FBI FD-204 report of Van Roe, *supra*.)

p. 20 The paper is a short memo: FBI report, Latent Fingerprint Sect., Mar. 10, 1976, Anna Mae Aquash, 275 229 P1.

p. 21 According to the FBI, "immediately" on learning: (Associated Press, "FBI denies coverup in death," *The Sunday Columbian*, Mar. 14, 1976, p. 16. See also FBI teletype, from Rapid City to Director, Mar. 11, 1976, *supra*; letter from A. Robert Walsh, FBI Acting Unit Chief, Office of Public and Congressional Affairs (for John E. Collingwood, Assistant Director), to U.S. Sen. Tom Daschle, Jan. 27, 1998; "Body to be exhumed for further study," *Rapid City Journal*, Mar. 10, 1976, p. 3.)

p. 21 But neither the FBI nor the office: FBI Rapid City claimed that Wood contacted the U.S. attorney's office on March 4, but there are no papers to support the claim. (FBI teletype from ASAC Rapid City to Director, May 25, 1976, *supra*.) The U.S. attorney's office refuses to release most of its files in the matter.

p. 21 March 8 happened to be the day a lawyer: FBI FD-302 report, interview of

Bruce Ellison by SA Thomas H. Greene, Rapid City, S.D, RC 70-11023, interviewed Mar. 8, 1976, transcribed Mar. 12, 1976. It has often been said, apparently wrongly, that Ellison demanded Aquash be exhumed and re-autopsied, or that he said WKLDOC would proceed with that course.

p. 22 . . . page-one exposés about the case: Oppenheimer, *supra*; McKiernan, "Indian woman's death," *supra*. Levi made his announcement after Oppenheimer's article ran in the *Star* but before McKiernan's piece ran in the *Tribune* the next day. (United Press International, "Levi Orders Probe Of Aquash Slaying," *The Oregon Journal*, May 25, 1976, p. 11; "Levi asks review of Indian death," *Minneapolis Tribune*, May 25, 1976.)

p. 22 But when Kelley spoke to the public: Kelley's statement was the FBI press release, Kelley "Statement," *supra*.

p. 22 What General Crimes investigated: Even years later, the FBI would only say that it "found no evidence of any attempt to conceal the cause of death and no evidence of misconduct by the FBI." (FBI report, "Inquiry Concerning Indian Matters," *supra*.)

p. 22 When USCCR persisted, Assistant Attorney General Richard Thornburgh: Letter from Richard L. Thornburgh, Assistant Attorney General (apparently written by Alfred L. Hantman, Chief, General Crimes Sec.), to John A. Buggs, U.S. Commission on Civil Rights Staff Director, Oct. 14, 1976. See also Flemming letter, May 10, 1976, *supra*; letter from Richard L. Thornburgh, Assistant Attorney General, to Arthur S. Flemming, Chairman, U.S. Commission on Civil Rights Chairman, July 12, 1976; letter from John A. Buggs, U.S. Commission on Civil Rights Staff Director, to Edward Levi, U.S. Attorney General, Sept. 16, 1976; Webster letter, *supra*.

p. 23 . . . and the legislators in turn asked: Rep. Les AuCoin, e.g., had written Attorney General Levi in April. (Letter from U.S. Rep. Les AuCoin, to Edward Levi, U.S. Attorney General, Apr. 23, 1976.) Kelley replied three months later. (Letter from Clarence M. Kelley, FBI Director, to U.S. Rep. Les Au Coin, July 26, 1976). Letters from Assistant Attorney General J. Stanley Pottinger to AuCoin (on July 19) and from AuCoin in reply are discussed in James Goodman, "FBI Chief Denies Oregon Times Charge," *Oregon Times Magazine*, Sept. 1976, p. 14ff. Per Goodman, AuCoin asked House Judiciary Chair Peter Rodino to probe the handling of Aquash's body; the committee did not.

p. 23 . . . unless a lone phone call from Norman Zigrossi: Zigrossi interview, *supra*. Zigrossi's account to me essentially matches what he claimed at the time. (FBI teletype from ASAC Rapid City to Director, May 25, 1976, *supra*.)

p. 23 "I don't think anything could come of it": FBI Authorization Hearings (testimony of James Frier), *supra*.

CHAPTER 2

p. 25   On that winter Friday a quartet of men: My account of the Yellow Thunder episode and related events is taken largely from articles in the *Rapid City Journal* of 1972: "Nebraska death linked to 'cruel practical joke,' " Mar. 3, p. 2; "AIM leader says Gordon will be in 'spotlight.' " Mar. 4, p. 2; "Indian demonstration set at Gordon; 1,300 expected," Mar. 7, p. 1; "Angry Indians name their own 'grand jury,' " Mar. 8, p. 1; "No mutilation of Yellow Thunder, but no answers about rumors, mistreatment, death, race relations,' " Mar. 10, p. 1; "Tension said easing at Pine Ridge," Mar. 11, p. 1; "Massive gathering at Pine Ridge planned," Mar. 12, p. 1; "Discrimination national problem, not localized, says BIA official," Mar. 13, p. 1; "AIM authority considered," Mar. 14, p. 1; "AIM hopes unrest continues," Mar. 15, p. 1; "BIA ignores charge they want Indians divided," Mar. 16, p. 1; "One charged in Indian death tells of beating," Mar. 25, p. 1; "Kleindienst says Yellow Thunder action not seen," Apr. 15, p. 1; "Venue change granted for Yellow Thunder suspects," Apr. 25, p. 1; "Yellow Thunder jury selection begins in Alliance," May 24, p. 2; "Yellow Thunder death trial stirs Nebraska town," May 25, p. 2; "Yellow Thunder case expected to go to jury," May 26, p. 1; "Two convicted of manslaughter in death of Yellow Thunder," May 27, p. 1; "Alliance Indian, white communities express relief at end of Hare trial," May 28, p. 3. See also "Yellow Thunder's death centered attention on Indian discrimination," Jan. 27, 1973, p. 5. Of several secondary sources, the most reliable are Rolland Dewing, *Wounded Knee II*, Great Plains Network/Pine Hills Pr., 1995, p. 29–32, and Paul Chaat Smith and Robert Allen Warrior, *Like a Hurricane: The Indian Movement from Alcatraz to Wounded Knee*, The New Press, 1996, p. 113–6. Other sources are Robert Burnette and John Koster, *The Road to Wounded Knee*, Bantam, 1974, p. 193; Associated Press, "AIM Director Reports Recklessness, Lawlessness of White[s] on Reservations," *Daily Capital Journal* (Pierre, S.D.), Mar. 31, 1972; Lakota Coalition, *Wounded Knee Bulletin #3*, Mar. 19, 1973, in WKLDOC Archives; untitled WKLDOC statement explaining why Wounded Knee occurred, ca. spring 1973, in WKLDOC Archives.

p. 26   At midnight, they stopped at the Legion Hall: Some weeks earlier the Hares had been blacklisted from the Legion Hall by a manager who thought them disruptive to other patrons. On this Friday, they decided to have their revenge on the manager by foisting Yellow Thunder on him. Yellow Thunder's humiliation apparently lasted not more than a minute or two; most of the patrons apparently did not even see it.

p. 28   . . . the Oglala Sioux Tribe: The name "Sioux" was enshrined in the tribe's BIA-written constitution. A constitutional amendment would be needed to change the name to "Oglala Lakota Tribe," and the tribe has never passed such an amendment.

p. 28   "It is isolated from modern facilities": Smith and Warrior, *supra*, p. 29.

p. 30   "For every rifle on the street": Associated Press, "Banks issues 'call to arms'; Guard in Custer," *Rapid City Journal*, Feb. 10, 1973, p. 1.

p. 31 . . . **"killing the Indian to save the man":** The dictum was that of Captain Richard C. Pratt, who pioneered the use of boarding schools to "educate" Indians.

p. 32 **"If the federal government once again":** "Penthouse Interview: Russell Means," *Penthouse*, Apr. 1981, p. 136.

p. 33 **Today the rumors are still spoken of:** *A Tattoo on My Heart: The Warriors of Wounded Knee 1973,* film by Charles Abourezk and Brett Lawler, 2005.

p. 34 **The Points called on the United States:** The Twenty Points contained other heresies, like a call to replace the BIA with a more responsive office of Indian relations.

p. 34 . . . **"as long as the rivers shall run":** This phrase was stock language in many Indian treaties. The literal phrase does not appear in the Fort Laramie Treaty of 1868, although the promise that the Indians could keep their land in perpetuity did.

p. 35 **"A more ripe and rank case":** It was the Indian Court of Claims that said thus. (207 Ct.Cl., at 241, 518 F.2d, at 1302, cited in *U.S. v. Sioux Nation of Indians*, U.S. Sup. Ct., June 30, 1980, 448 U.S. 388, 100 S.Ct. 2716.)

p. 35 **During World War II . . . the Oglalas lost 525:** American Indian Leadership Council, "About the 'Gunnery Range,'" *The Indian*, vol. 2, no. 3, Aug. 6, 1970; American Indian Policy Review Commission, *Report on Tribal Government, Task Force Two: Tribal Government*, Final Report to the American Indian Policy Review Commission, U.S. Govt. Printing Ofc., 1976, p. 342; House Report 1328, 90th Congress, 2nd Session, p. 1 and Senate Report 1349, 90th Congress, 2nd Session, p. 4, both quoting Letter from S. Bobo Dean, to Louis Bruce, Commissioner of Indian Affairs, reprinted in *Oglala Lakota*, Apr. 14, 1970. On August 8, 1968, Congress passed PL 90-468, which gave most of the bombing range to the Badlands National Monument.

p. 36 **Those Indians who held onto their land tended:** AIPRC report, *supra*, p. 352–3. See also Letter from Dave Long and Eddie White Wolf, Oglala Sioux Civil Rights Organization, to whom it may concern (explaining grievances behind the takeover of Wounded Knee), Aug. 16, 1973, in WKLDOC Archives; Untitled report, Oglala Sioux Landowners Association, ca. 1973, in WKLDOC Archives.

p. 36 **Tom Conroy . . . became the third-largest landowner:** The largest private landowner on the reservation was the Catholic Church. (Long and White Wolf Letter, *supra*.)

p. 36 **When the General Accounting Office . . . examined Conroy's:** The GAO study was requested by Sen. Henry M. Jackson, chair of the Senate Committee on Interior & Insular Affairs, on March 19, 1973. (Letter of Elmer B. Staate, Comptroller General of the United States, to Sen. Henry M. Jackson, May 7, 1973. See also Letter from Hank Adams, Survival of American Indians Association Director, to Dennis Banks and Russell Means, May 14, 1974, in WKLDOC Archives; WKLDOC report, "Witnesses Re: Land," in WKLDOC Archives; AIPRC report, *supra*, p. 352.

p. 37 **"Indian male life expectancy is 44.5 years":** Lakota Coalition, *supra*. Hank Adams, referring principally to the Staate letter, *supra*, wrote, "the level of federal expenditures [is] $2000-plus per capita; $11,000-almost per family . . ." (Adams letter, *supra*.)

p. 38 **But three weeks before . . . Harrison Loesch forbade:** Loesch's order was given by memo of October 11, 1972. (Smith and Warrior, *supra*, p. 147.) Quotations from Smith and Warrior below and the rest of their account of the BIA occupation appear on pp. 147–71 of their history.

p. 41 **. . . the Natives had backed a U-Haul:** The stack of BIA documents was said to have measured 178 cubic feet. (Smith and Warrior, *supra*, p. 171.)

p. 41 **Dennis Banks later said his people first:** Banks, *supra*, p. 139.

p. 42 **The sting was the work of John Arellano:** The spelling of the agent's name varies by source: Arrellano and Areliano are two common variants. (Richard LaCourse, "The FBI's 'Racial Intelligence' and the American Indian Militants," undated manuscript, in WKLDOC Archives; "Portrait of an Informer," *Akwesasne Notes*, early summer 1973, p. 47; Smith and Warrior, *supra*, p. 177.) A fine article about the sting and its aftermath that came to me as this book was going to press is Mark Feldstein, "The Jailing of a Journalist: Prosecuting the Press for Receiving Stolen Documents," *Communication Law and Policy*, v. 10, no. 2 (spring 2005), p. 137–77. Feldstein intends to include the episode in his forthcoming book, tentatively titled *Poisoning the Press: Richard Nixon, Jack Anderson, and the Rise of Scandal Media*, Ferrar, Straus & Giroux.

p. 42 **He later testified in court:** This was at a trial of an Indian who was prosecuted for possession of some of the BIA documents.

p. 43 **By one report, the National Guard of Washington:** Hank Adams said the war games were the work of 540th Aviation Unit of the Washington National Guard; he cited Captain Chris Lane for his source. (Adams statement, *supra*.)

p. 43 **Means, however, said he had been searched:** Russell Means, *Where White Men Fear to Tread*, St. Martin's Griffin, 1995, p. 240–1.

p. 44 **"I vass horrivied":** Interview of Richard Erdoes by author, Santa Fe, N.M., Nov. 2005.

p. 46 **"Nothing but a bunch of sponges":** "Tribe Leader Says Militants Give Indians A Bad Name," *Minneapolis Tribune*, Nov. 26, 1972. Wilson's other observations can be found in an article of uncertain title, *Sioux Falls Argus-Leader*, Nov. 11, 1972; Interview of Dick Wilson, *Newslines*, undated transcript, in WKLDOC Archives; and Interview of Dick Wilson by Cheryl McCall and Dee McGuire, Apr. 5, 1975, in WKLDOC Archives.

p. 46 **"The long-awaited Dick Wilson":** I have condensed this quotation slightly. (Terri Shultz, "Bamboozle Me Not at Wounded Knee, *Harper's*, June 1973, p. 48.)

McKiernan's observation is from Interview of Kevin McKiernan by author, Santa Barbara, Cal., July 2003.

p. 47 Wilson . . . helped himself to another $5,000: For this and other accusations against Wilson, see "Partial Transcript of Taped Interview with [Tribal Councilman] Richard Little," Nov. 16, 1973, in WKLDOC Archives; Letter of Eugene White Hawk, Inter-District Council president, and Hildigarde Catches, IDC secretary, to Oglala Sioux Tribal Council, Jan. 17, 1973; Statement of Rufus Fast Horse, trainee mechanic, Feb. 24, 1974, in WKLDOC Archives. Wilson's base salary of $13,500 would be worth about $50,000 in 2006. Wilson's critics also charged him with using the tribal station wagon for personal errands and drinking sprees and with using tribal mechanics to repair his own car.

p. 47 . . . an accounting firm that studied the tribe's books: Burnette and Koster, *supra*, p. 283. See also untitled article, *Shannon County News*, July 21, 1972, in WKLDOC Archives; interview of Delores Swift Bird, former tribal judge, date appears to be Jan. 1974, in WKLDOC Archives.

p. 48 In one egregious example, the tribal secretary: AIPRC report, *supra*, p. 354.

p. 48 Wilson called the council into its first session: For details on how Wilson ran the council in 1972, see Affidavit of Delores Swift Bird, former Oglala Sioux Tribal Judge, Apr. 8, 1974, in WKLDOC Archives; Long and White Wolf letter, *supra*. The tribal constitution did not anticipate the use of the executive committee for governance between sessions (special sessions of the council were supposed to be called for those), and any act of the committee was supposed to be ratified by two-thirds of the council at its next regular session, but Wilson ignored such formalities. In October 1972, when he was required to call the council into its second session, he did not. When he finally did in November, he refused to seek the council's approval for the executive committee's deeds. Again the BIA saw nothing wrong.

p. 48 "The Tribe is to be complimented": Letter from Dan Y. Jensen, Bureau of Indian Affairs Area Director [Dakota area], to Richard Wilson, Oglala Sioux Tribal President, Sept. 14, 1972, in WKLDOC Archives.

p. 49 If Wilson's critics were right, ordinance 72-55: Long and White Wolf letter, *supra*; Adams statement, *supra*. The quotation that follows is slightly condensed.

p. 49 While in jail, a turnkey who knew Means: Swift Bird interview, *supra*.

p. 49 Dennis Banks was also arrested: Article of unclear title, *Mitchell* (S.D.) *Republic*, Nov. 30, 1972; Letter of Long and White Wolf, *supra*.

p. 49 One was Vice President Long: Memorandum from Dick Wilson, Oglala Sioux Tribal President, to Dave Long, Oglala Sioux Tribal Vice President, Nov. 21, 1972, in WKLDOC Archives. Severt Young Bear, another tribal councilman, was also kicked off the reservation.

p. 49 The prosecutors said they would give: Long eventually won reinstatement to his seat, although only by appeal to the tribal council, not by the help of the federal government. (Editorial, *Shannon County News*, Dec. 15, 1972, p. 8.)

p. 50 Colhoff said the goons were a public nuisance: John O'Connell, "Note re Richard G. Colhoff," in WKLDOC Archives; "Partial Transcript of Taped Interview with Richard Little," *supra*; Long and White Wolf letter, *supra*.

p. 50 Colhoff was no saint: For example, Leroy Pumpkin Seed attested that in November 1972 he was arrested, driven into the country, and beaten by a police officer. (WKLDOC report, "Statement from complaint conference, April 2 and 3, 1973," which consists entirely of an excerpt from an FBI report, FBI file MP 70-6832, p. 50–51, in WKLDOC Archives.)

p. 50 . . . others out of fear of losing their jobs: Marvin Richard, e.g., said that George Wilson, Dick Wilson's brother, was his boss in the tribe's water works and well-repair department and he and his co-workers were afraid not to go to the training. (Statement of Marvin Richard, Apr. 6, 1973, in WKLDOC Archives.)

p. 50 But by the end of 1972 . . . called on Wilson and Lyman: WKLDOC report, "Time-line re: Wilson Impeachment," in WKLDOC Archives; Long and White Wolf letter, *supra*.

p. 51 . . . Wesley Bad Heart Bull was knifed to death: Wesley Bad Heart Bull was killed on January 21, 1973. Accounts of the killing and events of the next three weeks conflict badly, particularly in the secondary sources. The most accurate accounts are probably from the *Rapid City Journal* of 1973: "Custer man, 30, charged in death of Springs man," Jan. 23, p. 1; "Schmitz bound over on fatal stabbing charge," Jan. 24, p. 2; "AIM calling Indians to Custer rights day," Jan. 31, p. 2; "Indian group claims 'rampant discrimination,' " Feb. 3, p. 2; "Custer protest doesn't materialize by noon," Feb. 7, p. 1; "Confrontation first, then 'everything broke loose,' " Feb. 8, p. 1ff; "Thirteen arraigned on riot, arson charges," Feb. 9, p. 1; "Banks, 23 other AIM defendants arraigned," Feb. 10, p. 1; "Violence flares in city; 16 hurt, 40 arrested," Feb. 12, p. 1; "Different versions of stabbing offered," May 1, p. 1; "Schmitz says stabbing to protect him, others," May 2, 1973; "Schmitz found innocent in Bad Heart Bull death," Feb. 3. Further accounts are found in the *Journal* during the trial of Sarah Bad Heart Bull in 1974: "State witnesses say Custer trial defendants in incident," May 24, p. 1; "Three eye-witnesses tell of Custer incident," May 25, p. 2; "Gates testifies about AIM, demonstration," May 30, p. 1; "Custer deputy testifies about violence," May 31, p. 2; "Custer trial jury viewing disturbance film," June 4, p. 2; "Patrolmen take stand at Custer trial," June 6, p. 32; "Custer trial prosecution rests case," June 7, p. 1; "Bellecourt on stand for defense," June 8, p. 1; "Testimony centers on Bad Heart Bull death," June 11, p. 2; "Custer defendants say they had peaceful aims," June 12, p. 3; "Custer trial in hands of jury," June 19; "Three convicted at Custer trial," June 20; "Three get prison terms in Custer incident case," July 30, p. 1. Among the more reliable secondary sources (if biased in favor of the government) is Rolland Dewing, *Wounded Knee II*, *supra*, p. 40ff. See also Rolland Dewing, "South Dakota Newspaper Coverage of the 1973 Occupation of Wounded Knee," *South Dakota History*, vol. 12, no. 1, spring 1982; Smith and Warrior, *supra*, p. 183ff; Burnette and Koster, *supra*, p. 221ff; Peter Matthiessen, *In the Spirit of Crazy Horse*, Viking Pr., 1991, p. 62ff.

p. 53   AIM probably started it: After the riot, more than one Indian would claim to be the instigator. David Hill, who was inside the courthouse, told me he started the riot, while Russell Means, in his autobiography, claimed the honor. For other information on the riot, see Smith and Warrior, p. 184ff.

p. 54   "It was a different era": The chief of police was Thomas Hennies. (*Native Americans in South Dakota: An Erosion of Confidence in the Justice System*, South Dakota Advisory Committee to the U.S. Commission on Civil Rights, Mar. 2000 (www.usccr.gov/pubs/sdac/ch2.htm, viewed Apr. 2003).)

p. 55   SOG, in the words of its director: Wayne Colburn was the director. (Ed Meagher, Los Angeles Times News Service, "Special marshals' group on duty at Pine Ridge," *Rapid City Journal*, Mar. 21, 1973.) The marshals arrived on February 13 (WKLDOC report, "Time-line re: Wilson Impeachment," *supra*; see also Letter from Rogers C. B. Morton, U.S. Secretary of the Interior, to Richard G. Kleindienst, U.S. Attorney General, Feb. 13, 1973; FBI FD-302 report by SA Ray W. Gammon, Pine Ridge, S.D, MP 70-6832, events of Mar. 10, 1973, transcribed Mar. 16, 1973; Terry De Vine, "U.S. marshals doing their job," *Rapid City Journal*, Apr. 2, 1973, p. 8.)

p. 55   "There was an elaborate radio": I have condensed this diary entry for February 22, 1973. (Stanley Lyman, *Wounded Knee 1973: A Personal Account*, Univ. of Neb. Pr., 1991, p. 4–8.)

p. 56   He was also supposed to recuse himself: Tribal ordinance 26 of June 6, 1941, governed impeachment proceedings. ("Partial Transcript of Taped Interview with Richard Little," *supra*.)

p. 57   The next morning, BIA police escorted: Lyman, *supra*, p. 12–5.

p. 57   . . . had asked the marshals of Fort Wilson: (Memorandum from Oglala Sioux Civil Rights Organization to Mr. Cash [sic: Reese Kash], U.S. Marshall [sic], Feb. 19, 1973, in WKLDOC Archives.) In theory, the marshals were empowered to protect only federal property, personnel, and prisoners, but as events would show, they interpreted their mandate more broadly when it suited their purpose.

p. 57   "Whether the tribal president is corrupt": Lyman, *supra*, p. 19–20.

CHAPTER 3

p. 59   On Pine Ridge, the Oglalas called the superintendent: Much of my account of the massacre at Wounded Knee comes from Francis Paul Prucha, *The Great Father: The United States Government and the American Indians*, vols. I & II unabridged, Univ. of Neb. Pr., 1995, p. 727–9. Prucha's massive work is a valuable touchstone but overly sympathetic to the U.S. government.

p. 61   In 1975, Senator James Abourezk: John William Sayer, *Ghost Dancing the Law: The Wounded Knee Trials*, Harvard Univ. Pr., 1997, p. 216; Rolland Dewing, *Wounded Knee II*, Great Plains Network/Pine Hills Pr., 1995, p. 11.

p. 61   Its owners, the Gildersleeve: The Gildersleeves were Clive and Agnes; the Czywczynskis were Jim and his wife, whose name I did not discover. Their billboards are recalled in many publications, e.g., Mary Crow Dog and Richard Erdoes, *Lakota Woman*, Grove Pr., 1990, p. 129.

p. 61   A Catholic priest once watched: WKLDOC report, "Interview of Father Charles," in WKLDOC Archives.

p. 62   Years later Clive Gildersleeve was called to testify: Interview of Karen Northcott by author, Minneapolis, Minn., Aug. 2003. For the many alleged crimes of those who ran the trading post, see Russell Means with Marvin J. Wolf, *Where White Men Fear to Tread: The Autobiography of Russell Means*, St. Martin's Griffin, 1995, p. 262 (on illegal trading of government food commodities); Associated Press, "AIM Director Reports Recklessness, Lawlessness of White[s] on Reservations," *Daily Capital Journal* (Pierre, S.D.), Mar. 31, 1972 (on operating without a license) (see also *Rapid City Journal* of same date); Dewing, *supra*, p. 33, 106 (on the choking of teenager Ross Red Feather); Robert Burnette and John Koster, *The Road to Wounded Knee*, Bantam, 1974, p. 194 (on ditto).

p. 63   "The cavalry captain in charge": I have condensed this quotation slightly. (Means and Wolf, *supra*, p. 263.)

p. 63   . . . but Father Paul Manhart, vicar of Sacred Heart: Means and Wolf, *supra*, p. 259; Crow Dog and Erdoes, *supra*, p. 129.

p. 63   . . . the FBI had cultivated moles inside: Memorandum from Ralph E. Erickson, Deputy Attorney General, to Acting Director, FBI, Nov. 21 (or 23: the number is hard to read), 1972.

p. 64   . . . a pair of undercover agents infiltrated meetings: FBI teletype from Acting Director FBI, to SAC, Minneapolis (176-87), re "URTEL 2/19/73," Feb. 20, 1973; FBI teletype from SAC Minneapolis (157-1509) (P), to Acting Director FBI, re "Disorders by American Indians in South Dakota, E[xtremist] M[atters]," Feb. 23, 1973; U.S. Government Memorandum from G. C. Moore to Mr. E. S. Miller, re "Disorders by American Indians in South Dakota, Extremist Matters," Feb. 23, 1973; FBI FD-302 report by SA

Stanley R. Keel and SA Charles P. Stephenson, events of Feb. 22, 1973, Rapid City, S.D., MP 157-1509, transcribed Feb. 25, 1973; James M. Wall, "Wounded Knee Comes to Trial," *The Christian Century*, Mar. 6, 1974, p. 251.

p. 64 ... the FBI monitored Russell Means: *Voices From Wounded Knee*, self-published by *Akwesasne Notes* newspaper, 1974, p. 32; Smith and Warrior, *supra*, p. 194; Adams statement of Apr. 19, 1973, *supra*; *U.S. v. Dennis Banks and Russell Means*, U.S. Dist. Ct., W. Div. S.D., CR 73-5034 and 5035, CR 73-5062 and 5063, transcript p. 5,347.

p. 64 That evening, two hours before the congregants: For surveillance of the caravan, see FBI FD-302 report by SA Ray W. Gammon and SA James W. Dick, events of Feb. 27, 1973, Pine Ridge, S.D., MP 70-6832-48, transcribed Mar. 6, 1973; *Voices From Wounded Knee*, *supra*, p. 32.

p. 65 They empowered a junta: Banks, Means, Clyde Bellecourt, Carter Camp, and Pedro Bissonette were the main members of the junta. Medicine man Leonard Crow Dog was a quasi-member.

p. 65 By the reckoning of historians Paul Smith and: "Alcatraz and the BIA takeover had been the subject of intense local interest in San Francisco and Washington, and sporadic national interest, but neither event had completely penetrated the national consciousness." (Smith and Warrior, *supra*, p. 207.)

p. 65 "The American Indian commands respect": John G. Bourke, *On the Border with Crook*, 1892.

p. 65 Not all the press, however, was favorable: Later, several senior AIMers, looking to their legacy, would variously say they never took hostages, never used the word "hostages," and/or never encouraged their white "guests" to think they were hostages—the guests were merely being held for their own protection. This was all nonsense. AIM leaders at the time spoke openly of the whites as hostages (e.g., "The hostages," Russell Means said, "are in no danger from the Indian people. The only danger is if the federal troops attack—their bullets are indiscriminate."), and the list of detainees that AIM gave the FBI was titled "Hostages, Wounded Knee." (*Voices From Wounded Knee*, *supra*, p. 37–8.)

p. 65 "It is ridiculous to talk about": I have condensed this quotation. (Marge Buckley, "Justice in America," news article clipped from unknown publication, p. 16, in WKLDOC Archives.) McGovern is also quoted in Burnette and Koster, *supra*, p. 262. See also Letter from Hank Adams, Survival of American Indians Association National Director, to Senator George McGovern, Sept. 6, 1973, in WKLDOC Archives.

p. 66 "We asked to see Senator Abourezk": Burnette and Koster, *supra*, p. 228.

p. 66 "The fact is," octogenarian Wilbur Reigert: *Voices From Wounded Knee*, *supra*, p. 39.

p. 66 **"Do not let newspaper personnel in":** *Voices From Wounded Knee, supra,* p. 42; see also Dewing, *supra,* p. 57.

p. 67 **. . . the AIM pack trains that resupplied:** The packers were clever. They tantalized the government's tracking hounds with trails of urine that ended in mounds of Tabasco. One snort, and the dogs were out of operation for hours.

p. 67 **The Justice Department . . . tried to justify:** "We have discovered," the Justice Department's Ralph Erickson said, "the Indians have an automatic weapon which could wipe out a group of men. We believe it's an M-60 machine gun." (*Voices From Wounded Knee, supra,* p. 41.)

p. 67 **"Don't you think that destroys":** *Voices From Wounded Knee, supra,* p. 41–4. The claims about the M-60 and AK-47 appear in *Voices* too.

p. 67 **Invariably the agents on the roadblock:** Dewing, *supra,* p. 83.

p. 67 **The harassment was worse for reporters:** Lyman, *supra,* p. 21; Affidavit of Marc Kay Dinsmore, Apr. 1973, WKLDOC Archives; Carol Talbert, "Experiences at Wounded Knee," *Human Organization,* vol. 33, no. 2, Summer 1974, p. 216; WKLDOC memorandum, "Illegal Arrests,"1973, in WKLDOC Archives. The quotation about "no constitutional rights on the reservation" is drawn from the last of these sources.

p. 68 **"I published a story in *Ebony*":** Interview of Paul Collins by author, via phone, Jan. 2004.

p. 69 **. . . an estimated 500,000 by the end:** Peter Harriman, "One minute calm, the next chaos," *Sioux Falls Argus-Leader,* Mar. 16, 2003. McGovern is quoted in Sayer, *supra,* p. 114.

p. 69 **"I'm sure as hell planning on changing":** Burnette and Koster, *supra,* p. 238–9.

p. 69 **"Any spies who violate our borders":** Burnette and Koster, *supra,* p. 230; Dewing, *supra,* p. 89.

p. 71 **Wilson . . . tried to throw them off the reservation:** Dewing, *supra,* p. 89; Return of Service Writ by Server Pat Kelly, *James Fennerty et al. v. Dick Wilson et al.,* U.S. Dist. Ct., W. Div. S.D., Civ 73-5046, May [possibly Mar.] 14, 1973.

p. 71 **"Dope pushers," Wilson said:** Adams represented the National Council of Churches. His and Wilson's quotations are found in Dewing, *supra,* p. 88–9.

p. 71 **"At the spillway," Brave attested:** Affidavit of Corraine Brave, Apr. 1973, in WKLDOC Archives.

p. 72 **"But I remembered I was on":** I have condensed this quotation slightly. (Affidavit of Edward A. Cooper, alias Thomas White Bear, May 19, 1973, in WKLDOC Archives.) Cooper's friend was also interviewed; their accounts matched.

p. 72 **Gary Thomas . . . reported:** Associated Press, "Lawyer Says At AIM Trial He

Was Threatened With Death If He Didn't Leave Reservation," *Sioux Falls Argus Leader*, undated clipping from 1974, in WKLDOC Archives.

p. 72   For years the government left his post unfilled: Sayer, *supra*, p. 107.

p. 73   Judge Richards, in her last job as clerk: The many sins alleged against Judge Richards and the tribal court can be found in Interview of Delores Swift Bird, former tribal judge, ca. Jan. 1974, in WKLDOC Archives; Affidavit of Ethel Merrival, tribal attorney, *Oglala Sioux Civil Rights Organization v. Wilson*, U.S. Dist. Ct., W. Div. S.D., Civ. 73-5036, undated; Affidavit of Delores Swift Bird, former tribal judge, Apr. 8, 1974, in WKLDOC Archives; Statement of Barbara Means, Apr. 4, 1973, in WKLDOC Archives; Affidavit of Victoria Wounded Foot, Apr. 13, 1973, in WKLDOC Archives; WKLDOC memorandum, "Proposed testimony of Edward White Dress," 1973, in WKLDOC Archives.

p. 73   "The judge said she had just made": I condensed this quotation slightly. (Lyman, *Wounded Knee 1973*, p. 127–8. See also Barbara Means statement, *supra*.)

p. 74   Activists of the Oglala Sioux Civil Rights Organization: The complex discussion between activists and government about the petition is traced in Letter of Stanley D. Lyman, Pine Ridge Reservation Superintendent, to Barbara Means et al., Mar. 19, 1973, in WKLDOC Archives; Letter of Marvin L. Franklin, Assistant to the Secretary of the Interior, to Louis Bad Wound et al., May 3, 1973, in WKLDOC Archives; Letter of Elmer B. Staate, Comptroller General of the United States, to Sen. Henry M. Jackson, May 7, 1973; Letter of Ken Tilsen, WKLDOC, to Kent Frizzel[l], Dept. of the Interior Solicitor General, July 10, 1973, in WKLDOC Archives; Letter from Charles M. Soller, Acting Assoc. Solicitor for Indian Affairs, U.S. Dept. of the Interior, to Kenneth E. Tilsen, WKLDOC, Aug. 6 [or 16], 1973, in WKLDOC Archives; Letter from White Hawk, to Charles M. Soller, Acting Asst. Solicitor for Indian Affairs, U.S. Dept. of the Interior, Sept. 29, 1973, in WKLDOC Archives; Dewing, *supra*, p. 132; Lyman book, *supra*, p. 62–105.

p. 75   . . . on so grand an issue as an constitutional referendum: On this point, an analogy could be made to allowing a native Texan who had moved to New York fifty years before and who had never in his life registered to vote, to vote on throwing out the Texas constitution. It is also worth noting that in all of this affair, the BIA's position on whether to involve itself in tribal politics was exactly the opposite of what it had been a decade before. In 1962 agitators on Pine Ridge had petitioned for an election to recall the entire tribal council and the council had refused to hold the election. The agitators appealed to the BIA, but the BIA said resolutely that it could not get entangled in what were clearly intra-tribal political squabbles and the tribe would have to sort it out itself. (American Indian Policy Review Commission, *Report on Tribal Government, Task Force Two: Tribal Government*, Final Report to the American Indian Policy Review Commission, U.S. Govt. Printing Ofc., 1976, p. 340, 353.)

p. 75 **"It looks to me," Senator Jim Abourezk observed:** Burnette and Koster, *supra*, p. 257.

p. 75 **. . . "march into Wounded Knee and Kill":** This statement has sometimes been attributed to Wilson (e.g., Dewing, *supra*, p. 98), but it was sent out in a "Newsletter" of uncertain provenance. ("Newsletter," Mar. 26, 1973, source not identified, in WKLDOC Archives.)

p. 75 **the goons, who stuck their guns in the faces:** Ted Elbert, "Wounded Knee: A Struggle for Self-Determination," *The Christian Century*, Mar. 28, 1973, p. 357.

p. 76 **The agents caucused with Wilson:** Lyman book, *supra*, p.22–9, 55; *Voices From Wounded Knee*, *supra*, p. 129.

p. 76 **The FBI complied by giving:** Dewing, *supra*, p. 98. On the APC, see Dewing, *supra*, p. 106.

p. 76 **. . . the goons turned away mediators:** The two confrontations between Wayne Colburn and the goons at the roadblock, and the arrests and debate that followed, are discussed in Lyn Gladstone, "Man arrested at roadblock says FBI agents were assisting them," *Rapid City Journal*, Apr. 27, 1973; *Voices From Wounded Knee*, *supra*, p. 189, quoting FBI radio log of Apr. 23 saying the FBI tipped the goons; Lyman book, *supra*, p. 109–15, quoting *inter alia* "If there is going to be bloodshed"; FBI FD-302 report, interview of William E. Hall, associate director, USMS, by SA W. Gordon Gibler and SA John H. O'Neill, Jr., Pine Ridge, S.D., MP 70-6832-V-2, interviewed Apr. 23, 1973, transcribed Apr. 23, 1973; FBI FD-302 report, interview of Wayne B. Colburn, by SA W. Gordon Gibler and SA John H. O'Neill, Jr., Pine Ridge, S.D., MP 70-6832-V-3, interviewed Apr. 23, 1973, transcribed Apr. 23, 1973; Dewing, *supra*, p. 117–8.

p. 77 **In a press conference after the arraignment:** Hussman was probably referring to the deputization months before, when AIM was returning from the Trail of Broken Treaties. (WKLDOC report, "Notes on Goon Deputization," *supra*.)

p. 78 **"We came this far from shooting Frizzell":** Smith and Warrior, *supra*, p. 254–6.

p. 79 **. . . the White House would send a delegation:** The White House sent a staff member of low rank to a single meeting with the Lakotas.

p. 79 **(Frank Clearwater was buried elsewhere):** Lamont was a native of Pine Ridge and thus entitled to burial on Pine Ridge. Wilson would not permit the burial of the non-native Clearwater on the reservation.

CHAPTER 4

p. 81 **The house of Paul Thunder Horse:** The shooting of Mary Ann Little Bear on the night of August 24–25, 1973, and its aftermath are discussed in Affidavit of

Dallas Little Bear, Aug. 1973, in WKLDOC Archives; Affidavit of Roselyn Little Bear, Aug. 1973, in WKLDOC Archives; Statement of Robert Thunder Horse, Aug. 25, 1973, in WKLDOC Archives; Statement of Alex Bad Bear, Aug. 25, 1973, in WKLDOC Archives; Statement of Leo White Hawk, Aug, 26, 1973, in WKLDOC Archives; Statement of Edward White Dress, Aug. 1973, in WKLDOC Archives; WKLDOC report, "Chronology" (of Little Bear Shooting), undated, ca. Sept. 1973, in WKLDOC Archives. Robert Thunder Horse, his wife Lorene, and their three children were in the second car, which was driven by Anthony Good Lance. Bad Bear was in the first car, driven by Dallas Little Bear. Crooked Eyes was inside his house when he first heard the shots.

p. 82　**"He showed me two plastic bags":** I have condensed this quotation slightly. (Affidavit of Roselyn Little Bear, *supra*.)

p. 82　**The night . . . was not the first time guns:** Statement of Ellis Crooked Eyes, Aug. 25, 1973, in WKLDOC Archives.

p. 83　**The government . . . now mustered fourteen BIA police:** WKLDOC newsletter, Sept. 10, 1973, in WKLDOC Archives.

p. 83　**A second bullet had pierced the driver's side:** Affidavit of James Cecil Normandin, Aug. 1973, in WKLDOC Archives.

p. 84　**The government declined them all:** WKLDOC Motion, *U.S. v. Russell Means and Dennis Banks*, U.S. Dist. Ct., W. Div. S.D., CR 73-5035, 73-5034, 73-5062, 73-5063, p. 9; Russell Means and Mark Lane, "Wounded Knee Defendant and Attorney Doubt Sincerity of Grand Jury Investigation," WKLDOC news release, Dec. 12, 1973, in WKLDOC Archives.

p. 84　**The Civil Rights Division . . . had started its investigation:** Robert Burnette and John Koster, *The Road to Wounded Knee*, Bantam, 1974, p. 257–8; *Voices from Wounded Knee*, self-published by the newspaper *Akwesasne Notes*, 1974, p. 224-30.

p. 84　**There was no brutality in Wilson's dominion:** In the summer of 1973, after the siege of Wounded Knee, Senator Jim Abourezk held hearings in Rapid City about brutality on Pine Ridge. BIA police officers sat outside the hearing taking photographs and writing down names and license plates of Indians who attended. "This is one of the most reprehensible things I've seen," Abourezk said, but he was powerless to extract even so much as an explanation from the BIA. (Burnette and Koster, *supra*, p. 257.)

p. 86　**On the roadbed above, Clifford took aim:** It is not entirely clear that Clifford's gun failed too. The stories are confused. It is possible that only Rencountre's gun failed and that Clifford got off a shot without difficulty. The most reliable accounts of the shooting are probably: memorandum from Dennis Ickes, Ofc. of Indian Rights, to Carlton R. Stoiber, Ofc. of Indian Rights Director, "Shooting of Pedro Bissonette," Oct. 1973;

memorandum from R. Dennis Ickes, Deputy Director, Ofc. of Indian Rights, Dept. of Justice to J. Stanley Pottinger, Asst. Atty. Gen., Civil Rights Div., Dept. of Justice, "Prosecutive Summary," Nov. 5, 1973.

p. 88 . . . secure permission from Bissonette's mother: "Authorization of Susie Bissonette," Oct. 18, 1973, in WKLDOC Archives.

p. 88 Cavise said WKLDOC wanted . . . Clayton agreed: WKLDOC Motion, *supra*, p. 73; "Bissonette's death said surrounded in secrecy," *Rapid City Journal*, Oct. 18, 1973, p. 3.

p. 88 But shortly before 5:00 a.m., a nurse: At 4:50 a.m., Kay Hudson called the Bissonette house to say Pedro's body missing from morgue. At 4:55 Mark Lane went to the hospital. Police were watching the house and followed Lane to the hospital.

p. 88 It was produced, but the blanks: IHS's "Disposition of Body" form records the body's arrival the night of October 17 and its return from autopsy the night of October 18 but not the removal of the body for autopsy in the early morning of October 17. (IHS 523A form, "Clinical Record, Disposition of Body: Pedro Bissonette," Oct. 17 and 18, 1973, from IHS medical file of Bissonette.)

p. 88 "If you're going to say I told you that": WKLDOC phone log, Oct. 17-18, 1973, in WKLDOC Archives.

p. 89 An aide to Brown refused to answer: WKLDOC phone log, October 17-18, *supra.*

p. 89 (This was later proven untrue): Cavise had called Brown's office at 7:20 a.m.; Brown, by his own account, did not start the autopsy until 7:30. (FBI FD-302 report, interview of ▮▮▮▮, West Nebraska Hospital, by SA ▮▮▮▮, Scottsbluff, Neb., OM 44-522, interviewed Oct. 19, 1973, transcribed Oct. 25, 1973.)

p. 89 "Eastman insisted only one bullet": I have condensed Lane's recollection slightly. (Walter Gallacher, "Was Pedro Bissonette Slain? an interview with Mark Lane," *Shannon County News*, Dec. 21, 1973, vol. 34, iss. 42, p. 3. See also WKLDOC press release, Oct. 20, 1973, in WKLDOC archives.) Mark Lane refused to be interviewed for this book.

p. 90 "That's when they changed the story": Per the WKLDOC phone log, *supra*, the story changed sometime before 5:55 a.m. on the morning after Bissonette's death; at that time, Eastman said the killing wound was from a single shotgun shell. Lane did not consider that Eastman might have been confused or that Eastman, in the early hours after the shooting, might simply have not had all the facts before him.

p. 90 Later he seems to have said . . . a high-powered rifle: Ickes memo, Nov. 5, 1973, *supra.*

p. 90 Lane turned up two Pine Ridge residents: Statement of Verlean Ice, Oct. 19, 1973, in WKLDOC Archives.

p. 90   Another Pine Ridge couple, John and Cordila: WKLDOC memorandum, unsigned, "John and Cordila Attack Him," undated, in WKLDOC Archives. See also WKLDOC phone log, Oct. 17-18, 1973, *supra*, entry for 2:20 a.m.

p. 91   Bissonette was also a hothead: "He was not a sensitive, new age guy," reporter Kevin McKiernan remembered. "During Wounded Knee, he tried to lay all the sins of the white man on me—personally. Just when it was about to get physical, Clyde Bellecourt stepped in and said, 'That's racism, Pedro. Back off.' Pedro did, and later he wanted to make up with me. So he says, 'Hey, let's go out and take a piss.' That was his way of making up— taking a communal leak in the darkness by the sweat lodge. I almost wasn't able to deliver." (Interview of Kevin McKiernan by author, Santa Barbara, Cal., July 2003.)

p. 91   "I hear you're the toughest guy around": Interview of Poker Joe Merrival by author, Pine Ridge, S.D., Aug. 2003.

p. 92   . . . Merrival was one of Wilson's most trusted goons: Among other services Merrival provided Wilson, he was Dick Wilson's "personal observer in and around Custer, Wanblee, and Kadoka for an indefinite period beginning February 6, 1973." (Letter from Dick Wilson, Oglala Sioux Tribal President, to Joseph Merrival, Feb. 8, 1973, in WKLDOC Archives.)

p. 92   . . . indictments that Bissonette did before Wounded Knee: He was, for example, charged on September 9, 1970, with grand larceny, which was later reduced to petty larceny and assault and battery. On June 2, 1971, he was charged with making a false statement but the charge was dismissed.

p. 92   Some months before the assault, Theresa Perkins: Medical records of Pedro Bissonette, chart dates Oct. 4-7, 1972, Pine Ridge Hospital, S.D., Indian Health Service; Memorandum of Roger Finzel, WKLDOC, "Statement of facts in outstanding cases against Pedro," early Aug. 1973, in WKLDOC Archives.

p. 92   Bissonette went to the police station: FBI FD-204 report to USA, Sioux Falls, S.D., and U.S. Secret Service, Minneapolis, Minn., "Pedro Aloyious Bissonette," field office file no. 89-132, Nov. 13, 1972. See also FBI FD-36 form, teletype from SAC, Minneapolis (89-132) (P), to Acting Director, FBI, "Pedro Bissonette," Nov. 9, 1972.

p. 92   The next night BIA police stopped the pair: Accounts of the event are included in Marge Buckley, "Justice in America," from unknown periodical, p. 16, in WKLDOC Archives; WKLDOC notes re "Poker Joe Merrival," undated, in WKLDOC Archives; Untitled, undated document, labeled "16" in left corner, first line "Lt. Wayne Brewer" [sic: Duane Brewer], in WKLDOC Archives; FBI teletype, from Minneapolis (89-NEW) (P), to Acting Director, Nov. 7, 1972, 4:17 p.m.; FBI FD-376 form, from L. Patrick Gray III, Acting Director, to Director, US Secret Service, re "Pedro Aloyious Bissonette," Nov. 15, 1972; FBI FD-204 report to USA, Sioux Falls, S.D., and U.S.

Secret Service, Minneapolis, Minn., re "Pedro Aloyious Bissonette," field ofc. file 89-132, Bureau file 89-2317, Apr. 4, 1973; Unidentified report, apparently from FBI to U.S. Attorney, probably from file no. PR-73-96, Nov. 8, 1972, p. 6. The last report is a partial report released to me by the FBI, on referral from the Exec. Ofc. of U.S. Attys. under FOIA request 1022150, July 27, 2005.

p. 94 So Bissonette was appointed a lawyer: The accusations by Bissonette and WKLDOC against Warder and Bogue are included in Affidavit of Pedro Bissonette, *U.S. v. Russell Means, et al.*, U.S. Dist. Ct., S.D., CR 73-5035, 73-5063, June 2, 1973; WKLDOC Motion, *supra*, p. 17–23; Buckley, *supra*; Emergency Petition for Writ of Mandamus, *Pedro Bissonette v. Hon. Andrew Bogue*, U.S. Ct. of Appeals, 8th Cir., 73-1356; Gallacher, *supra*, p. 2.

p. 94 The judge was apparently not concerned: Nor, if Bissonette's account of what Warder told him was true, was Judge Bogue fazed by helping to broker deals for witnesses to testify against defendants who were to be tried in his court. Judge Bogue declined to be interviewed for this book.

p. 94 "I will stand with my brothers and sisters": I have condensed this quotation slightly. (Bissonette affidavit, *supra*.)

p. 94 . . . Bissonette received an unexpected jailhouse visit: WKLDOC memorandum, "Pedro Bissonet [sic] Interview by Robert J. Doyle," May 19, 1973, in WKLDOC Archives; WKLDOC Motion, *supra*, p. 19; WKLDOC memorandum from John Taylor to file, May 19, 1973, in WKLDOC Archives.

p. 95 WKLDOC lawyers who tried to visit Bissonette: On the day of Bissonette's trial, WKLDOC lawyers Mark Lane and Ramon Roubideaux tried to visit him in jail in Pierre, but no sooner had they sat down with him than a deputy sheriff ushered them out. The deputy explained he had been ordered to bar anyone, specifically including lawyers from WKLDOC, from visiting Bissonette. Later that day in a hallway in the federal courthouse, Judge Bogue swished up to Lane and Roubideaux in his black robes and demanded to know if they had been "tampering with our witnesses." When Lane said they had not but that they had tried to see Bissonette (and had done so briefly), Bogue pointed a finger at Lane's chest and said, "I gave strict orders that nobody was to bother him. I'll look into that." A short while later, prosecutor R. D. Hurd told Lane and Roubideaux that Bogue had just asked him whether he thought an appellate court would reverse him if he did not let Bissonette dump Warder for WKLDOC. Hurd had said no, and Bissonette's trial was gaveled into session.

p. 95 The panel made clear that if Bissonette: Order, *Pedro Bissonette v. Hon. Andrew Bogue*, U.S. Ct. of Appeals, 8th Cir., 73-1356.

p. 96 Bissonette allegedly fired a shot over the heads: The incident of September 22, 1973, in Whiteclay is discussed in Affidavit of David R. Gienapp, Assistant U.S.

Attorney, *U.S. v. Pedro Bissonette*, U.S. Dist. Ct., CR 73-5032, CR 73-5066, Sept. 25, 1973; Dewing, *supra*, p. 136–7; Order Revoking and Forfeiting Bond and for Issuance of a Bench Warrant, *U.S. v. Pedro Bissonette*, U.S. Dist. Ct., CR 73-5032, CR 73-5066, Sept. 25, 1973.

p. 96 . . . **a particularly senseless murder:** The homicide was Byron DeSersa. See chapter 11.

p. 96 **But the police discovered his whereabouts:** A tribal judge told the manager of a hotel where Bissonette was staying that a conversation between Bissonette and Banks had been tapped. (Statement of Beverly Geary, hotel manager, Oct. 22, 1973, in WKLDOC Archives.)

p. 96 **Bissonette told Poker he was going to turn:** Statement of Joseph F. Merrival, Oct. 18, 1973, in WKLDOC Archives.

p. 97 **When they did so, Bissonette fired a shot:** FBI FD-302 report, interview of ▇▇▇▇▇, BIA, Pine Ridge, S.D., by SA ▇▇▇▇▇ and SA ▇▇▇▇▇, Pine Ridge, S.D., MP 44-763, interviewed Oct. 18, 1973, transcribed Oct. 20, 1973. (There are two reports with the same citation but different content; they are interviews with each of the BIA officers.)

p. 97 **A few minutes later Bissonette came racing:** WKLDOC phone log, Oct. 17-18, 1973, *supra*; Dewing, *supra*, p. 136–7.

p. 97 **By one account, the officers were instructed to shoot:** Marei Kingi, a BIA police officer at the time, told several people that the police had orders to shoot to kill Bissonette. (Merrival interview, *supra*.) Kingi declined my several offers to interview him. A bartender in Rushville, Nebraska, told Gladys Bissonette that he overheard police officer Hobart Ecoffey say, "They wanted Pedro to testify against AIM. He should have done it. Then they wouldn't have had to kill him."

p. 97 **The hitchhiker, for one, told the FBI:** FBI FD-302 report, interview of ▇▇▇▇▇ by SAs ▇▇▇▇▇ and ▇▇▇▇▇, Pine Ridge S.D., MP 44-763, interviewed Nov. 8, 1973, transcribed Nov. 8, 1973. The FBI inspected the BIA radio log, which was titled "Pine Ridge Police Department Summary of Shift and Radio Station and Activity Log for October 17, 1973." (FBI FD-302 report, interview of ▇▇▇▇▇, BIA, Pine Ridge, by SA ▇▇▇▇▇ and SA ▇▇▇▇▇, Pine Ridge S.D., MP 44-763, interviewed Oct. 18, 1973, transcribed Oct. 19, 1973.)

p. 98 **"Mark [Lane] got on the phone":** Interview of Sand Brim by the author, via phone, Jan. 2004.

p. 98 **"The Oglala Sioux have organized":** Statement of Dick Wilson, undated but appears to be Oct. 18, 1973, in WKLDOC Archives.

p. 98 **"If you have to shoot them":** Statement of Lou Beane, Oct. 22, 1973, WKLDOC Archives.

p. 98 The police stopped mourners as they came: Statement of Hazel Little Hawk and Linda Brings, Oct. 21, 1973, in WKLDOC Archives; Statement of Jim Bordeaux, Oct. 24, 1973, in WKLDOC Archives; Statement of Floyd Running Hand, Oct. 25, 1973, in WKLDOC Archives; Statement of John Iverson, Oct. 24, 1973, in WKLDOC Archives.

p. 99 At the wheel was a drunken teenager: WKLDOC memorandum, "Incident at Bissonette Property—October 24, 1973," in WKLDOC Archives; WKLDOC press release, "Pine Ridge Lawyer, Bissonette Family File Criminal Complaint Against Richard Wilson," Oct. 29, 1973, in WKLDOC Archives. For the dispute about the filing of a complaint, see Associated Press, "Tribe Refutes Charge Claim," *Denver Post*, Oct. 30, 1973, p. 16.

p. 99 Perhaps the FBI was too busy investigating the mourners: For just a few examples of the widespread FBI spying on the caravan, see FBI urgent teletype, from Minneapolis 157-1458 P, to several offices, re "Minneapolis Tel to Bureau 10/18/73," Oct. 19, 1973, 7:10 p.m.; FBI Memorandum from SAC, San Francisco (157-9726) (RUC), to Director, FBI, "Proposed Caravan to Pine Ridge, South Dakota on 10/22/73, Relative to the Shooting of Pedro Bissonette, Sponsored by the American Indian Movement," Nov. 5, 1973.

p. 100 Decades later Ickes confirmed that he spoke: In fact, lawyers in the Civil Rights Division often requested that agents interview specific witnesses.

p. 100 But even so, the FBI's limited investigation . . . disturbed Ickes: Ickes memo, Oct. 1973, *supra*. The FBI will not release its diagram of how the participants were supposedly standing or its photos of the crime scene. (FBI FD-302 report by SA ████████ and SA ███████, events of Oct. 20, 1973, Pine Ridge S.D., MP 44-763, transcribed Oct. 19, 1973; FBI FD-302 report, interview of ███████, BIA, by SA ███████, Pine Ridge S.D., MP 44-763, interviewed Oct. 22, 1973, transcribed Oct. 23, 1973.)

p. 100 . . . a second autopsy Mark Lane commissioned by: Summary of interview of Dr. Perber by Len Cavise and Marty Fassler, WKLDOC, Nov. 13, 1973, in WKLDOC Archives. Perber apparently could neither confirm nor deny Dr. Brown's claim that Bissonette's blood alcohol level was .23 percent. (FBI FD-302 report, interview of ████████ [W. O. Brown], West Neb. Hospital, by SA ███████, Scottsbluff, Neb., OM 44-522, interviewed Oct. 19, 1973, transcribed Oct. 25, 1973.)

p. 102 "Since January, 1973, we have investigated": Ickes memo, Oct. 1973, *supra*. Ickes's boss passed Ickes's recommendations about Bissonette up the line dispassionately. (Memorandum from Carlton R. Stoiber, Ofc. of Indian Rights Director, to J. Stanley Pottinger, Assistant Attorney General for Civil Rights, "Proposed Investigative Grand Jury in Pine Ridge Cases," Nov. 5, 1973.)

p. 103 "It's good that we finally heard from": WKLDOC Motion, *supra*, p. 74; Gallacher, *supra*, p. 2.

p. 103 Charles said he had recently been menaced: "Joe Clifford Resigns," *Shannon County News*, Feb. 1, 1974.

p. 105 Not long before this book went to press, the FBI gave: The key documents in the newly released papers were the FBI's interviews of Rencountre and Clifford: FBI FD-302 report, interview of ▮▮▮ [Evans Rencountre], by SA ▮▮▮ and SA ▮▮▮, Hot Springs, S.D., MP 44-763, interviewed Oct. 18, 1973, transcribed Oct. 22, 1973; FBI FD-302 report, interview of ▮▮▮ [Joseph Clifford], by SA ▮▮▮ and SA ▮▮▮, Hot Springs, S.D., MP 44-763, interviewed Oct. 18, 1973, transcribed Oct. 20, 1973. See also, FBI FD-302 field report, interview of ▮▮▮, BIA, Pine Ridge, by SA ▮▮▮ and SA ▮▮▮, Pine Ridge S.D., MP 44-763, interviewed Oct. 18, 1973, transcribed Oct. 19, 1973.)

p. 105 But another FBI document ... summarized their claims: FBI FD-204 report from ▮▮▮, Minneapolis, to USA, Sioux Falls, title "▮▮▮, ▮▮▮, BIA Police Officers, Pine Ridge, South Dakota; Pedro Aloyisious Bissonette—Victim (Deceased)," field ofc. file MP 44-763, Oct. 23, 1973.

p. 106 Another FBI document said ... the FBI tested his hands: FBI FD-302 field report, interview of ▮▮▮, Scottsbluff Police Dept., by SA ▮▮▮, Scottsbluff, Neb., OM 44-522, interviewed Oct. 19, 1973, transcribed Oct. 25, 1973.

CHAPTER 5

p. 107 Anna Mae Pictou was born: For the outlines of Aquash's life, Johanna Brand's *The Life and Death of Anna Mae Aquash* (James Lorimer & Co., 1993) is valuable. Some additional information is available at "Anna Mae Pictou Aquash: Timeline," *News From Indian Country*, www.indiancountrynews.com/aquashlegacy.cfm, viewed Apr. 2003. Unfortunately, Aquash's family declined to be interviewed for this book, so I was unable to verify several details of her biography. For example, it is not entirely clear that Aquash was inside the BIA building when AIM occupied it during the Trail of Broken Treaties; she may have participated only in an earlier part of the Trail.

p. 109 ... Bill Means, brother of Russell, drove them: Interview of Bill Means by author, St. Paul, Minn., Aug. 29, 2003.

p. 110 "She was carrying a pack filled": Open letter of Michael Denny, ca. Mar. 2004, posted at AIM Grand Governing Council, www.aimovement.org/moipr/letters.html, viewed May 2004.

p. 110 "Most of the people at Wounded Knee": Interview of Kevin McKiernan by author, Santa Barbara, Cal., Aug. 2003.

p. 111 "They were loud-mouth city women": Mary Crow Dog and Richard Erdoes,

Lakota Woman, Grove Pr., 1990, p. 138. The Pie Patrollers now say they either liked Aquash just fine or did not much think about her.

p. 112 On April 25 . . . they walked out of the new nation: Interview log, either BIA or FBI, "Annie Mae Aguash," 70-6832-A-438, Apr. 26, 1973, in WKLDOC Archives; Undated FBI report, "Alleged Purchase of Weapons by Nogeeshik Aquash for the American Indian Movement (AIM)"; FBI FD-204 report from Charles E. Stephenson, Minneapolis, "RESMURS; Anna Mae Aquash," field office file 70-10239, Bureau file 89-3229, July 16, 1975.

p. 113 . . . Nogeeshik later said the story was not true: FBI FD-302 report, interview of Nogeeshik Aquash, *supra.*

p. 114 Today he acknowledges having had nothing more: "Silenced: The Execution of Anna Mae," *The Fifth Estate* television program, Canadian Broadcasting Corp., aired Nov. 8, 2000; Interview of Richard Erdoes by author, Santa Fe, N.M., Nov. 2005.

p. 114 Her liaison with Banks, her rise to AIM's: A report a few months later noted, "Source felt that the subject, through her association with BANKS, may rise to an influential position in the AIM movement." (FBI memorandum, from SAC, Minneapolis (157-4323) (P), to SAC, Los Angeles (157-11137), re "Joanna Jason, aka Anna Mae Aquash," Mar. 11, 1975.)

p. 115 Nearly all of the informers' reports on her: See, e.g., FBI FD-263 report of Charles P. Stephenson, Minneapolis, "RESMURS; Anna Mae Aquash," investigative period June 26, 1975—July 16, 1975, report issued July 16, 1975; FBI FD-306 informant report, received ████████, received by SA Gilbert R. Cordova, Los Angeles, Cal., prepared Dec. 12, 1974.

p. 115 "Our biggest problem," a spy quoted Aquash: I have condensed this quotation. (FBI FD-306 informant report, received ███████, received by SA Gilbert R. Cordova, SA Martin A. Gonzales, Los Angeles, Cal., prepared Jan. 9, 1975.)

p. 115 FBI agents prevailed on state officials: FBI FD-36 report, airtel from SAC, Los Angeles (157-11137) (P), to SAC, Minneapolis, "Joanna Jason, aka Anna Mae Aquash," Feb. 25, 1975; see also FBI report, "Anna Mae Aquash, also known as Joanna Jason," Los Angeles, Cal., July 11, 1975.

p. 115 When she handed out leaflets at an art exhibit: For the spying on petty activities, see, e.g., FBI FD-306 informant report, received ███████, received by SA Gilbert R. Cordova, SA Martin A. Gonzales, Los Angeles, Cal., prepared Feb. 24, 1975. FBI FD-306 informant report, "Messages & Bills taken from South West Regional AIM Office, Los Angeles, Cal.," received ███████, received by SA Martin A. Gonzales, SA Gilbert R. Cordova, Los Angeles, Cal., prepared Jan. 13, 1975; FBI report, "Anna Mae Aquash, also known as Joanna Jason," *supra.*

CHAPTER 6

p. 117 "When I took office, there was two hundred": "Interview with Dick Wilson," *Shannon County News*, Feb. 1, 1974. The $24 million helped support "a system of patronage for the 900 jobs available—on a reservation with 70 percent unemployment." ("Pine Ridge—1976," *Akwesasne Notes*, early spring 1976, p. 8.)

p. 117 But in the primary Means drew 150: Robert Burnette and John Koster, *The Road to Wounded Knee*, Bantam, 1974, p. 283.

p. 118 Means asked the Justice Department: "Statement of Russell Means," Jan. 22, 1974, in WKLDOC Archives.

p. 118 . . . disturbing reports began trickling into AIM: The election fraud is documented in Memorandum from Steve Trecker, WKLDOC, "Election Suit Report," July 1975, in WKLDOC Archives; Burnette and Koster, *supra*, p. 283; "A New Ally in the Election Suit," WKLDOC newsletter, Aug. 6, 1974, in WKLDOC Archives; Transcript of interview of Cecilia Martin by Kevin McKiernan, Feb. 9, 1974, in WKLDOC Archives, quoting Martin saying a BIA policeman in mufti ordered her out of the tribal office while the ballots were being counted.

p. 118 "No," the president said, "I'd still like to challenge": Peter Matthiessen, *In the Spirit of Crazy Horse*, Viking Pr., 1991, p. 135.

p. 118 . . . the council, which by law had five days . . . did nothing: Letter from William G. Hoerger and Carol Schapira, WKLDOC, to supporters, Apr. 6, 1974, in WKLDOC Archives.

p. 119 Judge Bogue had made clear his views: Bogue is quoted in *U.S. v. Gilbert Clarence Young*, Feb. 8, 1973, in chambers, transcript p. 2ff; Affidavit of David N. Rockwell, May 31, 1973, in WKLDOC Archives; "Reply to Answer to Petition for Writ of Mandamus," *Carter Camp, et al. v. Hon. Andrew Bogue, etc.*, U.S. Ct. of Appeals, 8th Cir., 73-1478 through 73-1483, July 31, 1973; Affidavit of Steven J. Trecker, Jan. 6, 1975, in WKLDOC Archives.

p. 119 . . . a group like WKLDOC that had sixty to eighty attorneys: Memorandum Opinion, *Russell Means, et al. v. Dick Wilson, etc., et al.*, U.S. Dist. Ct., W. Div. S.D., CV74-5010, Apr. 5, 1974. In all of South Dakota, WKLDOC had only seven lawyers, and all of these were either part-time or pro bono. ("Needs of the Committee," WKLDOC newsletter, Aug. 13, 1973, p. 4, in WKLDOC Archives; Hoerger and Schapira letter, *supra*.)

p. 120 He did not claim the vote had been free and fair: John William Sayer, *Ghost Dancing the Law: The Wounded Knee Trials*, Harvard Univ. Pr., 1997, p. 202. For the text of Bogue's decision, see *Russell Means et al. v. Dick Wilson, etc., et al.*, U.S. Dist. Ct., W. Div. S.D., CV74-5010, Apr. 5, 1974 (383 F.Supp. 378).

p. 120 . . . there had been "massive irregularities": Quoted in Darwin Olofson, "Rights Commission: Sioux Vote Invalid," *Omaha World Herald*, Jan. 8, 1975; Jan Sack, "New Pine Ridge Reservation Election Unlikely," *Lincoln Journal*, Jan. 9, 1975.

p. 121 A night or two after the foot patrols began: WKLDOC Motion, *U.S. v. Russell Means and Dennis Banks*, U.S. Dist. Ct., W. Div. S.D., CR 73-5035, 73-5034, 73-5062, 73-5063, p. 58ff. Each of the encounters between WKLDOCkers and FBI agents is discussed in the WKLDOC Motion. See also WKLDOC newsletter, Aug. 13, 1973; "Information Statement of Lake Headley & Mark Lane," Rapid City Police Dept., Aug. 6, 1973, 4:30 p.m., in WKLDOC Archives; "Information Statement of Anthony C. Muller," Rapid City Police Dept., Aug. 6, 1973, 4:30 p.m., in WKLDOC Archives.

p. 122 "After they had both tried to force Mr. Headley": I have condensed this quotation slightly. (WKLDOC Motion, *supra*, p. 60.)

p. 123 "This is a trumped-up charge": Harley Sorenson, "FBI not harassing Indians, agents say," *Minneapolis Tribune*, Sept. 19, 1973.

p. 124 "If you don't get that girl out of town": Affidavit of David W. Cohoes, Aug. 15, 1973, in WKLDOC Archives.

p. 124 "Those who harbor this fugitive": I have condensed this quotation slightly. (American Indian Movement, "All Points Bulletin," Aug. 1973, in WKLDOC Archives.)

p. 124 The phone lines in the fraternity sometimes gave off: Mary Anne Maul, undated note, "Surveillance, Tues., 9:50 a.m.," in WKLDOC Archives; Affidavit of Arlynn Gurwitz, Aug. 12, 1973, in WKLDOC Archives.

p. 124 "Bob Warder—that's your job": The voices were all male, from five to eight in number; they seemed to be having different conversations but to be all present in the same room. (Affidavit of Mary Anne Maul, May 29, 1973, in WKLDOC Archives.)

p. 124 On another night WKLDOCkers noticed: Interview of Roger Finzel by author, via phone, Mar. 2004.

p. 125 The case went to Judge Bogue, who said: "Memorandum Decision," *Wounded Knee Legal Defense/Offense Committee, etc., et al. v. Federal Bureau of Investigation, etc., et al.*, U.S. Dist. Ct., W. Div. S.D., CIV 73-5082, Aug. 16, 1973.)

p. 125 Dennis Banks and Russell Means were the first: An indispensable guide to the Banks-Means trial is John Sayer's *Ghost Dancing the Law: The Wounded Knee Trials*, *supra*, from which my account draws heavily. Another very helpful summary is included in a long letter from Larry Leventhal, Esq., to Henry Wolf, Fish Creek, Wis., Aug. 22, 1976, in WKLDOC Archives. The case was *U.S. v. Dennis Banks and Russell Means*, U.S. Dist. Ct., W. Div. S.D., CR 73-5034 and 5035, CR 73-5062 and 5063.

p. 125 To the question "What should be done": "If you think Mississippi was bad . . . visit South Dakota," WKLDOC newsletter, v. II, n. 16, Aug. 6, 1974.

p. 126 Perhaps there had been a clerical error: Prosecutor Hurd agreed that the mistake was innocent—no doubt caused by the mass of evidence the FBI had collected.

p. 126 "I used to think the FBI was one of the greatest": This and other quotations from Nichol are in Sayer, *supra*, p. 108ff.

p. 127 "He was a goon," WKLDOC's Sand Brim: Author interview of Sand Brim, via phone, Jan. 2004.

p. 130 . . . FBI knew the tap was illegal but had decided: Other documents later came to light that discussed the contents of conversations the FBI had eavesdropped on via the wiretaps. The documents were variously written or received by Joseph Trimbach.

p. 132 . . . "the grossest kind of a fluke": *U.S. v. Banks and Means*, *supra*, trial transcript p. 13,343–65. Some of the information about military involvement came out at other Wounded Knee trials, particularly those before Judge Warren Urbom in Lincoln, Nebraska. (Martin Garbus, "General Haig of Wounded Knee," *The Nation*, Nov. 9, 1974, p. 454.)

p. 132 "Rifles," he was supposedly told: *Voices From Wounded Knee*, self-published by the newspaper *Akwesasne Notes*, 1974, p. 44–5.

p. 132 All of this activity . . . had been approved secretly: Regarding Buzhardt's involvement, marshals' logs showed that the marshals asked the Air Force for photo reconnaissance. The request went through Buzhardt's office. On March 3, 1973, the Pentagon obliged, and Air Force F-4 Phantom jets flew a low sortie over the village. (*Voices From Wounded Knee*, *supra*, p. 44–5.)

p. 133 . . . the Defense Department released a report: Norman Kempster, "Military Ran the Show, Restrained FBI at Wounded Knee Siege," *Washington Star*, Dec. 1, 1975, p. A1; Rolland Dewing, *Wounded Knee II*, Great Plains Network/Pine Hills Pr., 1995, p. 104, 112; Matthiessen, *supra*, p. 72; Paul Chaat Smith and Robert Allen Warrior, *Like a Hurricane: The Indian Movement from Alcatraz to Wounded Knee*, The New Pr., 1996, p. 213.

p. 133 "Congress could have passed and may yet pass": Quoted in Garbus, *supra*, p. 454.

p. 133 WKLDOC did, naming as defendants: *Agnes Lamont v. Alexander Haig*, Civ. 75-0271, U.S. Dist. Ct., D.C.; U.S. Ct. of Appeals, D.C. Cir., 75-2006 (590 F.2d 1124).

p. 134 . . . the case was transferred to Dakota anyway: In South Dakota's federal courts, the case was first *Agnes Lamont, et al. v. Alexander Haig, et al.*, then *Gladys Bissonette, et al. v. Alexander Haig, et al.*, U.S. Dist. Ct., W. Div. S.D., 81-5048 (539 F.Supp. 552). On appeal, it was *Bissonette v. Haig*, U.S. Ct. of Appeals, 8th Cir., 84-2617 (776 F.2d 1384, 800 F.2d 812) and *Bissonette v. Haig*, U.S. Sup. Ct., 86-987 (485 U.S. 264). See also Memorandum Opinion, *Bissonette v. Haig*, U.S. Dist. Ct., W. Div. S.D., Oct. 18, 1984; and Memorandum Opinion, *Bissonette v. Haig*, U.S. Dist. Ct., W. Div. S.D., Feb. 3, 1989.

p. 136 . . . his many criminal charges—which included: Dennis Banks and Richard Erdoes, *Ojibwa Warrior: Dennis Banks and the Rise of the American Indian Movement*, Univ. of Okla. Pr., 2004, p. 220.

p. 137 . . . Mark Lane asked R. D. Hurd at a bench conference: *U.S. v. Banks*, trial transcript, p. 20,044–9. A detailed and mostly reliable account of events related to the alleged rape is Paula Giese, "Rape Cover-up in River Falls," *North Country ANVIL*, July 1975, p. 58ff.

p. 137 "Were you arrested in Wisconsin": This colloquy is as quoted in Banks and Erdoes, *supra*, p. 223.

p. 138 "Nichol found the behavior of the FBI": I have condensed this quotation. (Deposition of Kenneth Tilsen, *David Price v. Viking Press*, U.S. Dist. Ct., 4th Div. Minn., Civ. 4-85-819, Feb. 27, 1987, p. 85, 181–3.)

p. 140 Hurd told reporters he thought the jury: *Minneapolis Star*, Sept. 14, 1974, p. 1.

p. 140 "To a public saturated with misconduct": I have slightly condensed this quotation, which refers particularly to the Moves Camp affair but holds true for the trial as a whole. (Sayer, *supra*, p. 170.)

p. 140 . . . the Justice Department named R. D. Hurd: Hurd was later honored by being elevated to a judgeship by his friend Bill Janklow, South Dakota's longtime governor. (Deposition of William Janklow, *William Janklow v. Viking Press and Peter Matthiessen*, S.D. Circ. Ct., 2nd Circ., Civ. 83-1385, July 13, 1987, p. 478.) Hurd replaced the judge who imprisoned Russell Means for riot. "Judge Richard Braithwaite, who convicted me," Means said, "was busted this year for shoplifting, except in his case it was called a sickness, and he is receiving treatment instead of serving time." Reporter Kevin McKiernan said that when he requested his FBI file years later, he discovered that Hurd had asked the FBI to investigate him, and the FBI had.

p. 141 Of the 562 arrests and 185 federal indictments: Johanna Brand, *The Life and Death of Anna Mae Aquash*, James Lorimer & Company, 1993, p. 90.

p. 141 "To some extent, the prosecutions accomplished": Sayer, *supra*, p. 228.

p. 141 "AIM's most militant leaders and followers": Smith and Warrior, *supra*, p. 270; Sayer, *supra*, p. 228.

p. 141 FBI Director J. Edgar Hoover had used just such: Susanna McBee, "Hoover Ordered FBI to Plant Spies, Forge Papers Against Extremists," *Washington Post*, Mar. 8, 1974, p. A1.

CHAPTER 7

p. 143 He had also successfully sued both the nearby: Janklow's career and character are summarized in Molly Ivins, "It's Rarely Politics as Usual to South Dakota Governor,"

New York Times, Aug. 30, 1980, p. 6; Deposition of William Janklow, *William Janklow v. Viking Press and Peter Matthiessen*, S.D. Circ. Ct., 2nd Circ., Civ. 83-1385, July 13, 1987.

p. 144 . . . "put American Indian Movement leaders": Bruce Johansen and Roberto Maestas, *Wasi'chu: The Continuing Indian Wars*, Monthly Review Pr., 1979, p. 87, quoting WKLDOC mimeograph, "How South Dakota's Dual System of Justice Works," Rapid City, 1975.

p. 144 Wesley's killer, Darld Schmitz, had faced ten years: Robert Burnette and John Koster, *The Road to Wounded Knee*, Bantam, 1974, p. 223.

p. 144 . . . "a jump-suited tactical squad": The Sioux Falls Courthouse riot took place on April 30, 1974. (Peter Matthiessen, *In the Spirit of Crazy Horse*, Viking Pr., 1991, p. 106–7.) Judge Bottum, not incidentally, was running for reelection.

p. 145 "Janklow was standing outside the doors": Interview of Karen Northcott by author, Minneapolis, Minn., Aug. 2003.

p. 146 . . . Bill Means, brother of Russell, received a call: Interview of Bill Means by author, St. Paul, Minn., Aug. 2003.

p. 146 On a Saturday night in January 1967: The date of the alleged rape was January 14, 1967. Most of the information about Eagle Deer's story is contained in Case report R-67-22, *U.S. v. William Janklow*, "Statutory Rape," BIA Rosebud Agency, Special Officer Peter P[eter] Pitchlynn, Jan. 18, 1967.

p. 150 . . . "there is insufficient evidence to support": Letter from Assistant U.S. Attorney Ronald Clabaugh (for U.S. Attorney Harold Doyle) to Richard G. Held, FBI SAC Minneapolis, in re "William John Janklow," Mpls 70-4483, Feb. 27, 1967.

p. 150 In 1974 AIM reconstructed much of the story: The story that Eagle Deer told in 1974 varied in a few details from the story she told in 1967. For example, in 1967 she said the hush money Janklow gave her was three dollars; in 1974 she remembered it as twenty dollars.

p. 150 Much more probably, Banks was given a copy: Banks said AIM had seen the report on the alleged rape (probably meaning the BIA report) in an interview with Louis Cook, North Country Public Radio, Canton, N.Y., early Feb. 1983 (quoted in Leonard Peltier Defense Committee newsletter, Rapid City, S.D., undated). I have also been given notes, apparently in Banks's hand, that make clear AIM had seen the BIA report: the report's five-character case number and several phrases were quoted verbatim from the report.

p. 151 . . . Banks also accused Janklow of drunken driving: Memorandum Decision, *In re: Disbarment of William Janklow*, Rosebud Sioux Tribal Ct., Oct. 31, 1974; "Exhibits and Affidavits in Support of Newsweek's Motion for Summary Judgment," *William Janklow v. Newsweek, Inc.*, U.S. Dist. Ct., S.D., Civ. 83-4023, in National Archives and Records Administration, Rocky Mountain Region, Denver.

p. 151 **"The only way to deal with these kinds":** Affidavit of John Gridley III, May 27, 1975; "Janklow Justice," *In These Times*, Mar. 2-8, 1983.

p. 151 **. . . Attorney General Kermit Sande held:** "Sande, Janklow trade verbal punches at news conference," *Rapid City Journal*, Oct. 24, 1974, p. 3. See also, "States attorney admits removing Janklow file," *Rapid City Journal*, Oct. 26, 1974, p. 5.

p. 152 **. . . weekly newspaper . . . called a press conference:** The press conference was held on October 28, 1974. The quotations that follow are from a transcript of the press conference whose recorder is not identified, on file with the author.

p. 155 **"It looked like a trap to me":** Deposition of Peter Pitchlynn, *William Janklow v. Peter Pitchlynn*, U.S. Dist. Ct., S. Div. S.D., May 29, 1975, p. 27.

p. 155 **. . . but the officer's superiors ordered him:** Telegraphic message, Harley D. Zephier, acting BIA area director, to Mr. Norman Beare, special officer, Oct. 30, 1974.

p. 156 **. . . Janklow had prosecuted a tribal official:** This claim, unlike some of the others, was backed by documents that seemed to prove the case.

p. 156 **. . . "in obvious discomfort at reliving old horrors":** Memorandum Decision, *In re: Disbarment of William Janklow, supra*.

CHAPTER 8

p. 159 **To this port . . . a team from WKLDOC flew:** Reliable accounts of the beating at the airport include the following (most of which are in the WKLDOC Archives): Affidavit of Martha Copleman, Mar. 3, 1975; Affidavit of Bernard Escamilla, Mar. 2, 1975; Affidavit of Roger A. Finzel, Mar. 9, 1975; Affidavit of Eda Gordon, March 1975; interview of Eda Gordon by author, via phone, Jan. 2004; interview of Roger Finzel by author, via phone, Mar. 2004. See also FBI FD-302 report, interview of Duane Brewer by SA Edward A. Skelly Jr. and SA David F. Price, Pine Ridge, S.D., MP 70-9729, interviewed Feb. 28, 1975; FBI FD-302 report, interview of Duane Brewer by SA John E. McCarty and SA Edward A. Skelly, Pine Ridge, S.D., MP 70-9734, MP 70-9729, MP 149-467, interviewed Mar. 1, 1975; Deposition of Elizabeth Kingi, *U.S. v. Richard Wilson, Sr., et al.*, CR 75-5040, U.S. Dist. Ct., W. Div. S.D., Dec. 8, 1975; Partial transcript of jury trial, *U.S. v. Wilson, supra*, Dec. 15-18, 1975, on file with court; interviews of Eda Gordon and Duane Brewer, raw footage for *Spirit of Crazy Horse*, film by Kevin McKiernan and Michel Dubois, 1990, in Academy Film Archive, Los Angeles.

p. 163 **"We will go anywhere, at any time":** The speaker was FBI agent Noel Castleman. (*Voices From Wounded Knee*, self-published by *Akwesasne Notes* newspaper, 1974, p. 225.)

p. 163 **. . . but as they ran inside, all the officers ran out:** This was not the first time Wilsonites had run roughshod over the jail. The previous fall, Wilson and his goons took the jail by arms and released many of the prisoners. No one was prosecuted or arrested. (WKLDOC press release, Council Bluffs, Iowa, May 4, 1975, in WKLDOC Archives.) "The release from jail last fall of several Indians by Oglala Sioux tribal president Dick Wilson was acknowledged by [BIA Commissioner Morris] Thompson as being a problem. But he said the BIA 'could only act within the scope of the law and refer charges on the case.' " (United Press International, "BIA Head Will Increase Pine Ridge Police Force," *Omaha World-Herald*, Mar. 22, 1975.) Presumably the charges were referred to the U.S. attorney, who declined to prosecute.

p. 164 "We *investigate* violations of the federal law": The emphases are mine; they accurately reflect both the letter and spirit of Agent Enlow's remarks. ("FBI says we are not law enforcement agency," *Rapid City Journal*, Mar. 11, 1975.)

p. 164 Even these did not deter goons from cruising: Finzel affidavit, *supra*.

p. 165 Forty-eight hours after the beating, the FBI got: FBI FD-302 interview of Brewer by SAs Skelly and Price, Feb. 28, 1975, *supra*.

p. 165 Years later Brewer would say he was: *Spirit of Crazy Horse*, film by McKiernan and Dubois, *supra*.

p. 165 Agents also made a tardy visit to Dick Wilson: FBI FD-302 report, interview of Richard Wilson Sr., by ASAC Philip F. Enlow and SA John E. McCarty, Pine Ridge, S.D., MP 70-9729, MP 70-9734, MP 149-167, interviewed Mar. 4, 1975. Wilson also said, "Most of my people just want to lead peaceful lives. I'm constantly trying to prevent violence. This reservation is a powder keg, and it could blow at any moment."

p. 165 Earlier that afternoon Dick Marshall: Accounts of the events at the courthouse and during the running shootout that followed can be found in WKLDOC memorandum on the day's events, undated, unsigned, in WKLDOC Archives; Deposition of Marei Kingi, *U.S. v. Wilson*, *supra*, Dec. 8, 1975; FBI FD-302 interview of Brewer, by SAs Skelly and Price, Feb. 28, 1975, *supra*; FBI FD-302 interview of Brewer, by SAs McCarty and Skelly, Mar. 1, 1975, *supra*; FBI FD-302 report, interview with Orlin Wayne Wilson, aka Dick Wilson, by SA John E. McCarty and SA Ronald E. Brugger, Pine Ridge, S.D., MP 70-9734, MP 70-9729, MP 149-467, Feb. 28, 1975; Russell Means and Marvin J. Wolf, *Where White Men Fear to Tread*, St. Martin's Pr., 1995, p. 337.

p. 166 A small crowd of police and goons had: Duane Brewer told the FBI in one of his interviews that he had been tipped to the approach of the "AIM caravan."

p. 168 "Since we have no data": Associated Press, "Wilson denies AIM beating allegations," *Rapid City Journal*, Feb. 28, 1975, p. 2.

p. 168 The WKLDOCkers asked Judge Bogue: WKLDOC news release, Feb. 27, 1975, in WKLDOC Archives.

p. 168 Instead he offered for U.S. marshals: Finzel affidavit, *supra*.

p. 168 Clayton called a grand jury into session: WKLDOC newsletter, Apr. 1975, in WKLDOC Archives.

p. 169 Five days after Anderson started raising: The indictments are discussed in Jack Anderson, "A throwback to the Old West," *Newark Standard Ledger*, May 7, 1975; Associated Press, "Oglala Sioux President, Six Others Are Indicted," *Omaha World-Herald*, May 6, 1975, p. 34; Universal Press International, "Wilson, 6 Others Plead Innocent," *Omaha World-Herald*, May 10, 1975, p. 20; Memorandum of Law in Support of Defendants' Motion to Strike Surplusage from Indictment, *U.S. v. Wilson, supra*, undated. The others indicted were Tony Mousseaux, Chanfield Folson, and brothers Fred and Everett Brewer.

p. 169 In the year before the beating, twenty-six people: Cheryl McCall, "Life Is Cheap At Pine Ridge," *Berkeley Barb*, Apr. 11-17, 1975.

p. 170 . . . like the case of the Eagle Hawk family: WKLDOC newsletter, Apr. 1975, *supra*; Joe Fine, "Terror Drive Launched Against AIM Leaders," *Worker's Power*, Apr. 23, 1975, p. 3; WKLDOC report, "Chronological Fact Summary of Reservation Horror Stories," p. 3, in WKLDOC Archives.

p. 170 . . . federal charges against them were so light: Brief in Support of Motion to Dismiss, *U.S. v. Wilson, supra*, undated; Paul Riley, "Wilson, supporters denied dismissal motion," *Rapid City Journal*, Oct. 16, 1975, p. 2.

p. 171 But Ickes said . . . the statements "contained nothing": Memorandum in Support of the Motion of the United States to Limit Witnesses on Admissibility of Admissions, *U.S. v. Wilson, supra*, Dec. 3, 1975.

p. 171 . . . they reneged on their plea agreements: Memorandum in Opposition to the Defendant Everett Brewer's Motion to Withdraw His Plea of Nolo Contendere, *U.S. v. Wilson, supra*, Dec. 18, 1975.

p. 171 But WKLDOC could not convince either Judge Joseph Bottum: Memorandum Decision, *David Hill v. Kermit Sande et al.*, U.S. Dist. Ct., W. Div. S.D., Civ. 73-4080, Jan. 15, 1974.

p. 172 . . . (transcripts do not survive): More precisely, only a tiny sliver of a transcript survives, but it deals less with the trial proper than with the student protestors discussed elsewhere.

p. 172 . . . there were a pistol and rifle in the trunk: Roger Finzel freely admitted that on February 26 a .22 pistol, a .22 rifle, and .12-gauge shotgun shells were in the trunk of the convertible. (Partial transcript of jury trial, *U.S. v. Wilson, supra*, p. 39.)

p. 172 "That's the most ridiculous, most asinine": For this and similar discussion, see Partial transcript of jury trial, *U.S. v. Wilson, supra*, p. 2–6, 9, 27; Trial minutes, *U.S. v. Wilson, supra*, Dec. 15, 1975.

p. 172 . . . the goons were discharged from probation: It had been five months since the first plea. (Report and Order Terminating Probation Prior to Original Expiration Date, *U.S. v. Anthony Edward Mousseau, U.S. v. Chanfield Clark Folson, U.S. v. Everett Brewer, U.S. v. Fred Brewer, U.S. v. Duane James Brewer, U.S. v. Richard Wilson, Jr.*, U.S. Dist. Ct., W. Div. S.D., CR 75-5040, July 14, 1976.)

CHAPTER 9

p. 173 Committee staff searched the Capitol: Janklow's whereabouts were a matter of some dispute. The Associated Press said he had been excused before leaving, but the *New York Times* said he had disappeared without a word. Janklow's confirmation hearing was May 21, 1975. ("3 More Nominees of Ford in Peril," *New York Times*, May 22, 1975; Associated Press, "Janklow Walks Out on Interview for Legal Board," unlabeled newspaper clip, May 21, 1975, in file of *William Janklow v. Viking Press and Peter Matthiessen*, S.D. Circ. Ct., 2nd Circ., Civ. 83-1385, July 13, 1987, Minnehaha Co. Courthouse, Sioux Falls, S.D.)

p. 173 The presenter was Jimmy Durham: Jimmy Durham was no relation to Doug Durham.

p. 174 "Once it becomes clear that the federal": "Janklow: state taking offensive to end armed Indian takeovers," *Huron Plainsman*, May 5, 1975.

p. 174 . . . Abourezk told his colleague Alan Cranston: Abourezk said in 2005 that although he gave Cranston his opinion on the groundlessness of the rape charge, he did not otherwise help Janklow get a new hearing with the committee. (Interview of Jim Abourezk by Jenny Rich, author's assistant, via phone, Dec. 2005.) Janklow, however, told the committee that Abourezk was strongly behind him and had intended to testify on his behalf at his rescheduled hearing but that Abourezk was unable to because of a scheduling conflict. (Hearing of the Senate Committee on Labor and Public Welfare, 94th Congress, June 11, 1975, p. 415–31.)

p. 174 "This investigation included 45 substantive": The quotations from the hearing are in Senate Labor Committee Hearing, June 11, 1975, *supra*, p. 415–31.

p. 175 . . . the full Senate confirmed Janklow: *Congressional Record*, July 8, 1975, p. 21,823.

p. 175 . . . Banks and fellow AIMer Vernon Bellecourt drove: Durham gave the date of the confrontation at his house as March 7, 1975. (WKLDOC notes, "Defense notes on testimony of Doug Durham, *U.S. v. Alvarado et al.*," May 31, 1975, Lincoln, Neb., in WKLDOC Archives.)

p. 176 "We showed Doug a 302 FBI document": I have condensed the exchange slightly. (Dennis Banks with Richard Erdoes, *Ojibwa Warrior: Dennis Banks and the Rise of* *the American Indian Movement*, Univ. of Okla. Pr., 2004, p. 281). See also Nick Lamberto, "What it's like to be a spy—undercover agent tells all," *Des Moines Sunday Register*, Apr. 27, 1975, p. 3A.

p. 177 Douglass Frank Durham joined the Marine Corps: For the outline of Durham's biography, see Lamberto, "What it's like to be a spy," *supra*; "Anatomy of an Informer," *Akwesasne Notes*, early summer 1975, p. 14; "Anatomy of an Informer, Part 2," *Akwesasne Notes*, early winter 1975, p. 10 (both "Anatomy" articles were almost certainly based on the research of AIM's Paula Giese); Letters of Dennis Durham to author, Nov. 2003–Feb. 2004; Interview of Dennis Durham by author, Newton, Ia., Nov. 2005; Interview of Len Cavise by author, via phone, Mar. 2004; Alan Stang, "Red Indians," *American Opinion*, Sept. 1975, p. 1; "Defense notes on testimony of Doug Durham," *supra*; Dennis Cassano, "Wounded Knee informer has scandal-ridden past," *Minneapolis Star and Tribune*, Apr. 20, 1975, 1A; Associated Press, "Tells plan to spirit AIM leader to Cuba," *Des Moines Register*, first week of June 1975; WKLDOC report, "Excerpts from the 'Chicago Tapes,' " Mar. 1975, transcript, in WKLDOC Archives; Gene Raffensperger, "D.M. man tells of spying for FBI against AIM," *Des Moines Register*, ca. Mar. 14, 1975, p. 1; John Kifner, "Security Aide for Indians Says He was F.B.I. Informer," *New York Times*, March 13, 1975; John Adams, "AIM and the FBI," *Christian Century*, Apr. 2, 1975, p. 325ff; John Adams, "AIM, the Church and the FBI: The Douglass Durham Case," *Christian Century*, May 14, 1975, p. 489ff.; *Revolutionary Activities Within the United States: The American Indian Movement*, Hearing before the Subcommittee to Investigate the Administration of the Internal Security Act, U.S. Senate, 94th Congress, Apr. 6, 1976.

p. 178 "There was no evidence of foul play": I condensed this quotation slightly.

p. 178 . . . had quarreled and he had beaten her: By one account whose reliability is hard to judge, Donna was convulsed that Doug was taking bribes from burglars and pimping a string of women from a café called the Y Not? ("Anatomy of an Informer, Part 2," *supra*.)

p. 179 . . . to have seen two different death certificates: Dennis Durham interview, *supra*. No cause of death is listed in "Donna Durham is Dead at 27," *Des Moines Register*, July 7, 1964.

p. 179 Instead he became a restaurateur: Bill Bryson gives a hilarious account of one of Durham's restaurants, the Y Not, as a grease pit with sickly ex-cons for cooks and a steel-hearted matron for a waitress in his *Neither Here Nor There: Travels in Europe* (Harper Perennial, 1999, p. 69).

p. 179 Giese was . . . credulous in matters Durham: The sources for Giese's more extravagant claims about Durham are now mostly lost.

p. 179 . . . Durham was given other covert work: Durham seems to have worked undercover for state police in Iowa; for local police in Des Moines, Cedar Rapids, Sioux City, Omaha, and Lincoln; and possibly for federal drug and customs agencies. His free-lancing was probably abetted by the Law Enforcement Intelligence Unit, a national intelligence network run by state and local police departments of dubious methods and legality.

p. 180 In 1969 he was charged with receiving stolen: "Excerpts from the 'Chicago Tapes,' " *supra*. The fact that Durham had a "nice Italian" lawyer may have fueled the speculation that he was tied to the Mob.

p. 180 . . . indicted again, this time for extorting: *State of Iowa v. Douglas Frank Durham*, 196 N.W.2d 428, Apr. 13, 1972; Louise Swartzwalder, "Iowa Supreme Court Overturns D.M. Man's Larceny Conviction," *Des Moines Register*, Apr. 4, 1972, p. 6. See also Lamberto, "What it's like to be a spy," *supra*.

p. 180 . . . grand jury publicly chastised ten police: Various articles, *Des Moines Register*, Apr. 12–June 30, 1972, particularly Nick Lamberto, "Urges Censure for Nichols: Grand Jury's 10-X Report Chides City," June 21, p. 1; WKLDOC report, "An Excerpt from the Polk County, Iowa (Des Moines) Grand Jury Report on the '10-X' Police Corruption Scandal, Involving Durham," in WKLDOC Archives; Lamberto, "What it's like to be a spy," *supra*; Cassano, *supra*.

p. 182 "One minister suggested to me that Doug": I have condensed this quotation. (Adams, *supra*.)

p. 182 He had urged . . . the kidnapping of governors: For example, Dennis Banks wrote of Durham, "On a flight over Pierre he remarked casually, 'What we ought to do is bomb this place. We could get Janklow right from here with one good bomb.' He always made suggestions of that kind." Banks and Erdoes, *supra*, p. 268.

p. 183 When Congress created a Bureau of Investigation: Most of the facts about the FBI's spying on "subversives" can be found in Ronald Kessler, *The Bureau: The Secret History of the FBI*, St. Martin's, 2003; Richard Gid Powers, *Secrecy and Power: The Life of J. Edgar Hoover*, Free Press, 1988. Kessler's may be the one of the most accessible accounts, but it is also one of the least documented and in many places credits the FBI with more benign intentions than the facts warrant.

p. 184 It was a model of evasion Hoover would resort to: A similar dodge of Hoover's was to turn off all but a handful of the FBI's wiretaps before he testified before Congress. When committee members asked how many phones the FBI had tapped, Hoover would own up to only the small number that had been left on. After his testimony, he would have all the other taps turned back on.

p. 184 Hoover gave similar files to every president: The presidents were not just passive recipients of Hoover's information. In 1964, when Lyndon Johnson feared the Mississippi Democratic Freedom Party (the black wing of the Mississippi Democratic Party) would upset the Democratic national convention, he asked Hoover to spy on them. Hoover did, with a team of thirty agents. Richard Nixon made many illegal demands of the FBI. Among them was digging up dirt on the sexual proclivities of critical reporters as well as whatever might help Nixon impeach Supreme Court Justice William O. Douglas. (A different impeachment interrupted Nixon's plans.)

Hoover did not restrict such services to presidents. When Senator Joe McCarthy lied that he had a list of spies inside the State Department, Hoover ordered agents to give McCarthy any information in their files that might support him. They found nothing of weight but gave McCarthy what they had. Hoover also assigned FBI speechwriters to McCarthy.

p. 185 By the end of the 1950s, the FBI had amassed 432,000: Johanna Brand, *The Life and Death of Anna Mae Aquash*, James Lorimer & Co., 1993, p. 69.

p. 185 "If you have good intelligence": The espionage chief was George Moore, supervisor of the FBI's Racial Intelligence Section. (Brand, *supra*, p. 78, quoting testimony of Nov. 3, 1975.)

p. 186 "We must mark him now, if we have not": The aide was William Sullivan, head of the domestic intelligence division. Quoted in Brand, *supra*, p. 72.

p. 186 Agents provocateur were sent among the Panthers: Susanna McBee, "Hoover Ordered FBI to Plant Spies, Forge Papers Against Extremists," *Washington Post*, Mar. 8, 1974, p. A1.

p. 186 "Shootings, beatings and a high degree of unrest": Brand, *supra*, p. 79.

p. 187 "The COINTELPRO attack on her": Powers, *supra*, p. 459–60. Not long after Seberg killed herself, her former husband, Romain Gary (father of her dead child), killed himself in grief.

p. 187 One of the unfamous and unwhite was Geronimo Pratt: Pratt's story is very well told in Jack Olsen, *Last Man Standing: The Tragedy and Triumph of Geronimo Pratt*, Doubleday, 2000.

p. 189 "Every message I try to get through": Adams, *supra*.

p. 190 "Vernon called a meeting": I have condensed this quotation slightly. (Banks and Erdoes, *supra*, p. 276.) Bill Means said Durham was exposed when AIM found microfilm that Durham had mislaid in the St. Paul AIM office. Means's recollection is probably incorrect. (Peter Matthiessen, *In the Spirit of Crazy Horse*, Viking, 1991, p. 120.) By other accounts, there was a plot to execute Durham at the Menominee takeover in January 1975, but Durham's early departure foiled the plan: "In a recorded interview, Herb Powless described the plan AIM leadership had to kill Durham, but said Durham got away from the Novitiate before the plan could be executed . . ." (Indigenous Women for Justice, "The Lies of John Graham," indigenouswomenforjustice.org, viewed Feb. 1, 2004.)

p. 190 "One of the proofs that Durham was a provocateur": Interview of Kevin McKiernan by author, Santa Barbara, Cal., July 2003.

p. 191 On March 13, 1975, AIM held a press conference: The FBI discussed the conference in FBI airtel from SAC, Chicago, to Director, FBI, "American Indian Movement (AIM)," Mar. 13, 1975. See also Kifner, *supra*.

p. 192 Hurd's excuse was irrelevant: Nichol's order to the government, issued March 21, 1974, required the prosecution to reveal any evidence that was even "arguably relevant" to whether government informers had invaded—or even merely had "contact with"—the defense apparatus, which included the legal offices in both St. Paul and Rapid City. (John M. Crewdson, "Judge Says F.B.I. Withheld Data on Indians," *New York Times*, Apr. 5, 1975.) After Nichol issued his order, prosecutor Hurd and agent Trimbach flew to Washington and on March 28, 1974, met with Attorney General William Saxbe and FBI Director Clarence Kelley to discuss the order. After Hurd returned and went to court, he said there were no informers who met the criteria of Nichol's order. Later Durham said that while all of this was going on, he met with three agents—his handlers Ray Williams, Doug Hoffer, and Bob Taubert—in Minneapolis to see if he would be exposed. The agents said they would not expose him to Hurd. Hurd and Clayton later denied to Nichol that they had any knowledge of Durham. (Affidavit of Kenneth E. Tilsen, *U.S. v. Bernard Bravo Escamilla*, U.S. Dist. Ct., W. Div. S.D., CR 73-5138; Letter from Larry B. Leventhal, WKLDOC, to Henry Wolf, Aug. 22, 1976, in WKLDOC Archives.)

p. 192 . . . one of his subordinates, Agent Ray Williams, said: John William Sayer, *Ghost Dancing the Law: The Wounded Knee Trials*, Harvard Univ. Pr., 1997, p. 116–9, 207–11; Brand, *supra*, p. 99; Matthiessen, *supra*, p. 123.

p. 192 "I recognize that a court may": I have condensed this quotation slightly. (Letter from Fred J. Nichol to Kenneth E. Tilsen, re *U.S. v. Banks and Means*, Apr. 23, 1975, in WKLDOC Archives.) Nichol said he thought that the FBI had withheld the information about Durham from the prosecution, not that prosecution had the information and withheld it from the court. (Crewdson, "Judge Says," *supra*.)

p. 193 The very week that Nichol declined to punish: Mary Jo Cook said that for seventeen months in 1973 and 1974 she supplied the FBI as many as forty reports a month on the Attica defense committee. She said, "I realized I could seriously be undermining the courtroom process in the country . . . It was as if I were a TV monitor in people's lives." (William Claiborne, "Attica Trial Witness Admits FBI Spy Role," *Washington Post*, Apr. 22, 1975, A3.) For another example, Amnesty International concluded the FBI planted informers in the defense team of Black Panther Geronimo Pratt. ("FBI Misconduct in Trials of Militants," *Encore*, Jan. 1982, p. 8.)

p. 193 The Schafers . . . immediately started badgering: Interview of Sand Brim by author, via phone, Jan. 2004; Giese, "Anatomy of an Informer," *supra*.

p. 193 *The New York Times* exposed: John M. Crewdson, "U.S. Citizens Used by F.B.I. Abroad: Bureau Confirms Practice—Authorities Say It Does Not Violate the Law," *New York Times*, Feb. 16, 1975, p. 1; John M. Crewdson, "F.B.I. Reportedly Harassed Radicals After Spy Program Ended," *New York Times*, Mar. 23, 1975, p. 33. Other articles discussing the Schafers are Jack Davis, "Orleans couple: 'extremists' for the FBI," *New Orleans States-Item*, Mar. 6, 1975; Crewdson, "Judge Says," *supra*; Liberation News Service, "Uncovering the Undercovered," *WIN*, Mar. 6 or 23, 1975; Jack L. Schwartz, "Anti-War Activists Exposed As Agents Provocateur," Zodiac News Service, Washington, D.C., Feb. 23, 1975, in WKLDOC Archives. There is also a police intelligence card on Gi: "Schafer, Harry Eugene III," b. Aug. 21, 1943, New Orleans, FBI #332 243 H, Law Enforcement Intelligence Unit card, in WKLDOC Archives.

p. 193 Their names, like Durham's, were on the list: Gi Schafer also told the *Times* that in addition to setting up a fundraising front, he and Jill reported regularly to the FBI on the activities of WKLDOC. (Crewdson, "Judge Says," *supra*.) Gi was with Pedro Bissonette when he was arrested after slipping out of Wounded Knee in the spring of 1973. It was almost certainly Schafer who alerted the FBI to Bissonette's whereabouts.

p. 193 But Judge Nichol found no more cause: In addition to WKLDOC's attempt to elicit sanctions from Judge Nichol in *U.S. v. Banks and Means*, WKLDOC tried to elicit them from Judge McManus in *U.S. v. Crow Dog, Holder and Camp*, from Judge Bogue in *U.S. v. Escamilla*, and from Judge Urbom in *U.S. v. Cooper, Fleury, Wesaw, Dodge, Alvarado, and Williams*. Apparently all of these judges reviewed the informer files of Durham and the Schafers *in camera*. The same issue came before panels of the Eighth Circuit Court of Appeals in *U.S. v. Fleury, Wesaw and Johns*; *U.S. v. Alvarado and Williams*; and *U.S. v. Crow Dog*. None of WKLDOC's efforts bore fruit. (Affidavit of Kenneth E. Tilsen, Feb. 1976, in WKLDOC Archives; Leventhal letter, *supra*; Associated Press, "Dismissals Denied in 7 Siege Case," *Omaha World-Herald*, June 21, 1975, p. 28.)

p. 194 On the night of Friday, April 4, 1975: The death of Jancita Eagle Deer is recounted in Paula Giese, "Secret Agent Douglass Durham and the Death of Jancita Eagle Deer," *North Country Anvil* (Millville, Minn.), Mar./Apr. 1976, p. 2ff; "Anatomy of an Informer, Part 2," *supra*; "South Dakota Women Killed In Accident," *Aurora News-Register*, Apr. 10, 1975, p. 1; "Iowa Woman Killed at Aurora," *Grand Island* (Neb.) *Daily Independent*, Apr. 5, 1975, p. 1; "Investigator's Motor Vehicle Accident Report," State of Nebraska, driver Terry L. Scott, victim Jancita Marie Sheldahl, by William G. Gage, Hamilton County deputy sheriff, Apr. 4, 1975.

p. 196 . . . forgot all about it until he showed up at her house: When Durham came to Eagle Deer in 1974, he gave her a letter from her stepfather, Johnny Arcoren, which read, "Trust this man. Do what he tells you. He knows all about everything. . . . Indian families are depending on you."

p. 196 In all likelihood Durham took Eagle Deer's picture in an effort: After Durham was exposed, he said in court that he gave pictures of Indians to the FBI. ("Defense notes," *supra*; "Informers Cloud AIM Verdicts," *supra*.) Giese believed Durham had been casing Eagle Deer for some time. She suspected that he had a long-range scheme to get AIM to accuse Janklow of rape. But in fact in 1973, when Durham took Eagle Deer's picture, neither he nor AIM knew about the rape, and Janklow was an unknown legal aid lawyer with no obvious political prospects.

p. 196 "About fifteen seconds after I first": I condensed this quotation slightly. (Giese, "Secret Agent," *supra*, p. 2–7.)

p. 197 Meanwhile, Durham revived her rape claim: It seems it was Durham who turned up the investigative report of Eagle Deer's rape claim that helped convince Banks to bring his claim against Janklow.

p. 198 . . . in December 1975, Giese drove to Des Moines: The details of Giese's harassment by police in Iowa can be found in Letter from Paula Giese, WKLDOC, to Claudia Morrissey, Iowa Civil Liberties Union, Dec. 15, 1975, in author's files.

p. 198 The Sheldahls said that the FBI had questioned them: It is not clear that it was in fact the FBI that asked the Sheldahls about the address book, although both Twila Sheldahl and Jancita's daughter, Anette Sheldahl Claus, told me so. It may have been a state investigative agency.

CHAPTER 10

p. 201 She had worked in many of the same places: Senior AIMers would later say that they told Aquash that Durham had been sent west because he was under suspicion; they wanted her to keep an eye on him. But this was probably not true. AIM had almost certainly not yet discovered Durham.

p. 201 Bellecourt ordered Bob Robideau: Bellecourt has always denied having ordered the interrogation of Aquash. Bob Robideau has accused Bellecourt of making the order on several occasions (e.g., "Silenced: The Execution of Anna Mae," *The Fifth Estate* television program, Canadian Broadcasting Corp., aired Nov. 8, 2000; interview of Bob Robideau by author, via phone, Mar. 2006). Russell Means has said so as well: "Vernon ordered the interrogation. And if they were convinced that she was an agent, they were told by Vernon to kill her. They were satisfied she was not an informer and exonerated her." (Transcript of press conference held by Russell Means and Robert Pictou Branscombe, Nov. 3, 1999, Denver Fed. Bldg., posted at "Annie Mae Aquash, Special Issue—November

1999," www.indiancountrynews.com/aquashspecial.cfm, viewed Apr. 2003.) Paul DeMain has said, "That she was taken off to the mesa was also confirmed by Mark and Mickey Aquash, who were with Anna Mae and Nogeeshik when they went to Farmington. And I've spoken to at least two of Anna Mae's female friends in the last couple years, who have confirmed that Anna Mae said that Leonard was part and parcel of her interrogation out on the mesa." (Interview of Richard Two Elk, Native American Journalists Association conference, June 16, 2000, posted at www.dickshovel.com/lenanna.html, viewed Apr. 2003.) Aquash's daughter, Denise Maloney, has written, "Keep in mind she did recant [sic: recount] to her family in 'her own words' an incident where a well known activist held a gun to her head during one of their so called 'non violent' interrogations." (Denise Maloney, message board posting, vancouver.indymedia.org/news/2003/12/93080.php, Dec. 22, 2003, & ff. dates; see also postings of Paul DeMain at same site.) The claim that Peltier stuck a pistol in Aquash's mouth is made by Iris Thundercloud: "Thundercloud indicates to journalist Minnie Two Shoes that immediately after the interrogation, Annie Mae tells her that Peltier had stuck a pistol in her mouth during the interrogation." (Paul DeMain, "Aquash Murder Trial Timeline," Justice for Anna Mae and Ray Web site, jfamr.org/trialtime.html, updated Mar. 28, 2005, viewed May 2006.) Peltier's story about the interrogation, which I believe to be untrue, was recorded by Peter Matthiessen in *In the Spirit of Crazy Horse*, Viking Pr., 1991, p. 146. Bob Robideau, although not a witness to Peltier's methods, also portrays the aftermath of the interrogation as genial. (Interview of Bob Robideau by author, *supra*.)

p. 202 **"I was at this big party outside":** Interview of Paul DeMain by author, Hayward, Wisc., Aug. 2003. See also Deborah Kades, "Native Hero," *Wisconsin Academy Review*, Winter 2005, p. 11; Mike Mosedale, "Bury My Heart," *City Pages*, Feb. 16, 2000, front cover. DeMain has said of another reporter who was suspected of informing, "Richard LaCourse, Yakama, recounts having someone in AIM security put a gun next to his balls, and threatening to shoot—and he was well known amongst Native people as a straight shooter in terms of writing about events." (Email from Paul DeMain to author, Dec. 1, 2003.) Iris Thundercloud was another AIMer accused at Gresham.

p. 203 **"COINTELPRO program . . . as sophisticated as":** Paul DeMain, message board web posting, vancouver.indymedia.org/news/2003/12/93080.php, Dec. 18, 2003 & later dates.

p. 203 **. . . headquarters in St. Paul, where informers said she:** FBI FD-306 informant report, received ■■■■, received by SA Gilbert R. Cordova, SA Martin A. Gonzales, Los Angeles, Cal., prepared Feb. 19, 1975. See also Johanna Brand, *The Life and Death of Anna Mae Aquash*, James Lorimer & Company, 1993, p. 119.

p. 203 **The FBI monitored Aquash on her way to Shiprock:** FBI FD-36 form, teletype, from Los Angeles (157-11208), to Director Attn: INTD, re "Takeover of Fairchild Plant, Shiprock, New Mexico, February 24, 1975," Feb. 27, 1975; FBI FD-263 report of Stephenson, July 16, 1975, *supra*. For evidence that the FBI lost track of her afterward, see FBI memo, from SAC, Los Angeles (157-11137)(P), to Director, FBI, re "Anna Mae Aquash, aka Joanna Jason," June 23, 1975; FBI memo, from SAC, Albuquerque (157-960), to Director, FBI, re "Anna Mae Aquash," Sept. 9, 1975.

p. 204 After Shiprock, Aquash . . . went to the Pine Ridge: Aquash probably did not return to Los Angeles because the money stream there had been more trickle than flood.

p. 204 . . . the Royal Canadian Mounted Police had had him: Aquash's brother-in-law was Earl Lafford, married to Mary Pictou Lafford. "Lafford said in a telephone interview last week that he was surprised when a Royal Canadian Mounted Policeman from the Antigonish Detachment told him that a year ago, and was also able to tell him about detailed movements of the Lafford family, which was under surveillance. At least one other Canadian friend of Ms. Aquash was asked about her at the same time, said Mary Lafford. Norman Zigrossi, supervisor of the South Dakota FBI office in Rapid City, declined to comment when asked whether the FBI had initiated or was aware of any surveillance for the FBI by Canadian authorities." (Kevin McKiernan, "Indian woman's death raises many questions," *Minneapolis Tribune*, May 30, 1976, p. 1B.) The FBI has refused to release its files on Aquash from the FBI attaché's office in Ottawa.

p. 204 "AQUASH had brought in funds": "This information was never verified," the report continued. The information was given to the FBI around January 1975. (FBI FD-263 report of Stephenson, July 16, 1975, *supra*.) For the "special" or "secret" AIM project, see FBI NITEL, from Rapid City (70-10239) Resmurs, to Director, FBI (Attn: INTD & GID), July 10, 1975, 10:45 p.m.; FBI NITEL, from Rapid City (70-10239) Resmurs, to Director, July 26, 1975, 8:21 p.m.; FBI report, "Anna Mae Aquash, also known as Joanna Jason," Los Angeles, Cal., July 11, 1975.

p. 205 "Anna Mae left her home and her two kids": David Weir and Lowell Bergman, "The Killing of Anna Mae Aquash," *Rolling Stone*, Apr. 7, 1977, p. 51ff.

p. 205 "She was a quiet person when she lived": Interview of Ellen Moves Camp by author, near Wanblee, S.D., Nov. 2003.

p. 206 To this day the FBI will not disclose whether Aquash: At the time this book was published, I continued to sue the FBI to obtain the report on Price's interview with Aquash. The Bissonette murder has never been solved.

p. 206 At a quarter to noon on June, 26, 1975: Peter Matthiessen gives the seminal account of the shootout in *In the Spirit of Crazy Horse, supra*, p. 154ff.

p. 206 When Agents Ron Williams and: Williams had been David Price's partner in the Louis Moves Camp fiasco during the Banks-Means trial.

p. 207 "It looks like these guys are going": Williams's precise words in his last minutes are remembered differently by various people who overheard them. His transmissions were not recorded.

p. 207 . . . a BIA police officer and an FBI agent arrived: The BIA patrol car was driven by Frank Two Bulls. A few minutes after they arrived, several more BIA and FBI men appeared on the scene. Their arrival was so swift that Indians would say the FBI incursion must have been premeditated. This was unlikely: Williams and Coler, who had to fetch arms from their trunks and who were not wearing bulletproof vests, were utterly unprepared for a firefight. Also, the town of Pine Ridge, where the BIA police were based and where several FBI men were on duty that day, was only ten minutes away from the scene of the firefight. It would not have taken them long to arrive. On the other hand, a BIA SWAT team was on maneuvers not far from the Jumping Bull land on the day of the shootout, and the FBI was massing agents in the area in response to the "secret AIM project" in Oglala.

p. 209 This was the same FBI that . . . claimed to be a mere investigative: The FBI claimed no contradiction in its words and deeds. It said that the agents who massed in such numbers and with such armament in the minutes and days after the shootout at Oglala were not enforcing the law—merely investigating a crime.

p. 210 "cold-blooded ambush": Most of the quotations in this paragraph appear in Matthiessen, *supra*, p. 194. See also Joel Weisman, "About That 'Ambush' at Wounded Knee," *Columbia Journalism Review*, September–October 1975, p. 28ff.

p. 210 "It is patently clear," the U.S. Commission: Letter from Arthur S. Flemming, U.S. Commission on Civil rights Chairman, to U.S. Attorney General Edward Levi, July 24, 1975, which includes USCCR memo from William Muldrow, Mountain States Regional Ofc., to Shirley Hill Witt, Regional Director, July 9, 1975.

p. 210 "Sobsisters," Janklow said: I have condensed this quotation. ("Janklow Says He Is Fed Up," *Minot News*, June 28, 1975. See also Deposition of William Janklow, *William Janklow v. Viking Press and Peter Matthiessen*, S.D. Circ. Ct., 2nd Circ., Civ. 83-1385, July 13, 1987, p. 392, in which Janklow denies having said "sobsisters.")

p. 210 "The Oglalas don't like what happened": *Warrior: The Life of Leonard Peltier*, film by Suzie Baer, Cinnamon Productions, Westport, Conn., 1991; CBS Evening News, June 30, 1975, transcript in WKLDOC Archives.

p. 211 The manhunt for the agents' killers spread: Details about the manhunt can be found in Matthiessen, *supra*, p. 192ff.

p. 211 . . . "full-scale military-type invasion": Said USCCR, "They [the Oglalas] point out that little has been done to solve numerous murders on the reservation, but when two white men are killed, 'troops' are brought in from all over the country at a cost of hundreds of millions of dollars." The only hyperbole here was hundreds of millions of dollars. Flemming letter, *supra*.

p. 212 She had left the day before, June 25: She returned to Oglala on June 27 with Jean Day, Theda Nelson Clarke, and John Graham. (Paul DeMain, "Arlo Looking Cloud Trial Outline," Jan. 30, 2004, www.indigenouswomenforjustice.org, viewed Feb. 2004.) Clarke and Graham were soon to become important in Aquash's life.

p. 212 Aquash was not on the second list, but she was: See, e.g., FBI NITEL from Rapid City, July 10, 1975, 10:45 p.m., *supra*.

p. 212 "One day in July of '75": Author interview with Candy Hamilton, Oglala, S.D., Aug. 2003.

p. 213 Aquash kept a low profile through July: Aquash was discreet enough that the FBI believed she had gone or was going to Canada "in the company of Dennis James Banks." (FBI memo, re "Anna Mae Aquash et al," Minneapolis, Aug. 19, 1975.) The FBI asked the Royal Canadian Mounted Police for information, but what the Mounties told the Bureau, the Bureau will not say. (FBI FD-36 Airtel, from LEGAT, Ottawa (89-10) (P) RESMURS, to Director, FBI, re "Anna Mae Aquash," date uncertain but ca. Aug. 27, 1975.)

p. 214 Crow Dog called her an informer: "Anna Mae Pictou Aquash: Timeline," *supra*; Matthiessen, *supra*, p. 222; Brand, *supra*, p. 129.

p. 214 "She was scared of everybody": I condensed this quotation. (Mike Anton, "Dreams of Justice: 24-year-old murder keeps Pine Ridge Reservation on edge," Feb. 27, 2000, dickshovel.com/lenanna.html, viewed Apr. 2003.)

p. 214 A series of confrontations had preceded: The conflicting stories of the Beck-McCloskey affair can be found in WKLDOC press release, "Leonard Crow Dog and Six Arrested on Rosebud," Sept. 11, 1975, in WKLDOC Archives; Kenneth Tilsen, "Fair and Equal Justice: The FBI, Wounded Knee and Politics," *Quare: Student newspaper of the University of Minnesota Law School*, Sept. 1976, v. 3, n. 1, p. 1ff.; FBI teletype, from Rapid City (70-10488), to Bureau, re " ▪▪▪▪▪ [Leonard Crow Dog]—Fugitive," Sept. 5, 1975, 7:30 p.m.; FBI memo, from SAC, Minneapolis (70-10488)(P), to Director, FBI (Attn: FBI Laboratory, Latent Fingerprint Sec.), re "Leonard Crow Dog et al.," Sept. 8, 1975; FBI memo, General Investigative Div., re "RESMURS," Sept. 6, 1975 (date is obscured; could be Sept. 16 or Sept. 26); Rolland Dewing, *Wounded Knee II*, Great Plains Network/Pine Hills Pr., 1995, p. 166. Crow Dog was convicted of the assault on Beck and McCloskey and sentenced to five years, of which he served about two.

p. 215 He had once been convicted of menacing: Crow Dog had put the chainsaw blade to Roger Pfersick, whom Crow Dog accused of being an informer, on March 25, 1975. R. D. Hurd had prosecuted Crow Dog. (Dewing, *supra*, p. 166.)

p. 215 . . . he regularly and fiercely beat his wife Mary: "We saw the bruises on her," WKLDOC's Roger Finzel said, "but we didn't do anything. We were just locked in the time. It's something I'll never forgive myself for." (Interview of Roger Finzel by author, via phone, Mar. 2004.)

p. 215 AIM's version of their meeting: Price's words are quoted variously in Weir and Bergman, *supra*; Matthiessen, *supra*, p. 300; WKLDOC press release, Sept. 11, 1975, *supra*.

p. 216 "They were all over the place, dumping things": I have condensed Aquash's recollections. (Interview of Anna Mae Aquash by Candy Hamilton, Sept. 1975, transcript in WKLDOC Archives.)

p. 216 "Hey, you know who you got there": This conversation appears in Matthiessen, *supra*, p. 225; WKLDOC press release, Sept. 11, 1975, *supra*.

p. 217 . . . "a human hair found therein": FBI NITEL, from Rapid City (70-10239) (P) RESMURS, to Director (89-3229), Sept. 20, 1975, 9:54 p.m.; FBI FD-204 report, from William Van Roe, Minneapolis, to US Atty., Sioux Falls (Attn: Asst. US Atty. Bruce Boyd), re "Anna Mae Aquash," field office file 4-38, Sept. 11, 1975.

p. 217 "You know what that guy said": Matthiessen, *supra*, p. 228.

p. 218 "PICTOU put her head down on the desk": I condensed this quotation slightly. (FBI FD-302 report, interview of Annie Mae Pictou, by B. Jeanette Morgan and Frederick Coward, Jr., Pierre, S.D., MP 70-10238, interviewed Sept. 5, 1975, transcribed Sept. 9, 1975.)

p. 218 . . . "the agent told me that I could not make my call": I condensed this quotation slightly.

p. 219 "Price tried to get her to roll over": Interview of John Trudell by author, via phone, Sept. 2003. Aquash told Hamilton the same thing, although not during their recorded interview. (Interview of Candy Hamilton by author, via phone, Dec. 2005.)

p. 219 "But I went before the magistrate": For the FBI's summary of her refusal to talk, her bail, her release, and her indictment, see FBI teletype, from Rapid City (70-10488), to Bureau, re "Leonard Crow Dog et al.", Sept. 9, 1975; FBI NITEL, from Rapid City (70-10239) (P) RESMURS, to Director, Sept. 15, 1975, 11:15 p.m.; FBI memo from SA Olen Victor Harvey, to SAC, Pine Ridge (70-10239) (P), re "RESMURS," Sept. 9, 1975; FBI teletype, from Rapid City (70-10488), to Director, FBI, re ██████, Sept. 10, 1975, 3:30 p.m.; Indictment, *US v. Annie Mae Pictou, a/k/a Annie Mae Aquash*, U.S. Dist. Ct., Central Div. S.D., CR 75-[unnumbered], filed Sept. 17, 1975. See also FBI FD-204 report of Beinner, Nov. 17, 1975, *supra*.

p. 219 It still took four days for her friends to raise: Later, as the stories of Aquash's easy escapes from the law were inflated, she was said to have gotten out of jail on the same day as her arrest. This was not true.

p. 219 . . . her jailmates, who had all been indicted: More precisely, they had either been indicted or arrested on more serious grounds. Dino Butler, for example, was held for killing the agents. Leonard Crow Dog, Gerald Millard, Owen Young, and Frank Running were indicted for the alleged kidnapping and torture of McCloskey and Beck. (Loose FBI page marked "TRASH," perhaps from FBI FD-263 report of William Van Roe, Minneapolis, investigative period Sept. 3-5, 1975, re "Changed Leonard Emanuel Crow Dog et al.," Sept. 8, 1975. See also WKLDOC press release, Sept. 11, 1975, *supra*.)

p. 220 "These men that are in the woods": Letter from Rebecca Julian, to Robert C. Levy, Nova Scotia Legal Aid, June 4, 1976, in WKLDOC Archives.

p. 220 "If you could see the people": Brand, *supra*, p. 133.

p. 220 . . . an informer named John Stewart: By some accounts, Stewart was known as Darryl Blue Legs, not Darryl Blue Lake.

p. 220 They were arrested as they stepped off the plane: Much later, FBI documents proved that an informer (certainly Stewart) had been behind the arrest of Butler and Aquash at L.A. International. (FBI FD-209 memo, from SA Gregory J. Hoeschen, SA Eugene L. Crouch, to SAC, Minneapolis, re ■■■■■ [Nilak Butler], Sept. 12, 1975.)

p. 221 . . . Banks and Leonard Peltier were in Los Angeles: Matthiessen, *supra*, p. 223.

p. 221 "SA CORDOVA will attempt to surveil": FBI memo, from SA Arthur H. Turner, to SAC, Pine Ridge (4-39) (P), Subject RESMURS, Sept. 12, 1975.

p. 221 . . . under the watchful eyes of informers: See, e.g., FBI FD-306 informant report, received by Gilbert R. Cordova, Los Angeles, received Oct. 23, 1975, prepared Oct. 30, 1975.

p. 221 "It has been determined that ■■■■■■": I have condensed this report slightly. (FBI memo, from SA Gilbert R. Cordova, to SAC, Los Angeles, re ■■■■■■, Sept. 29, 1975; FBI FD-204 report of Beinner, Nov. 17, 1975, *supra*. See also FBI FD-306 informant report, received by Gilbert R. Cordova, Los Angeles, received Oct. 1, 1975, prepared Oct. 3, 1975; FBI background report, re "Anna Mae Aquash," 4-38-97, Dec. 23, 1975; FBI FD-36 report, airtel, from Acting ADIC, Los Angeles (157-11137) (P), to Director, FBI (157-34110), subject Anna Mae Aquash, Oct. 23, 1975; FBI FD-306, informant's report, received by SA Gilbert R. Cordova, Los Angeles, received Oct. 8, 1975, prepared Oct. 9, 1975; FBI FD-306 informant report, received by Gilbert R. Cordova, Los Angeles, received Oct. 23, 1975, prepared Oct. 30, 1975.

p. 222 They visited actor Marlon Brando, who gave: Dennis Banks and Richard Erdoes, *Ojibwa Warrior: Dennis Banks and the Rise of the American Indian Movement*, Univ. of Okla. Pr., 2004, p. 301.

p. 222 In early October, Banks, Peltier, and Aquash: Banks and Peltier probably drove the motor home part of the way back to Pine Ridge, and Aquash and an AIMer named Dave Hill drove the motor home the rest of the way. There are conflicting accounts.

p. 222 "She doesn't trust him because he tried": I have condensed this quotation slightly. (FBI FD-306, informant's report, received by SA Gilbert R. Cordova, Los Angeles, received Oct. 8, 1975, prepared Oct. 9, 1975.) "I think Riter really thought it was a good deal," said WKLDOC attorney Bruce Ellison, who was defending others who had been arrested at Crow Dog's and Running's. (See Brand, *supra*, p. 134–5; Weir and Bergman, *supra*.)

p. 222 AIM fingered Dick Wilson: " 'Reichstag' in Pine Ridge," WKLDOC newsletter, date uncertain but late 1975, in WKLDOC Archives.

p. 223 "We decided that the time had come": Matthiessen, *supra*, p. 221–2.

p. 223 By and by, friends came to Port Madison: Banks and Erdoes, *supra*, p. 303.

p. 224 . . . a judge issued a bench warrant for her arrest: FBI NITEL, from Portland (89-94) (P) RESMURS, to Director, Nov. 16, 1975, 4:24 p.m.; FBI NITEL, from Minneapolis (70-10488) (P), to Director, FBI 70-66344, Nov. 11, 1975, 9:16 p.m.

p. 224 The AIMers took the plane, correctly: Kenneth S. Stern, *Loud Hawk: The United States versus the American Indian Movement*, Univ. of Okla. Pr., 1994, p. 208ff, citing an evidentiary hearing in June 1980 in *U.S. v. Loud Hawk et al.*, U.S. Dist. Ct., Ore., 75-CR-296-RE.

p. 224 Banks would later say that the FBI had let them: Banks and Erdoes, *supra*, p. 304.

p. 224 At ten o'clock that night, they were approaching: Accounts of the encounter with Griffiths can be found in Crime report of Kenneth Griffiths, Ore. State Police, "Attempted Murder," occurred Nov. 14, 1975, 10:05 p.m., I-80N, eastbound lanes, milepost 377, Malheur Co.; Information report, Ore. State Police, "Attempted Murder," occurred Nov. 14, 1975, 10:05 p.m., Malheur Co., Clayton Kramer; FBI FD-302 report, interview of Kenneth Griffiths, Ore. State Patrol, by SAs Daniel S. Jacobs and R. Keith Bond, Ontario, Ore., PD 89-94, interviewed Nov. 15, 1975, transcribed Nov. 19, 1975; FBI FD-302 report, interview of Corporal Clayton Kramer, Ontario Police Dept., by SAs Daniel S. Jacobs and R. Keith Bond, Ontario, Ore., PD 89-94, interviewed Nov. 15, 1975, transcribed Nov. 19, 1975; FBI FD-302 report, interview of ███████, Ontario Police Dept., by SA Daniel S. Jacobs, Ontario, Ore., PD 89-94, interviewed Nov. 15, 1975, transcribed Nov. 19, 1975; Affidavit for Search Warrant of Clayton C. Kramer, Justice Court, Dist. of Ontario, Malheur Co., Ore., Nov. 15, 1975; Affidavit for Search Warrant of Kenneth Griffiths, Ore. State Police trooper, Justice Court, Dist. of Ontario, Malheur Co., Ore., Nov. 15, 1975; Stern, *supra*, p. 5ff. I condensed quotations from Griffiths's report slightly.

p. 226 . . . "was examined and found to contain": FBI FD-204 report from Wayne C. Barlow, Portland, to USA, Portland (Attn: AUSA Tommy Hawk), re "Anna Mae Aquash et al.," field office file 89-94, bureau file 89-3229, Jan. 21, 1976.

p. 226 . . . the caravanners had been quite bold: Banks and Erdoes, *supra*, p. 303; DeMain, "Arlo Looking Cloud Trial Outline," *supra*.

p. 226 "Anna Mae only had one thing to tell me": Weir and Bergman, *supra*.

p. 227 "I'm sure that as soon as I return": I have combined more than one quotation here. (McKiernan, "Indian woman's death," *supra*; Jerry Oppenheimer, "FBI Under Fire For Conduct in Indian's Death," *Washington Star*, May 24, 1976, p. A1.)

p. 227 . . . he set her free on her own recognizance: FBI FD-204 report from William Van Roe, Minneapolis, to USA, Sioux Falls (Attn: AUSA David R. Gienapp), re "Anna Mae Aquash," field ofc. file 4-38, Feb. 18, 1976.)

p. 227 . . . a furious Mehrige issued a warrant: FBI intel, from Minneapolis (70-10488) (P), to Director, Nov. 26, 1975, 11:07 p.m.

p. 227 . . . "she would not run because whatever": Julian letter, *supra*.

p. 228 "We were all staying in the same": I have condensed this quotation. (Bruce Ellison, diary entry, Nov. 25, 1975, in WKLDOC Archives.)

CHAPTER 11

p. 229 Russell Means . . . was preoccupied with various trials: "Means had been declared ineligible to run in this year's election after a Wilson challenge that he was a 'non-resident.' Means has spent most of the past two years facing trial in a dozen different court-rooms, and the ineligibility ruling was handed down just late enough to make protest impossible." ("Pine Ridge—1976," *Akwesasne Notes*, early spring 1976, p. 8.)

p. 229 . . . "needed straightening out": The lieutenant was the chairman of the district that included the town of Pine Ridge, Wilson's mainstay. (Kevin McKiernan, "The Killing of Byron DeSersa," KSJN, Minnesota Public Radio, Apr. 1 1976, tape in author's collection; Peter Matthiessen, *In the Spirit of Crazy Horse*, Viking Pr., 1991, p. 254. Other sources for the killing of Byron DeSersa are Transcript of Preliminary Hearing, *U.S. v. Charles David Winters, a/k/a Elmer Winters*, U.S. Dist. Ct., W. Div. S.D., CR 76-62M, Magistrate James H. Wilson, Feb. 20, 1976; Associated Press, "Wanblee man shot to death," *Rapid City Journal*, Feb. 1, 1976, p. 2; Associated Press, "Wanblee group asks BIA, FBI help in expelling 'outsiders,'" *Rapid City Journal*, Feb. 2, 1976, p. 1; United Press International, "FBI, BIA swarm Pine Ridge area looking for killer," ["swarm" was a gross exaggeration] *St. Paul Pioneer Press*, Feb. 2, 1976, p. 3; "Man shot to death in Pine Ridge outbreak," *Minneapolis Tribune*, Feb. 2, 1976, p. 2B; and other documents cited below.)

p. 229 **"Richard Lee was in Pine Ridge":** Interview of Charlie Abourezk by author, Rapid City, S.D., Aug. 2003.

p. 230 **"In those days," Guy Dull Knife said:** Interview of Guy Dull Knife by author, Potato Creek, S.D., Aug. 3, 2003.

p. 230 **The goons, for all their dubious reliability:** A typical account from the goons was that Dull Knife had walked out of his house, leveled what seemed to be an automatic rifle at people across the way, and opened fire. (FBI FD-302 report, interview of ███████ by SA ███████ [probably Fred Coward], MP 70-10945, interviewed Feb. 19, 1976, transcribed Feb. 26, 1976.) The goons' accounts on other matters, for example whether they had guns (as they clearly did), are badly conflicting. (FBI FD-302 report, interview of ███████ by SAs ███████ [one of whose initials were H.Q.C.], MP 70-10944, MP 70-10950, interviewed Feb. 3, 1976, transcribed Feb. 11, 1976.)

p. 230 **. . . and Dull Knife's father:** Guy Sr. was not fluent in English, so the interview was conducted through an interpreter, which might have allowed the FBI to color what he said. Also, it is clear from the FBI reports that the FBI was biased against the Dull Knifes. (FBI FD-302 report, interview of ███████ [Guy Dull Knife Sr.] by SAs ███████ [one of whom was probably George Haffner], MP 70-10944, interviewed Feb. 2, 1976, transcribed Feb. 16, 1976.) The friend who told a similar story may have been Richard Lee Lamont. (FBI FD-302 report, interview of ███████ by SAs ███████ [one of whom was probably George Haffner], MP 70-10944, interviewed Feb. 2, 1976, transcribed Feb. 16, 1976.)

p. 231 **. . . Byron DeSersa had fired no shots at all:** As the FBI wrote on February 4, 1976, "This investigation has determined that several of the reported victims (excluding Byron DeSersa) participated in acts of violence themselves, including shooting incidents during that weekend."

p. 231 **. . . seized Guy's gun and DeSersa's too:** The police said the guns were being taken to prevent further violence—AIM violence at least. The goons were allowed to keep their guns. ("This News Release Is Late 'But' For The Killers It Is Not Forgotten," *Crazy Horse News,* prepared by the Oglala Communications Center, May 29, 1976, in Byron DeSersa's FBI file.)

p. 231 **. . . the BIA officers did not even walk across the street:** FBI FD-302 report, interview of ███████, BIA police officer, by SAs ███████ (one of whom was probably Tom Greene), MP 70-10946, MP 70-10947, MP 70-10949, MP 70-10950, MP 70-10945, MP 70-10944, interviewed Feb. 2, 1976, transcribed Feb. 16, 1976; FBI FD-302 report, interview of ███████ by SAs ███████ (one of whom was probably Edward Diem), MP 70-10944, MP 70-10945, interviewed Feb. 2, 1976, transcribed Feb. 6, 1976.

p. 231 **. . . Webster Poor Bear ventured over to the goon house:** Webster Poor Bear was from the same extended family as Myrtle Poor Bear, of perjury fame. The story of Poor Bear going to the goons' house is from the goons. (Paul Riley, "Defendant testifies in DeSersa murder trial," *Rapid City Journal*, Feb. 25, 1977, p. 3.)

p. 233 "The black car that shot us up went past": I have condensed this quotation slightly. (McKiernan, *supra*.) Other accounts of the shooting are found in FBI FD-302 report, interview of ■■■■■ by SA ■■■■■ [probably Fred Coward], MP 70-10945, interviewed Jan. 31, 1976, transcribed Feb. 3, 1976. See also multiple reports with the same citation: FBI FD-302 report, interview of ■■■■■ by SA ■■■■■ [probably George Haffner], MP 70-10945, interviewed Jan. 31, 1976, transcribed Feb. 10, 1976; FBI FD-302 report, interview of ■■■■■ [George Bettelyoun] by SA ■■■■■ [probably Edward Diem], MP 70-10945, interviewed Jan. 31, 1976, transcribed Feb. 5, 1976, MP 70-10945; Transcript of Preliminary Hearing, *U.S. v. Winters, supra*, p. 40.

p. 235 Dr. Alvin Armstrong concluded that DeSersa: Autopsy report of Byron DeSersa, Alvin A. Armstrong, Jr., W.O. Brown, M.D. & Associates, P.C., Scottsbluff, Neb., received Jan. 31, 1976, reported Feb. 21, 1976. See also Paul Riley, "Doctor says DeSersa shouldn't have died," *Rapid City Journal*, Feb. 24, 1977, p. 3; FBI FD-302 report, interview of ■■■■■, BIA criminal investigator, by SA ■■■■■ [probably Fred Coward], MP 70-10945, interviewed Feb. 2, 1976, transcribed Feb. 3, 1976; FBI FD-302 report, interview of ■■■■■ [Dr. Alvin Armstrong], by SA ■■■■■, OM 70-1894, interviewed Feb. 20 & Mar. 1, 1976, transcribed Mar. 2, 1976; FBI teletype, from Rapid City, 70-NEW, Feb. 1, 1976, 12:10 p.m., *supra*.

p. 236 His boss was Bill Janklow: Associated Press, "Man arrested, charged with murder in shooting death of S.D. Indian," *Minneapolis Tribune*, Feb. 3, 1976, p. 1B.

p. 236 . . . Janklow would claim him for one of his informers: Deposition of William Janklow, *William Janklow v. Viking Press and Peter Matthiessen*, S.D. Circ. Ct., 2nd Circ., Civ. 83-1385, July 13, 1987, p. 308.

p. 236 One mole whom DeSersa mistook for a friend: The informer's name is censored in FBI documents released to me. (Handwritten FBI memo, from MPLS 70-NEW, UNSUBS: Byron DeSersa–Victim, CIR–Murder, to ASAC Rapid City, Feb. 1976; FBI memo, from SA ■■■■■, to SAC, Richard G. Held (70-New), re "Byron DeSersa, CIR," May 3, 1973.)

p. 236 . . . "described DECIRSA [sic] as the one": FBI report, title redacted, Oct. 15. 1973, p. 66.

p. 236 DeSersa traveled to Seattle, where he wound up: FBI nitel, from Seattle (157-1948), to Acting Director, re "Disorders by American Indians in South Dakota, Extremist Matters, American Indian Activities," June 1, 1973, 6:32 p.m.

p. 236 . . . almost certainly Gi or Jill Schafer: The reason one of the informers was almost certainly a Schafer is that the main informer apparently lived in New Orleans, whence the Schafers hailed and because the Schafers were quite familiar with DeSersa.

p. 237 . . . Chuck Richards had put a gun to the throat: In the FBI's version of Richards's threat to Amelia Lamont, a rifle-wielding Richards said, "You better get out of here, you bitch, or I'll kill you." He backed off when friends told him to leave her alone. (FBI FD-302 report, interview of ███████ by SAs ███████ [one of whom has initials M. C. S.], MP 70-10945, MP 70-10946, MP 70-10949, MP 70-10951, interviewed Feb. 4, 1976, transcribed Feb. 11, 1976.) In AIM's version, "Richards held a gun to her throat and said if he couldn't kill her husband, he would killer her. Some of his friends dragged him away." ("This News Release Is Late," *supra*.)

p. 237 "They were still shooting," Lamont later told: McKiernan asked, just to be sure, what precisely the policeman had said. Lamont answered, "He said, 'Well, get the hell out of there.' He said, 'They're shooting at you.'" (McKiernan, *supra*.) Gerald "Buddy" Brown was the officer who had the colloquy with Lamont. Both Brown and Lamont are dead. There were reports that BIA police cars had been shot at in Wanblee that night; naturally, the cops did not return fire or investigate or arrest the shooters.

p. 238 The FBI would eventually decide that Lamont: FBI FD-302 report, interview of ███████ by SAs ███████ [one of whom has initials J. W. G.], MP 70-10949, MP 70-10948, MP 70-10950, interviewed Feb. 4, 1976, transcribed Feb. 10, 1976. The FBI's insistence on trying to find fault with Lamont, the evidence notwithstanding, is a prime example of how agents often reported the facts of a case accurately but in such a way as to cast disfavor on people they disliked.

p. 238 ". . . it is clear that Federal officers": Letter from William H. Webster, FBI Director, to Elizabeth W. Robbins, Minneapolis, May 1, 1978, in WKLDOC Archives.

p. 239 Bettelyoun had drawn the agents' attention to: McKiernan, *supra*. The FBI's records verify that Bettelyoun described the cars and their owners for the FBI. (FBI FD-302 report, interview of ███████ [George Bettelyoun], *supra*.)

p. 239 "After the FBI left," Abourezk said: Abourezk interview, *supra*. See also FBI FD-302 report, interview of ███████ [probably Charlie Abourezk] by SA ███████, MP 70-10946, MP 70-10944, MP 70-10945, MP 70-10947, MP 70-10948, MP 70-10949, MP 70-10950, MP 70-10951, interviewed Feb. 2, 1976, transcribed Feb. 10, 1976. There is no doubt that the goons were shooting throughout the night, nor that Lonnie Bettelyoun was one of the most active shooters. For example, per one goon, "At one point in the ███████ house, ███████ he observed ███████ [Lonnie Bettelyoun] with a big handgun which was kept in a brown leather holster and strapped to ███████ [Bettelyoun's] right side, take this big revolver outside of the house while it was dark and shot it. ███████ that he did not know if ███████ [Bettelyoun] shot it at anything or if he shot it into the air." (FBI FD-302 report, interview of ███ by SAs ███ [one of whom was probably Fred Coward], MP 70-10945, interview date Feb. 9, 1976, transcribed Feb. 13, 1976. See also FBI FD-302 report, interview of ███ by SAs ███ [one of whom was probably Fred Coward], MP 70-10945, interviewed Feb. 19, 1976, transcribed Feb. 26, 1976; FBI FD-302 report, interview of ███ [Lonnie Bettelyoun] by SA ███ [initials L. L. D.], MP 70-10945, interviewed Feb. 3, 1976, transcribed Feb. 5, 1976.)

p. 240 Later that night a firebomb was thrown: FBI FD-302 report, interview of ███, BIA police officer, by SAs ███ [one of whom was probably Tom Greene], MP 70-10946, MP 70-10947, MP 70-10949, MP 70-10950, MP 70-10945, MP 70-10944, interviewed Feb. 2, 1976, transcribed Feb. 16, 1976; FBI FD-302 report, interview of ███ by SAs ███ [one of whom has initials H. Q. C.], MP 70-10944, MP 70-10947, interviewed Feb. 4, 1976, transcribed Feb. 11, 1976.

p. 241 ". . . was the captain, Skee Jacobs": His given name was Joseph Jacobs. FBI agent Fred Coward said Captain Jacobs was one of the lawmen on the scene in Wanblee on January 31 who did nothing about the goons. (Transcript of Preliminary Hearing, *U.S. v. Winters, supra,* p. 44–5.)

p. 241 "Her brother, Ted Big Crow, was": Ted Big Crow declined to speak with me.

p. 242 "I'll be the first to admit": Associated Press, "Officials admit mistakes in handling murder case," *Rapid City Journal,* Feb. 4, 1976, p. 2.

p. 242 The mistakes, however, were the BIA's: Associated Press, "Official denies BIA mishandled Wanblee shooting incident," *Rapid City Journal,* Feb. 17, 1976, p. 2.

p. 242 . . . the FBI was "an investigative agency and is not": Associated Press, "Man held without bond in shooting," *Rapid City Journal,* Feb. 3, 1976, p. 1.

p. 242 The distinction was again lost on Oglalas: Also, the FBI was not shy about calling the law-enforcement shots in the Oglala firefight: As Rolland Dewing noted, "The BIA police were ready to assault the Jumping Bull encampment and were frustrated almost to the point of physically confronting the FBI agents who stopped them." (Rolland Dewing, *Wounded Knee II,* Great Plains Network/Pine Hills Pr., 1995, p. 159.)

p. 242 . . . Zigrossi, who soon retracted even his criticism: Zigrossi was offended at even having to answer the charges—a waste, he wrote, of his agents' "investigative and administrative time which could best be put forth into the conducting of business as an investigative agency." (FBI report, "Inquiry from U.S. Commission on Civil Rights Concerning Law Enforcement on Pine Ridge Indian Reservation, South Dakota," Rapid City, S.D., May 27, 1976, p. 30–2.)

p. 242 "The officers who responded handled": Associated Press, "Officials admit mistakes," *supra.* (The officials of the headline who admitted mistakes were not of the BIA.)

p. 242 "There is nothing at the present time": Associated Press, "Official denies BIA mishandled," *supra*. Sayers said he would not investigate his officers. Nor would he let citizens question them. See also "Wanblee meeting reset," *Rapid City Journal*, Feb. 12, 1976, p. 3.

p. 243 . . . Charles Winters . . . told his uncle: Complaint for violation of USC 18, Sections 1153 and 1111, 1st Degree Murder, *U.S. v. Charles David Winters, a/k/a Elmer Winters*, U.S. Dist. Ct., W. Div. S.D., Feb. 2, 1976; Transcript of Preliminary Hearing, *U.S. v. Winters, supra*, p. 14 (testimony of Joseph "Skee" Jacobs); FBI FD-302 report, interview of ██████ by SA ██████ [probably Fred Coward], MP 70-10945, interviewed Feb. 2, 1976, transcribed Feb. 3, 1976.

p. 243 . . . he told a clutch of BIA and FBI men: FBI FD-302 report, interview of Elmer Winters, by SA ██████ [probably Fred Coward], MP 70-10945, interviewed Feb. 2, 1976, transcribed Feb. 3, 1976.

p. 243 . . . "apprehended through the investigative efforts": FBI press release, FBI Minneapolis, Feb. 2, 1976. Also, "The FBI said that Winters was arrested near Wanblee Saturday evening"—when in fact he was not arrested until Monday. (Associated Press, "Officials admit mistakes," *supra*.)

p. 244 Agents knew (because AIMers told them on Saturday): FBI report, "Inquiry from U.S. Commission on Civil Rights," *supra*, p. 3; FBI nitel, from Rapid City, 70-NEW, Feb. 1, 1976, *supra*.

p. 244 . . . the FBI was in no hurry to interview: Eventually, in the coming days and weeks, the FBI sought interviews with the suspects, but not in the first days after the shooting. The FBI's field reports said Lonnie Bettelyoun was interviewed on February 2. The FBI's report on the "Inquiry from U.S. Commission on Civil Rights" (*supra*) said February 3.

p. 244 . . . "what appears to be an indentation as a result": FBI airtel, from SAC, Minneapolis (70-10945), to Director, FBI (Attention: FBI Laboratory), re ██████ Dale Francis Janis, Charles David Winters, Byron Carl De Sersa, aka—Victim (deceased), Feb. 20, 1976.

p. 245 The FBI belatedly took their statements: FBI report, "Inquiry from U.S. Commission on Civil Rights," *supra*, p. 3; FBI FD-302 report, interview of ██████ by SAs ██████ [one of whom was probably Fred Coward], MP 70-10945, interviewed Feb. 10, 1976, transcribed Feb. 17, 1976; FBI FD-302 report, interview of ██████ by SAs ██████ [one of whom was probably Fred Coward], MP 70-10945, interviewed Feb. 9, 1976, transcribed Feb. 13, 1976; FBI FD-302 report, interview of ██████ by SA ██████ [probably Fred Coward], MP 70-10945, interviewed Feb. 17, 1976, transcribed Feb. 26, 1976; FBI FD-302 report, interview of ██████ by SAs ██████ [one of whom was probably Fred Coward], MP 70-10945, interviewed Jan. 31, 1976, transcribed Feb. 3, 1976; FBI FD-302 report, interview of ██████ by SA ██████, MP 70-10945, interviewed June

3, 1976, transcribed June 8, 1976; FBI airtel, from SAC, Minneapolis (70-10945), Feb. 20, 1976, *supra*.

p. 245 The ballistics evidence eventually confirmed: Report from FBI Laboratory, to SAC, Minneapolis (70-10945), FBI file 70-67421, May 13, 1976.

p. 245 The prosecutors in turn let five months: FBI memo, Rapid City, S.D., field ofc. file 70-10945, Apr. 16, 1976; FBI memo, from ASAC, Rapid City (70-10945)(P), to SAC, Minneapolis, re "Charles David Winters, aka; et al; Byron Lee De Sersa, aka—Victim (deceased); CIR—Murder," May 25, 1976; FBI FD-204 report of Rapid City, S.D. Ofc., 70-10945, Title "▓▓▓▓▓▓ [Lonnie Dean Bettelyoun et al]; Byron Lee DeSersa—Victim (deceased)," June 18, 1976; Indictment, *U.S. v. Dale Francis Catches a/k/a Dale Francis Janis, Lonnie Dean Bettelyoun, Billy Dean Wilson*, U.S. Dist. Ct., W. Div. S.D., CR 76-5054, undated but date appears to be July 30, 1976.

p. 245 . . . only after Winters recanted his confession: When he recanted for the last time, Winters told prosecutors what AIM had suspected: he had only confessed to the murder after being threatened by Chuck Richards and Billy Wilson. To the stick of threatened violence, Richards and Wilson had added the carrot of money and lawyers to defend Winters. But after Winters confessed, none of the promised goods materialized—the bastards, he said, hadn't even visited him. (*U.S. v. Charles David Winters, a/k/a Elmer Winters*, U.S. Dist. Ct., W. Div. S.D., CR 76-5027-1, various pleadings, 1976. See also Statement of Charles D. Winters to FBI, Sioux Falls, S.D., July 28, 1976; FBI notes re Charles D. Winters, file 70-10945, date uncertain; Transcript of Hearings, *U.S. v. Charles David Winters, a/k/a Elmer Winters*, U.S. Dist. Ct., W. Div. S.D., CR76-5027-1, Aug. 13, 1976, and Oct. 21, 1976, p. 12.)

p. 246 . . . file shows that a lawman . . . arrived at the goons': The lawman's statement is recorded in FBI FD-302 report, interview of ▓▓▓▓▓▓, interviewed Feb. 19, 1976, transcribed Feb. 20, 1976, MP 70-10945-103, MP 70-10944, MP 70-10946, MP 70-10947, MP 70-10948, MP 70-10949, MP 70-10950, MP 70-10951, MP 70-10981, MP 70-10982.

p. 246 The lawman was either the sheriff: AIMers said it was a sheriff: "On January 31, just prior to the shootings the sheriff from the county in which Wanblee is located was meeting with the goons at Rita Bettelyoun's house." ("This News Release Is Late," *supra*.)

p. 246 "At no time while he was in Wanblee": Apparently, when the lawman said he had heard of no firing in Wanblee, this included even the shooting of the Dull Knifes' house, about which everyone in Wanblee was talking. After the shooting at the goons' house that evening died down, the lawman neither called the Pine Ridge police nor took statements himself although he was cross-deputized to enforce the law on the reservation.

Neither the BIA nor the FBI recorded any rounds having hit the goons' house. (FBI FD-302 interview of ■■■■■■, Feb. 19, 1976, *supra*.)

p. 246 "We just warmed up a car": The statements of the goons can be found in FBI report, "Inquiry from U.S. Commission on Civil Rights," *supra*, p. 5–6; FBI FD-302 report, interview of ■■■■■■ by SAs ■■■■■■ [one was probably Fred Coward], interviewed Feb. 10, 1976, transcribed Feb. 13, 1976, MP 70-10945; FBI FD-302 report, interview of ■■■■■■ by SAs ■■■■■■ [one was probably Fred Coward], interviewed Feb. 10, 1976, transcribed Feb. 17, 1976, MP 70-10945; FBI FD-302 report, interview of ■■■■■ by SAs ■■■■■■ [one of whom was probably Fred Coward], interviewed Feb. 18, 1976, transcribed Feb. 26, 1976, MP 70-10945; Memo from ASAC, Rapid City (70-10945)(P), to SAC, Minneapolis, Subject Charles David Winters et al; Byron Lee DeSersa—victim (deceased); CIR—Murder, May 25, 1976.

p. 247 Of the two who said otherwise: The one who lied out of fear is discussed by the FBI in FBI FD-302 report, interview of ■■■■■■ by SAs ■■■■■■ [one was probably Fred Coward], interviewed Feb. 9, 1976, transcribed Feb. 13, 1976, MP 70-10945.

p. 247 . . . his presence at the festivities was never again mentioned: When the FBI's Norm Zigrossi reported on the events at Wanblee to his bosses at the Justice Department, he did not mention the lawman at all. (Memo from ASAC, Rapid City (70-10945)(P), to SAC, Minneapolis, May 25, 1976, *supra*.)

p. 247 . . . Elmer Winters struck a deal: Statement of Charles D. Winters, July 28, 1976, *supra*; FBI notes re Charles D. Winters, date uncertain, *supra*. For Winters's plea and sentencing, see Transcript of Hearings, *U.S. v. Winters*, *supra*, p. 5; FBI FD-36 form, teletype from Rapid City (70-10945)(P), to Director (70-67421)(Routine), Aug. 17, 1976; FBI FD-36 form, teletype from Rapid City (70-10945)(P), to Director (70-67421)(Routine), Jan. 12, 1977.

p. 247 R. D. Hurd was among his prosecutors: Hurd's performance in convicting Janis would seem to indicate that the prosecutors were not always in league with the goons. AIMers, however, have argued that the conviction of the minor Janis allowed prosecutors to say they had done their work—thereby giving them cover for botching the convictions of the adult goons, for whom a murder conviction would have meant much longer sentences. The FBI gave commendations to assistant U.S. attorneys Hurd and William Boyd for their work on all of the DeSersa cases. (Letter from FBI Director Clarence M. Kelley, to U.S. Attorney William F. Clayton, Feb. 8, 1977.)

p. 247 . . . but apparently Janis admitted firing: "Janis found guilty in murder case," *Rapid City Journal*, January 12, 1977, p. 2.

p. 247 . . . Judge Bogue permitted the murderer to remain at large: FBI FD-36 form, from Rapid City, to Director, Jan. 12, 1977, *supra*.

p. 247 When Janis was finally incarcerated: "Convicted slayer sentenced Monday," *Rapid City Journal*, May 17, 1977, p. 8; FBI report, missing cover page, RC 70-10945, undated but sometime between May 16 and May 26, 1977, p. 2.

p. 247 . . . expected that Bettelyoun and Wilson would take a plea: On January 25, 1977, agents in Rapid City wrote, "there is every indication they will enter pleas in the immediate future." (Memo, from ASAC Rapid City, to FBI Director (Attn: Finance & Personnel), subject either missing or redacted, Jan. 25, 1977.)

p. 248 They said they had shot to kill: "I was afraid he was going to kill me," Bettelyoun explained. ("Murder trial defendants say they 'would do it again,'" *Rapid City Journal*, Mar. 2, 1977, p. 2. See also "Jury finds two innocent of killing in DeSersa case," *Rapid City Journal*, Mar. 3, 1977, p. 2; Paul Riley, "Defendant testifies in DeSersa murder trial," *Rapid City Journal*, Feb. 25, 1977, p. 3.)

p. 248 (The lone witness who said otherwise also claimed): This lying witness is quoted in FBI FD-302 report, interview of ■■■■■ by SA ■■■■■ [probably Fred Coward], interviewed Mar. 9, 1976, transcribed Mar. 11, 1976, RC 70-10945. The FBI had examined DeSersa's car for signs of a sideswiping and found none. (FBI FD-302 report, by SAs ■■■■■ [one was probably Fred Coward], events of Mar. 3, 1976, transcribed Mar. 10, 1976, RC 70-10945.)

p. 248 . . . the U.S. attorney supported his cry: United States' Response to Defendant's Motion for Reduction of Sentence, *U.S. v. Charles David Winters, a/k/a Elmer Winters*, U.S. Dist. Ct., W. Div. S.D., CR 76-5027-1, Jan. 17, 1977.

p. 248 . . . and Bogue lopped two years off his term: Order, *U.S. v. Charles David Winters, a/k/a Elmer Winters*, U.S. Dist. Ct., W. Div. S.D., CR76-5027, Mar. 3, 1977. At the time, federal judges were allowed to reconsider sentences within six months of issuing them.

p. 248 Like Janis, Winters ended up serving: Peter Matthiessen, *In the Spirit of Crazy Horse*, Viking, 1991, p. 254–5.

CHAPTER 12

p. 249 . . . the sheriff's office . . . received a distress call: David Maruffo called the police around 11 p.m. (Defense notes, Skyhorse/Mohawk Legal Defense Fund, 1977 or 1978, in Center of Southwest Studies, record group 1: Theodore Hetzel Personal Papers, series 1.2, file 28, Fort Lewis College, Durango, Colo.)

p. 249 The deputies searched the camp's buildings: Details about the arrests made that night and about the events of the next few days are in "Your Information Might Save Their Lives," *Akwesasne Notes*, early spring 1976, p. 7; "Trial Update #30," Skyhorse/Mohawk Defense Committee, undated but ca. Jan. 1978, p. 2; "Trial Update

#31," Skyhorse/Mohawk Defense Committee, undated but ca. Jan. 1978, p. 1; "Judge Finds Murder Trial Humorous," *Akwesasne Notes*, late autumn 1976, p. 8.

p. 251 So the group urged the lawyers to disband: Peter Matthiessen, *In the Spirit of Crazy Horse*, Viking Pr., 1991, p. 113, 609. Note, however, that Matthiessen is wrong about many of the details of the Skyhorse/Mohawk case. See also Skyhorse/Mohawk Offense/Defense Committee newsletter, Jan. 19, 1978, p. 2; Affidavit of Paula Giese, *State of California v. Paul Durant and Richard B. Mohawk*, Ventura Co. Cir. Ct., Cal., Apr. 15, 1976, p. 7.

p. 251 . . . "he had beaten an elderly Indian woman": "Your Information Might Save Their Lives," *supra*; Giese affidavit, *supra*. See also "Free Paul Skyhorse & Richard Mohawk," pamphlet, 1977 or 1978, in Indians of North America: Skyhorse/Mohawk Defense Committee Collection, Special Collections Library, Univ. of Michigan; International Indian Treaty Council, "The Human Rights Case of Paul Skyhorse and Richard Mohawk," pamphlet, in WKLDOC Archives. Robert Morgan appears not to have been at Camp 13 at the time of the murder.

p. 252 . . . Banks and Durham . . . took an afternoon to inspect the camp: Matthiessen, *supra*, p. 113.

p. 252 . . . two of the campers robbed a neighbor: On October 8, 1974, Robin Louis Black Cloud, a.k.a. David Cloud West, and Clinton Jerome Rising Sun, a.k.a. Red Sun, robbed Herrell A. Wood. They were later convicted. (Giese affidavit, *supra*, p. 3.) After Rising Sun's conviction, he found unexpected friends. The BIA wrote Rising Sun's judge, "It is recommended that he be turned over to the Bureau of Indian Affairs program for training in his future endeavors. Our office is willing to assist him with the following services: financial assistance while in school, to include monies for transportation, food, housing, and clothing. Upon completion of training, assistance in locating a job." The judge agreed. Wrote one observer, "This solicitude on the part of the BIA is astonishing." AIMers suspected Rising Sun was treated well in exchange for helping with the prosecution of Skyhorse and Mohawk. ("Your Information Might Save Their Lives," *supra*.)

p. 252 . . . Redshirt, Broussard, and Eaglestaff did not appear to be AIM: Redshirt said at the trial of Skyhorse and Mohawk that he had not been active in AIM since about 1971. ("Trial Update #3: Major Prosecution Witness Admits Lying over 1000 Times," Skyhorse/Mohawk Defense Committee, June 17, 1977, p. 4; see also Giese Affidavit, *supra*.)

p. 253 Durham claimed a PhD in psychology: The sanity hearing was on December 3, 1974. Durham may have been found out by AIM's leadership by this point, but he had yet to be publicly exposed. (Giese affidavit, *supra*, p. 10; "Free Paul Skyhorse & Richard Mohawk," *supra*. See also "Notice of Motion and Motion for Dismissal of Evidence and for Other Appropriate Sanctions Because of Governmental Misconduct; Declaration;

Memorandum of Law," *State of California v. Paul Skyhorse and Richard Mohawk*, CR-10965, Ventura Co. Cir. Ct., Cal., Mar. 8, 1977, p. 2.)

p. 253 . . . AIMers tried to have him charged with perjury: Skyhorse and Mohawk also filed a civil rights lawsuit accusing prosecutors of conspiracy to solicit perjury against them. The lawsuit failed. ("The Skyhorse/Mohawk Trial," pamphlet, in Center of Southwest Studies, record group 1: Theodore Hetzel Personal Papers, series 1.2, file 29, Fort Lewis College, Durango, Colo.)

p. 254 "We have spoken with Richard Erwin": ("Judge Finds Murder Trial Humorous," *supra*.)

p. 254 . . . "insane troublemakers," that judge called them: This was Judge Ben Ruffner. ("Judge Finds Murder Trial Humorous," *supra*.)

p. 255 "My acquaintances have questioned my": I have condensed this quotation slightly. ("Your Information Might Save Their Lives," *supra*.)

p. 255 The informer was Virginia DeLuce: Information about DeLuce can be found in Michele Toulan, "Pin-up girl leaves wartime legacy," Mar. 11, 2004, iBerkshires.com, newmarlborough.iberkshire.com/story.php?story_id=13729, viewed Apr. 2004; Rolland Dewing, *Wounded Knee II*, Great Plains Network/Pine Hills Pr., 1995, p. 151; "Your Information Might Save Their Lives," *supra*; note by Paula Giese on webpage "Navajo-Hopi Dispute Links," www.kstrom.net/isk/maps/az/navhoplinks.html, viewed Apr. 2004; Matthiessen, *supra*, p. 112; "Dirty Trick One: Mohawk and Skyhorse," *Akwesasne Notes*, Sept. 1977, p. 21.

p. 256 . . . she may have written a book about the Diné: The book was said to have been titled *Life Among the Navajo*, which I have never succeeded in finding.

p. 256 . . . AIMers suspected her of continuing to pay: Skyhorse/Mohawk Offense/Defense Committee newsletter, Jan. 19, 1978, p. 2.

p. 256 . . . DeLuce had driven Skyhorse and Mohawk: The rally was at the federal building. It was called to demand the release of Sarah Bad Heart Bull, and Anna Mae Aquash was probably in attendance. ("Dirty Trick One," *supra*; Skyhorse/Mohawk Offense/Defense Committee newsletter, Jan. 19, 1978, p. 2.)

p. 257 The government disclosed DeLuce: The behind-the-scenes debate about whether DeLuce should be revealed is discussed in "Dirty Trick One," *supra*. Neither John Dobroth, the district attorney, nor Michael Bradbury, his assistant, responded to requests to be interviewed for this book. For Dobroth in particular, it was possible I did not have his correct contact information.

p. 257 "Before this," one of the investigators said: "Dirty Trick One," *supra*.

p. 257 She tracked down their lawyers and offered: Marsh told Giese he did not regard the case as having any political implications. ("Your Information Might Save Their Lives," *supra*.) Neither Kosmo nor Marsh responded to requests to be interviewed for this book.

p. 258 In the summer of 1976 the entertainment: The events surrounding the bar association performance can be found in "Judge Finds Murder Trial Humorous," *supra*; "Free Paul Skyhorse & Richard Mohawk," *supra*.

p. 258 The skit's author was the lawyer: The lawyer was Stephen V. Perren.

p. 259 She had shared a cell with Holly Broussard: The witness was Norma Gonzalez. ("Judge Finds Murder Trial Humorous," *supra*.) Gonzalez's story about Eaglestaff's comments was seconded at trial by another woman, Ramona Bland, who had shared a cell with Eaglestaff for three months. She said Eaglestaff confessed the murder to her and that Eaglestaff never said Skyhorse or Mohawk was present. ("Trial Update #35," Skyhorse/Mohawk Defense Committee, undated but ca. Feb. 1978, p. 1.)

p. 259 . . . jailed three days before the matter was sorted out: "Trial Update #21," Skyhorse/Mohawk Defense Committee, undated but ca. Nov. 1977, p. 1.

p. 259 . . . the accused were admitted to a hospital: They were admitted to the county hospital on February 23, 1977. (Article, title unknown, *Seven Days*, Apr. 11, 1977, reproduced by Natl. Council of Churches, in Center of Southwest Studies, record group 1: Theodore Hetzel Personal Papers, series 1.2, file 31, Fort Lewis College, Durango, Colo.) According to several documents, in May doctors forced the court to hospitalize both men after finding evidence of malnutrition, eye damage from multiple Macings, and possible blood-clotting in Mohawk's head. It is possible, however, that these sources were conflating the medical evaluations of May with the hospitalization of February since the trial, after all, began in May. (See, e.g., "Free Paul Skyhorse & Richard Mohawk," *supra*.)

p. 260 . . . behind bars longer than any pretrial defendants: "Free Paul Skyhorse & Richard Mohawk," *supra*; untitled, undated pamphlet, Skyhorse-Mohawk Defense Committee, late 1977 or early 1978; defense notes, Skyhorse/Mohawk Legal Defense Fund, *supra*. For at least part of their trial, the defendants were isolated behind a bulletproof glass shield that ran the width of the courtroom, which made them seem rather dangerous. (Letter from Natl. Council of Churches, Div. of Church and Society, undated, in Center of Southwest Studies, record group 1: Theodore Hetzel Personal Papers, series 1.2, file 28, Fort Lewis College, Durango, Colo.)

p. 260 Carradine had a vigorous social relationship: "Your Information Might Save Their Lives," *supra*.

p. 261 On cross-examination, defense lawyers reminded Redshirt: Redshirt's testimony can be found at "Trial Update #2: Prosecution's Key Witness Implicates A.I.M. Members," Skyhorse/Mohawk Defense Committee, June 14, 1977; "Trial Update #3: Major Prosecution Witness Admits Lying over 1000 Times," Skyhorse/Mohawk Defense Committee, June 17, 1977; "Free Paul Skyhorse & Richard Mohawk," *supra*.

p. 262 Defense lawyers suggested that the judge's salary: Dodson said he had no financial interest in the continuation of the trial. ("Trial Update #4: Judge Refuses to Release Skyhorse & Mohawk Despite Agreement," Skyhorse/Mohawk Defense Committee, June 14, 1977, p. 1; "Free Paul Skyhorse & Richard Mohawk," *supra*; untitled, undated pamphlet, Skyhorse-Mohawk Defense Committee, late 1977 or early 1978.)

p. 262 Holly Broussard admitted to joining in: Asked if she had enjoyed herself during the assault on Aird, Broussard said she had, "otherwise I wouldn't have done it." Like Redshirt, she confessed or was caught in a catalog of lies.

p. 263 . . . the D.A. told her that the original knife had been lost: "Skyhorse/Mohawk Case," typed transcription of article, *supra*; "Trial Update #4," *supra*; "Trial Update #5," Skyhorse/Mohawk Defense Committee, July 1, 1977. The detective who took the knife from Broussard at the crime scene was Austin Chafee, Ventura County Sheriff's Department.

p. 263 But a lone officer followed his colleagues: Detective Roger Kerr said he saw a folded pocketknife with a black handle—Broussard's knife—when he was at the East Valley Sheriff's Station. Kerr also saw Broussard's purse and bloody gloves, which also later went missing. His supervisor was Harvey Taylor. ("Trial Update #29," Skyhorse/Mohawk Defense Committee, undated but ca. Jan. 1978, p. 2; "Trial Update #32," Skyhorse/Mohawk Defense Committee, Jan. 27, 1978, p. 1.)

p. 263 . . . deputies said they had meant to send it to the lab: "Trial Update #11," Skyhorse/Mohawk Defense Committee, Aug. 12, 1977, p. 1.

p. 263 . . . Carmella Fish, said prosecutors had badgered her: "Trial Update #5," *supra*; defense notes, Skyhorse/Mohawk Legal Defense Fund, *supra*.

p. 264 . . . the investigator "mentally forced" her to say: The investigator was Cruz Reyna. "I felt his vibes that I'd best cooperate with what he [Reyna] wanted to hear," Fish said. "I just wanted him to leave. I wanted the interview to end." (United Press International, "Indian Trial Witness Calls Testimony 'Forced,'" *New York Times*, July 7, 1977.) Fish was not treated kindly in court. Judge Dodson called her testimony "evasive." He appears to have said no such thing about Broussard's or Redshirt's mendacious testimony. During one court recess, she did not return immediately; she had taken a walk to compose herself. The prosecutor asked Dodson to issue an order for her arrest, and he did. She returned on her own after a few minutes. ("Trial Update #5," *supra*, p. 3.)

p. 264 Six guards were called to the stand: "Trial Update #19," Skyhorse/Mohawk Defense Committee, undated but ca. Oct. 1977, p. 1–2; "Trial Update #21," Skyhorse/Mohawk Defense Committee, undated but ca. Nov. 1977.

p. 264 "If you kill Skyhorse and Mohawk": The inmate was Ronald Escobedo; he said inmates in nearby cells heard the proposition. ("Trial Update #19," Skyhorse/Mohawk Defense Committee, undated but ca. Oct. 1977, p. 2; Richard C. Paddock, "Jail Inmate

Says Deputy Solicited Murder of Skyhorse," *Los Angeles Times*, Oct. 19, 1977; Richard C. Paddock, "Jail Death Threat Reported by Indian," *Los Angeles Times*, Oct. 21, 1977.)

p. 264 The prosecution rebutted by producing an inmate: The prosecution's inmate was Robert Granger. The two supposed witnesses were inmates Roy Richards and Larry Steiner. ("Trial Update #22," Skyhorse/Mohawk Defense Committee, Nov. 11, 1977, p. 2; defense notes, Skyhorse/Mohawk Legal Defense Fund.)

p. 264 Judge Dodson weighed the evidence and said: Dodson ruled that "all allegations of misconduct or wrongdoing on the part of any Deputy Sheriff were and are false" and "none of the inmate witnesses was credible." Dodson scolded judges for meddling in the internal affairs of jails: "Too many Courts with no known expertise or qualification have too often made orders affecting the operation of schools, hospitals and jails. . . . It is not for judges to administer but to judge." ("Trial Update #21," *supra*, p. 2.) The California Supreme Court stayed Dodson's order revoking Skyhorse's and Mohawk's rights. ("Trial Update #25," Skyhorse/Mohawk Defense Committee, undated but ca. Dec. 1977, p. 1.) Months later, Skyhorse asked Dodson to restore their rights as co-counsels. Dodson denied the request. ("Trial Update #29," Skyhorse/Mohawk Defense Committee, undated but ca. Jan. 1978, p. 1.)

On December 19, a couple of months after Dodson opined that judges should not tinker with jails, Skyhorse arrived in court with an egg-sized contusion on his forehead, with some of his hair pulled out, with his nose and brow bloodied, and with his "unbreakable" prison-issue glasses broken. He had been beaten by sheriff's deputies in the courthouse parking garage. Dodson accepted the deputies' story that Skyhorse, cuffed at the hands, shackled at the ankles, and further hobbled by a waist chain to which all the other restraints were linked, had "viciously attacked a sheriff's deputy" while "he was being unhandcuffed." Skyhorse's story was that he had tried to lift the sagging waist chain, which was causing the handcuffs to dig into his wrists, when a deputy objected. Before Skyhorse could respond, the deputy hit him in the ribs with a blackjack and shoved him to the ground. Grabbing Skyhorse by his hair, the deputy slammed his head against the concrete several times. The sheriff's office described Skyhorse's injuries as "a small bump over his left eye and a scratch on the bridge of his nose." The lawmen told Judge Dodson that Skyhorse had been X-rayed but that the tests found no broken ribs or facial bones. Skyhorse said he was never X-rayed. ("Trial Update #28," Skyhorse/Mohawk Defense Committee, Dec. 23, 1977, p. 1.)

p. 265 . . . Frank Sexton, who testified that he had seen: "Trial Update #27," Skyhorse/Mohawk Defense Committee, Dec. 15, 1977, p. 2–3; "Trial Update #30," Skyhorse/Mohawk Defense Committee, undated but ca. Jan. 1978. The defense produced witnesses who had not been on benders and who had seen Skyhorse's pants that day and said there was no blood on them. ("Trial Update #27," *supra*, p. 1; "Trial Update #29," *supra*, p. 1.)

p. 265 The defense had only one important matter: The truth about Skyhorse and Mohawk's involvement in the night's events was probably the story (or one like it) put forward by the defense team. Namely: Skyhorse and Mohawk had been listening to music in the upstairs of one of the camp's buildings with Amy Broken Leg. Broken Leg went downstairs and saw Marvin Redshirt crouching over the cab driver, who had been brought into the building after the beating. She came back upstairs and told Skyhorse and Mohawk about it. Afraid, Skyhorse and Mohawk went out a back way and hid in a cave while they decided what to do. They returned to camp briefly, saw blood all over the camp kitchen, and fled. (Defense notes, Skyhorse/Mohawk Legal Defense Fund, *supra*.)

p. 265 The defense put the question to a police sergeant: The sergeant was Charles Rudd. He had introduced the FBI agents to Detectives McCoy and McKinley, who also admitted that Rudd had done so. ("Trial Update #34," Skyhorse/Mohawk Defense Committee, undated but ca. Feb. 1978, p. 4.)

p. 265 He also quashed every other attempt by the defense: Dodson once explained his abhorrence for political defenses by saying he did not want the trial to be "turned into a political circus." (Skyhorse/Mohawk Offense/Defense Committee newsletter, Jan. 19, 1978, p. 2.)

p. 265 On May 24, 1978, the jury acquitted: "Trial Update #42," Skyhorse/Mohawk Defense Committee, undated but ca. May 1978.

p. 266 "incompetent in the utter, utter, utter, ultimate": Hultman made his remark to an appellate court on April 12, 1978. (Quoted in *David Price v. Viking Penguin, Inc.*, 881 F.2d 1442, U.S. Ct. of Appeals, 8th Cir., 1989.)

CHAPTER 13

p. 271 The Cadillac that killed Randy Scott: Accounts of the crash can be found in Steve Young, "Strangers' lives entwine at crash site," *Sioux Falls Argus Leader*, Dec. 3, 2003; Richard Meryhew, "Witness: Before crash, Janklow raced past another vehicle," *Minneapolis Star Tribune*, Dec. 3, 2003; P. J. Huffstutter, "Tape Shown Jury Captures Janklow's Words, Horror," *Los Angeles Times*, Dec. 3, 2003; Jon Walker and Steve Young, "At crash scene, Janklow said blood sugar 'fine,' " *Sioux Falls Argus Leader*, Dec. 4, 2003; Jon Walker, "Debris, dust, 'body flying into the air,' " *Sioux Falls Argus Leader*, Dec. 3, 2003; Ben Shouse, "'95 Cadillac's black box offers scant speed data," Sioux Falls Argus Leader, Dec. 5, 2003; Denise Ross, "Accident expert calls speed estimate wrong," *Rapid City Journal*, Dec. 2003; Jon Walker, "Janklow didn't eat, witnesses say," *Sioux Falls Argus Leader*, Dec. 5, 2003.

p. 272 "I was going south, going to Brandon": David Kranz, "Janklow told cop: I wasn't speeding," *Sioux Falls Argus Leader*, Nov. 19, 2003; Walker, "Debris, dust, 'body flying into the air,' " *supra*.

p. 273 "We feel there is a beacon in California": I have condensed this quotation slightly. For five of the program's seven years, ninety-three people were transported from Dakota to California for alleged crimes including forgery, burglary, theft, and indecent exposure. (Deposition of William Janklow, *William Janklow v. Viking Press and Peter Matthiessen*, S.D. Circ. Ct., 2nd Circ., Civ. 83-1385, July 13, 1987, p. 424. Discussed in the deposition is "South Dakota Exporting Suspects," *New York Times*, Jan. 4, 1982.)

p. 274 . . . he declared that anyone found with dynamite: Later he claimed that he had not said that anyone caught with dynamite should be detonated: "What I did say is any-body caught trying to set off dynamite, it would detonate on them, and if it blew up, we would arrest what was left for possession of dynamite." (Janklow Deposition, *supra*, p. 100.)

p. 274 . . . blacklisted at state agencies: (Janklow deposition, *supra*, p. 468; Molly Ivins, "It's Rarely Politics as Usual to South Dakota Governor," *New York Times*, Aug. 30, 1980, p. 6.)

p. 275 . . . and, time again, judged unfounded: Associated Press, "Supreme Court Upholds Dismissal of Damage Suit Against 3 Lawyers," *Sioux Falls Argus Leader*, Mar. 27, 1976; Janklow deposition, *supra*, p. 35–6; Plaintiff's Answers to Defendants' First Set of Interrogatories and Request, *William Janklow v. Newsweek, Inc.*, U.S. Dist. Ct., S.D., Civ. 83-4023, June 14, 1983, p. 50.

p. 275 Such was the case with . . . *Newsweek*: The story was "Dennis Banks's Last Stand," *Newsweek*, Mar. 21, 1983, p. 28. The lawsuit was *William Janklow v. Newsweek, Inc.*, *supra*.

p. 275 Janklow demanded millions: *Janklow v. Viking and Matthiessen*, *supra*. Janklow sued not only Matthiessen and Viking but also bookstores that sold *Crazy Horse* in South Dakota—a blatantly frivolous claim.

p. 276 . . . he made the decisive argument: Associated Press, "S.D. governor claims he derailed Peltier pardon," Feb. 3, 2001.

p. 276 "Had we known that pardons were for sale": I condensed Bellecourt's quota-tion slightly. Said Janklow, "I'm probably the one who's responsible for Leonard Peltier not getting out." (Associated Press, "S.D. governor claims," *supra*.)

p. 276 The Native press, however, gave him a trace: Suzan Shown Harjo, "Questions from the past follow Janklow into the House," *Indian Country Today*, Jan. 17, 2003.

p. 276 . . . I also presumed he would share them with me: Janklow had once sworn, "I have never failed to consent to anybody looking at my records as far as I know. Had Mr. Matthiessen called me or Viking Press called me, I would have been more than happy to try to help them get the information so they wouldn't continue on the course they deliberately set on to libel me." (Janklow deposition, *supra*, p. 232. See also Continued Deposition of William Janklow, *Janklow v. Viking and Matthiessen*, Dec. 7, 1987, p. 693, 803.)

p. 276 The press secretary said Janklow would gladly: E-mails between Marshall Damgaard and author, Feb. 2003.

p. 277 . . . his alibi for the rape was deeply flawed: The FBI report about Eagle Deer's rape claim is FBI FD-263 report of John Penrod, Minneapolis, "William John Janklow; Jancita Eagle Deer—victim," Minneapolis file 70-4483, Headquarters file 7-44194, investigative period Jan. 17, 1967–Feb. 6, 1967, report issued Feb. 21, 1967. The BIA's is BIA case report R-67-22, *U.S. v. William Janklow*, "Statutory Rape," BIA Rosebud Agency, Special Officer Peter P[eter] Pitchlynn, Jan. 18, 1967.

Not incidentally, the court papers showed that Janklow was endlessly at odds with the truth on other topics. He claimed, for just a few examples, that he never said force should be used against AIM, that he never admitted that when he was a teenager he had assaulted a girl as a "preliminary to" rape, and that he never, not once, had been accused of being anti-Indian. Meanwhile, Jancita Eagle Deer was "a liar," Peter Pitchlynn was one of the "lyingest human beings who ever lived," Rosebud president Bob Burnette was such a liar that Janklow would have jailed him if he could have, and Dennis Banks could not order coffee without lying. (Janklow deposition, *supra*, p. 22, 262, 288–9).

p. 278 "You'd wait to see if he wanted to prosecute": Interview of John Penrod by author, via phone, Nov. 2003. Penrod said that had he seen contradictions in an alibi, he would have drawn attention to them in his report.

It would not surprise Indians that the FBI's investigative standards for crimes against them compared poorly with those for other crimes. Wesley Swearingen, a retired FBI agent of twenty-five years and author of the whistleblowing *FBI Secrets*, told me, "When we'd investigate bank robberies, a squad of maybe half a dozen would go immediately to the bank. Two of the agents would do nothing but dust for prints and look for fibers. Others would interview witnesses. Another would work the street outside." On the other hand, Swearingen said, "If the U.S. attorney isn't hot on prosecuting rape on a reservation, the agent could feel he's wasting his time." (Interview of Wesley Swearingen by author, via phone, Nov. 2003.)

p. 279 . . . gross, ongoing under-prosecution of reservation rapes: When Smith sifted through every criminal prosecution on one mid-sized reservation for the year 2000, she found no rape charges. A Justice Department official under Clinton once told her that there were only two U.S. attorneys nationwide who would bother to prosecute rape charges on reservations. Rape falls under federal jurisdiction only when it occurs on Indian reservations and similar federal land. Because state prosecutors deal with most rapes, federal prosecutors view it as a less glamorous crime to prosecute: a U.S. attorney with the chance to prosecute a drug kingpin will not generally be inclined to focus on a rapist instead. "If it's this bad today," Smith said, "imagine what it must have been back in the '70s." (Interview of Andrea Smith by author, via phone, Nov. 2003.)

p. 280 . . . the FBI did not bother to re-interview: My claim is based on both the court papers and on interviews by me with Penrod and Clabaugh, and by another investigator with Kaye Lord.

p. 280 The senators who cleared Janklow had been snowed: Donald Elisburg, who reviewed the FBI's work for the Democratic Senate committee, said in 2003 that he did not remember much about the review but that he was certain the charge was taken seriously. "But it would also be fair to say," he allowed, "that the level of intensity of scrutiny was definitely not where it is now. It was much more, not casual, but collegial in dealing with nominations." (Interview of Donald Elisburg by author, via phone, Nov. 2003.)

p. 281 The court ignored him: Janklow's license to practice law was finally suspended after he was convicted of killing Randy Scott. (Terry Woster, "Janklow's law license suspended," *Sioux Falls Argus Leader*, Dec. 17, 2003.)

p. 283 . . . Bill Janklow might be the George Wallace: I suggested to editors that if the FBI had looked the other way when, say, a black girl accused the virulently anti-black George Wallace of rape, they would probably consider it newsworthy. The editors were not moved by my argument. Months later, when Strom Thurmond's daughter—who was begat from Thurmond's statutory rape of a black teenaged servant—stepped forward from half a century of silence, every newspaper that turned me down ran the Thurmond story on or near page one. I eventually published an article with the small-circulation newsletter *CounterPunch* (Dec. 16–31, 2003).

p. 283 He is wont to offer reporters to listen: Which is what Gonzalez and his lawyer Sid Flores of San Jose, California, did to me.

p. 284 "It was Governor Janklow": Richard Meryhew, "Janklow had another close call at same intersection as deadly collision" *Minneapolis Star Tribune*, Aug. 31, 2003. Tony Aas was the deputy who stopped the white car that day. He would later say that when he first saw the car, his radar tracked it at ninety-two miles per hour and finally "locked on" at eighty-six. Aas did not give Janklow so much as a warning. At trial, the prosecution did not ask Aas or other officers why they did not ticket Janklow. See David Kranz, "Woman: Janklow nearly hit my pickup," *Sioux Falls Argus Leader*, Nov. 5, 2003; David Kranz, "Janklow jury won't see tickets," *Sioux Falls Argus Leader*, Nov. 11, 2003; Steve Young, "Trent woman: No regrets 'for telling truth'," *Sioux Falls Argus Leader*, Dec. 4, 2003; Richard Meryhew, "Janklow's passenger: It 'happened in a second or two,' " *Minneapolis Star Tribune*, Dec. 4, 2003; T. R. Reid, "Janklow Jury Told of Earlier Near-Accident," *Washington*

Post, Dec. 4, 2003, p. A03; Jon Walker, "'You can't imagine what this is like,' " *Sioux Falls Argus Leader*, Dec. 7, 2003; "The week in review," *Sioux Falls Argus Leader*, Dec. 7, 2003; "Janklow on the witness stand," *Sioux Falls Argus Leader*, Dec. 7, 2003; Steve Young, "Range of emotion reflected in testimony," *Sioux Falls Argus Leader*, Dec. 7, 2003; Denise Ross, "Janklow testifies, says he has 'probably' run stop signs in the past," *Rapid City Journal*, Dec. 8, 2003; Denise Ross, "Janklow jury seated in Janklow trial," *Rapid City Journal*, Dec. 9, 2003; Denise Ross, "Aide: Janklow hadn't eaten," *Rapid City Journal*, Dec. 9, 2003.

p. 284 . . . validated by other reportorial discoveries: Joe Kafka, Associated Press, "Janklow has a need for speed," *Rapid City Journal*, Aug. 19, 2003; "Janklow style has been fast," *Sioux Falls Argus Leader*, Aug. 19, 2003; David Kranz, "Janklow has a history of accidents while driving," *Sioux Falls Argus Leader*, Aug. 20, 2003; Corrine Olson, "Janklow reported swerving to avoid vehicles in other traffic accidents," *Sioux Falls Argus Leader*, Aug. 21, 2003; John-John Williams IV, "Emergency lights found in Janklow car," *Sioux Falls Argus Leader*, Aug. 21, 2003; Corrine Olson, "No evidence of 3rd vehicle," *Sioux Falls Argus Leader*, Aug. 22, 2003; Bob von Sternberg, "Some in South Dakota think accident will end Janklow's political career," *Minneapolis Star Tribune*, Aug. 24, 2003; Michelle Malkin, "Janklow should go; GOP ought to say so," *Washington Post* (weekly edition), Sept. 4, 2003, p. 7B; Associated Press, "Janklow Given Neb. Warning," *Washington Post*, Sept. 5, 2003, p. A02; "Janklow case timeline," *Sioux Falls Argus Leader*, Nov. 30, 2003; Jon Walker, "Reckless or confused: Janklow jury to decide," *Sioux Falls Argus Leader*, Dec. 2, 2003; Richard Meryhew, "Witness: Before crash, Janklow raced past another vehicle," *Minneapolis Star Tribune*, Dec. 3, 2003; P. J. Huffstutter, "An Emotional Janklow Takes Stand in Trial," *Los Angeles Times*, Dec. 7, 2003; Doug Grow, "Doug Grow: A stunning verdict in Janklow case" *Minneapolis Star Tribune*, Dec. 9, 2003; Denise Ross, "Witnesses describe Janklow accident scene," Rapid City Journal, Dec. 9, 2003; Denise Ross, "Janklow quotes," *Rapid City Journal*, Dec. 2003; Terry Woster, "Janklow: Didn't ask for special treatment," *Sioux Falls Argus Leader*, July 1, 2004.

p. 284 "How many times have you been stopped": I have condensed this exchange slightly. Continued deposition of Janklow, *supra*, p. 547–50.

p. 285 . . . they showed that state troopers had showered: The investigation examined only those stops made by the state patrol. Stops by local police were another matter, and the press could not discover their number with any precision. (Terry Woster, "Highway Patrol's report on Janklow will remain sealed," *Sioux Falls Argus Leader*, Dec. 12, 2003; letter, from Colonel Dan Mosteller, to Gov. M. Michael Rounds, Jan. 7, 2004; T. R. Reid, "Janklow Sentenced to 100 Days in Jail," *Washington Post*, Jan. 23, 2004, p. A03; Terry Woster, "16 stops, no tickets," *Sioux Falls Argus Leader*, June 30,

2004; Terry Woster, "Janklow: Didn't ask for special treatment," *Sioux Falls Argus Leader*, July 1, 2004.)

p. 285 . . . the state's attorney for Moody County: Bill Ellingson was only a part-time state's attorney (Moody County being small of population). The rest of the time he was a tax lawyer.

p. 285 Come the trial, Janklow mounted a defense: Events surrounding the trial can be found in David Kranz, "Janklow medical defense raised," *Sioux Falls Argus Leader*, Nov. 26, 2003; Kevin Dobbs, "Defense case touchy for diabetics," *Sioux Falls Argus Leader*, Dec. 3, 2003; Monica Davey, "His Jury Sees Rep. Janklow Placing Blame," *New York Times*, Dec. 3, 2003; Jon Walker, "Diabetes had effect, doctor says," *Sioux Falls Argus Leader*, Dec. 6, 2003; Monica Davey, "Rep. Janklow Says He Recalls Nothing of Fatal Car Crash," *New York Times*, Dec. 7, 2003; Denise Ross, "Janklow twice mentioned he saw stop sign," *Rapid City Journal*, Dec. 9, 2003; and other articles cited in this chapter.

p. 286 "Always," he said. But he added: "Janklow on the witness stand," *Sioux Falls Argus Leader*, Dec. 7, 2003; Richard Meryhew, "An emotional Janklow testifies in his manslaughter trial in South Dakota," *Minneapolis Star Tribune*, Dec. 7, 2003; Denise Ross, "Janklow testifies, says he has 'probably' run stop signs in the past," *Rapid City Journal*, Dec. 7, 2003; T. R. Reid, "In Testimony, Janklow Remembers Little," *Washington Post*, December 7, 2003, p. A06; Denise Ross, "Analysis: whom will jurors believe," Rapid City Journal, Dec. 8, 2003.

p. 287 "I felt he was honest": The jury foreman was James Mitchell. Juror Debra Garamaker, fifty, a beautician, said, "My gut reaction was he was speaking from his heart. I really felt what he had to say was what he believed and what he could remember." (Randy Furst, "Diabetes defense may have backfired for Janklow," *Minneapolis Star Tribune*, Dec. 9, 2003. See also Monica Davey, "Lawmaker Guilty of Manslaughter," *New York Times*, Dec. 9, 2003)

p. 287 Janklow's sentencing hearing followed: Details of Janklow's sentencing can be found in Denise Ross, "Janklow sentenced to 100 days in jail," *Rapid City Journal*, Jan. 23, 2004; Jon Walker, "Janklow gets jail time, fine, 3 years probation," *Sioux Falls Argus Leader*, Jan. 23, 2004; P. J. Huffstutter, " 'Remorseful' Janklow Gets 100 Days in Jail," *Los Angeles Times*, Dec. 9, 2003. See also Brenda Wade Schmidt, "Drivers can face variety of charges in fatalities," *Sioux Falls Argus Leader*, Aug. 20, 2003; Peter Harriman, "Man who will decide on charges called earnest, fair," *Sioux Falls Argus Leader*, Aug. 20, 2003; Kevin Woster, "Prosecutors weigh possibilities," *Rapid City Journal*, Aug. 23, 2003; Terry Woster, "Prosecutors: Similar charges might not fit similar crashes," *Sioux Falls Argus Leader*, Aug. 24, 2003.

CHAPTER 14

p. 289 "Ladies and gentleman, on a December": The opening statement of James McMahon can be found in *U.S. v. Fritz Arlo Looking Cloud*, U.S. Dist. Ct., S. Div. S.D., CR 03-50020, Feb. 2004, transcript, p. 2–13. I have condensed it.

p. 289 . . . she had jumped bond—had called a friend: The friends who gave Aquash a ride to Denver were Evelyn Bordeaux and her boyfriend (later husband) Ray Handboy. They arrived in Pierre about ten o'clock at night, picked up Aquash at the St. Charles Hotel, and drove all night to Denver. Bordeaux died some years ago. (Handboy's testimony is in *U.S. v. Looking Cloud, supra*, p. 199–207.)

p. 291 "Arlo Looking Cloud didn't kill anybody": The opening statement of Timothy Rensch can be found in *U.S. v. Looking Cloud, supra*, p. 13–22. I have condensed it. Looking Cloud sometimes went by the name Frank Dillon.

p. 292 "And what does Arlo do, the twenty-two": Looking Cloud, born March 25, 1951, was actually twenty-four at the time of the murder.

p. 295 . . . Joseph Trimbach, who had interrupted a Floridian: Trimbach attended the trial because he was working on a book about his FBI days, which has not yet been published.

p. 296 The prosecution called for Nathan Merrick: Merrick's testimony is in *U.S. v. Looking Cloud, supra*, p. 31–49.

p. 296 For twenty-eight years, the government had said: For a recent example of the government's ongoing denial: "There was no identification on the body, and the cause of death was not immediately apparent." (Letter from A. Robert Walsh, Acting Unit Chief, for John E. Collingwood, Asst. Director, FBI Ofc. of Public & Congressional Affairs, to U.S. Sen. Tom Daschle, Jan. 27, 1998.)

p. 296 Not then, nor for the rest of the trial, would jurors: The extent of the jury's knowledge about the handling of Aquash's body was that the first autopsy had, in McMahon's word, been "botched." He said only that the coroner had first determined the cause of death to be exposure but that then the body had been exhumed and the bullet found.

p. 297 Nor did reporters bring Merrick's revelation: AIMers accused the media of malice in their coverage of the trial, but the media's slant was less personal. Few reporters knew enough about AIM's history to know what they were hearing.

p. 297 . . . Merrick would say that he could not recall: Interview of Nathan Merrick by author, Macy, Neb., Nov. 2005.

p. 297 How much blood—whether microscopic: Given Merrick's claim to have seen blood on her head, one would presume that the blood on her clothes was obvious as well. Aquash's clothes were not sent to the lab until March 10. In the teletype accompanying the clothes, the Rapid City office wrote, "Laboratory is requested to examine enclosed items, specifically for any evidence of blood or semen." (FBI airtel, from ASAC Rapid City (70-11023) (P), to Director, FBI (attn: FBI Laboratory, Serology Sec.), "Unsub; Anna Mae Aquash (Deceased)—Victim, CIR—Possible manslaughter," Mar. 10, 1976.) The serologists received the clothing on March 13, whereupon they found the blood but no semen. (Report of the FBI Laboratory, to ASAC, Rapid City (70-11023), FBI file 70-67632, Lab file PC-M6264 OJ MC, re "Unsub; Anna Mae Aquash (Deceased), Victim," Apr. 16, 1976.) Dr. Brown, for his part, said the clothes were "soiled, but showed no other distinctive finding." He did not say with what the clothes were soiled. (W. O. Brown, pathologist, autopsy of Anna Mae Aquash, performed Feb. 25, 1976, reported Mar. 15, 1976.)

p. 297 Donald Dealing, retired from twenty-six: Dealing's testimony is in *U.S. v. Looking Cloud, supra,* p. 54–62.

p. 297 Whereas the Bureau held that he was the only: Dozens of FBI reports had said Dealing had been the only agent of record at the crime scene. On the stand he said, "I actually was the first agent that was present at the scene." *First* rather suggested others followed, but Rensch did not ask Dealing about it. However, I found an FBI report, through unofficial channels, that said of the day Aquash's body was found, "Bureau of Indian Affairs (BIA) Police along with Special Agents ███████ of the FBI, recovered the body . . ." The plurality of "Special Agents" was damning. Eventually I received a duplicate of this paper from the FBI. The "s" of "Agents" was cutely censored: "Special Agent███████ of the FBI". When I discussed this censorship with an FBI lawyer and an FBI censor, both referred to the "Special Agents" mentioned in the document and to the "names" of the "agents" that had been censored. But they refused to release them. Also, it appears that Donald Dealing was not one the agents whose name was censored. I say this because the FBI told me it would release the name or names of any agent whose name had already been released in connection with events at the scene. Since Dealing's name had been released in many other documents, I conclude that his name was not one of those censored. (FBI FD-36 form, teletype from ASAC, Rapid City (70-11023), to Director, FBI, re "Unsub, Anna Mae Aquash," May 25, 1976.)

p. 298 . . . Bill Wood, who turned out to be: Wood's testimony is in *U.S. v. Looking Cloud, supra,* p. 80–96.

p. 299 This answer had the advantage of agreeing: Bob Ecoffey, the director of BIA police nationwide and the man who worked the case the longest, seconded the government line at trial. He was asked how he had come to work on the case. He said the FBI had invited him to get involved in the early 1980s when the FBI needed help interviewing Indian witnesses in Denver. He had gone to Denver and helped with the case, but the leads had gone nowhere. Ecoffey had stayed with the case, mostly informally and wholly without luck until 1993, when he got a tip that broke the case open. Ecoffey was not asked at trial to explain why he said the case was broken open in 1993 when the FBI's files showed that the basics of the murder were known in 1976. (Ecoffey would not respond to my several requests to interview him.) Ecoffey's testimony is in *U.S. v. Looking Cloud, supra*, p. 408–65.

In a hyper-literal sense, Wood's answer may have been correct. He probably did not receive the report of December 19, 1975, from the informer that December; an FBI agent in Denver did. Wood was probably given the report a few months later. But this answer and others like it very strongly implied that Wood knew nothing about the December reports, which was untrue.

p. 299 "On December, 19, 1975": FBI teletype, from Denver (70-4623), to Director, re "Unsub; Anna Mae Aquash, aka (Deceased)," Apr. 28, 1976, 7:02 p.m. Importantly, the FBI knew soon after Aquash disappeared from Pierre that she had gone to Denver. (Kevin McKiernan, "Indian woman's death raises many questions," *Minneapolis Tribune*, May 30, 1976, p. 1B.)

p. 299 . . . and had been arrested over the summer: The mention of the arrest at the Crow Dog–Running raid was slightly garbled in the FBI teletype, which referred to "the group of Indians arrested in Nebraska last summer." The Crow Dog and Running properties were near, but not in, Nebraska. The reference, however, was surely to the raid on their properties.

p. 300 "█████ source advised Anna Mae Aquash": FBI FD-209 report, memorandum from SA William Van Roe (P), to SAC, Minneapolis, Subject ██████, Dec. 8, 1975.

p. 300 Certainly the only legal justification: The FBI claimed that if it revealed what was in this fragment, the informer's identity could be exposed and her or his life jeopardized. This was an almost certainly bogus claim. Aquash was surrounded by a great many people at the time of this informer's report, so whatever the informer reported was in all likelihood known to several people and could not be traced back to any one source.

p. 300 Yet it . . . did nothing: At least, to judge from what documents the FBI has released to me, the FBI did nothing. Conceivably the FBI is withholding documents that show it acted on this information. On the other hand, further evidence that the FBI had the case solved much earlier than admitted arose from the testimony of Troy Lynn Yellow Wood (below). Yellow Wood, according to the prosecution, was approached by law enforcement officers about Aquash's murder only two years after it occurred.

p. 300 . . . "negative results concerning any positive": Wrote Wood in one report, "Numerous individuals who are either former associates of ANNIE MAE AQUASH or persons believed to have knowledge regarding AQUASH's death have been interviewed with negative results concerning any positive information regarding AQUASH's death." Wood attached about sixty pages of mostly dead ends that the FBI had pursued in Minneapolis, Los Angeles, Oklahoma, and South Dakota. (FBI FD-263 report of William B. Wood, Rapid City, investigative period Mar. 29–Aug. 23, 1976, re "Unsub; Annie Mae Aquash, aka (Deceased)—Victim," Sept. 9, 1976. See also FBI FD-204 report from William B. Wood, Rapid City, to USA, Sioux Falls, S.D. (Attn: AUSA Bruce W. Boyd), re "Unknown Subject, Annie Mae Aqush [sic] (Deceased)—Victim," field office file 70-11023, bureau file 70-67632, Sept. 9, 1976.)

p. 300 . . . even though he knew . . . it was accurate: No later than two months after Aquash's body was found, the FBI concluded that the tip it had received on December 19, 1975, from the Denver source was accurate. The proof is a report from April 1976 that discusses the tip and concludes, "It, therefore, appears that the incident which occurred ▆▆▆▆ the murder of Aquash." The censored text, no doubt, contains an affirmation. (FBI teletype, from Denver (70-4623), to Director, re "Unsub; Anna Mae Aquash, aka (Deceased)," Apr. 29, 1976, 5:56 p.m.)

p. 301 . . . several amateurs solved the case: One amateur who did so was Robert Pictou-Branscombe, a distant cousin of Aquash who re-mortgaged his house to pay for his investigation and whose work confirmed Paul DeMain's. Robert Pictou-Branscombe publicly fingered Clarke, Looking Cloud, and Graham in 1999; DeMain published their names the same year.

p. 301 "For years the identity of Anna Mae's killers": Interview of Paul DeMain by author, Hayward, Wisc., Aug. 2003.

p. 301 (Theda Clarke has escaped indictment): Although Clarke claimed Alzheimer's, she appeared entirely lucid when I visited her in 2003. For example, she had no trouble recalling a letter I had sent her months before, she easily understood what I wanted to talk about, and she shouted me from her room with knowing vigor.

p. 302 (His file said the opposite): And Wood's boss Norm Zigrossi said Aquash had rebuffed the FBI in its attempts to recruit her: "We would have loved to have had her as an informant," Zigrossi said. "But she didn't want any part of us."

p. 302 Kamook Nichols was a casting director: Nichols's testimony is in *U.S. v. Looking Cloud, supra,* p. 112–81.

p. 303 Permitted to speak, Nichols: Judge Piersol told jurors they were not to judge the truth or falsity of whatever Aquash had told Nichols, only Aquash's state of mind. The instruction was more easily given than followed. Several times during the trial, when the prosecution wanted to introduce evidence that (intended or not) was damning to AIM, Piersol allowed it with the same instruction.

p. 303 . . . "and they were making her make bombs": Candy Hamilton later told the same story. Said Hamilton, "Cheyenne Nichols, Kamook's mother, told me before she died that Dave Hill made Annie Mae make the bombs. He kept calling her a snitch. 'So if we get caught, you're gonna be the one that made them, and you'll have to take the fall.' " (Interview of Candy Hamilton by author, Oglala, S.D., Aug. 2003; e-mail from Candy Hamilton to author, Nov. 2003.) Viola "Cheyenne" Nichols died in 2002.

p. 305 . . . Nichols's sister, Bernie Lafferty, said: More precisely, Lafferty made this statement before trial, but it was not made public until after trial. ("Bernie Nichols Speaks Regarding Leonard Peltier," Feb. 19, 2005, Justice for Anna Mae and Ray Web site, jfamr.org/didit.html, viewed Mar. 2005, citing interview by unknown source of Mar. 9, 2001.) Paul DeMain has also reported that "several people" have told him of hearing Peltier boast of killing the agents, and other people (or perhaps the same) have told him of seeing Peltier flourishing Agent Coler's revolver as a trophy. (Paul DeMain, "Arlo Looking Cloud Trial Outline," Jan. 30, 2004, www.indigenouswomenforjustice.org, viewed Feb. 2004.)

p. 305 The FBI wired her for sound and sent her: Prosecutor McMahon said he would call her back to the stand to discuss what was said in some of those wired conversations, but he never did. Nichols refused to be interviewed for this book.

p. 305 Forty-odd thousand dollars seemed: When Rensch asked if $49,000 was a lot of money, Nichols said no, although it was twice her normal annual income. She also denied having witnessed crimes in her AIM days, though she had just testified to watching bombs being made. She was evasive in other respects as well.

AIM denounced Nichols as a turncoat and liar, but there was proof only of the former—if one can be called a turncoat for speaking what was probably the truth. AIMers speculated that Nichols had been brainwashed, or was selling movie rights, or was writing a book, or had been cowed into informing by having her children threatened. Few AIMers said (not aloud anyway) that Indians might be better served by hearing the truth from her (if truth she was telling) than by a continuation of the cover-up of AIM's role in Aquash's murder. Nichols did not help matters. In addition to her evasiveness, she refused to say publicly that the FBI had a long history of sabotaging AIM or that the government might be using her for the less than noble end of burying Peltier.

p. 306 Mathalene White Bear of El Monte: White Bear's testimony is in *U.S. v. Looking Cloud, supra,* p. 181–90.

p. 307 After the trial, White Bear would say: Interview of Mathalene White Bear by author, El Monte, Cal., Nov. 2005.

p. 308 . . . a WKLDOC lawyer had smuggled it out: The lawyer was Beverly Axelrod, now dead.

p. 309 Twenty-nine years before Angie Janis: Janis's testimony is in *U.S. v. Looking Cloud, supra,* p. 209–35.

p. 309 Rios owned the empty apartment: Rios has denied knowing her apartment was used to hold Aquash. She said plenty of friends used her apartments; if some of them committed crimes there, what was that to her? (Interview of Thelma Rios by author, Rapid City, S.D., Feb. 2004.)

p. 310 . . . two or three members of the Latino rights group: The members of the Crusade for Justice alleged by multiple sources to have been at the meeting were George Pilfe and Ernesto Vigil.

p. 310 "Do you remember what was being discussed": Tim Rensch, fearing prejudicial information, asked for the jurors to be excused for the discussion about what the members of the Crusade said. Judge Piersol agreed, and the jurors never heard it.

p. 311 The prosecution called Candy Hamilton: Hamilton's testimony is in *U.S. v. Looking Cloud, supra*, p. 299–326. I have supplemented her testimony with interviews from 2003 and 2005.

p. 312 Hamilton didn't see the people in the room: Another WKLDOCker, Jeanette Eagle Hawk, said she was barred from the front room that day, but she looked in briefly and saw Ellison, Rios, the Meanses, and Clyde Bellecourt. It was the only occasion she could recall in which she was ever prevented from going into a part of the house. Eagle Hawk's testimony is in *U.S. v. Looking Cloud, supra*, p. 326–32.

p. 313 According to Bob Robideau, Bruce Ellison: Transcript of conversation between Robert Robideau and John Trudell, Dec. 3, 1994, Albuquerque, N.M.

p. 313 "Madonna Gilbert?": Before the trial, Madonna Gilbert, now Madonna Thunder Hawk, told me that she had nothing to do with an interrogation of Aquash. "I barely even knew who Anna Mae Aquash was," she said before changing the subject. (Interview of Madonna Thunder Hawk by author, Cheyenne River Reservation, S.D., Nov. 2003.) Peter Matthiessen wrote in *In the Spirit of Crazy Horse* that Thunder Hawk was "rather unwilling" to talk about Aquash. (Viking Press, 1991, p. 436.) When I asked Thunder Hawk about Matthiessen's comment, she said, "When I saw that, I knew the man didn't know anything. I put the book down right then and never read it." But I agreed with Matthiessen's assessment. John Trudell later said that when Arlo Looking Cloud confessed the murder to him, he (Looking Cloud) had said that when the kidnappers first arrived in Rapid City, "Lorelei Means and Madonna Thunder Hawk and Thelma Rios and John Boy and himself, between them, somebody always stayed with her, and she was kept in that house, not free to leave."

p. 314 . . . Cleo Gates looked more like: Gates's testimony is in *U.S. v. Looking Cloud, supra*, p. 333–43. Gates was the sister of Joe Morgan, the drinking buddy whom Arlo Looking Cloud had gone to find on the afternoon that he knocked on Troy Lynn Yellow Wood's door. Gates's then-husband, Dick Marshall, was the AIMer who shot Martin Montileaux in the bathroom of the Longhorn Saloon and became a cause célèbre until he belatedly confessed to the crime.

p. 315 "I didn't think anything of it": Author interview with Cleo Gates, Manderson, S.D., Nov. 2003.

p. 315 Troy Lynn Yellow Wood took the stand: Yellow Wood's testimony is in *U.S. v. Looking Cloud, supra,* p. 235–92. McMahon asked whether Aquash had told Yellow Wood about Peltier's interrogation of her in Farmington. Yellow Wood told substantially the same story that Nichols had told.

p. 315 "He said that she told him they were deciding": I have condensed this exchange slightly.

p. 317 John Trudell had chaired AIM from: Trudell's testimony is in *U.S. v Looking Cloud, supra,* p. 380–408.

p. 317 . . . saying flatly, "That is Annie Mae": Trudell said this in June 1976 at the trial of Dino Butler and Bob Robideau for the murder of the FBI agents in Oglala. (Quoted in Matthiessen, *supra,* p. 301.) Trudell has said Vernon and Clyde Bellecourt were in the car when Banks made his revelation.

In 2004, Banks claimed that it was Trudell who had told him, in a meeting with several people, that the Jane Doe was Aquash: "It was during a meeting in Los Angeles, California, that John Trudell came over to me and said, 'Annie Mae's body has been found.' The news devastated me. It was only the presence of so many people that prevented me from bursting into tears. There was absolute silence in the committee room. I left in order to regain my composure." Banks could have supported the claim by naming the other people at the meeting. He did not. (Banks and Erdoes, *Ojibwa Warrior: Dennis Banks and the Rise of the American Indian Movement,* Univ. of Okla. Pr., 2004, p. 220.) Trudell called Banks's claim "total fucking bullshit." (Interview of John Trudell by author, via phone, Dec. 2005.)

p. 317 "When you were speaking to him," Rensch said: I have condensed this exchange. Rensch also asked Trudell, "If you were friends with Anna Mae, why, if Arlo said these things to you in '88, didn't you call the police and do something about it?" Trudell answered, "Because I told Arlo that what he said to me, he said it in confidence. And go to police? I mean no offense, but my relationship with the United States government isn't a real good one. I have no basis to be trusting police."

p. 318 Ecoffey did not ask how "little": There was no sign at trial that Ecoffey or the Denver police gave Looking Cloud a breath (or other) test to see if he was drunk. Ecoffey refused to be interviewed for this book.

p. 319 . . . by summoning David Price: Price's testimony is in *U.S. v. Looking Cloud, supra,* p. 465–9. Price refused to be interviewed for this book.

CHAPTER 15

p. 321 In 1988 a Montana ranch foreman: Clausen's story—both of his own travails and of his relationship with the Durham brothers—can be found in his obscure, self-published, and often entertaining book *Burning Rage: The Growing Anger Within My Country* (Sail Away Press, 2000), of which the Durham episode is a single chapter. Most of the book is a rant against liberal ills that Clausen believes are ruining America. Clausen's main career in 2006 was promoting himself as an expert on environmental "extremists." His veracity has frequently, and rightly, been called into doubt (e.g., Bob Ortega, "Clausen's 'Eco-Probes' Draw Suspicion, But He Still Turns up on TV, in Papers," *Wall Street Journal*, Mar. 2, 1999). I have restricted my use of his claims to those that I could corroborate with other sources, with a few exceptions that should be obvious to the reader (e.g., conversations in which only Durham and Clausen were present and so are unverifiable). Clausen refused several offers to speak with me. One of the legacies of the FBI's refusal to shed light on its operatives is that reporters are often forced to get information about those operatives from sources like Clausen whom they would just as soon ignore.

p. 321 "You know Doug Durham?" the sheriff said: According to Clausen, the sheriff was Lee Edmisten of Madison County, and the FBI agent in Butte was Gary Lincoln.

p. 322 So well did Durham and the sheriff get along: Durham had worked on the sheriff's election campaign. (Interview of Dennis Durham by author, Newton, Ia., Dec. 2005.)

p. 323 . . . plenty of lawmen liked crooks—their crooks: Revelations have piled up in recent years about FBI agents who got too close to the bad guys and became bad guys themselves. One of the worst examples came from Boston, where agents helped cover up murders committed by their mafia friends. See Dick Lehr and Gerard O'Neill, *Black Mass: The Irish Mob, the FBI, and a Devil's Deal*, Public Affairs Press, 2000.

p. 323 "It was a glorified pyramid scheme": Dennis Durham interview, *supra*.

p. 325 Durham had lowered his profile: The information on this scandal comes from Dennis Durham. (Dennis Durham interview, *supra*.)

p. 326 "No," he wrote back. "My dad taught": Information from Dennis is in Dennis Durham interview, *supra*; various letters from Dennis Durham to author, 2003–4.

p. 326 Policemen and FBI agents were always stopping by: Dennis said shortly before his father's death, "I know that to this day Doug has a relationship with the FBI. In the '80s, several times we would pull right into the FBI office, get buzzed in and greeted and go right to [Special Agent in Charge Dave] Gillis's office. Doug would talk for hours while I got shown around. I don't know if Doug was still on the job [for the FBI] in Dallas or not, but he could get what he wanted."

p. 327 "Doug's dead," his next letter began: Durham died on February 22, 2004, at Sunrise Hospital in Las Vegas. His remains were to be shipped to his hometown of Galatia, Illinois, for burial in a family plot.

p. 328 In May 2000 the FBI compiled a report: FBI report, Minneapolis field office, "Accounting for Native American Deaths, Pine Ridge Reservation, South Dakota," May 2000.

p. 328 . . . a hearing of the U.S. Commission on Civil Rights: South Dakota Advisory Committee to the U.S. Commission on Civil Rights transcript, "Native Americans and the Administration of Justice in South Dakota," Dec. 6, 1999, Rapid City, S.D.

p. 328 USCCR eventually concluded: Technically speaking, it was not USCCR proper that concluded thus; it was the South Dakota Advisory Committee to the USCCR, which in March 2000, four months after the hearing in Rapid City, issued a report called *Native Americans in South Dakota: An Erosion of Confidence in the Justice System.* In careful but firm language, the committee damned prosecutors, police, and especially the FBI for what was at best a strong appearance of dereliction of duty.

p. 328 ("Garbage," Governor Janklow said): Terry Woster, "Janklow: Civil rights report is 'garbage,' " *Sioux Falls Argus Leader*, April 5, 2000. Janklow then commissioned a report of his own, which also found evidence that Indians were treated worse than whites by South Dakota's justice system. (Richard Braunstein and Steve Feimer, "South Dakota Criminal Justice: A Study of Racial Disparities," *South Dakota Law Review*, vol. 48, 2003, pp. 171ff.)

p. 329 . . . aside from a few "nonspecific rumors": As the FBI wrote in its May 2000 "Accounting for Native American Deaths," "The names of murder victims were not attached to the rumors and addressing the allegations could not be accomplished." Only in December 1999, "for the first time," did complainants "provide the FBI with specific information to address."

p. 329 "I am not overwhelmed": USCCR transcript, *supra*, p. 30.

p. 329 The truth, as scores of FBI documents show: FBI report, "Inquiry from U.S. Commission on Civil Rights Concerning Law Enforcement on Pine Ridge Indian Reservation, South Dakota," Rapid City, S.D., May 27, 1976, p. 13ff. The report discusses investigations since July 1, 1975. Another list (or perhaps the same) was compiled for Senator Jim Abourezk, who demanded the FBI and U.S. attorney give him a list of outstanding felonies on Pine Ridge. There were, of course, many other instances over the years in which the FBI was told of the alleged crimes. For examples of these, see Letter from Hank Adams, Director of Survival of American Indians Association, to Dennis Banks and Russell Means, May 14, 1974, in WKLDOC Archives; untitled, unsigned WKLDOC memo, Mar. 10, 1975, in WKLDOC Archives); FBI memo from SA Noel A. Castleman, to SAC Minneapolis (70-6332) (P), re "Wounded Knee Information Received from Geraldine Mae Janis," April 12, 1973, in WKLDOC Archives.

p. 330 The list was expanded and republished: Churchill and Vander Wall published the expanded list in *The COINTELPRO Papers: Documents from the FBI's Secret Wars Against Domestic Dissent* (South End Pr., 1991), and Churchill republished the list in two more books: *Indians Are Us?: Culture and Genocide in Native North America* (Common Courage Pr., 1993) and *From a Native Son: Selected Essays on Indigenism*, 1985–1996 (South End Pr., 1996). Churchill is often unreliable on facts, but his list of unsolved violent crimes was more accurate than not.

p. 330 Only after reporters learned of its existence: Reporters learned of the report by word of mouth on the thirtieth anniversary of the takeover of Wounded Knee. (Heidi Bell Gease, "FBI report responds to claims of unsolved Indian deaths," *Rapid City Journal*, Feb. 27, 2003.) The FBI's "Accounting" received page-six coverage in the newspapers of the Plains and no important coverage in any major media outlet.

p. 333 The FBI did and does have jurisdiction: And in any case, lack of jurisdiction often did not stop the FBI from investigating AIM, as its forays into the Skyhorse and Mohawk case and Dick Marshall's killing of Martin Montileaux show.

p. 334 "I told Dennis, 'We think he's a fed' ": Mike Mosedale, "Bury My Heart," *City Pages* (Minneapolis–St. Paul), Feb. 16, 2000, p. 1.

CHAPTER 16

p. 335 Bissonette wanted the occupiers: Rolland Dewing, *Wounded Knee II*, Great Plains Network/Pine Hills Pr., 1995, p. 100.

p. 335 . . . a fight over the disposition of a load of dynamite: Peter Matthiessen, *In the Spirit of Crazy Horse*, Viking Pr., 1991, p. 578. Martinez's widow confirmed for me that he wanted to kill Banks. (Interview of Vicki Thunder Hawk by author, Porcupine, S.D., Nov. 24, 2003.) Bob Free told me, "I was offered gifts, but killing each other wouldn't have been good publicity. So I said no thanks on this one." (Interview of Robert Free by author, via phone, Nov., 2003.)

p. 336 . . . whether to assassinate Vernon Bellecourt: An FBI informer who went into Wounded Knee on April 21, 1973, accompanied by Byron DeSersa, "advised that an individual by the name of ▮▮▮▮ [almost certainly Vernon Bellecourt] who was to secure a shipment of arms and ammunition for the occupants of Wounded Knee, apparently 'blew the gun deal' and now ▮▮▮▮ and other individuals are planning to assassinate him. . . ." (FBI memo from SA ▮▮▮▮, to SAC, Minneapolis (70-6832)(P), re "Wounded Knee," date uncertain but the informer was interviewed Apr. 23, 1973.)

When DeSersa was interviewed by the FBI in a Seattle hospital bed a month later, he confirmed there had been a split inside Wounded Knee and that both Vernon and Clyde Bellecourt had been accused of misusing funds. DeSersa did not admit knowledge of an assassination plot. (FBI nitel from Seattle [file numbers unclear], to Acting Director FBI

(157-15434) [numbers are very fuzzy and may be wrong], re "Disorder by American Indians in South Dakota, Extreme Matters, American Indian Activities," June 1, 1973.)

The FBI has told me that it has other reports from the time of the siege that contain "a reference to certain third parties who had been identified to be murdered by certain AIM members." The FBI will not release those reports. (Defendant FBI's Second Preliminary Vaughn Index, *Stephen Hendricks v. FBI et al.*, U.S. Dist. Ct. Mont., Helena Div., CV 0361-H-CSO, May 19, 2005, p. 17.)

p. 336 . . . a goon foot patrol captured twelve men: *Voices From Wounded Knee*, self-published by *Akwesasne Notes* newspaper, 1974, p. 190ff.

p. 336 The government . . . sent agents and marshals: The government documents, heavily censored, do not say where or how thoroughly the government men searched.

p. 337 "Because I could not fight the white man": I have condensed this quotation and the one in the next paragraph slightly. (Barbara Deming, *Prison Notes*, Grossman Pubs., 1966, p. 113.)

p. 337 He found what he was looking for in 1964: Accounts of Robinson's activism can be found in Deming, *Prison Notes*, *supra*, p. 113; Barbara Deming, *We Cannot Live Without Our Lives*, Grossman Pubs., 1974; Carson Walker, Associated Press, "A follower of Martin Luther King Jr. might be buried at Wounded Knee: Slain activist had roots in civil rights movement," Jan. 15, 2004; e-mails from Cheryl Buswell-Robinson to author, 2003–5; interviews of Cheryl Buswell-Robinson by author, via phone and in Detroit, Mich., 2003–5. The Québec-to-Guantánamo walkers resorted to boat for the last few hundred miles; Robinson did not take part in the oceanic leg.

p. 338 "And goddamn if the next day": Interview of Cheryl Buswell-Robinson by author, Detroit, Mich., Dec. 2005.

p. 338 "While I was speaking to Clark": I have condensed this quotation slightly. (E-mail from Hank Adams, to author and Paul DeMain, Dec. 3, 2003.)

p. 339 . . . on the front page of the *New York Times*: Ray Robinson, Cheryl Buswell-Robinson, and James Washington (the last of Cincinnati) "had intervened when Supreme Court security officers were attempting to take into custody youths who were tampering with the flag." (Earl Caldwell, "High Court Building Stormed In Demonstration by the Poor," *New York Times*, May 30, 1968, p. 1.)

p. 339 . . . Robinson might be an agent provocateur: Hank Adams said he thought that it was someone in either the Alianza headed by Reies Tijerina or the Crusade for Justice headed by Corky Gonzales who first suggested that Robinson was an agent provocateur. The Crusade for Justice was the same group whose members were allegedly at Troy Lynn Yellow Wood's when Aquash was taken from Denver to Rapid City—and one of whose members, in the claim of Angie Janis at the Looking Cloud trial, suggested slitting the throats of provocateurs.

p. 339 He drove with friends to Rapid City: The friends were Janie Waller, who lived with the Robinsons on the People's Farm in Alabama; Emily Gordon; and Herschel Joiner, Gordon's boyfriend. I have not found Gordon or Joiner. Waller, as noted elsewhere, is dead.

p. 339 His hike seems to have gone poorly: As best Cheryl and others could recollect, he hiked into Wounded Knee on or about April 20.

p. 339 By at least two accounts, the deep-voiced Robinson: Cheryl Buswell-Robinson was told this story when she investigated Ray's death. I was told it by Allen Cooper, a friend of Ray's inside Wounded Knee. (Interview of Allen Cooper by author, Albuquerque, N.M., Nov. 2005.) When Robinson's hiking companions urged him to be quiet, he may have replied that the feds were nothing to be afraid of.

p. 340 Robinson was overcome and: Interview of Lenny Foster by author, via phone, Nov. 2005. Foster took part in the sweat. He remembered Robinson by skin color, not name; Robinson was the only black man in Wounded Knee at the time.

p. 340 "If he's the guy I'm thinking of": Interview of Kevin McKiernan by author, via phone, Mar. 2004. A woman who walked out of Wounded Knee on April 20, 1973, told the FBI there were two hundred Indians, eleven whites, and two blacks inside. (Walker, *supra*.) The black woman was almost certainly Robinson's friend Janie Waller; the man was almost certainly Robinson. Of the many people I have spoken to who were inside Wounded Knee at the time, Robinson and Waller were the only black people they remember.

p. 340 "He seemed to have difficulty": Two Elk's recollections can be found in Richard Two Elk, "Wounded Knee April 1973 . . . Forward Edge of Battle . . ." [ellipses in original], posted to alt.native Google newsgroup, Jan. 16, 2004; and Walker, *supra*. I have condensed some of Two Elk's quotations.

p. 341 There was much in Two Elk's account that was self-serving: Before Two Elk made his revelation, he had had a bitter falling out with AIM. His hatred of AIM's leaders, particularly Dennis Banks, was absolute. Many AIMers in turn came to hate Two Elk for testifying on behalf of the prosecution at the trial of Arlo Looking Cloud. Looking Cloud and Two Elk had grown up together, and the former confessed the murder of Aquash to the latter several times over the years. Two Elk's testimony is in *U.S. v. Fritz Arlo Looking Cloud*, U.S. Dist. Ct., S. Div. S.D., CR 03-50020, Feb. 2004, p. 347–79.

p. 341 . . . at the end of 2003 published a story about it: Stephen Hendricks, "Man Missing at Wounded Knee, 1973," *Black Hills People's News*, Dec. 12, 2003, p. 9. Paul DeMain of *News from Indian Country* was working on the story simultaneously but separately.

p. 342 "My uncle Stanley Hollow Horn": Interview of Marlette Thunder Horse by author, via phone, Nov. 2005.

p. 342 ". . . Carter Camp that took him . . . and Leonard Crow Dog": Camp refused to speak to me about the claim (e-mails from Carter Camp to author, Mar. 2006), and Crow Dog, who has no fixed address but receives messages through his family, did not respond to my request in 2006 for an interview on the matter. I had set up an interview with Crow Dog in 2003, but he stood me up.

p. 342 In another version of Ray's last moments: This version apparently originated with Keith DeMaris, who later ran the International Indian Treaty Council and who was told the story after inquiring of friends about Robinson's death. (DeMaris told his story to Barbara Deming, a friend of the Robinsons, discussed elsewhere.) More than one person has told me off the record that Banks was Robinson's summoner. Richard Two Elk has said so to Paul DeMain (E-mail from Paul DeMain to author, Jan. 19, 2004), and Cheryl Buswell-Robinson was told the same thing when she inquired into Ray's killing in 1974.

p. 342 . . . run by Madonna Gilbert and Lorelei DeCora: Both Gilbert (now Thunder Hawk) and DeCora have declined to talk either to me or to Cheryl Buswell-Robinson about Ray's killing.

p. 343 . . . Janie Waller, hiked into Wounded Knee: By some accounts, Robinson may have been alive when Waller entered. She stayed in Wounded Knee until the stand-down two weeks later.

p. 343 "I'd patrolled with these guys, man": Cooper interview, *supra*.

p. 343 ". . . questioned me while Stan Holder": Stan Holder declined to talk to me about the matter.

p. 344 . . . "there is a young white male locked up": FBI memo from SA ▮▮▮▮, to SAC, Minneapolis (70-6832)(P), re "Wounded Knee," date uncertain but ca. Apr. 23, 1973. According to another informer's report, "The third individual mentioned by source was an unknown whitemale [sic] who was being held in the Wounded Knee jail. He was told by ▮▮▮▮ that ▮▮▮▮ had informed ▮▮▮▮ that the fellow in jail was going to be tried and shot for being a traitor." The suspected traitor was supposedly caught with a notebook and camera, apparently on April 21, 1973, but possibly on April 22, 1973; either date roughly coincides with the killing of Robinson and interrogation of Cooper. (FBI FD-204 report from ▮▮▮▮, Minneapolis, to USA, Sioux Falls, and to AUSA, Rapid City, field ofc. file 70-7085, Bureau file 70-58959, Sept. 15, 1973.)

p. 344 Deming made an investigation: Cheryl Buswell-Robinson told me about Deming's investigation.

p. 344 "When I heard, and I am emphasizing heard": Interviews of Sand Brim by author, via phone and in Venice, Cal., Dec. 2003, Nov. 2005.

p. 345 The Wounded Knee veterans . . . would not admit even: Another WKL-DOCker, Gail Sullivan, told me, "In 1975, I heard a story about Ray being killed and asked around, but every time I asked, the door was shut in my face. Nobody had ever seen him, which just wasn't believable: he was tall and black and would have stood out. It left me with the unsettled feeling that someone on our side could have been responsible for his death." (Interview of Gail Sullivan by author, via phone, Dec. 2003.)

p. 346 "I don't know who you're talking about": Walker, *supra*; e-mail from Carson Walker to author, Feb. 2004.

p. 346 The letter, from Dennis Banks to an envoy: Letter from Dennis Banks to Manny Salinas, Community Relations Service, U.S. Justice Department, Oct. 17, 1974, copy in author's files. Dennis Banks and Clyde Bellecourt declined my offers to talk about this and related matters.

p. 346 This is a WKLDOC memo: Davies's note about Robinson read, "VVAW has had two post cards in last 2 days." (WKLDOC memo, from Jeanne Davies, to Ken Tilsen, re "Current Information Concerning the Defense Committee's File on Missing Persons," July 14, 1973, in WKLDOC Archives.) When Cheryl Buswell-Robinson visited AIM in 1974, she was not told about this memo or the investigation it described.

p. 348 . . . in 1965, when Viola Liuzzo . . . was murdered: The FBI operative who was involved in the murder was Gary Thomas Rowe. The story is well told in Gary May, *The Informant: The FBI, the Ku Klux Klan, and the Murder of Viola Liuzzo*, Yale Univ. Pr., 2005.

p. 348 Just one example of the intelligence: The FBI has not released Ray Robinson's file, but it has released Cheryl Buswell-Robinson's. Her file includes reports of spying on Ray.

p. 348 A CIA report from 1965: The report appears to have been based wholly or mostly on surveillance by the FBI. James Bernard Wilcott, an FBI infiltrator of civil rights groups in Miami and elsewhere, briefed the CIA (or briefed the FBI, which briefed the CIA) on Robinson. (CIA document, from Deputy Chief of Personnel Security Division, to Deputy Director of Security for Personnel Security, re "Wilcott, James Bernard Jr. #109 301," Aug. 31, 1965, text at www.ajweberman.com/nodules/nodule3.htm, viewed Oct. 2003.)

p. 349 . . . agents were only too pleased to learn of his murder: Or perhaps agents feared that if they investigated the case of someone murdered on suspicion of informing for the FBI, the story of COINTELPRO might come out in open court.

p. 349 . . . other reporters asked Dennis Banks: Walker, *supra*.

p. 349 Stan Holder, the security chief: Holder's wife during Wounded Knee, Leola One Feather, said that a "close connection" of hers had told her about Robinson's killing at the hands of AIMers inside Wounded Knee. (Interview of Leola One Feather by author, Wounded Knee, S.D., Nov. 2003.)

p. 349 Nor did . . . Madonna Thunder Hawk: Thunder Hawk had, however, spoken with me on previous occasions. Our conversations came to an abrupt end when I began asking about Ray Robinson. Among the messages she did not answer was one in which I asked if she would tell Cheryl what she knew, if anything, about Ray's last minutes.

p. 349 Of the several people allegedly involved: Russell Means and Pedro Bissonette, the other principal leaders of Wounded Knee, were not in the village when Robinson was shot. Anna Mae and Nogeeshik Aquash left Wounded Knee shortly after Robinson was killed. Whether they knew about the killing is not known.

p. 349 Camp first spoke publicly about Robinson: See Debbie Lang, "Leonard Peltier Freedom Month: The Spirit of Wounded Knee," *Revolutionary Worker*, n. 1,030, Nov. 14, 1999, posted at alt.native Google newsgroup, Nov. 24, 2003.

p. 351 They said they had an open investigation: Agent Vukelich told me too, in late 2003, that the investigation into Robinson's death was open and, therefore, the FBI could not discuss it.

p. 351 "Then they brought in this racist-ass": According to Cheryl, the assistant U.S. attorney said that looking for Ray's body would be a problem on Pine Ridge because Indians thought *everything*—his tone implied everything from toothpicks to mountains—was sacred. He rolled his eyes as he said it. The same assistant U.S. attorney told me that he suspected that authorities in 1976 had buried Aquash's body quickly not because of mischief on the part of the government but because "Indians get spooked by things like dead bodies." His tone implied Indians were feeble of mind. (He also had his facts wrong: when Aquash's body was buried, it was not in the possession of Indians but of a white mortician in Nebraska.) This assistant U.S. attorney is intimately involved in prosecuting (or not) cases that originate on Indian reservations.

CHAPTER 17

p. 353 But it is certain that in late November: Most of the events in the last weeks of Aquash's life can be found in Paul DeMain, "Annie Mae Pictou Aquash Time Line: An Investigation by News from Indian Country," www.indiancountrynews.com/aquash.cfm, viewed Apr. 2003.

p. 353 "When Madonna [Gilbert] told me": Interview of Candy Hamilton by author, Oglala, S.D., Aug. 29, 2003.

p. 354 . . . Ted Means, Web Poor Bear, and the man: I was unable to locate Ted Means or Webster Poor Bear for comment.

p. 354 . . . Russell Means, who got the story from: Means said at a press conference, "Vernon Bellecourt made the phone call to the house on Rosebud, which"—and here Means choked up—"is my brother's house—and Clyde Bellecourt took the call from Vernon and then issued the order for her death, for her murder, in 1974—in 1975. . . . One of the three that took Anna Mae to her death has told me that it was Vernon Bellecourt, and that's why I'm coming forth." (Transcript of press conference, Russell Means and Robert Pictou Branscombe, Denver Federal Bldg., Nov. 3, 1999, posted at "Annie Mae Aquash, Special Issue—November 1999," www.indiancountrynews.com/aquashspecial.cfm, viewed Apr. 2003. See also Robert Weller, Associated Press, "AIM leader says other AIM members killed woman activist," at same Web site.)

p. 354 . . . editor Paul DeMain, who got the story: "Annie Mae Pictou Aquash Time Line," *supra*. DeMain has speculated that Aquash was killed not because AIMers thought she was an informer but because they feared she would become an informer. The chief fear was that she would testify that Leonard Peltier had killed one of the agents at Oglala. DeMain speculates that Aquash was also a threat because she knew many other dark secrets within AIM, perhaps including Ray Robinson's murder. Both speculations are plausible. But like the prosecutors of the Aquash murder, DeMain has shown little interest in the possibility that the FBI was involved in the conspiracy to kill Aquash.

p. 355 . . . Aquash's wallet turned up in the hands: Tilsen returned the wallet to Aquash's family. The cover letter he enclosed is Letter from Kenneth E. Tilsen to Robert C. Levy, May 17, 1976, in WKLDOC Archives. Levy wrote back that he had received the wallet and had given it one of Aquash's sisters, who was grateful to receive it. (Letter from Robert C. Levy, Nova Scotia Legal Aid, to Kenneth E. Tilsen, July 16, 1976, in WKLDOC Archives.)

p. 355 . . . "we needed someone who was not wanted": Dennis Banks with Richard Erdoes, *Ojibwa Warrior*, Univ. of Okla. Pr., 2004, p. 303.

p. 355 . . . a canard since several other people: Indeed, FBI reports show that several of the other AIMers went into gas stations and restaurants. Also, Banks has boasted that during the time he was a fugitive, he almost never tried to hide his movements and freely frequented public places.

p. 356 "You know, we believe the FBI set us up": "Anna Mae Pictou Aquash Time Line," *supra*.

p. 356 "It just didn't happen," he said: Interview of Bill Means by author, St. Paul, Minn., Aug. 2003.

p. 357 "The American Indian Movement is no more": Interview of Vernon Bellecourt by author, Minneapolis, Minn., Aug. 2003.

p. 357 I had heard that Bellecourt had been: I had heard so from more than one source. See also Interview of Richard Two Elk by members of the Native American Journalists Association, NAJA annual meeting, June 16, 2000, published at www.indiancountrynews.com/2elk1.cfm, viewed Apr. 2003.

p. 358 The Bellecourtian speaker said: Carson Walker, Associated Press, "Aquash exhumed, now going home," *Rapid City Journal*, Apr. 22, 2004. Vernon's brother Clyde "said he often stays at Means' house when he's in South Dakota but was never present for a conversation that included orders to kill Aquash. 'Everyone in the movement knows I would not allow anything like that to take place,' he said."

p. 358 "I . . . enclose Anna Mae's billfold": Tilsen letter, May 17, 1976, *supra*.

p. 358 "You know—boy—I've never seen that": Interview of Ken Tilsen by author, Troy, Wisc., Aug. 2003.

p. 359 Peter Matthiessen told me Tilsen had lied: According to Matthiessen, Tilsen led him to believe that AIMer Richard Marshall did not kill Martin Montileaux even though Tilsen knew Marshall had killed him. (Conversation between Peter Matthiessen and author, via phone, Mar. 2006. The Marshall-Montileaux affair can be found in Matthiessen's *In the Spirit of Crazy Horse*, Viking Pr., 1991.)

p. 359 . . . he replied with insults to my intelligence: E-mails between author and Ken Tilsen, Mar. 2006.

p. 361 But he is best known for dynamiting: Hill's FBI file was released to Barry Bachrach, attorney for Leonard Peltier, on October 31, 2005 (FOIA release 989352-000), and was made available to me just as this book was going to press—too late to cite the many documents inside it. The great majority of the documents relate to the Mt. Rushmore bombing, which is file 174-927 in the FBI's Rapid City office and file 174-6240 at headquarters in Washington. In addition to the papers in Hill's file showing he was the bomber, several sources inside AIM have confirmed the same, including Bob Robideau in "I for one applaud the verdict of guilty," Justice for Anna Mae and Ray Web site, www.jfamr.org/rob.html, Feb. 13, 2004, viewed Feb. 2004. When I asked Hill in 2003 about making bombs, he said, somewhat uncomfortably, that he would prefer not to answer. See also "Bombing Case, Firearms Arrests Made by FBI," *Rapid City Journal*, July 7, 1975; Paul DeMain, "Arlo Looking Cloud Trial Outline," Jan. 30, 2004, www.indigenouswomenforjustice.org, viewed Feb. 2004.

p. 363 In 2003 I spoke with Hill: Interview of David Hill by author, via phone, Nov. 2003. Hill has no fixed address, and I have found him only once. One of the matters we discussed was the X incident. In 1991, several years after the demise of AIM and the imprisonment of Leonard Peltier, a ski-masked figure who identified himself only as X told writer Peter Matthiessen that Peltier had not killed the agents at Oglala—X had. Bob Robideau, who had watched the agents die, set up X's meeting with Matthiessen and vouched for X's tale. Matthiessen published X's claim (see his *In the Spirit of Crazy Horse, supra*, p. 580ff.), but it was shortly exposed for a scam: Robideau and X had merely been trying to win Peltier's liberty. When the fraud was laid bare, it hurt Peltier more than it helped him. X, it turned out, was David Hill. Whether Hill had been sincerely trying to help Peltier or trying to sabotage him is a question still debated. When I spoke with Hill in 2003, he claimed he was not X, although he most assuredly was.

p. 363 He even claimed he had met Aquash only once: In addition to the accounts of AIMers (including Hill's friend Bob Robideau) who said Hill had driven Marlon Brando's motor home back from Los Angeles to Pine Ridge with Aquash, and those who said Hill had forced Aquash to make the Columbus Day bombs, Hill's ex-wife Thelma Rios said, "I knew Anna Mae, of course. I saw her there at our old place on Milwaukee Street. But it was David Hill who took her away. . . . I saw him take her out to the car, his hand on her arm, putting on that charming act of his. But he was squeezing her arm hard. She was so scared and crying." (David Seals, "Interviews with Thelma Rios," published Jan. 10, 2004, at John Graham Defense Committee Web site, www.grahamdefense.org, interviewed occured in late 1990s, interviews occurred in the late 1990s, viewed Jan. 2004.) John Graham has also said Hill was in Rapid City during Aquash's last hours there. ("The Lies of John Graham," indigenouswomenforjustice.org, viewed Feb. 2004.) Another source has told me he saw Hill at Rios's house the night before the interrogation, and Paul DeMain has also reported that Hill was in Rapid City at the time, possibly relying on the same source as me. ("Annie Mae Pictou Aquash Time Line," *supra*.) Hill told me he was not in Rapid City at the time Aquash was being interrogated there.

p. 363 In 2004, Seals published excerpts: Seals, *supra*.

p. 363 . . . I asked her to explain exactly how: Interview with Thelma Rios by author, Rapid City, S.D., Feb. 2004.

p. 363 A year later I chanced into a lunch date: Interview with Norman Zigrossi by author, Knoxville, Tenn., Dec. 2005.

p. 365 Then again, maybe Zigrossi . . . only wanted me to think: Two other reporters said of Zigrossi's motivations three decades ago, "Zigrossi worried about the possibility that FBI informers played a role in Aquash's death. If so, he said, 'I'd throw an informer's ass in jail so fast he wouldn't know what hit him.' Still, the prospect was not likely to help his career. And, as the Aquash case dragged on, it became obvious that Zigrossi was not eager to plunge into the shadowy world of informers and double agents that haunts the Left and the FBI." (David Weir and Lowell Bergman, "The Killing of Anna Mae Aquash, *Rolling Stone*, Apr. 7, 1977, p. 51ff.)

p. 365 . . . Russell Means and family drove by: "People were really mad about Russ at the time," Candy Hamilton said, "but I didn't see any reason to expect them to stop. I mean, that's the crowd that never liked Annie Mae and always gave her a hard time." (Hamilton interview, *supra*.) Means said he must not have been on the reservation at the time; he must have been on trial somewhere—although no records have been produced that bear him out. (Matthiessen, *supra*, p. 262.)

p. 365 On Sunday, March 14, in a driving snow: For information about Aquash's second burial, see Kevin McKiernan, "Indian woman's death raises many questions,"

Minneapolis Tribune, May 30, 1976, p. 1B; Johanna Brand, *The Life and Death of Anna Mae Aquash*, James Lorimer & Company, 1993, p. 18, 143; Matthiessen, *supra*, p. 262.

p. 366 . . . neither he nor any of AIM's other leaders attended: "Anna Mae Pictou Aquash Time Line," *supra*.

p. 366 "I've been to Annie Mae's grave sixty, seventy": Interview of Dennis Banks by Serle Chapman, Rapid City, S.D., Sept. 1999, in e-mail from Paul DeMain to author, Jan. 7, 2004.

p. 366 "We don't want Vernon Bellecourt holding": Carson Walker, Associated Press, "Aquash exhumed, now going home," *Rapid City Journal*, Apr. 22, 2004.

p. 366 "We have complete faith that those": Denise Maloney Pictou, "A Voice for Anna Mae, Family Statement," Dec. 23, 2003, in e-mail from Catherine Martin, occasional family spokesperson, to author, Dec. 23, 2003. Maloney Pictou's many statements that she does not care about the political overtones of her mother's death and that she wants only to convict the person or persons who pulled the trigger coincide nearly exactly with the view of the FBI. (See Denise and Deborah Maloney Pictou, "A Statement from the Family of Anna Mae Pictou Aquash," in e-mail from Catherine Martin and Paul DeMain to author, Dec. 19, 2003; Denise Maloney, message board Web posting, vancouver.indymedia.org/news/2003/12/93080.php, Dec. 22, 2003 & later dates.)

POSTSCRIPT

p. 367 . . . who is believed to be Bernie Lafferty: Lafferty did not respond to requests to be interviewed for this book.

INDEX